Informatik aktuell

Herausgeber: W. Brauer
im Auftrag der Gesellschaft für Informatik (GI)

Springer
*Berlin
Heidelberg
New York
Barcelona
Hongkong
London
Mailand
Paris
Singapur
Tokio*

Ulrich Killat
Winfried Lamersdorf (Hrsg.)

Kommunikation in Verteilten Systemen (KiVS)

12. Fachkonferenz
der Gesellschaft für Informatik (GI)
Fachgruppe „Kommunikation und Verteilte
Systeme" (KuVS)
unter Beteiligung des VDE/ITG
Hamburg, 20.–23. Februar 2001

Die Deutsche Bibliothek – CIP-Einheitsaufnahme

Kommunikation in verteilten Systemen: (KiVS); …Fachkonferenz der Gesellschaft für Informatik (GI), Fachgruppe Kommunikation und Verteilte Systeme (KuVS) unter Beteiligung des VDE/ITG. – 1979 – . – Berlin; Heidelberg; New York; Barcelona; Hongkong; London; Mailand; Paris; Singapur; Tokio: Springer, 1979 (Informatik aktuell) ISSN 0720-5503 Erscheint zweijährl. – Bibliographische Deskription nach 12 (2001) 12. Hamburg, 20.–23. Februar 2001. – 2001

CR Subject Classification (2001): C.2

ISBN 978-3-540-41645-6   ISBN 978-3-642-56675-2 (eBook)
DOI 10.1007/978-3-642-56675-2

Springer-Verlag Berlin Heidelberg New York
ein Unternehmen der BertelsmannSpringer Science+Business Media GmbH

© Springer-Verlag Berlin Heidelberg 2001

Satz: Reproduktionsfertige Vorlage vom Autor/Herausgeber
Gedruckt auf säurefreiem Papier   SPIN: 10719253   33/3142-543210

Vorwort

Hauptthemen der alle zwei Jahre stattfindenden Tagung „Kommunikation in Verteilten Systemen" (KiVS) der GI-Fachgruppe „Kommunikation und Verteilte Systeme" (KuVS) sind verteilte Anwendungen und die sie unterstützende Kommunikationsinfrastruktur. Die „KiVS" ist auf diesem Gebiet die bedeutendste regelmäßig stattfindende deutschsprachige Konferenz.

Nachdem die lange Reihe bisheriger KiVS-Tagungen im „letzten Jahrhundert" bis zur erfolgreichen KiVS '99 in Darmstadt führte, beginnt nun die KiVS '01 in Hamburg das 21. Jahrhundert als Zwölfte in dieser inzwischen schon traditionsreichen Reihe. Die Tagung wird gemeinsam ausgerichtet von der AG „Verteilte Systeme" des FB Informatik der Universität Hamburg und vom Arbeitsbereich „Kommunikationsnetze" der Technischen Universität Hamburg-Harburg. Dieser Brückenschlag über die Elbe markiert nicht nur die Kooperation Hamburger Hochschulen im IT-Bereich, sondern auch die Spannbreite der Forschungsgebiete, die im interdisziplinären Diskurs traditionell die KiVS befruchten.

Die im Rahmen der KiVS behandelten Fragestellungen erfreuen sich vor dem Hintergrund der schnell wachsenden Bedeutung von Kommunikationstechniken - man denke z.B. an Mobilfunk und das Internet - sowie der darauf basierenden verteilten Anwendungen - man denke z.B. an E-Commerce - einer großen Aufmerksamkeit seitens der Fachwelt und seitens einer interessierten Öffentlichkeit. Das gilt sowohl für die akademische und industrielle Forschung als auch für den - gerade im Hamburger Umfeld bedeutsamen - Einsatz derartiger Systeme in der betrieblichen Praxis.

Dies lässt sich auch am Programm der KiVS '01 ablesen: Es spannt einen Bogen von multimedialen Anwendungen über Middleware-Konzepte und Protokolle bis hin zu modernen Netztechniken mit ihren jeweiligen Mobilitäts- und Sicherheitsfragen.

Der Programmausschuss der KiVS '01 hat aus ca. 80 eingereichten Beiträgen aus Wissenschaft und Industrie insgesamt 28 Voll- sowie 8 Kurzbeiträge (Work in Progress) zur Präsentation ausgewählt. Die thematische Ausrichtung reicht dabei von Mobilen Kommunikationssystemen über Fragen der Dienstgüte, des Dienstmanagements und des Verkehrmanagements bis hin zu Sicherheit in Rechnernetzen, Multimedia, Groupware und Workflow Management-Systemen. Daneben wird in 6 Tutorien in aktuelle Technologien und Anwendungen wie Java 2 Enterprise Edition, Componentware, UMTS, Next Generation IP, Active Networks und Electronic Commerce eingeführt. Höhepunkte des Tagungsprogramms bilden schließlich auch die eingeladenen Vorträge aus drei unterschiedlichen Bereichen (Digitale Informationsräume, neue Steuerungskonzepte im Internet sowie innovative Firmengründungen im Bereich drahtloser Anwendungen), die Podiumsdiskussion zum Thema „Jobmaschine Internet", die traditionellen Präsentationen der Preisträger der GI-Fachgruppe KuVS aus den vergangenen beiden Jahren sowie der abschließende Workshop zum Thema „Erstellen und Wiederverwenden von multimedialen Kurseinheiten".

Nicht nur den Autoren und Vortragenden, sondern auch dem Programmausschuss sowie allen direkt oder indirekt an der inhaltlichen Vorbereitung der Tagung Beteiligten sei an dieser Stelle für ihre Mitwirkung gedankt. Zudem gilt unser Dank natürlich auch den vielen an der lokalen Organisation Beteiligten; stellvertretend für diese seien hier vor allem Herr Dr. Matthias Pätzold von der Technischen Universität Hamburg-Harburg sowie Herr Harald Weinreich von der Universität Hamburg als Hauptverantwortliche für die lokale Organisation genannt. Last but not least gilt unser Dank natürlich auch den Sponsoren für ihren finanziellen Beitrag, ohne den gerade in Zeiten knapper Kassen eine derartige Konferenz nicht (oder zumindest nicht in dieser Form) hätte stattfinden können.

Hamburg, im November 2000   Ulrich Killat und Winfried Lamersdorf

Inhaltsverzeichnis

Eingeladener Vortrag I

Resource Pricing for Differentiated Services 3
  P. B. Key; Microsoft Research

Session 1: Verkehrsmanagement I

Policy-basiertes Metering für IP-Netze 21
  G. Carle, S. Zander, T. Zseby; GMD FOKUS

PCR Policing: A Comparison of Fuzzy Policers vs. GCRA 35
  *L. Battaglia, F. Guardado, U. Killat; TU Hamburg-Harburg &
  Alcatel SEL AG*

Wegewahl in hierarchischen Netzen: Erweiterte Gütebewertung 47
  P. Jocher, A. Kaspar, B. Quendt; TU München & Siemens AG

Session 2: Mobile Computing

Paketfilter- und Tunnelkonfiguration
zur Firewall-verträglichen Mobilitätsunterstützung in IP-Netzen 59
  F. Pählke, G. Schäfer, J. Schiller; Uni Karlsruhe & TU Berlin

Service Awareness in Mobile Ad Hoc Networks 69
  J. Wu, M. Zitterbart; TU Braunschweig

Entwicklung von WAP-Anwendungen 81
  *A. Schmidt, H.-W. Gellersen, M. Beigl, O. Frick; Uni Karlsruhe &
  SAP AG*

Session 3: Sicherheit in Rechnernetzen

Verteiltes Filtern mit Contags und Sicherheits-Labeln 93
  M. Kabatnik, R. Sailer; Uni Stuttgart & T. J. Watson IBM Research

Sicherheitskonzept für eine durch Kunden steuerbare
Dienstmanagement-Architektur 103
  *Z. Nochta, G. Augustin, M. Becker, M. Friedmann, S. Abeck;
  Uni Karlsruhe*

Session 4: Groupware und Workflowmanagement

Communication Support for Mobile Virtual Groups 117
  U. Walther, S. Fischer; Internationale Uni Bruchsal

Using XSL to Coordinate Workflows.................................... 127
  R. Tolksdorf, M. Stauch; TU Berlin

Eingeladener Vortrag II

Wireless Handheld Devices and the Web 141
  A. Paepcke; Stanford University

Session 5: Verkehrsmanagement II

Signalling Support for Scalable Group Communication
over ATM Networks 147
  A. Böger, M. Zitterbart; TU Braunschweig

Auswirkung drahtloser Netzsegmente auf die Transporteffizienz
von TCP/IP-Verbindungen.. 159
  M. Matthes, U. Krieger, O. Drobnik; Uni Frankfurt &
  Deutsche Telekom Innovationsgesellschaft mbH

Improving the Performance of TCP
on Guaranteed Bandwidth Connections 173
  H. Ritter, K. Wehrle, L. Wolf; Uni Karlsruhe

Session 6: Multimedia

Architektur für eine integrierte Training Online Plattform 187
  C. Rueß, M. Wolf, R. Eberhardt, J. Hördt; DaimlerChrysler AG

Fehlertolerante Videokommunikation
über verlustbehaftete Paketvermittlungsnetze.......................... 201
  K. Heidtmann, J. Kerse, T. Suchanek, B. Wolfinger, M. Zaddach;
  Uni Hamburg

Document Specification and Dissemination
with an Extensible Multimedia System 215
  J. Hauser, K. Rothermel; Uni Stuttgart

Session 7: Work in Progress - Anwendungsunterstützung

Eine integrierte Dienstmanagementarchitektur
für den qualitätsgesicherten Betrieb von vernetzten Systemen............ 229
  S. Abeck, C. Mayerl, M. Schauer, D. Feuerhelm, L. Dolling;
  Uni Karlsruhe

A CORBA Domain Management Service............................... 233
  G. Brose, H. Kiefer, N. Noffke; Freie Uni Berlin

An Approach to Reduce Delay and Jitter for Time-Critical Data in IEEE
802.11 Wireless Local Area Networks 237
  V. Kahmann; Uni Karlsruhe

Telekommunikationsnetze in CORBA-basierten Echtzeit-Systemen
am Beispiel wirklichkeitsnaher Telepräsenzanwendungen 241
  G. Lin, T. Unterschütz, V. Vogel;
  Deutsche Telekom Innovationsgesellschaft mbH

Session 8: Work in Progress - Anwendungen

Einsatz von LDAP in einer Telekooperationsumgebung 247
  R. Faust, U. v. Lukas; Zentrum f. Graph. Datenverarbeitung e.V.

Sicheres Nomadic Computing in Intranet-Umgebungen -
Problemstellungen und Lösungskonzepte 251
  C. Link, N. Luttenberger; Uni Kiel

My Home is my Network or how to HAVi 255
  R. Baier, C. Gran, A. Zisowsky; GMD FOKUS

Verteilte Kommunikation in der Praxis:
Ein neuer Verkehrstelematik-Dienst „Parken und Leiten" 259
  R. Hinz; DaimlerChrysler AG

Session 9: Mobile Kommunikationsnetze

Lokalisierung mobiler Teilnehmer unter
Berücksichtigung regelmäßigen Verhaltens 265
  T. Ziegert; TU Dresden

High Quality Mobile Communication 279
  H. Hartenstein, A. Schrader, A. Kassler, M. Krautgärtner,
  C. Niedermeier; NEC Europe Ltd. & Uni Ulm & Siemens AG

Evaluating the GPRS Radio Interface
for Different Quality of Service Profiles 291
  C. Lindemann, A. Thümmler; Uni Dortmund

Session 10: Softwaretechnologien für Verteilte Systeme

Sicherheitdienste für mobile Agentenanwendungen 305
  J. Bohn, G. Karjoth; ETH Zürich & IBM Forschungslabor Rüschlikon

Performance Evaluation of Various Migration Strategies
for Mobile Agents 315
  P. Braun, C. Erfurth, W. Rossak; Uni Jena

Generative Softwarekonstruktion auf Basis typisierter Komponenten 325
  F. Griffel, C. Zirpins, S. Müller-Wilken; Uni Hamburg

Eingeladener Vortrag III

Der Wireless Application Service Provider: „Chance im m-Commerce" 341
  M. Lübbehusen; smapCo GmbH

Session 11: Dienstgüte

Layer4+ Supported Class of Service 349
  T. Harbaum, H. J. Stüttgen, M. Zitterbart; TU Braunschweig &
  NEC Europe Ltd.

Active QoS Routing 359
  M. Welzl, A. Cihal, M. Mühlhäuser; Uni Linz & TU Darmstadt

Real-Time Support on Top of Ethernet 369
  R. Koster, T. Kramp; Uni Kaiserslautern

Fun Factor Characterization of User Perceived Quality of Service
for Elastic Internet Traffic 377
  J. Charzinski; Siemens AG

Session 12: Dienstmanagement

Signalisierungsplattform zur netzübergreifenden Dienststeuerung
in heterogener TIME Infrastruktur 391
  W. Kellerer, P. Sties; TU München

Management-Aufgaben bei komponentenbasierten verteilten Systemen
im Fahrzeug-Telematikbereich 403
  V. Feil, M. Stümpfle; Uni Stuttgart & DaimlerChrysler AG

Reduzierung der Anzahl von Übertragungen
in „Floating Car Data"-Diensten 415
  W. J. Franz; DaimlerChrysler AG

CIM/CORBA-basiertes Management
verteilter kooperierender Managementsysteme 425
  A. Keller; T. J. Watson IBM Research

Preisträger

Entwicklung und Leistungsbewertung einer ATM-Funkschnittstelle 439
  D. Petras; RWTH Aachen

Konzeption und Bewertung einer TINA-konformen Architektur
für das Mobilitätsmanagement von UMTS 455
  F. Imhoff; RWTH Aachen

Spezifikations- und Meßmethodik
für ein adaptives Dienstgütemanagement 467
   J.-P. Richter; Uni Hamburg

Service Separation and QoS in ATM Networks:
The RCC+ Multiplexer 479
   D. Abendroth; TU Hamburg-Harburg

Index der Autoren 491

Eingeladener Vortrag I:

P. B. Key; Microsoft Research

Resource Pricing for Differentiated Services

Peter B. Key

Microsoft Research, St George House, Cambridge, CB2 3HN, UK
http://research.microsoft.com/users/pbk/

Abstract. In paper we present an overview of recent work on resource pricing for differentiated services in the Internet. This approach is based upon encouraging cooperation between the end-systems and the network by use of the correct feedback signals. These signals reflect the congestion shadow prices at a resource, and their use means then even 'selfish' end-systems, acting in their own best interests, will push the system to a global or social optimum. In contrast to most current Diffserv proposals, little is required from resources in the network; they just have to mark packets correctly, while the end-system can use complex or simple strategies. All that is needed is for the end-systems to have an incentive to react to the feedback signals, and then we have a distributed resource sharing mechanism. We give examples of typical end-system behaviour, and show how this approach can also implement Distributed Admission Control, where the decision is in the hand of the end-system. We comment on how ECN (Explicit Congestion Notification) could be used as an enabling technology. Lastly we outline how guarantees can be constructed with this framework.

1   Introduction

The current Internet is based upon a single class of service (Best Effort), with a limited range of end-system behaviour. But different applications, particularly real-time services, may have different requirements from the network, in other words demand a different Quality of Service, (QoS), and the IETF is seeking to evolve the Internet to meet these demands. Quality of Service has layers of meaning, but at its most basic says something about the level and quality of bandwidth delivered, and the delay seen by packets traversing the Network. Telephony networks assure quality of service by dimensioning for a peak load, using signalling, reserving bandwidth for connections and denying access to connections if the network is congested. The IntServ proposal for the Internet incorporates some of these ideas to give reservations some assured bandwidth. Current DiffServ proposals look at ways of giving differentiated services by defining marking packets with various labels (code points), treating packets differently on a per-hop basis and using service level agreements to give some form of end-to-end performance guarantees across domains. Traffic shapers and policers are needed at the edges and gateways to enforce contracts, with priority queueing or some other form of scheduling needed in the routers to produce the different per-hop behaviours.

There is a growing body of work that looks at a simpler framework for providing differential QoS, using ideas from economics and optimisation based upon 'Resource Pricing' or 'Congestion Pricing'. This is the approach we explore in this paper. The basic idea is to encourage co-operation between the users and the network by sending the correct signals to the users. These reflect the damage that the users cause to the network by entering the system, or the 'congestion costs'. For example, if the network is lightly loaded, these are negligible, but increase with the network loading. A network comprises a set of linked resources, each of which calculate their own 'Resource Price' or 'Congestion Cost', which are aggregated across routes by users. The users (end-systems or applications) are then free to act as they wish, subject to the constraint that there is an incentive to react to feedback signals. In economic terms congestion is a (negative) externality, and if this information is fed back to the users as a cost or tax, then the externality is internalised and users acting in their own self-interest will push the system to the global or system optimum.

This framework enables a distributed resource sharing approach to QoS, where the end-systems play a key role in the resource allocation, and cooperate with each other and the network through the feedback signals that the network provides. It can also be seen as a practical way of implementing a version of the 'smart-market' approach proposed by Mackie-Mason and Varian [16]. Much less is required of the network than current DiffServ proposals, and more of the intelligence is placed in the end-systems or edge devices. Moroever, some interesting recent work by Bonald and Massoulié [2] shows some specific disadvantages of using 'unfair' priority mechanisms (as proposed in Diffserv), which do not occur with the 'fair' allocation we advocate here.

In section 2 we explore the theoretical background to this work, which is based of the work on Kelly and co-workers [8, 4]. Section 3 uses a simple model of TCP to relate the theory to current practice, while Section 4 briefly considers implementation issues and what is required of routers. It should be stressed that in this paper we do not address the issue of how to charge for services: resource pricing only reflects congestion costs, which may or may not be translated into real monetary costs to the user, and other considerations have to be taken into account when setting tariffs or prices. Our approach can be thought of as a distributed game between the users and the network, which we look at in Section 5, while Section 6 looks at end system behaviour, for adaptive applications and file transfers. It is also possible to deal with demands that have a fixed bandwidth requirement, putting admission control in the hands of the user, which we describe in Section 7. Lastly we comment on the relationship between guarantees and this approach, and make some concluding remarks.

2　Motivation and Theoretical Background

We now explain how the feedback signals can be derived, and how they link to notions of 'fairness'. For convenience in what follows we use the term 'user' to denote any end-system or application.

A network is a set of linked resources, and a path through the network will use some subset of these resources in a specific order. The description is general, but it may help to think of the current Internet where typical resources are bandwidth and service rate or buffer capacity in a router output port. We shall assume fixed routing, so a route determines a specific subset of the resources. Let J be a finite set of resources indexed by j, and R a finite set of users (end-systems), indexed by r, where the 0–1 incidence matrix $A = A_{jr}$ indicates whether user r uses resource j or not. Suppose further that we can characterise a user's preference for bandwidth by a concave, non-decreasing utility function, $U_r(x)$, which is appropriate for 'elastic' traffic [23]. For convenience assume U_r is everywhere differentiable and $U_r(x_r) \downarrow -\infty$ as $x \downarrow 0$. It is natural for users to attempt to pursue their own ends, and seek to maximise $U_r(x_r)$ over $x_r \geq 0$. But resources are (usually!) finite, so this behaviour will tend to overload certain resources. To counteract this, suppose that when the load on resource j is y_j, the resource incurs a cost at rate $C_j(y_j)$. Then a social planner would seek to

$$\text{Maximise} \quad \sum_r U_r(x_r) - \sum_j C_j \left(\sum_r A_{jr} x_r \right) \qquad \text{over} \quad x_r \geq 0 \ ; \quad r \in R \ . \tag{1}$$

At the optimum,

$$U_r'(x_r) = \sum_{j \in r} p_j(y_j) \tag{2}$$

where p_j is the derivative or shadow price $p_j(y_j) = C_j'(y_j)$ with a corresponding load on resource j given by

$$y_j = \sum_r A_{jr} x_r \ . \tag{3}$$

Suppose now we send feedback signals to the user. We want signals to be additive, and if signals are to be carried on packets, signals need to be proportional to load, suggesting a feedback signal of the form $t_r x_r$. If these reflect a 'charge' to the User, the user wants to maximise the net return, that is

$$\text{Maximise} \ U_r(x_r) - t_r x_r \qquad \text{over} \quad x_r \geq 0 \ . \tag{4}$$

hence if these 'prices' are set correctly, that is if

$$t_r = \sum_{j \in r} p_j(y_j) \tag{5}$$

the users acting independently will drive the system towards the social optimum [8]. Note that the tax or congestion price t_r internalises the congestion costs, and is sum of the resource prices along the route.

Under this identification, and writing $p_r = \sum_{j \in r} p_j(y_j)$, a natural user adaptation is to adapt the rate x_r according to

$$\frac{d}{dt} x_r(t) = \kappa_r \left(x_r(t) U_r'(x_r(t)) - x_r(t) \sum_{j \in r} p_j(y_j(t)) \right) \tag{6}$$

in which case provided U_r is strictly concave and each C_j is convex then each user will converge to the unique (system). It is possible to show by Lyapunov techniques that all trajectories converge to the unique fixed point [8, 11].

We now show that is it possible for the Network to mandate all users to use a particular update rule (perhaps by mandating a specific protocol stack), which will impose a particular form of fairness, and still recover the same results. Part of the motivation for this is that, in general, the network does not know the utility functions of the users (which are an abstraction in any case). Suppose that each user has to use the 'willingness-to-pay' update rule

$$\frac{d}{dt}x_r(t) = \kappa_r \left(w_r - x_r(t) \sum_{j \in r} p_j(y_j(t)) \right) . \tag{7}$$

This is equivalent to using a utility function of the form

$$F_r(x) = w_r \log x_r \tag{8}$$

and hence the Network is implicitly maximising $\sum_r w_r \log x_r - \sum_j C_j(y_j)$. It can be shown that such an allocation is weighted Proportionally Fair [8]. [1] At the optimum,

$$w_r = p_r x_r \tag{9}$$

hence w_r is the amount user r is prepared to pay per unit time. If the user adapts the parameter w_r over time according to

$$w_r = x_r U_r'(x_r) \tag{10}$$

then the User Optimum and Social optimum again coincide, based upon an underlying 'Proportional Fairness' model. Updating w_r according to (10) is equivalent to the user seeking to

$$\text{Maximise} \quad U_r\left(\frac{w_r}{p_r}\right) - w_r \quad \text{over} \quad w_r \geq 0 . \tag{11}$$

We shown in the appendix that the same results hold under different mandated behaviours dictated by choosing a different function F. But much of the literature has concentrated on the 'willingness to pay' algorithm, which is equivalent to $F_r(x_r) = w_r \log x_r$. This which is appealing since firstly, w_r has a ready interpretation, secondly the behaviour of aggregates is linear with respect to w_r (in other words a single stream with value $w = w_1 + w_2$ behaves as the sum of the two streams with w_1 and w_2) and thirdly the underlying fairness model, weighted 'Proportional Fairness' [8], in economic terms is 'Nash fair' and results in an Nash arbitration scheme [21, 19]. In the bandwidth sharing case it is possible to show that this is only allocation that produces a Nash arbitration scheme.

---

[1] Normally fairness is used in the context of fixed capacity constraints, where resource j has capacity c_j; this fits in the above by taking $C_j(\cdot)$ as a penalty function.

3 TCP as an Optimisation

The above description laced with talk of utility functions may seem very abstract. However, consider the current TCP protocol. When in congestion avoidance mode, the congestion window W increases by 1 per round trip time, and halves its window if a packet loss is detected. If the same behaviour occurs when a packet is marked (rather than lost), then in a window of size W, if packets are marked with probability p, there will be pW packet marks each potentially halving the window. Now scale the systems so that W is large, then for small p the rate of packet sending $x = W/T$, where T is the (assumed constant) round trip time (RTT) can approximated by

$$\frac{dx(t)}{dt} = \frac{1}{T}\frac{dW(t)}{dt} = \frac{1}{T^2} - \frac{x(t)^2 p}{2} \tag{12}$$

At the equilibrium this gives the familiar inverse square root dependence on p

$$x = \frac{1}{T}\sqrt{\frac{2}{p}} \ . \tag{13}$$

This is the same *as if* each user was trying to maximise their *net* utility, that is utility minus cost, where the utility function is

$$U(x) = K - \frac{2}{T^2 x} \tag{14}$$

for K an arbitrary constant, and where the cost function is just the linear rate of charge, px. This utility function can be interpreted as a weighted version of the time taken to transfer a file of unit size [12]. Note how this utility function penalises long round-trip times (weights round trip times more heavily than bandwidth), and that squared dependence on x in the decrease behaviour means that the behaviour of aggregates is not linear.

4 Implementation Issues and Marking

4.1 End-system Reactions

To implement the resource pricing ideas, a way of generating feedback signals is needed, and users (end-systems or applications) must be able to adapt. Resources generate feedback signals, and we explore various ways of setting these marks below. If the feedback signals can be represented by a single bit, then the current IETF Explicit Congestion Notification (ECN) RFC [22] provides a suitable mechanism: this sets a flag in the IP header, which can be used to indicate congestion or not. The current RFC concentrates on TCP behaviour, and specifies how TCP should behave in response to marked packets, by essentially requiring the same behaviour as if the packet had been lost. By allowing a much more general behaviour, we lay the framework for truly differential quality of service. For responsive flow-aware applications, such as TCP, the feedback signals can be fed back to the receiver in the ACK packet (as in the ECN RFC). For other applications (such as current UDP-type applications) the feedback needs to be returned to the source. One approach that enables existing applications to be used is to create some form of 'Congestion Manager', which sits between the application and the network stack and interprets the feedback signals to the application, together with a mechanism for reflecting the marks back to the source. The reflection may either be done on a per-resource basis, or reflected by an edge device. Prototype operating systems stacks exist which support ECN, and ECN-capability is likely to be in future versions of Operating Systems such as Windows and Linux, thus laying the foundations for building new adaptive applications, which can react directly to the feedback information without the need for a Congestion Manager.

It is an open question as to whether single bit marking is sufficient: if more bits are required then the ECN proposal is not sufficient, and either IPv6 would have to be used for a general solution, or the Congestion manager approach for IPv4.

4.2   Resource Marking

The question of how to mark packets depends on the cost function $C(y)$ that is used. Current marking in the Internet is based around marking lost packets, where the marking function, $p(y)$ (the derivative of $C(y)$) represents the rate of loss. But it is more natural to regard the *cost* function $C(y)$ as reflecting the rate of loss; for example if a resource has capacity c_j then the cost should reflect the rate of loss, $(y_j - c_j)^+$, or $\mathbb{E}\left[(y_j - c_j)\right]$ if we interpret y_j as a random variable, If y_j is Poisson [4] or Gaussian, then the derivative is given by

$$p_j(y_j) = \Pr\{y_j \geq c_j\} \equiv \mathbb{E}\left[1_{y_j \geq c_j}\right] , \tag{15}$$

in other words we mark all the packets when the load exceeds capacity. This is the probability of resource saturation, which typically marks at least an order of magnitude more packets than the loss rate (which is $\mathbb{E}\left[(y - c_j)^+\right]/\mathbb{E}[y]$). Note the difference here: loss marking marks those packets which suffer as a result of congestion, whereas the alternative approach advocated here marks all those packets *responsible* for congestion.

Current generation routers are reasonably approximated by an output buffered switch, with packets dropped (marked) at an output port when the buffer exceeds its maximum value B. Recent proposals such as RED (Random Early Detection) [3], start marking packets before loss occurs, when some threshold $b < B$ is met, and try to avoid synchronisation effects that occur when loss is used as a feedback signal by marking some proportion of packets at levels below b. A related proposal (REM, Random Early Marking) [14] marks a packet with probability $1 - \phi^{-W})$ where W is a congestion measure based on current workload and $\phi > 0$ a parameter.

The choice of an appropriate $p(\cdot)$ is the subject of current research, see for example [26]. The beginning of this section suggested marking on arrival rate, which is a more reactive signal than marking schemes based on queue length, since the queueing process integrates the arrival rate. A virtual queue marking scheme [4] which marks as though the queue had a smaller service rate (capacity) and potentially smaller buffer size is able to provide early warning of problems. Moreover by a suitable choice of parameters [7], we can track the derivate of the real queue, which is related to the arrival rate, and the real object of interest.

More generally, the function $C(y)$ might represent the costs associated with delay, in which case the price functions p reflect the shadow price of delay.

5   Distributed Games

With the network providing the correct feedback signals (the shadow prices), users or end-systems can do as they please, provided that they have an incentive to react to these prices or 'costs'. The signals encourage cooperation, while the users seek to do the best they can subject to the cost they incur. We can then view the whole system as an environment, where users 'compete' against each other. This is reminiscent of a multi-user, multi-objective game where users may have very different objectives, and seek the best way of achieving them. For example, one user may wish to maximise throughput whilst ensuring the rate of charging, the cost, is less than some amount, while some users may be prepared to adapt the rate in response to price signals, and another may not.

The 'best' algorithm for a user will be one that performs well in a mixed environment: the strategy has to do well against all sorts of other strategies. Consequently, one way to discover 'good' strategies is to create an environment where strategies can compete against each other. A first step is to construct strategies that do well for a specific object, and then see how robust they are. A good algorithm can then be embedded in a protocol, which adapts the rate of sending packets in response to feedback received from the network.

Microsoft Research in Cambridge has built such an environment [10, 11], where such ideas can be tried out: a network simulator simulates certain key features of a real network (transmission of packets, routers, etc) and a simple text-based protocol allows users to communicate with the network. This enables users to write strategies in any language, and communicate with the network remotely via a TCP connection. In other words this is a distributed game environment, where users 'compete' against each other and the network. The network topology, router functionality and marking functions can be freely altered to allow general experiments to be conducted.

In the next section we describe certain user strategies.

6 End-system behaviour

The simplest form of user behaviour is an unreactive source, which just continues at a fixed or varying rate, regardless of the feedback. These can be interpreted as users who are insensitive to price, and have the effect of forcing the price up (price setters). We now look at those adaptive applications that adapt their sending rate in response to feedback signals, which can be thought of as generalisations of TCP.

6.1 Rate Control

Suppose users adjust their rate according to the Gibbens and Kelly 'willingness-to-pay' strategy [4] described earlier,

$$\frac{d}{dt}x_r(t) = \kappa_r\left(w_r - p_r(t)x_r(t)\right) \tag{16}$$

where as in Section 2, $p_r(t)$ is the feedback along the route, the sum of the resource prices $p_r(t) = \sum_{j\in r} p_j(t)$. Then w_r is the amount user r is prepared to pay per unit time, or the maximum rate of marking the user can tolerate, and κ_r is a gain parameter. The user increases the sending rate at rate κ_r times the difference between what the user is prepared to pay (w_r) and the network charges $p_r x_r$. In the steady state equilibrium, users have a throughput proportional to w_r, i.e. $x_r = w_r/p_r$, hence those that are prepared to pay twice as much receive twice as much. Note the dependence on $1/p_r$, in contrast to the square root dependence of TCP. Simulation studies [4, 11, 13] have shown that this relative throughput is indeed attained in practice and also show [11, 13]how such strategies can co-exist with TCP [11]. Therefore this simple mechanism has given a way of giving relative shares. Recall that this algorithm is equivalent to using a logarithmic utility function, $U_r(x_r) = w_r \log x_r$ hence the resulting allocations are weighted proportionally fair. This algorithm with a packet scheduling policy that conforms to the rate equation can define a rate control protocol.

The parameter κ_r affects the rate of convergence. Equation (16) always converges to the equilibrium point, however this assumes instantaneous feedback. In practice, there is a delay D_{sj} from source s to resource j, and a delay in the message travelling from resource j back to the sender, D_{js}. Let T_r be the round-trip time for user r, and assume that $D_{rj} + D_{jr} = T_r$ then the delayed version of equation (16) is

$$\frac{d}{dt}x_r(t) = \kappa_r\left(w_r - p_r(t - T_r)x_r(t - T_r)\right) \tag{17}$$

where now $p_r(t-T_r)$ is shorthand notation for $\sum_{j\in r} p_j(\sum_{s:j\in s} x_s(t-D_{jr}-D_{sj}))$. Recent work by Massoulié [17] has proved a version Tan's conjecture [25] that this system is stable if

$$\kappa_r T_r \left(p_r + \sum_{j\in r} p'_j \bar{y}_j\right) < 1 \; , \quad r \in R \tag{18}$$

where $\bar{y}$ the equilibrium vector of loads. This says that κ_r must be less than some fraction of the inverse round trip time, $1/T_r$. Note that the multiplier only depends on quantities along route r. The larger the κ_r, the faster the convergence, but if κ exceeds the bound the system may be unstable. Note that the system can still oscillate — the right hand side of (18) has to be smaller than 1 to avoid oscillation, and in the single resource case less than $1/e$. See [6] for illustrations for specific marking functions.

The above evolutions are gradual adaptations designed to adjust the load to its equilibrium point. When a connection first enters, it can take some time to reach this point, and there are good reasons to use something like TCP slow-start behaviour to find a good operating point: for example doubling the sending rate until say w_r packets are marked, and then using the slow evolution. Equivalently, use the parameter κ_r as a time dependent parameter, $\kappa_r = \kappa_r(t)$ with κ_r starting out from a high (unstable) value and decaying to a stable value. [9] gives an interpretation of slow-start like algorithms in terms of risk-averse behaviour.

6.2 Window Based Control

Current TCP is a window based control, which has useful self-clocking features. Writing $x_r = W_r T_r$, and $\kappa_r = \gamma_r/T_r$ gives the window evolution for W_r as

$$\frac{d}{dt}w_r(t) = \gamma_r \left(w_r - \frac{p_r(t)}{T_r} W_r(t) \right) \tag{19}$$

with γ_r a suitable fraction to give stability. This can be implemented by increasing the window $W_r(t)$ by $\gamma_r w_r T_r$ every round trip time (equivalently increasing the window by $\gamma_r w_r T_r/W_r$ every ACK), and decreasing by γ_r for every marked ACK. This gives an expected throughput which is independent of the round trip time: if an inverse dependence on the round trip time is required (to be TCP like) then the updating can be modified to

$$\frac{d}{dt}w_r(t) = \gamma_r \left(\frac{w_r}{T_r} - \frac{p_r(t)}{T_r} W_r(t) \right) \tag{20}$$

where now the window increases by $\gamma_r w_r/W_r$ every ACK, and where for stability $\gamma_r < 1/\left(p_r + \sum_{j\in r} p'_j \bar{y}_j \right)$. This is closest to a direct modification of TCP: the throughput is given by

$$\bar{x}_r = \frac{1}{T_r}\frac{w_r}{p_r} \ . \tag{21}$$

6.3 File Transfers

File transfers have rather different objectives: example objectives might be to transfer a file F by a given time T at minimum cost, or transfer a file F at a cost of no more than W. These have very different behaviour: in the first case, [5] used the simulation environment to look at simple strategies, where the sending rate could vary between a high peak rate (sending packets close together) or a low rate. Simple strategies, such as sending at the high rate if the last sent packet was not marked performed well in bake-off experiments. This is not surprising, and echoes results found by Axelrod [1] for the repeated prisoner's dilemma where simple strategies proved the most robust in a mixed environment (despite not being 'optimal' when considered in isolation). Massoulié and Key [18] looked at a more sophisticated estimation procedure that could be used to try and estimate marking periods and react accordingly.

If instead the user wants to send the file size F at a cost of no more than W, then users are prepared to pay a maximum amount per packet, $W(t)/F(t)$, where $W(t)$ denotes the amount of W remaining at time t and $F(t)$ the amount still to be transferred. Hence a user will enter the system if the price is below this, and will drop out if the predicted price means that they cannot afford to send the amount left. This encourages a start-stop behaviour where a sender can stop sending in the middle of a file, and wait until the price drops again before re-entering. This can be fitted into a 'willingness to pay' strategy [4], where the willingness to pay, $w(t)$, is a function of time and updated by relating it to $W(t)x(t)/F(t)$.

For a general user, whose utility function is a decreasing function of the time to transfer T, with a maximum bearable price $p^* = W/F$, Key and Massoulié [9] show that for a large system, where users and capacity are scaled together, the optimal strategy for a user is to send at the peak rate, if the price is less than p^* and otherwise to wait. This provides some linkage between the previous two strategies.

7 Distributed Admission Control

So far we have concentrated on concave utility functions. If the utility function is 's-shaped', with a convex initial region, followed a concave region, then if the price is too high, the user will not enter (this happens if px never intersects the curve $U(x)$), otherwise the user will ideally choose the point rate x where $U'(x) = p$, and the convex initial region has no influence on the allocation. Let us now concentrate on a users who only want to enter if the price is less than some value p^*, and want to have fixed amount of bandwidth, x_f (f for fixed) . This could correspond to users who have a utility function which is approximates to a step function, appropriate for non-adaptive real time traffic. Now suppose each connection sends a number of probe packets through the network, and only enters if none of these packets are marked. This creates a distributed admission scheme studied by Kelly et al [7], where the users, rather than the network, decide if it they should enter or not.

Let m_f be the number of probe packets user f send through the network. The larger m_f, the less likely user r will enter: in effect the user is trading off the cost of entering the network and being marked more than they want to be against not entering and losing utility. Key and Massoulié [9] suggest a Bayesian framework for choosing m_f. Suppse we have a set of such users, F, that connections of type f arrive as a Poisson process of rate ν_f, last for a mean time μ_f and when connected generate packets at rate λ_r when connected. If mean holding times and packet generation rates are equal, and if this set of users are the only users of a network or sub-network, then the distribution of the number of connections n_f has a product form solution. As we relax these assumptions, the product form disappears but we can write down differential equations that approximate the system behaviour, and which become exact as the system size grows.

For example, suppose we now mix the adaptive and non-adaptive traffic, and that instances of adaptive traffic of type r arrives with Poisson rate ν_r and have a mean holding time of μ_r. Then the evolution of the system is described by the system of equations,

$$\dot{n}_r(t) = \nu_r - n_r(t)\mu_r \tag{22}$$

$$\dot{x}_r(t) = \kappa_r \left(w_r - p_r(t)x_r(t) \right) \tag{23}$$

$$\dot{n}_f(t) = \nu_f(1 - p_f(t))^{m_f} - n_f(t)\mu_f \tag{24}$$

where

$$p_r(t) = \sum_{j \in r} p_j(y_j(t)) \tag{25}$$

$$y_j(t) = \sum_{r \ni j} n_r(t)x_r(t) + \sum_{f \ni j} n_f(t)\lambda_f \tag{26}$$

The last equation implies that when a new type r connection arrives it uses the common sending rate of the type r connections.

We can easily write down a Lyapunov function in the case where $m_r \equiv 1$ or in the case when the system load is small, in which case $(1 - p_f)^m \approx 1 - m_f p_f$. As $t \uparrow$, $n_r(t) \to \nu_r/\mu_r$, hence for by considering sufficiently large t, we can show that the function

$$\mathcal{U}(x,n) = \sum_{r \in R} \frac{\nu_r}{\mu_r} \log x_r \tag{27}$$

$$+ \sum_{f \in F} \frac{1}{m_f \lambda_f} \left(\nu_f n_f - \mu_f \frac{n_f^2}{2} \right) - \sum_{j \in J} \int^{\sum_{r \ni j} \frac{\nu_r}{\mu_r} x_r + \sum_{f \ni j} n_f(t)\lambda_f} p_j(y)dy$$

is a Lyapunov function for the system. Hence with mild constraints on p, all trajectories converge to the unique fixed point.

Notice at this fixed point,

$$p_j = p_j \left(\sum_{r \ni j} \frac{\nu_r}{\mu_r} \frac{w_r}{p_r} + \sum_{f \ni j} \frac{\nu_f}{\mu_f} (1 - p_f))^{m_f} \lambda_f \right) \tag{28}$$

thus given the load upon the network, we can calculate the appropriate equilibrium rejection probabilities for type f calls, namely $(1 - p_f)^{m_f}$.

8   Guarantees

For adaptive traffic, traffic streams are allocated resource in proportion to what they are prepared to pay. So an end-system prepared to pay twice as much as another user, e.g. $w_1 = 2w_2$, receives twice as much. (We can without loss of generality assume all uses are willingness-to-pay users, since more general users can be thought of has having load dependent w_r — see Section2). We can go further than this if we bound the total demand of the network: consider the example of the last section, but where there is no fixed traffic (i.e. $\nu_f \equiv 0$). First, notice that

$$x_r = w_r/p_r \tag{29}$$

hence user r has a throughput of at least w_r provided the system 'price-matched', that is provided $p_r < 1$ for all r. To expand this: suppose each resource is a form of buffered resource, which can serve packets at maximum rate c_j, hence a resource will be overloaded if the load exceeds c_j. Then a sufficient condition for resource j not to be overloaded is

$$\sum_{r \ni j} \frac{\nu_r}{\mu_r} w_r < c_j \tag{30}$$

which says that resource j can mark more packets than the users passing through it are willing to bear. This is a strong condition with $|J|$ constraints, but lays the groundwork for guarantees to be given. Not that the constraint is the *the maximum the users can pay*, rather than the maximum loading on the network. There are corresponding conditions for the users, and corresponding necessary 'max-flow' type bounds: if a flow denotes the vector of 2-tuples n_r, x_r, then we require

$$\sum_{r:x_r>0} n_r w_r < \sum_{j:y_j>0} c_j \tag{31}$$

In practice, for a 'properly-sized' network, we would like the probability of marking to be reasonably small, $p_r < p_{max}$, say not more than 10% on average across routes. In this case, user r will achieve a throughput of a least w_r/p_{max}. Necessary conditions then are that

$$\sum_{r:x_r>0} \frac{1}{p_{max}} n_r w_r < \sum_{j:y_j>0} c_j \tag{32}$$

or stricter conditions are given by

$$\sum_{j \in r} p_j \left(\sum_{r \ni j} \frac{\nu_r}{\mu_r} \frac{w_r}{p_{max}} \right) < p_{max} \quad \forall r \ . \tag{33}$$

Analogous equations hold in the case that $\nu_f > 0$: a sufficient condition for stability is

$$\sum_{r \ni j} \frac{\nu_r}{\mu_r} w_r + \sum_{f \ni j} \frac{\nu_f}{\mu_f} \lambda_f < c_j \tag{34}$$

while if we want the probability of marking to be less than p_{max}, which is a lower bound on the probability of *rejecting* a type f call, then necessary conditions are that

$$\sum_{j \in r} p_j \left(\sum_{r \ni j} \frac{\nu_r}{\mu_r} \frac{w_r}{p_{max}} + \sum_{f \ni j} \frac{\nu_f}{\mu_f} \lambda_f \left(1 - p_{max}\right)^{m_f} \right) < p_{max} \quad \forall r \ . \qquad (35)$$

The use of the above equations mean that is possible to give 'hard' or 'soft' guarantees provided we constrain or bound the users' ability to respond to marks appropriately.

9 Concluding Remarks

We have described a general framework that builds a differentiated services model from simple components: resources in a network (e.g. routers) mark packets when they are congested and the end-systems react to these marks. The end-systems can react as they please provided they have an incentive to react to marks, that is marked packets count as a cost to the user. This may represent real money, but initially at least is more likely to be some form of distributed mint or credit system. For example, we could bound the rate at which users or a particular application can spend consume marks. By bounding the aggregate rate offered to the network, the last section showed how it is possible to give guarantees on quality of service. An edge device may constrain the aggregate marking for a group of systems, in which case it is possible to trade-off marks between applications or end-systems in the same aggregate [11]. For example, in a multimedia application we may choose to preserve the audio quality at the expense of the video, by passing the audio's marks to the video stream.

In optimisation terms (see Section 2) we are solving the Primal problem, where the users average information from the resources (with averaging parameter κ_r), but the resources send back instantaneous information. A complementary approach is used by Low et al [15], who use a Primal-Dual approach where the resources also use an updating function, much as RED uses an average of the queue length to mark packets rather than the instantaneous value. It is interesting to note that for the user, the optimal gain parameter depends on T_r, the reciprocal of the round-trip time, which can be found by the user; one could conjecture that it may be hard for a resource to correctly average information for sources which have very different round trips times, suggesting that averaging at a resource may be difficult and even slow convergence.

If packet marking can be accomplished with a single bit, then the current ECN RFC provides a suitable mechanism for marking packets. The RFC is targeted specifically at TCP: we suggest broadening its scope so that ECN is seen as an IP level mark, and passed up the network stack so that all applications can potentially react to the marks, and not just those based on TCP. Moreover, we wish to allow a variety of reactions to marks, rather than just TCP behaviour.

It is an open question as to whether a single bit is sufficient. Strictly speaking, we should add marks across resources, however little is lost by taking the maximum of the marks along a route rather than the sum provided that the network is lightly loaded (congestion is low). There are other reasons why multiple bits may be useful: for example for identifying where congestion occurs as a packet traverses different domains, or perhaps to communicate an average rate to flows just starting, or when the number of flows is small. Barham and Stratford [24] describe an experimental implementation built on top of Windows2000 which uses a 3rd party traffic controller to alter the rates of the Windows2000 traffic shapers in response to feedback signals, and uses multiple bit marking.

References

[1] Robert Axelrod. *The Evolution of Cooperation*. Basic Books, NY, 1984.

[2] T. Bonald and L. Massoulié. Impact of fairness on Internet performance. Submitted for publication, 2000.

[3] S. Floyd and V. Jacobson. Random Early Detection gateways for congestion avoidance. *IEEE/ACM Transactions on Networking*, 1(4):397–413, 1993. http://www-nrg.ee.lbl.gov/floyd/red.html.

[4] R. J. Gibbens and F. P. Kelly. Resource pricing and the evolution of congestion control. *Automatica*, 35:1969–1985, 1999. http://www.statslab.cam.ac.uk/~frank/PAPERS/evol.html.

[5] R. J. Gibbens and P. B. Key. The use of games to assess user strategies for differential quality of service in the internet. In *Workshop on Internet Service Quality Economics*, MIT, December 1999. http://research.microsoft.com/research/network/publications/gibkey1999.ps.

[6] F. P. Kelly. Models for a self-managed internet. *Philosophical Transactions Royal Society*, pages 2335–2348, 2000. www.statslab.am.ac.uk/~/smi.html.

[7] F. P. Kelly, P. B. Key, and S. Zachary. Distributed admission control. *IEEE Journal on Selected Areas in Communications*, 18(12), December 2000. http://research.microsoft.com/research/network/publications/dac.htm.

[8] F. P. Kelly, A. K. Maulloo, and D. K. H Tan. Rate control in communication networks: shadow prices, proportional fairness and stability. *Journal of the Operational Research Society*, 49:237–252, 1998.

[9] P. B. Key and L. Massoulié. User policies in a network implementing congestion pricing. In *Workshop on Internet Service Quality Economics*, MIT, December 1999. http://research.microsoft.com/research/network/publications/ISQElm.ps.

[10] P. B. Key and D. R. McAuley. Differential QoS and pricing in networks: where flow control meets game theory. *IEE Proceedings Software*, 146(2):39–43, March 1999.

[11] Peter Key, Derek McAuley, Paul Barham, and Koenraad Laevens. Congestion pricing for congestion avoidance. Microsoft Research Technical Report MSR-TR-99-15, MSR, 1999. http://research.microsoft.com/pubs/.

[12] S. Kunniyur and R. Srikant. End-to-end congestion control schemes: Utility functions, random losses and ECN marks. In *INFOCOM 2000*, 2000.

[13] Koenraad Laevens, Peter Key, Derek McAuley, and Paul Barham. An ECN-based end-to-end congestion-control framework: experiments and evaluation. Microsoft Research Technical Report MSR-TR-2000-104, MSR, 2000. http://research.microsoft.com/research/network/publications/MSRTR2000_104.pdf.

[14] D. E. Lapsley and S. H. Low. Random Early Marking: an optimisation approach to Internet congestion control. In *Proceedings of IEEE ICON'99*. IEEE, 1999. Brisbane, Australia.

[15] S. H. Low and D.E. Lapsley. Optimization flow control – I: Basic algorithm and convergence. *IEEE/ACM Transactions on Networking*, 7(6):861–874, December 1999.

[16] J. K. MacKie-Mason and H. R. Varian. Pricing congestible network resources. *IEEE Journal of Selected Areas in Communications*, 13(7):1141–1149, 1995.

[17] L. Massoulié. Stability of distributed congestion control with heterogeneous feedback delays. Tech Report MSR-2000-111, Microsoft Research, 2000.

[18] Laurent Massoulié, Peter B. Key, and Koenraad Laevens. End-user policies for predicting congestion patterns in data networks. In *13th ITC Specialist Seminar on Internet Traffic Measurement*, September 2000. http://research.microsoft.com/research/network/publications/monterey.ps.

[19] R. Mazumbdar, L.G. Mason, and C. Douglieris. Fairness in network optimal control: optimality of product forms. *IEEE Trans. Communications*, 39:775–782, 1991.

[20] J. Mo and J. Walrand. Fair end-to-end window based congestion control. In *SPIE 98, International Symposium on Voice, Video and Data Communications*, 1998.

[21] John F Nash. The bargaining problem. *Econometrica*, 1950.

[22] K. Ramakrishnan and S. Floyd. A proposal to add explicit congestion notification (ECN) to IP. RFC 2481, IETF, January 1999. ftp://ftp.isi.edu/in-notes/rfc2481.txt.

[23] S. Shenker. Fundamental design issues for the future Internet. *IEEE J. Selected Area Communications*, 13:1176–1188, 1995.

[24] Neil Stratford. Congestion pricing: A testbed implementation. In *Multi-Service Networks 2000*, July 2000. http://research.microsoft.com/research/network/talks/Neil_S_Cos2k.pdf.

[25] D. K. H. Tan. *Mathematical models of rate control for communication networks*. PhD thesis, University of Cambridge, 1999. http://www.statslab.cam.ac.uk/ dkht2/phd.html.

[26] Damon Wischik. How to mark fairly. In *Workshop on Internet Service Quality Economics*. MIT, December 1999.

Appendix: Fairness and Mandated Controls

We can generalise the approach of Section 2 by letting the Network mandate that users should adjust their rates according to the update rule

$$\frac{d}{dt}x_r(t) = \kappa_r \left(x_r(t)\, F_r'(x_r(t)) - x_r(t) \sum_{j \in r} p_j(y_j(t)) \right) \tag{36}$$

where F_r is a function of the form

$$F_r(x) = w_r \frac{x^{1-\alpha}}{1-\alpha} \tag{37}$$

for some fixed $\alpha \neq 1$. The Network implicitly maximises $\sum_r F_r(x_r) - \sum_j C_j(y_j)$, and the resulting allocation will correspond to a Maximum Utilisation allocation if $\alpha = 0$, corresponds to Proportional Fairness if $\alpha \to 1$ and Max-Min fairness as $\alpha \uparrow$ [20], and weighted variants of these for general w_r. At the optimum,

$$F_r'(x) \equiv w_r x_r^{-\alpha} = p_r \ . \tag{38}$$

If the user adapts the parameter w_r over time according to

$$w_r = x_r{}^{\alpha} U_r'(x_r) \tag{39}$$

or equivalently is seeking to solve

$$\text{Maximise} \quad U_r\left(\left(\frac{w_r}{p_r}\right)^{\frac{1}{\alpha}}\right) - p_r \left(\frac{w_r}{p_r}\right)^{\frac{1}{\alpha}} \quad \text{over} \quad w_r \geq 0 \ , \tag{40}$$

then we can show that the User Optimum and Social optimum again coincide, based upon an underlying 'α-Fairness' model.

In this case w_r has the interpretation that $w_r x_r{}^{1-\alpha}$ is the amount the user is prepared to pay per unit time. The case $\alpha = 1$ is equivalent to $F_r(x_r) = w_r \log x_r$

Session 1:

Verkehrsmanagement I

Policy-basiertes Metering für IP-Netze

Georg Carle, Sebastian Zander, Tanja Zseby

GMD FOKUS
Kaiserin-Augusta-Allee 31
D-10589 Berlin
`[carle, zander, zseby]@fokus.gmd.de`
`http://www.fokus.gmd.de/glone/`

Abstract. Die kommerzielle Erbringung von IP-Diensten macht neben der Kontrolle des Zugangs zu Diensten über Authentifizierung und Autorisierung eine leistungsfähige Messinfrastruktur zur Erfassung der Ressourcennutzung erforderlich. In Differentiated Services Netzen müssen dazu messtechnische Lösungen zur Erfassung von Accounting-Daten und zur Überprüfung der im Service Level Agreement zugesagten Grenzwerte der Dienstqualität bereitgestellt werden. Die häufig heterogene Messinfrastruktur und die effiziente Aufteilung von Messaufgaben im Netz erfordern eine flexible Architektur zur Ansteuerung und Verteilung. Es wird eine policy-basierte Architektur für verteiltes Metering zur Erbringung der geforderten Messaufgaben vorgestellt. Messaufgaben werden dazu in einer einheitlichen Meterkonfigurationssprache ausgedrückt, und eine automatische Verteilung sowie Umsetzung auf spezifische Meter-Konfigurationen für unterschiedliche Meter unterstützt. Hierdurch kann auf dienstspezifische Accounting-Anforderungen und dynamische Änderungen der Verkehrscharakteristik unter Berücksichtigung von Funktionalität, Auslastung und maximaler Leistungsfähigkeit einzelner Meter eingegangen werden.

Einleitung

Innerhalb der IETF-Arbeitsgruppe AAA (Authentication, Authorization, Accounting) und der IRTF-Forschungsgruppe AAAARCH (Authentication, Authorization, Accounting Architecture) wird an Lösungen zur Bereitstellung einer generischen AAA-Architektur [Laat00] für IP-Dienste und anwendungsorientierte Dienste gearbeitet. Nach Authentifizierung und Autorisierung eines Kunden erfolgt die Konfiguration des geforderten Dienstes. Handelt es sich bei dem Dienst z.B. um die bevorzugte Weiterleitung von IP-Paketen in einem Differentiated Services Netzwerk, so beinhaltet dies die Konfiguration der Marker und Scheduler. Die AAA-Architektur sieht sogenannte Application Specific Modules (ASMs) für die Konfiguration von Service Equipment [Voll00a] und Accounting Equipment [CaZZ00] vor. Bei Differentiated Services IP-Netzen ist neben der messtechnischen Erfassung des Ressourcenverbrauchs auch eine kontinuierliche oder auf Stichproben basierende Überprüfung der erbrachten Dienstqualität wichtig. In Netzen mit differenzierten Dienstgüten fallen also zwei unterschiedliche Messaufgaben an:

- Messung des Ressourcenverbrauchs für eine verursachergerechte Abrechnung
- Messung von Dienstqualitätsparametern zur Validierung der vereinbarten Qualitätsstufe

Um diese Messaufgaben zufriedenstellend zu bewältigen, wird eine Infrastruktur mit Messinstanzen an verschiedenen Punkten im Netz benötigt. Die Parameter zur Durchführung der Messung wie die jeweils benötigten Messwerte, Genauigkeit der Messung, Messintervall, etc. können dabei für verschiedene Tarife, Dienstklassen, Kundentypen, Tageszeiten oder andere Faktoren variieren. Viele der Parameter lassen sich aus dem zwischen Kunden und Provider vereinbarten Service Level Agreement (SLA) ableiten. Ein weiterer wichtiger Punkt stellt die meist heterogene Infrastruktur in vielen Provider-Netzen dar. Um das Zusammenspiel der vorhandenen Komponenten zu ermöglichen, muss eine konsistente Ansteuerung der unterschiedlichen Messwerkzeug-Typen unterstützt werden.

In diesem Beitrag stellen wir eine Architektur vor, in der Konfigurationsparameter in Form von Meter-Policies zur Ansteuerung einer verteilten heterogenen Messarchitektur eingesetzt werden. Die Meter-Policies werden aus den im SLA festgelegten Kenngrößen (z.B. Tarif, Messverfahren, Messhäufigkeit) abgeleitet. Damit wird die Erfassung der Ressourcennutzung über Accounting-Meter und die Überprüfung der im SLA vereinbarten QoS-Parameter über passive Messungen realisiert.

Das Dokument gliedert sich wie folgt: Kapitel 2 gibt einen Überblick über existierenden Lösungen zur messtechnischen Erfassung von Daten über den Ressourcenverbrauch und der bereitgestellten Qualität. In Kapitel 3 wird das Konzept des policy-basierten Metering vorgestellt. Dabei wird die Anwendung zur Erfassung der Ressourcennutzung und der Validierung von SLAs verdeutlicht. In Kapitel 4 wird die Meter-Architektur zur Ansteuerung verschiedener Messkomponenten vorgestellt. Kapitel 5 zeigt anhand von Messungen, wie die Leistungsfähigkeit eines Meter durch hierarchische policy-basierte Filterung verbessert werden kann. Kapitel 6 fasst die erzielten Ergebnisse zusammen und gibt einen Ausblick auf zukünftige Arbeiten.

Metering für Accounting

Algorithmen zur Filterung und Klassifikation von IP-Paketen werden nicht nur in Accounting-Metern, sondern auch in verschiedenen anderen Anwendungen und Einsatzgebieten benötigt (z.B. Routing, Firewalling, Dienstdifferenzierung, etc.). Daher müssen bei der Beurteilung geeigneter Algorithmen die speziellen Anforderungen, die sich durch das Einsatzgebiet Accounting ergeben, berücksichtigt werden. Accounting stellt die Basis für die Rechnungserstellung dar. Daher sollten neu auftretende Datenströme von Beginn an erfasst werden. Spätestens nach erfolgreichem Abschluss der Autorisierung müssen daher die entsprechenden Filter-Regeln im Accounting-Meter zur Erfassung des Datenstromes existieren.

Eine Möglichkeit zur Erfüllung dieser Anforderung besteht in der permanenten Erfassung aller auftretenden Datenströme. Das von Cisco entwickelte Meter NetFlow [Cisc99] arbeitet nach diesem Prinzip. Auch das konfigurierbare Meter NeTraMet [RFC2063] stellt einen Modus zur Verfügung, in dem eine automatische Klassifikation aller Datenströme erfolgt. Die Erfassung aller Flows kann allerdings besonders bei feiner Granularität zu hohen Datenmengen führen. In Szenarien, in denen die Weiterleitung bestimmter Pakete (z.B. Best Effort Verkehr) umsonst ist oder durch eine Flat Rate abgedeckt wird, führt dies meist zu unnötigem Klassifikationsaufwand und zu überflüssigen Einträgen in der Flow-Tabelle des

Meters. Ein weiterer Nachteil dieser Variante ist die notwendige feste Definition der Attribute zur Eingruppierung der Pakete. Damit ist die Granularität der Erfassung fest vorgegeben und für alle Datenströme identisch. Die zweite Variante ist das schnelle dynamische Hinzufügen und Entfernen von Klassifikations-Regeln. Dies erfordert einen flexiblen Klassifizierer, der eine Veränderung der Regeln zur Laufzeit unterstützt.

Je nach eingesetztem Tarifmodell kann Accounting neben der Behandlung einer großen Anzahl an Filterregeln, auch die Klassifizierung anhand mehrerer Header-Felder erfordern. In [NARUS] wird ein System vorgestellt, in dem sogar eine semantische Verkehrs-Analyse zur Auswertung von Applikations-Informationen stattfindet, um Datenströme einzelnen Sessions auf Anwendungsebene zuzuordnen. Die Klassifikationsanforderungen für Accounting machen eine Aufteilung von Mess-Aufgaben auf verschiedene Messinstanzen zweckmäßig. So können zum Beispiel Filter-Regeln auf verschiedene Messinstanzen die der Datenstrom durchquert verteilt werden, (z.B. auf Ingress- und Egress-Router) um die Belastung der einzelnen Meter zu reduzieren.

Accounting Meter

Das Accounting-Meter NeTraMet [RFC2063] ist aus der Arbeit der IETF Arbeitsgruppe Real-Time Traffic Flow Measurement (RTFM) entstanden. Die RTFM Architektur setzt sich aus einem Meter, einem Meter Reader und einem Meter Manager zusammen. Das Meter lässt sich über SNMP konfigurieren und auslesen.

Cisco NetFlow [Cisc99] ist ein Router-internes Meter speziell für Cisco Router. Es setzt das Betriebssystem Cisco IOS voraus und bietet im Vergleich zu NeTraMet nur wenige Konfigurationsmöglichkeiten. Es werden alle IP-Flows in der feinsten Granularität gemessen und nur einige vorgegebene Aggregierungs-Schemata zur Verfügung gestellt.

Linux Netfilter [Netf00] ist ein Klassifizierer im Linux Kern, der zur Realisierung verschiedener Anwendungen wie Firewalling, NAT und Accounting verwendet werden kann. Pakete können an verschiedenen Stellen im Netzwerk-Kern erfasst und klassifiziert werden. Der Klassifizierer wird über die Kommandozeile konfiguriert. Tabelle 1 vergleicht die Hauptmerkmale der vorgestellten Meter.

	NeTraMet	NetFlow	NetFilter
Flow-Definition	Bidirektional (optional unidirektional)	Unidirektional	Variabel
Flow-Granularität	Variabel	Festes Set von Attributen, einige feste Aggregation-Schemata	Variabel
DiffServ Codepoint	JA	JA	JA
RSVP Flowspec	Erweiterungs-Konzept in [CaMM98]	NEIN	NEIN
Ipv6 Adressen	JA	NEIN	JA
Multicast Attribute	Geplant	Geplant für Cisco IOS 12.0(7)T	NEIN
Sampling	JA	NEIN	NEIN
QoS Messungen	JA (RTT)	NEIN	NEIN
Unterstützte Betriebssysteme	DOS, Linux, BSD, Solaris, IRIX	Cisco IOS	Linux
Kosten	Frei erhältlich	ca. $ 5000,- pro Lizenz	Frei erhältlich

Tabelle 1: **Vergleich der Accounting-Meter NeTraMet, NetFlow und Netfilter**

NeTraMet bietet die höchste Flexibilität der vorgestellten Meter. Die Definition von Verkehrsklassen kann über die Klassifikationsregel frei gewählt werden. Da die Klassifizierung im User Space stattfindet, kann NeTraMet auf verschiedenen Betriebssystemen eingesetzt werden. Cisco NetFlow ist ein vergleichsweise statisches Meter. Die Attribute, mit der die Klassen unterschieden werden, sind fest vorgegeben. Ausserdem ist das Meter ausschließlich zusammen mit Cisco IOS verfügbar. Dafür kann bei der Klassifikation eine höhere Leistungsfähigkeit erzielt werden. Bezüglich zusätzlicher Funktionalität schneidet NetFlow im Vergleich zu NeTraMet eher schlecht ab. Eine Erklärung dafür ist mit Sicherheit die freie Verfügbarkeit des NeTraMet-Quellcodes, die eine Weiterentwicklung des Tools durch interessierte Entwickler ermöglicht. Dies trifft auch auf den Linux-Klassifizierer Netfilter zu. Da Netfilter jedoch - anders als NeTraMet und NetFlow - primär für Anwendungen wie Firewalling konzipiert wurde, sind hier bisher nur wenige Erweiterungen für Accounting und Messzwecke verfügbar.

Paket-Klassifikation

Accounting Meter benötigen im Kern einen Paket-Klassifizierer. Aufgrund der vielfältigen Einsatzgebiete für Paket-Klassifizierer stellt die Weiterentwicklung und Verbesserung von Algorithmen zur Paket-Klassifikation ein aktives Forschungsgebiet dar, bei dem in der Regel ein Kompromiss zwischen Klassifikationsgeschwindigkeit, Speicherbedarf und Flexibilität gefunden werden muss.

In [GuMc99] wird basierend auf der Analyse von derzeit verwendeten Filterregeln (für Routing, Firewalling und Bereitstellung von QoS-Diensten) ein einfacher heuristischer Algorithmus mit dem Namen Recursive Flow Classification (RFC) entworfen. Dieser nutzt die Struktur in den Filterregeln aus, um zusammenhängende Bereiche zu identifizieren und diese in sogenannte equivalent Class IDs zu gruppieren. Damit wird der Klassifikationsprozess auf Kosten eines etwas höheren Speicherbedarfs beschleunigt. Aufgrund der notwendigen Vorausberechnung bietet der Algorithmus jedoch nur eine sehr eingeschränkte Flexibilität bezüglich des Hinzufügen und Entfernens von Filterregeln. Außerdem basiert der Ansatz stark auf den in den untersuchten Beispiel-Filterregeln gefundenen Regel-Strukturen und ist daher nicht ohne weiteres auf beliebige Einsatzgebiete erweiterbar.

In [EnKa96] wird ein Dynamic Packet Filter (DPF) vorgestellt, der eine dynamische Code-Generation verwendet, um einen auf dem PathFinder-Filter [BaGP94] basierenden Paket-Filter zu optimieren. Der Filter-Code wird dabei direkt in Maschinensprache kompiliert. Dies ermöglicht zwar das schnelle Hinzufügen und Entfernen von Regeln, schafft aber auch eine Abhängigkeit vom verwendeten Betriebssystem. DPF ist ein Paket-Filter, eine Klassifizierung von Paketen ist daher nicht möglich.

Policy-basiertes Metering

Um eine verursachergerechte Tarifierung zu realisieren, müssen Informationen über die Ressourcenreservierung und –nutzung im Netz erfasst und gesammelt werden. Auch für die Überprüfung der im SLA vereinbarten Grenzwerte sollte eine messtechnische Erfassung der erbrachten Qualität erfolgen. Provider können sich durch unterschiedliche Dienstangebote und Tarifkonzepte sowie durch Bereitstellung spezieller Accounting-Dienste (z.B. detaillierte Rechnungen, permanente Information über die momentane Ressourcennutzung, etc.) gegeneinander abgrenzen. Auf welche Weise die Ressourcennutzung erfasst werden soll, hängt unter anderem ab von der Größe und dem Zweck des Provider Netzes, den angebotenen Dienstklassen, den verwendeten Tarifierungsverfahren, den zu unterstützenden Accounting-Diensten sowie der Möglichkeit, vorhandene Infrastruktur (z.B. MIBs) nutzen zu können. Die Metering-Infrastruktur muss an die jeweilige Messaufgabe anpassbar sein und einen hohen Grad an Flexibilität bezüglich der Datenerfassung, -sammlung, -weiterleitung und -speicherung aufweisen. Ein Beispiel für die Ableitung der Messaufgabe aus dynamischen DiffServ-SLAs findet sich in [ShSt00].

Im folgenden stellen wir eine Architektur für policy-basiertes Metering vor. Die Architektur erlaubt eine Anpassung an unterschiedliche Messaufgaben für Accounting und SLA-Überprüfung. Die Verwendung von Meter-Policies ermöglicht zum einen den Austausch von Konfigurationsinformationen zwischen Providern. Zum anderen kann über Meter-Policies die Ansteuerung verschiedenartiger Meter-Typen in einer heterogenen Messumgebung realisiert werden.

Das SLA kann dabei als Basis für Informationen zu den benötigten Tarifvariablen und den vereinbarten Qualitätsparametern dienen. Diese bilden den Ausgangspunkt, um Policies für das Accounting und die QoS-Messungen zu definieren. Über AAA-Server können diese Informationen an andere Provider weitergeleitet werden. Über ein Application Specific Modul (ASM) wird dann das Mess-Equipment konfiguriert [CaZZ00].

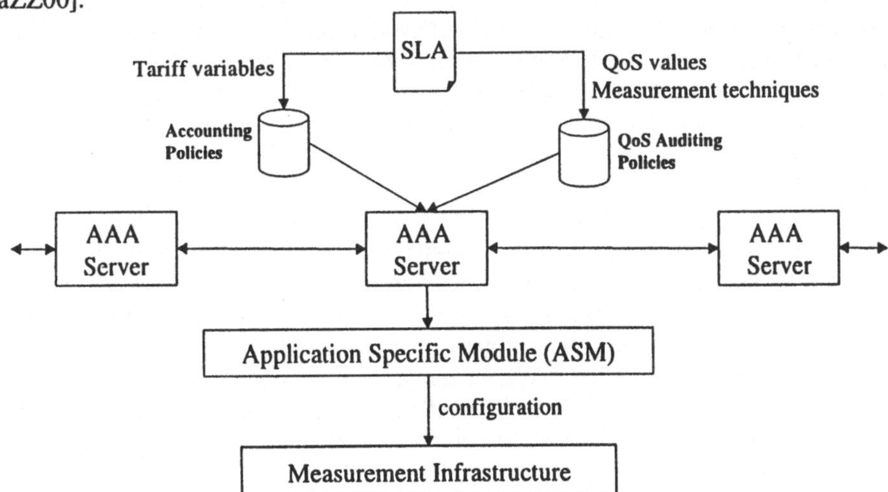

Abbildung 1: Konfiguration der Mess-Infrastruktur über Policies

Meter-Policies beschreiben die Regeln für die Erzeugung, den Transport und das Speichern der gemessenen Daten in einer standardisierten Form und können in die entsprechende Konfiguration der einzelnen Messelemente der Accounting-Infrastruktur umgewandelt werden. Meter-Policies erlauben die Konfiguration folgender Datenstrukturen und Parameter:

Meter-Records: Die im Meter-Record enthaltenen Messdaten (relevante Attribute) lassen sich aus dem verwendeten Tarifierungsverfahren bzw. der im SLA vereinbarten QoS-Überprüfung ableiten. Meter-Policies lassen sich einsetzen, um einem benachbarten Anbieter mitzuteilen, was dieser messen muss, z.B. im Fall von Roaming.

Meter-Record-Ziel: Das Ziel eines Meter-Records beschreibt, wohin ein Record gesendet werden soll. Das Ziel kann ein nachfolgender Billing-Prozeß, ein benachbarter Provider, ein Kunde (Hot Billing) oder eine Auditing-Datenbank sein.

Meter-Intervall: Das Meter-Intervall beschreibt, in welchen Abständen Meter-Records generiert und an das Ziel gesendet werden.

Aufbewahrungszeit: Die Aufbewahrungszeit beschreibt, wie lange der Record (z.B. für Auditing-Zwecke) gespeichert werden muss.

Zugangskontroll-Liste: Diese Liste spezifiziert die Zugangsrechte zu den gemessen Daten, d.h. wer Lese- und/oder Schreibrechte auf die Daten hat.

Meter-Genauigkeit: Die Meter-Genauigkeit gibt an, mit welcher Genauigkeit die Daten erfasst bzw. gespeichert werden.

Meter-Granularität: Das Metering kann sich auf aggregierte Flows sowie auf einzelne Flows (spezifiziert durch Schicht-3-Informationen, sowie optional durch Informationen höherer Schichten) beziehen.

Überprüfung des SLAs durch QoS Messungen

Service Level Agreements (SLAs) beschreiben den Vertrag zwischen Nutzer und Provider. SLAs enthalten die vereinbarte Qualität, mit der ein Dienst vom Provider erbracht werden muss. Sie können darüber hinaus auch Vorschriften enthalten, wie die vereinbarte Qualitätsstufe kontrolliert wird. Auch genaue Angaben über die verwendeten Messverfahren und Reglungen über die Konsequenzen bei Nicht-Einhaltung der vorgegebenen Qualitätsgrenzen können Bestandteil des SLAs sein. [Verm99].

Zur Ermittlung der momentanen Qualität einer Verbindung sind permanente Messungen erforderlich. Bei der Verwendung von aktiven Messverfahren werden Test-Pakete auf die zu messende Strecke gesendet. Diese Testpakete führen zu unerwünschter Zusatzlast, welche die Messungen verfälschen kann. Bei Messungen über Providergrenzen hinweg ergibt sich eventuell zusätzlich das Problem, dass ein benachbarte Provider den Test-Verkehr nur ungern in das eigene Netz weiterleitet, insbesondere wenn besondere Paketformate verwendet werden. Passive Messverfahren besitzen den Vorteil, ohne zusätzlichen Verkehr die Qualität der Verbindung zu überprüfen.

Im Differentiated Services Model werden unidirektionale Datenströme betrachtet. Außerdem können sich Performance-Kenngrößen wie Paket-Verlustrate und Verzögerungszeit für die Hin- und Rückrichtung stark unterscheiden. Daher sollten bei der Ermittlung der Qualität einer Verbindung One-Way-Metriken gemessen werden. Dies erfordert mindestens zwei Messpunkte im Netz. Es müssen also mindestens zwei Messpunkte entsprechend den im SLA spezifizierten Messanforderungen konfiguriert werden. Die im folgenden beschriebene Messarchitektur dient dazu, die Messanforderungen aus dem SLA abzuleiten und anhand einer Meter-Datenbank die Verteilung der Messaufgabe auf die unterschiedlichen Instanzen zu automatisieren.

Meter Architektur

Dieses Kapitel beschreibt die entwickelte Messarchitektur zur Erfassung der Accounting-Daten und zur Überprüfung der Dienstqualität. Abbildung 2 zeigt die einzelnen Komponenten der Architektur und deren Kommunikation untereinander.

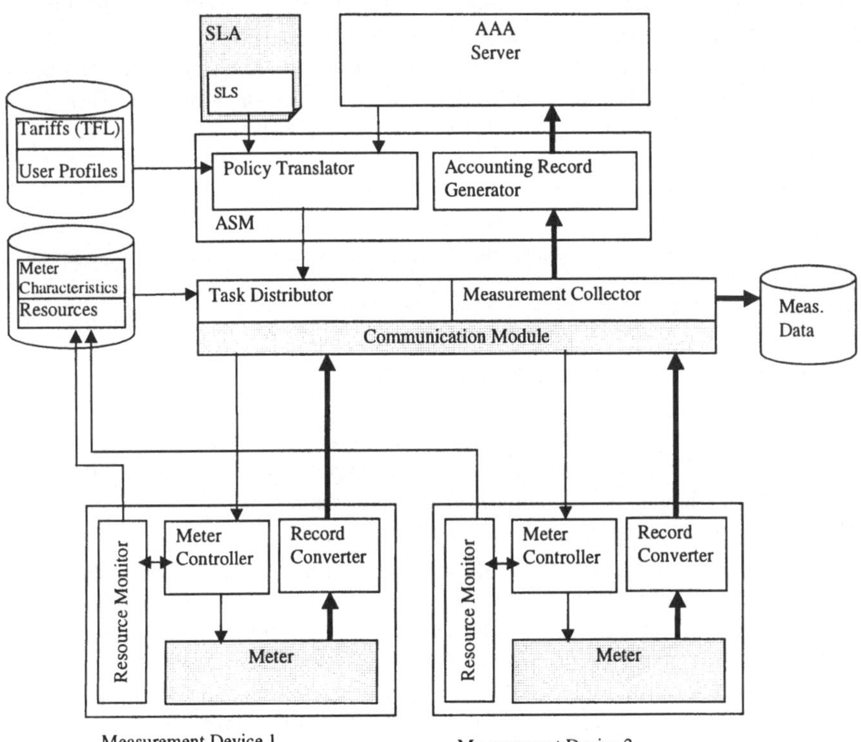

Abbildung 2: Meter-Architektur

Der Policy Translator generiert anhand der Service Level Specification (SLS) [BeSB00], des Tarifs und des Kunden Profils die entsprechende Meter Policy. Zur Beschreibung des Tarifs wird die Tarifbeschreibungssprache TFL (Tariff Formula Language, [CaHZ99]) eingesetzt. Soll das Metering für einen Kunden eines anderen Anbieters konfiguriert werden, erhält der Policy Translator Anweisungen über den AAA-Server. Der Task Distributor verteilt die Meter-Policies an die entsprechenden

Messgeräte. Er entscheidet über die Verteilung anhand der vorhandenen Meter und deren Position in bezug auf den Pfad des zu messenden Verkehrs, der Ressourcenauslastung der einzelnen Meter, sowie der Funktionalität der Meter. Auch die Messergebnisse vorangegangener Messungen können eine Änderung der Konfiguration veranlassen. So ist es z.B. möglich QoS-Werte zunächst mit einer relativ einfachen Messmethode nur grob zu erfassen (z.B. Erfassung der Round-Trip-Time statt des geforderten One-way-delays) und nur falls die ungenaueren Messwerte bestimmte Grenzwerte überschreiten, eine präziserer Messung (z.B. zur Bestimmung des One-way-delays) zu starten. Das Communication Module übernimmt die Verteilung der Meter-Policies an die einzelnen Meter und den Transport der gemessenen Werte von den Metern zum Collector. Der Meter Controller wertet die empfangenen Policies aus und wandelt sie in entsprechende Konfigurations-anweisungen für das jeweilige Meter sowie den Resource Monitor um. Der Resource Monitor misst die verfügbare Ressourcen auf dem Meter System (CPU-Auslastung, Speicher) und sendet diese in regelmäßigen Abständen an ein zentrales Repository und an den Meter Controller. Der Meter Controller ist in der Lage, lokal Maßnahmen bei einer kritischen Ressourcenauslastung zu ergreifen, z.B. lediglich priorisierte IP-Flows zu vermessen. Ermittelte Messwerte werden vom Meter Controller über das Record Converter Module an den Measurement Collector gesendet. Der Record Converter konvertiert die gemessenen Meter-spezifischen Records in ein standardisiertes Format. Der Measurement Collector speichert die empfangenen Werte in einem Repository. Wurden Daten für einen Kunden eines anderen Anbieters gemessen, werden im Accounting Record Generator Accounting Records generiert. Der AAA-Server sendet die Accounting Records dann an den AAA-Server des Kunden.

Umsetzung von SLA-Angaben in Meter Policies

Das folgende Beispiel verdeutlicht, wie SLA-Angaben in Meter-Policies umgesetzt werden. Die Meter-Informationen enthalten Ort, Typ und andere Kenngrößen der im Netz verfügbaren Meter. Die Nutzer-Informationen enthalten Informationen über den verwendeten Dienst und den anzuwendenden Tarif.

Diese Informationen werden vom Policy-Translator ausgewertet und daraus Meter-Policies generiert. Anhand der Flow-Angaben aus dem Kundenprofil und den benötigten Tarifvariablen aus der Tarif-Datei wird eine Klassifikationsregel für den Datenstrom des Nutzers generiert. Diese wird anhand der in den Meter Characteristics spezifizierten Adressen für Meter und Reader an die entsprechende Komponenten des Meter Systems übertragen. Auf diese Weise wird die neue Klassifikationsregel beim entsprechenden Meter eingefügt. Hierfür wurde eine einfache Meter-Policy-Sprache definiert, die das Setzen von Parametern sowie das Hinzufügen und Entfernen von Meter-Rules erlaubt. Da die Überprüfung der erbrachten Dienstleistung in der Regel Teil der Dienstleistungsvereinbarung ist, sollten SLAs präzise Angaben zur messtechnischen Ressourcenerfassung und Überprüfung der erbrachten Qualität enthalten. Mess-Parameter, die nicht durch das SLA vorgegeben sind, werden durch Voreinstellungen des Providers festgelegt.

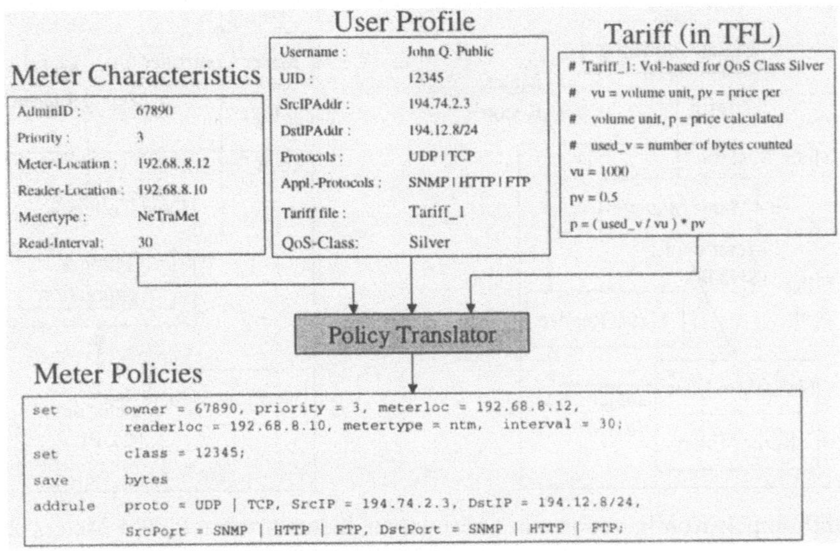

Abbildung 3: Umsetzung von SLA-Angaben (Kundenprofil und Tarif)
in Meter-Policies

Konfiguration unterschiedlicher Meter-Typen

Die Benutzung von Meter-Policies ermöglicht die einheitliche Konfiguration unterschiedlicher Meter-Typen. Die Meter-Policies werden vom Meter Controller in die für den entsprechenden Meter passende Konfiguration umgewandelt. Abbildung 4 zeigt die policy-basierte Konfiguration von zwei unterschiedlichen Meter-Typen (NeTraMet und Cisco NetFlow) dar.

Das NeTraMet Meter wurde zusätzlich erweitert, um den Klassifizierer mit einem Filter im Kernel (BPF) kombinieren zu können [CATZ00]. Policies können hierbei dazu benutzt werden, das Kernel-Filter so zu konfigurieren, dass Pakete von IP-Flows, die nicht gemessen werden sollen, gar nicht erst an den Klassifizierer im User Space weitergereicht werden. Hierdurch kann eine Überlastung des Meters vermieden werden. Die Meter-Policies für die relevanten Flows und die zu messenden Attribute werden vom Meter Controller in die Meter-spezifische Konfiguration (NeTraMet ruleset) übersetzt. Außerdem wird der Meter Reader, der die gemessenen Daten per SNMP ausliest, entsprechend konfiguriert. Während beim NeTraMet Meter konfiguriert werden kann, welche Flows gemessen werden, liefert das NetFlow Meter grundsätzlich Messergebnisse für alle Flows. Nicht benötigte Messergebnisse müssen verworfen werden. Meter Policies können im Meter Controller in Filter-Anweisungen für den Flow Collector umgewandelt. Der Meter selbst ist hier statisch und deshalb nicht von der Konfiguration betroffen.

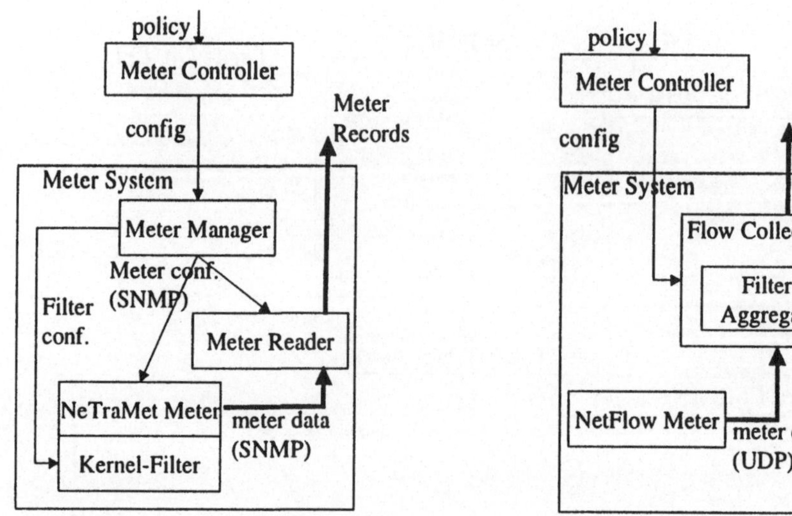

Abbildung 4: Konfiguration eines erweiterten, hierarchischen RTFM-Meters und eines erweiterten NetFlow-Meters

Verteilung der Messaufgaben und Sammeln der Messergebnisse

Zum Verteilen der Messaufgaben in Form von Meter-Policies und zum Sammeln der Messergebnisse in Form von Meter-Records wird eine Erweiterung des National Internet Measurement Infrastructure (NIMI) Systems verwendet [PaAM00]. NIMI stellt ein System zur Ansteuerung verschiedener Messtools dar. NIMI Probes stellen die Mess-Funktionen zur Verfügung, die über Kontroll-Instanzen konfiguriert und ausgelesen werden können. Die Ansteuerung der Messtools erfolgt zur Zeit über Skripte, die als NIMI-Wrapper dienen. NIMI unterstützt die Sammlung von Meter-Daten über das TCP-Protokoll und verfügt über Zugangskontrollmechanismen.

Durch Verteilung von Messaufgaben auf mehrere Meter lässt sich eine Überlastung einzelner Meter vermeiden. Wenn durch Aggregierung von IP-Flows sehr hohe Daten- und Paketraten anfallen, bei der die Leistung eines einzelnen Meters nicht ausreicht, so kann die gleiche Messaufgabe auf mehrere hierarchische Meter verteilt werden. Jedes beteiligte Meter muss hierbei nur noch einen Teil der IP-Flows vermessen, während die restlichen Flows jeweils durch ein Kernel-Filter entfernt werden können.

Messungen

Nachfolgend präsentieren wir Ergebnisse unserer Leistungsuntersuchungen unter Verwendung des NeTraMet-Meters. Wir demonstrieren den Einfluss unterschiedlicher Verkehrscharakteristiken auf die benötigten Meter-Ressourcen. Anschließend zeigen wir, wie bei unserer Erweiterung von NeTraMet die policy-basierte Konfiguration eines Kernel-Filters dazu genutzt werden kann, eine Überlastung des Meters zu vermeiden.

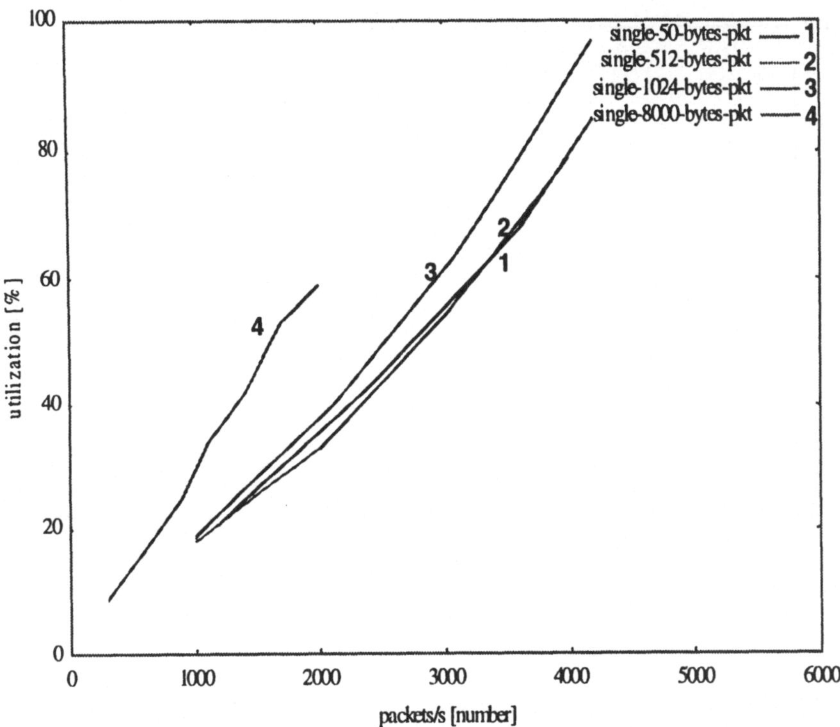

Abbildung 5: CPU-Last in Abhängigkeit der Paketrate für
unterschiedliche Paketgrößen (NeTraMet)

Die erste Messung wurde auf einer SUN Ultra 1 unter Solaris 2.6 durchgeführt. Zur Messung der CPU-Last wurde das Programm vmstat eingesetzt. Abbildung 5 zeigt das Anwachsen der CPU-Last eines Meters (NeTraMet) bei wachsender Paketrate für vier unterschiedliche Paketgrößen. Es wird deutlich, dass beim betrachteten Szenario die Leistungsfähigkeit des Meters in erster Linie von der Paketrate abhängt. Die Paketgröße und damit auch die Datenrate hat demgegenüber einen deutlich geringeren Einfluss. Dieses Ergebnis entspricht den Erwartungen, da die Verarbeitungsschritte beim Metering sich überwiegend auf den Paketkopf beziehen, und weil die Anzahl der Kontextwechsel des Betriebssystems mit wachsender Paketrate zunimmt.

Die zweite Messung wurde auf einem PC unter FreeBSD (Filtering mit BPF im Kernel) durchgeführt. Abbildung 6 zeigt das Experiment, bei dem Accounting durch ein hierarchisches Meter (NeTraMet mit aktiviertem BPF-Kernel-Filter) durchgeführt wird. Variiert wird hierbei die Anzahl der Flows, die durch das Kernel-Filter herausgefiltert werden. Die Anzahl der vorhandenen IP-Flows ist konstant. Der NeTraMet-Prozess im User-Bereich muss hierbei nur die Flows verarbeiten, die durch den Kernel nicht herausgefiltert werden. Bei sinkender Anzahl herausgefilterter IP-Flows nimmt die Systemlast des Benutzerprozesses, und damit auch die gesamte CPU-Last zu. Das Experiment zeigt, dass bei geeigneter Konfiguration des Kernel-Filters sowie der Filter-Regeln im User-Bereich eine Überlast einzelner Meter abgewendet werden kann.

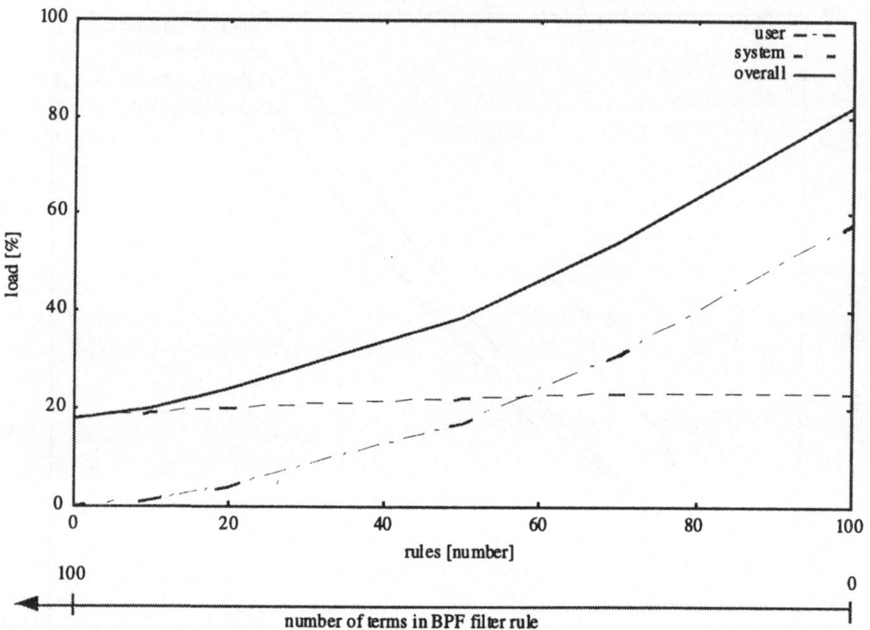

Abbildung 6: CPU-Last in Abhängigkeit der Filterregeln in Userspace und Kernel (NeTraMet mit BPF-Erweiterung)

Zusammenfassung und Ausblick

In IP-Netzen mit differenzierter Dienstqualität fallen vielfältige Messaufgaben an, um verursachergerechte Tarifierung, sowie eine Überprüfung von Dienstqualitätsparametern zu ermöglichen. Wir stellen für die hierzu erforderliche Messinfrastruktur eine Architektur für policy-basiertes Metering vor, die geeignet ist, einen Accounting-Dienst konform mit der generischen AAA-Architektur [Laat00] der IRTF-AAAARCH-Gruppe zu realisieren. Ein Policy-Translator setzt SLA-Angaben mit Kundenprofil und Tarifformel in Meter-Policies um, die von einem Task-Distributor an geeignete Meter weitergeleitet werden. Aus Ausdrücken der Meter-Policy-Sprache werden Meter-spezifische Konfigurationsinformationen generiert. In zukünftigen Arbeiten wird untersucht, inwieweit sich SLA Angaben in Abhängigkeit von den Eigenschaften der verfügbaren Meter in Meter Policies umsetzen lassen.

Die Verwendung von Meter-Policies erlaubt eine effiziente Verwaltung von Netzen mit heterogenen Messkomponenten.

Bei dem erweiterten, auf NeTraMet basierenden hierarchischen RTFM-Meter kann ein Kernel-Filter so konfiguriert werden, dass auch bei begrenzten Systemressourcen eine Überlastung des Meters vermieden werden kann. Messergebnisse für das NeTraMet-Meter zeigen, dass hohe Paket-Raten zu einer Überlastung des Meters führen können und wie sich durch geeignete Konfiguration eines Kernel-Filters die CPU-Last des Meters verringern läßt.

Ein flexibles Meters für Accounting und QoS-Messungen basierend auf dem Linux Klassifizierer Netfilter, das sich über Policies ansteuern läßt, ist zur Zeit in Entwicklung. Eine erste Vergleichs-Messung mit NeTraMet zeigte bereits eine deutlich bessere Leistungsfähigkeit des Linux-Klassifizierers.

Die vorgestellte Architektur für policy-basiertes Metering erweist sich somit als geeignet, um eine heterogene, flexible und leistungsfähige Messinfrastruktur in IP-Netzen bereitzustellen. Im Rahmen des von DFN-Verein und deutscher Telekom geförderten Projektes QUASAR wird die Eignung der policy-basierten IP-Meter-Architektur für das G-WIN untersucht werden.

Literaturangaben

[AbAH00] Bernard Aboba, Jari Arkko, David Harrington, "Introduction to Accounting Management", <draft-ietf-aaa-acct-03.txt>, Work in Progress, 2 May 2000

[BaGP94] Mary L. Bailey, Burra Gopal, Michael A. Pagels, Larry L. Peterson, Prasenjit Sarkar: PATHFINDER. A Pattern-Based Packet Classifier, In Proceedings of the 1rst Symposium on Operating System Design and Implementation, Monterey, California, November 1994. (BGP+94)

[BeSB00] Y. Bernet, A. Smith, S. Blake, D. Grossman, "A Conceptual Model for Diffserv Routers", draft-ietf-diffserv-model-03.txt, Work in Progress, May 2000

[BrBl00] Nevil Brownlee, Alan Blount, "Accounting Attributes and Record Formats", Internet-Draft draft-ietf-aaa-accounting-attributes-03.txt, Work in Progress, 14 April 2000

[CaHZ99] Georg Carle, Felix Hartanto, Michael Smirnow, Tanja Zseby, "Charging and Accounting for QoS-enhanced IP Multicast", IFIP Sixth International Workshop on Protocols For High-Speed Networks (PfHSN '99), August 25-27, 1999, Salem, MA, U.S.A.

[CaMM98] Massimiliano Canosa, Martino De Marco, Alessandro Maiocchi, "Traffic accounting mechanism for Internet Integrated Services", Technical Report, CEFRIEL, Politecnico di Milano, 1998

[CATZ00] Georg Carle, Jens Tiemann and Tanja Zseby. Assessment of accounting Meters with Dynamic Traffic Generation based on Classification Rules. The First Passive and Active Measurement Workshop (PAM2000), pages 127-133. Hamilton, New Zealand, April 2000.

[CaZZ00] G. Carle, S. Zander, T.Zseby, Policy-based Accounting, draft-irtf-aaaarch-pol-acct-00.txt, Work in Progress, June 2000

[Cisc99] NetFlow Services and Applications, White Paper, Cisco Systems, 1999

[EnKa96] D. Engler, M. F. Kaashoek, DPF: Dynamic Code Generation Packet Filter, SIGCOMM 96, pp. 53-59.

[GuMc99] Pankaj Gupta and Nick McKeown: Packet Classification on Multiple Fields, Proc. ACM Special Interest Group on Data Communication - SIGCOMM 1999, Cambridge, Massachusetts, USA, September 1999

[Laat00] C. de Laat, G. Gross, L. Gommans, J. Vollbrecht, D. Spence, "Generic AAA Architecture", draft-irtf-aaaarch-generic-01.txt, Work in Progress, March 2000

[NARUS] NARUS Building the business of the Internet:Technical Note: NARUS System, http://www.narus.com

[Netf00] The Netfilter Project HomePage: http://www.samba.org/netfilter/

[PaAM00] Vern Paxson, Andrew K. Adams and Matt Mathis, "Experiences with NIMI", Passive & Active Measurement Workshop PAM 2000, Hamilton, New Zealand, April 2000

[RFC2063] N. Brownlee, C. Mills, G. Ruth, "Traffic Flow Measurement: Architecture", RFC2063, IETF, Jan. 1997

[ShSt00] Syed Shaah and P. Steenkiste, "Cooperative Metering for Receiver Initiated Service Level Agreements", Proceedings of NOSSDAV 2000, Chapel Hill, North Carolina, U.S.A., June 2000

[Voll00a] John Vollbrecht, et al, "AAA Authorization Framework", draft-irtf-aaaarch-authorization-framework-00.txt, January 2000

[Voll00b] John Vollbrecht et al., "AAA Authorization Application Examples", draft-irtf-aaaarch-authorization-apps-00.txt, Work in Progress, Jan. 2000.

PCR Policing: A Comparison of Fuzzy Policers Versus GCRA

Lorenzo Battaglia[1], Francisco Guardado[2], Ulrich Killat[1]

[1] Department of Communication Networks, AB 4-06, Technical University of
Hamburg-Harburg, Denickestr. 17, D-21073 Hamburg, Germany (e-mail
Postmaster@Battaglia.de, Killat@TU-Harburg.de; Tel.: +49 40 42878 3249;
FAX: +49 40 42878 2941).
[2] Alcatel SEL AG (e-mail F.Guardado@alcatel.de).

Abstract. Any Call Admission Control algorithm and any Network Dimensioning depend on the reliability of the chosen Usage Parameter Control algorithm. The standardized ATM Usage Parameter Control algorithm is the GCRA. An ideal ATM PCR policer should guarantee a very low cell loss probability (10^{-9}) for the cells of a well-behaved user and police contract violation as rigidly as possible. All this independently of the characteristics of the monitored stream and of the background traffic. In this paper we compare the selectivity performance and the dynamic behaviour of the GCRA to those of one of the most famous Fuzzy Policers. This, in a realistic scenario: the PCR policing of a video stream passing through an ATM multiplexer, with a self-similar background traffic.

1 Introduction

Call Admission Control (CAC), Network Dimensioning and Usage Parameter Control (UPC) are very important issues in ATM technology. They all depend on how input traffic is described and on how cell streams' characteristics change when passing through an ATM queueing system. CAC and Network Dimensioning strongly depend on the reliability of the chosen UPC algorithm. The standardized ATM UPC algorithm is the Generic Cell Rate Algorithm (GCRA). The GCRA depends on two parameters: the Increment I and the Limit L.

One of the main criteria to dimension an ATM policer is to minimize cell loss. The loss of a single ATM cell would cause the loss of a higher layer's packet, resulting in wasted bandwidth and loss of QoS. At the same time it is very important for the network provider that any malicious user is policed as rigidly as possible. Any charging system as well as any network dimensioning to guarantee a desired QoS and any CAC algorithm is valid only if all cell streams entering the network do comply with the traffic contract. An ideal ATM policer should then guarantee a very low cell loss probability (10^{-9}) for the cells of a well-behaved user and police contract violation as rigidly as possible. This property is called selectivity. An ideal policer shall be selective independently of the characteristics of the monitored stream and of the cell delay variations due to the other ATM applications whose cells pass through the same ATM queueing systems (see Fig.1). When a source sends at a higher rate than negotiated, a policer shall also react fast. It has to quickly reach such a rejection ratio of the monitored cells, that the rate of the stream let into the netwotk is at most the negotiated one. How fast the policer reacts is called dynamic behaviour. To be able to protect all network resources, the policing function must be located as close as possible to the actual traffic source [24] and obviously be under direct control of the network provider. Since this function must be available for every connection during the entire active phase and must operate in real time, the policing algorithm used must be fast, simple and cost-effective.

Since the dimensioning of GCRA parameters was left to the user without clear guidelines, several alternative policing methods have been introduced in the literature. Most of them have been evaluated against their capability to enforce the Peak Cell Rate (PCR) of ON-OFF sources. All have been compared to the GCRA. Fuzzy Logic [13]-[16], Neural Networks [28] and Finite State Automata [22] control methods have been presented. Even "improved" versions of the GCRA [3], [5], [19], [20] have been tested. Of all the alternative policers, the Fuzzy Logic-based one presented in [15], that we in the sequel denote by FP, was recognized to be the best one. Simulation results based on the assumption that the monitored stream at the output of a multiplexer can be described as a renewal process had shown that the FP performs better than the GCRA, in terms of selectivity and dynamic behaviour. This renewal assumption is clearly unrealistic. Therefore we decided to compare the selectivity performance and the dynamic PCR policing behaviour of the GCRA to those of the FP, in a realistic scenario. We didn't try to describe the monitored stream at the output of a multiplexer through a simplified model. Nor did we choose a cushy unrealistc background traffic: we used realistic Long Range Dependent (LRD) traffic. This paper is organized as follows. We model the problem (Section II), recall some important concepts of the GCRA (Section III), present the FP (Section IV) and finally compare their performances (Section V).

2 Modelling the problem

Figure 1 shows the ATM PCR policing reference model [4]. A user network consists of a FIFO multiplexer with N input lines and one output link equipped with a buffer of length B. Time slots on each of the input lines are of the same length and synchronized to each other.

Every new cell is assumed to arrive at the beginning of a slot and can be transmitted at once if no predecessor exists. The output of the multiplexer is sent to the provider's User Network Interface (UNI) and passes through the Network Termination (NT) before entering the network. In the NT the PCR of each connection is policed by a GCRA.

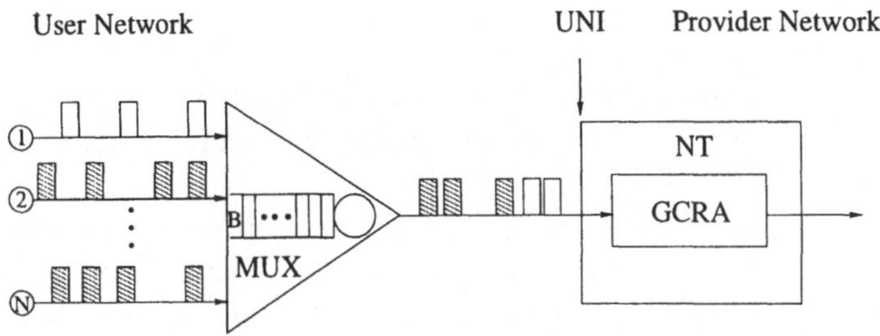

Fig. 1. The ATM PCR policing reference model. The unmarked cells belong to the monitored connection.

3 The Generic Cell Rate Algorithm

We assume the reader to be familiar with the GCRA and only briefly recall some useful concepts. In the ensuing discussion we refer to a $GCRA(I, L)$ for the monitored stream. Let's consider a possible realisation of the departure process of a monitored stream from an ATM queueing system. Let's denote by $t_a(i)$ the discrete time instant in which the ith cell of the monitored stream arrives at the policer and by $TAT(i)$ its Theoretical Arrival Time. Whenever $t_a(i) > TAT(i)$ the cell is accepted and the following TAT is given by

$$TAT(i + 1) = t_a(i) + I.$$

If $t_a(i) \leq TAT(i)$ the cell is accepted if

$$TAT(i) - L \leq t_a(i)$$

holds and the new TAT is given by

$$TAT(i + 1) = TAT(i) + I.$$

In [6] we showed that setting I to the inverse of the negotiated PCR and L to the buffer length B, transforms the GCRA into an ideal PCR policer. We used this dimensioning for our simulations.

4 The FP

Fuzzy logic fascinates for its capacity to capture human expertize and to formalize approximate reasoning processes. For this reason it was also investigated if fuzzy logic can be a good answer to the many challenges of UPC. Before going into details, a short insight into fuzzy logic will be provided.

4.1 Fundamentals of Fuzzy Logic

Fuzzy logic is more based on quality than on quantity. It allows a system to make rational decisions in complex and not clearly defined environments. It is based on the concepts of fuzzy sets and linguistic variables.

Let U be the universe of discourse. A fuzzy set F is represented as a set of ordered pairs $(u, m_F(u))$, where u is a generic element of U and $m_F(u)$ is its degree of membership. The membership function assumes values in the interval $[0, 1]$. A linguistic variable x in U is characterized by a set $W(x) = (W_{1x}, ..., W_{nx})$ and a set $M(x) = (M_{1x}, ..., M_{nx})$. $W(x)$ is the term-set, the set of names the linguistic variable x can assume. It is constructed by means of primary terms, e.g. *high, medium, low*, and modifiers, e.g. *very, quite*, which can be placed before the primary terms according to a defined syntax. Each W_{ix} is a fuzzy set, with a membership function M_{ix}. Linguistic variables can be used to form propositions with operators OR, AND, and NOT, and with conditional rules of the type IF...THEN..., to formalize the empirical rules by which a human operator is able to describe a process. A fuzzy controller is basically defined through the definition of

1. inputs and outputs,
2. the way fuzzification of the inputs is performed,
3. which fuzzy outputs correspond to which fuzzy inputs,
4. the way defuzzification of the output is performed.

A fuzzy controller, then, receives a set of numbers as inputs, transforms them into qualitative fuzzy inputs (fuzzification), decides which fuzzy outputs are the right ones and finally produces output numbers (defuzzification), using the (few) numbers obtained through the fuzzification of the inputs.

4.2 The Fuzzy Policer

The proposed fuzzy policer allows a maximum number N_i of cells that can be accepted in the window i, of length W. This policer has three input variables and one output variable. At the end of the ith window, the input variables are

- A_{oi}, the average number of cell arrivals per window since the start of the connection,
- A_i, the number of cell arrivals in the ith window,
- N_i, the number of cells that at most would have been accepted during the last window,

and the output variable is

- ΔN_{i+1}, the variation to be made to the threshold N_{i+1}, the threshold of window $i + 1$.

The variable A_{oi} gives an idea about the long-term trend of the source, A_i indicates its current behaviour, and N_i shows if the source is fully using its credit or not.

The input variables are fuzzified in three categories: Low (L), Medium (M), and High (H). For the output variable, seven categories are proposed: Zero (Z), Positive Small (PS), Positive Medium (PM), Positive Big (PB), Negative Small (NS), Negative Medium (NM), and Negative Big (NB). The membership functions for each variable are depicted in figures 2, 3, and 4. The membership functions for the input variables are used to fuzzify. That of the output variable, to defuzzify.

A thorough description of this system is out of the scope of this manuscript. For our purposes, it's enough to cite that this model, comprising the control rules and the term sets of the variables with their related fuzzy sets, was obtained through a tuning process, that had the task to make a generic source respect the negotiated cell rate.

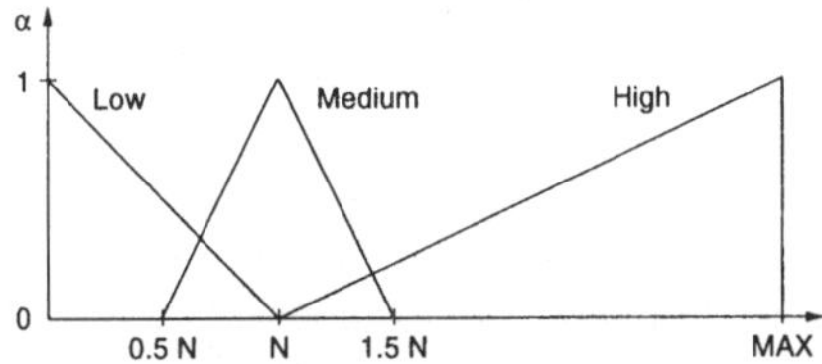

Fig. 2. Membership function for the A_{oi} and A_i input variables.

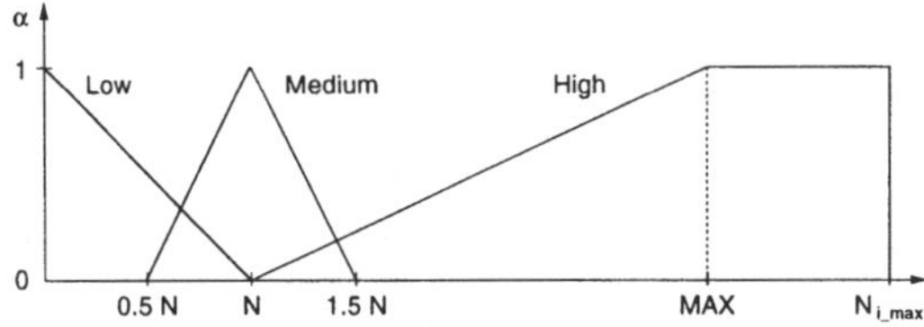

Fig. 3. Membership function for the N_i input variable.

Table 1 shows the fuzzy conditional rules of the policer. There, each of the possible 27 input configurations (three variables each with three possible values) is mapped to the corresponding ΔN_{i+1} output (seven possible values). The authors show that only 18 of these 27 configurations can occur. These rules are the core of the policer. For details we refer to [15].

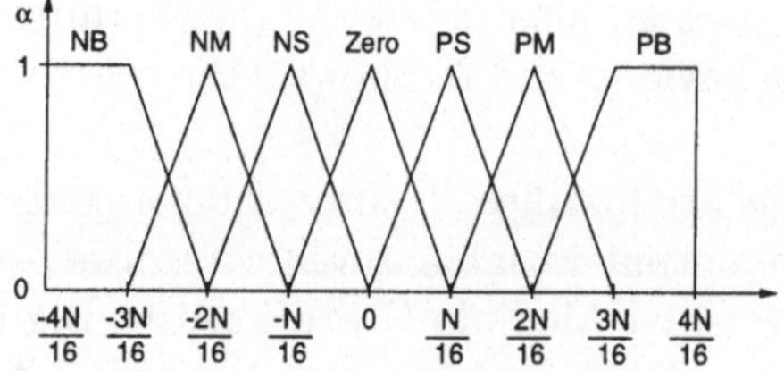

Fig. 4. Membership function for the ΔN_{i+1} output variable.

	A_{oi}	N_i	A_i	ΔN_{i+i}
1	L	H	L	PB
2	L	H	M	PS
3	L	H	H	Z
4	M	M	L	PB
5	M	M	M	PS
6	M	M	H	Z
7	M	H	L	PB
8	M	H	M	Z
9	M	H	H	NB
10	H	L	L	PB
11	H	L	M	PM
12	H	L	H	PS
13	H	M	L	PB
14	H	M	M	PM
15	H	M	H	Z
16	H	H	L	NS
17	H	H	M	NM
18	H	H	H	NB

Table 1. Fuzzy Policer Rules

5 Performance Comparison

We decided to compare the performance of these two policers in a real environment. We chose then to simulate the policing of a source connected to a Gbit/sec ATM network, through a multiplexer at the user side. In order not to be dependent on an arbitrarily chosen number of input lines to the multiplexer, we considered, as e.g. [18], a multiplexer with one input fed by the monitored source S and one multi-input, fed by a source which, alone, simulates the background traffic. As monitored source we considered the worst case for a source having a negotiated PCR, i.e. a CBR sending at rate PCR. We assumed the source has a rate of 2 Mbit/sec, which could nowadays be accepted as video rate. About the background traffic model: it is widely recognized that traditional traffic models developed for circuit-switched and early data networks have failed to capture the complexity of the traffic observed in today's networks. Traditional traffic models assumed independence between successive arrivals (Poissonian Process, PP). Due to the discovery of the role correlation plays, models like the Markov Modulated Poisson Process (MMPP) were proposed. Those could capture the short-range correlation structure. Today's traffic exhibits a long-range correlation structure, with a far bigger burstiness. We used then as background traffic generating source the Sup-FRP [25]. This source was successfully employed as a flexible, high-speed fractal ATM traffic generator on a real-time traffic generation and monitoring system built in Columbia University [26]. We dimensioned the source so to generate what mostly measured in high speed networks: a LRD traffic with a Hurst parameter $H = 0.8$. As load, it was chosen a background traffic load of 80% of the link rate. The buffer length B was set to 300. The window size W of the FP was set to ten times the period of the monitored source. This value gave the best results for both performance measures, selectivity and dynamic behaviour.

5.1 Selectivity Performance

From a user point of view, the policer has to discard no cell of a complying source. From a provider point of view, the policing mechanism has to rigidly police any misbehaving source. These two requirements translate to what Fig. 5 shows. On the x-axis is the ratio of the used rate over the negotiated rate. On the y-axis is the rejection ratio, i.e. the ratio of the number of discarded cells over the total number of cells sent. In the region with abscissa bigger than one, the curve is the plot of the lowest rejection ratio a policer shall guarantee in the case the source uses more bandwidth than negotiated. Any source using less than its assigned rate shall not experience any losses in the policer. This holds also for a source using exactly its rate, note the vertical asymptote at one. Any source exceeding its assigned rate shall experience losses of at least the excessive rate. Let's consider, for instance, a source constantly using twice its assigned bandwidth. Over any interval of time, it will then send twice the amount of acceptable cells. That means that at least 50% of the sent cells has to be discarded, which is exactly what the curve shows at abscissa two.

As in [15] we measured the policer selectivity right after the source has emitted 1500 cells. The FP proved to fairly approximate the solid curve. The GCRA almost exactly approximates it, at all measured points. The FP rejection probability for the cells of a misbehaving source is always lower than that of the GCRA. If the monitored source uses 1.1 times the negotiated rate, for instance, virtually no cells are discarded by the FP. Our analyses in [6] showed that with our dimensioning the GCRA discards no cells of a well-behaved user. No analytical results are available for the FP in this case. In longer (feasible) simulations (10^6 cells), the FP didn't discard any cell of a well-behaved user. All the given simulation results were obtained with a 95% confidence interval of the true value. This interval is so slight to be already included in the marker vertical dimension.

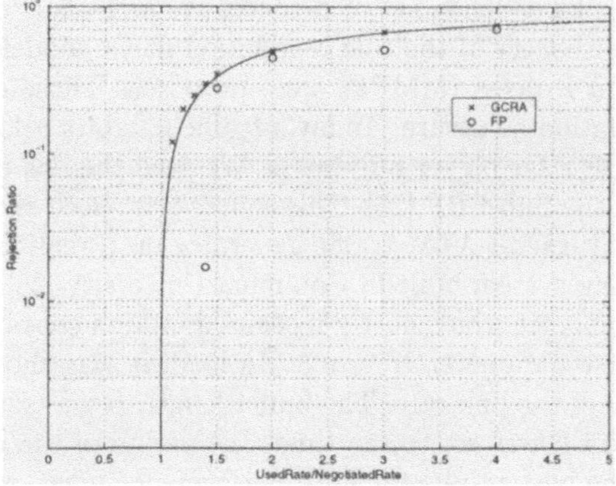

Fig. 5. Selectivity performance versus cell rate variations.

5.2 Dynamic Behaviour

A further requirement for a policer is its speed in detecting misbehaviour. Ideally, it should react already from the second cell a source sends. Figure 6 shows the time response of both policers if the monitored source sends at twice the negotiated rate. This dynamic behaviour remains qualitative identical also if the source emits at a different (higher than negotiated) rate. Both policers proved to be robust, also in this case the curves were obtained with a 95% confidence interval of the true value. This interval is so slight to be already included in the line width. The FP reacts slowly to contract violation, whereas the GCRA behaviour is practically ideal.

6   Conclusions

We have compared the selectivity performances and the dynamic behaviours of the GCRA and of the FP in a realistic scenario: the PCR monitoring a video source with a negotiated peak rate of 2 Mbits/sec, whose cells pass through an ATM multiplexer connected to a Gbit/sec ATM network. As background traffic we used realistic LRD traffic with $H = 0.8$ and a link utilization of 80%. Both policers proved to be robust and to perform reliably. The GCRA, however, performs better. It has an almost ideal selectivity performance and quickly reaches the necessary rejection probability when a source misbehaves. The problem of monitoring and enforcing a traffic contract is not limited to ATM networks but is also a corner stone in the Differentiated Services Arquitecture of QoS over IP networks, which, therefore can also benefit from our results.

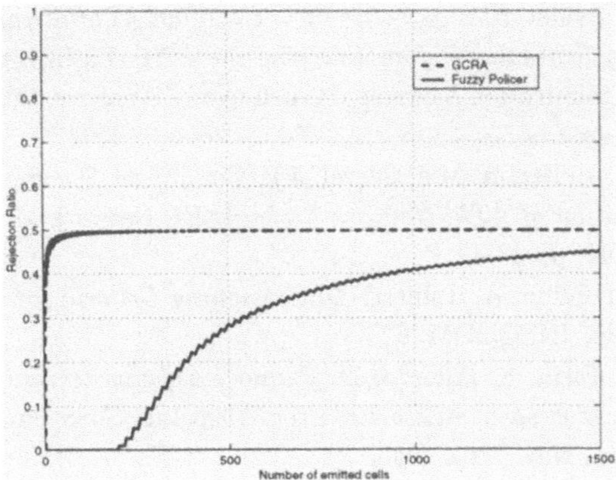

Fig. 6. Dynamic behaviour if the source sends at twice the negotiated rate.

References

1. R. Ahmad, *Next Generation of Broadband Network Architectures-Traffic Flow Control and End-to-End Performance*, IFIP ATM '98, 20th-22nd July 1998, Craiglands Hotel, Ilkley, UK.
2. G. Ascia, V. Catania, *A VLSI parallel architecture for fuzzy expert systems*, Int. J. Pattern Recognition Artificial Intelligence, vol. 9, no. 2, 1995.
3. A. Atlasis, G. Stassinopulos, A. Vasilakos, *Leaky bucket mechanism with learning algorithm for ATM traffic policing*, IEEE Symp. on Comp. and Commun. - Proc. 1997. IEEE Los Alamitos, CA, pp 68-72
4. ATM Forum, Traffic Management Specification, Version 4.0, af-tm-0056.000, April 1996.
5. W. Bao, S. Cheng, *Parameter adaptation mechanism for ATM traffic policing*, Chinese Journal of Electronics, vol. 6, no. 1, Jan. 1997.
6. L. Battaglia, Z. Bažanowski, U. Killat *Dimensioning GCRA Parameters to Fairly Police a CBR Stream Passing an ATM Multiplexer Equipped with a Traffic Shaper*, Proceedings IFIP ATM '98, 20th-22nd July 1998, Ilkley, UK.
7. L. Battaglia, U. Killat *QoS of IP over ATM: The PCR and ACR Policing Issue*, IEEE IWS '99, 18th-20th Feb. 1999, Osaka University Convention Center, Japan.
8. L. Battaglia, U. Killat *How to Dimension two Sets of GCRA Parameters to Fairly Police PCR and SCR of Connections Passing an ATM Multiplexer*, AEÜ, International Journal of Electronics and Communications, 53 (1999) No. 3, 129-134, Urban & Fischer Verlag.
9. L. Battaglia, U. Killat *On the PCR Policing of an Arbitrary Stream Passing Through a Private ATM Network Before Reaching the Public UNI*, IFIP TC 6 Fifth Int. Conf. on Broadband Communications '99, 10th-12th Nov. 1999, Hong Kong, Kluwer Academic Publishers.

10. L. Battaglia, U. Killat *How to Police the PCR of an ATM Stream Passing Through a Fair Queueing Scheduler Before Entering the UNI*, Eigth International Conference on Telecommunication Systems, Modeling and Analysis, 9th-12th March 2000, Nashville, Tennessee.

11. P. Boyer, F.M. Guillemin, M.J. Servel, J.P. Coudreuse *Spacing Cells Protects and Enhances Utilization of ATM Network Links*, IEEE Network Magazine, Vol. 6, No. 5, September 1992, pp 38-49.

12. P. Castelli, A. Forcina, A. Tonietti *Dimensioning Criteria for Policing Functions in ATM Networks*, INFOCOM '92.

13. V. Catania, G. Ficili, S. Palazzo, D. Panno, *A fuzzy decision maker for source traffic control in high speed networks*, Proc. 1995 Int. Conf. on Network Protocols (ICNP 95), Tokyo, Nov. 7-10, 1995.

14. V. Catania, G. Ficili, S. Palazzo, D. Panno, *A fuzzy expert system for Usage Parameter Control in ATM networks*, Proc. GLOBECOM '95, Singapore, Nov. 13-17, 1995.

15. V. Catania, G. Ficili, S. Palazzo, D. Panno, *A Comparative Analysis of Fuzzy Versus Conventional Policing Mechanisms for ATM Networks*, IEEE/ACM Transactions on Networking, Vol. 4, no. 3, June 1996.

16. C. Douligeris and G. Develekos, *A Fuzzy Logic Approach to Congestion Control in ATM Networks*, Proc. IEEE ICC '95, Seattle, WA, June 1995.

17. J. Heinanen, F. Baker, W. Weiss and J. Wroklawski, *Assured Forwarding PHB Group*, Internet Draft, January 1999.

18. F. Huebner, *Dimensioning of a Peak Cell Rate Monitor Algorithm Using Discrete-Time Analysis*, ITC 14 / J. Labetoulle and J.W. Roberts (Editors).

19. Z. Jiang, Z. Liu *Improved algorithm of usage parameter control in ATM networks*, Int. Conf. on Commun. Tech. Proc., ICCT vol. 1, 1996. IEEE, Piscataway, NJ, pp 24-27.

20. Z. Jiang, Z. Liu *Fuzzy leaky bucket for policing mechanism in ATM networks*, Neural Networks for Signal Processing. Proc. IEEE Workshop 1996, Piscataway, NJ, pp 510-517.

21. K. Kang, B. Steyaert and C. Kim *Service Separation in ATM Networks Using a Hardware Efficient Rate-Controlled Cell Multiplexer*, ITC 16 Proceedings, Elsevier Science 1999.

22. L. Mason, A. Pelletier, J. Lapointe *Toward optimal policing in ATM networks*, Computer Communications, vol. 19, no. 3, Mar 1996, pp 194-204.

23. R. O. Onvural, *Asyncronous Transfer Mode Networks: Performance Issues*, Norwood, MA: Artech House, 1994.

24. E. P. Rathgeb, *Modeling and Performance Comparison of Policing Mechanisms for ATM Networks*, IEEE J. Select. Areas Commun. vol. 9, no. 3, pp. 325-334, Apr. 1991.

25. B. K. Ryu, S. B. Lowen, *Point Process Approach to the Modelling and Analysis of Self-Similar Traffic: Part I - Model Construction*, in Proc. IEEE INFOCOM'96, San Francisco, March 1996.

26. B. K. Ryu, *Fractal Network Traffic: From Understanding to Implications*, PhD Thesis, Columbia University, 1996.

27. J. Sairamesh and N. Shroff, *Limitations and pitfalls of leaky bucket, a study with video traffic*, Proc. 3rd Int. Conf. Comput. Commun. Networks, Sept. 1994.

28. A. Tarraf, I. Ibrahim, and T. Saadawi, *A novel neural network traffic enforcement mechanism for ATM networks*, IEEE J. Select. Areas Commun., vol. 12, no. 6, pp. 1088-1096, Aug. 1994.

Wegewahl in hierarchischen Netzen: Erweiterte Gütebewertung

Peter Jocher, Andreas Kaspar und Bernhard Quendt

Lehrstuhl für Kommunikationsnetze, TU München, Arcisstr. 21, D-80333 München
{Jocher,Kaspar}@lkn.ei.tum.de

Siemens AG, Hofmannstr. 51, D-81359 München
Bernhard.Quendt@icn.siemens.de

Abstract. Die prognostizierte Entwicklung des Internets macht deutlich, dass die zukünftigen Kommunikationsnetze eine immer größere Zahl an Teilnehmern und Verkehr bewältigen müssen. Damit die Verkehrslenkungsverfahren ihre Aufgaben in einem solchen Umfeld in skalierbarer Weise bewältigen können, empfiehlt es sich, Netzzustandsinformationen hierarchisch zu strukturieren. Das ATM-Forum hat im Bereich privater Netze mit der Anfang 1996 veröffentlichten Spezifikation des Private Network-to-Network Interface (PNNI) [1] bereits einen Schritt in diese Richtung unternommen. Ein physikalisches Netz wird dort sukzessive in Gruppen untergliedert und in weitere virtuelle Ebenen abstrahiert, um zu einer hierarchischen Netzabbildung zu gelangen. Dadurch wird es möglich, dass ein einzelner Vermittlungsknoten nicht mehr das vollständige Netz kennen muss, sondern auf Basis einer reduzierten Teilsicht seine Verkehrslenkungsaufgaben durchführt.

Die mit der Hierarchisierung einhergehende Reduzierung der Netzzustandsinformationen hat einen Genauigkeitsverlust zur Folge. Er erfordert effiziente Aggregationsverfahren, die ein ausgewogenes Verhältnis zwischen der Verringerung der Datenmenge und der damit einhergehenden Unschärfe in der Datenbasis erreichen. In einer früheren Veröffentlichung [2] wurden bereits erste Gütebewertungen für zwei ausgewählte Aggregationsverfahren - die Simple Node Representation [1] und die Full Mesh Representation [6] - anhand einfacher regelmäßig strukturierter Modellnetze vorgestellt. Durch Erweiterungen in der verwendeten Messsoftware sind nun auch Untersuchungen an unregelmäßig strukturierten Netzen möglich geworden. Die dabei gewonnenen Ergebnisse werden in diesem Beitrag vorgestellt und einer kritischen Bewertung unterzogen.

Einleitung

Verteilte, multimediale Anwendungen führen zu einem erheblich ansteigenden Datenaustausch zwischen den beteiligten Netzeinheiten und Endgeräten. Wegewahl- bzw. Routing-Verfahren, die die optimalen Datentransportpfade über ein Kommunikationsnetz bestimmen, sind vor diesem Hintergrund von großer Bedeutung.

Das ATM-Forum hat Anfang 1996 die Spezifikation des Private Network-to-Network Interface (PNNI) veröffentlicht (vgl. [1]) und damit eine skalierbare und flexible Routing-Architektur bereitgestellt.

Durch die Verwendung einer quellenbasierten, dynamischen Wegewahl (Source-Routing) kann PNNI auf Änderungen im Netz reagieren und schleifenfrei Verbindungen aufbauen. Vorraussetzung dafür ist, dass die aktuellen Netzzustandsinformationen im Quellknoten vorliegen. In großen Netzen kann dies schnell zu einem intensiven Datenaustausch sowie zu Speicherplatz- und Zeitproblemen führen. Deshalb werden die benötigten Topologieinformationen in jedem Knoten in Form eines hierarchisch strukturierten Netzabbildes gespeichert. Da die einzelnen Ebenen durch eine sukzessive Gruppierung und Aggregation von Teilnetzen entstehen, sind die Informationen über entfernte Bereiche auf höheren Hierarchieebenen angesiedelt und damit stark zusammengefasst.

Durch ein erweitertes, sogenanntes hierarchisches Source-Routing-Prinzip werden dann, ausgehend von den Quellknoten, die Wege zu den Zielen mit abnehmendem Detaillierungsgrad festgelegt.

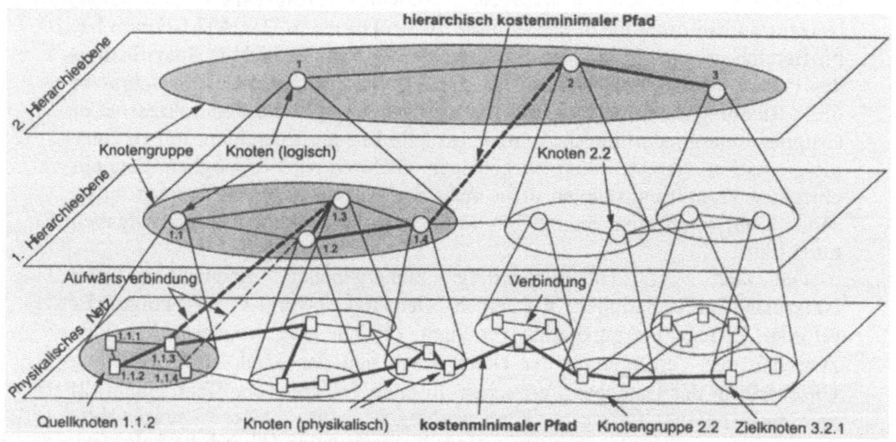

Abb. 1. PNNI-Beispielnetz mit zwei Hierarchieebenen

Wie beispielhaft in Abbildung 1 zu sehen ist, bildet das physikalische Netz mit seinen Vermittlungsknoten die unterste Ebene. Die einzelnen Knoten sind Gruppen zugeordnet, die auf der darüber liegenden Ebene zu einem Knoten zusammengefasst werden. Die rekursive Anwendung dieses Prinzips führt letztlich zu einem vollständigen hierarchischen Abbild, von dem die physikalischen Knoten aber nur eine Teilsicht besitzen.

In Abbildung 1 sind die Bereiche grau hervorgehoben, die der Knoten 1.1.2 und seine Gruppenmitglieder kennt. Die Aufwärtsverbindungen (Uplinks) markieren diejenigen Knoten bzw. Gruppen, die physikalische Verbindungen zu hierarchisch entfernteren Abschnitten unterhalten.

Basierend auf seiner hierarchischen Netzsicht nähert ein Quellknoten den kostenminimalen Pfad zu einem Ziel durch einen hierarchisch kostenminimalen Pfad an. Dieser setzt sich aus einer Kette von Teilpfaden auf den betroffenen Ebenen und den sie verbindenden Uplinks zusammen. Für das Knotenpaar 1.1.2-3.2.1 ist in

Abbildung 1 der kostengünstigste Pfad im physikalischen Netz und der hierarchische Pfad der Netzsicht hervorgehoben. Letzterer besteht aus den Pfadabschnitten 1.1.2-1.1.3, 1.3-1.2-1.4 und 2-3.

Die Gruppierung von Netzbereichen und deren Zusammenfassung sind die Kernprozesse bei der Bildung einer hierarchischen Netzsicht und beeinflussen die Wegewahl maßgeblich. Wie leicht einzusehen ist, sinkt die Güte der hierarchischen Wegewahl mit wachsender Informationsreduktion, da die Kosten für die Durchquerung von Teilnetzen und für Wegeabschnitte zu Zielknoten im Inneren von Teilnetzen immer ungenauer abgeschätzt werden können.

Die Gruppenbildung wurde bereits ansatzweise unter dem Aspekt der Routing-Komplexität in [3] und weiterführend in [4] untersucht, während sich [5] mit der optimalen Aufteilung lokaler Netze in Verkehrsbereiche befasst hat. Vorschläge für Aggregationsverfahren finden sich in [1, 6].

Vorliegender Beitrag möchte, basierend auf den Erkenntnissen aus [2], weiterführende Gütebewertungen der hierarchischen Wegewahl in Abhängigkeit der Netzzusammenfassung vorstellen. Neben dem Grad der Hierarchisierung, ausgedrückt durch die Zahl der Hierarchieebenen eines Netzes und dem Aggregationsverfahren, ist es nun möglich, den Einfluss unregelmäßig strukturierter Topologien auf die Güte zu erfassen.

Im nachfolgenden Abschnitt werden die untersuchten Verfahren zur Teilnetzzusammenfassung beschrieben, um im Anschluss den verwendeten Gütebegriff zu definieren. Nach der Beschreibung des Netzmodells werden die Ergebnisse vorgestellt und die gewonnenen Erkenntnisse abschließend zusammengefasst.

Beschreibung der Aggregationsverfahren

Die hierarchische Netzsicht führt aufgrund der Teilnetzzusammenfassung zu einer Informationsreduktion in den Knoten. Maßgeblichen Einfluss darauf hat das verwendete Verfahren zur Teilnetzzusammenfassung. Es verdichtet die Verbindungsinformationen eines Teilnetzes zu wenigen repräsentativen Daten. Für die vorliegenden Untersuchungen wurden die folgenden beiden Aggregationsverfahren gewählt.

Full Mesh Representation

Ausgehend von der untersten Hierarchieebene stellt die Full Mesh Representation (FMR) ein Teilnetz in der darüber liegenden Schicht durch einen Mehrportknoten dar, der eine vollständige Vermaschung zwischen seinen Ports aufweist (vgl. Abbildung 2, 1. Schritt). Die Ports selbst bilden sich aus den Grenzknoten des zu aggregierenden Netzbereichs. Dabei handelt es sich um diejenigen Knoten, die zu benachbarten Netzabschnitten Links unterhalten.

Die Eigenschaften der Verbindungsstrecke zwischen zwei Ports in der FMR bilden sich aus den möglichen Wegen, die zwischen den beiden zugrundeliegenden Grenzknoten existieren. Die gewählte Berechnungsvorschrift sollte dabei das bei der Wegewahl angewandte Kriterium berücksichtigen. In unserem Fall lag es deshalb nahe, einzig den kostengünstigsten Pfad zwischen den beiden Grenzknoten für die Charakterisierung zu nutzen. Die Eigenschaften der nach außen führenden Links des Mehrportknotens werden aus dem zu aggregierenden Netzbereich übernommen.

Bei der Ermittlung höherer Hierarchieebenen ($n \geq 2$) sind die Grenzknoten selbst Mehrportknoten, weshalb die Bestimmung der internen Verbindungsstrecken (Intraknotenverbindungen) und der externen Anbindungen (Interknotenverbindungen) schwieriger wird. In einem ersten Schritt werden deshalb die Grenzknoten B_j des zu aggregierenden Netzbereichs der Ebene n bestimmt. Sie bilden die Ports P_j des neuen Mehrportknotens K_i^{n+1} auf der nächsten Hierarchieebene n+1. Die Kosten C_{P_j,P_l} der internen Verbindungen zweier Ports P_j und P_l berechnen sich aus den kostenminimalen Pfaden zwischen allen Ports der Grenzknoten B_j und B_l:

$$C_{P_j,P_l} = f(C_{P_r(B_j),P_s(B_l)}, \forall r,s) \tag{1}$$

Im Rahmen dieser Arbeit wurde als Funktion der Durchschnittswert betrachtet. Besitzt ein Mehrportknoten der Hierarchieebene n mehrere Verbindungsstrecken zu einem Nachbarbereich, so werden sie in der darüber liegenden Ebene zusammengefasst. Die Kosteneigenschaften bestimmen sich über eine Mittelwertbildung.

Zusammenfassend kann festgestellt werden, dass die FMR durch den Wegfall der internen Knoten in der nächst höheren Hierarchieebene in der Regel eine Verringerung der Topologieinformationen erreicht. Ist jedoch in dem zu aggregierenden Netzbereich die Zahl der internen Verbindungsstrecken geringer als für die Vollvermaschung der Ports notwendig, so müssen bei diesem Verfahren mehr Link-Informationen weitergegeben werden als im ursprünglichen Netzbereich vorhanden waren. Eine zusätzliche Informationsreduktion tritt auf den höheren Ebenen ein, wenn die externen Verbindungen der Mehrportknoten zusammengefasst werden.

Simple Node Representation

Die Simple Node Representation (SNR) fasst einen Netzbereich auf der nächsten Hierarchieebene zu einem einzelnen Knoten zusammen. Da sie im Gegensatz zur FMR keine internen Links aufweist, müssen die Durchgangskosten bei der Charakterisierung der externen Anbindungen berücksichtigt werden. Ansonsten würden diese Informationen nicht mehr für das Routing zur Verfügung stehen.

Abbildung 2 zeigt anhand eines einfachen Beispiels die Bildung der SNR. In einem ersten Schritt wird die Full Mesh Representation der Netzbereiche bestimmt. Im Anschluss erfolgt die Umwandlung in eine Sterndarstellung, bei der sich die internen Verbindungskosten zwischen einem Port und dem Sternpunkt aus dem halbierten Mittelwert aller Durchgangskosten der FMR bestimmen. Dies hat zur Folge, dass die Durchgangskosten des Teilnetzes unabhängig von der Wahl des Eingangs- und Ausgangsports sind. Im dritten Schritt werden die externen Verbindungen bis zum Sternpunkt verlängert und mit den zusätzlichen Kosten beaufschlagt. Besitzen zwei Netzbereiche untereinander mehrere Verbindungen, so werden sie im letzten Schritt zu einem einzigen Link zusammengefasst, der die gemittelten Eigenschaften besitzt.

Im Gegensatz zur FMR ist die Informationsreduktion durch die Simple Node Representation wesentlich größer. Neben den fehlenden internen Verbindungen sorgt die Zusammenfassung der externen Anbindungen der Netzbereiche für eine zusätzliche Minimierung der Datenmenge.

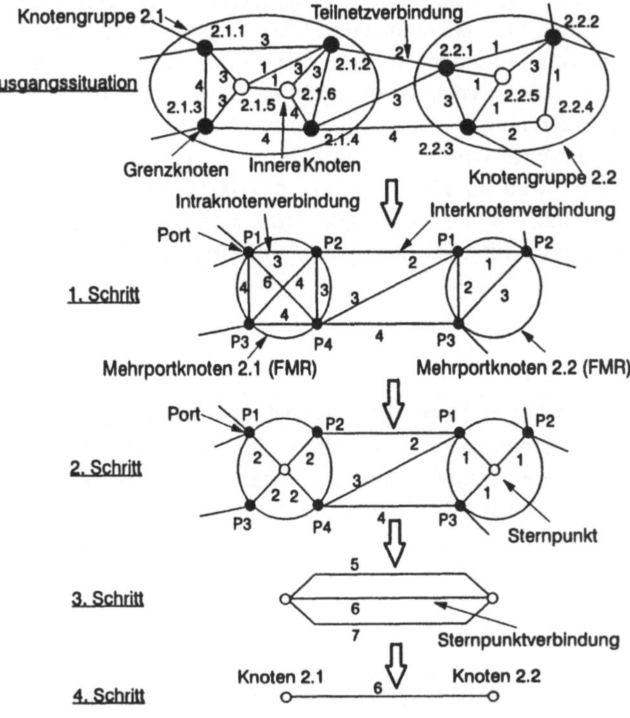

Abb. 2. Bildung der SNR

Definition des Gütebegriffs

Es ist zu erwarten, dass die Präzision der Wegewahl infolge der Teilnetzaggregation abnimmt, da letztere die Topologieinformationen reduziert, die einem Quellknoten für die Wegewahl zur Verfügung stehen. Dieser Effekt wird in vorliegender Arbeit durch ein Gütemaß erfasst. Um es zu bestimmen, müssen für jedes Knotenpaar (i, j) die Kosten $C_{iH(j)}$ des kostenminimalen hierarchischen Pfads ermittelt werden. Dieser Wert wird den Kosten C_{ij} des kostenminimalen Pfads gegenüber gestellt, die sich bei vollständiger Kenntnis des physikalischen Netzes ergäben. Ergebnis sind das Fehlermaß pro Knotenpaar ε_{ij} und die hierarchische Güte Γ_H:

$$\varepsilon_{ij} = \frac{\left| C_{iH(j)} - C_{ij} \right|}{C_{iH(j)}} \tag{2}$$

$$\Gamma_H = 1 - \frac{1}{N} \cdot \sum_i \sum_j \varepsilon_{ij} \tag{3}$$

Güteeinfluss der Teilnetzaggregation

Die bisherigen Untersuchungen in [2] beruhen auf Netzen, die sowohl in der physikalischen Schicht als auch auf den höheren Hierarchieebenen eine regelmäßige gitterähnliche Struktur besitzen. Weitere Einschränkungen bestehen hinsichtlich der Größe der zusammengefassten Knotengruppen und der Art der Vermaschung. So besteht in [2], unabhängig von der betrachteten Ebene, jede Gruppe aus vier untereinander vollvermaschten Knoten mit entsprechender Anbindung an die Nachbarbereiche. Durch eine Erweiterung des Netzmodells ist es in vorliegender Arbeit möglich, unter Angabe beliebiger Gruppengrößen unregelmäßig strukturierte Netze zu erzeugen und Gütemessungen durchzuführen (siehe hierzu [7]).

Netzgenerator

Die Erzeugung zufälliger Netzstrukturen erfolgt durch einen Netzgenerator. Als Eingabeparameter stehen neben der Zahl der physikalischen Knoten und der Vermaschungsparameter auch die Art der Linkkostenzuweisung und die Gruppengröße bzw. Ebenenzahl zur Verfügung.

In der ersten Phase der Netzerzeugung wird die gewünschte Anzahl an Knoten auf der physikalischen Ebene zufällig verteilt und mit Hilfe eines auf [8] basierenden Linkgenerators die Vermaschung der Knoten vorgenommen[1]. Anschließend wird der Kostenparameter jedes Links mit einem zufälligen Wert konfiguriert.

Tabelle 1. Phasen der Gruppenbildung

Phase	Bemerkung
Initialisierung	Verteilung der Gruppenreferenzpunkte auf der Netzebene.
Zuweisung I	Zuweisung eines Erstknotens zu jedem Referenzpunkt. Kriterium: Geometrische Entfernung
Zuweisung II	Sukzessive Zuweisung weiterer Knoten, wenn möglich bis zur geforderten Gruppengröße. Kriterien: - Anzahl der Links zu den Gruppen - Geometrische Länge der Linkanbindung
Waisen	Zuweisung der noch ungruppierten Knoten. Kriterien: - Gruppengröße - Anzahl der Links zu den Gruppen - Geometrische Länge der Linkanbindung
Umgruppierung	Angleichung der Gruppengröße durch Knotentausch. Kriterien: - Gruppengröße - Anzahl der Links zu den Gruppen - Geometrische Länge der Linkanbindung

[1] Für die Generierung der Links wird die gleiche Wahrscheinlichkeitsfunktion wie bei Waxman [9] genutzt, mit dem Unterschied, dass das hier verwendete Verfahren von Salama schon nach einem Durchlauf sicher stellt, dass neben einer Mindestkonnektivität von 2 je Knoten auch die geforderte mittlere Konnektivität erreicht wird.

Die Teilnetzzusammenfassung erfordert anschließend die Einteilung der Knoten in Knotengruppen. Dabei ist als wichtige Nebenbedingung zu beachten, dass das durch die Gruppenknoten geformte Teilnetz zusammenhängend sein muss. Zusätzlich wurde definiert, dass die Gruppengröße auf allen Ebenen, soweit dies durch die jeweilige Zahl der Knoten möglich ist, gleich sein soll. Mit Hilfe eines mehrphasigen Algorithmus (Tabelle 1) kann diese Vorgabe eingehalten werden.

Auf eine weitere Optimierung der Gruppenbildung wird bewusst verzichtet, da in erster Linie der Einfluss verschiedener Netzszenarien mit unterschiedlichen Gruppenformen auf die Güte der hierarchischen Wegewahl untersucht werden soll. In einem weiteren Schritt ist es sicherlich notwendig, ein an das Aggregationsverfahren angepasstes Verfahren zur Gruppenbildung zu entwerfen, um zusätzliche Informationsverluste aufgrund einer nicht optimalen Topologie zu vermeiden.

Die gewonnenen Knotengruppen werden gemäß den zuvor vorgestellten Verfahren (SNR bzw. FMR) aggregiert. Die weiteren Hierarchieebenen entstehen schließlich durch die sukzessive Anwendung des geschilderten Gruppierungsverfahrens auf die Mehrportknoten der FMR bzw. auf die SNR-Knoten.

Ergebnisse der Gütemessungen bei unregelmäßigen Topologien

Im Rahmen der Messungen wurden unregelmäßig aufgebaute Topologien aus 1024 Knoten und einer mittleren Konnektivität von 8 untersucht.

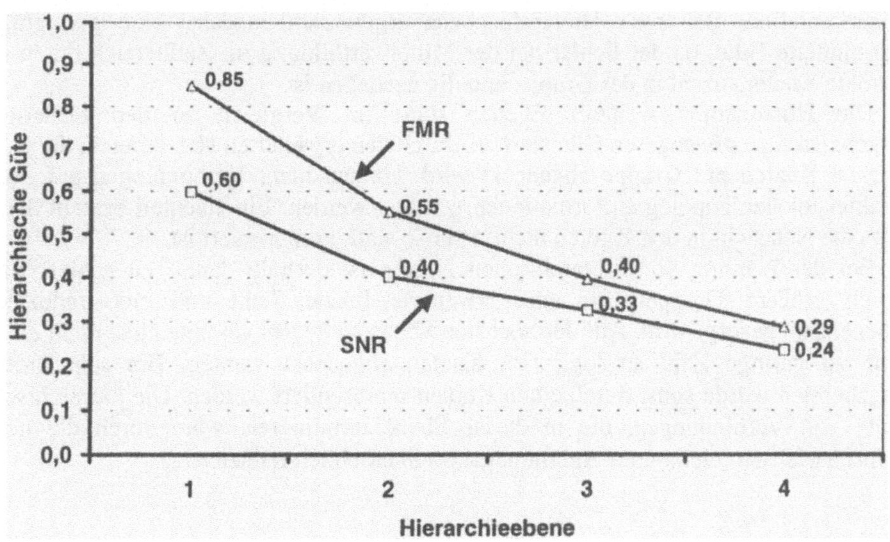

Abb. 3. Hierarchische Güte bei SNR und FMR (1024 Knoten; Ø 4 Knoten je Gruppe)

In Abbildung 3 sind die Ergebnisse für Netze aufgetragen, die in Knotenzahl (1024) und Gruppengröße (4) mit den in [2] vorgestellten Messungen übereinstimmen[2]. Bedingt durch die unregelmäßige Topologie fallen die Gütewerte schlechter aus. Wurde in [2] bei vier virtuellen Ebenen und der Simple Node Representation noch eine hierarchische Güte von 0,64 erzielt, so führt die nun aus Sicht des Aggregationverfahrens nicht mehr „angepasste" Topologie[3] auch bei der Full Mesh Representation zu schlechteren Werten.

Ursache dieses Ergebnisses sind nicht nur die zusammengefassten Transitkosten. Beide Aggregationsverfahren bieten zusätzlich keine exakten Informationen über die Anbindungskosten der einzelnen Knoten im Zielbereich.

Bei der FMR kann zwar über den halbierten Mittelwert der Durchgangskosten eine Abschätzung vorgenommen werden; diese führt aber zu höheren Kosten des hierarchisch optimalen Weges und einer Abnahme der Güte. Dies ist in Abbildung 3 besonders deutlich bei einer Hierarchieebene zu erkennen. Bei der FMR ist die reduzierte Güte dort nur durch die Anbindungskosten im Zielbereich bedingt, da die Transitkosten auf dieser ersten Ebene noch ohne Informationsverlust abgebildet werden. Die SNR „leidet" zusätzlich unter den ungenauen Kosten im Durchgangsbereich.

Durch ein detailliertes Wissen der Anbindungskosten in Verbindung mit einer Erweiterung der eingesetzten Dienstsignalisierung (siehe hierzu [2] bzw. [10]) kann eine erhebliche Verbesserung der Gütewerte erzielt werden.

Einfluss der Gruppengröße auf die hierarchische Güte

Abbildung 4 vergleicht die Auswirkungen vergrößerter Gruppen bei der Full Mesh Representation. Bei einer Hierarchieebene ergibt sich zunächst eine geringfügig verminderte Güte, da der Fehler bei der Mittelwertbildung im Zielbereich durch die erhöhte Knotenanzahl in der Gruppe anteilig gestiegen ist.

Die Hinzunahme weiterer Ebenen führt im Vergleich zu den bisherigen Ergebnissen zu günstigeren Gütewerten. Durch den erweiterten Netzbereich, der bei 6 bzw. 8 Knoten pro Gruppe abgedeckt wird, können mehr Verbindungen auf Basis exakter lokaler Topologieinformationen geroutet werden. Ein Nachteil besteht darin, dass die Netzsicht in den Knoten nicht mehr so stark komprimiert ist.

Bei der Planung von hierarchischen Netzen ist deshalb darauf zu achten, dass durch größere Gruppen für eine erweiterte lokale Sicht und eine reduzierte Ebenenzahl gesorgt wird. Auf der höchsten Ebene sollte das gesamte Netz nicht durch eine zu geringe Zahl an logischen Knoten abgedeckt werden. Ein sehr großer Netzbereich würde sonst durch einen Knoten repräsentiert werden. Die hierarchische Güte von Verbindungen, die in dieser Ebene terminieren, wäre durch die hohe „Unschärfe" der Zielknoten-Anbindungskosten erheblich reduziert.

---

[2] Für die einzelnen Messpunkte in den nachfolgenden Abbildungen wurde auf die Angabe eines Konfidenzintervalls verzichtet, da keine nennenswerten Streuungen aufgetreten sind.

[3] In [2] tritt der Effekt ein, dass die Gitterstruktur einer Netzebene (n) jener der FMR-aggregierten Netzebene (n+1) gleicht. Die Topologie wird daher als „an das FMR-Aggregationsverfahren angepasst" bezeichnet.

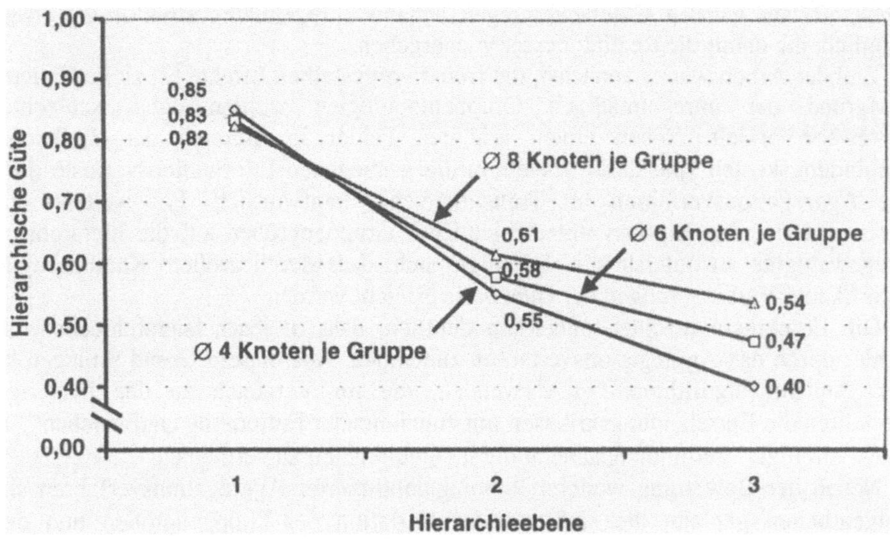

Abb. 4. Hierarchische Güte FMR (1024 Knoten)

Rückwirkung auf die Verbindungsannahmeentscheidung

Abschließend sei auf den Zusammenhang zwischen hierarchischer Wegewahl und Verbindungsannahmekontrolle (Connection Admission Control, CAC) in den Quellknoten hingewiesen.

Auf Basis der Wegewahlergebnisse entscheidet der CAC-Algorithmus über die Annahme einer Verbindung. Wie deutlich zu sehen war, sind die Routing-Ergebnisse fehlerbehaftet. Es ist daher nicht einsichtig, warum für Verbindungen in entfernte Netzbereiche die gleichen strengen Annahmeentscheidungen getroffen werden sollten, wie für lokale Verbindungen. Vielmehr wird ein hierarchischer Annahmealgorithmus vorgeschlagen, der mit zunehmender Entfernung weichere Annahmekriterien definiert.

Denkbar wäre, in Abhängigkeit der Hierarchiestufe eines Verbindungsabschnitts das Entscheidungskriterium durch einen Schwankungsbereich „aufzuweichen". Die zugelassene Abweichung vom ursprünglichen Annahmekriterium ist dabei um so größer, je höher man sich gerade in der Hierarchie befindet. Auf diese Weise kann vermieden werden, dass Verbindungen aufgrund nur vermeintlich ungünstiger Wegeeigenschaften abgelehnt werden.

Zusammenfassung

Im Rahmen dieser Arbeit wurden die in [2] begonnenen Messungen an ausgewählten Aggregationsverfahren fortgesetzt. Durch Erweiterungen in der verwendeten

Messsoftware wurden Gütebewertungen anhand unregelmäßig strukturierter Netze möglich, die damit die Realität besser wiedergeben.

Ziel der Arbeit war es zunächst, die früher vorgestellten Effekte [2] zu verifizieren. Aufgrund der unregelmäßigen Gruppentopologien wurden dabei schlechtere Gütewerte erzielt. Neben einem erhöhten Fehler im Bereich der Zielknoten-Anbindungskosten sind dafür vor allem die gestiegenen Informationsverluste durch die Aggregationsverfahren im Transitbereich verantwortlich. Ein weiteres Ziel bestand darin, den Einfluss unterschiedlicher Gruppengrößen auf die hierarchische Wegewahlgüte zu untersuchen. Es zeigte sich, dass durch größere Knotengruppen signifikante Verbesserungen der Gütewerte erreicht wurden.

Die Ergebnisse machten außerdem deutlich, dass in jeder Hierarchieebene die Fehler durch das Aggregationsverfahren zunehmen. Aus diesem Grund schlagen wir vor, Annahmealgorithmen zu verwenden, die im Vergleich zu den bisherigen Verfahren die Entscheidungskriterien mit zunehmender Entfernung „aufweichen", um eine „voreilige" Verbindungsablehnung im Quellknoten zu vermeiden.

Neben der Bewertung weiterer, topologieoptimierter Aggregationsverfahren sind Folgearbeiten geplant, die sich mit der Variation der Gruppengrößen und dem Entwurf eines hierarchischen Annahmealgorithmus beschäftigen.

Referenzen

[1]   ATM-Forum. Private Network-Network Interface Specification Version 1.0 (PNNI 1.0). *af-pnni-0055.000*, 1996.

[2]   B. Quendt, B. Zumbusch. Güte hierarchischer Wegewahl in PNNI. In *Proceedings of the KiVS '99 (ITG-Fachtagung Kommunikation in Verteilten Systemen)*, Darmstadt, 1999.

[3]   P. Van Mieghem. Estimation of an optimal PNNI topology. In *Proceedings of the IEEE ATM '97 Workshop*, Lisbon, 1997.

[4]   P. Van Mieghem. Dividing a network into peer groups to build a hierarchical structure. In *Proceedings of the DRCN '98 (Workshop on the Design of Reliable Communication Networks)*, Brugge, 1998.

[5]   E. C. Alves, B. Liau. Partitioning networks into areas of traffic. In *Proceedings of the Networks '98 (International Telecommunication Network Planning Symposium)*, Sorrento, 1998.

[6]   W. C. Lee. Topology Aggregation for hierarchical routing in ATM networks. In *ACM SIGCOMM Computer Communication Review*, 1995.

[7]   A. Kaspar. Güteruntersuchung ausgewählter Aggregationsverfahren für Kommunikationsnetze mittels eines modifizierten Software-Tools. Diplomarbeit, Lehrstuhl für Kommunikationsnetze, Technische Universität München, 2000.

[8]   H. F. Salama. Multicast routing for real-time communication on high-speed networks. Dissertation, Department of Electrical and Computer Engineering, North Carolina State University, 1996.

[9]   B. Waxman: Routing of Multipoint Connections: IEEE Journal on Selected Areas in Communications, Vol. 6, Nr. 9, S. 1617-1622, Dezember, 1988.

[10]   B. Quendt. Agentenunterstützte Steuerung von Multimediadiensten. Dissertation, Lehrstuhl für Kommunikationsnetze, Technische Universität München, 2000.

Session 2:

Mobile Computing

Paketfilter- und Tunnelkonfiguration zur Firewall-verträglichen Mobilitätsunterstützung in IP-Netzen

Frank Pählke[1], Günter Schäfer[2], Jochen Schiller[1]

[1] Institut für Telematik, Universität Karlsruhe (TH), D-76128 Karlsruhe
`[paehlke|schiller]@telematik.informatik.uni-karlsruhe.de`
[2] Institut für Nachrichtentechnik und Theoretische Elektrotechnik, TU Berlin,
Einsteinufer 25, 10587 Berlin, `schaefer@ee.tu-berlin.de`

Zusammenfassung Mobile IP gemäß RFC 2002 kann aus Sicherheitsgründen in den wenigsten Netzen eingesetzt werden. Ein wesentliches Problem ist hierbei die Zusammenarbeit mit Firewalls. Damit der Ansatz von Mobile IP auch in Firewall-geschützten Netzen eingesetzt werden kann, wurde die Architektur FATIMA entwickelt, in welcher ein mobilitätsunterstützendes Gateway in die Firewall eines Netzes integriert wird. Der vorliegende Artikel befasst sich speziell mit den Auswirkungen dieser Mobilitätsunterstützung auf die Filterregeln der Firewall-Router sowie mit der Konfiguration der zwischen FATIMA-Infrastrukturkomponenten bestehenden Tunnel. Außerdem werden Möglichkeiten zur Optimierung der Datenpfade innerhalb eines Netzes aufgezeigt und bewertet.

1 Einleitung

Die Bedeutung der mobilen Internet-Kommunikation wird in Zukunft stark zunehmen, nicht zuletzt durch die kommenden Mobilfunknetze der dritten Generation. Das Mobile-IP-Protokoll nach dem Standard RFC 2002 [8] unterstützt die Mobilität von Endsystemen in der IP-Schicht. Dabei ist ein mobiles Endsystem immer unter derselben IP-Adresse erreichbar, sodass es für die höheren Schichten keine Rolle spielt, wo sich das Endsystem gerade befindet. Ein mögliches Anwendungsszenario hierfür ist z.B. die transparente Einbindung „nomadischer" Mitarbeiter in das Intranet einer Firma. Auch die Unterstützung mobiler Endgeräte in Peer-to-Peer-Anwendungen (z.B. Multimedia-Konferenzwerkzeuge nach H.323) sowie die Realisierung mobiler Server (z.B. einer Kamera mit eingebautem WWW-Server) werden wesentlich vereinfacht.

Allerdings kann Mobile IP nach dem usprünglichen Standard RFC 2002 aus Sicherheitsgründen nur in den wenigsten Netzen eingesetzt werden. Ein wesentlicher Grund hierfür ist das Senden von Datenpaketen eines sich in einem fremden Netz aufhaltenden Rechners mit einer topologisch falschen Adresse (ein mobiler Knoten behält bei Mobile IP seine IP-Adresse und sendet mit dieser IP-Adresse auch in einem fremden Netz). Diverse Lösungen dieses Problems, wie z.B. das Rücktunneln (Reverse Tunneling) nach RFC 2344 [6], lassen sich ebenfalls nicht nutzen, da hier beispielsweise ein ungesicherter Tunnel durch eine Firewall gelegt werden müsste.

Damit der Ansatz von Mobile IP auch in Netzen mit Sicherheitsarchitekturen wie Firewalls eingesetzt werden kann, wurde die Architektur FATIMA entwickelt. Ein Überblick über FATIMA und verwandte Ansätze findet sich in [4]. Der vorliegende Artikel befasst sich nach einer kurzen Einführung in die generelle Architektur speziell mit den Auswirkungen der Mobilitätsunterstützung durch FATIMA auf die Filterregeln der Firewall-Router sowie mit der Konfiguration der zwischen FATIMA-Infrastrukturkomponenten bestehenden Tunnel.

2 Die Firewall-Aware Transparent Internet Mobility Architecture (FATIMA)

Dieser Abschnitt gibt einen Überblick über die Architektur von FATIMA. Beim Entwurf der Architektur standen die folgenden Ziele im Vordergrund:

- *Transparenz:* Alle Erweiterungen gegenüber Mobile IP müssen transparent für Endgeräte und für die Infrastruktur entfernter Netze sein, damit die Architektur nahtlos in das vorhandene Internet eingebettet werden kann.
- *Zentralisierung sicherheitskritischer Funktionen:* Diese Eigenschaft ist einer der großen Vorteile einer Firewall im Vergleich zu verteilten Schutzmechanismen, welche auf jedem Endsystem konfiguriert werden müssten.
- *Vollständige Authentisierung:* Alle Komponenten der Architektur müssen sich gegenseitig authentisieren können.
- *Unterstützung von Mikromobilität:* Bewegt sich ein mobiler Rechner zwischen verschiedenen Subnetzen eines Netzes, so sollte die Übergabe effizienter unterstützt werden als bei einer Bewegung zwischen verschiedenen Netzen. Hierdurch verbessert sich die Skalierbarkeit gegenüber normalem Mobile IP erheblich, da dort alle Subnetzwechsel stets einen umfangreichen Signalisierungsverkehr und eine erneute Authentisierung verursachen. Einige existierende Ansätze zur Mikromobilitätsunterstützung werden in [5] gegenübergestellt und aus dem Blickwinkel der Sicherheit bewertet.

Das wesentliche Merkmal von FATIMA ist die Konzentration aller sicherheitskritischen Funktionen in einem Gateway, welches in die Firewall eines Netzes integriert wird. In den einzelnen Subnetzen werden anstelle der Heimat- und Fremdagenten von Mobile IP wesentlich einfachere Stellvertreteragenten (home/foreign agent proxy, HAP/FAP) eingesetzt. Zwischen allen Infrastrukturkomponenten werden alle übertragenen Daten durch ESP-Tunnel (Encapsulating Security Payload [3]) authentisiert und optional verschlüsselt. Durch die ESP-Tunnel wird innerhalb des lokalen Netzes ein abgeschottetes virtuelles Netz gebildet, in welchem sich alle FATIMA-Infrastrukturkomponenten sowie alle anwesenden Mobilrechner (Mobile Nodes, MNs) befinden. Hierdurch wird einer gegenseitige Beeinflussung zwischen den mobilen und ortsfesten Teilen des Netzes entgegengewirkt.

Die grundlegende Architektur von FATIMA ist in Abb. 1 gezeigt. Die Funktionalität der gezeigten Infrastrukturkomponenten teilt sich wie folgt auf:

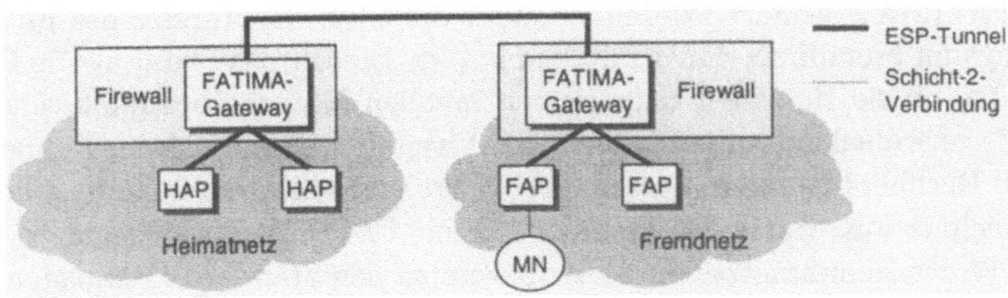

Abbildung 1. FATIMA-Komponenten: Minimale Konfiguration

- *FATIMA-Gateway (FGW):* Das FGW ist die zentrale mobilitätsunterstüt- zende Instanz in einem Netz. Es gehört zur Firewall des Netzes und ist von innen wie außen erreichbar. Alle sicherheitskritischen Funktionen (z.B. Regi- strierung von MNs und Entkapselung getunnelter Datenpakete) werden vom FGW erbracht und können daher zentral administriert werden. Nach außen hin erscheint das Gateway als der einzige Fremdagent und gleichzeitig als der einzige Heimatagent des Netzes. Jedem besuchenden MN wird als COA (Care-Of Address) die Adresse des FGW zugewiesen.
- *Foreign Agent Proxy (FAP):* Alle Fremdagenten werden durch wesentlich einfachere Stellvertreter, die FAPs, ersetzt. Gegenüber einem besuchenden MN verhält sich der FAP exakt wie ein normaler Fremdagent. Er bearbeitet die Kontrollnachrichten z.B. bei der Registrierung allerdings nicht selber, sondern leitet sie an das FGW weiter, welches die eigentliche Registrierungs- funktionalität erbringt. Die Antworten des FGW werden umgekehrt an die MNs weitergeleitet, welche den FAP daher nicht von einem gewöhnlichen Fremdagenten unterscheiden können.
- *Home Agent Proxy (HAP):* Alle Heimatagenten werden ebenfalls durch ein- fachere Stellvertreter, die HAPs, ersetzt. Diese werden durch Kontrollnach- richten des FGW aktiviert, fangen dann alle für abwesende Mobilrechner bestimmten Datenpakete ab und tunneln sie zum FGW des Heimatnetzes. Das Heimat-FGW tunnelt die Pakete weiter zur COA und wickelt den ge- samten Mobile-IP-Kontrolldatenverkehr mit dem Fremdnetz ab.

Eine detailliertere Beschreibung weiterer Komponenten und Funktionen der Ar- chitektur, die sich im Wesentlichen auf die Skalierbarkeit, Wegeoptimierung und sichere Registrierung beziehen, findet sich in [4].

2.1 Paketweiterleitung

In einem FATIMA-erweiterten Heimatnetz werden alle Datenpakete, welche für einen gerade abwesenden mobilen Rechner gedacht sind, im Heimat-Subnetz des mobilen Rechners durch einen HAP abgefangen und zum FGW des Heimat- netzes weitergeleitet. Das FGW kapselt die Datenpakete und leitet sie so in einem Tunnel an die aktuell gültige COA weiter. Ist das Fremdnetz ebenfalls durch FATIMA erweitert worden, so stellt die COA die Adresse des FATIMA-Gateways im Fremdnetz dar. In diesem Fall entkapselt das Gateway die Pakete, überprüft, ob sie für einen registrierten mobilen Rechner bestimmt sind, und leitet sie anschließend an denjenigen FAP weiter, welcher sich im Subnetz des mobilen Rechners befindet. Dieser FAP liefert schließlich die Pakete an den mobilen Rechner aus. Hätte das Fremdnetz keine FATIMA-Erweiterung, so würde das FGW des Heimatnetzes die Datenpakete an den Standard-Fremdagenten im aktuellen Subnetz des mobilen Rechners weiterleiten.

Alle Pakete, die von einem mobilen Rechner im Fremdnetz gesendet werden, leitet ein FAP an das FATIMA-Gateway des Netzes weiter. Dort werden diejenigen Pakete herausgefiltert, deren Quelladresse nicht zu einem registrierten mobilen Rechner gehört. Die verbleibenden Pakete werden entweder direkt oder über einen Rücktunnel zum HA bzw. FGW im Heimatnetz an den Kommunikationspartner (Correspondent Node, CN) weitergeleitet.

- Im Fall einer *direkten Weiterleitung* muss dem FGW im Fremdnetz erlaubt werden, Pakete mit topologisch falscher Quelladresse zu senden, da es nach der Sicherheitsüberprüfung Pakete von MNs weiterleitet, deren Quelladresse nicht zum Fremdnetz gehört (In Mobile IP ist die Situation vergleichbar, jedoch findet dort keinerlei Sicherheitsüberprüfung statt). Da das FGW die einzige Komponente mit dieser Anforderung ist und als Bestandteil der Firewall der direkten Überwachung durch die Systemverwaltung untersteht, werden dadurch bei geeigneter Konfiguration der Paketfilter keine unkontrollierbaren Risiken in das Fremdnetz eingebracht, was bereits einen wesentlichen Fortschritt gegenüber Mobile IP darstellt.
- Es gibt aber auch, neben einer erhöhten Sicherheit, gute Gründe, die von einem MN in Richtung Internet gesendeten Pakete ebenfalls durch einen *Tunnel (Rücktunnel)* in Richtung HA bzw. Heimat-FGW weiterzuleiten (Reverse Tunneling gemäß RFC 2344). Nimmt der MN beispielsweise an einer Multicast-Übertragung teil, so könnte es sein, dass das Fremdnetz entweder gar keine Anbindung an das MBone besitzt oder die Lebensdauer (TTL) der Pakete vom Fremdnetz aus nicht mehr ausreicht, um alle Gruppenteilnehmer zu erreichen. Dann muss das Paket über einen Rücktunnel geleitet werden, sodass es scheinbar aus dem Heimatnetz kommt. Ein weiterer Grund könnten bereits etablierte Vertrauensverhältnisse zwischen Netzen sein, z.B. dass ein Netz dem Heimatnetz vertraut, nicht aber Daten aus einem beliebigen Fremdnetz. Auch in diesem Fall muss es nach außen so aussehen, als kämen die Pakete des mobilen Rechners aus dem Heimatnetz, um die Forderung nach Transparenz aufrechtzuerhalten.

Unter Effizienzgesichtspunkten ist es wünschenswert, dass Pakete zwischen den Rechnern eines Netzes und den in diesem Netz anwesenden MNs innerhalb dieses Netzes weitergeleitet werden, anstatt zu einem u.U. weit entfernten Heimatnetz und wieder zurück zu laufen. Verschiedene Möglichkeiten einer entsprechenden Optimierung der Datenpfade sind Gegenstand des Abschnitts 3.3.

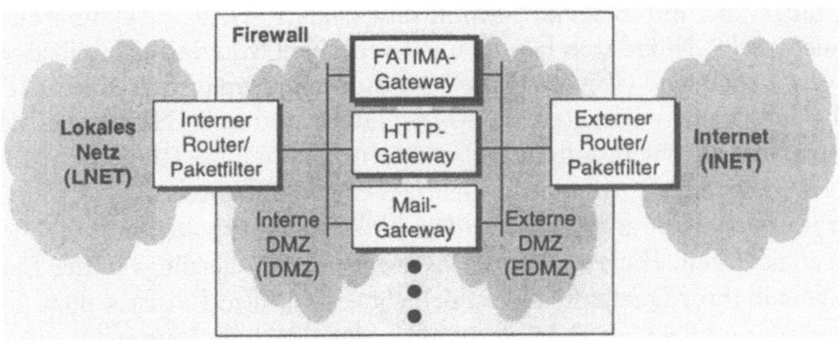

Abbildung 2. Firewall-Konfiguration mit zweigeteilter DMZ

3 Paketfilter- und Tunnelkonfiguration

Es gibt verschiedene Typen von Firewalls, welche sich in ihren Sicherheitseigenschaften unterscheiden (vgl. [1, M 2.73]). Wie in Abschnitt 3.1 erläutert wird, ist
für den Einsatz von FATIMA eine Firewall mit einer zweigeteilten „de-militarized
zone" (DMZ) empfehlenswert (Screened Subnet mit Dual-homed Gateways, siehe Abb. 2); dies ist auch generell die sicherste Konfiguration. Die interne DMZ
(IDMZ) gehört hierbei logisch zum lokalen Netz (LNET) und die externe DMZ
(EDMZ) zum Internet (INET). Wenn das lokale Netz private Adressen verwendet, dann benutzt die interne DMZ ebenfalls private Adressen, die externe DMZ
hingegen öffentliche Adressen.

3.1 Interner und externer Router

Damit das FATIMA-Gateway über die ESP-Tunnel mit den FAPs und HAPs im
lokalen Netz kommunizieren kann, müssen die zugehörigen Pakete vom internen
Router durchgelassen werden. Da die ESP-Tunnel gegebenenfalls verschlüsselt
sind, kann die Firewall keine Informationen (z.B. Portnummern) auswerten, welche nicht im äußeren IP-Kopf enthalten sind, sodass sich für den Paketfilter des
internen Routers die folgenden zusätzlich zulässigen Regeln ergeben:

Richtung	Protokoll	Quelladr.	Quellport	Zieladr.	Zielport
LNET → IDMZ	ESP	LNET	—	FGW	—
IDMZ → LNET	ESP	FGW	—	LNET	—

Wenn der interne Router ausreichend leistungsfähig ist, lässt sich die Sicherheit
noch verbessern, wenn die obigen generischen Regeln durch je ein Regelpaar
pro HAP und pro FAP ersetzt werden, welches genau den Austausch von ESP-
Paketen zwischen diesem HAP/FAP und dem FGW erlaubt. Die Anzahl der
zusätzlichen Regeln ist dann proportional zur Anzahl der HAPs/FAPs, d.h. zur
Anzahl der Subnetze innerhalb des lokalen Netzes.

Beim externen Router muss für einkommende Pakete berücksichtigt werden,
dass das FGW Kontrolldaten mit entfernten FATIMA-Gateways durch einen

ESP-Tunnel und mit Standard-Mobilitätsagenten (HAs, FAs) über normales UDP austauscht. Nutzdaten kommen entweder von Standard-Mobilitätsagenten (oder von beliebigen CNs im Falle von Routenoptimierung) durch IP-in-IP-Tunnel [7] oder von entfernten FATIMA-Gateways durch ESP-Tunnel herein.

Wenn es möglich sein soll, ausgehende Nutzdaten ohne Rücktunnel direkt an den CN weiterzuleiten, so muss es dem FGW gemäß Abschnitt 2.1 als einzigem System im lokalen Netz erlaubt werden, Pakete mit topologisch falscher Quelladresse zu schicken. Hierzu muss der externe Router allerdings in der Lage sein, Pakete gemäß ihrer Quelladresse auf Schicht 2 zu filtern. Existiert diese Möglichkeit nicht, dann bleibt als einziger Ausweg, den externen Router für ausgehende Pakete vollständig zu öffnen. Dies ist der Hauptgrund, weshalb ein FGW nur in einer Firewall mit zweigeteilter DMZ wie in Abb. 2 verwendet werden sollte: Nur so ist sichergestellt, dass alle Pakete, die den externen Router von innen nach außen passieren, von einem der vertrauenswürdigen Gateways innerhalb der Firewall stammen und somit gefahrlos durchgelassen werden können. Insgesamt ergeben sich für den externen Router die folgenden zulässigen Regeln:

Schnittstelle	Protokoll	Quelladr. *[Schicht 2]*	Quellport	Zieladr.	Zielport
EDMZ → INET	alle	alle *[FGW]*	alle	INET	alle
INET → EDMZ	ESP	INET	—	FGW	—
INET → EDMZ	IP-in-IP	INET	—	FGW	—

Da der externe Router keine Informationen über besuchende MNs und deren Heimatnetze besitzt, ist er nicht in der Lage, die einkommenden getunnelten Pakete (ESP oder IP-in-IP) mit feinerer Granularität zu filtern. Dies ist Aufgabe des FATIMA-Gateways. Theoretisch wäre es denkbar, dass das FGW über eine Management-Schnittstelle die Filterregeln des externen Routers dynamisch beeinflusst. Wir halten diesen Ansatz allerdings sicherheitstechnisch für bedenklich. Außerdem wäre die große Zahl an zusätzlichen Filterregeln (im ungünstigsten Fall gleich der Anzahl der besuchenden MNs) mit einer erheblichen Mehrbelastung des externen Routers verbunden, welcher den gesamten Datenverkehr zwischen lokalem Netz und Internet filtern muss. Das FATIMA-Gateway ist nur für den normalerweise viel geringeren Datenverkehr von und zu den lokalen MNs zuständig, sodass eine feingranulare Filterung auch unter Effizienzgesichtspunkten auf dem FGW durchgeführt werden sollte.

3.2 FATIMA-Gateway

Das FATIMA-Gateway führt selbst ebenfalls Filterfunktionen aus. Alle eingehenden Pakete müssen durch einen Tunnel in das FGW kommen: aus dem lokalen Netz durch einen ESP-Tunnel, aus dem Internet durch einen ESP- oder IP-in-IP-Tunnel. ESP-Pakete, deren Authentisierung fehlschlägt, werden verworfen.

Danach überprüft das Gateway anhand seiner Tabellen mit den COAs abwesender eigener MNs sowie mit den HA-Adressen besuchender fremder MNs, ob die einkommenden Pakete zulässig sind. Die gilt sowohl für die Registrierungsnachrichten von lokalen HAPs bzw. FAPs sowie externen HAs, FAs oder FGWs als auch für getunnelte Datenpakete. Bei der Weiterleitung von Datenpaketen ergeben sich die folgenden Fälle (ein *besuchender* MN ist dabei ein im lokalen Netz anwesender fremder MN, und ein *abwesender* MN ist ein eigener MN, der sich in einem entfernten Fremdnetz aufhält):

- *Datenpakete von besuchenden MNs:* Diese Pakete kommen durch einen Tunnel von einem lokalen FAP. Die entkapselten Pakete werden entweder durch einen Rücktunnel zum Heimatnetz geschickt, oder sie werden ohne erneute Kapselung in die externe DMZ ausgegeben.

  Falls die Zieladresse innerhalb des lokalen Netzes liegt, erreichen die Pakete im zweiten Fall sofort das zuständige Anwendungs-Gateway innerhalb der Firewall, ohne dass sie die Filtermechanismen des externen Routers passiert haben. Da die Pakete jedoch logisch gesehen von einem externen Rechner stammen, müssen die Filterregeln des externen Routers im FGW repliziert werden, um die Schutzwirkung der Firewall zu erhalten.

  Falls die Zieladresse außerhalb des lokalen Netzes liegt, werden die Pakete aus der externen DMZ über den externen Router in das Internet geleitet. Auf Grund der Filterkonfiguration aus Abschnitt 3.1 können die Pakete den externen Router problemlos passieren.

- *Datenpakete von eigenen MNs:* Im Falle lokaler MNs, welche sich zwar innerhalb ihres Heimatnetzes, aber außerhalb ihres Heimat-Subnetzes befinden, kommen diese Pakete ebenfalls durch einen Tunnel von einem lokalen FAP. Im Falle abwesender MNs kommen die Pakete durch einen Rücktunnel von einem entfernten FA oder FGW.

  Falls die Zieladresse innerhalb des lokalen Netzes liegt, dürfen die Pakete die Firewall nicht durchlaufen. Um die Routing-Semantik zu erhalten, müssen sie daher durch einen Rücktunnel zum jeweils zuständigen HAP geleitet werden, der sie entkapselt und in das Heimat-Subnetz ausgibt.

  Falls die Zieladresse außerhalb des lokalen Netzes liegt, müssen die Pakete ohne erneute Kapselung in die interne DMZ ausgegeben werden, damit sie die Gateways der Firewall korrekt durchlaufen. Genau symmetrisch zum obigen Fall der Datenpakete von besuchenden MNs an Zieladressen innerhalb des lokalen Netzes müssen hierbei die Filterregeln des *internen* Routers im FGW repliziert werden, um die Schutzwirkung der Firewall zu erhalten. Als Alternative können die Pakete auch durch einen Rücktunnel zum HAP geleitet werden, sodass sie die Firewall auf jeden Fall von innen passieren.

- *Datenpakete für besuchende MNs:* Diese Pakete kommen durch einen IP-in-IP-Tunnel von einem entfernten HA oder durch einen ESP-Tunnel von einem entfernten FGW und werden, sofern der betreffende MN existiert und anwesend ist, zum zuständigen FAP weitergetunnelt. Für die Sicherung gegen Angriffe sind die MNs selbst verantwortlich. Das lokale FGW kann nicht filtern, da es die Filterregeln des entfernten Heimatnetzes anwenden müsste, über welche es keine Informationen besitzt. Inwiefern die Filterfunktionalität teilweise von der Firewall des Heimatnetzes an das FGW des Fremdnetzes delegiert werden könnte, ist Gegenstand weitergehender Untersuchungen.

- *Datenpakete für eigene MNs:* Diese Pakete kommen durch einen Tunnel von einem lokalen HAP. Der CN befindet sich entweder innerhalb des lokalen

Netzes, oder die Pakete haben die Firewall auf dem Weg zum HAP bereits durchlaufen. Sie müssen daher nicht gefiltert werden, sondern können direkt an die jeweils zuständige Instanz weitergetunnelt werden. Bei Paketen für abwesende MNs handelt es sich bei der zuständigen Instanz um einen entfernten FA oder ein entferntes FGW. Bei Paketen für lokale MNs, welche sich zwar innerhalb ihres Heimatnetzes, aber außerhalb ihres Heimat-Subnetzes befinden, handelt es sich bei der zuständigen Instanz um einen FAP des lokalen Netzes.

3.3   Verkürztes Routing von Datenpaketen

Will ein lokal anwesender (eigener oder besuchender) MN einem CN innerhalb eines FATIMA-erweiterten Netzes Daten senden, so müssen diese Daten über das FGW des Netzes geleitet werden, damit sie von der Firewall des Netzes so behandelt werden können, als kämen sie von außen. Danach werden sie jedoch, wie in Abschnitt 3.2 beschrieben, direkt an den CN weitergeleitet. Dieses Vorgehen ist zwar nicht so effizient wie Mobile IP mit Routenoptimierung, jedoch bietet es einen Schutz des Fremdnetzes vor Angriffen durch besuchende MNs. In Mobile IP ist ein solcher Schutz nur durch das Rücktunneln gemäß RFC 2344 möglich, wobei alle Datenpakete zunächst zum Heimatnetz getunnelt werden, bevor sie wieder zurück zum Fremdnetz fließen. Insbesondere wenn zwischen Heimat- und Fremdnetz Weitverkehrsverbindungen liegen, ist der bisherige Standard also entweder unsicher oder inakzeptabel aus Sicht der Netzbelastung und Verzögerung; der FATIMA-Ansatz ist demgegenüber wesentlich leistungsfähiger.

In der umgekehrten Richtung, also beim Senden von Daten von einem Rechner innerhalb des Fremdnetzes an einen besuchenden MN, ist die Optimierung des Datenpfades wesentlich schwieriger, da das FGW die einzige Instanz im lokalen Netz ist, welche die Informationen über alle anwesenden MNs besitzt. Da die MNs aus beliebigen Heimatnetzen stammen können, sind die entsprechenden Pakete nicht anhand ihrer Zieladresse zu erkennen.

Der Ansatz, den gesamten Datenverkehr zwischen lokalem Netz und Internet über das FGW zu leiten, scheidet aus Effizienzgründen i.d.R. aus. Statt dessen könnte das FGW bei allen Registrierungen und Deregistrierungen über ein Routing-Protokoll den externen Router umkonfigurieren, welcher dann alle Pakete für lokal anwesende MNs an das FGW und nicht in das Internet weiterleitet. Eine solche dynamische Umkonfigurierung von Firewall-Komponenten ist allerdings sicherheitstechnisch bedenklich. Auch die Effizienz und Skalierbarkeit dieses Ansatzes sind fraglich, da die Routingtabelle des externen Routers enorm vergrößert wird (im ungünstigsten Fall um einen Eintrag pro besuchendem MN).

Eine Möglichkeit, die geschilderten Sicherheits- und Effizienzprobleme zu umgehen, bestünde in der Einführung zusätzlicher Infrastrukturkomponenten, im Folgenden „Agent Proxy" oder AP genannt, in allen Subnetzen eines Netzes (also auch in solchen mit ausschließlich ortsfesten Endsystemen). Ein AP ähnelt funktionell einem HAP, d.h. er fängt Pakete ab, welche für MNs bestimmt sind, und tunnelt sie zum FGW, welches sie dann an den zuständigen FAP weitertunnelt. Hierzu meldet das FGW sämtliche Registrierungs- und Deregistrierungsvorgänge an alle APs innerhalb des Netzes. Über ein Routing-Protokoll oder eine andere geeignete Schnittstelle bringt dann jeder AP den für das jeweilige Subnetz zuständigen Router dazu, alle für besuchende MNs bestimmten Pakete an den AP zu tunneln. Bei diesem Ansatz muss zwar jeder Router im ungünstigsten Fall einen eigenen Routingeintrag für jeden MN anlegen. Da die lokalen Router aber i.d.R. ein wesentlich geringeres Datenaufkommen zu bewältigen haben als der externe Firewall-Router, können sie potenziell größere Routingtabellen verwalten, sodass sich die Skalierbarkeit erhöht. Zudem sind die lokalen Router weniger sicherheitskritisch als der externe Firewall-Router. Ein neues Problem hinsichtlich der Skalierbarkeit ist allerdings der bei jeder (De-)Registrierung anfallende Signalisierungsverkehr zwischen FGW und APs, welcher proportional zur Anzahl der APs, d.h. zur Anzahl der Subnetze des lokalen Netzes ist. Es ist noch zu untersuchen, inwiefern sich die Skalierbarkeit durch diesen Ansatz tatsächlich erhöhen lässt.

Ein grundsätzliches Sicherheitsproblem für MNs und deren Heimatnetze ergibt sich bei jeder Form verkürzten Routings innerhalb eines Fremdnetzes: Da die Firewall des Heimatnetzes umgangen wird, muss der MN wesentlich besser gegenüber Angriffen aus dem Internet abgesichert werden, als dies innerhalb des Heimatnetzes der Fall wäre. Verkürztes Routing innerhalb eines Fremdnetzes sollte daher auf keinen Fall aktiviert werden, wenn vom MN oder vom Heimatnetz Reverse Tunneling angefordert wurde, denn hierdurch wird signalisiert, dass unter anderem aus Sicherheitsgründen alle Pakete über den HA bzw. das heimatliche FGW geleitet werden sollen. Wurde kein Reverse Tunneling angefordert, so werden ohnehin manche Pakete am Heimatnetz vorbeigesendet, sodass durch das verkürzte Routing keine zusätzlichen Gefahren enstehen.

4 Zusammenfassung und Ausblick

Aufbauend auf der allgemeinen Architekturbeschreibung in [4] wurde in diesem Artikel ein detaillierter Einblick in die Paketfilter- und Tunnelkonfiguration gegeben, welche innerhalb der FATIMA-Architektur notwendig ist, um in Zusammenarbeit mit der Firewall eines Netzes eine sichere Mobilitätsunterstützung zu bieten. Die Integration einer FATIMA-Infrastruktur benötigt unabhängig von der Zahl der zu unterstützenden Mobilrechner eine konstante, relativ geringe Anzahl zusätzlicher Filterregeln in den internen und externen Firewall-Routern. Die Filterregeln dieser Router wiederum müssen z.T. innerhalb des FATIMA-Gateways repliziert werden, damit Pakete von und zu mobilen Rechnern genauso gefiltert werden wie alle übrigen ein- und ausgehenden Pakete.

Der Nutzdatenverkehr von mobilen Rechnern zu anderen Rechnern innerhalb eines Fremdnetzes kann in FATIMA komplett innerhalb des Fremdnetzes abgewickelt werden, sofern MN und Heimatnetz dies aus Sicherheitsgründen erlauben. Bei Mobile IP ist eine direkte Zustellung solcher Pakete zwar ebenfalls möglich, eröffnet den MNs aber Angriffsmöglichkeiten auf das Fremdnetz. Für die wesentlich schwierigere Gegenrichtung (Pakete an einen MN von einem CN im Fremdnetz) wurden mehrere potenzielle Lösungsansätze mit unterschiedlicher

Sicherheit und Skalierbarkeit aufgezeigt. Es ist geplant, die Ansätze mit Hilfe einer Simulationsumgebung für verschiedene Mobilitätsszenarien zu bewerten.

Ein Gegenstand für weitergehende Forschungsarbeiten ist der Schutz von Mobilrechnern und ihren Heimatnetzen. Idealerweise sollte es unter Sicherheitsgesichtspunkten gleichgültig sein, ob ein MN sich in seinem Heimatnetz oder in einem Fremdnetz befindet. Dies kann z.B. durch zusätzliche kryptographische Tunnel wie in [2] erreicht werden. Ein wesentlich radikalerer Ansatz für den Fall, dass das Heimatnetz dem Fremdnetz in gewissem Umfang vertraut (z.B. weil es sich um zwei Standorte einer Firma handelt), wäre, die Filterregeln des Heimatnetzes durch ein geeignetes Protokoll in der Firewall des Fremdnetzes zu replizieren. In zukünftigen Forschungsarbeiten wird die Machbarkeit dieses Ansatzes überprüft werden.

Literatur

[1] Bundesamt für Sicherheit in der Informationstechnik. *IT-Grundschutzhandbuch*, July 2000. http://www.bsi.bund.de/gshb/.

[2] V. Gupta and G. Montenegro. Secure and Mobile Networking. *Mobile Networks and Applications*, 3(4):381–390, Jan. 1999.

[3] S. Kent and R. Atkinson. *IP Encapsulating Security Payload (ESP)*. IETF, Nov. 1998. RFC 2406.

[4] S. Mink, F. Pählke, G. Schäfer, and J. Schiller. FATIMA: A Firewall-Aware Transparent Internet Mobility Architecture. In *Proc. of ISCC 2000*, pages 172–179, Antibes, France, July 2000. IEEE Computer Society.

[5] S. Mink, F. Pählke, G. Schäfer, and J. Schiller. Towards Secure Mobility Support for IP Networks. In *Proc. of ICCT 2000*, pages 555–562, Beijing, China, Aug. 2000. IFIP.

[6] G. Montenegro. *Reverse Tunneling for Mobile IP*. IETF, May 1998. RFC 2344.

[7] C. E. Perkins. *IP Encapsulation within IP*. IETF, Oct. 1996. RFC 2003.

[8] C. E. Perkins. *IP Mobility Support*. IETF, Oct. 1996. RFC 2002.

Service Awareness in Mobile Ad Hoc Networks

Jidong Wu* and Martina Zitterbart

Institute of Operating Systems and Computer Networks
Technical University of Braunschweig
{wu|zit}@ibr.cs.tu-bs.de
http://www.ibr.cs.tu-bs.de

Abstract. With the increasing availability of mobile devices, mobile ad hoc networks become a hot research topic. They are characterized by not having a fixed infrastructure — all nodes are potentially mobile. Moreover, we assume that these mobile nodes can provide services to other nodes in a mobile ad hoc network. This results in services being mobile and, consequently, requires a concept for *service awareness*. Mobile nodes need to gain knowledge about the services that are available and need to select a proper service provider out of the list of available providers. We present a concept of service awareness that explicitly copes with the high dynamics in mobile ad hoc networks.

1   Introduction

Currently, mobility is a vital research area with many new aspects being under development including ubiquitous computing and multi-hop ad hoc networking. The latter is appealing in environments without pre-existing communication infrastructure. Mobile ad hoc networks are autonomous systems of mobile routers (and associated hosts) connected by wireless links — the union of which forms an arbitrary graph [1]. All nodes in such a network are potentially mobile. Since the topology in mobile ad hoc networks is inherently dynamic, suited support with respect to routing is needed. This issue is currently investigated in the IETF working group Mobile Ad Hoc Networking (MANET).

On mobile devices currently being used in mobile communications, mainly three different applications can be listed: telephony, SMS messages, and web surfing based on WAP [2]. Web surfing based on WAP incorporates a typical client/server application with the server assumed to be located in the fixed network. Recently, web servers on embedded devices are discussed, and wireless connectivity among embedded devices appears to be extremely desirable [3]. The approach presented in this paper extends this scenario by placing web servers or web proxies not only on nodes in the fixed network, but also on mobile nodes in wireless domains. Consequently, these servers are mobile as well and some support is needed in order to keep track of the current location of such a mobile node and the services located on it.

---

* The author holds a scholarship from Hanns-Seidel-Stiftung.

The basic idea for the support of service mobility is to use a proactive mechanism to inform the neighbors of a node about the awareness of a service in an ad hoc network. This is performed through service announcements which are sent at service set-up and tear-down. Based on such service information, mobile nodes can build up a service awareness cache. The service awareness (SA) functionality presented in this paper makes use of the routing protocol Dynamic Source Routing (DSR) [4, 5], which was developed in the context of MANET.

Generally, the issue of service location is also being discussed in the context of other networking environments, such as Service Location Protocol (SLP) [6], MIT's Intentional Naming System (INS) [7], Bluetooth Special Interest Group's Service Discovery Protocol (SDP) [8]. SLP provides a flexible way of discovering heterogeneous network resources within a site. INS uses an overlay network of INS resolvers in order to discover resources and to locate services for dynamic and mobile network environments. SDP is used in Bluetooth environments to let a device in motion find available services dynamically in the radio-frequency proximity of this device (i.e. in one hop range). Unlike SLP, INS and SDP, our work mainly emphasizes special communication issues arising out of *multi-hop* mobile ad hoc networks. For example, SLP assumes that a fixed infrastructure is available. In INS the overlay network can be "self-configurating", but it still needs a resolver list maintained centrally and an underlying routing protocol with periodic exchange of updates.

The rest of the paper is structured as follows. Section 2 provides an example scenario with service mobility. Section 3 introduces the concept of service awareness in some detail and outlines the mechanisms used. Simulation results are analyzed in section 4. Section 5 concludes the paper.

2 Networking with Service Mobility

Traditionally, servers (or proxies) are arranged in a fixed hierarchy and are known to the hosts via IP addresses. However, such a pre-configuration is not suited in mobile ad hoc networks because all nodes are potentially mobile and a dedicated node may only temporarily provide a specific service to others (e.g., due to battery limitation).

Figure 1 shows a scenario with mobile nodes providing services to other mobile nodes. Rectangles, so-called *mobile servers*, represent mobile nodes that currently provide services. Circles depict "regular" mobile nodes. Four mobile nodes, namely S_1, S_2, S_3 and S_4, act as web proxies. Furthermore, the mobile nodes m_1 and m_2, currently access the web and, thus, use one of the web proxies. Assume that S_3 serves as web proxy for m_2 and S_1 is the current web proxy of m_1. Due to mobility, m_2 changes its position to a location that is closer to the web proxy S_2 than to S_1. Therefore, it would be reasonable that m_2 now uses S_2 as its web proxy. The mobile node providing the web proxy can also change its physical location. For example, the node S_1 in Fig. 1 moves to a different location. As a result, m_1 may prefer using the web proxy S_2 to continuing to use the web proxy S_1.

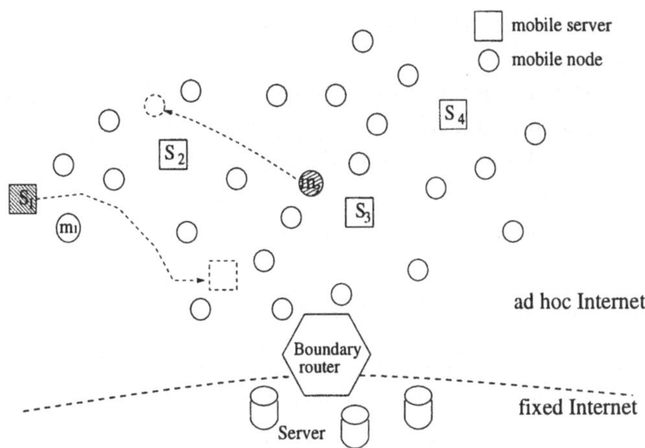

Fig. 1. Service awareness scenario in mobile ad hoc networks

Even if S_1 would remain at its current location, it could be possible that it is no longer willing to act as web proxy, e.g., due to limitations of the battery lifetime. In this case, m_1 would have to select another web proxy. Therefore, it needs information about available web proxies. The concept of *service awareness* presented in this paper provides such information to mobile nodes. It is specifically designed for a highly dynamic networking scenario. It is assumed that no static structure considering the placement and interaction among servers is available in mobile ad hoc networks.

3 The Concept of Service Awareness

The basic question that service awareness tries to answer is: Which service is available on which node? Due to the high dynamics assumed in mobile ad hoc networks, the answer to this question might change rapidly. Our concept for service awareness aims at finding a good answer to this question, i.e., finding a node providing the required service that is located close to the mobile node requesting the service. Thereby we focus on service dynamics — routing protocols, in contrast, cope with node mobility.

Service awareness is tightly coupled to routing protocols, since a path to the selected server is required. Routing protocols known from the fixed Internet are not directly applicable for operation in mobile ad hoc networks. Basically, every mobile node functions as both, host and router, in order to operate an ad hoc network robustly and efficiently. Mobile IP [9] is not sufficient, since it relies on the existing routing infrastructure in fixed networks. Specific routing protocols are needed, such as DSR, Temporally Ordered Routing Algorithm (TORA) [10], and Ad Hoc On-Demand Distance Vector (AODV) [11]. Since our focus is not on routing protocols, we selected one of these protocols, DSR, and place the service awareness functionality above it. However, service awareness is not dependent on this routing protocol.

It is assumed that in mobile ad hoc networks each node operates as a router. As such, each node has information on the current network topology which is provided through the routing protocol. This information is utilized by the service awareness functionalities. As an implication, inter-layer communication inside networking nodes gains even more importance.

3.1 Management of Service Awareness Information

Before going into the details of the service awareness protocol, management of service awareness information in the mobile nodes is outlined. Keeping some information in the nodes increases the memory requirements, but, on other hand, decreases the amount of information that needs to travel through the network. The latter is critical in mobile ad hoc networks that typically consist of low speed wireless links.

The following data structures are maintained in each mobile node for the provision of service awareness:

Awareness cache Within the *awareness cache* information about available services and the respective service providers is cached. This information has been introduced by a server into the network and, subsequently, forwarded hop-by-hop to the mobile node. An entry in the cache consists of the *service ID* and the provider list. The service ID unambiguously identifies a service, such as a web proxy. The provider list collects the known providers of a particular service. It may not necessarily list all providers that are available, but gives a decent list for selection. An entry in the provider list consists of the following fields: *provider ID, service status, update time.*

The service status field is updated as the result of one of the following events:

- reception of a service awareness packet,
- updated routing information,
- reception of data packets originated by servers that are already known to the node.

Service list The *service list* provides information about which service should be acquired and distributed by a mobile node. Additionally, the service list in a mobile server contains the services provided by this mobile server.

Advertisement table A mobile node stores its recent received advertisements in the *advertisement table*. When a node receives a service advertisement, in addition to storing the service information in its awareness cache, it also saves the pair <provider ID, advertisement sequence> in its advertisement table. A mobile node can recognize a new service advertisement from a re-broadcasted advertisement by comparing the pair <provider ID, advertisement sequence> in the packet to the entries in its advertisement table. Advertisement tables prevent re-broadcasting the same advertisement multiple times.

3.2 Service Awareness Protocol

One of the basic characteristics of mobile ad hoc networks is that the underlying topology may change rapidly. Therefore, the service awareness protocol needs to be independent of the network topology.

The following procedures are part of the service awareness concept:

Service Advertisement Servers issue service advertisements if changes in their service offering occur, i.e., if a new service is created or an existing service is terminated.

A neighboring node that receives a service advertisement with newly advertised services, creates a corresponding entry in the service awareness cache. The mobile node that has received an advertisement of a new service will propagate this information further into the ad hoc network, i.e., to its neighbors that will apply the same procedure. Duplicates do not cause any changes to the service awareness cache.

The propagation time of new service information depends on the number of hops to be passed. Since the diameter of a mobile ad hoc domain is considered to be limited, this does not cause a major problem.

Service Discovery When a mobile node does not own any information about a specific service, service discovery is needed. That is, for example, the case if a mobile node joins an ad hoc network or if all corresponding service information is out-dated at that node. For service discovery, a node broadcasts a service discovery packet to its neighbors. They reply in order to provide it with the requested information.

Neighbors that do not have the requested information simply ignore the service discovery packet. However, these nodes will issue a service discovery to their neighbors in order to find information about the requested service. If this is the case, they eventually reply to the original discovery request.

Service Information Update For updating service information, a mobile node can use one of the following alternatives: implicit service confirmation, reception of a service poll reply, reception of a "no service" indication from the node on which the expected services are no longer available.

Implicit service confirmation is based on snooping into received or bypassing data packets. If a server address is contained in the packet, this is implicitly considered as a confirmation that the corresponding server can still be reached by the mobile node and, thus, the advertised service can be utilized. Moreover, service information can be derived from routing information. For example routing update information may confirm that a specific server can still be reached, or may report that the path to a server is interrupted and, thus, the server cannot be reached. The service status field in the service awareness cache will be updated accordingly.

The service status field is used to determine the up-to-dateness of the service information. If an entry is outdated, i.e., a timeout in the service status field is reported, it is simply deleted from the service awareness cache. Thus, a soft-state approach is applied in the concept of service awareness.

Since service discovery is somewhat time consuming and costly (broadcasts), the mobile host will also try to receive new information concerning out-dated services. Therefore, IP options are utilized. The node can include a *service poll* request as an IP option in data packets being currently sent. The data packet which transports the service poll request will be selected randomly. In order to avoid a storm of piggybacked service poll requests, a maximum number of pending poll requests as well as a minimum time interval between consecutive poll requests is defined.

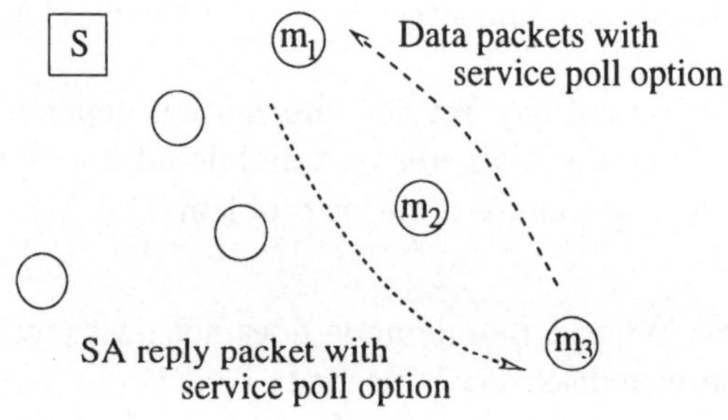

Fig. 2. Service status refresh using piggybacked option

The service poll request is carried as IP option in a data packet. Intermediate nodes will ignore the service poll request, and only the destination node of the data packet will process this request. The destination node will prepare a service awareness packet which is addressed to the source of the poll request and has a "service poll reply" IP option. The poll reply will, in contrast to the poll request, be processed by all intermediate mobile nodes. This service awareness packet may carry service information that is not available in these nodes, i.e., they can benefit from this situation and update their service awareness cache. Additionally, the intermediate nodes will check the service provider ID list included in the service awareness packet. Intermediate nodes may add new entries to the provider ID list if they have service information about additional services. As a result, the mobile node that has issued the service poll request will receive service information not only from the destination node but also from all intermediate nodes on the path.

Suppose node m_3 in Fig. 2 sends a data packet with the service poll option to node m_1. After m_1 receives this data packet it will process the service poll option and return a reply packet to node m_3. This packet contains a active service list known in node m_1. The active service list may be empty if there is no up-to-date service information available in node m_1. This reply packet carries the service poll reply as IP option. A direction flag in service poll IP option is set to indicate that it is a reply packet. All nodes located between m_1 and m_3 will process this reply packet.

Service information update is complemented by another mechanism that addresses services which are no longer available. If a data packet destined for a service that is not active on the server is received, the service awareness component is informed. It will construct an indication to the mobile node that the requested service is not available. The node requesting the service then updates its service awareness cache accordingly.

4 Service Awareness Performance

The evaluation of the service awareness is based on simulation experiments in network simulator ns [12]. The CMU Monarch research group developed wireless and mobility extensions to ns, which included node mobility, a realistic physical layer, the IEEE 802.11 Medium Access Control (MAC) protocol using the Distributed Coordination Function (DCF), and some ad hoc routing protocols [13]. The physical radio characteristics were chosen to approximate the Lucent Wave-LAN direct sequence spread spectrum radio with a raw capacity of 2Mb/s and a 250m nominal transmission range. For our simulation purpose the simulator ns was enhanced with simulation code of the service awareness function proposed in the section 3.

In each simulation experiment 50 wireless nodes forming an ad hoc network move over a $1500m$ x $300m$ space for a total 900 seconds simulation time. Nodes move according to the model "random waypoint" [4]: Each node stays stationary for *pause time* seconds after the simulation begins, then selects a random destination and moves to that destination. After reaching that destination, each node stays for the same pause time seconds, selects a new destination and moves. This behavior is repeated until the end of the simulation. The speed of node movement is randomly selected and is less than 20m/second. In our simulation experiments we selected 7 different pause times: 0, 30, 60, 120, 300, 600, and 900 seconds and generated 70 different movement scenario files, 10 for each value of the pause times. This setup is comparable to the one used for DSR performance evaluation reported in [13]. Furthermore, two different communication patterns, which correspond to 20 and 30 sources producing constant bit rate (CBR) traffic, were used in simulations respectively. Seven other nodes were selected as servers and acted as data sinks.

In order to evaluate the effect of service awareness, two sets of simulation experiments were conducted: with and without service awareness. In the former case ("with SA"), all those seven nodes are considered as alternative and intermittent data sinks. But only 5 of them are available at the same point of time, and totally 5 turn-overs of servers take place in each experiment. In the latter case ("without SA"), each data source is randomly chosen to connect with one of the 7 servers at simulation start and keeps this association until the end of the simulation. The goal of the simulation experiments is to evaluate the effectiveness of service awareness by comparing it with results from experiments without the function of service awareness.

The following metrics were selected for performance evaluation: data packet delivery ratio, ratio of control protocol overhead, average path length for delivery of data packets. It should be noted that the results collected with different pause times but plotted as points of the same curve might not be compared directly with each other, because the corresponding movement patterns used are different.

Packet delivery ratio Data packet delivery ratio is the ratio of the packets originated by the CBR sources to the packets received by the server sink agents at nodes providing the corresponding service.

Figure 3 shows the fraction of the delivered application data packets, as a function of both node mobility rate (pause time 0 stands for high mobility and 900 for static topology) and network load (number of sources). In the simulations with service awareness, the packet delivery ratio is above 97%.

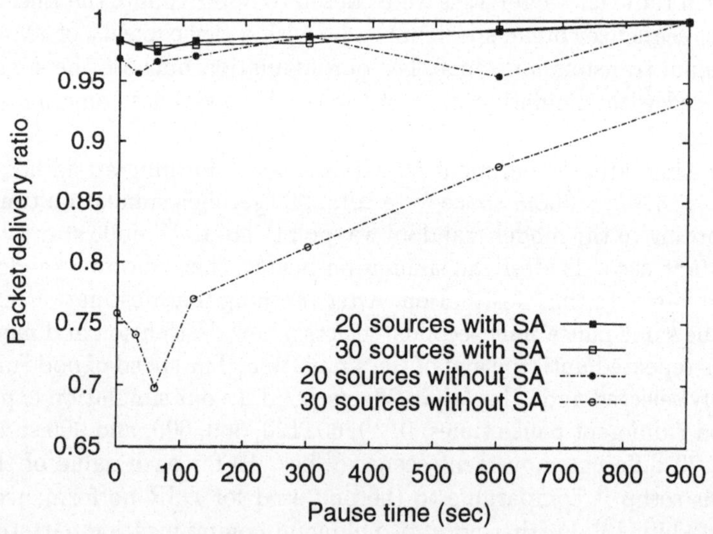

Fig. 3. Packets delivery ratio.

In the case of 30 sources, an obvious difference can be observed between the curves with and without service awareness (cf., Fig. 3). In this case the delivery ratio is noticeably lower than in the other cases, and it is different from what was reported in the CMU's paper [13], in which all packet delivery ratio of DSR routing are above 95%. The reason for this difference can be found in the packet sizes used. We used 512 bytes packets, whereas CMU used 64 bytes packets. In the latter case, congestion is mostly avoided. Using a packet size of 64 bytes, we observed results similar to those reported in [13].

The results clearly depict that service awareness can help improve the packet delivery rate. As we can see later, in the case of using service awareness the data packet delivery path length can be considerably reduced, resulting in less congestion within the network.

Ratio of Control protocol overhead The ratio of control protocol overhead is the ratio of the transmitted non-data packets, such as the service awareness packets or the routing packets, to the all transmitted packets including data and non-data packets. In the simulation experiments without service awareness functionality, non-data overhead includes only the transmission of routing packets. Packets that are forwarded across multiple hops are accounted as follows: one transmission is accounted for each transmission of the packet across a hop. This means that transmissions are considered on a per-hop basis and not on a per-path basis.

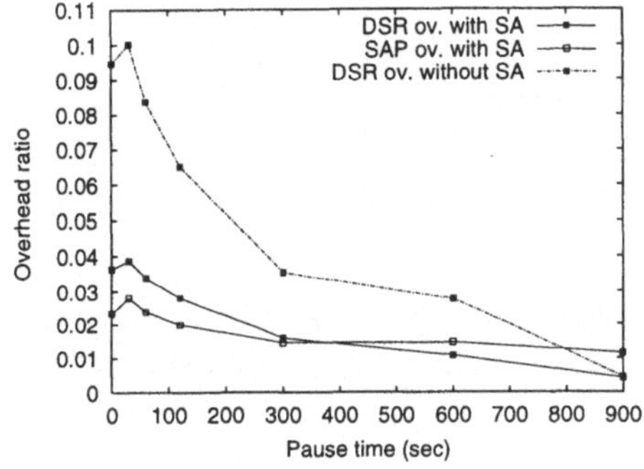

Fig. 4. Control overhead ratio

Figure 4 shows the ratio of service awareness overhead in the simulations with 20 data sources (in Fig. 4 SAP stands for service awareness protocol). To enable a comparison, the routing overhead ratios in both cases, with and without service awareness, are also illustrated. In the simulations with 30 sources the comparable results have been obtained. Note that, in high mobility situations of the simulations with service awareness functionality, the service awareness overhead is slightly lower than the DSR routing overhead. On the other hand, the overhead of DSR routing is lower than the service awareness overhead in low mobility situations. The reason is that DSR is an on-demand routing protocol and, therefore, in lower mobility situations less route searching procedures are required. The service awareness concept, however, uses proactive mechanisms to achieve service awareness. These mechanisms are applied during service discovery and service information update. They generally help keep the service information up to date.

Furthermore, it can be observed that in most mobile situations the control overhead in the cases using service awareness (routing overhead plus service awareness overhead) is still lower than the control overhead in the cases without service awareness (only routing overhead). The following two reasons are mainly responsible for that. Firstly, because routing information is used to update service status, less service awareness packets need to be sent. It should be noted, however, that this increases processing requirements per packet on the nodes. Secondly, with service awareness the route to servers is available with a higher probability than without service awareness. Thus, the need for route searching is reduced.

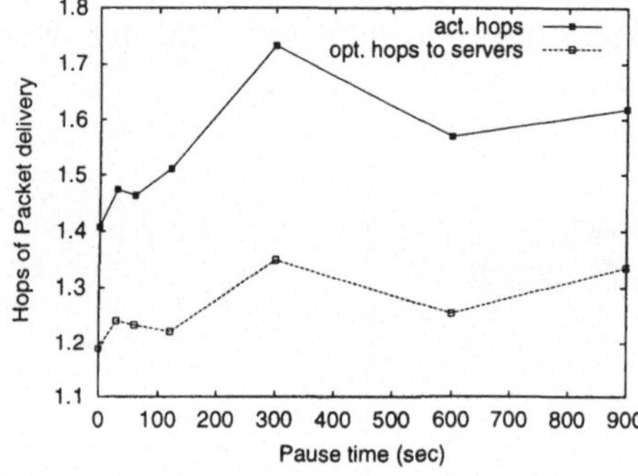

Fig. 5. Average actual hops while sending data packets to servers with SA

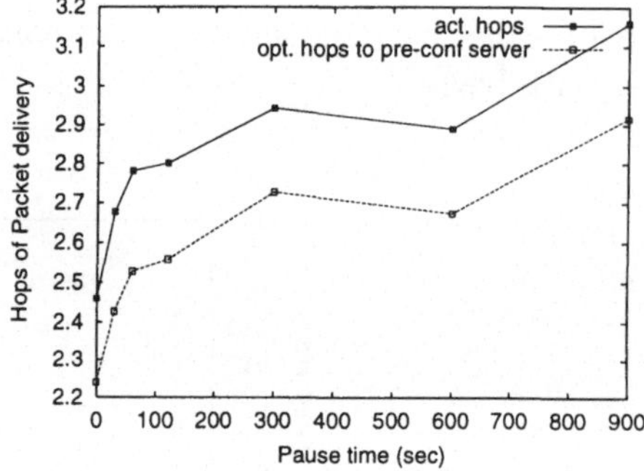

Fig. 6. Average actual hops while sending data packets to servers without SA

Average data packets delivery path length The path length of data delivery refers to the number of hops that a packet has passed in order to reach its destination node. The lower the average path length for data delivery is, the fewer transmissions are needed. Keep in mind that transmissions are accounted on a per-hop basis.

Figure 5 and Figure 6 show the average length of the actual and optimal data packets delivery path (measured as hops) in the cases of 20 data sources. Again, the cases of applying service awareness and not applying service awareness are considered. Comparing the two figures, it can be noticed that the average hops (both actual and optimal) in cases with service awareness are reduced almost to half of those without service awareness. The transmissions of data packets are almost doubled correspond to experiments without service awareness, because each transmission is counted when a data packets traverses multiple hops. Since wireless transmission media is a scare resource that all nodes share, more transmissions refer to a higher possibility of congestion in the network. Service awareness reduces the traffic in an ad hoc network.

5 Summary

In this paper, we propose a concept that is called *service awareness*. The basic idea is that mobile nodes in a mobile ad hoc network may provide services to other mobile nodes. Currently, service provision is more or less assumed to run on nodes in the fixed network where fixed hierarchical structures are implemented. Examples are web servers or domain name servers. We push this paradigm one step further and place the client as well as the server on mobile nodes. However, this leads to the problem, that not only clients but also servers are potentially mobile. The concept of service awareness presented in this paper especially addresses this issue of *service mobility*. Service awareness comprises mechanisms related to service advertisements, service discovery and service information update. We decouple service mobility from node mobility. Node mobility is addressed by proper routing protocols. Service mobility makes use of the routing information stored in routing tables, i.e., it needs access to this information.

In order to evaluate our approach, some simulation experiments have been conducted. We used the network simulator *ns*, mobility extensions provided by CMU and applied further extensions addressing service awareness. The results show, that mobile ad hoc networks can benefit from service awareness. For example, the packet delivery ratio can be improved. Moreover, the number of hops needed for transmission can be reduced and, thus, the overall traffic in the ad hoc network can be reduced.

Our present design of service awareness uses broadcasting to advertise service information. An enhanced concept that reduces broadcasts is currently under development. We plan to enhance the simulation framework in oder to contain more realistic examples (e.g., web caching), so that we can characterize the class of applications that will benefit from the concept of service awareness.

References

[1] Scott Corson and Joseph Macker. Mobile ad hoc networking(MANET): routing protocol performance issues and evaluation considerations. RFC 2501, January 1999.

[2] Wireless Application Protocol Forum Ltd. Wireless application protocol, October 1999. `http://www.wapforum.org/what/WAP_white_pages.pdf`.

[3] Gaetano Borriello and Roy Want. Embedded computation meets the world wide web. *Communications of the ACM*, 43(5):59–66, May 2000.

[4] David B. Johnson and David A. Maltz. Dynamic source routing in ad hoc wireless networks. In *Mobile computing*, pages 153–182. Kluwer academic publishers, 1996.

[5] Josh Broch, David B. Johnson, and David A. Maltz. The dynamic source routing protocol for mobile ad hoc networks, December 1998. draft-ietf-manet-dsr-01.txt(work in progress).

[6] Erik Guttman, Charles E. Perkins, John Veizades, and Michael Day. Service location protocol, version 2. RFC 2608, June 1999.

[7] William Adjie-Winoto, Elliot Schwartz, Hari Balakrishnan, and Jeremy Lilley. The design and implementation of an intentional naming system. *Operating Systems Review*, 34(5):186–201, December 1999. 17th ACM Symposium on Operating System Principles(SOSP'99).

[8] Bluetooth Special Interest Group. Specification of the bluetooth system - core: Part e service discovery protocol (SDP), November 1999. `http://www.bluetooth.com/link/spec/bluetooth_e.pdf`.

[9] Charles E. Perkins. IP mobility support. RFC 2002, October 1996.

[10] Vincent D. Park and M. Scott Corson. A highly adaptive distributed routing algorithm for mobile wireless networks. In *Proceedings of INFOCOM'97*, pages 1405–1413, April 1997.

[11] Charles E. Perkins, Elizabeth M. Royer, and Samir R. Das. Ad hoc on demand distance vector (aodv) routing, March 2000. draft-ietf-manet-aodv-05.txt(work in progress).

[12] Kevin Fall and Kannan Varadhan, editors. *ns Notes and Documentation*. July 1999. `http://www-mash.cs.berkeley.edu/ns/`.

[13] Josh Broch, David A. Maltz, David B. Johnson, Yih-Chun Hu, and Jorjeta Jetcheva. A performance comparison of multi-hop wireless ad hoc network routing protocols. In *Proceedings of ACM/IEEE MOBICOM'98*, pages 85–97, October 1998.

Entwicklung von WAP-Anwendungen

Albrecht Schmidt[#], Hans-W. Gellersen[#], Michael Beigl[#] und Oliver Frick[+]

[#]Telecooperation Office (TecO), Universität Karlsruhe
[+]SAP-CEC Karlsruhe, Corporate Research, SAP AG

{albrecht|hwg|michael}@teco.edu, o.frick@sap.com

Der Anspruch des Wireless Application Protocolls (WAP) und der Wireless Markup Language (WML) sowie darauf basierender Systeme ist es, mobile Geräte mit Informationen und verteilten Anwendungen zu versorgen. Oft wird dabei der Vergleich zum World-Wide Web gezogen. In diesem Bericht wird exemplarisch anhand von fünf von uns verwirklichten WAP-Anwendungen aufgezeigt, welche Parallelen gerechtfertigt sind und wo die spezifischen Unterschiede liegen. Insbesondere werden Schwächen und Probleme konzeptioneller und technischer Art der derzeitigen Implementierung des WAP Netzwerks genannt. Teile der hier vorgestellten Anwendungen sind als Lösungen für die Überwindung dieser Probleme konzipiert, andere dienen als Testfeld, um die Einsatzmöglichkeiten von WAP-Anwendungen auszuloten. Auf der Basis der hierbei gesammelten Erfahrungen werden abschließend Hinweise für die Entwicklung von WAP-Anwendungen für mobile Endgeräte gegeben.

1. Einleitung

Mobile Endgeräte, welche das *Wireless Application Protokol* (WAP) einsetzen, eröffnen neue und vielfältige Möglichkeiten auf Informationen, Daten und Anwendungen im Internet zuzugreifen. Es läßt sich jedoch beobachten, dass der anfänglichen überschwenglichen Begeisterung für das neue Medium eine Ernüchterung folgte. Die Frustration der Benutzer mit der neuen Technologie und insbesondere mit der Bedienung scheint das gesamte Konzept in Frage zu stellen [2].

In diesem Beitrag analysieren wir die technischen Möglichkeiten von WAP, Informationen und Anwendungen auf Mobiltelefonen und PDAs verfügbar zu machen. Darüber hinaus geben wir einen Überblick über die grundsätzlichen Probleme, welche sich aus der Benutzerschnittstelle von kleinen tragbaren Geräten ergeben.

An verschiedenen WAP-Anwendungen, die im Rahmen von verschiedenen Forschungsprojekten entwickelt wurden, zeigen wir exemplarisch, welche Arten von Anwendungen sich sinnvoll auf WAP anbieten lassen. Abschließend führen wir die gesammelten Erfahrungen zusammen, diskutieren die Implikationen, die sich daraus ergeben und schlagen Richtlinien für den Entwurf und die Umsetzung von WAP-Anwendungen vor.

2. WAP – Einführung und Analyse

Mit WAP steht eine weitere Technologie zur Verfügung, welche die Vision des *Informationszugriffs immer und überall* [8], der Realität ein Stück näher bringen kann.

2.1. Architektur

Die Netzwerkarchitektur basiert auf dem Client-Gateway-Server-Prinzip. Beim Server handelt es sich um einen Web-Server, welcher statische oder dynamische Ressourcen über das HTTP-Protokoll zur Verfügung stellt. Das Gateway setzt Anfragen vom mobilen Endgerät (z.B. Telefon über GSM) auf HTTP um, beschafft die angefragte Ressource, codiert diese für das Endgerät (z.B. Kompression von Daten oder Kompilieren von WMLScript) und überträgt diese zum Client, siehe auch [7].

2.2. Ressourcen - WML, WMLScript und Bilder

Für den Einsatz mit WAP sind drei Typen von Ressourcen von besonderem Interesse: Wireless Markup Language (WML), die Skriptsprache WMLScript und das Bildformat WBMP. Die Ressourcen werden über MIME-Types spezifiziert. Für die technische Umsetzung auf Serverseite unterscheidet sich WAP somit kaum von anderen Dokumententypen im WWW. Ressourcen werden als Dokumente auf dem Server abgelegt oder mit Hilfe von serverseitigen Technologien, wie Server-Side-Include, Server-Side-Scripting (z.B. ASP, PHP) oder CGI dynamisch generiert. Für die Entwicklung lassen sich die Vorgehensweisen, das Wissen und unter Umständen auch Programmbibliotheken, die vom WWW bekannt sind, einsetzen.

Die Wireless Markup Language (WML) ist eine Anwendung von XML und wird genutzt, um Dokumente zu beschreiben. WML bietet Konstrukte zur formatierten Ausgabe von Daten, zum Einlesen von Benutzereingaben in verschiedener Form und zur Navigation. Ein Dokument wird als *Stapel* (engl. *Deck*) bezeichnet und kann eine oder mehrere *Karten* (engl. *Cards*) enthalten. Die Navigation innerhalb eines Dokuments bezieht sich auf diese Karten. Sie sind somit im Entwurf die kleinste logische Einheit. Ereignisse (engl. *Events*) und Zeitgeber (engl. *Timer*) sind weitergehende Konzepte im WML, die es ermöglichen, den Ablauf von Dokumenten zu steuern. Um die Navigation über verschiedene Karten hinweg konsistent zu halten, ist das Konzept der Schablonen (engl. *Templates*) vorhanden, mit welcher sich die Navigationseigenschaften für alle Karten innerhalb eines Decks definieren lassen.

Mit WMLScript steht eine vollwertige Skriptsprache zur Verfügung. Die Sprache wurde so entwickelt und optimiert, dass sie für Geräte mit begrenzten Ressourcen verwendet werden kann. Der Entwickler schreibt dabei ein Skript, welches auf dem Server als Dokument liegt. Der Compiler befindet sich im Netz (i.allg. im Gateway) und übersetzt das Script in Bytecode, der dann an das Endgerät übertragen wird. Der Zugriff auf spezifische Funktionen des Mobiltelefons, wie z.B. das Initiieren eines Gesprächs, wird über die *Wireless Telephone Architecture (WTA)* ermöglicht.

2.3. Konzeptbedingte Probleme

WAP soll Geräten mit sehr kleinen Displays den Zugang zum Internet ermöglichen. Neben dem Potential des weltweit unbeschränkten Zugangs zu Informationen ergeben sich aber auch Probleme, insbesondere hinsichtlich der Bedienoberfläche. Typische Displaygrößen von Mobiltelefonen liegen bei ca. 100 x 70 Pixel, womit die Menge der Information, die sich darstellen lässt, sehr begrenzt ist. Überlegungen, die Anzeige zu vergrößern, um mehr Information darstellen zu können, sind konträr zum allgemeinen Trend im Design der Miniaturisierung mobiler Endgeräte.

Das Angebot von Geräten auf denen WAP-Browser eingesetzt werden, reicht von Handheld Computern mit halber VGA-Auflösung (z.B. Ericsson MC218, Psion, 640x240 Pixel), über PDAs (z.B. PalmPilot 160x160 Pixel) bis hin zu Mobiltelefonen und Armbanduhren (z.B. Nokia 7110, 96x65 Pixel). Betrachtet man das Verhältnis der Bildschirmfläche von 24:1 so erkennt man, dass eine Entwicklung von Anwendungen, die sinnvoll auf allen Geräten angezeigt werden können, mit besonderen Schwierigkeiten verbunden ist.

Die Möglichkeiten, welche mobile Geräte zur Benutzerinteraktion und insbesondere zur Eingabe von Daten offerieren, unterscheiden sich sehr stark. Handheld Computer bieten meist eine Tastatur und oft auch einen Touchscreen, wohingegen PDAs meist keine Tastatur besitzen. Beide Arten von Geräten unterstützen die direkte Manipulation, wie z.B. das Klicken auf einen Link. Mobiltelefone hingegen zwingen den Benutzer zur Verwendung des Tastenfeldes für die Navigation. Allerdings bieten die meisten Telefone sehr gute Möglichkeiten (oft eigene Tasten) für das einfache Scrollen durch Listen.

Die Eingabe von Freitext bereitet den Benutzern auf den meisten kleinen Geräten große Schwierigkeiten [3]. Telefone sind beispielsweise aufgrund ihres traditionellen Haupteinsatzzwecks auf die Eingabe von Zahlen optimiert. In einer Studie haben wir die Effizienz der Eingabe von Text und Zahlen über ein Mobiltelefon quantifiziert. Dazu haben 19 Versuchspersonen jeweils einen Block von entweder 100 Zahlen oder 100 Buchstaben über ein Mobiltelefon (Nokia 7110) eingeben. Aufgezeichnet wurden dabei die Fehlerrate sowie die Dauer der Interaktion, siehe Tabelle 1.

Das Experiment hat gezeigt, dass die Eingabe von Textkolonnen mehr als doppelt so lange dauert wie die Eingabe einer gleichlangen Zahlenkolonne (148 s gegenüber 376 s) und die Fehlerrate bei der Texteingabe knapp fünf mal so hoch ist (0,7 gegenüber 3,5). Selbst bei Berücksichtigung der Tatsache, dass die Eingabe von Text

	Numerisch	Textuell
Anzahl der Tastenanschläge	100	217
Durchschnittliche Zeit (sec)	148	376
Durchschnittliche Zeit / Tastenanschlag (sec)	1,47	1,69
Durchschnittliche Fehlerrate	0,7	3,5
Durchschnittliche Fehlerrate / Tastenanschlag	0, 7 %	1,6 %

Tabelle 1: Bewertung der Eingabe von Text und Zahlen über ein Mobiltelefon.

gegenüber der Eingabe von Zahlen etwa die doppelte Anzahl der Tastenanschläge erfordert, ist die Zeit pro einzelnem Tastenanschlag bei der Texteingabe immer noch grösser und die Fehlerrate doppelt so hoch. Weiter zeigte sich, dass die Benutzer zur Eingabe von Zahlen kaum auf das Tastenfeld sahen, wohingegen nahezu alle Probanten zur Eingabe von Buchstaben eine visuelle Kontrolle benötigten. Dadurch lässt sich beispielsweise ableiten, dass die Benutzerinteraktion über Mobiltelefone textuelle Eingabe vermeiden und wo immer möglich numerische Eingabetechniken verwenden sollten.

2.4. Technische Probleme

Betrachtet man die aktuell verfügbaren Systeme und Implementierungen, insbesondere Endgeräte (z.B. Mobiltelefone), Gateways und Entwicklungswerkzeuge, so müssen weitere Probleme betrachtet werden.

Die meisten der verfügbaren Implementierungen sind nur bedingt konform zu den aktuellen Standards oder implementieren nur eine Untermenge der definierten Eigenschaften. Es ergeben sich somit häufig Situationen, in denen WML/WMLScript-Anwendungen nur auf einem Endgerät-Typ funktionsfähig ist. Ein unserer Erfahrung nach schwerwiegenderes Problem ergibt sich, wenn Anwendungen nur mit einem bestimmten Gateway funktionieren, da hier Fehlerfälle für den Entwickler oder Benutzer schwer nachvollziebar sind. Für den Entwickler ist des deshalb unumgänglich, die Anwendung während des Entwicklungsprozesses mit verschiedenen Gateways zu testen. Die Beschränkung der Länge von URLs und der Größe von Dokumenten stellen zwei weitere Problembereiche dar.

Die Fehlertoleranz der Clients und Gateways ist minimal. Dies läßt sich einerseits darauf zurückführen, dass WML als XML-Anwendung weiterergehende Anforderungen an das Markup stellt als dies für HTML der Fall ist. Andererseits kann es teilweise auf schlechte Implementierungen zurückgeführt werden. Erschwert wird die Fehlersuche durch die fehlende Möglichkeit des Debuggens und die Eigenschaft der Mobiltelefone, nicht verstandene Anweisungen zu ignorieren und keine Fehlermeldung auszugeben. Deshalb sind derzeit nach unseren Erfahrung die Entwicklungskosten im Bereich WAP wesentlich höher als die für vergleichbare WWW-Anwendungen.

Die Art der Einwahl und das Abrechnungsmodell stellen weitere Problemfaktoren dar. Insbesondere die sehr lange Zeit des Verbindungsaufbaus (bis zu 30 Sekunden) stellen eine Hemmschwelle dar, kleine Informationsmengen abzurufen. Durch das zeitbezogen Abrechnungsmodell entstehen sehr hohe Kosten, z.B. für den Zugriff auf das aktuelle Kinoprogramm und die Navigation (Übertragungszeit drei Sekunden bei 9600Kbit/s) ist eine Verbindungszeit von mindestens einer Minute notwendig. Die eigentliche Bandbreite selbst stellt, insbesondere bei den Geräten mit kleinen Displays, kein Problem dar.

3. WAP Anwendungen

In diesem Abschnitt stellen wir exemplarisch verschiedene WAP-Anwendungen vor, welche wir in den letzen 18 Monaten im Rahmen verschiedener Projekte entwickelt haben. Sie zeigen das Spektrum der Möglichkeiten und Grenzen von WAP auf.

3.1. Personal WAP

Das Verwalten von Information auf einem WAP-Endgerät ohne Tastatur ist sehr mühsam, die Eingabe einer einzelnen URL kann eine Minute oder länger dauern. Im Projekt *Personal WAP* (pWAP) wurde deshalb das vom WWW bekannte Portalkonzept für die neuen Anforderungen angepasst und exemplarisch implementiert.

Die grundlegende Idee des Portals besteht darin, dass der Benutzer eine auf seine Bedürfnisse ausgerichtete Startseite benutzt, um an weitere Informationen zu gelangen. Der Benutzer besitzt die Möglichkeit dieses Portal an seine persönlichen Präferenzen anzupassen. In pWAP besteht das Portal aus zwei Zugängen, einem WWW-Zugang, der als WWW-Anwendung die Verwaltung des Portals auf sehr einfache und benutzerfreundliche Art ermöglicht, und dem WAP-Zugang, der das persönliche Portal für WAP-Geräte zur Verfügung stellt. Die Auswahl der Darstellung geschieht abhängig vom Gerät mit dem auf die Seite zugegriffen wird.

Mit Hilfe eines Web-Browsers kann der Benutzer im Portal auf einfache Weise Lesezeichen (Bookmarks) speichern, Informationskanäle abonnieren oder Notizen, die vom mobilen Gerät aus zugreifbar sein sollen, ablegen. Auf dem WAP-Gerät muss nur einmal der URL der persönlichen Portalseite eingetragen werden. Alle Änderungen werden dann via Webzugang durchgeführt. Eine genaue technische Beschreibung findet sich in [6], siehe auch Bild 1.

Eine besondere Anwendung, die hier realisiert wurde, ist das *Kopieren und Einfügen* von Standardanwendungen (z.B. E-Mail) auf das Mobiltelefon. Der Benutzer hat auf seinem Arbeitsplatzrechner eine WWW-Anwendung, die einen Notizzettel darstellt. Alles was in diesen Notizzettel eingefügt wird, ist dann auch auf der persönlichen Portalseite auf dem WAP-Endgerät verfügbar. Ein einfaches Beispiel soll die Anwendung der Funktionalität illustrieren: Der Benutzer erhält eine E-Mail mit der Wegbeschreibung zum Kunden. Er kopiert diesen Text und fügt ihn in den Notizzettel ein. Diese Notiz ist nun auch auf dem Mobiltelefon zugreifbar.

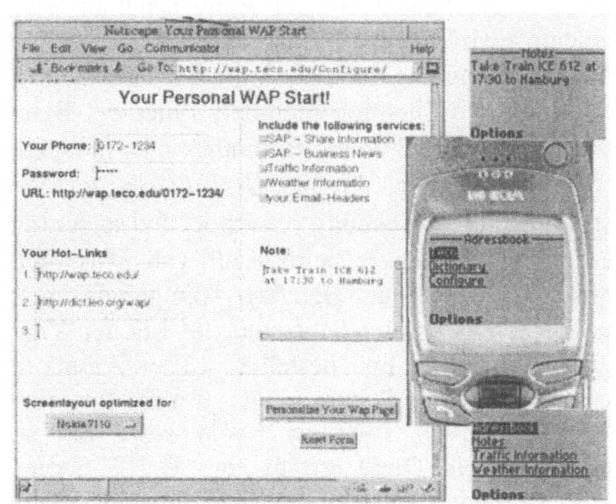

Bild 1: pWAP. Browser und Telefon.

Grundlegende Konzepte, die sich für die Entwicklung von Anwendungen ableiten lassen, sind:

- Co-Design von WWW und WAP Anwendungen
  Es ist oft sinnvoll, Anwendungen mit zwei Zugängen zu erstellen: einen Zugang über das WWW, der für Standardbrowser ausgelegt ist und mit dem die Verwaltung erledigt werden kann, sowie ein weiterer Zugang, der auf das mobile Endgerät zugeschnitten ist und auch nur die Funktionen enthält, welche für den mobilen Einsatz sinnvoll sind.
- Personalisierte Anwendungen
  Um den relativ hohen Aufwand für die Navigation auf den mobilen Endgeräten zu minimieren ist es sinnvoll, Anwendungen stark auf die Bedürfnisse eines einzelnen Benutzers abzustimmen.
- Einfache Metaphern
  Um den Umgang mit den Geräten zu erleichtern ist es notwendig, sehr einfache Bedienmetaphern zu verwenden (Beispiel Notizzettel).

3.2. Situationsbezogene Anwendungen - E-Commerce mit WAP

Wird statt eines PC-Browsers ein mobiles Endgerät wie ein WAP Handy verwendet, ergeben sich Erweiterungen und zum Teil völlig neue mobile E-Commerce Anwendungen (M-Commerce). Diese Einsatzgebiete sowie die verwendeten mobilen Geräte stellen neue Anforderungen an die Anwendungen. So limitieren z.B. die geringen Displaygrößen die Ausgabe und die problematische Navigation sowie Dateneingabe erfordern eine Beschränkung auf die absolut notwendige Information.

Im Gegensatz zu stationären Anwendungen mit eher universellem Charakter haben wir in unseren Forschungsprojekten die Erfahrung gemacht, dass sinnvolle M-Commerce-Anwendungen situationsabhänig sind. Daher ist eine situationsbezogene Reduktion der Informationen möglich.

Ähnlich dem in [1] beschriebene „Pocket Bargain Finder" haben wir eine WAP-Anwendung entwickelt, die nach Eingabe einer ISBN-Nummer die Angebote der verschiedene Versandanbieter für dieses Buch auflistet. Der Benutzer kann dann einen Anbieter auswählen und direkt bestellen – oder sich gegen die Online-Bestellung entscheiden und das Buch direkt im Buchgeschäft mitnehmen. Die Interaktion ist für eine bestimmte Situation optimiert - hier der Benutzer hat die ISBN Nummer zur Hand, da er sich z.B. in der Bibliothek oder in einem Buchgeschäft befindet.

In einem weiteren Projekt *GetThatSong* werden situationsabhängige Daten zur Anpassung der Anwendung verwendet und so der Interaktionsaufwand verringert. Die Idee ist, den Benutzer beim Kauf von Musik-CDs oder MP3s zu unterstützen. Typische Situation: ein Benutzer hört gerade im Radio ein Lied, das er in seiner persönlichen Sammlung haben möchte. Mit der WAP-Anwendung *GetThatSong* kann er genau diese ad hoc bestellen. Unser Ansatz verwendet dabei das verfügbare situationsabhängige Datum „Zeit", um die Interaktion zu reduzieren. Der Benutzer ruft, während das Lied im Radio läuft, mit seinem Mobiltelefon die WAP-Anwendung auf. Diese erfrägt vom WWW-Server der Radiostation den zur Zeit gerade laufenden Titel (diese Funktionalität ist z.B. bei SWR3 vorhanden). Mit diesem Titel wird dann entweder eine Anfrage an Online-CD-Händler gestellt und dirckt auf die Bestellung verzweigt, oder das MP3 im Web gesucht. Die zur Bestellung benötigten Adress- und Abrechnungsdaten sind in den Profilen hinterlegt, die vom Benutzer über eine separate Webseite gepflegt werden.

Die folgenden Konzepte sind von uns als grundlegend für die Entwicklung von WAP-Anwendungen identifiziert worden:

- Situationsabhängige Anwendungen erstellen
  Der Interaktionsaufwand mobiler Anwendungen kann durch Verwendung situationsabhängiger Daten - der Ort, die Zeit, das momentane Umfeld des Benutzers - wesentlich reduziert werden. Hierzu zählt auch der Zugriff auf Daten an anderer Stelle.

- Personalisierung der Anwendung
  Benutzerprofile und die Historie des Benutzers können die notwendige Interaktion weiter verringern, beispielsweise durch die Automatisierung von Standardvorgängen oder das Vorgeschlagen von Defaultwerten.

3.3. WAP als Terminal zur Gerätebedienung

Eine Vielzahl von Geräten verfügen heute über Schnittstellen zur entfernten Steuerung und Konfiguration. Die entsprechenden Protokolle sind dabei in der Regel proprietär, was eine Systemintegration stark erschwert. In letzter Zeit zeichnet sich dabei ein Übergang zu TCP/IP bzw. HTTP ab, verschiedene Haussteuerungssysteme bieten inzwischen beispielsweise Gateways zur Steuerung der Geräte über das WWW an. Mit WAP kann dieser Entwicklung ein weiteres Element hinzugefügt werden: die Möglichkeit der ortsunabhängigen Fernbedienung von Geräten über Mobiltelefone.

In unserer Laborumgebung haben wir verschiedene einfache Geräte, die sich über HTTP steuern lassen: Türöffner, Lampen, Lüfter und eine Kaffeemaschine etc. Die Steuerfunktionen sind dabei zweifach ausgelegt, in HTML zur Steuerung über WWW, und in WML zur Steuerung mittels WAP. Die Funktionalität der Anwendung beschränkt sich dabei nicht nur auf die binäre Funktionskontrolle „An/Aus", sondern ermöglicht auch die detaillierte Statusüberprüfung und Konfiguration eines Geräts.

Ein in unserem Labor vorhandener Getränkeautomat beispielsweise verfügt ab Werk über eine Konfigurationsschnittstelle nach dem Standard der *European Vending Association (EVA)*. Diese wurde von uns um einen Protokollumsetzer erweitert, der das EVA-Protokoll in HTTP/HTML bzw. HTTP/WML übersetzt. Letzteres eröffnet nun die Möglichkeit, den Getränkeautomat von einem beliebigen Ort zu überprüfen und zu konfigurieren (Bild 2 zeigt die Konfiguration der Kühlung über WAP). Der Gerätezugriff erfolgt nun entweder direkt vor Ort um beispielsweise auf die Installation eines eingebauten Terminals zu verzichten, von einem dezentralen Auslieferungslager aus um den Füllstand des Automaten zu überprüfen und eine geeignete Route zu planen, oder unterwegs von einem Servicetechniker um kurzfristig und qualifiziert

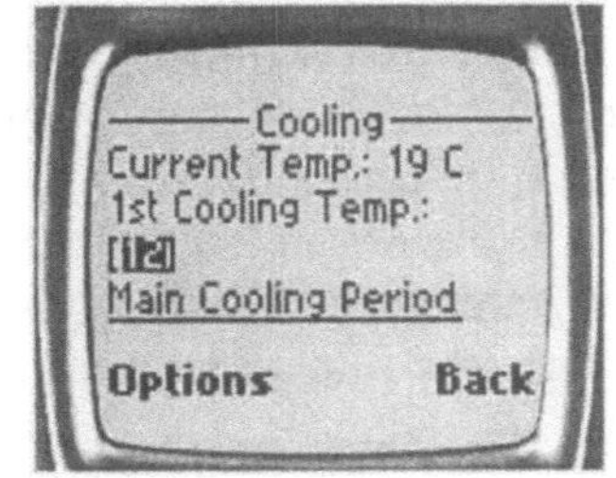

Bild 2: Fernkonfiguration der Temperatur eines Getränkeautomaten über WAP.

Serviceanfragen zu bewerten und zu planen.

Die Vorteile dieses Ansatzes liegen nun zum einen in einem einheitlichen Interface zur Konfiguration unterschiedlichster Geräte. Zum anderen können die Kosten des Systems reduziert werden, da keine zusätzliche Schnittstelle zur Wartung mehr benötigt wird. Schließlich besteht zu jedem Zeitpunkt von jedem Ort aus ein logischer Zugang zum Gerät, wodurch Geschäftsabläufe optimiert werden können. Als grundlegende Konzepte lassen sich hieraus ableiten:

- WAP-Anwendungen können als Schnittstellen zur Steuerung von Geräten implementiert werden und so die Funktionalität eines Mobiltelefons zu Fernbedienungen erweitert werden.
- In Embedded Systems, wie z.B. Verkaufsautomaten, welche ohnehin über eine Möglichkeit zur entfernten Steuerung verfügen, können WAP-Anwendungen eine Alternative zum eingebauten Terminal bieten. Hier bieten sich zusätzliche Möglichkeiten wie ortsunabhängige sowie rollenbezogene Zugänge oder Mehrsprachigkeit.

3.4. Context-Call

Primär werden Mobiltelefone für die Kommunikation zwischen Menschen eingesetzt. Betrachtet man die Kommunikation zwischen Personen, welche sich am gleichen Ort befinden, stellt man fest, dass eine Vielzahl von impliziten Konventionen bestehen und dass diese meist eingehalten werden. Ein wichtiger Aspekt ist der Beginn einer Konversation. Die Person, die das Gespräch eröffnen möchte, sucht hierfür einen möglichst günstigen Zeitpunkt. Dazu wird die Dringlichkeit des eigenen Anliegens und die Situation, in der sich der potentielle Gesprächspartner befindet, berücksichtigt. Insbesondere sind hierfür die Rollen der einzelnen Personen, ihre sozialen Beziehungen und die Umgebung von großer Bedeutung.

Betrachtet man nun die fernmündliche Kommunikation stellt sich das Problem, dass der Anrufer zwar sein eigenes Anliegen kennt, aber die Situation auf der Seite des Empfängers nur erraten kann. Mit Mobiltelefonen ist das Einschätzen der Situation noch schwieriger geworden, da sich nun auch der Rückschluss auf den Aufenthaltsort aus der Telefonnummer nicht mehr vollziehen lässt.

Um dem Anrufer die Möglichkeit zu geben einzuschätzen, ob der Zeitpunkt für den Anruf gut gewählt ist oder nicht, haben wir im Projekt ContextCall ein System bestehend aus einem Server und zwei WAP-Anwendungen entwickelt, welche es zulässt, Information über die eigene Situation dem Anrufer zur Verfügung zu stellen, siehe Bild 3. Der Anrufer kann auf Grund dieser Information dann entscheiden, ob er den Anruf durchführen, eine Nachricht hinterlassen, oder ob er den Vorgang abbrechen möchte.

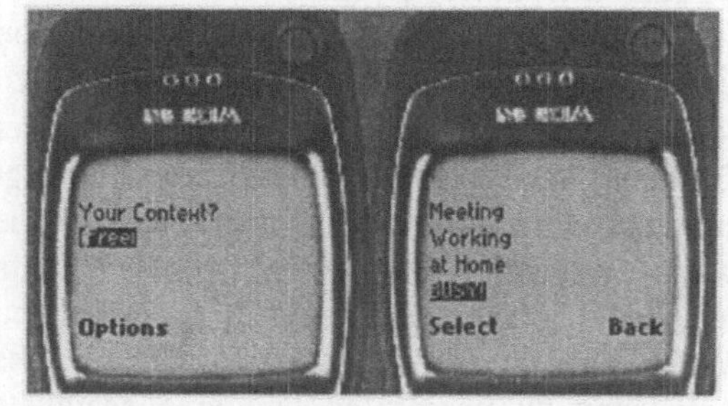

Bild 3: ContextCall, Kontext setzen

Das System besteht aus drei Teilen. Mit einer WAP-Anwendung kann ein Teilnehmer Informationen über seine Situation zur Verfügung stellen. Hierbei kann er aus einer Liste von vordefinierten Profilen (*zu Hause, Büro, Besprechung, beschäftigt,* etc) auswählen oder eine freie Texteingabe vornehmen. Wir arbeiten an

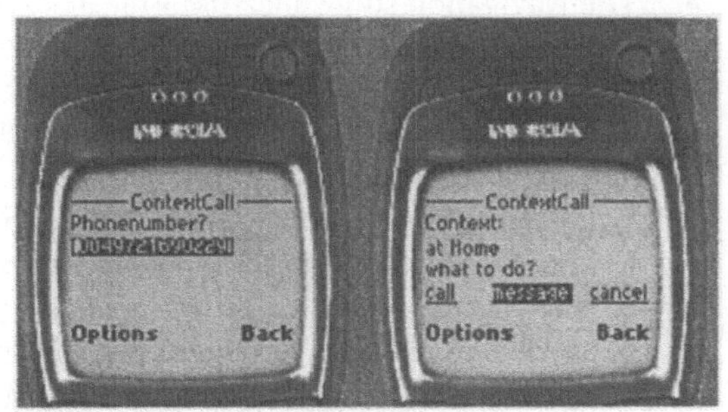

Bild 4: ContextCall. Ablauf eines Gesprächsaufbau.

Ansätzen diesen Schritt durch Sensorintegration und Perzeptionstechniken zu automatisieren [5]. Diese Kontextinformation wird dann auf dem Server gespeichert.

Kern des Systems ist eine WAP-Anwendung, die der Benutzer anstelle der vorhandenen Anruffunktion im Telefon verwendet, um die Eigenschaften von ContextCall zu nutzen. In Bild 4 ist der Ablauf eines Anrufs dargestellt. Der Anrufer wählt die Nummer oder den Namen des gewünschten Gesprächspartner. Daraufhin erhält er die Information über die Situation des Angerufenen als Entscheidungsgrundlage. In der Implementierung wird mit der Eingabe aus dem ersten Schritt eine Verbindung zum Server geöffnet und die Information über den potentiellen Empfänger zum Anrufer übertragen. Entscheidet sich der Anrufer, den Anruf fortzusetzen, wird die entsprechende WTAI Funktion im Telefon aufgerufen. Durch das Austauschen von Kontextinformation entstehen viele Fragen bezüglich des Datenschutzes. Diese haben wir in [4] angesprochen.

Durch die Öffnung des Telefons, z.B. durch WAP, ergeben sich folgende grundlegende Neuerungen:

- Es kann eine ganze Klasse von Anwendungen entstehen, welche die Funktionalität der Telefonanwendung erweitert oder an spezifische Anforderungen anpasst.
- Die Bedienoberfläche der Telefonsoftware (z.B. Anruffunktion, Kalender, Adressbuch, Spiele, etc.) kann unabhängig von der Telefon-hardware, basierend auf einem offenen Standard entwickelt und vertrieben werden.

4. Zusammenfassung

Durch die Einführung von WAP und dafür geeigneten Endgeräten werden die Möglichkeiten für den mobilen Informationszugriff wesentlich erweitert.

Beim Entwurf und der Implementierung von Anwendungen sollten die folgenden grundlegenden Regeln beachtet werden:

- Beim Aufbau der Anwendung ist das Konzept von Decks und Cards zu berücksichtigen, d.h. Informationseinheiten zu entwickeln und auszuwählen, die sinnvoll auf einer Card darstellbar sind. Einheiten die zusammen gehören sollen in einem Deck vereint werden.

- Die Navigation sollte spezifisch für die jeweiligen Geräte entwickelt werden. Z.B. ist es mit den meisten WAP-Telefonen einfacher durch eine lange Liste zu scrollen als Links zu folgen. Die Navigation sollte über die gesamte Anwendung hinweg einheitlich sein. Dazu kann das Konzept der Templates verwendet werden.

- Benutzereingaben sollten soweit dies möglich ist minimiert werden. Ansätze hierfür bieten Situationsbezogenheit, Personalisierung und Co-Design mit WWW-Anwendungen. Sind dennoch Eingaben notwendig, sollten diese so gestaltet sein, dass sie möglichst gut auf dem jeweiligen Gerät zu bewältigen sind, d.h. auf Telefonen ist es sinnvoll Ziffern Buchstaben vorzuziehen.

- Die Verwendung von Markup zur Gestaltung des Layouts ist für WAP-Anwedungen oft nicht möglich, da die Darstellung auf unterschiedlichen Geräten sehr verschieden ist. Ist es notwendig auf das Layout Einfluss zu nehmen, müssen für jede Klasse von Geräten (u.U. für jedes potentielle Gerät) spezifische Seiten entwickelt oder generiert werden.

- Anwendungen sollten ausgiebig getestet werden. Hierzu ist es wichtig verschiedene Endgeräte und verschiedene Gateways (bzw. Einwahlpunkte) zu verwenden.

WAP bietet eine Plattform für einen vielseitigen Einsatz und für verschiedenste Anwendungsfelder. Beim Entwurf ist jedoch die Überlegung anzustellen, worin der Vorteil einer WAP-Anwendung gegenüber einer WWW- Anwendung liegt. Hierzu ergeben sich insbesondere die Bereiche:

- Mobiler Informationszugriff und Datenerfassung
- Situationsbezogene Dienste und Anwendungen
- Anwendungen zur Steuerung und zur Kontrolle von Geräten
- Anwendungen, welche die Funktion des Telefons erweitern oder anpassen

5. Literatur

[1] Brody, A.B., Gottsman, E.J.: Pocket BargainFinder: A Handheld Device for Augmented Commerce, *Proc. Int. Symposium on Handheld and Ubiquitous Computing 1999*. Lecture notes in computer science; Vol 1707, Springer, 1999, Seite 44-51

[2] FAZ, Zu viele Funktionen in einem viel zu kleinen Kästchen. *Frankfurter Allgemeine Zeitung*, 2. November 1999.

[3] Goldstein, M., Book, R., Alsiö., Tessa, S. Non-Keyboard QUERTY Touch Typing: A Portable Input Interface For The Mobile User. *Proceeding of the CHI 99*, Pittsburg, 1999.

[4] Schmidt, A., Takaluoma, A., Mäntyjärvi, J.. Context-Aware Telefony over WAP. *Personal Technologies Volume 4(4)*, September 2000. Seite 225-229.

[5] Schmidt A., Aidoo K.A., Takaluoma A., Tuomela U., Van Laerhoven K., Van de Velde W.: Advanced Interaction in Context. *Proc. Int. Symposium on Handheld and Ubiquitous Computing 1999*. Lecture notes in computer science; Vol 1707, Springer, 1999, Seite 89-101

[6] Schmidt, A., Schröder, H., Frick, O. WAP - Designing for Small User Interfaces. *Extended Abstracts of the CHI 2000*, The Hague, Netherlands. 2000.

[7] WAP, Wireless Application Protocol. 2000. *http://ww.wapforum.org*

[8] Weiser, M., The Computer for the 21st Century; *Scientific American*, September 1991

Session 3:

Sicherheit in Rechnernetzen

Verteiltes Filtern mit Contags und Sicherheits-Labeln

Matthias Kabatnik[1], Reiner Sailer[2]

[1] Institut für Nachrichtenvermittlung und Datenverarbeitung, Universität Stuttgart
[2] IBM Research, T. J. Watson Research Center, Yorktown Heights, NY, USA

`kabatnik@ind.uni-stuttgart.de, sailer@watson.ibm.com`

Abstract

Im Zuge der Globalisierung von Netzdiensten haben sich sehr heterogene Netzstrukturen entwickelt. Teilnetze unterschiedlicher Technologien und unterschiedlicher Verantwortlichkeiten werden zusammengeschaltet. Dabei sind ernstzunehmende Sicherheitsprobleme entstanden, deren Lösung bis heute zu erheblichen Einschränkungen des über Netzgrenzen gelenkten Verkehrs führt.

Dieser Beitrag stellt ein neues Zugriffskontroll-Verfahren vor, das die Übergänge zwischen Teilnetzen mit feinerer Granularität absichert. Unser Verfahren arbeitet auf Netzebene und erweitert das bislang verwendete Filtern sowohl um Filterkriterien, z.B. basierend auf Integritäts- und Vertraulichkeitsklassen, als auch um Kontextinformation. Sicherheits-Label speichern Sicherheitsklassen für Daten im Datenpaket selbst. Sie bilden die Grundlage für ein Zugriffskontrollverfahren, das unabhängig von Benutzern und Rechnerknoten arbeitet. Context-Tags (Contags) speichern Kontext-Informationen (Meta-Information) direkt im Datenpaket, z.B. ob das Datenpaket geschützt empfangen wurde (z.B. durch IPSec/IKE) oder über welchen Link Daten empfangen wurden (z.B. Incoming Linkset). Contags ermöglichen verteiltes Filtern, da sie die für das Filtern relevanten Meta-Informationen erhalten (Historie). Das hier vorgestellte Zugriffskontroll-Verfahren implementiert eine verteilte und zustandslose Filterung. Wir wenden es auf IP-basierte Netze und auf Signalisiernetze an.

1 Einführung

Die Vernetzung von Computersystemen und der Einsatz verteilter Anwendungen ermöglichen eine Vielzahl neuer, flexibler Dienste. Gleichzeitig entstehen jedoch neue Herausforderungen bezüglich der Sicherheit der Information, die zwischen verteilten Anwendungen über Netze ausgetauscht wird. Insbesondere wenn die Vernetzung in großem, nicht mehr unmittelbar überschaubarem Maßstab erfolgt, müssen zusätzliche Schutzmaßnahmen getroffen werden.

Ein aktuelles Beispiel ist die Kopplung (Interconnection) verschiedener TCP/IP-Teilnetze einer Firma über den öffentlichen Bereich des Internets. Dort sind Schutzmaßnahmen notwendig, da sonst vertrauliche Daten ausgespäht oder manipuliert werden könnten oder Systeme durch unautorisiertes Einspielen von Daten in ihrer Integrität bedroht würden. Ein weiteres aktuelles Beispiel ist die Kopplung von SS7[1]-Signalisiernetzen eines Betreibers bei gleichzeitiger Anbindung von Fremdnetzen.

---

1. SS7: Das Signalisiersystem Nr. 7 wird zum Austausch von Steuer- und Management-Daten in öffentlichen Fernsprechnetzen angewendet, z.B. im ISDN und im GSM.

Wir stellen in diesem Beitrag ein Verfahren vor, das zum Schutz heterogener Netzstrukturen auf Netzebene eingesetzt werden kann. Das Verfahren basiert darauf, größere heterogene Netze in kleinere – aus Sicherheitssicht homogene – Teilnetze zu zerlegen. Diese Teilnetze werden intern unabhängig geschützt. Die Übergänge zwischen Teilnetzen werden durch zusätzliche Zugriffskontroll-Mechanismen überwacht. Zur Strukturierung von heterogenen Netzen wird das *Domänen-Konzept* herangezogen [10]. Dieses Konzept unterscheidet Domänen hinsichtlich sicherheitsrelevanter Eigenschaften, z.B. Verantwortlichkeiten, physikalischer Schutz, Steuerungs-Software, Zugangspunkte. Nachfolgend wird unter einer Domäne ein Bereich verstanden, der durch Einsatz von Sicherheitsmaßnahmen an den Bereichsgrenzen von seinen umgebenden Bereichen sicherheitstechnisch unabhängig ist (autonom). Beispiele autonomer Bereiche stellen durch Firewalls geschützte LAN-Segmente oder durch physikalische Separation und Nachrichtenfilter geschützte öffentliche Netze (z.B. SS7-Signalisiernetze des ISDN) dar.

Innerhalb einer Domäne lassen sich Schutzziele festlegen (Sicherheitsanforderungen bezogen auf Objekte), die durch innerhalb der Domäne implementierte Schutzvorkehrungen garantiert werden. Ein ISDN-Netzbetreiber kann beispielsweise Schutzziele innerhalb seines Netzes durch entsprechende Zugangskontrollen und Sicherheitsfunktionen autonom durchsetzen. An den Übergangspunkten zu *angrenzenden Domänen* muß sichergestellt werden, daß Informationsströme zwischen den Domänen keine Schutzziele des Ursprungs- oder Ziel-Bereiches verletzen. Z. B. sollen Management- oder Tarifierungsinformationen aus fremden Netzen nicht verarbeitet werden, falls sie ungeschützt über unsichere Bereiche übertragen wurden oder in nicht vertrauenswürdigen Bereichen entstanden sind.

Die Zusammenschaltung von unabhängig gesicherten Teilbereichen und der Schutz bereichsübergreifender Informationsströme und Ressourcen stellen die zentralen Punkte dieses Beitrags dar. Bild 1 veranschaulicht das Prinzip der Zusammenschaltung: Wird ein Datum von einem Netzbereich A in einen Netzbereich B übertragen und werden an dieses Datum bestimmte Anforderungen wie Vertraulichkeit oder Integrität gestellt, so muß der Übergangspunkt zwischen den Teilbereichen A und B sicherstellen, daß die Anforderungen trotz bereichsübergreifender Kommunikation eingehalten werden. Dies erfolgt entweder durch ein a-priori Wissen des Prüfpunktes (Policy-Information) oder durch entsprechenden vorsorglichen Schutz der Daten durch Verschlüsselung oder Signierung zur Überbrückung unsicherer Bereiche.

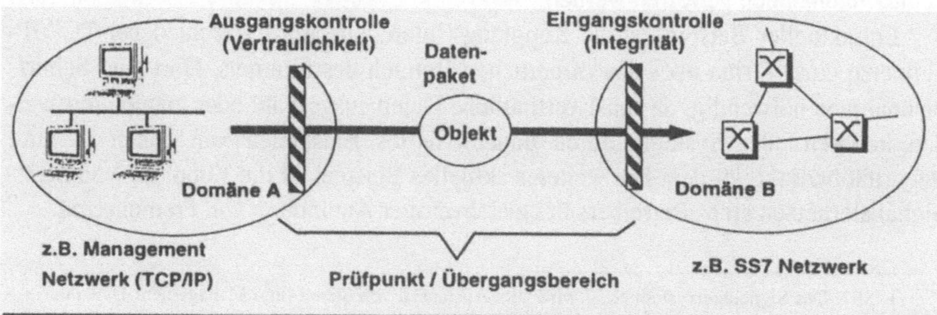

Bild 1:   Übergang zwischen separat gesicherten Teilnetzen (Domänen)

Wir verwenden eingangsseitig Integritätsanforderungen und ausgangsseitig Vertraulichkeitsanforderungen als Prüfregeln an den Domänen-Übergängen:

- *Integrität*: Jeder Nachricht oder jedem Parameter kann eine Integritätsklasse zugeordnet werden. Die Integritätsklasse von Daten beschreibt die "Vertrauenswürdigkeit" dieser Daten im Hinblick auf ihre Verarbeitung durch sensitive Netz- oder Anwendungsfunktionen.
- *Vertraulichkeit*: Jeder Nachricht kann eine Vertraulichkeitsklasse zugeordnet werden. So klassifizierte Nachrichten werden nur in jene benachbarten Domänen entlassen, die eine entsprechende Berechtigung (Clearing) besitzen.

Die Ursprungs-Domäne A prüft vor dem Weiterleiten von Daten an eine angrenzende Domäne B, ob die Vertraulichkeitsklasse der Daten diese Weiterleitung über B an den Zielbereich erlaubt oder nicht. Ausgangsseitig wird folglich die Vertraulichkeitsanforderung vor der Freigabe geprüft. Eingangsseitig prüft Bereich B, ob die Integritätsklasse der Daten eine Verarbeitung innerhalb des Bereiches zuläßt. Dadurch wird Manipulationen der bereichsinternen Steuerung durch extern eingeschleuste manipulierte Steuerungsdaten entgegengewirkt. Dies entspricht einer Annahme-Prüfung. Die Vertraulichkeits- und Integritätsklasse einer Nachricht passen sich an die Sicherheitsklassen der von dieser Nachricht durchlaufenen Domänen (im Sinne einer Verschärfung der Schutzanforderungen) an.

2 Verwandte Arbeiten

Bell und LaPadula führen in [3] allgemeine Zugriffskontroll-Modelle ein. Denning erweitert in [1] dieses Modell durch geordnete Mengen (Lattices) zur Beschreibung von Vertraulichkeitsklassen und legt den Grundstein für Mandatory Access Control-Modelle [7]. Biba führte in [6] Integritätsklassen ein. Gemein ist den Verfahren, daß ein Monitor alle Zugriffe auf geschützte Objekte überwacht.

Bei Mandatory Access Control-Modellen kann der Besitzer eines Objektes die Zugriffsrechte jedoch nicht ändern. Allen Instanzen (Subjekten) sind Sicherheits-Clearings zugewiesen (z.B. Clearing für vertrauliche Daten); alle geschützten Objekte sind Sicherheitsklassen zugeordnet (z.B. streng vertraulich). Ein Zugriff über den Monitor wird erlaubt, falls das Clearing der zugreifenden Instanz mindestens der Vertraulichkeitsklasse entspricht, die dem Objekt zugeordnet ist. Sensible Anwendung (mit Integritäts-Clearing) dürfen entsprechend nur auf Daten mit derselben oder höherer Integritätsklasse arbeiten.

Das sogenannte High Water Mark-Modell (Weissman [4]) ermöglicht das dynamische Klassifizieren von Objekten. In [4] erhält eine Datei jeweils die Vertraulichkeitsklasse der Anwendung, die zuletzt auf diese Datei zugegriffen hat. Für Integritätsklassen gilt entsprechend, daß Daten die Integritätsklasse der Anwendung erben, die das letzte Mal schreibend darauf zugegriffen hat. Die Integrität von Daten wird dabei gewöhnlich herunterklassifiziert, die Vertraulichkeitsklasse nach oben verändert. Karger et. al. stellen in [5] ein Zugriffskontroll-Modell mit Vertraulichkeits- und Integritätsklassen für Chipkarten vor.

Wir wenden das Mandatory Access Control-Modell für Vertraulichkeits- und Integritätsklassen auf den Nachrichtenaustausch zwischen zusammengeschalteten Kommunikationsnetzen an. Sicherheits-Label (eingeführt für IP in [2]) kennzeichnen die Vertraulichkeits- und Integritätsklasse von Nachrichten. Zusätzliche Tags speichern Kontext-Information (Incoming Linkset, etc.) zur späteren Verarbeitung. Eine dynamische Anpassung der Sicherheitsklassen von Nachrichten wird an den Übergängen zwischen den Netzen vorgenommen. Sicherheitsaspekte der Zusammenschaltung offener Telekommunikationsnetze werden in [11] und [12] behandelt. Die Verwendung von Sicherheits-Labeln in Signalisiernetzen wurde in [8] vorgestellt. Steve Bellovin beschreibt in [9] ein Verfahren, bei dem Firewall-Funktionen bis in die Benutzer-Terminals verlegt werden. Wir verteilen die Filterfunktionen auf Netzgrenzen und zielen auf sichere Übergänge von Kommunikationsnetzen ab, nicht auf Benutzersicherheit.

3 Verteiltes Filtern

An jedem Übergangspunkt zwischen sicherheitstechnisch eigenständigen Teilnetzen (Domänen) muß entschieden werden, ob bestimmte Datenpakete die Netzgrenze passieren dürfen. Diese Zugriffssteuerung (Access Control) besteht aus Entscheidungsfunktionen (Access Control Decision Functions) und Durchsetzungsfunktionen (Access Control Enforcement Functions). Wir beschreiben im nächsten Abschnitt die Kriterien, die in Entscheidungsfunktionen verwendet werden und behandeln anschließend die allgemeine Struktur von Filtern und deren Verteilungsaspekt.

3.1 Sicherheits-Label und Contags

Sicherheits-Label und Contags speichern Informationen, auf deren Grundlage entschieden wird, ob Datenpakete in einen Bereich eingelassen oder aus einem Bereich entlassen werden. Sie sind die Eingangsgrößen für die Entscheidungsfunktion.

Sicherheits-Label speichern Sicherheitsklassen eines Datenpaketes im Datenpaket selbst. Wir unterscheiden Vertraulichkeit und Integrität. Die Zuordnung von Sicherheitsklassen zu Datenpaketen und Domänen ist Aufgabe der sogenannten Sicherheits-Policy eines Unternehmens. Bezüglich *Vertraulichkeit* und *Integrität* können folgende Sicherheitsklassen unterschieden werden, die bezüglich ihrer Indizes geordnet sind:

V0 nicht vertraulich

V1 vertraulich, Nutzdaten oder Netzsteuerdaten (z.B. zum Schutz vor der Erzeugung von Dienstnutzungsprofilen durch Dritte)

V2 streng vertraulich, z.B. Management-Passwörter zum Remote-Management

I0 keine Integrität garantiert, z.B. Benutzereingaben

I1 minimale Integrität, z.B. Benutzer initiierte Steuerdaten (Verbindungswunsch)

I2 mittlere Integrität, z.B. netzintern / von anderen Netzbetreibern erzeugte Daten

I3 hohe Integrität, z.B. Netzmanagementdaten (nur intern, z.B. SNMP[2], OMAP[3])

Diese Klassen können anders gewählt werden, müssen aber an den Netzgrenzen von angrenzenden Bereichen konsistent interpretiert werden. Sicherheits-Label begleiten ein Datenpaket und können netzübergreifend verwendet werden.

---

2. SNMP: Simple Network Management Protocol

3. OMAP: Operation and Maintenance Application Part

Contags sind im Gegensatz zu Sicherheits-Labeln nur innerhalb einer Domäne von Bedeutung. Sie speichern Kontextinformation, die aus der Umgebung (Kommunikationskontext) abgeleitet wird. Beispiele für Kontextinformation sind Incoming Linkset/Network, Time of Arrival und Protection Level on Arrival (z.B. IPSec geschützt). Gewöhnlich ist diese Kontextinformation nur am Entstehungsort vorhanden und wird dort zum Filtern verwendet. Die sich bei unserem Verfahren durch Contags im Datenpaket ansammelnde Kontextinformation (Historie) kann zu einem späteren Zeitpunkt von einer Entscheidungsfunktion mit feinerer Granularität verwertet werden.

Aufgrund der Bedeutung, die Contags und Sicherheits-Label für die Entscheidungsfindung bei der Zugriffssteuerung haben, müssen sie beim Transport über unsichere Netzbereiche gegen Manipulation geschützt werden, beispielsweise durch Message Authentication Codes (kryptographisch gesicherte Nachrichten-Hashwerte). Zusätzlich werden in Entscheidungsfunktionen herkömmliche Datenpaket-Felder verwendet, beispielsweise die Ursprungs- oder Zieladresse oder der Datentyp einer Nachricht (Nutz-, Steuer- oder Management-Pakettyp, nationale Parameter).

3.2 Bausteine der Zugriffskontrolle an Netzübergängen

Aufbauend auf den Sicherheits-Labeln und Contags kann der Übergang zwischen Domänen mit Hilfe dreier aufeinander aufbauender Stufen beschrieben werden:

Eine *Eingangsprüfung* entscheidet, welchen Labels und Tags vertraut wird. Diese Entscheidung ist abhängig von der Sicherheits-Policy, die beschreibt welchen Netzbetreibern wieweit vertraut wird. Am Eingang muß die Integritätsklasse des Datenpaketes geprüft werden. Ist das Datenpaket P durch I(P) klassifiziert und ist die Domäne D der Klasse I(D) zugeordnet, so muß das Datenpaket in der Filterstufe (s.u., dritte Stufe) verworfen werden, falls I(P)<I(D). Dies schützt sensible Anwendungen der Domäne vor manipulierten Daten. Diese Prüfung macht nur dann Sinn, wenn der Klassifizierungsinformation im Datenpaket vertraut wird. Eventuell vorhandene Message Authentication Codes oder Signaturen können hier geprüft werden, um Vertrauen in die Daten zu erzeugen. Kann dem Datenpaket nicht vertraut werden, so wird das Datenpaket als nicht authentisch markiert und in der zweiten Stufe pessimistisch mit neuen Sicherheits-Labeln versehen.

Die zweite Stufe ist für das *Context-Tagging* und für die *Label-Anpassung* zuständig. Neue Contags können dem Datenpaket hinzugefügt werden, beispielsweise als Secure Header Option [2] in IP-Paketen oder in freien Feldern von Signalisiernachrichten des SS7. Außerdem werden die Sicherheitsklassen des Datenpaketes angepaßt. Besitzt die Domäne ein Clearing für die Vertraulichkeits-Klasse V(D) und ist ein Datenpaket P der Klasse V(P) zugeordnet, dann wird das Datenpaket neu klassifiziert und V(D) zugeordnet. V(D) >= V(P) gilt, da das Paket sonst am Ausgang der sendenden Domäne gefiltert worden wäre (s.u., Filter). Dieses Umklassifizieren ist notwendig, da Rechner innerhalb des Bereiches hoch klassifizierte Daten zum Datenpaket hinzufügen können. Ein nicht authentisiertes Datenpaket P mit Integritätsklasse I(P) aus der sendenden Domäne S mit I(S) erhält als neue Integritätsklasse I(P) := min(I(S),I(P)). Die Default-Integritätsklassen umgebender Domänen sind von der Unternehmens-Policy festzulegen.

Eine dritte Stufe (*Filter*) filtert Datenpakete aufgrund der Tags und Label sowie sonstiger Paketinformation. Eine Domäne hat immer Ein- und Ausgangs-Filter, sofern Bereichsübergänge bidirektionalen Verkehr erlauben. Am Eingang werden Datenpakete mit Integritätsklasse I(P) ausgefiltert (verworfen oder protokolliert), falls bzgl. der Integritätsklasse I(D) der Domäne gilt: I(D) > I(P), d.h. die Domäne eine höhere Datenintegrität fordert als das Paket anbietet. Am Ausgang werden Datenpakete ausgefiltert, deren Vertraulichkeitsklasse V(D) größer ist als die Vertraulichkeitsklasse der Domäne, an die das Paket geschickt wird, d.h. falls die Daten zu sensibel sind.

3.3 Verteilte Filterung

Das von uns vorgeschlagene Filterverfahren kann aufgrund der Strukturierung und Hinzunahme von Tags verteilt implementiert werden. Heute vorhandene Filter integrieren gewöhnlich alle drei Filterstufen. Bild 2 zeigt links einen herkömmlichen Filter. Für Daten aus den Quellbereichen Q1 oder Q2 werden zunächst die für Zugriffsentscheidungen relevanten Eigenschaften festgestellt. Danach wird aufgrund von Entscheidungsregeln das zu übertragende Datum entweder weitergeleitet oder verworfen. Eine solche Architektur findet sich beispielsweise in Firewall-Routern oder in Betriebssystemkernen. Implizite Informationen, z.B. der Incoming Link, sind in späteren Filtern nicht mehr sichtbar.

Auf der rechten Bildhälfte ist das verteilte Filtern zu sehen. Die Prüffunktion befindet sich am Eingang einer Domäne. Filterfunktionen sind verteilt; Eingangsfilter und Ausgangsfilter können auf impliziten Informationen arbeiten, die in den Contags gespeichert sind..

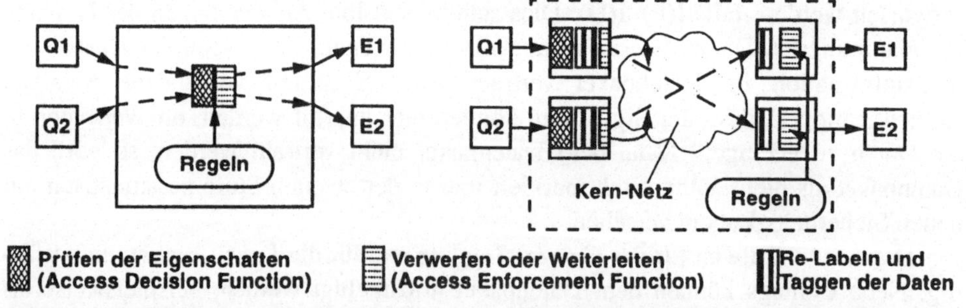

Bild 2:   Übergang zu verteilter Filterung basierend auf Contags und Labeln

Die Prüfung der Eigenschaften findet direkt am Übergabepunkt der Daten statt. Nicht authentische Daten werden markiert. Danach wird das Re-Labeln entsprechend Stufe 2 in Abschnitt 3.2 durchgeführt. In der Eingangsstufe wird die Integrität geprüft (siehe Stufe 3 in Abschnitt 3.2). Datenpakete, die innerhalb des Bereiches verarbeitet werden könnten[4], müssen hier gegebenenfalls verworfen werden. Vor der Ausgabe eines Datenpaketes an einen empfangenden Netzbereich (E1 oder E2) werden Vertraulichkeitsanforderungen geprüft und die Sicherheitsrichtlinien bezüglich der Klassifizierun-

---

4. Dies ist der Fall, wenn die Zieladresse innerhalb des Bereiches liegt oder nicht vollständig bekannt ist; z.B. bei Global Title-Adressierung.

gen durchgesetzt. Daten, die innerhalb einer Domäne erzeugt werden, erhalten beim Re-Labeln vor dem Ausgangsfiltern automatisch die Vertraulichkeitsklasse und Integritätsklasse dieser Domäne.

Der Vorteil dieses Verfahrens ist, daß die Entscheidung über die Zulässigkeit eines Informationsflusses zu einem späteren Zeitpunkt auf Basis von kumulierter Kontextinformation (Historie) erfolgen kann, die ohne Sicherheits-Label und Contags nicht mehr sichtbar wäre. Da der Übergangsbereich (gestrichelte Linie) vertrauenswürdig sein muß, müssen auch die darin liegenden Kommunikationspfade hinsichtlich ihrer Integrität und gegebenenfalls hinsichtlich ihrer Vertraulichkeit geschützt werden.

3.4 Sicherheitstechnische Kompatibilität von benachbarten Domänen

Das oben eingeführte Re-Labeln von Datenpaketen führt gewöhnlich zu "überklassifizierten" Datenpaketen. Um die Kommunikation nicht unnötig einzuschränken, werden Maßnahmen berücksichtigt, die den Zugriff auf hoch klassifizierte Daten in niedrig klassifizierten Transitbereichen verhindern (z.B. Verschlüsselung).

Wir unterscheiden bei der Kompatibilität von benachbarten Domänen folglich zwei Fälle: Wenn Daten des sendenden Bereiches im benachbarten Bereich verarbeitet werden, dann müssen die in Abschnitt 3.2 eingeführten Regeln für Integritäts- und Vertraulichkeitsklassen streng eingehalten werden. Ist der benachbarte Bereich jedoch nur ein übermittelnder Bereich, so können additive Schutzmaßnahmen (Verschlüsselung bzw. Integritätsschutz z. B. mit Hilfe von IPSec-Tunneln) zur sicherheitstechnischen Überbrückung der Domäne genutzt werden. Die Prüfung der Sicherheitsklassen erfolgt dann basierend auf dem über den geschützten Tunnel verbundenen entfernten Bereich. Daraus folgt, daß nicht vertrauenswürdige Transfer-Bereiche

- nicht zur "Herunterklassifizierung" der Integrität von Datenpaketen (in der empfangenden Domäne) führen, sofern die Pakete über einen integritätsgeschützten Tunnel empfangen werden. Das Tunneln kann in Contags für die spätere Auswertung gespeichert werden. Das Re-Labeln der Eingangsstufe berücksichtigt diese Tags beim Bestimmen der Integritätsklasse eines empfangenen Paketes.

- vertrauliche Daten übertragen können, wenn diese Daten über einen vertraulichkeitsschützenden Tunnel übertragen werden. Dieses wird beim Re-Labeln am Ausgang des Sendebereiches berücksichtigt. Nach dem Verschlüsseln wird die Vertraulichkeitsklasse *V0* in das umschließende Datenpaket geschrieben, so daß der Ausgangsfilter die Daten in den nicht vertrauenswürdigen Bereich senden kann.

Ob geschützte Kanäle verwendet werden, wird bei zentralen Policy-Datenbanken oder – beim Verwenden von IPSec – direkt bei der IPSec Policy-Datenbasis abgefragt.

3.5 Anwendungsbeispiel

Als Beispiel für den Einsatz verteilter Filterung mit Contags wird die Zusammenschaltung von ISDN-Signalisiernetzen mehrerer Betreiber (A, B und C) betrachtet. Ein Zwischensignalisiernetz ZSN unter der Kontrolle von Betreiber A verbindet die Netze A, B und C. Die erlaubten Verkehrsarten zwischen den Netzen sind durch Verträge zwischen den Netzbetreibern festgelegt. A akzeptiert von B und C jegliche ISUP-Signalisiernachrichten zur Rufsteuerung[5]. Jedoch soll nur B auf höherwertige Netzdienste (z.B. Dienste des Intelligenten Netzes) zugreifen dürfen; das ZSN erlaubt den Austausch von Signalisiernachrichten zur Steuerung höherwertiger Dienste (z.B. IN Dienste) nur zwischen B und A.

Eine Auswertung von Informationen höherer Protokollschichten (z.B. SS7-Anwenderteile wie Intelligent Network Application Protocol, INAP) ist am Zugangspunkt zum ZSN wegen des hohen protokolltechnischen Aufwandes jedoch nicht praktikabel (Performance-Verlust). Beim Filtern am Übergang zum Zielnetz kann der Absender aber nicht zweifelsfrei festgestellt werden, da die Korrektheit der Absenderadresse (Origination Point Code, OPC) zu diesem Zeitpunkt (ohne Contags) nicht mehr überprüft werden kann.

Daher wenden wir hier verteiltes Filtern mit Sicherheits-Labeln und Contags an. Wir prüfen die Authentizität der Absenderadresse einer Nachricht schon am Eingang des ZSN und vermerken das Prüfergebnis anhand eines Contags in der Signalisiernachricht. Bei den betrachteten Nachrichten handelt es sich um Schicht 3-Nachrichten des SS7 (Message Transfer Part-Nachrichten). Sicherheits-Label und Tags werden auf "Sparebits" des Service Indicator Octets der MTP-Nachrichten abgebildet, wie in Bild 3 dargestellt [13].

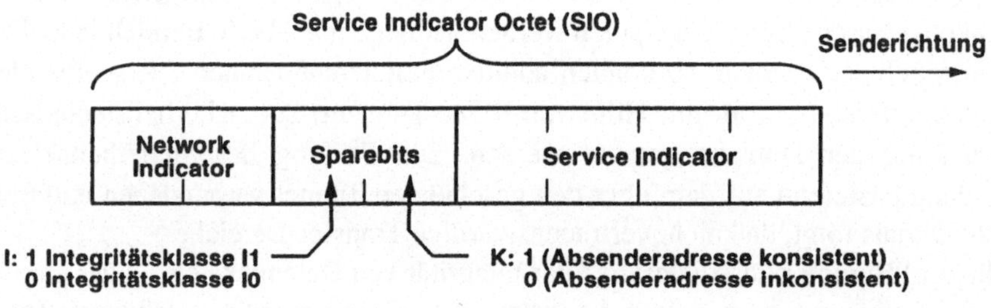

Bild 3:   Nutzung des Service Indicator Oktets für Contags

Zunächst wird Netz A logisch in zwei Teilnetze A1 und A2 zerlegt, die über eigene Zugangspunkte mit dem ZSN verbunden werden (vgl. Bild 4). Während der Zugangspunkt A1 nur ISUP-Verkehr behandelt (Service Indicator SI=5) wird der übrige Verkehr über den Zugangspunkt A2 geführt. Den Netzen B und C werden unterschiedliche Integritätsklassen (I0 und I1) zugeordnet.

Bei Entgegennahme einer Nachricht durch das ZSN wird zunächst die Korrektheit der Absenderadresse (OPC) bezüglich des Incoming Link geprüft und als Contag im Adress-Header der Nachricht vermerkt (K=1: konsistent). Sofortiges Ausfiltern der Nachrichten ist nicht möglich, da bezüglich des Verkehrs zwischen B und C unter Umständen andere Anforderungen hinsichtlich zulässiger OPCs bestehen[6]. Die Integritätsklasse des Ursprungsnetzes wird durch ein Integritäts-Label I in der MTP-Nach-

---

5. Der ISDN User Part (ISUP) unterstützt die Steuerung der leitungsgebundenen Kommunikation im digitalen Telefonnetz. Dies geschieht über Signalisiernachrichten, die über den Message Transfer Part (MTP), ein paketvermittelndes Netz, ausgetauscht werden.

6. Dieser Fall kann beispielsweise auftreten, wenn das ZSN eine Transitfunktionalität (Signalling Transfer Point, STP) für Signalisierverkehr zwischen B und C bereitstellt.

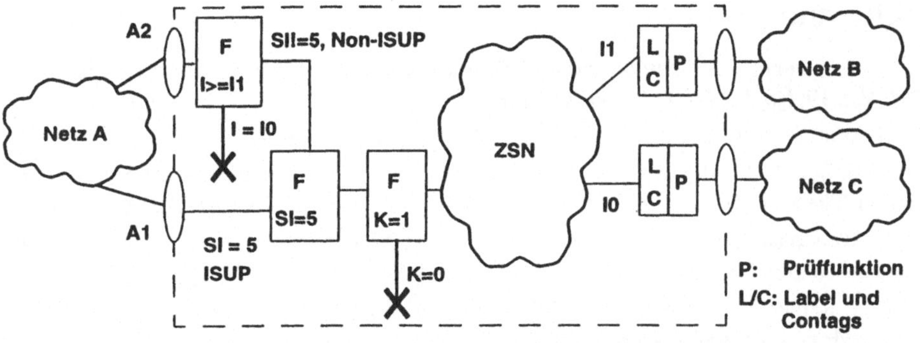

Bild 4:   Verteilte Filterung bei der Kopplung von SS7-Signalisiernetzen

richt (weiteres Sparebit im SIO, vgl. auch Bild 3) abhängig vom Incoming Link festgehalten.

An den Zugangspunkten des Netzes A werden Pakete mit inkonsistenten OPCs durch Ausfiltern des Contags K=0 verworfen (Schutz vor OPC Spoofing). Der restliche Verkehr wird durch Auswertung des Service Indicators in ISUP und Nicht-ISUP-Verkehr aufgeteilt. Bei letzterem wird durch Filterung sichergestellt, daß nur MTP-Nachrichten der Integritätsklasse I1 das Zielnetz erreichen. Am Eingang zum Zielnetz können nicht mehr benötigte Labels und Contags entfernt werden.

Die Verwendung von Contags und Sicherheits-Label in der vorgestellten Weise ermöglicht somit eine verteilte, intelligente Filterung und damit eine partielle Öffnung des Netzes A, z.B. für IN-Dienste, gegenüber anderen Betreibern. Durch die Einschränkung des Gültigkeitsbereiches auf das ZSN ist dieser Mechanismus vollständig transparent gegenüber den bestehenden Signalisierprotokollen und benötigt keine Veränderungen der MTP-Protokollinstanzen in den angeschlossenen Netzen A, B und C.

4 Zusammenfassung

Das vorgestellte Filter-Verfahren integriert bestehende lokale Sicherheitsmechanismen und netzübergreifende Sicherheits-Policies zum Schutz von Netzübergängen. Es schützt somit bestehende Investitionen. Verteiltes Filtern ermöglicht die kontrollierte Öffnung schutzwürdiger Teilnetze und eröffnet Möglichkeiten der Globalisierung sensitiver Netzdienste. Es unterstützt insbesondere das zentrale Management von Netzinseln. Bei entsprechender Definition der Sicherheits-Policy wirkt das Verfahren trotz Fehlverhalten von Benutzern und Netzelementen solange die Ausgangs- und Eingangskontrollen sicher sind und alle Bereichsübergänge abdecken. Anwendungsbeispiele für IP-basierte Netze sind aus dem gegebenen Beispiel ableitbar.

5 Literatur

[1]   D. E. Denning: A Lattice Model of Secure Information Flow. Communications of the ACM, Vol. 19, No. 5, May 1976, pp. 236-243.

[2]   S. Kent: Security Options for the Internet Protocol. Nov 1991. RFC 1108.

[3]   D. E. Bell, L. J. LaPadula: Computer Security Model Unified Exposition and Multics Interpretation, The MITRE Corp., ESD-TR-75-306, Ma., June 1975. (NTIS # AD A023588)

[4]   C. Weissman: Security Controls in the ADEPT-50 Time Sharing System. 1969 Fall Joint Computer Conference, AFIPS, Vol 35, AFIPS Press, Montvale, N. J., 1969, pp. 119-133.

[5]   P. A. Karger, V. R. Austel, D. C. Toll: Using a Mandatory Secrecy and Integrity Policy on Smart Cards and Mobile Devices. EUROSMART Security Conference, June 2000.

[6]   K. J. Biba: Integrity Considerations for Secure Computer Systems. ESD-TR-76-732, HQ Electronic Systems Division, Hanscom AFB, Ma., April 1977.

[7]   R. S. Sandhu: Lattice-Based Access Control Models. IEEE Computer, Vol. 26, No. 11, November 1993, pages 9-19.

[8]   M. Kabatnik, R. Sailer: Modelling of Secure Interconnection. Communication Fraud Control Association, 1999 Spring International Conference in Ismaning/Germany, May 1999.

[9]   S. Bellovin: Distributed Firewalls. login, Nov 1999, pp. 37-39.
URL: http://www.research.att.com/~smb/papers/distfw.pdf

[10] Sailer, R., Kühn, P.: Ein Domain-Konzept zur systematischen und wirtschaftlichen Integration von Sicherheit in Kommunikationsnetzen. Informationstechnik und Technische Informatik. Bd. 38 (1996) Heft 4, S. 30-33.

[11] K. Ward: The Impact of Network Interconnection on Network Integrity. British Telecommunications Engineering, Vol. 13, January, 1995.

[12] Sailer, R.: Security Services in an Open Service Environment. Proc. 14th ACSAC, Phoenix, Arizona, IEEE Computer Society, Los Alamitos, pp. 223-234.

[13] ITU-T Recommendation Q.704: Specification of Signalling System No. 7 — Message transfer part — Signalling network functions and messages; ITU, 1996.

Sicherheitskonzept für eine durch Kunden steuerbare Dienstmanagement-Architektur

Z. Nochta, G. Augustin, M. Becker, M. Friedmann und S. Abeck

Universität Karlsruhe (TH), Institut für Telematik,
Forschungsgruppe Cooperation & Management
Zirkel 2, D-76128 Karlsruhe

E-mail:zoltan.nochta@cooperation-management.de

Zusammenfassung. Dieser Beitrag beschäftigt sich mit Sicherheitsfragestellungen einer auf CORBA basierenden Dienstmanagement-Architektur. Diese erlaubt Dienstnehmern die Verwaltung der von ihnen in Anspruch genommenen IT-Dienste. Aus diesem Szenario ergeben sich erhöhte, spezifische Sicherheitsanforderungen. Zur Erfüllung dieser Anforderungen wurde ein Konzept entwickelt, das neue und standardisierte Ansätze der Public-Key Technologie (Public-Key Infrastruktur und Privilege Management Infrastruktur) in die vorgestellte Managementarchitektur integriert. Die praktische Umsetzung dieses Konzepts wird durch eine prototypische Implementierung demonstriert.

Einführung

Eine der Hauptaufgaben der heutigen Informationstechnologie (IT) ist die Bereitstellung von Diensten, die wichtige wirtschaftliche und gesamtgesellschaftliche Prozesse der modernen Informationsgesellschaft unterstützen. Ein konkreter IT-Dienst ist hierbei eine komplexe Funktion oder Leistung, die ein Dienstgeber (Betreiber) seinen Dienstnehmern (*Kunden*) zur Verfügung stellt. IT-Dienste werden durch heterogene, miteinander logisch und physisch verbundene Komponenten (Ressourcen) erbracht.
Das *Dienstmanagement* beschäftigt sich mit der Integration und dem Management dieser Komponenten, um bestimmte Dienstqualitätsmerkmale sicherstellen zu können [HAN99]. Die einzelnen diensterbringenden Komponenten müssen mit adäquaten *Managementwerkzeugen* (MW) verwaltet werden. Diese Managementwerkzeuge werden i.d.R. in geschützten Umgebungen (z.B. Intranets) durch Fachpersonal betrieben.
Im Rahmen eines Forschungsprojekts werden in Kooperation mit einem der größten deutschen Netzbetreiber die unterschiedlichen Aspekte einer durch Kunden steuerbaren *Dienstmanagement-Architektur* (DMA) untersucht. Dieses Szenario impliziert, dass potenziell gefährliche Dienstanwender über unsichere Netze die von ihnen in Anspruch genommenen Dienste - und damit indirekt die IT-Ressourcen des Betreibers - überwachen und konfigurieren. Eine der größten Herausforderungen ist hierbei der möglichst weitgehende Schutz der diensterbringenden Systeme vor unbefugten Zugriffen und anderen möglichen Gefährdungen.

In diesem Beitrag wird im ersten Teil eine auf der *Common Object Request Broker Architecture* (CORBA) [OMG99] basierende, durch Kunden steuerbare Dienstmanagement-Architektur vorgestellt. Der zweite Teil beschäftigt sich mit den Sicherheitsanforderungen, deren Erfüllung den sicheren Betrieb dieser Architektur erlauben soll. Der dritte Abschnitt spezifiziert ein umfassendes, auf *Public-Key Verfahren* basierendes *Sicherheitsmanagementsystem*, das die gestellten Anforderungen erfüllt. Der abschließende Teil beschreibt wichtige technische Aspekte der Integration des spezifizierten Sicherheitsmanagementsystems in die vorgestellte CORBA-Architektur.

Eine durch Kunden steuerbare Dienstmanagement-Architektur

Die vom Betreiber angebotenen Dienste werden zumeist durch eine große Anzahl von heterogenen, vernetzten Netz-, System-, und Softwarekomponenten erbracht. Die einzelnen Komponenten können mit verschiedenen, räumlich verteilten Managementwerkzeugen verwaltet werden, die in Abhängigkeit von den besonderen Eigenschaften der gemanagten Ressourcen entwickelt und konfiguriert werden.

Um die getrennte Verwaltung einzelner Komponenten durch das einheitliche Management ganzer Dienste abzulösen, ist die Integration existierender MW in eine Dienstmanagement-Architektur erforderlich. Eine solche DMA überlässt den spezialisierten Werkzeugen die Überwachung und Konfiguration der zugrundeliegenden Ressourcen und sorgt auf einer höheren, logischen und technischen Ebene für die Integration des Managements. Arbeiten wie z.B. [MN+00] beschäftigen sich mit der technischen und organisatorischen Problematik der Integration heterogener Managementsysteme in eine DMA. Abb. 1 illustriert eine auf CORBA basierte, durch Kunden steuerbare DMA.

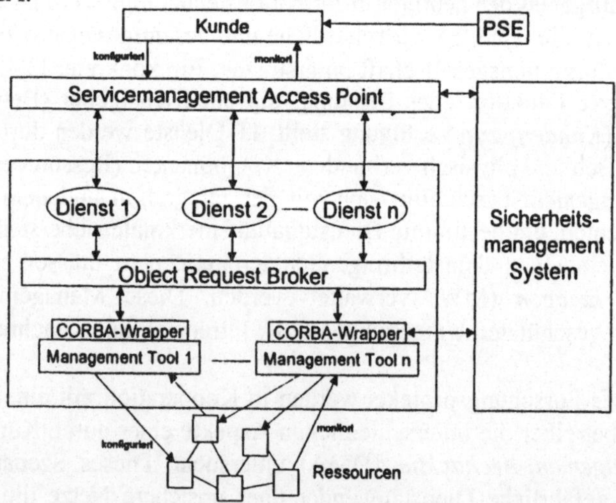

Abb. 1: Eine auf CORBA basierte, durch Kunden steuerbare Dienstmanagement-Architektur

Die Middleware-Plattform CORBA unterstützt die hier benötigte Integration von Managementanwendungen, indem sie u.a. Kommunikationskanäle und geeignete, standardisierte Schnittstellen zur Verfügung stellt. Mit Hilfe dieser Mechanismen können entfernte Kunden über die DMA indirekt auf die verteilten MW zugreifen, die ursprünglich ein solches Nutzungsszenario nicht vorsehen.

Die von den einzelnen Diensten benutzten Ressourcen werden durch dedizierte MW konfiguriert bzw. überwacht. Falls die MW selbst keine CORBA-Anwendungen sind, werden sie durch sogenannte *Wrapper-Objekte* erweitert. Diese Wrapper transformieren die CORBA-Methodenaufrufe in Funktionsaufrufe der Programmierschnittstellen (API) der MW. Der Aufwand, solche Wrapper zu realisieren, ist relativ gering.

Die mit „Dienst 1...n" bezeichneten CORBA-Objekte bieten die Dienstmanagement-Funktionalität in Form von Methodensammlungen an, die letztendlich Funktionen der verteilten MW aufrufen. Das CORBA-Objekt „*Servicemanagement Access Point*" (SAP) bietet einen einheitlichen Web-Zugangspunkt zur DMA. Auf Kundenseite kommen CORBA-Clients zum Einsatz, die jeweils in einem Web-Browser als JAVA-Applet ausgeführt werden. Der SAP empfängt Funktionsaufrufe der Clients und leitet diese an die Dienstobjekte weiter. Die interne Struktur der DMA und der dahinterliegenden Ressourcen bleiben für die Kunden verborgen.

Bei den Zugriffen über den SAP werden die Benutzer zuerst authentifiziert. Nach einer erfolgreichen Anmeldung erfolgt die Autorisierung für jeden einzelnen Zugriff.

Die Architektur benutzt dabei Funktionen des Sicherheitsmanagementsystems. Hierbei ist zu erwähnen, dass der SAP und die darunterliegenden Systeme (z.B. Web-Server) durch zusätzliche Sicherheitsvorrichtungen zu schützen sind, beispielsweise Firewalls und Intrusion Detection Systeme.

Jeder Benutzer verfügt über ein *Personal Security Environment* (PSE), das seine Identität sicher speichert und gegen Manipulationsversuche schützt. Dieses PSE wird zur Anmeldung beim Sicherheitssystem benutzt, wobei sensible Daten (Passwörter) immer verschlüsselt übertragen werden.

Anforderungen an das Sicherheitsmanagementsystem

Zur Absicherung der DMA muss das Sicherheitsmanagementsystem eine Reihe von Anforderungen erfüllen. Diese sind im Folgenden ohne Rücksicht auf ihre jeweilige Wichtigkeit aufgeführt. Abhängig von der Natur des konkreten Dienstes kann ihr Stellenwert variieren.

1. **Gegenseitige Authentisierung**: Um die missbräuchliche Nutzung der DMA durch Dritte zu verhindern, muss sowohl für den Betreiber als auch für den Kunden die Identität der jeweiligen Gegenseite nachprüfbar sein. Das fälschliche Vorspielen einer fremden Identität (z.B. mittels eines abgefangenen Passworts) soll ausgeschlossen sein. Im Falle der Kompromittierung von PSEs soll deren Gültigkeit außer Kraft gesetzt werden können.

2. **Autorisierung**: Den authentisierten Benutzern (Kunden und Mitarbeitern) sind nach vordefinierten Richtlinien (*Policies*) individuelle Berechtigungsprofile zugeordnet. Benutzer sollen Transaktionen (z.B. bzgl. Monitoring und Konfiguration) nur dann ausführen können, wenn diese nach den vorgegebenen Zugriffsrechten zulässig sind. Das Sicherheitsmanagementsystem muss die entsprechenden Rechte verwalten und bei initiierten Transaktionen die Überprüfung ihrer

Zulässigkeit unterstützen. Die Überprüfung selbst soll durch dedizierte Komponenten - sogenannte *Verifier* - erfolgen.

3. **Vertraulichkeit der Kommunikation**: Sensible Informationen müssen zwischen Kunden und Betreibern sicher ausgetauscht werden (z.B. Kontoverbindungen, Konfigurationsparameter u.ä.). Ein Zugriff von unbefugten Dritten auf diese Informationen ist durch Verschlüsselung der Kommunikation auszuschließen.

4. **Integrität der übertragenen Daten**: Die Verfälschung der übertragenen Daten kann die ausgeführten Transaktionen erheblich beeinträchtigen und ist deswegen zuverlässig auszuschließen.

5. **Unabstreitbarkeit (Non-Repudiation)**: Der Neuerwerb von Diensten, deren Umkonfigurierung sowie ggf. deren Abbestellung können erhebliche Auswirkungen haben, insbesondere auf die Erbringung des Dienstes und somit auf die Erfüllung des Vertrages zwischen Kunde und Betreiber. Es besteht somit dringender Bedarf, die Auslösung von Transaktionen den jeweiligen Akteuren sicher zuzuordnen.

6. **Trennung des Dienstzugangspunktes von den Ressourcen**: Motiviert durch potenzielle Denial-of-Service-Angriffe soll deren Wirkung zumindest auf den Zugangspunkt des Dienstmanagements beschränkt bleiben. Sie dürfen die eigentlichen Dienstfunktionalitäten nicht beeinträchtigen, sondern nur deren aktuelle Konfigurierbarkeit. Zugriffe auf Ressourcen (v.a. ihre Konfiguration) sollen ausschließlich durch die abgesicherte Plattform erfolgen. Bei den diensterbringenden Ressourcen ist des Weiteren von dazugehörigen, nicht gesicherten Managementwerkzeugen auszugehen, die i.d.R. nicht gesicherte Managementprotokolle verwenden (z.B. SNMPv1).

Spezifikation des Sicherheitsmanagementsystems

Als Nächstes werden die Komponenten des Sicherheitsmanagementsystems aus Abb. 1 detailliert beschrieben. Ziel ist es, die oben aufgeführten Anforderungen zu erfüllen. Das System verwendet dazu standardisierte kryptographische Algorithmen [PKS95].
Secret-Key (symmetrische) Verfahren werden wegen ihrer leistungsfähigen Implementierbarkeit zur Verschlüsselung der zu übertragenen Daten verwendet. Die gängigsten Algorithmen sind DES und IDEA bzw. ihre Varianten. *Public-Key* (asymmetrische) Verfahren kommen zum Einsatz beim Austausch eines geheimen (symmetrischen) Sitzungsschlüssels und zur Erstellung von digitalen Signaturen. Beispiele hierfür sind die Algorithmen RSA und Diffie-Hellman. Die *Einweg-Hash-Funktionen* wie z.B. MD5, SHA-1 sorgen für die Integrität der digital signierten Daten. Das Protokoll *Secure Sockets Layer* (SSL) wurde ursprünglich von der Firma Netscape entwickelt [SSL96]. Es sichert die komplette Kommunikation oberhalb von TCP/IP ab. Darum eignet sich SSL für die vertrauliche Kommunikation zwischen Endpunkten auf der Anwendungs- und Plattformebene. Die aktuelle Version des Protokolls unterstützt die gegenseitige Client-Server Authentisierung: Die Kommunikationspartner identifizieren sich gegenseitig beim Verbindungsaufbau mittels asymmetrischer Verschlüsselung und vereinbaren einen gemeinsamen geheimen Schlüssel,

mit dem die ausgetauschten Daten verschlüsselt werden. Hierbei kommen digitale Zertifikate (z.B. X.509) und Signaturen (z.B. mittels MD5 und RSA) zum Einsatz. Die Datenströme werden zusätzlich mit einer Prüfsumme (MAC) versehen, um die Integrität der Daten zu schützen.

In SSL wird vorausgesetzt, dass beide Kommunikationspartner im exklusiven Besitz ihres jeweiligen privaten Schlüssels sind und über ein sicheres Medium den öffentlichen Schlüssel oder ein Zertifikat des Kommunikationspartners erhalten haben. Letzteres ist einer der wichtigsten Schritte bei der Authentisierung mit asymmetrischer Verschlüsselung und einer der Hauptgründe für den Einsatz einer *Public-Key Infrastruktur* (PKI). Die sichere, unmodifizierbare Speicherung der Identität der Subjekte, repräsentiert durch den privaten Schlüssel, soll durch ein oben erwähntes PSE umgesetzt werden. Beispiele für PSE-Implementierungen sind Smart-Cards oder von PKIs exportierte, proprietär verschlüsselte Dateien.

Authentisierung mit Hilfe einer Public-Key Infrastruktur

Die oben erwähnten kryptographischen Verfahren alleine können keine zuverlässige Authentisierung und Autorisierung der Subjekte leisten. Kommunikationspartner müssen in den Besitz des öffentlichen Schlüssels der Gegenseite kommen, um das jeweilige Gegenüber mit Hilfe von digitalen Signaturen authentisieren zu können. Es muss verhindert werden, dass ein unbefugter Dritter durch den Austausch eines öffentlichen Schlüssels eine falsche Identität vorspielen kann.

Die zentrale Instanz einer PKI, die *Certification Authority* (CA), erstellt für jeden Benutzer ein individuelles Dokument, das *Public-Key Zertifikat* oder kurz Zertifikat. Das genaue Format der Zertifikate wird im Standard [ITU99] festgelegt. Ein Zertifikat beinhaltet u.a. den Namen und den öffentlichen Schlüssel des Zertifikatinhabers und wird von der CA digital signiert. Verbindungspartner müssen nur noch den öffentlichen Schlüssel der PKI über einen sicheren Kanal (offline) erhalten, um die Echtheit eines von der CA signierten Zertifikats überprüfen zu können und (vorbehaltlich des Widerrufs des Zertifikats) dem darin enthaltenen öffentlichen Schlüssel vertrauen zu können.

Die wichtigsten Dienste einer PKI sind: Erzeugung der Schlüsselpaare, Erstellung und Signierung von Zertifikaten, Veröffentlichung und Widerruf der Zertifikate, Verwaltung der öffentlichen und privaten Schlüssel, Zertifizierung von anderen CAs (cross-certification) und der Zeitstempeldienst [AL99]. Diese Dienste und die sie unterstützenden Protokolle wurden von der IETF Working Group PKIX definiert und in zahlreichen RFCs veröffentlicht [PKIX]. Sie gelten mittlerweile als etablierter Standard.

Im Zusammenspiel mit der DMA ist es die Aufgabe der PKI, die Zertifikate der Subjekte (Kunden, Betreiber, CORBA-Objekte usw.) auf technischer Ebene zur Verfügung zu stellen. Dies bedeutet, dass jedem Beteiligten ein Schlüsselpaar und ein individuelles Zertifikat zugeordnet werden muss. Die Subjekte authentisieren sich gegenseitig mit Hilfe ihres Zertifikats und des darin enthaltenen öffentlichen Schlüssels. Die PKI überprüft jeweils im Auftrag des zugegriffenen Objekts die Echtheit und Gültigkeit des präsentierten Zertifikats. Die privaten Schlüssel sind geschützt in einer PSE gespeichert, können jedoch in dieser Umgebung über kryptographische Funktionen verwendet werden, wodurch der tatsächliche Besitz des privaten Schlüssels nachgewiesen wird, was seinerseits auf die Identität des Kommunikationspartners schließen lässt. Weiterhin übernimmt die PKI im Rahmen der DMA die Aufgabe einer zentralen Benutzerverwaltung.

In unserer prototypischen Implementierung wird eine PKI der Firma Entrust verwendet. Diese bietet eine adäquate API zum Überprüfen der Zertifikate an.

Autorisierung mit Attributzertifikaten: Privilege Management Infrastructure

Attributzertifikate (*Attribute Certificates*, AC) sind digital signierte Dokumente, die zu Autorisierungszwecken benutzt werden [ITU99]. Die Einträge dieser Zertifikate beschreiben die dem jeweiligen Inhaber zugeordneten Sicherheitsattribute (z.B. Zugriffsrechte, zeitliche Einschränkungen, Rollenzugehörigkeiten). Die ACs (und damit die Zugriffsrechte) werden durch eine andere Instanz, die *Privilege Management Infrastructure* (PMI) verwaltet. Ein wichtiger Grund hierfür ist die zumeist kürzere Gültigkeitsdauer von Zugriffsrechten (typischerweise Wochen, Monate) im Vergleich zur Lebensdauer von Public-Key Zertifikaten (Jahre). Wichtige Komponenten einer PMI sind die *Attribute Authorities* (AAs), die die ACs erstellen und unterschreiben. Sie sind somit verantwortlich für den korrekten Inhalt der ACs und der damit implizierten (Benutzer-) Rechte. In einer verteilten Umgebung können gleichzeitig mehrere AAs existieren (z.B. Abteilungen eines Unternehmens). Standardgemäß setzt die Autorisierung mittels Attributzertifikaten den Einsatz einer PKI in der vorausgehenden Authentifizierung voraus. Abb. 2 verdeutlicht in diesem Kontext das Zusammenspiel einer PKI und einer PMI.

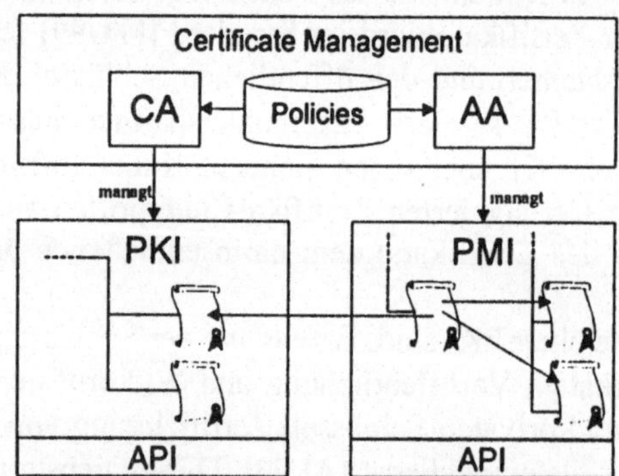

Abb. 2: Sicherheitsmanagement mittels X.509 Zertifikaten

Die Dienste einer PMI unterstützen die zentralisierte Verwaltung der X.509-Attributzertifikate. Zu den Diensten einer PMI gehören: Erstellung, Signierung, Veröffentlichung und Widerruf von Attributzertifikaten. Die Historie aller ausgegebenen und ggf. schon abgelaufenen ACs unterstützt u.a. die Unabstreitbarkeit ausgeführter Aktionen.

Für jede in der PKI registrierte Instanz (z.B. für jeden Kunden) existiert i.d.R. mindestens ein AC, das von einer AA unterschrieben ist. In einem AC ist eine Referenz auf das Public-Key Zertifikat der Instanz gespeichert. Ferner sind in den Attributen des AC konkrete Rechte bzw. Verweise auf weitere ACs enthalten, die ihrerseits die

Rechte von Benutzergruppen (Rollen) beschreiben. Der Verweis auf das AC einer Benutzergruppe weist den Inhaber implizit als Mitglied dieser Benutzergruppe aus. Lesezugriffe auf die PMI haben als Parameter die Identität einer Instanz (d.h. den Verweis auf ihr Public-Key Zertifikat) und überprüfen ob ein Benutzer ein bestimmtes Privileg besitzt. Alternativ kann die Liste sämtlicher Gruppenzugehörigkeiten und Rechte erstellt und durch eine API zurückgegeben werden. Schreibzugriffe auf die PMI werden ausschließlich durch die AAs durchgeführt. Nach jeder Änderung muss das betroffene AC erneut unterschrieben und veröffentlicht werden. Unter Umständen kann die CA der PKI die Rolle einer AA übernehmen.

Die ursprünglichen Informationen zur (automatisierten) Erstellung der ACs können in Form von Policies festgelegt und in einer geeigneten Datenbank (*Policy Repository*) abgelegt werden. Diese Policies definieren die Richtlinien für die Rechte von Subjekten und Rollen, die Zugriffskontrolle auf Objekte, den Schutz von übertragenen Daten vor Ausspähung und Verfälschung, die Überwachung von Zugriffen (Auditing) und die Unabstreitbarkeit von Transaktionen (Non-repudiation).

Das Zertifikatmanagementmodul kontrolliert und überprüft die strukturierte und automatisierte Umsetzung der Policies in die erforderlichen Zertifikate. Hierbei können spezielle Werkzeuge eingesetzt werden, mit denen die Konsistenz und Effizienz der erzeugten Prüfstrategien sichergestellt wird.

Überprüfung von Zugriffsrechten

Jedem CORBA-Objekt der verteilten Managementarchitektur wird eine als Verifier bezeichnete Komponente zugeordnet. Diese kontrolliert die Zugriffe von Subjekten auf die Funktionen des betroffenen Objekts (s. Abb. 3).

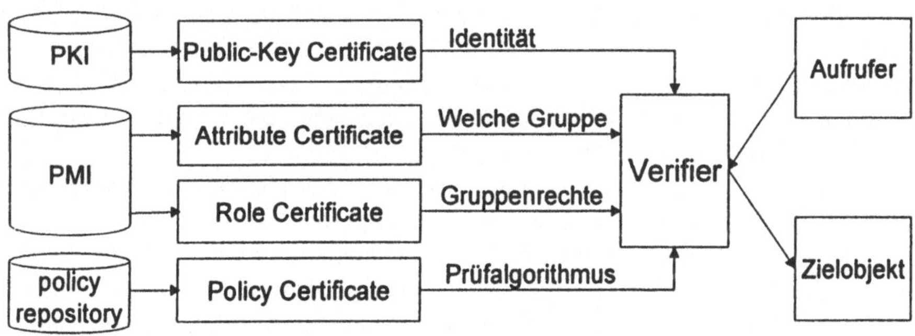

Abb. 3: Verifier-Mechanismus

Die Entscheidung über die Zulässigkeit des Zugriffs wird anhand von Informationen getroffen, die von der PKI und PMI bereitgestellt werden: Die Identität eines Subjekts wird über die PKI ermittelt. Anschließend werden seine aktuellen Rechte direkt oder indirekt (über seine Rollenzugehörigkeiten) mit Hilfe der PMI festgestellt. Die für den Zugriff erforderlichen Rechte werden aus der für das betroffene Objekt gültigen Zugriffs-Policy ermittelt. Diese Policy definiert auch die Vergleichsfunktion, die aufgrund der aktuellen und erforderlichen Rechte über den Erfolg des Zugriffsversuchs entscheidet.

Verifier sind innerhalb der Sicherheitsarchitektur Instanzen mit eigener Identität und spezifischen Rechten. Damit wird ein erweiterter Schutz des gültigen Rechte- und Rollenkonzepts, der Rollenbelegung und der Zugriffskontrollfunktionen möglich. Der Zugriff auf diese Informationen wird auf die Menge der ausgewiesenen Verifier-Objekte beschränkt.

Prototypische Implementierung

In diesem Teil wird die Integration der vorgestellten Sicherheitstechniken und –systeme in die DMA beschrieben. Tiefergehende Details zur Implementierung der DMA und des spezifizierten Sicherheitsmanagementsystems werden an dieser Stelle nicht betrachtet. Grundbausteine dieses Prototyps sind eine kommerzielle, auf JAVA aufbauende *Object Request Broker* (ORB) Implementierung (Inprise Visibroker) und eine kommerzielle PKI (Entrust/PKI).

Die CORBA-Spezifikation wurde um einen Sicherheitsdienst (*CORBA Security Service*, CSS) erweitert [OMG98]. Diese Erweiterung sieht eine API für Public-Key Verfahren vor, aber wichtige praktische Aspekte wie z.B. die Integration der Dienste einer PKI wurden in diesem Standard nicht berücksichtigt.

Zur Absicherung des CORBA-Kommunikationsprotokolls (*Internet Inter-ORB Protocol*, IIOP) wurde eine sichere Protokollschicht (SECIOP) und als Alternative die sogenannte IIOP over SSL Kommunikation (SSLIOP) spezifiziert. Kommerzielle und Open-Source ORB Implementierungen (z.B. Inprise Visibroker oder JacORB) realisieren bislang meistens SSLIOP [IC98] [BRO00]. Beispielsweise wird bei Inprise der ORB um das Objekt SSLCertificateManager ergänzt. Dieses Objekt verwaltet die im Dateisystem abgelegten Zertifikate und benötigt den privaten Schlüssel der beteiligten Instanzen in *Klartextform*, um eine SSL-Verbindung aufbauen zu können. Die von einer PKI ausgestellten privaten Schlüssel sollten aber ausschließlich in PSEs geschützt gespeichert werden. Uns bekannte Implementierungen erlauben aber keine Einbindung von solchen PSEs. Folglich musste bislang auf die Prüfung der Zertifikate durch eine PKI verzichtet werden.

Abb. 4 zeigt eine Lösung zur Behebung dieser Defizite. Hierbei wird angenommen, dass der ORB nicht geändert werden kann, weil z.B. der Quellcode nicht zur Verfügung steht. In diesem Fall werden die CORBA-Objekte der DMA (z.B. die Wrapper) um einen *Interceptor* ergänzt. Interceptors sind Erweiterungen des ORB. Sie erlauben die Überwachung von Bindevorgängen und Methodenaufrufen, sowohl auf der Client- als auch der Serverseite, bei ankommenden und ausgehenden Aufrufen [OMG99].

Die Aufgabe eines Interceptors besteht in diesem Prototyp darin, die Kommunikation zwischen Objekten über einen, bei der Instanziierung der Objekte bereits initialisierten SSL-Kanal zu leiten. Zum Aufbau dieses SSL-Kanals werden die aus JAVA-Klassen bestehenden *PKI-Adapter* verwendet [ETK00]. Diese sind in der Lage, die in PSEs (Entrust Profile File) gespeicherten privaten Schlüssel zu benutzen. Die Gültigkeit der Zertifikate wird dabei von der PKI (durch die Klasse EntrustChainVerifier) bei jedem SSL-Verbindungsaufbau automatisch überprüft.

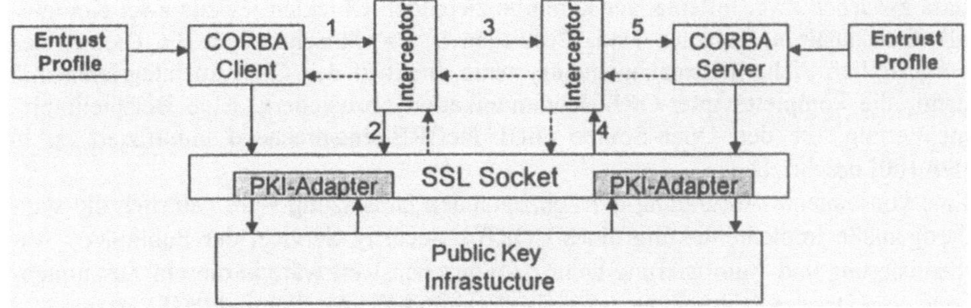

Abb. 4: Implementierung der Integration einer PKI in die DMA

Wenn eine Methode des Objekts „CORBA Server" (z.B. der SAP) vom Objekt „CORBA Client" ausgeführt werden soll, ruft der ORB die Methode `send_request` des Client-Interceptors auf (1). Dieser Methode wird unter anderem ein Stream übergeben, der die Nutzdaten des Aufrufs (z.B. ein Passwort) enthält. Der Interceptor leitet diese Daten über den bei der Initialisierung aufgebauten SSL-Kanal (2). Dem ORB werden die anderen Parameter des Aufrufes (z.B. IIOP-Header) und eine aus Füllzeichen bestehende Zeichenkette übergeben (3) (letztere ist der „Platzhalter" für die über den SSL-Kanal übertragenen Nutzdaten). Der ORB ruft dann auf der Serverseite die Methode `receive_request` des Interceptors auf. Als Eingabeparameter bekommt diese den Platzhalter der Nutzdaten übergeben, den der Interceptor durch die aus dem SSL-Kanal erhaltenen, entschlüsselten Nutzdaten ersetzt (4). Zum Schluss wird der Aufruf mit den korrekten Daten an das Server-Objekt weitergereicht (5). Somit wird erreicht, dass die Nutzdaten der von den Objekten generierten IIOP-Paketen über einen sicheren SSL-Kanal übertragen werden. Über solche Aufrufe hinausgehende ORB-spezifische Kommunikation bleibt unverschlüsselt.

Nach Eingehen eines Methodenaufrufs müssen noch die Rechte des Aufrufers (CORBA Client) überprüft werden. Hierzu werden die ACs des bereits authentisierten Aufrufers verwendet. Der Verifier des aufgerufenen Objekts prüft mit Hilfe des öffentlichen Schlüssels der ausstellenden AA die Gültigkeit der Signatur der präsentierten ACs und ermittelt daraus die Rechte (Gruppenzugehörigkeiten) des Aufrufers. Falls der Aufrufer die erforderlichen Rechte besitzt, darf die Methode ausgeführt werden. Ansonsten erhält der Aufrufer eine Fehlermeldung. Im momentan vorhandenen Prototyp werden die Rechte durch eine Erweiterung der oben erwähnte JAVA-Klasse `EntrustChainVerifier` überprüft.

Ausblick

Beim vorgestellten Prototyp wurde davon ausgegangen, dass der ORB unabgesichert funktioniert und sein Quellcode unzugänglich ist. Die benötigte Sicherheit ist durch die Interceptor-Technik realisiert, indem die Kommunikation zwischen den CORBA-Objekten manipuliert wird, wobei die Dienste externer Sicherheitssysteme benutzt werden. Ein Vorteil dieses Ansatzes besteht darin, dass existierende Anwendungen ohne interne Änderungen abzusichern sind. Ein großer Nachteil dieser Lösung ist, dass zwischen zwei miteinander kommunizierenden Objekten jeweils zwei Kommunikationskanäle aufzubauen sind. Deswegen ist es wünschenswert die Dienste des vorgestellten Sicherheitsmanagementsystems direkt in den ORB zu integrieren und damit die komplette inter-ORB Kommunikation abzusichern. Eine Beispielimplementierung, die den Open-Source ORB JacORB entsprechend modifiziert ist in [NA+00] beschrieben.

Eine konsequente Abrundung der konzeptuellen Umsetzung wäre natürlich die standardgemäße Implementierung eines CORBA Security Service, der Public-Key Authentisierung und Autorisierung benutzt. Wünschenswert wäre in diesem Zusammenhang eine Standardisierung der fehlenden Schnittstellen zu PKI und PMI Systeme.

Ein nächster geplanter Schritt in der Weiterentwicklung des Prototyps ist die Integration von PSEs in Form von Smart Cards.

Literatur

[AL99]   Carlisle Adams, Steve Lloyd:
            Understanding Public-Key Infrastructure: Concepts, Standards, and Deploy-
            ment Considerations
            Macmillan Technical Publishing, 1999

[BRO00]   Gerald Brose:
            JacORB 1.0 Programming Guide, Revision 1.17
            April 2000

[ETK00]   Entrust Technologies
            Entrust/Toolkit for Java Programmers' Guide
            June 2000

[HAN99]   H.-G. Hegering, S. Abeck, B. Neumair: Integrated Management of Networked
            Systems: Concepts, Architectures, and Their Operational Application
            Morgan Kaufmann Publishers, 1999.

[IC98]   Inprise Corporation
            Visibroker 3.3 SSL Pack – Programmer's Guide
            1998

[ITU99]   ITU-T Recommendation X.509
            Information Technology – Open Systems Interconnection – The directory:
            Public-Key and Attribute Certificate Frameworks, September 1999

[KPS95]   Charlie Kaufman, Radia Perlman, Mike Spencer:
            Network Security – PRIVATE Communication in a PUBLIC World
            Prentice Hall, 1995

[MN+00]   C. Mayerl, Z. Nochta, M. Müller, M. Schauer, A. Uremovic, S. Abeck:
            Specification of a Service Management Architecture to Run Distributed and
            Networked Systems, 3rd IFIP/GI International Conference on Trends towards a
            Universal Service Market, Munich, 2000

[NA+00]   Z. Nochta, S. Abeck, G. Augustin, M. Becker, M. Friedmann:
            Integration von Public-Key Infrastrukturen in CORBA-Systeme
            Eingereicht zur Arbeitskonferenz Kommunikationssicherheit der GI Fachgrup-
            pe 2.5.3, Klagenfurt, 2001

[OMG98]   Object Management Group
            Security Service Specification v1.5
            Document 98-12-03, December 1998

[OMG99]   Object Management Group
            The Common Object Request Broker: Architecture and Specification
            Revision 2.3.1, Oktober 1999

[PKIX]   The PKIX Working Group Charter
            http://www.ietf.org/html.charters/pkix-charter.html

[SSL96]   Transport Layer Security Working Group
            Alan O. Freier, Philip Karlton, Paul C. Kocher:
            The SSL Protocol Version 3.0
            Internet-draft November 18, 1996

Session 4:

Groupware und Workflowmanagement

Communication Support for Mobile Virtual Groups

Ulrich Walther and Stefan Fischer

International University in Germany, Campus 3, D-76646 Bruchsal
`{ulrich.walther,stefan.fischer}@i-u.de`

Abstract. With the increasing availability of wireless networks with different bandwidths, communication between mobile users plays a more and more important role. Today, voice communication between two users over mobile phones is the dominant application, but soon, multimedia group applications will likely get a good share of the market. The possibility to dynamically create and destroy mobile virtual groups will make a wealth of new applications possible. One of these applications, which we consider here, is the communication between a group of *tourists* (for instance, a family visiting a city), whose members are logically related, but who are located at different physical places. For this scenario, we have developed, in the framework of the DeepMap project, the group communication application *LocaPhone*, which allows the single members of a group to use one mobile device at the same time as an electronic tourist guide, a mobile (IP) phone, and an instrument for navigation and location detection. In this paper, we describe the design considerations behind this application and its implementation. We focus on the two components for voice communication and for location detection.

1 Introduction

Today, nearly 100% of the surface of at least the industrialized nations are covered by wireless network access points (mostly GSM). In addition, many organizations offer additional private wireless networks such as WLANs. Therefore, mobile users can, in many areas, access their resources in much the same way as they do in their offices or at home using fixed networks. Also, communication between mobile users plays an increasingly important role in today's and tomorrow's application scenarios. Still and increasingly yet, voice communication between two users (one-to-one) over mobile phones is the dominant application, but soon, multimedia group (one-to-many, many-to-many) applications will likely get a good share of the market, with UMTS as the new standard wireless network technology already becoming visible on the horizon. The possibility to dynamically create and destroy virtual groups of mobile users – we call them *mobile virtual groups* –, whose members communicate with each other, makes a wealth of new applications possible. With single group members being able to localize each other or themselves (location awareness [6]), the number of possible applications is increased further.

In the framework of the DeepMap project [7], a group of universities and research institutes under the leadership of the European Media Lab (EML) investigates a number of new technologies for the realization of geographical and historical information systems. Its most prominent sub-project deals with the implementation of an electronic tourist guide for the world-famous city of Heidelberg. But this tourist guide does not only provide information on this city; rather, it also serves as a powerful communication and navigation device. Our group at the International University is responsible for the implementation of both the communication infrastructure for DeepMap and applications that support group communication, navigation, and location detection of single group members. In this paper, we describe the design and the implementation of such an implementation as it is used in the electronic tourist guide of DeepMap.

The paper is organized as follows: in Section 2, we first introduce the DeepMap project and its most popular application, the electronic tourist guide. Section 3 then discusses the requirements on a communication application in a touristic environment. Based on these requirements, we developed the LocaPhone application which provides a number of useful communication features for tourists. This application is described in detail in Section 4. Finally, Section 5 presents conclusions and an outlook.

2   The Project DeepMap and its Electronic Tourist Guide

DeepMap [7] is a common project of a number of research groups mainly from Germany, but also from the US, which investigate various areas of computer science: geo-information systems, natural language processing, intelligent user interfaces, knowledge representation, etc. The goal of Deep Map is to develop information systems that can handle huge heterogeneous data collections, complex functionality and a variety of technologies, but are still accessible for untrained users. In its most prominent sub-project, the group develops a digital personal mobile tourist guide for the city of Heidelberg. The idea is that tourists can collect the device at a central point in the city and then take it with them on their sight-seeing tour. The guide provides the following features:

- pre-computation of tours, following the specific tourist's interests
- leading the tourist on this tour, possibly leading him/her back on the track when necessary
- presentation of information on sights when the tourist approaches them (in different media)
- allow for virtual tours through buildings (for instance the old castle), even in different historical times ("How did this castle look in 1450?")
- choose presentation media according to the specific situation and user (do not play loud audio clips in a church)
- allow for communication between tourists and human guides and among members of a group of tourists
- allow for location detection of other group members

The current proptotype is built on a Xybernaut wearable PC running Linux. The guide accepts as input human voice commands. Its output is either displayed on a head-set screen or a small monitor to be carried by the tourist, and through speakers. The following section describes the specific communication infrastructure available in Heidelberg and the requirements on a solution for the last two bullets of the above list.

3 Requirements on a Tourist Communication System

Heidelberg is completely covered by a number of GSM networks, so connectivity is available in every place. In addition, a number of touristic *hot spots* (e.g. at the Heidelberger Schloss, the station, Universitätsplatz) are covered by Wireless LAN networks. Tourists in these areas can make use of the higher bandwidth and have much better access to all data sources available. Streaming of video and audio streams, external rendering of 3D models and transmission of the resulting pictures to the mobile device, or voice communication is no problem in this area. Still, a communication solution should be usable outside these hot spots, making only use of the available GSM connection. In order to allow for this, the mobile device is equipped with both a GSM modem card and a Wireless LAN card.

What are now the requirements on a solution for the group communication problem? Let's first have a look at a typical situation: a family of four people, two adults, two children, are doing a trip through Heidelberg. Since the children have completely different interests than their parents, they both take different routes. Certainly, the parents would like to (a) still be able to communicate with the children, and (b) know where they are and possibly being guided to them. Therefore, the mobile guide should run an application that allows for voice communication, possibly among the whole group, and for location dectection of all group members. Taking the specific situation described above into account, we can derive the following requirements on a solution:

- Group voice communication should be possible even over a low-bandwidth GSM connection, since the group members might be located outside of hot spots.
- Still, regular touristic data transfer such as download of pictures etc. should run in parallel.
- Only one device should be used for all kinds of communication, in order not to have the tourist handle different devices such as the mobile guide and an additional cell phone. Different networks that might be used should also be hidden by one integrating technology, e.g. IP.
- A location detection mechanism has to be available.
- A group management mechanism has to be available that handles all members of a mobile virtual group, but has no information on non-group tourists. The reason is that personal data has to be protected, and not every user of the system should know where every other user currently is located.

The following section describes in detail how our solution takes these requirements into account.

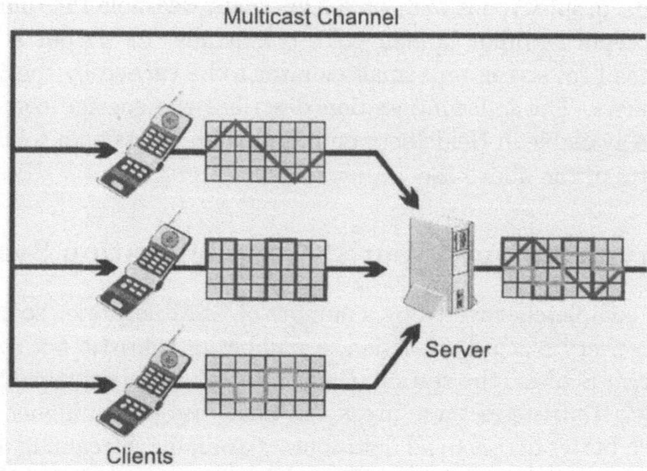

Fig. 1. System architecture. Three conferencing clients, one conferencing server.

4 An Integrated Application for Voice Communication, Navigation, and Location Detection

Our application is logically divided into two separate modules; one module that realizes the group voice communication, and the other component that enables access to location detection devices and processes user location information. The combination of those two functional entities results in an easy-to-use phone with built-in user location, the *LocaPhone*.

4.1 The Group Voice Component

The group voice communication component was designed to only use 50% of the total bandwidth of a GSM connection (as much as $B_{min} = 4.8$ kbit/s) while still allowing other applications to contact network services such as hotel reservation systems, routing plan servers or natural speech processing servers [13]. If we look at the general case where n participants of a group want to talk to each other, each client must receive the audio signals from the $n - 1$ other members in the group. Even for a small group with $n = 3$ this means that the audio signal must be transmitted at a data rate of $B_{min}/2 = 2.4$ kbit/s (including IP procotol overhead), which results in very bad audio quality considering today's best compression codecs available. For larger groups, audio quality is inacceptable [8, 10]. To achieve an integrated transmission system, IP is used as the network protocol, so both touristic information and voice are carried over IP.

Our solution to the problem of limited bandwidth is to use a dedicated *conferencing server* for each group. Its architecture is shown in Figure 1. The conferencing server receives the (IP/UDP-packetized) audio signals from all participants and computes one single audio signal by mixing together all incoming audio streams. The resulting audio stream is then sent back to the group members by using one IP multicast group, or by using unicast IP. Multicast may e.g. not make sense in MobileIP environments, where multicast routing causes problems. IP packets may experience high overheads and latency when the home agent is far from the best route between mobile host and corresponding host (triangle routing problem). Our server therefore supports both methods.

The resulting audio stream only requires the bandwidth of one single audio stream, thus solving the mentioned problems and offering better audio quality. As a tradeoff, the delay is increased considerably by longer communication paths and time needed for decoding, mixing, and coding MPEG audio packets. In [13], we show how this additional delay can be minimized in order to still allow for reasonable conference quality.

Since each client receives a mixture of all audio signals (containing the client's own contribution), it is desirable to suppress the annoying echo. Therefore each client manages a frame buffer of past contributions to be able to filter its own echo from the incoming audio signal. Voice compression at very low bitrates results in fundamental changes of mathematical properties of the signal (like frequency, phase shift), therefore filtering is difficult in that case. We do not focus on this issue in this paper, but refer the interested reader to [13].

The conferencing client uses the audio hardware to capture the audio signal and to playback the received audio signal concurrently. The captured audio signal is divided into packets of the same size, then each packet is compressed through an MPEG-4 audio encoder [9] and the header of our protocol is prepended. These packets are sent to the conferencing server. On the other side, the MPEG-4 compressed audio frames that are received from the server are decoded, the client's echo is cancelled by filtering the signal from the client's frame buffer, and the resulting signal is played back through the audio hardware. The client is implemented in Java using the Java Media Framework [2] for access to the audio hardware, and using a Java Native Interface [3, 1] for accessing the MPEG-4 codec.

4.2   The Navigation and Location Detection Component

To be able to compute the user's location, a Global Positioning System (GPS) device is integrated into the virtual tourist guide hardware. Since May 1st 2000, the Selective Availability (SA) that randomly mutilated GPS signals to decrease precision for civil users was switched off, enabling non-differential GPS devices to operate at an accuracy of about 10 meters in average [12].

We developed a Java GPS driver that enables programming of GPS devices and retrieval, parsing and processing of location and quality information to make it usable for applications. Based on that GPS driver, we designed a location agent that is executed on the user's device and sends location information upon request to the group management agent (see Figure 3). The location agent supports polling and also offers subscription to two types of location reporting [5]:

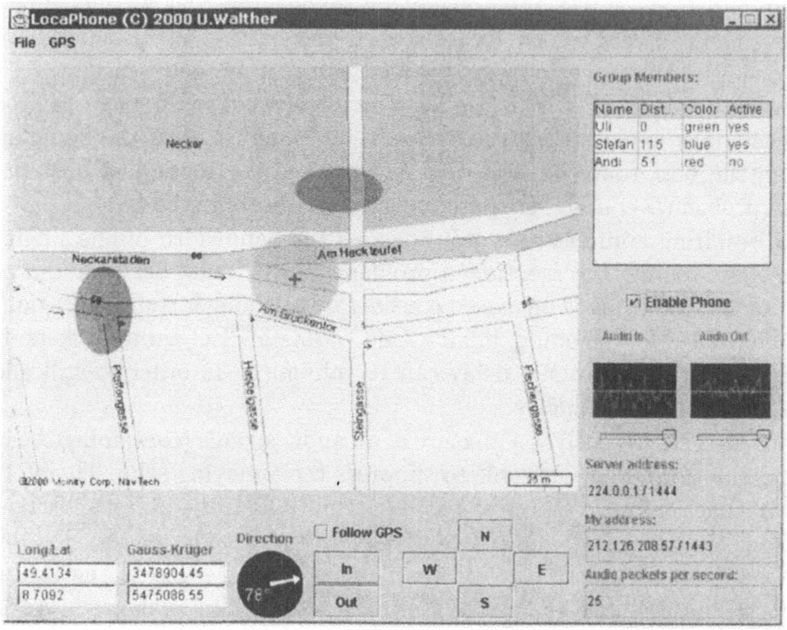

Fig. 2. Graphical User Interface of the LocaPhone application

- *distance-based reporting*, where the agent reports the new user location if a given distance threshold is reached, and
- *time-based/periodic reporting*, where the agent reports the user location in a periodic manner, or at a specific point of time.

The group management agent runs on a server and holds location information of all users. All location requests for users are processed by the management agent who only sends location requests to the location agents if necessary. The agents itself are written in Java and use the communication architecture that is defined within the DeepMap framework [7], as do all other DeepMap applications (like the hotel reservation system, routing agent, natural language processing etc.).

By using the GPS agent functionality, the LocaPhone (Location and Phone) application shows the members belonging to the same tourist group on a city map, thus allowing to e.g. safely trace one's children on their way to the city while being able to talk to them using the group communication functionality described in the previous section. All GPS agents that belong to the same tourist group subscribe to one agent group, therefore each GPS agent receives location information about all other members in the same group. Figure 2 shows the graphical user interface of the LocaPhone application showing three tourists in Heidelberg. Each tourist is displayed in a different color, the ellipses show the estimated user location area as computed by the GPS driver. Smaller ellipses on the display denote more accurate positions. By clicking on a user's ellipse on

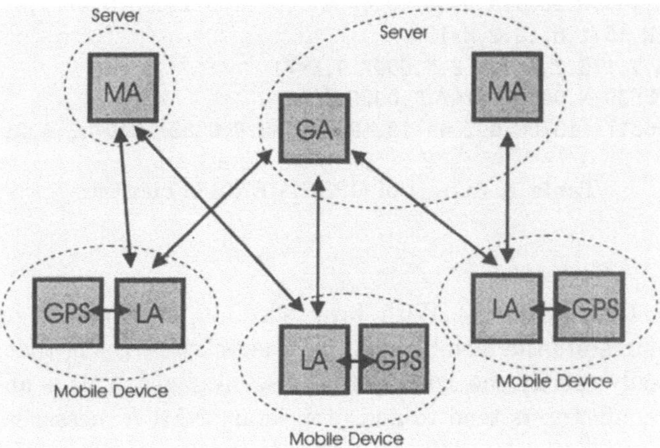

Fig. 3. Location Agents (LA) with GPS Drivers (GPS), the Map Agents (MA) and the Group Management Agent (GA)

the map display, his current position and direction are indicated. On the upper right, the list of members belonging to the user's group is displayed, and the user can start talking to the group by enabling the **Enable Phone** checkbox.

The map is calculated by a map agent that takes the Gauss-Krueger coordinates of the map center as input and returns a bitmap of the area. Since the map agent is currently under heavy construction, we used a dummy agent that retrieves maps over the internet using the `www.shellgeostar.com` site.

GPS receivers send the current position, number of satellites in view, accuracy and precision that can be expected from the measurement and many other information as messages in the standardized NMEA0183 format [11]. The receiver is connected to the wearable computer via a serial communication line (`COMx` in the Windows world or `/dev/ttySx` in Unix). A small extract of messages that a GPS receiver sends can be seen in Table 1. The NMEA message

```
$GPVTG,175.4,T,175.2,M,004.3,N,0007.9,K
```

e.g. means that the current true course of the user is in direction 175.4 degrees, the magnetic course is 175.2 degrees, and the user's speed is 4.3 knots or 7.9 km per hour. Due to the asynchronous way GPS devices send information, it is unpredictable when a certain information will be updated next, therefore to each data structure that represents a certain type of GPS data, we added a counter that represents the age of that information. Thus applications can decide up to which age a certain kind of information is still usable, or if it should be excepted from further processing instead of using imprecise values.

To enable access to serial communcation lines, the GPS driver uses the `javax.comm` library that is available as an extension to the Java Development Kit [4]. The design of the NMEA message parser uses the ability to reflect on Java

```
$GPGGA,092644,4909.5639,N,00837.9107,E,1,07,1.6,132.3,M,47.9,M,,*48
$PGRME,10.2,M,15.1,M,18.2,M*13
$GPVTG,175.4,T,175.2,M,004.3,N,0007.9,K*71
$LCGLL,4909.5639,N,00837.9107,E,092644,A
$PGRMF,46,206817,110700,092644,13,4909.5639,N,00837.9107,E,A,2,0,236,3,2*22
```

Table 1. Extract of GPS NMEA0183 messages

classes (`java.lang.reflect`). With Java reflection, it is (among other things) possible to enumerate the members and types of classes. Using that feature, we are able to easily specify the syntax of NMEA messages. This is an advantage, since GPS manufacturers tend to add proprietary NMEA messages to enhance functionality; so when using different GPS receivers it may be useful to include their definitions of additional proprietary messages.

5 Conclusions and Outlook

In this paper, we presented the LocaPhone application which is a useful tool for groups of tourists, since it provides voice group communication at acceptable quality over GSM connections and graphically locates the other members in the tourist group. We proposed the use of location agents for the realization of that service, the voice group communication is based on a centralized server. The Java-based implementation shows the feasibility of our approach.

In the future, we plan to investigate the situation where we have several hot spots in the city that are covered by wireless LAN, whereas the other areas still provide connectivity through the GSM network. Wireless LAN connections have far higher bandwidths, therefore the group communication component could be extended with video functionality. If certain hot spot areas are covered by more than one wireless access point, we want to analyze to which degree it is possible to enhance the accuracy of the user's location as computed by the GPS receiver, or even to only rely on that computation and being able to omit the GPS hardware, if we take into account the signal strengths that can be measured between the user and the various access points.

References

1. R. Gordon and A. McClellan. *Essential JNI: Java Native Interface.* Prentice-Hall, Englewood Cliffs, NJ 07632, USA, 1998.
2. R. Gordon and S. Talley. *Essential JMF: Java Media Framework.* P T R Prentice-Hall, Englewood Cliffs, NJ 07632, USA, 1999.
3. JavaSoft. Java Native Interface Specification, Nov. 1996. Release 1.1.
4. Java Development Kit 1.3. Sun Microsystems, 2000.
5. A. Leonhardi and K. Rothermel. A comparison of protocols for updating location information. Technical Report TR-2000-05, Universität Stuttgart, Fakultät Informatik, Germany, Mar. 2000.

6. U. Leonhardt. *Supporting Location-Awareness in Open Distributed Systems*. Phd thesis, Imperial College of Science, Technology and Medicine, Unversity of London, 1998.

7. R. Malaka and A.Zipf. DEEP MAP - Challenging IT Research in the Framework of a Tourist Information System. In *Proc. 7th International Conference in Information and Comm. Technology in Tourism*, 2000.

8. MPEG4. Very low bitrate audio-visual coding - Part 3: Audio. *ISO/IEC 14496-3*.

9. MPEG4. Very low bitrate audio-visual coding - Part 5: Reference Software. *ISO/IEC 14496-5*.

10. MPEG4. MPEG-4 Audio verification test results: Audio on Internet. *Atlantic City*, October 1998.

11. NMEA 0183. Standard for Interfacing Marine Electronics Devices.

12. U.S. Coast Guard Navigation Center. Global Positioning System Standard Positioning Service Specification. 2nd Edition, June 1995.

13. U. Walther and S. Fischer. Group Voice Communication for Mobile Environments. In *Proc. IEEE International Conference on Computer Communications and Networks (ICCCN)*, 2000.

Using XSL to Coordinate Workflows

Robert Tolksdorf[1] and Marc Stauch[2]

[1] Technische Universität Berlin, Fachbereich Informatik, FLP/KIT,
Sekr. FR 6–10, Franklinstr. 28/29, D-10587 Berlin, Germany,
mailto:tolk@cs.tu-berlin.de, http://www.cs.tu-berlin.de/~tolk
[2] *mailto:marc@stau.ch*

Abstract. Web-based workflow management can greatly benefit from Internet
technologies, as these offer required functionalities to support distributed and
cross-organizational workflows. It is, however, vital for any successful Internet
application to deliver its services via a standard protocol in a standard format.
The Workspaces architecture combines workflow management with standard Internet technology, namely the Extensible Markup Language XML and the Extensible Stylesheet Language XSL, with coordination technology. It is based on the
notion of *steps* as the basic kinds of activity. Several kinds of steps describe activities or their coordination. A workflow definition is compiled into a set of steps
that can be distributed individually. The implementation of Workspaces uses XSL
processing for the generation and execution of steps.
The Workspaces architecture and its implementation with standard Internet technologies is described. We report on the experiences made and draw conclusions
on the adequacy of XSL as a platform independent and standardized component
to build a Web-based workflow system.

1 Introduction

Workflow management systems are an application domain which can greatly benefit
from Internet technologies, as these offer required functionalities to support workflows
across heterogeneous and distributed organizations ([Wor98b]). Using Internet technologies implies the use of open standards. While the functionality of services is specific to the application-domain and the offering vendor, any successful Internet application must deliver that service via a standard protocol in a standard format.

Internet-based workflow management thus means to incorporate standard representation format for data and processes. The Extensible Markup Language XML currently
evolves into the dominating representation format for documents in the Internet and is
accompanied by a set of standardized associated technologies, such as the Extensible
Stylesheet Language XSL used to transform XML documents ([Tol99])[1]. We proposed
the *Workspaces* architecture ([Tol00a,Tol00b]) which uses XML and XSL processing to
implement a workflow system. It is described in more detail below and leads to several
insights about the adequacy of these standards in that application domain.

Workspaces also relies on coordination technology to provide services that support the smooth interplay of distributed and asynchronous work processes. It has been

---

[1] In the following we use "XSL" and "XSL-T" synonymously.

shown ([CTV$^+$98]) that the means provided by Web technology to start and execute active processing have to be accompanied by such a component to support the interplay of multiple activities. That role is taken by the *XMLSpace* in Workspaces which is a distributed repository for XML documents with associative access operations in the tradition of the coordination language Linda ([GC92]). For the purpose of this paper, however, the role of coordination technology in Workspaces is of lesser importance and will not be considered in the following.

The question we pose with this paper is to what extend the standard Internet technologies XML and XSL are suited to serve as a basis for the implementation of a Web-based workflow system such as Workspaces. We will base our answer on the experiences made with an implementation of our architecture.

In this paper we first give a brief overview on the Workspaces conception and architecture. Then, the details of the use of XSL in the implementation are given. Finally, we report on our experiences with that technology and draw conclusions.

2 Workspaces

In this section, we give an overview of the conception of *Workspaces*, which is an architecture for the coordination of workflows over the Internet. It is based on the notion of a *step* as the basic kind of activity. Each step is an activity that transforms one or more documents into a number of other documents which can, in turn, cause further activities to start. The coordinated execution of steps together is the workflow.

Workspaces combines workflow concepts with standard Internet technology. The documents involved in the workflow are assumed to use application specific markup languages expressed in the *Extensible Markup Language* XML ([Wor98d]). XML is a language to describe the grammar of a markup language and will be the dominant format for documents on the Internet. XML documents consist of plain text structured by markup-tags. As the tags must be well-balanced with one tag enclosing the whole document, XML documents form trees with the tags and contained text as nodes. Transforming XML documents is the very subject of the standardized *Extensible Stylesheet Language* XSL technology ([Wor99,Wor00b]). XSL uses (XML encoded) rules, referred to as stylesheets, describing the kind of transformations that are to be applied to an XML document. They contain templates that match to certain nodes in the document. The node and its content are then transformed into some replacement node.

In Workspaces, activity descriptions are represented as XSL rules that are executed by an XSL processor. It reads an XSL rule set which contains patterns and transformations, tries to match patterns in the input document and to apply transformations on the match that generate fragments in the output document.

We distinguish *basic steps* that describe the actual performance of work, *coordination steps* that change the course of work and *meta steps* that operate on a workflow description. There are three kinds of basic steps as follows:

- *Automatic steps* are pure document transformations and require only activity of some transformation component within the system. An example is a text formatter that transforms a document from some markup language into a formatted and print-able representation. They are implemented using normal XSL processing taking a document and producing an new one.

- *External steps* involve applications that take a document as input, let the user perform some activity on it, and generate an output document. An example is editing a text with an editor. They invoke an external application via the XSL processor.
- *User steps* are performed by a user without any support by a system. An example is the activity of reading a conference submission. The user has to report the completion of such a step using a GUI.

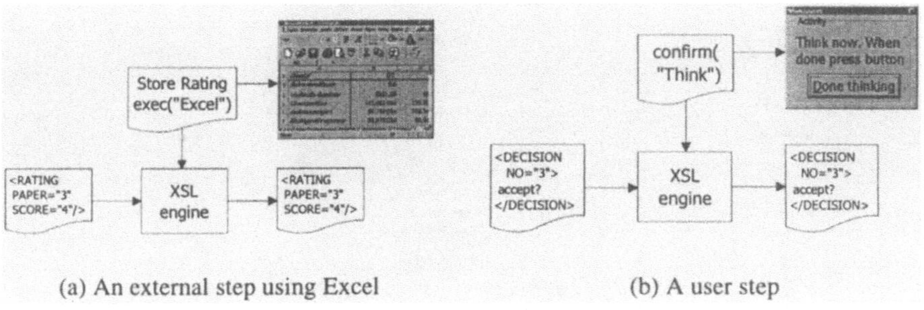

(a) An external step using Excel(b) A user step

Fig. 1. Steps with external effects

Coordination steps only coordinate the flow of work and thus are orthogonal to the basic steps. Workflow procedures describe temporal and causal dependencies among activities represented as steps. The management of these dependencies is the central issue for any workflow system. Following [MC94], we call this management activity *coordination*.

In the process model put forth by the WfMC ([Wor98a]) we find examples of explicit coordination steps with the ROUTE, LOOP and SUBFLOW activities. In addition, JOIN and SPLIT activities are implicitly embedded in the topology of the workflow graph. We also consider these as explicit steps. Together, these coordination activities play the role of the coordination language of the workflow, as opposed to the set of automatic, external, and user steps that represent the actual work performed.

A very simple kind of managing a dependency amongst two activities is their sequential execution which is represented in a workflow graph by one activity being the direct or indirect successor of the activity on which it depends. More complex coordination operations are ones that change the direction of threads of work such as OR-JOIN, start multiple such threads (SPLIT), or synchronize them with a single successor activity (JOIN) as show in figures 2(a) and 2(b).

Basic steps together with coordination steps form complete workflow graphs. Figure 3 shows such a graph where review forms on a paper submission are distributed,

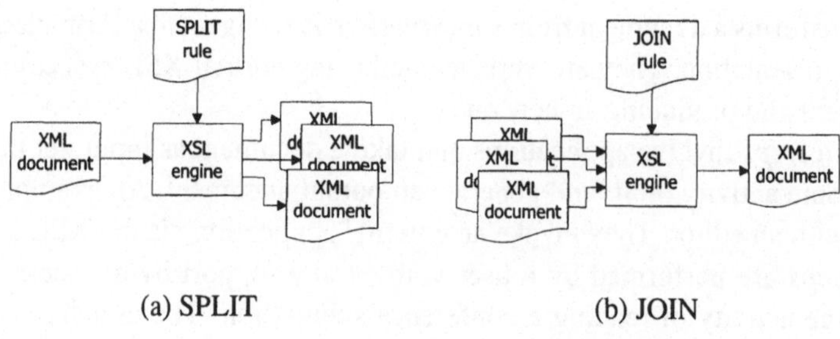

(a) SPLIT
(b) JOIN

Fig. 2. Coordination steps in Workspaces

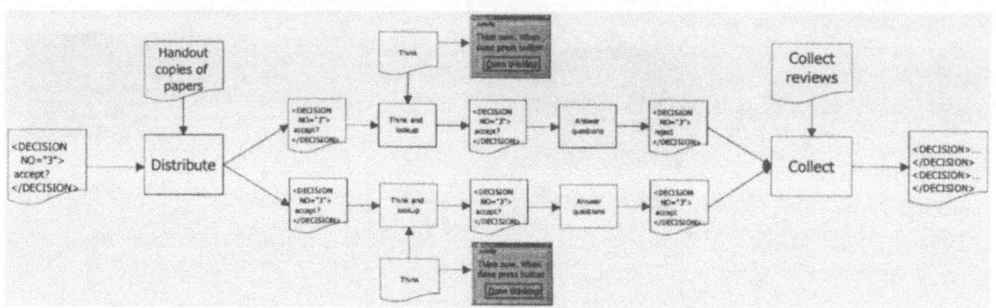

Fig. 3. A complete workflow graph

answered, and finally collected and merged. In the Workspaces system, the graph is represented as an XML document following the formal grammar of the *Workspaces Coordination Language*, WSCL. WSCL is based on the Workflow Process Description Language as defined by the WfMC in the Interface 1 of the Reference Model ([Wor98a]).

Meta steps change or generate the structure of the workflow. An example is the generation of a set of individual steps from a process description. While the workflow graph can be considered the "program" written in a higher level language, the execution of a workflow is the execution of individual steps, which resemble "instructions" in microprocessors. The "compilation" is performed by *meta steps* in Workspaces. XSL rule sets are by definition represented as XML documents following a syntax defined in the XSL standard. Thus, the compilation of the graph into steps is the transformation of one XML document into a set of XML documents, each containing an XSL rule for one step, as depicted in figure 4.

3   An XSL based Implementation of Workspaces

In this section we consider the issues regarding the implementation of Workspaces with XSL-technology. XSL transformations are performed by *XSL processors* – sometimes

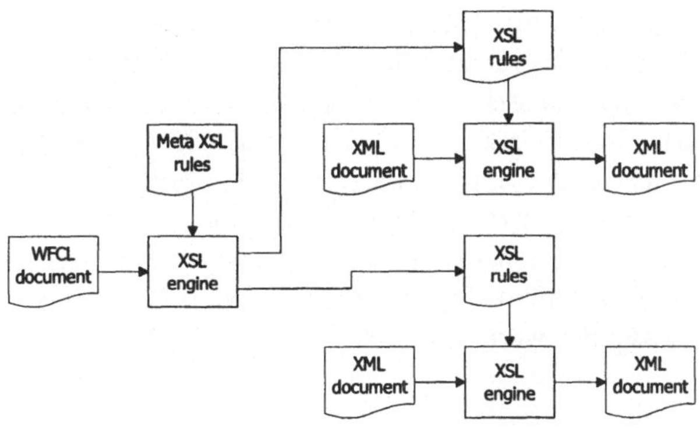

Fig. 4. Compiling a workflow graph into steps

called XSL engines – which are publicly available as Open Source. The *Workspaces engine* includes such an XSL processor as one component and complements it with additionally required functionality. The restrictions of XSL transformations and their primary use in document processing, made it impossible to build the Workspaces engine "within" a standard XSL engine through the use of external Java programs that could be called from the respective XSL stylesheets. Instead we had to wrap an XSL processor with the Workspaces engine, resulting in the architecture depicted in figure 5.

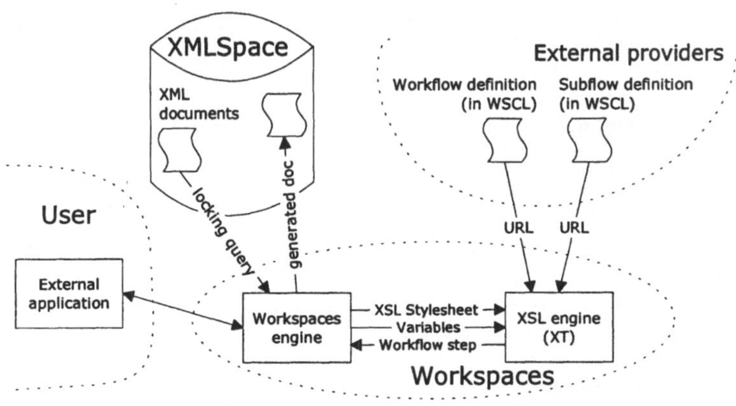

Fig. 5. Architecture of the Workspaces Implementation

The architecture is open and supports distributed storage of data by the use of URLs to access workflow definitions, and through the use of the distributed XMLSpace which acts as a database-like document space to access the workflow documents. Moreover, the use of XML as an interchange language between the different modules ensures a high level of adaptability and programmability.

The current implementation ([Sta99]) is based on an architecture of a Workspaces engine that launches and coordinates the local user processes and activities using a simple Java Swing graphical user interface. The Workspaces engine uses the XSL processor XT written by James Clark in Java ([Cla]) as an XSL stylesheet processor, IBM's XML4J Java XML parser that implements DOM 1.0 ([Wor98c]) and offers classes for parsing, manipulating and generating XML. Using these tools workflow definitions are transformed into XML files containing single steps with all the necessary information to run a single workflow activity. Figure 6 shows how the XSL engine is embedded in the processing of a step in a workflow instance.

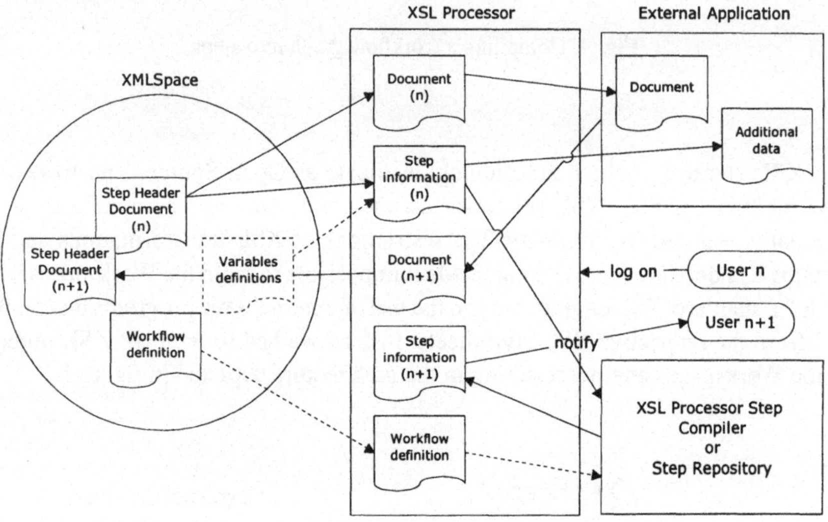

Fig. 6. Calculation of a Step in the Workspaces Engine

This information is then presented to the user who will choose which activities and hence external applications are to be launched. Figure 7 shows a screen shot of the graphical interface of the Workspaces engine.

3.1 Step Compilation with XSL

The workflow definition in WSCL represents a graph, consisting of transitions between activities. The necessary information for the execution of a single step refers to exactly one activity and its corresponding transitions. The XSL meta-step for compilation hence has to to find transitions that connect this last activity with new activities.

At the same time the XSL script should compile all the information that is needed to execute and coordinate the following new activities. This involves resolving variables within subflows with respect to their relative scope, and further extraction of elements from the XML tree according to their identifier attributes in the widest sense. The resulting step is an XML document that can be validated.

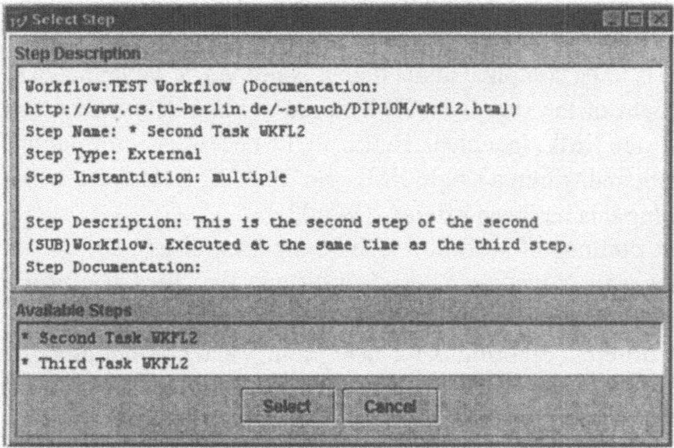

Fig. 7. Graphical User Interface of the Workspaces Engine

Two different scenarios are conceivable to implement this behavior. We refer to these two alternative modes of compilation as "eager" and "lazy", meaning either run- or start-time compilation of steps.

- *Eager Compilation:* In this scenario compilation takes place when or before the workflow is started. All the information about the possible steps and variables of a workflow are generated when the workflow is launched. Steps and variables are gathered in a step repository – either within XMLSpace or accessible through a URL. Steps await their execution until certain start conditions are reached. External subflow definitions have their own repositories – possibly at different locations –, and need not be compiled by the local engine.

  The concept of a repository allows it to share the step information across workflow instances. This is of specific interest when external subflow definitions have many instances. At the same time the control of updates of subflows is left to the provider of the subflow, ensuring soundness and completeness across large networks, since new versions of the steps are automatically used by the workflow participants.

  The notion of a step repository is of high interest when participating in the workflow while being detached from the net. Once the relevant steps have been detected, they can be packaged and transferred to the mobile system along with their respective pointer to documents within XMLSpace, thus enabling working offline.
- *Lazy Compilation:* This second scenario implies that compilation takes place as late in the running workflow instance as possible. The step information is generated at the time it is needed, after an activity is finished by the client.

  Since steps are only generated when needed there is no unnecessary space consumption by potentially unused steps. References to subflows (as URLs or possibly as documents within XMLSpace) are resolved as late as possible, thus if an external provider of a subflow changes its code it will automatically be used. The external provider is not required to compile his scripts, all compilation is client-side, minimizing the risk of potentially large scale server-side computation.

If the step is to be compiled at the time it is needed, it would make sense to extract the document of the step from XMLSpace at compilation time and to include it within the step XML document. Hence all the necessary information for an activity is to be gathered within a single XML file. With XML Namespaces a standardized way of doing this has been offered ([Wor00c]).

If relevant portions of workflow definitions as well as relevant documents from XMLSpace were copied onto detached systems the client-side lazy compilation of steps would guarantee the possibility of working offline in a mobile environment. But more different algorithms for determining and computing potential steps for future detached work within a workflow instance are conceivable but have not yet been explored in Workspaces.

In our implementation of the Workspaces engine the lazy mode of compilation has been chosen. The primary objective was to ensure consistency while still enabling a high degree of distribution. The advantages of a step repository seem to be at the expense of emphasizing server-side computation as in traditional client-server architectures. We favored ubiquitous engines depending on a ubiquitous XMLSpace that process documents and instructions themselves when needed.

Refer to figure 8 for an example of an XSL stylesheet template used in the workspaces engine. This very simple template illustrates the insertion of the responsible performer once an activity for a step has been determined.

```
<!-- Insertion of Performers -->
<xsl:template mode="insert-performer" match="*">
  <xsl:variable name="name" select="@PERFORMER"/>
  <xsl:choose>
    <!-- is the matching PARTICIPANT in the WORKFLOW ? -->
    <xsl:when test='ancestor::WORKFLOW/child::PARTICIPANT[@ID=$name]'>
      <xsl:copy-of
       select="ancestor::WORKFLOW/child::PARTICIPANT[@ID=$name][position()=1]"/>
    </xsl:when>
    <!-- is the matching PARTICIPANT in the MODEL ? -->
    <xsl:when test='/child::MODEL/child::PARTICIPANT[@ID=$name]'>
      <xsl:copy-of
       select="/child::MODEL/child::PARTICIPANT[@ID=$name][position()=1]"/>
    </xsl:when>
     <!-- so, where is the PARTICIPANT ? -->
    <xsl:otherwise>
      <xsl:text>NO MATCHING PARTICIPANT FOUND</xsl:text>
    </xsl:otherwise>
  </xsl:choose>
</xsl:template>
```

Fig. 8. Sample XSL stylesheet, insertion of performers

Execution of user steps has been implemented using Java threads that are monitored by the Workspaces engine. Termination of an activity initiates the compilation of successor steps. Refer to *http://www.cs.tu-berlin.de/~stauch/diplom* for further information on the implementation of Workspaces.

3.2 An Example of a Workflow instance

Refer to figure 9 for an example of the output of the Workspaces engine when starting a new workflow instance and exporting the first external step. It describes the engine's processes after a new workflow instance has been started.

Once the user has chosen to start a new workflow, the workflow definition and the initial document are read and parsed. A start time stamp is then created for future use (e.g. references to the current running instance from future subflows). References to external workflow definitions and variables in the current workflow definition are resolved and the first step is compiled using the `lazy.xsl` XSL-T script from figure 8 (the necessary parameters for the script to excerpt the first step of a workflow definition are also presented).

Once the step has been compiled it is made available. The step selection window subsequently opens automatically since the first step that has just been compiled in this case is a step for the same user that started the workflow instance.

In the following the output of the engine shows that the user selected this step for execution. Hence the step is extracted from XMLSpace and the document is extracted to a local temporary file, using the documents top level XML tag name. The local executable program file is then determined using a local preferences file. This program is executed with the current temporary copy of the document and any other parameters that were specified in the workflow definition.

The Workspaces engine now waits for the program to terminate, its output reminding the user that he or she will not be notified in the case of any new steps being generated for him or her during the execution of the current step.

4 Related work

[MSKP97] discusses a number of important issues for Web-based workflows and how these have been dealt with in several projects. This work places the Workspaces approach in its context.

XML has been considered for the use in workflow systems: SWAP was an activity to define a common abstraction over running workflows by providing an interface to workflow engines ([Swe98], [BK99]). These then were to exchange messages about the status of the workflow in an XML based representation. As a successor activity to SWAP, the WfMC is also considering XML as the appropriate encoding to exchange the status of currently running workflows ([Wor00a]).

Both approaches, however, concern the Interface 4 of the WfMC reference model and are thus not comparable to the Workspaces approach. Here, the processes as well as the data they work on are represented in XML and the Interface 1 of the reference model is the focus of work. To our knowledge, there is currently no documented system based on open Web-standards comparable to Workspaces.

```
Starting new Workflow
Workflow Definition read
Document read
Starting Workflow at: 20000114014214400
Creating local resolved Workflow Definition
Starting to resolve Workflow Definition File (HREFs)
Starting to resolve Workflow Definition File (VARIABLES)
Running XSL-T: (XT)
XT Arguments:
D:\ENGINE\WORK\Workflows\wkfl36097.xml
D:\ENGINE\WORK\XSLscripts\resolve.xsl
D:\ENGINE\WORK\Workflows\wkfl36098.xml
XSLT terminated
Created resolved Workflow Definition:
D:\ENGINE\WORK\Workflows\wkfl36098.xml
Running XSL-T: (XT)
XT Arguments:
D:\ENGINE\WORK\Workflows\wkfl36098.xml
D:\ENGINE\WORK\XSLscripts\lazy.xsl
getFirst=true
currentDoc=D:\Engine\Work\Workflows\initial.xml
stepDir=D:\ENGINE\WORK\Steps\
currentWorkflow=
date=20000114014214400
result=D:\ENGINE\WORK\Steps\start36099
XSLT terminated
Exporting First Step
First Step exported
Opening Stepselect Window
Found user Steps
Selected
One node DOCUMENT found in DOMSave.saveElement.
Correct.
Found a User Step for execution
Executing:D:\ENGINE\XMLSPACE\marc@stau.ch\startat20000114014214400.xml
Command line: D:\USR\textpad\Textpad.exe D:\ENGINE\WORK\Docs\doc36100.xml
Waiting for single program to terminate (NO Notification)
Executing User Step
```

Fig. 9. Sample Output of the Workspaces Engine

5   Conclusions

The initial question for this paper was if the standard Internet technologies XML and
XSL were suitable to serve as a basis for the implementation of a Web-based workflow
system such as Workspaces.

The current Workspaces engine has proved to be stable and has shown good performance in a restricted test environment. However this environment did not reflect all the
potential problems faced in real world applications. Scalability could clearly become
an issue of importance considering the memory and performance problems inherent in
implementations of the DOM Model and XSL transformation tools with respect to large
documents. Notably the syntax and semantics of XPath expressions calls for optimization or compilation of stylesheets before execution of XSL stylesheets.

With regard to the challenges of detached computing this seems to be an issue of real
importance, memory and computational power being limited in the currently available
portable devices. At the time of writing, there have been several announcements of new
XSL compilers that optimize performance and thereby our implementation.

Client-side browser support of XSL is another attractive option in the further development of the Workspaces model. A complete separation of the Workspaces engine from the XSL engine – which will be available within the next generation of standard browsers – will then become possible.

A major drawback is inherent in XSL itself: programming of XSL stylesheets is very clumsy. Major problems are caused by the unhandy XML notation and by the write-once definition of XSL variables. It is unclear whether direct XSL-programming should be the basis for software development. The problem is in part caused by the fact that we use technologies intended for document-markup and -processing for the compilation and execution of processes.

All in all, out experiences have shown that building on standard technologies is the right way to go. We benefited greatly from the existence of tools and libraries to process standard formats. While this is an implementation advantage, we also believe that the resulting system is of higher value by supporting standard formats and technologies. Thus, we believe that XML and XSL can in fact serve as a basis for the implementation of a complex application such as a Web-based workflow system. Further information about the current status of Workspaces is available on the Web at *http://www.cs.tuberlin.de/˜tolk/workspaces.*

References

[BK99]   Gregory Alan Bolcer and Gail Kaiser. SWAP: Leveraging the Web to Manage Workflow. *IEEE Internet Computing*, 3(1):85–88, 1999.

[Cla]   James Clark. XT. http://www.jclark.com/xml/xt.html.

[CTV⁺98]   Paolo Ciancarini, Robert Tolksdorf, Fabio Vitali, Davide Rossi, and Andreas Knoche. Coordinating Multiagent Applications on the WWW: A Reference Architecture. *IEEE Transactions on Software Engineering*, 24(5):362–375, May 1998.

[GC92]   David Gelernter and Nicholas Carriero. Coordination Languages and their Significance. *Communications of the ACM*, 35(2):97–107, 1992.

[MC94]   T.W. Malone and K. Crowston. The Interdisciplinary Study of Coordination. *ACM Computing Surveys*, 26(1):87–119, 1994.

[MSKP97]   J. Miller, A. Sheth, K. Kochut, and D. Palaniswami. The Future of Web-Based Workflows. In *International Workshop on Research Directions in Process Technology*, July 1997. http://lsdis.cs.uga.edu/lib/download/MS+97.ps.

[Sta99]   Marc Stauch. Design and Implementation of a System for Distributed Workflows using XML / XSL. Master's thesis, Technische Universität Berlin, 1999. http://www.cs.tuberlin.de/ stauch/diplom.

[Swe98]   K. Swenson. Simple Workflow Access Protocol (SWAP). Technical Report draft-ietf-swenson-swap-prot-00.txt, Netscape Communications Corp, 1998. INTERNET-DRAFT.

[Tol99]   Robert Tolksdorf. XML und darauf basierende Standards: Die neuen Auszeichnungssprachen des Web. *Informatik Spektrum*, 22(6):407–421, 1999.

[Tol00a]   Robert Tolksdorf. Coordinating Work on the Web with Workspaces. In *Proceedings of the IEEE Ninth International Workshops on Enabling Technologies: Infrastructure for Collaborative Enterprises WET ICE 2000*. IEEE Computer Society, Press, 2000.

[Tol00b]   Robert Tolksdorf. Coordination Technology for Workflows on the Web: Workspaces. In *Proceedings of the Fourth International Conference on Coordination Models and Languages COORDINATION 2000*, LNCS. Springer-Verlag, 2000.

[Wor98a] Workflow Management Coalition. Interface 1: Process Definition Interchange Process Model, 1998. http://www.wfmc.org.

[Wor98b] Workflow Management Coalition. Workflow and Internet: Catalysts for Radical Change. WfMC White Paper, 1998. http://www.wfmc.org.

[Wor98c] World Wide Web Consortium. Document Object Model (DOM) Level 1 Specification. W3C Recommendation, 1998. http://www.w3.org/TR/REC-DOM-Level-1.

[Wor98d] World Wide Web Consortium. Extensible Markup Language (XML) 1.0. W3C Recommendation, 1998. http://www.w3.org/TR/REC-xml.

[Wor99] World Wide Web Consortium. XSL Transformations (XSLT). W3C Recommendation, 1999. http://www.w3.org/TR/xslt.

[Wor00a] Workflow Management Coalition. Interoperability Wf-XML Binding. WFMC-TC-1023, May 2000. http://www.wfmc.org.

[Wor00b] World Wide Web Consortium. Extensible Stylesheet Language (XSL) Specification. W3C Working Draft, 2000. http://www.w3.org/TR/xsl.

[Wor00c] World Wide Web Consortium. Namespaces in XML. W3C Recommendation, 2000. http://www.w3.org/TR/REC-xml-names.

Eingeladener Vortrag II:

A. Paepcke; Stanford University

Wireless Handheld Devices and the Web
(Summary of Invited Presentation)

Andreas Paepcke

Stanford University
Paepcke@cs.stanford.edu

PDA access to the World-Wide Web pose a variety of difficulties for users. The small screen quickly renders Web pages confusing and cumbersome to peruse. Inputting information by pen is time consuming and error-prone. The download time for Web material to radio linked devices is still much slower than landline connections. The standard browsing process of downloading entire pages just to find the links to pursue next is thus poor for the context of wireless PDAs.

In searching out solutions for these problems, the Stanford Digital Library Project turned to principles of distributed systems, and combined them with information retrieval technologies. We place a proxy server in between wirelessly connected PDAs and the World-Wide Web (Figure 1). The proxy serves as a data cache, but it also performs Web site indexing, search keyword completion, and information summarization functions. In our work so far, we have designed, implemented, and tested several approaches to accomplishing these functions in a distributed environment.

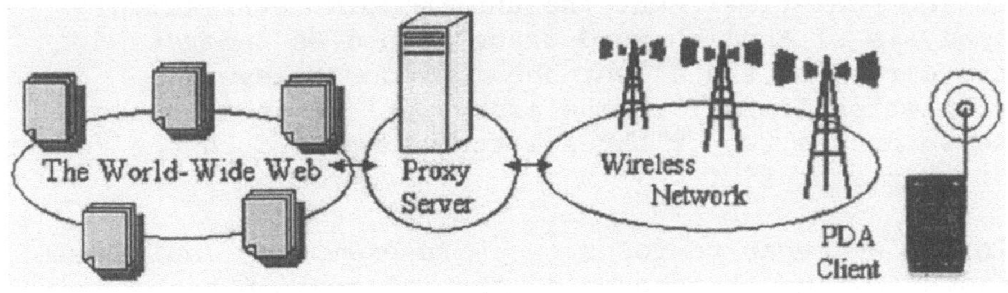

Figure 1: A Proxy Architecture Mediates Between
PDA and the World-Wide Web

In [1] we introduced support for the navigation phase of information seeking activities on the Web. As users navigate through pages, we show each page's link anchors

on the PDA. The rest of the pages' material is not
displayed. A left-to-right pen gesture over one
of the links causes a crawler at the proxy to fetch the
corresponding destination page. That page's link anchors
are extracted and displayed indented on the screen. This
approach is similar to how file browsers on common
operating systems display folders and files.

In [2] we addressed the search phase of information
tasks. Once users begin to explore a Web site, a crawler
at the proxy dynamically collects and indexes pages on
that site. The crawler continues its work until the user
browses out of the site. At that point the index is
retained, but not expanded. As soon as the same user, or
others, re-enter the site, the indexing activity is
resumed. The index enables us to provide site-specific.
searches from the PDA. Since the indexes are created and
maintained at the proxy, PDA clients can be kept very
small.

We also use the site indexes to enable search keyword
completion. After users have entered either one or two
characters of a search keyword, a proxy sends a list of
the words that occur on the current Web site, and begin
with the specified characters. This facility saves time,
because pen input on PDAs is slow and error prone. One
challenge of this keyword completion facility is its
distributed nature. The underlying machinery needs to be
tuned so that the round-trip delay of asking the proxy
for keyword lists is not so long that the user could
during that time input the entire word. Statistical
analysis of English word usage helped us understand
how early our PDA client should request keyword
completion lists from the proxy while a user inputs a
keyword. The two or three letter threshold is the result
of this analysis.

In [3] we began to focus on users examining individual
pages. During this phase of the information task, users
need to gain an overview of a given page, and they need
the ability to explore successive portions of the page in
more depth. Figure 2 shows a screen shot of the work
described in [3].

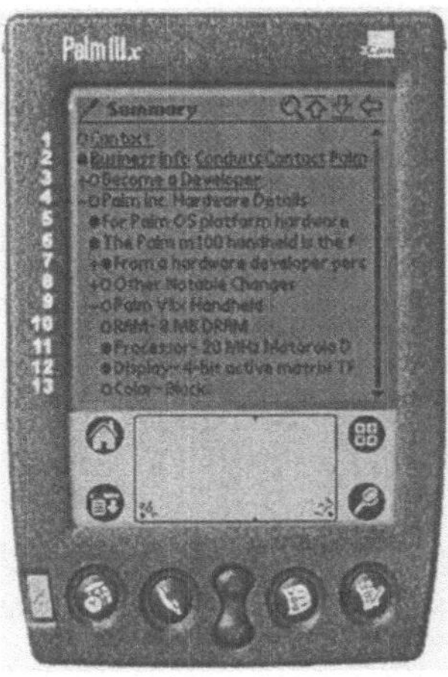

Figure 2: Screenshot of Our PDA Accordion Browser

We arrive at the page summary display of Figure 2 by partitioning an original Web page into 'Semantic Textual Units' (STUs). In summary, STUs are page fragments such as paragraphs, lists, or ALT tags that describe images. We use font and other structural information to identify a hierarchy of STUs. Initially, only the top level is shown. In Figure 2 this top level consists of lines 1-4. Users may use left-to-right pen gestures or the '+/-' nesting controls to open the hierarchy, as shown in lines 7-13. The lower-level STUs are shown indented. Lines 7-13 elaborate on the text "The Palm m100 handheld is the f" on line 6.

In [4] we expanded the browser of Figure 2 to include summarization. We began to allow users to hide most of the STUs most of the time, and to have the system progressively disclose the information contained in the STU's as it was needed. In this system, the proxy examines each STU and extracts both keywords and a representative sentence from the STUs. We implemented several approaches for the progressive information disclosure. One approach allows users to reveal progressively more of an STU's text. Other approaches first show a series of keywords for each STU. Users can then expand the respective STUs to see either the actual text, or summarizations.

In [5], finally, we examined how we an save screen real-estate and transmission time by having the proxy server summarize Web forms before transmitting them to the PDA.

The proxy attempts to extract appropriate text labels for each input element on the Web form. Only
those text labels are then displayed on the PDA. We tested a variety of algorithms that can isolate text labels from other text on HTML pages.

References

[1] Orkut Buyukkokten, Hector Garcia Molina, Andreas Paepcke, and Terry Winograd. Power Browser: Efficient Web Browsing for PDAs. In *Proceedings of the Conference on Human Factors in Computing Systems*, 2000.

[2] Orkut Buyukkokten, Hector Garcia-Molina, and Andreas Paepcke. Focused Web Searching with PDAs. In *Proceedings of the Ninth International World-Wide Web Conference*, 2000.

[3] Accordion Summarization for End-Game Browsing on PDAs and Cellular Phones. *CHI* 2001.

[4] Orkut Buyukkokten, Hector Garcia-Molina, and Andreas Paepcke. Seeing the Whole in Parts: Text Summarization for Web Browsing on Handheld Devices. *Submitted for publication*, 2000. Available at http://www-diglib.stanford.edu/cgi-bin/get/SIDL-WP-2000-0146.

[5] Oliver Kaljuvee, Orkut Buyukkokten, Hector Garcia-Molina, and Andreas Paepcke. Efficient Web Form Entry on PDAs. *Submitted for publication*, 2000. Available at http://www-diglib.stanford.edu/cgi-bin/get/SIDL-WP-2000-0145.

Session 5:

Verkehrsmanagement II

Signalling Support for Scalable Group Communication over ATM Networks

Axel Böger, Martina Zitterbart

Institute of Operating Systems and Computer Networks
Technical University of Braunschweig, Germany,
{boeger|zit}@ibr.cs.tu-bs.de

Abstract. In this paper an approach towards scalable group (many-to-many) communication across ATM networks is presented. Many network based applications rely on the concept of groups with dynamic membership. Todays ATM networks do not provide an adequate support for group communication as for example is available with IP multicast. In this document a hierarchical solution is described that adapts to the PNNI routing protocol. Based on a hierarchical group management, a scalable and efficient scheme for data transportation over ATM connections is presented. This scheme is based on a distributed signalling protocol, that allows group communication beyond local ATM network boundaries.

1 Introduction

The use of group communication is becoming increasingly important for todays networked applications. Typical examples are video conferencing, open distance learning, multi-user network games and distributed simulations. All these applications inherently imply the concept of groups. They, however, may rely on different requirements on group support, for example, considering group dynamics, openness of groups and reliability of group communication. Underlying networking and protocol technologies need to support these requirements adequately. An overview on group communication is given in [1].

This paper presents an approach on supporting group communication over large scale ATM networks. ATM offers point-to-multipoint connections, which allow a basic support for group communication. ATM connections need to have explicit knowledge of the group member address, since ATM does not offer group addresses for a set of participants that form a group. Generally it can be stated that todays ATM networks do not provide an adequate support for group communication as for example the Internet with IP multicast [2].

Groups can consist of a large set of participants, who can be geographically wide spread. To enable group communication over large scale ATM networks two prerequisites must be fulfilled: on the one hand a scalable management of groups and their participants is needed, and on the other hand an efficient data transfer of user data among group members is critical (both conditions have to be solved with a signalling protocol). Considering data transfer over ATM networks it is favorable to remain in the ATM layer as long as possible in order to utilize the ATM capabilities at its best. The target should be a 'short-cut' routing similar to NHRP [3].

This paper is organized as follows. Section 2 outlines related work. Based on a hierarchical approach for group management and administration (section 3) a concept for an efficient organization of ATM connections for group communication over large scale ATM networks is presented (section 4). The required signalling support and additional simulation results are described in section 5. Section 6 concludes the paper with a summary and an outlook on further issues to be considered.

2 Related Work

Existing approaches handle group communication in ATM by means of an emulation of IP multicast over ATM. Particularly the MARS (Multicast Address Resolution Server) is of interest, which provides a sound base for local ATM networks with a limited range and a limited number of members. Further enhancements of the MARS concept improve different deficits, like missing QoS support and the lack of scalability. MARS [4, 5] provides two emulation schemes (see figure 1): VC mesh and Multicast Server (MCS).

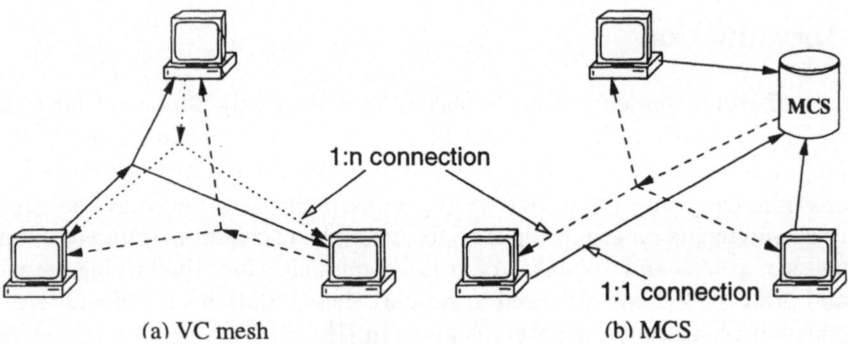

Fig. 1. MARS concept.

The basic MARS design is well suited for local ATM networks, but does not scale for large networks and large group sizes. There are a number of reasons which prevent efficient group communication with MARS:

- Only one MCS exists for a group. The MCS is a single point of failure and it can easily become a performance bottleneck in case of multiple senders per group [6]. A solution with multiple MCS is described in [7]. Load balancing between several MCS remains as an open issue.
- With VC mesh, changes in group membership lead to a high ATM signaling traffic because every sender has to modify its ATM connections.

– The MARS concept can only be applied to a local ATM network (LIS=Logical IP Subnet). Different subnets have to be connected with IP multicast routers. A solution to overcome LIS boundaries is presented with EARTH (EAsy IP multicast Routing tHrough ATM clouds) [8].

A more detailed description on the problems of extending MARS for large ATM networks can be found in [9]. None of the above concepts treats the problems of group communication over ATM networks, without an emulation. We further refer to this as direct group communication in ATM not involving an emulation of IP multicast over ATM. The approach presented here follows this way. Primary a group communication solution for ATM is discussed in order to improve efficiency. For the purpose of providing global group communication IP multicast can be emulated on top of the presented approach.

A number of other concepts (SEAM, SPAM, CRAM [10–12]) are considering a solution for many-to-many communication in the ATM layer. The main problem of these concepts is, that they are hard to realize, because almost any switch in an ATM network needs to be modified. In our approach the components communicate with ATM over the ATM Forum's UNI signalling specification (similar to MARS). This allows a smooth integration of our presented concept in existing ATM networks. The placement of components in an end system or in an ATM switch affects only the efficiency of the concept, but is completely independent from its functionality.

3 Hierarchical Group Management

In this section a management concept is described for the administration of groups in ATM networks. The basic idea is to hierarchical interconnect local groups (i.e. groups that can be served by MARS), in order to provide scalable group communication in large networks. The visibility of group addresses is also considered, whereby the range can be limited by a scope. A tree scheme is used to organize the management hierarchical.

The concept is oriented at the PNNI-Routing [13]. With PNNI, network segments are summarized and represented as one abstract network segment to the next level in the hierarchy. Hierarchical group management can be closely connected with PNNI Routing making use of its hierarchical organization. However PNNI is not mandatory to the presented approach towards scalable group communication. Nevertheless, an orientation at the PNNI hierarchy is helpful, in order to adapt to the administrative boundaries in an ATM network.

An example configuration of a logical hierarchy is shown in figure 2a. The leaves of the tree represent end systems connected to ATM. The components in the tree are so-called group controller (or simple: controller) which administer the group participants. An appropriate implementation in the ATM network is depicted in figure 2b. A controller is a network component similar to the MARS, but with several extensions. The controller resolves a group address to a set of ATM-addresses, and moreover it distributes and collects group information with other controllers.

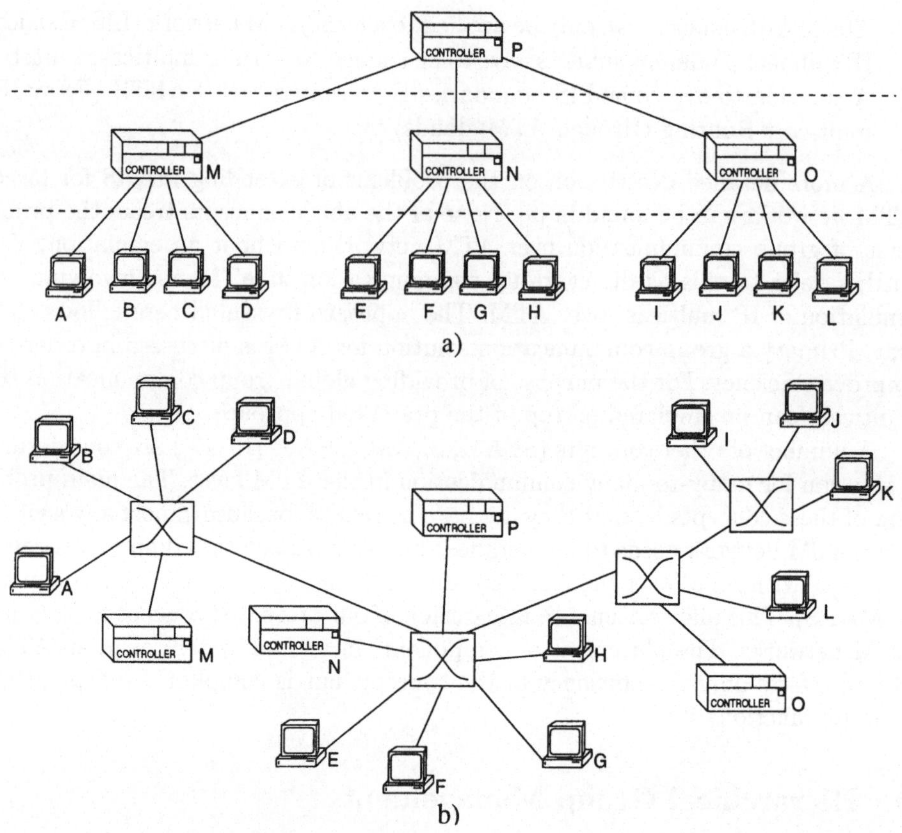

Fig. 2. Group Management: a) Example hierarchy for a large ATM network, b) Implementation of the example hierarchy.

As shown in figure 2b a controller is not fairly associated with an ATM switch. A controller can be similar to an end system connected to an ATM switch or it can also be integrated in an ATM switch. This is achieved by handling all communication between controller and ATM layer over the ATM-UNI.

The hierarchy levels orient themselves at the definition of the ATM Forum for UNI4.0. anycast address scopes [14]. These scopes can be regarded as an equivalent to IP multicast address scopes [15]. Through the additional declaration of a scope to an address the visibility can be limited to a predefined level of hierarchy.

Among the controllers in the tree ATM connections are established. These are SVCs (Switched Virtual Circuits), which transport all necessary signalling traffic. Details of the signalling can be found in section 5. For the establishment of ATM connections the addresses of the controllers in the levels of the hierarchy must be known. Therefore, ATM anycast is used. The controllers can be identified through 'well known' anycast addresses. This allows an easy configuration of all controllers, mainly two parameters are necessary: the hierarchy level and the associated anycast address.

Communication between controllers takes place only among neighbouring levels of the hierarchy. The already established management connections are used, i.e., no additional connections are needed. It is important to note, that this procedure is applied only for signalling messages. User data exchange within the groups uses separate connections. These connections between different MCS and end systems can be spanned over several levels of the hierarchy.

In local ATM networks group members explicitly join and leave the group as sender or receiver by sending a control message to the controller. When a join/leave-message arrives at a controller, the information is checked and the participant is added to or removed from the group. For this purpose each controller consists of two layers (see figure 3). The lower *detail-layer* contains the detailed group structure and is responsible for management of child nodes (either end system or controller nodes). For each child the groups are stored together with information if senders and/or receivers are available in this group. In case of a modification in one of the child nodes the *aggregation-layer* is informed about this modification. The task of the aggregation-layer is to summarize the information collected in the detail-layer. Here, the groups are managed independently of the lower subtrees. The concept with two layers, one for detailed and one for aggregated information can also be found in the PNNI routing with the logical group node abstraction. Figure 6 in section 5 shows the effect of this two layer approach on the signalling and on the reduction of the stored group informations.

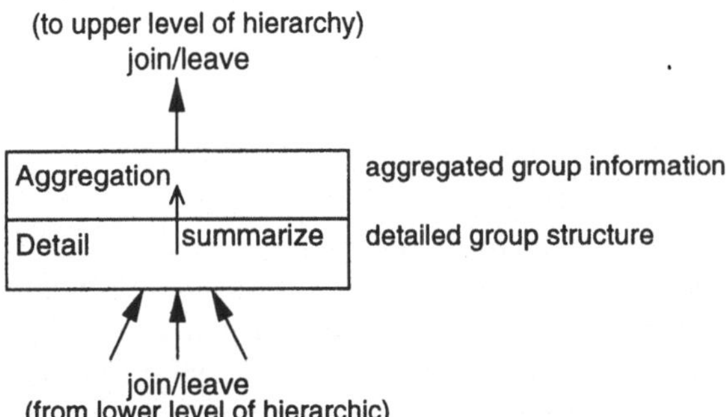

Fig. 3. Message processing scheme in the controller.

4 Group Communication Scheme

As described in the previous section the group management collects and stores information about the participants in the groups. Based on this, the data communication within a group needs to be set-up.

The introduction of a hierarchy forms an obvious possibility of supporting group communication in large scale networks, not limited to ATM. Similarly to the hierarchical group management presented above, data communication can be structured hierarchical in a tree. Figure 4 shows this methodology applied to the MCS scheme. A dedicated MCS exists for each level in the hierarchy. It distributes the data of the participants within the respective level. This requires the use of additional MCS components and the main disadvantage, that a MCS can become a bottleneck and single point of failure, is intensified with this scheme. Another disadvantage is in case of many active groups. A local MCS handles only data from local active groups, but a MCS in a higher hierarchy must serve all groups which are active in the tree leaves, and so the number of groups and the amount of data increases with the hierarchy level.

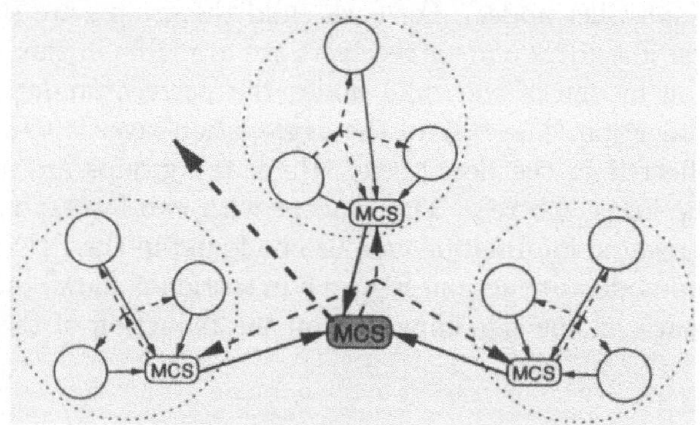

Fig. 4. A hierarchical MCS scheme.

The problem can be significantly reduced by using a local MCS for the functions of the superior MCS, as shown in figure 5a. This MCS will be called *primary* MCS, which serves the local group and is also responsible for higher levels of the hierarchy. But here also, data concentration at a MCS caused by many active groups could not be prevented. This can be prevented when a local MCS will not be selected as primary MCS for all groups in a higher level of the hierarchy. For each active group a new primary MCS will be individually selected. Thus several groups can be distributed over different MCS.

A further optimization exists in the reduction of the outgoing ATM connections of the primary MCS (see figure 5b). Only one outgoing ATM connection is needed at the coordinating MCS. With this the link utilization can be reduced, because transmission of duplicated data over a link is reduced. The *primary* MCS handle the other external MCS in the same manner as the local participants, and the external MCS can connect to the primary MCS in the same way, like the child nodes of the primary MCS does.

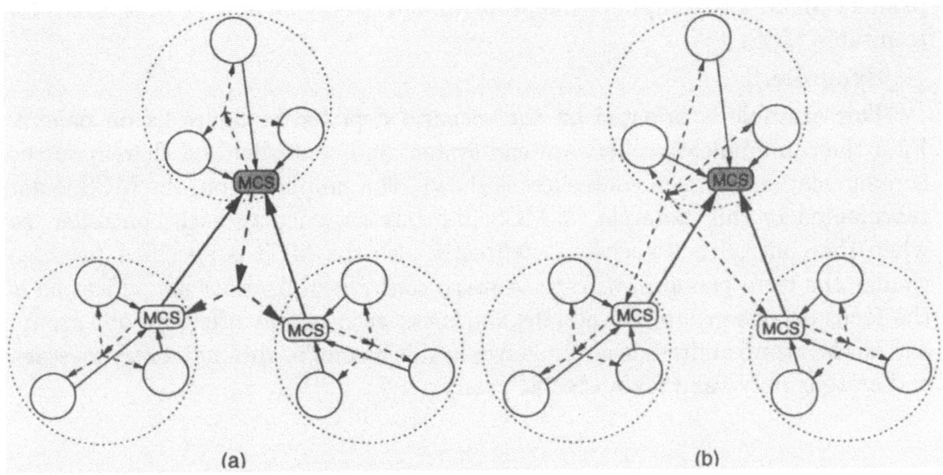

Fig. 5. Distributed hierarchical MCS scheme: a) use of an existing MCS for the next hierarchy level, b) reuse local SVCs for data distribution to other MCS.

5   Signalling Support

Signalling support is needed as the basic mechanism for the establishment of ATM connections for group communication. A distributed approach is presented, based on the management concept introduced in section 3 and based on the hierarchical group communication concept presented in the previous section.

5.1   Signalling Protocol

The signalling protocol is the basis for the establishment of ATM connections for group communication. Signalling is always initiated by group participants, e.g. sender or receiver, i.e., join/leave respectively. All signalling messages are transported by a reliable transport protocol. This protocol offers an exactly-once-semantic and acts like a stop-and-wait protocol. The signalling is subdivided into signalling between end system and controller and signalling between controllers. The protocol uses two different message types: one for communication between end system and controller, called *member_msg* and one for communication between controllers, called *update_msg*.

The discussion is focussed on the 'regular' signalling. Failures or breakdowns of components are not taken into account.

The main part of the signalling is betwen controllers. An example explains the basic mechanisms and message transfers, that construct a distributed hierarchical MCS scheme (as shown in figure 5b). Important for this is the election of the primary MCS. In the actual implementation of the signalling protocol always the first MCS which registers itself as a MCS for a group is elected as the primary MCS. This simplifies the protocol, but it may be not the best choice for a suitable MCS.

Example:

This example is oriented on the scenario depicted in figure 2a on page 4. First the communication between end system and controller and thereupon the communication between controllers is shown. For simplification, the MCS is not represented in this example. A MCS is firmly assigned to each controller, so when the controller is specified, indirectly also the MCS is specified (we also change the term *primary MCS* to *primary controller*). Another simplification is the focus on one group. All actions and messages are only affecting one group, and so the group address is never shown in this example, although every message and state is only valid for a specific group.

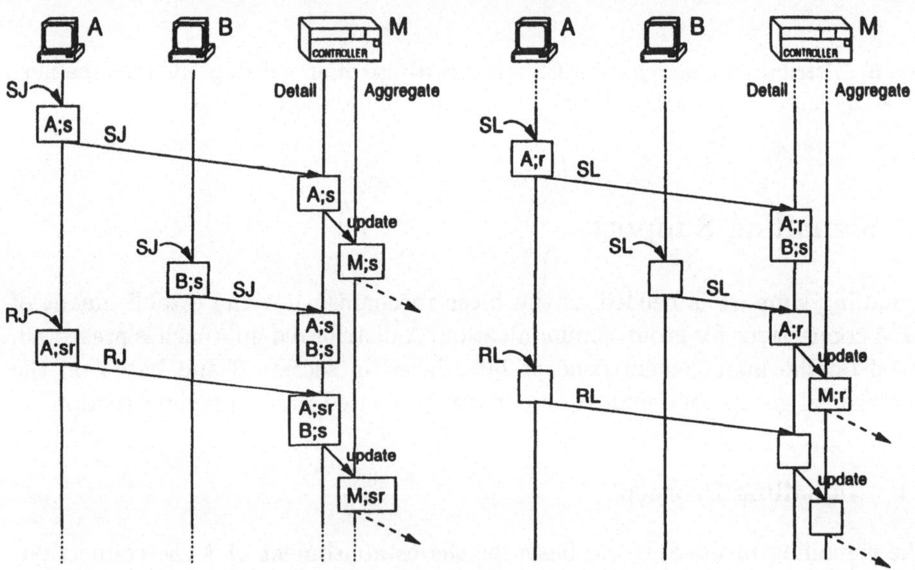

Fig. 6. Signalling between end system and controller.

Figure 6 shows the interaction between end systems and controllers. Both end systems (named A and B) join the group as sender (SJ = SenderJoin), then the first end system (A) joins as receiver (RJ = RecieverJoin). In the same order the end systems leave the group (SL = SenderLeave, RL = ReceiverLeave). The controller is drawn with two time lines, one for the detail layer (see section 3) and one for the aggregation layer. The boxes on the time lines indicate the actual state of the system in the group. The controller keep information about group members and their state (s = sender and r = receiver) in the detail layer. This information is not available in the aggregation layer.

In the aggregation layer the group members are summarized, i.e., the respective controller address is registered. This controller is responsible for the communication between local and external systems. An update from the detail layer to the aggregation layer takes place only if the number of the senders or receivers changes from 0 to 1 or from 1 to 0, this behaviour can be seen in figure 6 at the second sender join.

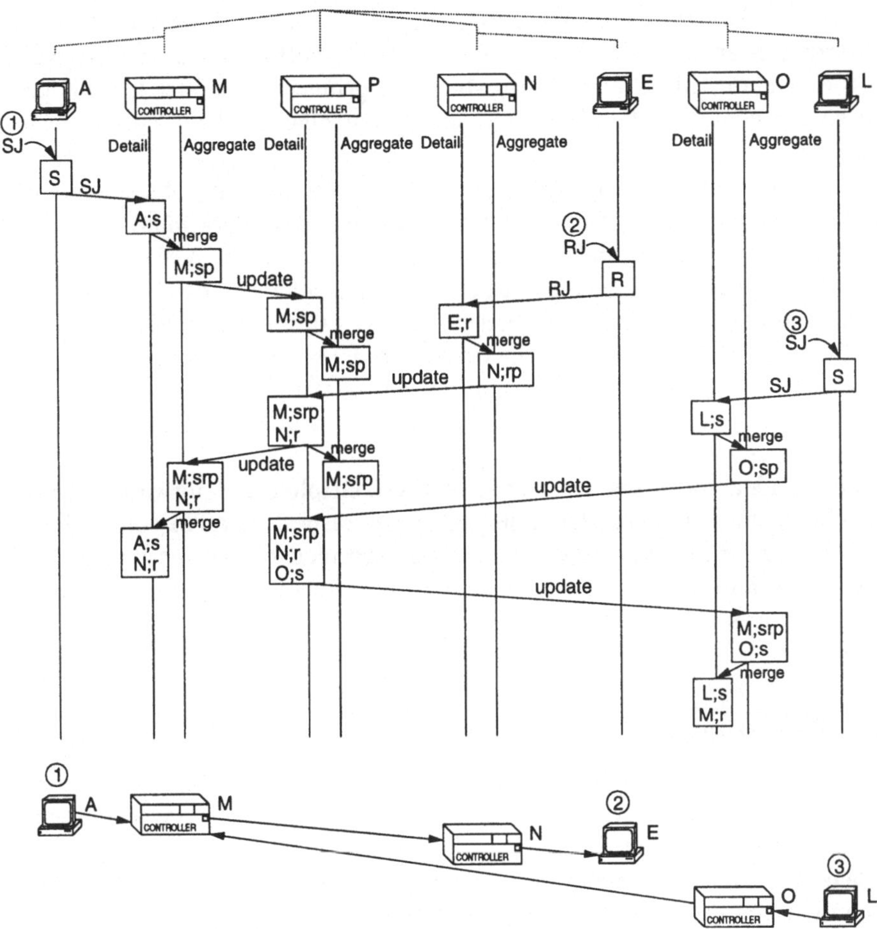

Fig. 7. Signalling between controllers.

The communication flow between controllers is depicted in diagram 7. The adumbrated lines at the top shows the controller hierarchy similar to figure 2 and at the bottom are the constructed SVC's for user data transportation shown. The new state p (*primary*) is introduced in the controller. It identifies the primary controller for the higher levels of the hierarchy. As can be seen in diagram 7, the controller M which joined first is always selected as primary controller. Furthermore sender and receiver joins are handled different. Upon a receiver join, the primary controller gets informed about the new receiver (see the receiver join of end system E in figure 7). Upon a sender join conversely the new sender gets informed about the primary controller (sender join of end system L in figure 7). Thereby it is achieved that sender transmit their data to the primary controller and the primary controller forwards it to the receivers.

An interesting point in figure 7 is the state of the controller O after the sender join from end system L. The controller declares itself as primary controller and forwards this state to the next higher controller P. However at the controller P another system (M) is already registered as primary controller for this group, and so the controller P informs the lower controller O of the correct primary controller.

An important fact is the division and separate handling of senders and receivers within a group. Contrary to IP multicast, senders must also register themselves for a group, before they can transmit data. In ATM networks this separation is caused by the fact that only the sender can establish ATM connections to receivers. The enhancement in UNI 4.0, the 'leaf initiated join' is no improvement in this case, since the leaf (receiver) must also know the sender address and the appropriate connection ID, before the leaf can start a connection establishment. Thus also in this case an address resolution of group address to sender addresses must occur.

The sender addresses are stored in the controller and forwarded to other controllers, since these senders must setup the respective ATM connections. To which systems the connections are setup is specified by the receiver addresses. Thus sender and receiver addresses have two completely different functions. The receiver addresses are distributed by the controllers in direction to the sender addresses.

5.2 Simulation

The protocol is implemented in a model for the OpNet Network Simulator [16]. To get an idea of the protocol efficiency the time between a receiver join and the reception of the first data packet was measured. In this scenario one group was modeled with one permanent active sender and hundred receiver. The receiver join and leave randomly during a time interval of hundred seconds. The network topology is fairly oriented at the German multicast backbone [17]. The simulation results in figure 8 show the connection delays for four different hierarchy levels, whereby level 0 is similar to the MARS-MCS scheme and level 1 is compareable to the example hierarchy in figure 2. All controllers have a constant processing delay of 10 ms per message and the MCS have additional queueing delays per data packet (< 1ms).

As can be seen in figure 8 the connection delays vary in the different levels. In level 0 the variation of the connection delay is high, and indepently of the number of receivers. The average connection delay is approx. 52ms (with a standard deviation of 19ms). The connection delays of level 1 and level 2 are quite similar

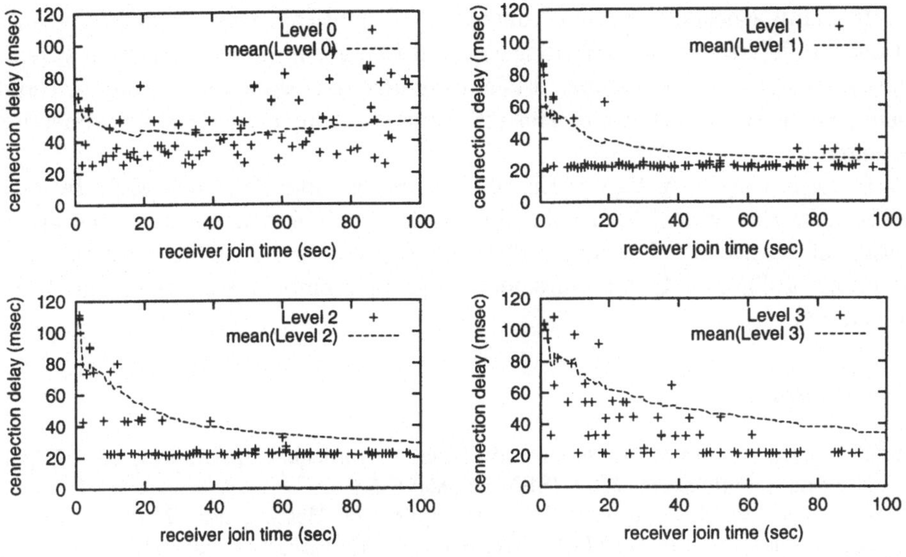

Fig. 8. Receiver connection delay.

and have an average delay of approx. 29ms. In level 3 the connection delays rise to approx. 35ms. This is in consequence of the involved mangement overhead: A three level hierarchy is an over engineering in relation to a number of hundred group participants. But even in this case it can be stated, that the hierarchical approach presented in this paper scales better than the original MARS concept when the group and network sizes increase.

6 Summary and Conclusions

In this paper an approach for supporting group communication over ATM networks was presented and a signalling protocol to enable this concept was described. The approach is based on a hierarchical concept for group management. Whereupon a scalable scheme for data communication within a group was developed that permits group communication between local participants, and also communication over longer distances. This scheme avoids data concentration, as it would arise with a strictly hierarchical concept. Different groups can be distributed over several systems (i.e. MCS). Furthermore no special components are needed for the realisation of the levels of hierarchy. Available components, that are already used for local group communication over ATM (MCS), can be integrated in this scheme. The simulation results show shorter connection delays in the hierarchical scheme than the centralized MARS concept. On the other hand too many levels of hierarchy in relation to the group size can also lead to a too long connection delay.

In many aspects, the group concept of IP multicast was adapted. The substantial difference is the explicit sender join to a group. In the presented scheme only closed groups are possible, it is not possible to transmit to a group, without being a member of this group. This difference is mainly caused by the connection oriented nature of ATM.

Current work investigates the application of more than one MCS in local ATM networks and of load balancing on these MCS. Furthermore, the application of several MCS within a distributed group is taken into account. The handling of different QoS requirements of group members is another topic to be considered.

References

1. R. Wittmann and M. Zitterbart. Multicast – Protocols and Applications. Morgan Kaufmann Publishers, 2000, ISBN 1-55860-645-9.
2. A. Böger and M. Zitterbart. Towards Support for Heterogenous Multipeer across ATM Networks. 9th LANMAN Workshop, Banff, Canada, May 1998.
3. J. Luciani, D. Katz, D. Piscitello, B. Cole and N. Doraswamy. NBMA Next Hop Resolution Protocol (NHRP). RFC 2332, April 1998.
4. Grenville J. Armitage. IP Multicasting over ATM Networks. IEEE JSAC, Vol.15, No.3, April 1997.
5. G. Armitage. Support for Multicast over UNI 3.0/3.1 based ATM Networks. RFC 2022, November 1996.
6. R. Talpade, G. J. Armitage, M. H. Ammar. Experience with Architectures for Supporting IP Multicast over ATM. In Proceedings of the IEEE ATM '96 Workshop, San Francisco, 1997.
7. R.Talpade and M. H. Ammar. Multicast Server Architectures for MARS-based ATM multicasting. RFC 2149, May 1997.
8. Michael Smirnov. EARTH - EAsy IP multicast Routing tHrough ATM clouds. Internet Draft, March 1997.
9. G. Armitage. VENUS - Very Extensive Non-Unicast Service. RFC 2191, September 1997.
10. M. Grossglauser and K. K. Ramakrishnan. SEAM: Scalable and Efficient ATM Multipoint-to-Multipoint Communication. Proceedings of the IEEE Infocom'97, Kobe, Japan, April 1997.
11. S. Komandur and D. Mossé. SPAM: A Data Forwarding Model for Multipoint-to-Multipoint Connection Support in ATM Networks. Proceedings of the 6th IC[3]N, Las Vegas, September 1997.
12. S. Komandur, J. Crowcroft and D. Mossé. CRAM: Cell Re-labeling at Mergepoints for ATM Multicast. Proceedings of the ICATM'98, Colmar, France, June 1998.
13. ATM Forum. *Private Network-Network Interface Specification Version 1.0 (PNNI 1.0)*. ftp://ftp.atmforum.com/pub/approved-specs/af-pnni-0055.000.pdf, March 1996.
14. ATM Forum. *ATM User-Network Interface (UNI) Signalling Specification Version 4.0*. ftp://ftp.atmforum.com/pub/approved-specs/af-sig-0061.000.pdf. July 1996.
15. D. Meyer. Administratively Scoped IP Multicast. RFC 2365, July 1998.
16. OPNET. http://www.opnet.com.
17. Mbone-DE. http://www.mbone.de.

Auswirkung drahtloser Netzsegmente auf die Transporteffizienz von TCP/IP-Verbindungen

Michael Matthes, Udo Krieger, Oswald Drobnik

Fachbereich Informatik, J.W. Goethe-Universität
Robert-Mayer-Str. 11-15, D-60054 Frankfurt/Main
email: {*matthes*, drobnik}@tm.informatik.uni-frankfurt.de

T-Nova Deutsche Telekom Innovationsgesellschaft mbH
Technologiezentrum, Am Kavalleriesand 3, D-64295 Darmstadt
email: udo.krieger@ieee.org

Zusammenfassung Ein Forschungsschwerpunkt in der Entwicklung von Kommunikationsinfrastrukturen stellt derzeit die Integration von drahtlosen Netzsegmenten in bestehende IP-basierte Festnetze dar. Bestehende Protokolle des Festnetzes berücksichtigen jedoch nur unzureichend die Einflüsse von funkbasierten Übertragungswegen (variierende Verbindungsqualitäten, Möglichkeit des Roamings). Eine effiziente multimediale Datenkommunikation bei Einbeziehung funkbasierter Übertragungswege erfordert Adaptionsfähigkeit auf mehreren Protokollebenen. In diesem Beitrag werden einige der zu berücksichtigenden Umgebungsbedingungen auf mehreren Protokollebenen anhand von Experimenten in einem drahtlosem LAN mit Mobile-IP auf der Netzwerkebene identifiziert und Hinweise zur Anpassung von Kommunikationsströmen formuliert.

1   Einführung

Aktuelle Forschungsbestrebungen im Bereich der mobilen Datenkommunikation befassen sich derzeit mit der Entwicklung von effizienten Transportmechanismen, die typische Eigenschaften von drahtlosen Netzsegmenten berücksichtigen. Der Einsatz von Protokollen, die für IP-Festnetze optimiert sind, hat in funkbasierten Netzwerkumgebungen hemmende Auswirkungen auf den Kommunikationsfluss von TCP/IP-Verbindungen. Dynamisch variierende Verbindungsqualität drahtloser Übertragungen, beispielsweise hervorgerufen durch Bewegung oder durch Roaming von mobilen Anwendern, machen Notifikationsmechanismen zwischen Protokollschichten erforderlich, die eine Anpassung an aktuelle Umgebungsbedingungen ermöglichen. Zukünftige Anwendungen müssen dafür in der Lage sein, auf "mobile Randbedingungen" angemessen reagieren zu können. Eine offene Frage hierbei ist, an welchen Umgebungsparametern sich eine Anwendung orientieren und auf welche Weise sie reagieren soll.

In diesem Beitrag werden eine Experimentumgebung für "mobile-aware" Anwendungen und die durchgeführten Experimente zur Identifizierung von anwendungsbeeinflussenden mobilen Umgebungsbedingungen vorgestellt. Die Experimentumgebung besteht aus einem Funk-LAN, dessen Komponenten zum

Standard IEEE 802.11 [1] kompatibel sind. In mehreren Experimenten wurden die Auswirkungen von Bewegung und Roaming mobiler Stationen beobachtet und ausgewertet. Für Subnetz-übergreifendes Roaming wurde das Mobile-IP-Protokoll eingesetzt. Diese Experimente liefern Hinweise auf die Entwicklung von "mobile-aware" Anwendungen.

Insbesondere wurde das Verhalten des TCP-Protokolls untersucht. TCP ist ein Protokoll der Transportebene, das verbindungsorientiert arbeitet und eine zuverlässige Übertragung garantiert [20]. Darüber hinaus sind Staukontrollmechanismen implementiert, die auf Änderungen in der Netzkapazität reagieren und bei Stausituationen die Übertragung von Paketen reduzieren. Stausituationen können von TCP jedoch nur indirekt anhand von ausbleibenden Quittungen erkannt werden, die auf den Verlust von Datenpaketen hinweisen. In Festnetzen entsteht ein Paketverlust im allgemeinen durch eine Überlast beispielweise in Vermittlungssystemen (*router*), die Pakete aufgrund überlaufender interner Puffer verwerfen. Da in einem solchen Fall die Übertragung von Paketen die Stausituation nur weiter forcieren würde, drosselt TCP die Einspeisung von Paketen in das Kommunikationsnetz. Dies geschieht mittels des sog. *Congestion-Avoidance* Mechanismus im Zusammenspiel mit dem *Slow-Start* Mechanismus. Ein sog. *Congestion-Window* gibt die Anzahl der Pakete an, die ohne Bestätigung in das Kommunikationsnetz verschickt werden dürfen. Bei einer Stausituation wird die Fenstergröße reduziert. Um das Netz nicht zu überlasten, wird das Congestion-Window nur schrittweise gemäß dem Slow-Start Mechanismus wieder geöffnet, um die optimale Fenstergröße für die aktuelle Netzsituation zu finden und einen effizienten Verkehrsfluss zu ermöglichen.

Die Annahme, dass Paketverluste auf Stausituationen zurückzuführen sind, gilt für Festnetze, da ein Verlust aufgrund fehlerhafter Übertragung mit großer Wahrscheinlichkeit ausgeschlossen werden kann. Die Mechanismen, die auf dieser Annahme beruhen, sind dementsprechend für die Anpassung an Stausituationen konzipiert. In drahtlosen Netzsegmenten gilt diese Annahme im allgemeinen nicht. Paketverluste sind eher auf Fehler bei der Übertragung über die Funkstrecke zurückzuführen. In funkbasierten Umgebungen können auch Paketverluste auftreten, wenn mobile Stationen den Zugangspunkt zum Festnetz wechseln (*roaming*) und Pakete einer Verbindung noch über den "alten" Zugangspunkt ausgeliefert werden. Eine Stausituation liegt in solchen Fällen nicht vor.

In diesem Beitrag sollen die Tauglichkeit der TCP-Mechanismen und die Auswirkungen auf die Transporteffizienz von TCP-Verbindungen in funkbasierten mobilen Umgebungen untersucht werden. Im Vergleich zu bereits durchgeführten Messungen (vgl. u. a. [4], [19]) und Simulationen (vgl. u. a. [16]) anderer Forschungseinrichtungen werden erstmals Dynamik-Messungen des TCP/IP-Protokolls beim Roaming von mobilen Stationen betrachtet.

Im folgenden werden die Experimentumgebung sowie die für die Experimente eingesetzten Messwerkzeuge vorgestellt. Daraufhin werden die durchgeführten Experimente beschrieben und ausgewählte Ergebnisse diskutiert und entsprechende Folgerungen aus den Ergebnissen formuliert. Abschließend folgt ein Ausblick auf die zukünftig geplante Forschungsarbeit.

2 Experimentumgebung

Das für die Experimente aufgebaute Funknetzwerk besteht aus IEEE 802.11 [1] kompatiblen Systemkomponenten der Firma Lucent Technologies. Zum Einsatz kommen Access-Points und PCMCIA-Funkkarten mit einer Übertragungsrate von 1 Mbit/s bzw. 2 Mbit/s. Die Experimentumgebung umfasst zwei sich überlagernde Funkzellen (s. Abbildung 1). Durch die Überlagerung der Funkzel-

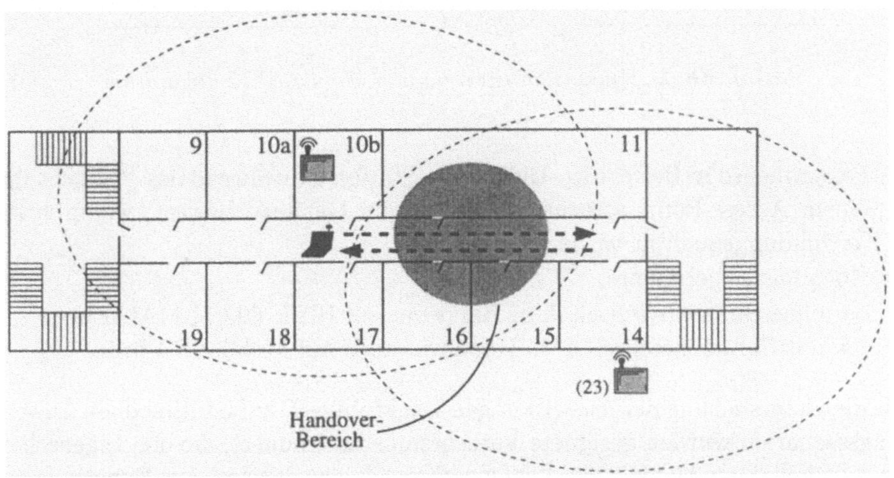

Abbildung1. *Experimentumgebung mit sich überlagernden Funkzellen.*

len sind Experimente mit Handover-Ereignissen durchführbar. Die Access-Points lassen sich für verschiedene Szenarien konfigurieren. Wenn beide Access-Points demselben Subnetz angehören, erfolgt Roaming auf Hardware-Ebene (Schicht 1 und 2), gehören sie verschiedenen Subnetzen an, ist darüber hinaus ein Handover auf Netzwerkebene (Schicht 3) erforderlich. Für Roaming-Experimente auf Netzwerk-Ebene wurde die *Dynamics* [12] Mobile-IP Implementierung für Linux der *Helsinki University of Technology (HUT)* eingesetzt. Die Dynamics-Implementierung ist die derzeit umfangreichste Umsetzung des Mobile-IP Protokolls [18] für aktuelle Versionen des Betriebssystems Linux, die neben "normaler" Mobile-IP Funktionalität auch über einige Optimierungen verfügt [9]. Die Konfiguration der Mobile-IP Komponenten (*Home Agent, Foreign Agent, Mobile Node*) kann Abbildung 2 entnommen werden, die einen Ausschnitt des Rechnernetzes zeigt. *Home Network* und *Foreign Network* sind über Fast-Ethernet-Switches miteinander verbunden. Folgende Versuche wurden in dieser Experimentumgebung durchgeführt:

- Stationäre Experimente: Die mobile Station wird während der Versuchsdurchführung nicht bewegt. Es werden mehrere Versuche in verschiedenen Abständen zum assoziierten Access-Point durchgeführt.

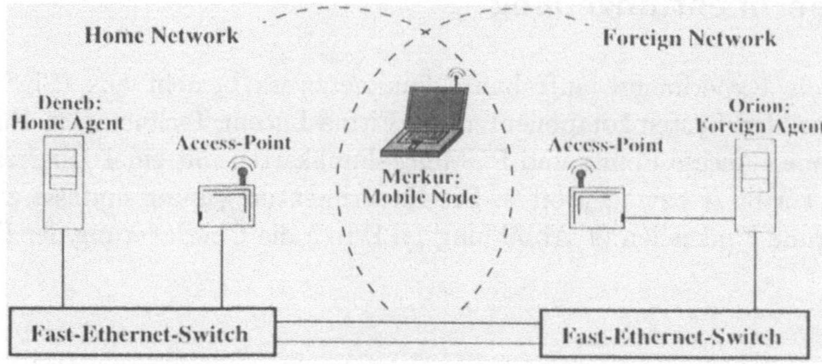

Abbildung2. *Funknetzintegration und Mobile-IP Konfiguration.*

- Experimente in Bewegung: Die mobile Station ist während des Versuchs mit einem Access-Point assoziiert und wird im Gebäude bewegt, wodurch die Verbindungsqualität variiert.
- Roaming-Experimente:
  - ohne Subnetzwechsel, d. h. Handover auf IEEE 802.11 MAC-Ebene,
  - mit Subnetzwechsel, d. h. Handover auch auf Mobile-IP Ebene.

Für die Untersuchung der Auswirkungen von Mobile-IP auf multimediale Anwendungsszenarien wurden geeignete Verkehrsmuster simuliert, die den Eigenschaften multimedialer Datenströme entsprechen. Es wurden bei den Experimenten verbindungslose und verbindungsorientierte Übertragungen beobachtet, wofür zwei unterschiedliche Software-Werkzeuge eingesetzt wurden.

3 Messwerkzeuge

Experimente in funkbasierten Umgebungen können nur schwer reproduzierbar durchgeführt werden, da Funkumgebungen nicht leicht zu isolieren sind und mit statistischen Störeinflüssen zu rechnen ist. Eine Auswertung der Experimentergebnisse sollte daher relativ zu den vorhandenen Umgebungsbedingungen erfolgen. Hierfür wurde ein Messwerkzeug zur Protokollierung der "Wireless-Statusinformationen" entwickelt, das für die Experimente mit verbindungsloser Kommunikation eingesetzt wurde. Für verbindungsorientierte TCP-Kommunikation wurde ein weiteres Messwerkzeug eingesetzt, das TCP-Statusinformationen protokolliert.

3.1 WVPing

Übliche Software-basierte Netzwerkmonitore berücksichtigen bislang keine Statusinformationen von Funkverbindungen. Aus diesem Grund wurde von uns das Programm "ping" [20] um die Protokollierung von Wireless-Statusinformationen erweitert. In der erweiterten Version – WVPing (Wave-Ping) – werden neben der Round-Trip-Time (RTT) auch Signalstärke, Rauschstärke, Signal-To-Noise-Ratio (SNR) und die Anzahl der fehlerhaften Pakete auf MAC-Ebene ausgegeben, so dass Round-Trip Zeiten in Abhängigkeit von der Qualität der Funkverbindungen erfasst werden können (s. Abbildung 3). Um die Auswirkungen von

PING 141.2.14.37: 1024 data bytes

Seq-No	RTT(ms)	Signal(dBm)	Noise(dBm)	SNR(x/92)	Discarded	Channel
1	17.9	-57	-82	26	1	6
2	17.8	-57	-82	26	1	6
...	...	...	...	...	...	...

—- 141.2.14.37 PING Statistics —-
1135 packets transmitted, 1132 packets received, 0.26% packet loss
round-trip (ms) min/avg/max = 17.6/18.1/71.9 (std. deviation = 2.62)

Abbildung3. *Ausgabe von WVPing.*

verschiedenen Paketgrößen zu beobachten, wurden die gleichen Versuchsabläufe stets mit unterschiedlichen Paketgrößen durchgeführt. Motivation hierfür sind die zu erwartenden burstartigen Fehler. Bei längeren Paketen, deren Übertragungszeit größer ist, besteht eine höhere Wahrscheinlichkeit für das Auftreten solcher Fehler.

3.2 Distributed Benchmarking System (DBS)

Auf der Basis eines umfangreichen Vergleichs verschiedener Messwerkzeuge wurde zur Beobachtung von TCP-Statusinformationen (z. B. Größe des Congestion-Window) das *Distributed Benchmarking System (DBS)* [15] des *Nara Institute of Science and Technology, Japan* ausgewählt, das verschiedenste Messparameter und Auswertungshilfen bereitstellt. DBS besteht aus einem Kontrollprogramm und einem Messprogramm. Auf jeder bei der Messung beteiligten Stationen läuft das Messprogramm. Das Kontrollprogramm läuft auf einer separaten Station und veranlasst die Messprogramme gemäß einer spezifizerten Versuchskonfiguration Messungen durchzuführen. In der Konfiguration werden Sender- und Empfängerstationen, die Art des Datenstroms (z.B. bestimmte Datenmuster), die Dauer des Experimentverlaufes sowie das Übertragungsprotokoll (UDP, TCP) bestimmt. Die Protokollierung der zu beobachtenden Parameter erfolgt während des Messverlaufs von jeder Station separat, wodurch kein zusätzlicher Netzverkehr während der Messung durch das Messwerkzeug erzeugt wird. Erst nach Experimentdurchführung werden die Ergebnisse miteinander verknüpft. Ein herausragender Vorteil des DBS-Systems ist die Angabe von Mustern für die zu übertragenden Daten. Beliebige Multimedia-Datenströme können nen somit simuliert werden. Die Experimente wurden mit repräsentativen Mustern für zwei typische Datenstromarten durchgeführt: Simulation von Streaming (z. B. GSM-Audiodaten mit konstanter Bitrate von 13 kbit/s) und Simulation von MPEG-Videodaten. Beim Streaming werden Datenpakete konstanter Größe kontinuierlich übertragen. Datenpakete unterschiedlicher Größe ergeben sich bei MPEG-Videodaten. Dadurch kann das in der Praxis häufig auftretende On/Off-Verhalten von Datenübertragungen nachgebildet werden. DBS verfügt nicht über die Einbeziehung von Wireless-Statusinformationen, so dass die Auswirkungen der Funkverbindung anhand der Messergebnisse eruiert werden müssen.

4 Experimente und Messergebnisse

4.1 Messungen ohne Bewegung innerhalb einer *Basic Service Area*

Für einen ersten Eindruck der Auswirkung einer drahtlosen Funkverbindung auf die Datenübertragung wurde die mobile Station in verschiedenen Entfernungen zum assoziierten Access-Point für den Zeitraum des Messvorgangs stationär aufgestellt. Dadurch bleibt die Signalstärke relativ konstant. Abbildung 4 zeigt die

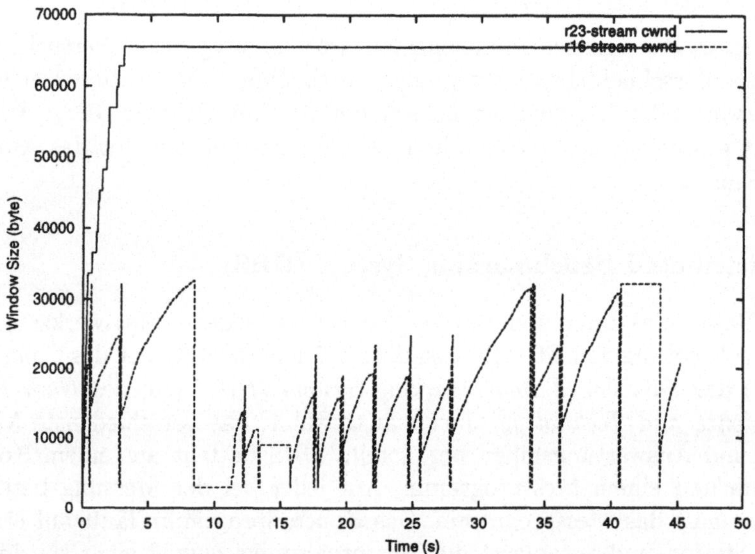

Abbildung4. *Stationäre Messungen des TCP-Congestion-Window mit DBS. Öffnung des TCP-Congestion-Window bei guter Link-Qualität (Raum 23, Mean SNR = 37 dBm), stets Zusammenfallen bei schlechter Link-Qualität (Raum 16, Mean SNR = 4 dBm).*

Ergebnisse des TCP-Experiments mit DBS in zwei unterschiedlichen Entfernungen zum ausgewählten Access-Point. Es ist das Congestion-Window in Raum 23 (vgl. Abbildung 1) und in Raum 16 bei Streaming-Mustern dargestellt. Während in Raum 23 das Congestion-Window von TCP bis zum maximalen Öffnungsgrad zunimmt, fällt es in Raum 16 aufgrund höherer Fehlerrate, die auf die schlechte Verbindungsqualität (Signal-to-Noise-Ratio) zurückzuführen ist, öfter abrupt auf den minimalen Öffnungsgrad zurück.

Bei Verwendung von Echtzeit-Multimedia-Anwendung wie beispielsweise Telekonferenz-Anwendungen sollte daher die Parametrisierung der Medienströme in Abhängigkeit von der Verbindungsqualität gewählt werden, also in Abhängigkeit von dem aktuellen Signal-To-Noise-Ratio. Außerdem muss insbesondere bei zeitkritischen Medienströmen wie Sprachdaten eine dynamische Pufferanpassung erfolgen, um eine kontinuierliche und störungsfreie Wiedergabe zu garantieren.

4.2 *Moving* innerhalb einer *Basic Service Area*

Bei der *Moving*-Versuchsreihe wurde die mobile Station auf einem Rollwagen stets einmal den gesamten Gang entlang bewegt. Gestartet wurde vor Raum 14 bei relativ geringer Signalstärke, die mit Annäherung an den Access-Point in Raum 10b zunahm und mit Entfernen vom Access-Point wieder abnahm (vgl. Abbildung 1). Mit Hilfe des WVPing-Werkzeuges konnten die Round-Trip Zeiten in Abhängigkeit der Wireless-Statusinformationen protokolliert werden.

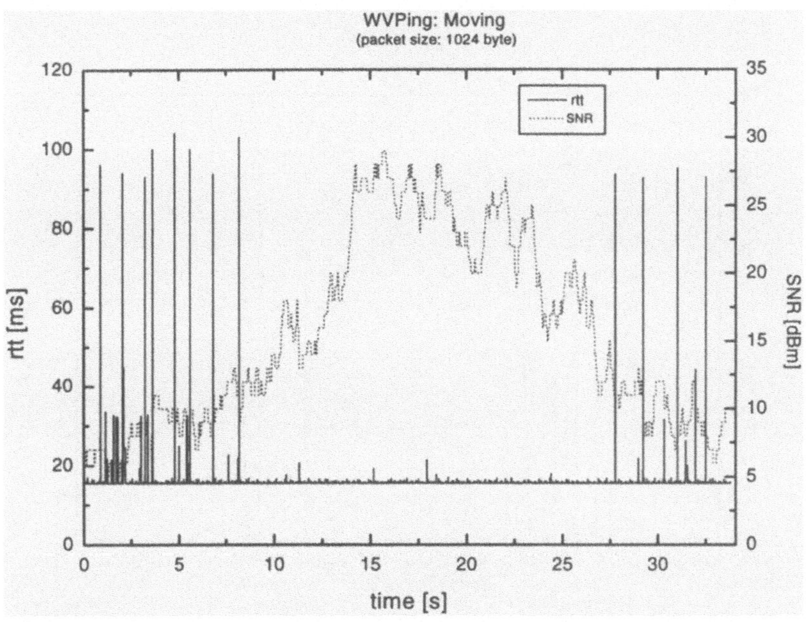

Abbildung5. *RTT und SNR bei Messung in Bewegung mit WVPing.*

Bei allen Messreihen ergeben sich bei Annäherung an den Access-Point weniger Paketverluste (s. Abbildung 5), sobald das Signal-to-Noise-Ratio über 15 dBm liegt. Anwendungen könnten somit ihr Übertragungsverhalten an das aktuelle Signal-to-Noise-Ratio der Funkverbindung anpassen. Gegebenenfalls könnte auch eine Statistik über die bisherigen SNR-Werte geführt werden, um zu entscheiden, ob aktuelle Werte längerfristig zu erwarten sind oder nur kurzzeitig auftreten.

Das Verhalten der drahtlosen Übertragungsstrecke nach Fehlerkorrektur kann auf IP-Ebene wie in Abbildung 5 ersichtlich relativ einfach durch ein On/Off-Modell beschrieben werden, das aufgrund der höheren Fehlerrate, die durch einen zu kleinen SNR erzeugt wird, zu einem vielfachen der Round-Trip-Time und somit zu einer extremen Verlangsamung der TCP-Dynamik führt.

4.3 *Roaming* ohne Subnetzwechsel

In dieser Versuchsreihe gehören beide Access-Points demselben Subnetz an, wodurch Roaming zwischen den beiden Funkzellen mit Umschaltung auf MAC-Ebene ermöglicht wird. Beim Handover muss die mobile Station die De-Assoziation mit dem Access-Point durchführen, dessen Funkzelle verlassen wird, und sich mit dem neuen Access-Point assoziieren. Die Experimentdurchführungen beinhalteten jeweils zwei Handover. Diese wurden erreicht, indem die mobile Station ausgehend von Raum 10b bis zum Raum 14 und wieder zurück bewegt wurde (vgl. Abbildung 1). Abbildung 6 zeigt die Verzögerungszeiten bei WVPing. Es

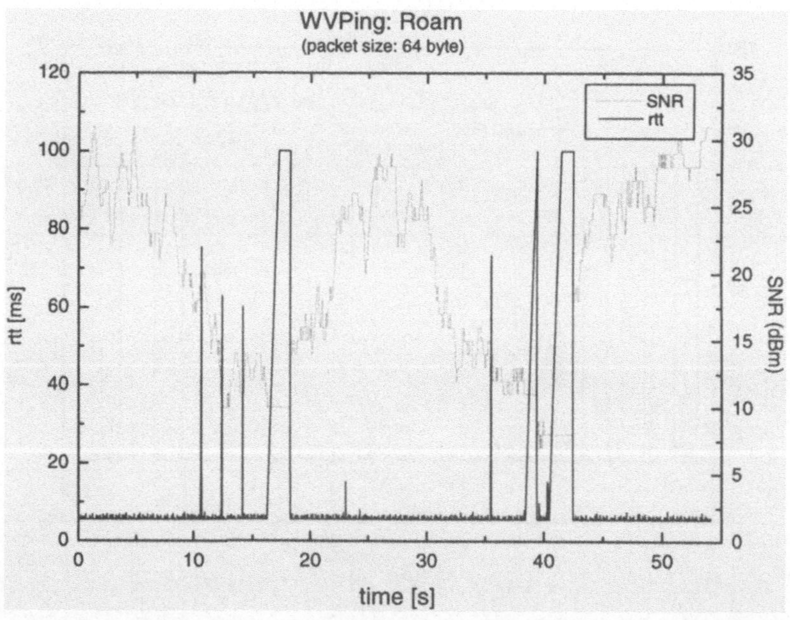

Abbildung6. *Roaming ohne Subnetzwechsel: Verzögerungszeiten mit WVPing.*

können beim Handover Übertragungsaussetzer von einigen Sekunden beobachtet werden. In Abbildung 7 ist das Congestion-Window des TCP-Experiments mit DBS dargestellt. Die Verbindungsunterbrechung beim Assoziationswechsel lag bei beiden Verkehrsmustern (Streaming und On/Off-Verkehrsmuster) im Bereich von 2-3 Sekunden. Teilweise treten schon vor dem eigentlichen Handover Verzögerungen der Übertragung auf, wodurch ein Einbruch des Congestion-Window

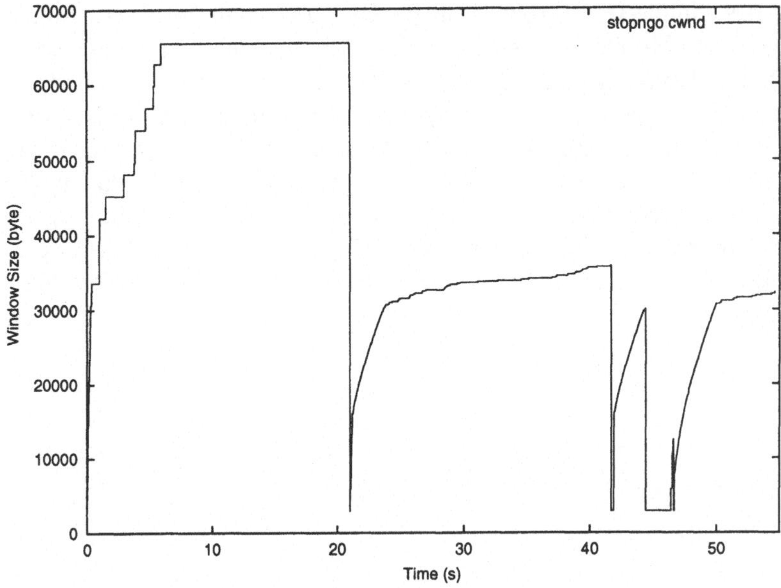

Abbildung 7. *Roaming ohne Subnetzwechsel: Congestion-Window bei OnOff-Verkehrsmuster mit DBS.*

verursacht wird. Der Einbruch erfolgt, da TCP innerhalb eines gewissen Timeouts ein *Acknowledgement* auf versandte Pakete erwartet. Die Mechanismen beim Handover sind verantwortlich für die Überschreitung dieses Timeouts. Das Congestion-Window wird auf den minimalen Wert von einem Segment zurückgesetzt (vgl. [20]) und der *Congestion-Avoidance* Mechanismus von TCP setzt ein (vgl. Abschnitt 1), um auf die vermeindliche Stausituation zu reagieren, wobei das Congestion-Window nur langsam wieder geöffnet wird (*Slow-Start*). Bei dem hier durchgeführten Assoziationswechsel liegt keine Stausituation vor. Nach dem Assoziationswechsel könnte das Congestion-Window wieder vollkommen geöffnet werden, da die Verbindungsqualität vor und nach dem Wechsel nahezu unverändert ist. Kurzzeitige Verbindungsunterbrechungen, wie sie bei Roaming von mobilen Stationen auftreten, werden also von TCP nicht berücksichtigt. Eine Lösung wäre hier ein Einfrieren des TCP-Zustandes, das durch ein Handover-Ereignis gesteuert wird, wie z. B. TCP-Snoop [2] oder Congestion-Awareness in neuen TCP-Varianten [17] [22].

4.4 *Roaming* mit Subnetzwechsel

Für die Durchführung von Roaming mit Subnetzwechsel wurden die beiden Access-Points für verschiedene Subnetze konfiguriert. Um bei diesem Subnetzwechsel die bestehenden Verbindungen weiterführen zu können, wurde die *Dynamics*-Mobile-IP Implementierung eingesetzt (s. Abschnitt 2). Zu den Mechanismen, die beim Wechsel des Zugangspunktes auf MAC-Ebene erfolgen, kommen

nun die des Mobile-IP Protokolls hinzu. Die *Movement-Discovery* (ohne Optimierungen) von Mobile-IP orientiert sich an empfangenen *Agent-Advertisements*
der Mobility-Agents (Home Agent oder Foreign Agent, vgl. Abbildung 2). Um
in unseren Experimenten die Verzögerung zu minimieren, die durch den "normalen" Mobile-IP Movement-Discovery-Mechanismus hervorgerufen wird, wurde das Agent-Advertisment-Intervall auf den kleinsten einzustellenden Wert von
einer Sekunde gesetzt, d. h. pro Sekunde wird von den Mobility-Agents eine
Nachricht ausgesandt, anhand der die mobile Station einen Subnetzwechsel erkennen kann. Mit unserem Experimentaufbau ließen sich Subnetzwechsel vom

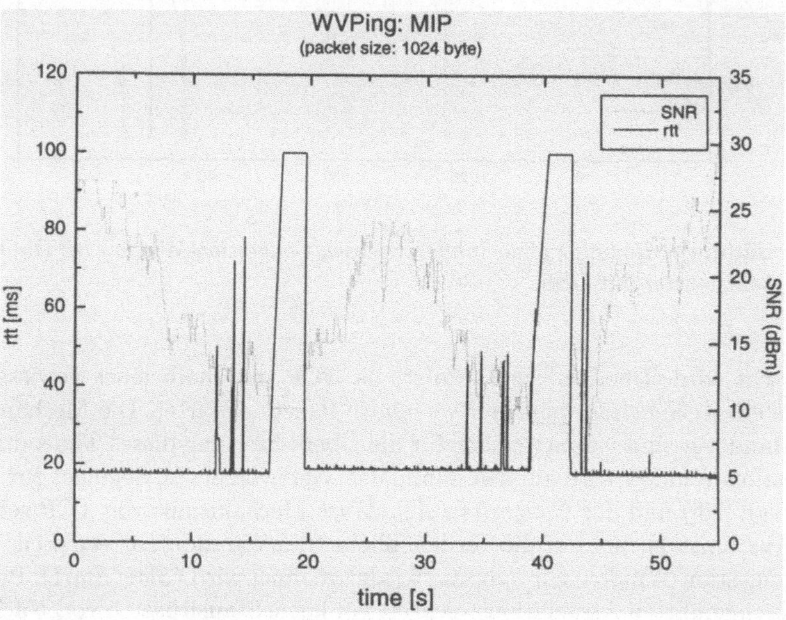

Abbildung 8. *Roaming mit Subnetzwechsel: Verzögerungszeiten mit WVPing.*

Home Network zum *Foreign Network* und wieder zurück durchführen. Hierfür
wurde die mobile Station zwischen Raum 10b und Raum 14 und wieder zurück
bewegt. In Abbildung 8 ist zu erkennen, dass die Ausfallzeiten während des Handovers erwartungsgemäß höher liegen als beim Roaming ohne Subnetzwechsel.
Ein Unterschied zwischen dem Wechsel vom Home Network ins Foreign Network
und dem Wechsel in umgekehrter Richtung konnte aber trotz unterschiedlicher
Vorgänge innerhalb des Mobile-IP Protokolls nicht beobachtet werden. Bei den
TCP-Experimenten mit DBS (s. Abbildung 9) sind ebenfalls größere Ausfallzeiten beim Handover als beim Roaming ohne Subnetzwechsel aufgetreten. Wie
schon beim Roaming ohne Subnetzwechsel kann der Einbruch des Congestion-
Window bereits vor dem Handover beobachtet werden. Außerdem sorgt der hier

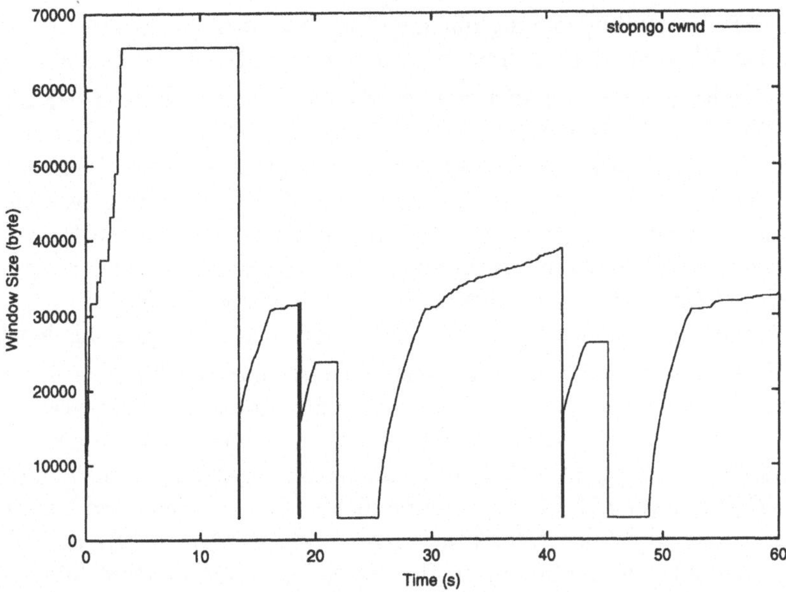

Abbildung 9. *Roaming mit Subnetzwechsel: Congestion-Window bei On/Off-Verkehrsmustern mit DBS.*

vorhandene längere Ausfall der Übertragung während des Handovers für den Einbruch des Congestion-Window.

5 Bewertung der Experimente

Die Arbeiten an verschiedenen Forschungseinrichtungen haben ergeben, dass die Leistung des TCP-Protokolls beim Einsatz in funkbasierten Netzen deutlich einbricht (u. a. [19], [8]). Dies konnte auch in den hier durchgeführten Experimenten mit dem TCP-Protokoll beobachtet werden. Das Congestion-Window brach dabei unmittelbar vor und während eines Handovers zusammen. Diese Reaktion erfolgt hierbei nicht aufgrund einer Stausituation, wie es vom TCP-Protokoll angenommen wird. Dies ist darauf zurückzuführen, dass TCP für die Charakteristika von verkabelten Netzwerken und nicht für kabellose Umgebungen ausgerichtet ist (vgl. [7]). Da nach einem Handover die mobile Station wieder ohne Beeinflussung erreichbar ist (in den hier durchgeführten Experimenten), wirken sich die Staubehebungsmechansimen von TCP hemmend auf den Kommunikationsfluss aus. Wünschenswert wäre die Wiederherstellung des Congestion-Windows auf den Wert vor dem Handover. Hierzu müßte aber das Protokoll um Mobilität unterstützende Mechanismen erweitert werden, wie beispielsweise in [2] oder [11] vorgeschlagen wird. Von besonderen Interesse wäre eine den Umgebungsbedingungen angepasste Kontrolle des Congestion-Window. In [22] wird eine Variante des Slow-Start-Mechanismus vorgestellt, der sog. *Smooth-Start*, der eine ensprechende Beeinflussung erlaubt. Eine Verbindung der aktuellen Eigenschaften der Funkumgebung mit der Kontrolle über die Reaktionsweise des Congestion-Window-Mechanismus von TCP erscheint vielversprechend.

Die Experimente haben auch gezeigt, dass bei der Beurteilung der Effizienz des TCP-Protokolls die Variabilität der Round-Trip-Time zur Auslieferung von Paketen, die durch Sendewiederholung bei Paketverlusten auftritt, von entscheidender Bedeutung ist (vgl. Abbildung 5). Eine Berücksichtigung verschiedener Fehlerursachen (verlorengegangene Pakete, teilweise übertragene Pakete oder Bitverfälschungen) wie in [6] beschrieben kann in diesem Zusammenhang helfen, geeignete Maßnahmen auszuwählen, die eine Reduktion der Fehlersituation bewirken können (z. B. dynamische Anpassung der Maximum-Transmission-Unit).

Die Experimente mit Mobile-IP weisen darauf hin, dass für Micro-Mobilität mit gleichzeitigem Einsatz des TCP-Protokolls Mobile-IP nicht geeignet ist, da die Ausfallzeiten der Übertragung als zu hoch angesehen werden können. Ähnliche Experimente in [8] haben ebenfalls die negativen Auswirkungen von Mobile-IP Handover auf TCP veranschaulicht. Um ein schnelleres Umschalten im Bereich der sog. Micro-Mobilität zu erhalten, werden in [21] und [5] Verfahren vorgeschlagen, die Mobile-IP für Macro-Mobilität vorsehen, aber für die Micro-Mobilität speziell optimierte Routing- und Caching-Mechanismen einsetzen, das sog. *Cellular IP*. In [10] wird ein Zwei-Phasen-Handover vorgestellt, der den Verlust von Paketen bei einem Mobile-IP Handover weitestgehend vermeidet. Hierbei wird zunächst der *Downstream* (Pakete zur mobilen Station) und dann der *Upstream* (Pakete von der mobilen Station) umgeleitet. Außerdem werden derzeit in der IETF Mobile-IP Working-Group weitere Verfahren für Fast-Handover diskutiert (s. [13], [14]). Die Notwendigkeit von beschleunigten Handover-Zeiten insbesondere für den Einsatz von Echtzeit-Multimedia-Anwendungen wurde durch die hier durchgeführten Experimente bestätigt.

6 Ausblick

Die entwickelte Experimentumgebung hat sich als tragfähig erwiesen, um die Einflüsse von Funkverbindungen auf die Transporteffizienz von Internet-basierten multimedialen Kommunikationsverbindungen messtechnisch zu erfassen. Geplant sind weitere Dynamik-Messungen des TCP-Protokolls beim Roaming von mobilen Stationen in Verbindung mit multimedialen Kommunikationsanwendungen, um einen subjektiven Eindruck der Auswirkungen der ermittelten Messergebnisse auf audiovisuelle Echtzeitströme zu erhalten. Hierzu stehen uns Anwendungen wie z. B. die kollaborative Lernumgebung CLE [3] zur Verfügung. Desweiteren sollen Experimente mit 11 Mbit/s Funkkarten erfolgen, die zum erweiterten Standard IEEE 802.11(b) kompatibel sind. Die Erfahrungen aus den Versuchsergebnissen zusammen mit dem Wissen über deren Auswirkungen in der Praxis stellen die Grundlage für die Entwicklung von geeigneten Notifikationsmechanismen für adaptive Kommunikationsverbindungen dar, die dynamisch auf Einflüsse von Funkverbindungen reagieren können: "mobile-aware" Anwendungen.

Literatur

1. IEEE 802. Part 11: Wireless LAN Medium Access Control (MAC) and Physical Layer (PHY) specifications. *The Institue of Electrical and Electronics Engineers, Inc., New Yourk, USA*, 1999.
2. H. Balakrishnan, S. Seshan, E. Amir, and R. Katz. Improving TCP/IP Performance over Wireless Networks. *Proeedings. of the 1st ACM Conference on Mobile Computing and Networking, Berkeley, CA*, November 1995.
3. J. Berghoff, M. Matthes, and O. Drobnik. Mobile-awareness in Collaborative Learning Envrionments. *Proc. of ISAS'99, Orlando, USA*, July 1999.
4. Benny Bing. Measured Performance of the IEEE 802.11 Wireless LAN. *Proc. of the IEEE Conference on Local Computer Networks, LCN'99, Lowell/Boston, Massachusetts, USA*, October 1999.
5. Andrew T. Campbell, Javier Gomez, and András G. Valkó. An Overview of Cellular IP. *First IEEE Wireless Communications and Networking Conference (WCNC'99), New Orleans, USA*, September 1999.
6. David A. Eckhard and Peter Steenkiste. A trace-based evaluation of adaptive error correction for a wireless local area network. *Mobile Networks and Applications 4, 273-287, Baltzer Science Publishers BV*, 1999.
7. A. Fieger and M. Zitterbart. Transport Protocols over Wireless Links. *Proc. of 2nd IEEE Symposium on Computers and Communications (ISCC'97), Alexandria, Egypt*, March 1997.
8. Anne Fladenmuller and Ranil De Silva. The effect of Mobile IP handoffs on the performance of TCP. *Mobile Networks and Applications 4, 131-135, Baltzer Science Publishers BV*, 1999.
9. D. Forsberg, J.T. Malinen, J.K. Malinen, T. Weckström, and M. Tiusanen. Distributing Mobility Agents Hierarchically under Frequent Location Updates. *Proc. of Sixth IEEE International Workshop on Mobile Multimedia Communications (MOMUC'99), San Diego*, November 1999.
10. Dan Forsberg. Communication availability with Mobile IP in wireless LANs. *Master's Thesis, Faculty of Information Technology, Helsinki University of Technology*, March 2000.
11. Daichi Funato, Shunichiro Okada, Hideyuki Tokuda, and Nobuo Saito. TCP Redirection for Adaptive Mobility Support in Stateful Applications. *IEICE Trans. Inf.&Syst., Mol. E82-D, No.4*, April 1999.
12. Dynamics Group. Dynamics - HUT Mobile-IP. *Helsinki University of Technology, Finnland*, 1999. http://www.cs.hut.fi/Research/Dynamics/.
13. James Kempf, Pat R. Calhoun, and Chandana Pairla. Foreign Agent Assisted Hand-off. *IETF Mobile-IP Working Group, Internet-Draft, draft-calhoun-mobileip-proactive-fa-01.txt*, June 2000.
14. Karim El Malki and Hesham Soliman. Fast Handoffs in Mobile IPv4. *IETF Mobile-IP Working Group, Internet-Draft, draft-elmalki-mobileip-fast-handoffs-02.txt*, July 2000.
15. Yukio Murayama and Suguru Yamaguchi. DBS: a powerful tool for TCP performance evaluations. *Performance and Control of Network Systems, Proc. of SPIE, Volume 3231*, November 1997.
16. Marek Natkaniec and Andrzej R. Pach. An Analysis of the Backoff Mechanismen used in IEEE 802.11 Networks. *Proc. of IEEE Symposium on Computers and Communications'2000 (ISCC)*, 2000.

17. Christina Parsa and J.J. Garcia-Luna-Aceves. Improving TCP performance over wireless networks at the link layer. *Mobile Networks and Applications 5, 131-135, Baltzer Science Publishers BV*, 2000.

18. C.E. Perkins. MobileIP - Design Principles and Practices. *Addison-Wesley Wireless Communications Series, Massachusetts, USA*, October 1997.

19. B. Rathke, M. Schläger, and A. Wolisz. Systematic Measurement of TCP Performance over Wireless LANs. *Telecommunication Networks Group, Technical Report TKN-01BR98, TU-Berlin, Germany*, December 1998.

20. W.R. Stevens. TCP/IP Illustrated, Volume 1 - The Protocols. *Addison-Wesley Professional Computing Series, Massachusetts, USA*, 1994.

21. András G. Valkó. Cellular IP: A New Approach to Internet Host Mobility. *SIGCOMM Computer Communication Review, Vol. 29, No. 1*, Januar 1999.

22. Haining Wang, Hongjie Xin, Douglas S. Reeves, and Kang G. Shin. A Simple Refinement of Slow-start of TCP Congestion Control. *Proc. of IEEE Symposium on Computers and Communications'2000 (ISCC)*, 2000.

Improving the Performance of TCP on guaranteed bandwidth connections

Hartmut Ritter, Klaus Wehrle, and Lars Wolf

Institute of Telematics, University of Karlsruhe,
Zirkel 2, D-76128 Karlsruhe, Germany
Phone: +49 721 608 6411, Fax: +49 721 388097
{ritter,wehrle,wolf}@telematik.informatik.uni-karlsruhe.de

Abstract. This paper discusses the performance of the Transmission Control Protocol under two aspects: First, the future Internet will provide some kind of service differentiation and bandwidth guarantees. Nevertheless, TCP connections often cannot fully exploit the reserved bandwidth over time. The congestion control mechanisms like slow start and congestion avoidance have to be revised in the context of guaranteed services, where no congestions occur for special flows.

Second, short-lived TCP connections have become more and more important in the Internet. Short-lived connections are needed in transaction-oriented network applications and client-server scenarios; a typical example is the common use of the World Wide Web. TCP has typical performance flaws in these cases.

Former approaches of improving the performance of TCP did not succeed because their objective was the adaption of all involved TCP stacks. This leads to a change in every TCP stack in the Internet – at least 80 millions hosts nowadays. In this paper another way has been chosen: only one host within a connection will be modified, particularly with regard to client-server communication. Within this context, several modifications to improve TCP's performance with given bandwidth guarantees and their evaluation will be presented in this paper.

1 Introduction

The provisioning of Quality of Service (QoS) has been intensively studied for ATM and IP networks. Whereas QoS support in ATM networks seems to be solved, in IP networks the technical details are not yet clear. The former Integrated Services Architecture [BrCS94] as well as the currently discussed Differentiated Services Architecture [NiJZ99] are still not broadly deployed in existing IP networks. Nevertheless, it seems to be obvious, that some kind of bandwidth guarantees will be available in the next generation Internet.

The transport protocol TCP, most likely to be used in the current Internet as well as in future networks, shows performance problems in an environment providing guaranteed bandwidth. These problems of TCP increase, when short-lived connections are considered, because the greatest loss of performance takes place in in the early stages of a connection.

Short-lived TCP connections have to be taken more into account nowadays. On the one hand Web traffic gains more importance, not at least due to the economic interests in the World Wide Web. On the other hand, legacy applications formerly using different networks, like online brokerage or typically transaction-oriented ticket reservation systems, tend to be integrated into the Internet.

But using TCP in the next generation Internet, where on the one hand short-lived connections dominate the traffic and on the other hand, Quality of Service mechanisms are used to assure the bandwidth, todays TCP will lead to performance problems as the following sections will indicate. TCP can not exploit the entire bandwidth that has been negotiated for the connection. This is not in the end user's interest, above all he has to pay for the value-added IP service.

To solve this problem, the Transmission Control Protocol has to be modified according to the new requirements. Nevertheless, it is impossible to change a transport protocol, that is used in over eighty millions hosts. Furthermore, it is impossible to change the underlying transport protocol of the mostly used applications in the Internet from TCP to another (more QoS friendly) protocol from one day to the next. TCP is the most used transport layer instance. This is the status quo and will not change within the next decade.

Consequently, the focus of this paper is not the change of the TCP instances in all Internet hosts, but a modification of a small amount of them, which have strategic positions in the Net as described in the next section. In the opinion of the authors, this would solve the described problems in the most use cases.

1.1   The Internet is a client-server network

Client-server communication, where the bigger part of the traffic is sent from the server to the client, is the most used communication pattern in the Internet, e.g. DNS, SMTP, FTP, and above all the World Wide Web. Only a small amount of traffic is really load-balanced between the two peers, e.g. chat traffic, IP-telephony, interactive audio/video-conferences.

In the following, the focus is put on Web communication, because it forms the majority of todays Internet traffic. TCP connections in this scenario are typically very short. Nevertheless, Quality of Service will also be introduced into this environment, enabling users to select the quality of the servers response. A framework for such a QoS-enabled web server, with focus on different kinds of signaling for the desired service level between client and server, is discussed in [RiPW00].

In such a scenario, the TCP implementation of the server has to be modified anyway for guaranteed rate connections on the downlink from the server to the client, e.g. a traffic shaper has to be used for limiting the outgoing traffic to the negotiated rate, and the server can initiate the reservation on behalf of the client. So, it is possible to modify also the TCP stack in the server to improve the behavior of the transport protocol on the leased line. The TCP implementation in the client remains *unchanged*. This is a necessary condition

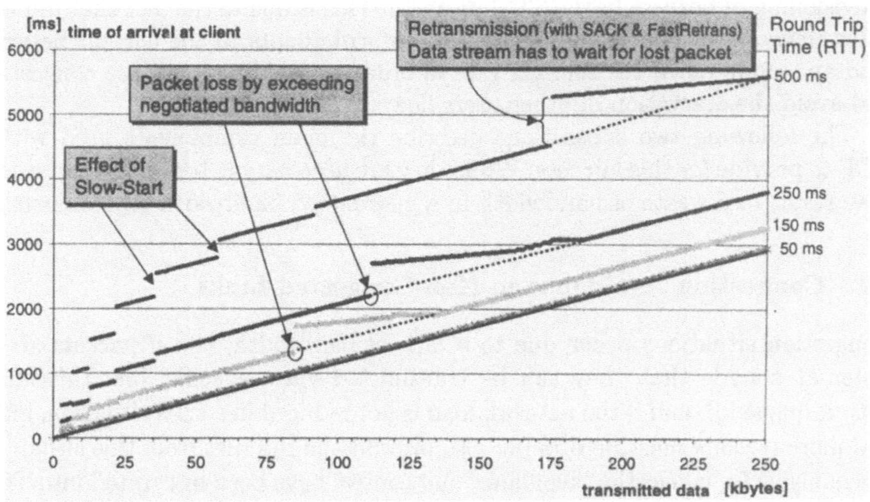

Fig. 1. Performance evaluation of a TCP connection using guaranteed bandwidth (with varying round trip times)

for a practical solution. The interoperability of modifications of TCP with legacy TCP implementations is therefore a main prerequisite for all approaches.

The next section discusses some reasons why TCP cannot use the whole bandwidth in the case of an environment providing bandwidth guarantees. The related TCP mechanisms will be discussed and analyzed in the context of short-lived connections and QoS-supporting networks. Section 3 provides a description of the testbed, describes the realized modifications of TCP and presents measurements. In section 4 the integration of the modifications in a single TCP implementation applicable in heterogeneous networks with and without guarantees is discussed.

2   Problems of TCP in a Guaranteed Rate Environment

TCP is one of the most frequently used transport protocols. It is almost twenty years old and several modifications have been integrated into TCP over the years, e.g., RFC1323. Moreover, many proposals have been made in order to enhance TCP (T/TCP (RFC1644), I/TCP [BaBa95], mobileTCP [BrSi97], etc.).

While the behavior of TCP in ATM networks with guaranteed bandwidth connections was studied by some research groups, e.g. [Bona98], [KJFG+96], the behavior of TCP in native IP networks with guaranteed bandwidth services has not been analyzed in detail so far. The problems of TCP in the context of guaranteed bandwidth services result from design decisions which target the provisioning of fairness in the TCP protocol. This is due to the fact that in best-effort networks it is necessary that the protocol adapts to the current network load and slows down the sending rate in order to avoid resp. reduce congestion and avoid the starvation of other users flows.

The following two subsections describe the main components used within TCP to provide for this fairness. While they are necessary in best-effort networks, they result in a waste of bandwidth in a guaranteed bandwidth environment.

2.1 Congestion Avoidance in Non-Congested Links

Congestion situations occur due to a lack of bandwidth, i.e., if packets arrive faster at a node than they can be transmitted via a specific link, this link's output queue fill, and if the network load is not reduced in such a situation, more and more packets must be dropped. To prevent the Internet from this situation, mechanisms for congestion avoidance and control have been integrated into TCP - the Slow Start algorithm and the Congestion Avoidance algorithm [Jaco88].

When congestion occurs and the communication partners note the resulting packet losses, they reduce the amount of data they are sending into the network by applying the Slow Start and Congestion Avoidance algorithm. A typical characteristic of the Slow Start algorithm is the sawtooth behavior of the congestion window (which is also reflected in the measurements given in Fig. 1). The behavior of Slow Start and Congestion Avoidance can be described briefly as follows:

- TCP starts with a congestion window of one segment and increases this after a successful transfer of the whole window.
- The congestion window and thus the send rate is further increased. In the slow-start-phase this window opens up exponentially, after exceeding a slow-start threshold, TCP enters the congestion avoidance phase where the further increase of the window size occurs linearly. The slow start phase can be seen in Fig. 1. With bigger round trip times the effect can be seen better, because the acknowledgements needed for opening up the congestion window suffer from higher delay.
- If a packet has been lost, TCP returns to a very low transmission rate. This is not the case, if the SACK option is used, like it was done in the example of Fig.. 1. The effect can be seen at the point of the curves, where a packet was dropped from the meter. In the case of SACK TCP the selective acknowledgement enables the sender to retransmit just the one lost packet. The packets sent after the transmission of the lost packet are cached on the receiver side and passed up to the receiving application not until the retransmitted packet arrives. As a result, the packets are passed to the receiving application in a burst with a higher rate.

These algorithms are necessary for the best-effort Internet in order to handle the offered traffic without collapse even if the principal transmission demand is much higher than the available bandwidth. Nevertheless, if a certain amount of bandwidth is guaranteed per connection, be it Expedited Forwarding (DiffServ) or Guaranteed Service (IntServ), then no congestion occurs and no packets are lost as long as the traffic conforms to the negotiated traffic contract, e.g., if the offered load of the connection stays below its reserved bandwidth. The critical point is that the Slow Start and Congestion Avoidance algorithms are not aware of the guarantees given by the network to a flow.

There are two problems resulting from the slow-start and congestion-avoidance mechanisms:

- Because TCP does not know anything about the guaranteed rate available to a particular connection, it always exceeds this rate in the congestion avoidance phase when increasing the send rate linearly, i.e., it does not comply to the negotiated rate. As a consequence, packet loss occurs in a policing unit of the network such as the traffic shaper of a DiffServ router or a similar meter of a different network technology which enforces the compliance between the generated traffic on the one side and the traffic contract and the negotiated rate on the other side.
- After such a packet loss has occurred, TCP lowers its transmission rate for this connection, usually returning to the slow start phase. However, since a much higher constant rate has been reserved and guaranteed for this connection, the reduction of the transmission rate is basically just a waste of resources because the guaranteed rate is not fully exploited.

2.2   Window-Based Flow Control

In order to avoid buffer overflow at the receiver side, TCP implements a Flow Control mechanism. The TCP sender and receiver negotiate a maximum amount of packets which can be sent without being acknowledged. The original specification allows a window size of up to 64kbyte. The TCP modifications specified in RFC1323 allow for window sizes larger than this value. These modifications have been designed with the intention to better support so called 'long-fat pipes', i.e., networks with a large bandwidth-delay product. This value is an upper limit for the amount of bytes the sender is permitted to send without having to wait for acknowledgements from the receiver, provided the congestion window is open. In a network with a large bandwidth-delay product, the sender cannot exploit the full rate if the Flow Control Window is not large enough. The reason is that a fast sender has sent all packets it is allowed to transmit very soon and has to wait for the acknowledgement from the receiver. Especially the performance of short-lived TCP connections will be impacted, because these connections will perhaps never leave the slow-start phase. At least, the percentage of time a connection does not exploit the reserved bandwidth is extremely high. The option for large window sizes is already part of most modern TCP implementations, especially in a guaranteed rate environment the option should be activated and used.

In different TCP variants additional mechanisms and enhancements were added to the basic TCP. The mechanisms of slow start and congestion avoidance were introduced in TCP Tahoe [Jaco88]. In TCP Reno and New Reno

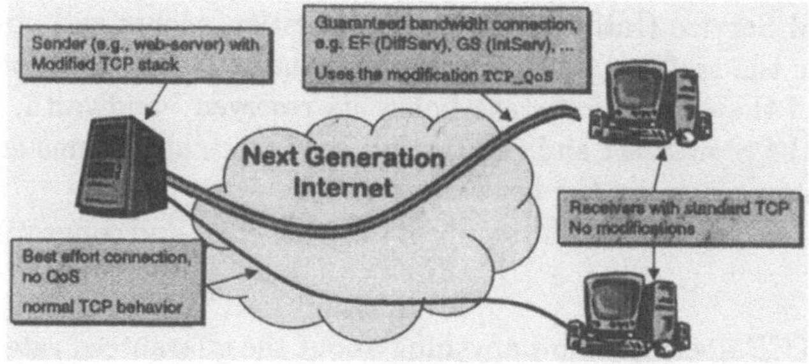

Fig. 2. Assumed scenario: TCP connections with QoS assurance can use modified TCP in the server. Normal connections are using standard TCP in the server (default). Clients always use standard TCP.

[FaFl96], a modified Fast Retransmit [Jaco90] and a Fast Recovery algorithm were introduced, which avoid the slow start in some situations, when there is an obviously very short network congestion. However, during the slow start phase the available bandwidth is not used. TCP New Reno is part of the standard Linux operating system, which has been used for measurements in this paper. TCP Vegas [BrPe95] introduces ways to detect incipient stages of congestion before losses occur. These mechanisms can also be used in the slow start phase. Nevertheless, as there is no exact information about the available bandwidth, it takes time to adapt to the maximum rate. In a guaranteed rate environment a rate based flow control as proposed in this paper can skip this adaptation phase.

3 Scenario

Some assumptions concerning the QoS support and the overall scenario have been done in the presented work (cf. figure 2):

- The realization of QoS support in the network is not focused. Instead, it is assumed, that some kind of reservation is issued before a TCP connection is set up, and it is additionally assumed, that this reservation is strong and holds during the connection time.
- Reservation is done per flow, i.e. in the case of DiffServ each TCP connection is provided with an unique EF flow from end to end. Multiplexing of many TCP connections to one EF flow is not considered at the moment, dynamic adaptation of reservations neither.
- Best-effort and better services like EF in DiffServ or Guaranteed Service in IntServ co-exist in one network, but the bandwidth reserved per flow can not be borrowed to best-effort traffic if not exploited by the better services.

In this scenario, improving the performance of TCP is done in the context of the following objectives:

- Improving the performance of TCP means in the context of guaranteed bandwidth connections, that a TCP flow exploits the full rate which was reserved and is not hindered by internal mechanisms.
- Only *one* TCP stack in a peer-to-peer connection has to be modified. This is a prerequisite for an incremental deployment of the modified TCP in the future Internet. It is obvious that not each TCP stack can be modified at once. Client-server scenarios are the main paradigm nowadays, for example in the world wide web. Modifying the server's stack without a need for changes in all the client's stacks requires full interoperability of the improved TCP stack of the server and the legacy TCP stacks of the clients.
- The modifications should only be put into execution when the bandwidth is really guaranteed. Therefore the modifications should be activated only when the bandwidth has been previously reserved and confirmed.

4 Modifications of TCP in the server

As indicated in section 2, TCP is well designed for today's Internet with its best effort characteristic. But when guaranteed services should be used, the behavior of TCP hinders full exploitation of them. In order to achieve an improvement of performance in this environment, the TCP stack has been modified. The modification meets the objectives given in the previous section:

- *Modification of the slow start and congestion avoidance algorithms:* As described in section 2.1 the slow start and congestion avoidance algorithms prevent from the immediate exploitation of a guaranteed bandwidth. Due to service guarantees there will be no congestion during the connection. Consequently, an algorithm for congestion avoidance is not needed in this case. Therefore, a new TCP socket option TCP_QoS was implemented in the Linux kernel, by means of which the slow start algorithm in the sender is switched on or off. As can be seen in figure 4, described in the following section, this will avoid the slow increase of the TCP sending rate. Especially in the case of short-lived TCP connections the slow start algorithm results in the phenomenon, that these connections never reach the maximum rate or at least rest a high percentage of the connection life time in the slow start phase, far below the reserved rate. In the example shown in Fig. 1 the overall throughput for transmitting 100kbyte has been 37% with a round trip time of 500ms.
- *Rate based flow control:* To avoid bursty traffic leaving the TCP stack because of the window based flow control, the sending window was increased up to the path capacity and a rate based flow control algorithm was integrated, which sends out TCP segments in a smoothed way, conforming to the negotiated rate. Increasing the sending window to the product of bandwidth and round trip time effects that TCP can continuously send data with the negotiated rate without waiting for acknowledges from the receiver caused by higher round trip times (RTTs). In order to avoid exceeding the sending

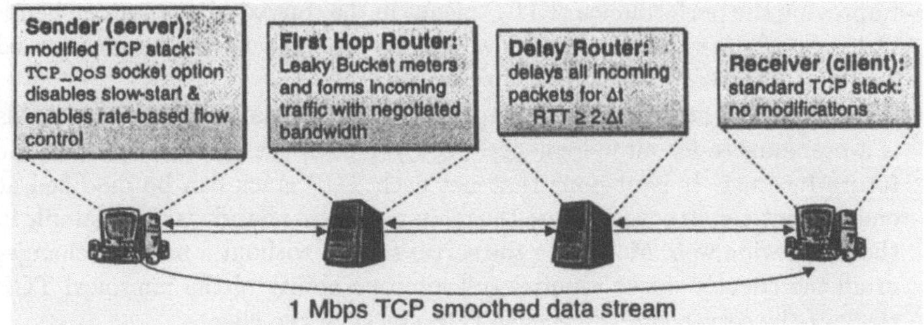

Fig. 3. Linux-Testbed with Differentiated Services- and Delay-Router

rate, the rate-based flow control is implemented by a token bucket model added to the TCP stack.

Supported by a fine-granular timer [RiWe00] the token bucket controls the outgoing rate in a byte-oriented way. The sending rate can be set as parameter of the socket option TCP_QoS mentioned above.

By implementing just these small modifications in one of the communication partners (in this case the server) the performance of the Transmission Control Protocol was improved up to nearly the maximum throughput. This has been proved by the measurements presented in the following section.

5 Evaluation of the performance improvement

The measurements and modifications of TCP have been done in a testbed environment illustrated in figure 3. Four standard PCs (Pentium III, 450MHz, 256 MB RAM) and full duplex 10BaseT network connections were used. TCP client and server are connected with a Differentiated Services router (using the KIDS implementation described in [BlWe99]) and another router realizing a delay queue. The DiffServ router implements a Traffic Shaper [RiWe00], based on a Leaky Bucket, as commonly used for limiting the bandwidth used by a flow. The delay queue in the second router just delays all incoming packets for a given amount of time in order to simulate different round trip times. The combination of DiffServ- and Delay-router therefore allows the testing of the behavior of TCP in networks with different bandwidth-delay products.

Several measurements were done with round trip times increasing from 10ms up to 500ms. In this paper only measurements with 500ms are presented, because they show most clearly the achieved performance improvement. The effects of smaller RTTs scales down linearly depending on the round trip time. In each measurement the server sent a smoothed TCP data stream with the negotiated rate to the receiver. In the QoS-Router an Expedited Forwarding [BHCD+97]

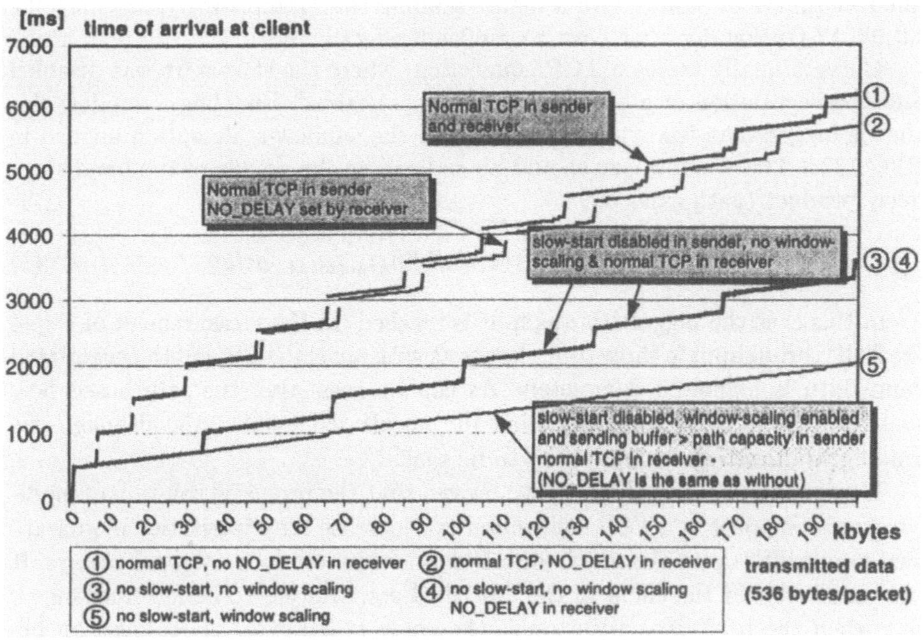

Fig. 4. Evaluation of modified TCP's performance with a round trip time of 500ms.

traffic profile with a reservation of 1,1 times of the sending rate has been installed with a burst size of 50.000 byte each.

Figure 4 shows different measurements done in this testbed with a RTT of 500ms. On the x-axis it shows the amount of data that has been sent downlink and received by the Host B. The y-axis shows the arrival times of the TCP segments (each about 536 bytes) of a TCP connection between client and server. The uppermost curve (curve 1) shows the normal behavior of a non-modified TCP. The typical behavior of TCP can be seen here: The fast arrival of a bunch of packets, followed by a time where no packets arrive due to the described slow start mechanism.

Curve 2 shows an also un-modified TCP where the socket option NO_DELAY was enabled in the client. Normally this delay allows the receiver to aggregate acknowledgements in order to prevent him from sending to much (small) acknowledge packets. This slows down the sender, but as it can be seen the throughput does not differ much. Curve 3 in figure 1 shows the behavior of a modified TCP, the slow start being disabled. Disabling the slow-start means here, that the congestion window of TCP is opened up to a threshold set by the new socket-option from the beginning of the connection. This socket option informs the TCP stack, that a guaranteed bandwidth exists for this socket, and that slow start is not needed. As can be seen, the throughput of this connection is higher due to the fact that TCP starts with a higher sending rate. Interestingly, enabling the NO_DELAY-Option does not have a significant effect here.

Curve 5 finally traces a TCP connection, where the slow-start was disabled and the negotiation of a big window size was enabled. Enabling a window size that is bigger than 64kbyte is possible with the window-scale option defined in RFC 1323. The window size should be as large as the double of the bandwidth delay product (path capacity):

$$window\ size \geq 2 \cdot bandwidth_{negotiated} \cdot delay \tag{1}$$

In this case the biggest throughput is reached. In the measurement of Fig. 4 the TCP throughput is three times larger as with normal TCP and the negotiated bandwidth is exploited completely. As can be seen also, the rate based flow control hinders TCP from exceeding the negotiated bandwidth, although the sending windows allows more data to be sent.

The measurements in Fig. 4 have proven that the proposed solution of modifying only one peer in a TCP connection can increase the exploitation of guaranteed bandwidth up to the maximum. But this solution does not work always. It was assumed that the client in the described scenario has to be left unchanged. But when the path capacity exceeds the value of 64kbyte, the connection between the two peers should use the window-scale option to increase the window size. When the receiver is not accepting the window-scale option of RFC 1323 it can only be reached a throughput of

$$throughput_{effective} = \frac{negotiated\ bandwidth}{64\ kbyte} \tag{2}$$

In the example of Fig.4 the throughput of curve 3 is only $512\ kbps = \frac{1\ Mbps}{32\ kbyte}$ because the client has rejected the window-scale option and offered only a window-size of 32kbyte (this has been manually set to the maximum window-size to avoid the automatic acceptance of the window-scale option). In curve 5, where the window-scaling has been accepted the throughput reached the maximum possible amount of $1\ Mbps$, because the window size could have been increased up to the path capacity. Most commonly used operation systems support the window-scale option (as required by RFC 1323), so this problem can be neglected in the future Internet.

6　Integration of the Modifications in a Universal TCP

The measurements show that disabling slow-start and using big window sizes allows a throughput up to three times better than with an unmodified TCP (New Reno) implementation. As said before, the problem of unfairness is not relevant in a guaranteed rate environment, because the usage of the reserved rate does not influence other flows.

However, using this modified TCP in today's best-effort Internet would create a very aggressive behavior and unfairness of this TCP connection in relation to connections of unmodified TCP implementations. Even in future QoS-supporting networks there will be a great amount of best-effort traffic. Thus, there is the need for a single TCP implementation which adapts its behavior, depending on the service guarantees the flow requires and the environment provides. The presented implementation realizes a single TCP stack, the modifications can be switched on or off at the socket interface, thus per flow, as described above. The only parameters needed for the modified TCP to work sufficiently are the reserved rate and the round trip time. Whereas the round trip time can be calculated by built-in TCP mechanisms at connection setup, the information about the reserved rate must be gathered from components outside of TCP.

7   Conclusion

This paper discussed the performance of TCP on guaranteed bandwidth connections provided by native IP mechanisms. The presented measurements illustrate that modifications of TCP are needed in order to make TCP more efficient in such an environment. The modifications discussed and proposed in this work consist of disabling the slow start and congestion avoidance algorithms for such connections and introducing a rate-based flow control.

For any modification to this dominant protocol it has to be considered how the changes affect the network in general and the deployed implementations. The mechanisms presented in this work must be integrated into a TCP entity which must be capable of supporting concurrently guaranteed bandwidth and regular best-effort network connections in an efficient manner. A basic requirement for the incremental deployment of such methods is the backward compatibility of the proposed modifications, i.e. that a server running a modified TCP stack can communicate with a client running a legacy stack. The mechanisms introduced in this work ensure both, the ease of deployment and the interoperability requirements because only one side of a connection must be changed, e.g., a web server, and the introduced changes are only local modifications, i.e., the peer is not affected.

The proposed modifications are especially well suited for web traffic where short-lived connections are prevalent and where the standard TCP mechanisms lower the reachable throughput. Not at least due to the increasing commercial and non-commercial interest in the Internet, the integration of QoS and web traffic is a very important issue. This integration requires further work such as to study how future QoS-architectures and existing components interoperate and can be better integrated. Elements in the end system which provide TCP with further information about the currently provided and needed QoS level will be necessary as well as information from the network about the load situation. Therefore, the presented modifications of TCP are currently integrated in an adaptive QoS architecture in the end system presented in [BeRS99].

References

BaBa95.   A. Bakre and B. Badrinath. I-TCP: Indirect TCP for mobile hosts. Proceedings of the 15th International Conference on Distributed Computing Systems (ICDCS), May 1995.

BeRS99.   M. Bechler, H. Ritter and J. Schiller. Integration of a Traffic Conditioner for Differentiated Services in End-systems via Feedback-loops. In *Proceedings of Broadband Communications*, Hong Kong, November 1999. IFIP.

BHCD$^+$97. F. Baker, J. Heinanen, M. Carlson, E. Davies, Z. Wang and W. Weiss. An Architecture for Differentiated Services. RFC 2475, IETF, June 1997.

BlWe99.   R. Bless and K. Wehrle. Evaluation of Differentiated Services using an implementation under Linux. In *Proceedings of the 7th IEEE/IFIP Workshop on Quality of Service (IWQoS99)*, London, October 1999. IEEE.

Bona98.   O. Bonaventure. A simulation study of TCP with the GFR service category. In *High-performance networks for multimedia applications*, Boston, October 1998. Kluwer Academic Publishers.

BrCS94.   R. Braden, D. Clark and S. Shenker. Integrated Services in the Internet Architecure: an overview. RFC 1633, IETF, June 1994.

BrPe95.   L. S. Brakmo and L. L. Peterson. TCP Vegas: End to End Congestion Avoidance on a Global Internet. IEEE Journal on Selected Areas in Communication, Vol. 13, No. 8, October 1995.

BrSi97.   K. Brown and S. Singh. mobileTCP: TCP for mobile cellular networks. ACM Computer Communications Review 27(5), May 1997.

FaFl96.   K. Fall and S. Floyd. Simulation-based Comparisons of Tahoe, Reno and SACK TCP. In *Computer Communication Review V.26 (N. 3)*, New York, July 1996. ACM.

Jaco88.   V. Jacobson. Congestion avoidance and control. In *Proceedings of SIGCOMM 1988*, Stanford, August 1988. ACM.

Jaco90.   V. Jacobson. Modified TCP Congestion Avoidance Algorithm. In *Technical Report, available at ftp://ftp.ee.lbl.gov/email/vanj.90apr30.txt*, Berkeley, April 1990. LBNL.

KJFG$^+$96. S. Kalyanaraman, R. Jain, S. Fahmy, R. Goyal, F. Lu and S. Srinidhi. Performance of TCP/IP over ABR. In *Proceedings of Globecom 1996*, London, November 1996. IEEE.

NiJZ99.   K. Nichols, V. Jacobson and L. Zhang. A Two-bit Differentiated Services Architecture for the Internet. RFC 2638, IETF, July 1999.

RiPW00.   H. Ritter, T. Pastoors and K. Wehrle. DiffServ in the Web: Different Approaches for Enabling better Services in the World Wide Web. In *Proceedings of Networking 2000 (joint conference of Broadband Communications, High Performance Networking and Performance of Communication Networks)*, Paris, May 2000. Springer.

RiWe00.   H. Ritter and K. Wehrle. Traffic Shaping in ATM and IP networks. In *Proceedings of Intern. Conference on ATM*, Heidelberg, June 2000.

Session 6:

Multimedia

Architektur für eine integrierte Training Online Plattform

C. Rueß, M. Wolf, R. Eberhardt, J. Hördt

DaimlerChrysler AG, Forschung und Technologie 3
Postfach 2360, 89013 Ulm, Germany

christian.ruess@daimlerchrysler.com
michael.m.wolf@daimlerchrysler.com
reinhold.eberhardt@daimlerchrysler.com
jan.hoerdt@daimlerchrysler.com

Abstract. Im Rahmen der innerbetrieblichen Qualifikationsentwicklung kommen innerhalb der DaimlerChrysler AG verschiedene Lehrmethoden zum Einsatz. Neben den „klassischen" Lehrmethoden sind momentan verstärkt Bemühungen auf den Aufbau eines globalen Online-Lernsystems gerichtet. Die in diesem Rahmen in Entwicklung und Evaluation befindlichen Teilsysteme werden hier vorgestellt und die Motivation, die Ziele sowie die Ansätze zur Integration in ein Gesamtsystem beschrieben. Dieses System soll für die verschiedenen Benutzerkategorien (wie z.B. Lernende, Ausbilder, Personalverantwortliche und Autoren) einen web-basierten Zugang zu den verschiedenen computer- bzw. web-basierten Lehrmethoden, sowie zu Kursangeboten und Lehrmaterialen bieten. Für Ausbilder, Autoren und Personalverantwortliche sollen Schnittstellen zur Verwaltung, Pflege, und Komposition von Lehr- bzw. Kursangeboten und deren Medien, sowie zur Benutzer- und Ressourcenverwaltung angeboten werden. Das Gesamtsystem wird nicht als Software-Entwicklung im „traditionellen" Sinne etabliert werden, sondern aus kommerziell verfügbaren Komponenten (sog. „Standardsoftware") zusammengefügt werden. Die darauf zurückzuführende Abweichung vom herkömmlichen Lebenszyklus einer Eigenentwicklung wird ebenfalls dargestellt.

1. Einleitung

Gegenwärtig kommt dem Bereich „Online Training" eine ständig wachsende Bedeutung zu. Die sich ständig verkürzenden Innovationszyklen im technischen Bereich und die fortschreitende Globalisierung erfordern die permanente Weiterbildung von Mitarbeitern. Diese Entwicklung erfordert die Verfügbarkeit von technischen Detailinformationen, didaktisch konzipierten Schulungen und Schulungsmaterialien für verschiedene Zielgruppen schon oft weit vor Markteinführung einzelner Produkte. Die angewandten Lehrmethoden haben sich dabei bereits in der Vergangenheit von der klassischen Ausbildung durch Printmedien und Präsenztraining ausgehend weiterentwickelt. Es werden zunehmend neue Medien wie Lehrvideos, TV-Übertragungen, computergestütztes Lernen (CUL) und Teleseminare verwendet. Seit der kommerziellen Entdeckung des Internets kommt verstärkt auch die webbasierte Schulung (web based training, WBT) als asynchrone Lehrmethode zum Einsatz. Werden WBT-Schulungen um synchrone Komponenten erweitert so spricht man von internet- und intranetbasierten Teleseminaren oder virtuellen Präsenzseminaren. Die ständig wachsende Verbreitung des Internets und die wachsenden Übertragungsraten der eingesetzten Netzwerktechnologien machen diese Methoden besonders interessant, da dadurch auch umfangreiche multimediale Schulungsangebote weltweit kostengünstig verbreitet werden können. Virtuelles Präsenztraining bietet darüber hinaus das Potential, gruppendynamische Prozesse des Lernens auch bei verteilten Lernprozessen durch Einsatz synchroner Elemente (virtuelles Klassenzimmer, Gruppeninteraktion [Man99] und virtuelle Präsenz) zu nutzen.

In einer Organisation, in der die genannten Lehrmethoden derzeit weitgehend isoliert zum Einsatz kommen, ist ein integriertes Konzept wünschenswert. Dabei soll einerseits der Mitarbeiter einen zentralen Zugang zu allen verfügbaren Lehrmethoden und -angeboten und deren Materialien erhalten; andererseits sollen Weiterbildungspläne für einzelne Individuen, Zielgruppen oder auch gruppenübergreifende Lehrpläne in Anlehnung an die Firmen- und Produktentwicklung erstellt werden können. Durch das integrierte System soll die Weiterbildung der Mitarbeiter gesteuert und beobachtet werden. Vor Markteinführung eines neuen Produktes kann sichergestellt werden, dass allen betroffenen Mitarbeitergruppen (wie z.B. Vertrieb oder Service) das erforderliche Wissen (z.B. Merkmale, Absatzwege und die technischen Details) über das Produkt vermittelt wurde. Die zentrale Verwaltung aller Ausbildungsressourcen wie Seminarräume, deren Ausstattung und der Mitarbeiter ist ein weiterer Vorteil eines Gesamtsystems. Der Erstellungsprozess neuer Lehrmaterialien profitiert durch einen solchen integrierten Ansatz durch die Wiederverwendbarkeit einzelner Medien in verschiedenen Granularitäten und der zentralen Verwaltung dieser Medien. Weiterhin können ggf. individuelle Kompositionen von Lehrmaterialen durch die Mitarbeiter oder Agentensysteme selbst erstellt werden.

2. Überblick über die eingesetzten Lehrmethoden

Im Folgenden wird eine kurzer Überblick über die Lehrformen gegeben, die im Umfeld von Mercedes-Benz zum Einsatz kommen und daher durch das integrierte System zu unterstützen sind (siehe Abbildung 1).

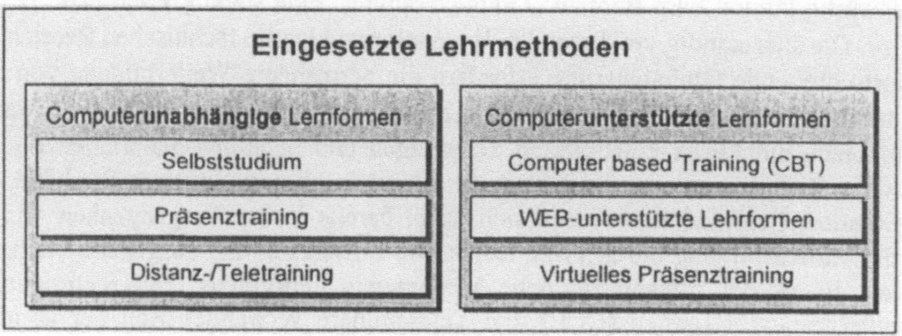

Abbildung 1: Überblick über die eingesetzten Lehrmethoden

2.1 Computerunabhängige Lehrformen

Im Bereich der computerunabhängigen Lehrformen kommt bei DaimlerChrysler neben Selbststudium und klassischem Präsenztraining bereits seit mehreren Jahren Distanz-/Teletraining zum Einsatz.

2.1.1 Selbststudium

Das Selbststudium (oder Selbstlernen) bezeichnet die Vermittlung von Wissen durch verschiedenste Medien wie z.B. Printmedien, Audios oder Videos. Der Lernende bestimmt hierbei i.d.R. Ort, Zeit, Länge und Anordnung der einzelnen Lerneinheiten selbst. Eine Interaktion mit einem Trainer findet nur indirekt, z.B. durch Anleitung zum Selbststudium, durch Wissenskontrolle und Beratung statt.

Das Selbststudium tritt bei Mercedes-Benz in verschiedenen Formen auf: Mittels Printmedien werden Teilnehmer von Lehrgängen durch die Vermittlung oder Auffrischung von Grundlagen auf einen gemeinsamen Wissenstand vor Lehrgangsbeginn gebracht. Durch Videos, welche jedoch nur in geringem Umfang vorhanden sind, können die Mitarbeiter ihr Fachwissen vertiefen oder sich auf Präsenztrainings vorbereiten.

Eine weitere Form stellt DCTV (DaimlerChrysler TV), eine konzerninterner Fernsehsender, dar. Über diesen werden Informationen über das Unternehmen und dessen Produkte und Dienstleistungen vermittelt.

2.1.2 Präsenztraining

Das Präsenztraining (oft auch „face-to-face training" genannt) stellt, neben dem Selbstlernen durch Printmedien, eine weitere „klassische" Lehrmethode dar. Während eines solchen Trainings kann der Trainer den anwesenden Lernenden sowohl theoretisches Wissen als auch praktische Fertigkeiten vermitteln. Die Inhalte können hierbei den Teilnehmern in unterschiedlichen Formen (Theorieunterricht, praktische Übung, Seminar usw.) und unter Verwendung verschiedenster Medien (wie z.B. Audio, Video, Printmedien) vermittelt werden. Ein wesentliches Merkmal des Präsenztrainings ist die Interaktionsmöglichkeit mit dem Trainer: Der Lernende (als einzelner oder als Gruppe) kann Einfluss auf den Ablauf der Lehreinheit nehmen, indem er z.B. Fragen stellt oder dem Trainer aktiv oder passiv Feedback gibt. Durch diese Interaktion kann die Wissensvermittlung individualisiert und dadurch der Lernprozess für den Lernenden effektiver gestaltet werden.

Ein weiterer, wichtiger Aspekt des Präsenztrainings ist die des Gruppenprozesses und der daraus resultierenden Effekte für den Lernprozess. Der direkte Kontakt der Teilnehmer untereinander ermöglicht Erfahrungsaustausch und Wissensvermittlung untereinander. Das Wissen der Gruppenmitglieder über die individuellen Neigungen und Fähigkeiten der einzelnen Teilnehmer lassen sie zu Ansprechpartnern für spezielle Fragen zu diesen Wissensgebieten werden. So können gezielt Kenntnislücken durch die Interaktion in der Lerngruppe geschlossen werden.

2.1.3   Distanztraining oder Teletraining

Als Distanztraining (oder auch „distance learning", DL) werden hier Lehrformen bezeichnet, welche die Vermittlung von Wissen durch einen Trainer über eine räumliche Distanz hinweg realisieren. Im Gegensatz zum Präsenztraining ist hier nicht gewährleistet, dass der Lernende weitere Teilnehmer wahrnehmen und mit diesen kommunizieren kann. Jedoch kann er mit dem Trainer in Interaktion treten und ggf. den Ablauf der Trainingseinheit beeinflussen. Dieses Merkmal unterscheidet diese Lehrformen vom einem Selbststudium, bei dem lediglich die Medien (evtl. zu festgelegten Sendeterminen) distribuiert werden bzw. das Selbststudium in einer Gruppe stattfindet.

Als Teletraining bezeichnet man i.d.R. ein Distanztraining, in dem ein Trainer unter Verwendung einer Audio- oder Videoübertragung Wissen vermittelt. Diese können beispielsweise über private oder öffentliche Radio- oder Fernsehübertragung realisiert werden. Diese Lehrform erzeugt eine gewisse Ortsunabhängigkeit, jedoch ist sie nicht zeitunabhängig, da die Übertragungszeiten wahrgenommen werden müssen. Der Lernende kann dabei entweder durch gezielte Interaktion oder Fragen zum Inhalt Einfluss auf den Ablauf der Lehreinheit nehmen.

Mit AKUBIS steht Mercedes-Benz seit mehreren Jahren ein solches Teletraining-System zur Verfügung. Durch dieses System wird europaweit ein siebensprachiges Programm per Satellit ausgestrahlt. Speziell eingerichtete Empfangsräume für ca. 20 Personen sind durch die Bündelung von 16 ISDN-Kanälen audiovisuell mit dem Sendezentrum verbunden und dadurch in der Lage, (Zwischen-) Fragen zu stellen oder evtl. den Ablauf zu ändern.

2.2   Computerunterstützte Lehrformen

Der Begriff des Computerunterstützten Lernens (CUL) bzw. des computer based trainings (CBT) beschreibt als Sammelbegriff alle Lernsituationen und -arrangements, bei denen der Computer als zentrales Hilfsmittel im Lehr- und Lernprozess eingesetzt wird. So definiert das IEEE LTSC:

> *computer-based training (CBT): 1) The use of computers to provide an interactive instructional experience. 2) In CMI, the use of instructional programs (also referred to as lessons) that are controlled by a CMI system.* [Glossary00]

Wobei der in der zweiten Alternative genannte Begriff „CMI" (computer managed instruction) hierbei den Einsatz von Computern bzw. Softwaresystemen für das Management des gesamten Lernprozesses bezeichnet, inkl. Nutzer- und Ressourcenverwaltung, sowie Lernerfolgskontrolle.

Hier wird der Begriff des computer based trainings (CBT) jedoch in Anlehnung an die Verwendung innerhalb Mercedes-Benz (und ähnlich zur zweiten Alternative aus der oben aufgeführten Definition) für eine Form des CUL verwendet, bei der eine Softwareapplikation eine Wissensvermittlung durchführt. Abweichend von o.g. Definition ist dabei jedoch die Kontrolle durch ein CMI-System optional.

CUL stellt in diesem Zusammenhang keine Lehrform im eigentlichen Sinne dar. Sie ist als computerunterstützte Variante des Selbststudiums oder des Distanztrainings zu sehen. In diesem Zusammenhang wird sie jedoch mit allen anderen computerabhängigen und –unabhängigen Lehrformen unter diesem Begriff subsummiert werden.

Der Einsatz von CUL im Selbststudium nimmt durch die Möglichkeit zur „Pseudointeraktion" eine besondere Stellung ein. Der Begriff der Pseudointeraktivität wird hier verwendet, da es sich bei der Interaktion des Lernenden mit einer Software nicht um eine Interaktion mit dem Trainer im Sinne des „klassischen" Lehrprozesses handelt. Der Autor der Lernsoftware kann beispielsweise mehrere alternative Lehrpfade anbieten oder den Ablauf der Lehreinheiten von den Reaktionen des Lernenden abhängig machen, jedoch sind dies i.d.R. vorgegebene und limitierte Alternativen, welche zum Zeitpunkt der Erstellung definiert werden müssen. Eine individuelle, didaktische und auf Lehrerfahrung basierende Reaktion der Lernsoftware ist momentan (wenn überhaupt) lediglich von speziellen Expertensystemen zu erwarten, welche in diesem Zusammenhang nicht zur Verfügung stehen. Jedoch umfasst der Sammelbegriff des Distanztrainings (bzw. der des distance learning) im Bereich des computerunterstützten Lernens auch diese Pseudointeraktivität, falls sie über ein Netzwerk kommuniziert wird: Der Begriff des „Trainers" ist dabei nicht auf eine Person beschränkt, sondern kann auch durch eine Softwareapplikation repräsentiert werden. So definiert das IEEE LTSC:

> *distance learning: A form of learning in which a learner communicates with a learning technology system or teacher via a network.* [Glossary00]

2.2.1 Computer based Training (CBT)

CBTs stellen im Umfeld und der Begriffsverwendung von Mercedes-Benz computerbasierte Medien für das Selbststudium dar. Sie sind i.d.R. als eigenständige, d.h. abgesehen vom erforderlichen Betriebssystem ohne zusätzliche Software ausführbare Applikationen auf kostengünstigen Tertiärspeichern wie z.B. CD-ROM oder DVD verfügbar. CBTs zeichnen sich oft durch den hohen Umfang an enthaltenen Medien wie Animationen, Audios, Videos usw. aus, welche sie für den Prozess der Wissensvermittlung besonders interessant machen. Der Datenaustausch mit spezieller Managementsoftware erlaubt das Erfassen und Verarbeiten von Daten über den Lernenden und dessen Interaktion mit der Lernsoftware, und damit die Überwachung und Auswertung des Lernfortschritts, sowie die Anpassung des Lernablaufs.

Für die Verkaufsniederlassungen von Mercedes-Benz steht ein produkt- und zielgruppenspezifisches eingeteiltes Angebot an CBTs für Schulungszwecke zur Verfügung, welches sie in verschiedenen Abonnements oder per Einzelanforderung auf CD-ROM beziehen können.

2.2.2 Web-unterstützte Lehrformen

Web-unterstützte Lehrformen stellen eine Sonderform des CUL dar und bezeichnen alle Internet- und Browser-basierenden Formen des computerunterstützten Selbststudiums oder Distanztrainings. Während jedoch beim web-basierten Selbststudium lediglich der Lerninhalt über das Internet übertragen und durch einen Browser dargestellt wird, erweitert die Nutzung des Internets die Möglichkeiten im Bereich des Distanztrainings maßgeblich.

Analog zur Verwendung des Begriffs CBT wurde der gebräuchliche Begriff „WBT (web-based training) für diese Lehrform übernommen: Er bezieht sich hier auf Lernmaterial, welches über das WWW verbreitet wird und darüber hinaus mit einem Managementsystem zum Austausch von Lerner- und Lernfortschrittsdaten kommuniziert.

In ihrer Grundform werden die Inhalte eines WBTs als HTML-Dokumente modelliert und können daher die unterschiedlichsten Medien (wie z.B. Bild, Text usw., siehe [HTML99]) beinhalten. Weiterhin ist der Einsatz von Skriptsprachen (wie z.B. ECMAScript [ECMA99], besser bekannt als JavaScript oder JScript) zur Generierung von dynamischen Inhalten möglich. Diese multimedialen Dokumente werden mittels des HTTP-Protokolls (Hypertext transfer protocol, siehe [HTTP99]) von einem sog. HTTP-Server zum anfragenden Klienten übertragen. Auf der Klientenseite ist zur Darstellung dieser Lehreinheiten (abgesehen vom Betriebssystem und der Internet-Anbindung) lediglich eine sog. Browsersoftware zur Darstellung des Dokumentes erforderlich. Unter Zuhilfenahme verschiedener Zusatzapplikationen, sog. Plug-Ins kann die Anzahl der durch den Browser darstellbaren Medien (um Animationen, VR-Modelle Medienströme usw.) erweitert werden.

Als herausragender Vorteil gegenüber den CBTs ist die Verfügbarkeit der WBTs über das Internet zu nennen: Nach ihrer Erstellung und Publikation können die einzelnen Lehreinheiten ohne weitere Verzögerung weltweit über Standardsoftware abgerufen und dargestellt werden. Weiterhin können über diese Netzanbindung Informationen über den Lernenden, dessen Lernweg und seinen Lernerfolg übertragen und zentral gespeichert bzw. verarbeitet werden. Nachteilig gegenüber den CBTs ist jedoch der mengenmäßig oft geringere Medienanteil, da die Übertragung von vergleichbare Datenmengen zu unerwünscht hohen Downloadzeiten bzw. Leitungsbelastungen führen würden.

Resultiert die Kommunikation der Lernfortschrittsdaten mit einem Dienst über das Internet in eine alternative Abfolge der Lerneinheiten, so entspricht diese Lehrform einem (internet-basierten) Distanztraining. Werden die Daten jedoch nur über das Netzwerk erfasst und es erfolgt keine Reaktion (über das Netzwerk), entspricht sie dem Selbststudium.

2.2.3 Virtuelles Präsenztraining

Als virtuelles Präsenztraining wird im Folgenden eine netzwerk- und computergestützte Form des Distanztrainings bezeichnet. Sie wird als „virtuell" bezeichnet, da sie nicht nur die Kriterien eines Distanztrainings erfüllt, sondern darüber hinaus einerseits die Interaktion mit einer Person als Trainer und andererseits die Wahrnehmung weiterer Teilnehmer erlaubt und deren Kommunikation mit- und untereinander ermöglicht. Daher ist sie in der Lage, den oben beschriebenen Gruppenprozess des Präsenztrainings, wenn auch eingeschränkt, zu ermöglichen.

In diesem Zusammenhang wird auch oft der Begriff des „virtuellen Klassenzimmers" verwendet. Er bezeichnet die Bündelung der verschiedenen Applikationen, welche die Durchführung der virtuellen Präsenzseminare ermöglichen. Sie realisieren die benötigten Dienste der Kommunikationen, der Präsentation der Lehrinhalte und die der virtuellen Präsenz.

3. Anforderungen an die Architektur

Für eine integrierte Systemarchitektur ergeben sich eine Reihe von Anforderungen. Im vorliegenden Umfeld sind dabei nicht nur funktionale Aspekte von Bedeutung, sondern auch eine Reihe nicht-funktionaler Anforderungen.

3.1 Nichtfunktionale Anforderungen

Eine der bestimmenden Anforderungen an die Architektur des Gesamtsystems ist (neben den funktionalen Anforderungen) die weitgehende Verwendung kommerzieller Standardsoftware zur Kostenreduzierung sowie die Erweiterbarkeit und die Skalierbarkeit des Systems. Letztere Punkte sollen vor allem durch Verwendung sog. „offener" Standards und Systeme erreicht werden. Die Vorgabe, einen größtmöglichen Einsatz kommerzieller Standardsoftware im Architekturprozess zu berücksichtigen, hat einen tiefgreifenden Einfluss auf diesen Prozess und wandelt ihn von einem Architekturprozess in einen Integrations- bzw. Kompositionsprozess (vgl. [Clements95] und [Vigder96]).

3.1.2 Einfluss kommerzieller Standardsoftware

Der Begriff „kommerzielle Standardsoftware" (oft auch als „COTS-Software" bezeichnet, wobei „COTS" für „commercial off-the-shelf" steht) bezeichnet eine Software, welche von einer kommerziell tätigen Einrichtung (d.h. einem Unternehmen) aus kommerziellen Gründen für die Öffentlichkeit (d.h. für den Markt) entwickelt und an den Markt gebracht wurde.

Die Verwendung von solchen kommerziellen Komponenten als Komplettlösung oder als Subsysteme komplexer Architekturen erfreut sich seit Anfang bzw. Mitte der 90er Jahre einer steigenden Beliebtheit. Die dadurch etablierten Systeme werden (je nach dem Einsatz dieser Komponenten) als „COTS-Lösung" oder „buy-and-adapt system" (wenn es auf einem Produkt basiert) bzw. als „COTS-integriertes" System oder „component integration" (wenn es mehrere heterogene Produkte integriert) bezeichnet (vgl. [Carney99] bzw. [Vigder96]).

Für die Verwendung von kommerziell verfügbaren Komponenten in einem System spricht eine Reihe von Vorteilen, welche maßgeblich zur Verbreitung dieser Praxis beigetragen haben. Auf die oftmals aufgeführten Gründe für die Verwendung von COTS-Software, deren Eigenschaften und die damit verbundenen Nachteile wird hier jedoch nicht eingegangen. Diese sind ausführlich in [Clements95], [Dean97], [Stavridou], [Kachmarik], [Vigder96] und [Vigder98] beschrieben. Deren Einfluss auf den Entwicklungsprozess sind hier aus Platzgründen lediglich in Stichpunkten in Abbildung 2 wiedergegeben.

Die Analyse muss abstrakt und flexibel genug gehalten werden, um eine Auswahl an COTS-Produkten als Komponenten zuzulassen. Die Detaillierung der Analyse erfolgt gemeinsam mit der Evaluation der COTS-Kandidaten. Dabei muss neben der Abdeckung der funktionalen Anforderungen auch die Anpassbarkeit/Integrierbarkeit der Komponenten berücksichtigt werden. Die Design und Implementierungsphase befaßt

Abbildung 2: Veränderter Entwicklungsprozess beim Einsatz von COTS-Komponenten

sich zu einem großen Teil mit der Anpassung und Integration der Komponenten. Beim Einsatz ist u.U. Tausch bzw. Update der verwendeten Komponenten erforderlich.

Abschließend ist anzumerken, dass die Verwendung kommerziell verfügbarer Komponenten hauptsächlich aus Gründen der Kostenreduzierung entschieden wird. Diese Reduktion der Kosten tritt jedoch nur dann auf, wenn die Möglichkeiten und Beschränkungen des eingesetzten Produkt (abgesehen von minimalen Anpassungen) akzeptiert werden (vgl. [Vigder96]). Müssen jedoch (wenn überhaupt möglich) aufwändige Änderungen am Produkt vorgenommen werden, und das ggf. wiederholt an jedem Update des Produkts, kann dieser Vorteil nicht genutzt werden. Daher sind die Funktionalitäten und Schnittstellen dieser Produkte i.d.R. als gegebene Faktoren anzunehmen, und nicht als Variablen, welche beliebig modifiziert werden können [Carney99]. Wird dieser Aspekt nicht beachtet und die Software modifiziert, kann diese ggf. nicht mehr als eine COTS-Software angesehen werden (vgl. [Dean97]).

3.2 Funktionale Anforderungen der Architektur

Die resultierende Architektur soll es dem Benutzer ermöglichen, von einem beliebigen Computerarbeitsplatz mit Anbindung an das Internet bzw. Intranet aus der ihm zur Verfügung stehenden Auswahl an Lehrangeboten auszuwählen bzw. die für ihn vorgeschriebenen oder empfohlenen Kurse zu belegen. Im einzelnen soll er seine Teilnahme an Seminaren anmelden, WBT- und CBT-Kurse wahrnehmen, Printmedien anfordern oder als Ausdruck erstellen, an (Live-)Übertragungen, Teleseminaren (DL) und virtuellen Präsenztrainings teilnehmen können und Informationen über weitere Lehrangebote erhalten. Zusätzlich zu den Lehrangeboten sollen Informations- und Diskussionsforen zur Verfügung stehen, welche den Austausch über einzelne Sachfragen einerseits mit anderen Mitarbeitern, andererseits auch mit Ausbildern und Experten ermöglichen. Weiterhin soll er Einfluss auf seinen individuellen Lehrplan nehmen können, indem er weitere Ausbildungsmöglichkeiten wahrnimmt und dadurch seine Karriereplanung unterstützt. Die Übertragungen der Sendungen von DCTV sollen ebenfalls live zu verfolgen sein. Seinem individuellen Lerninteresse soll der Benutzer durch verschiedene Suchmöglichkeiten über den Datenbestand nachkommen können. Dadurch kann er Lehrmedien außerhalb der Einbettung in komplette Kurse betrachten und somit gezielt eigene Informationslücken ausfüllen.

Ausbilder und Personalverantwortliche sollen von einem solchen Arbeitsplatz aus Lehrpläne zusammenstellen können. Im einzelnen soll dabei für bestimmte Zielgruppen (wie z.B. Vertrieb oder Service) aber auch für einen individuellen Mitarbeiter ein Lehrplan als empfohlener oder vorgeschriebener Ablauf von Lehr- und Testeinheiten erstellt werden können. Die Teilnahme an den Angeboten und der Erfolg bei den einzelnen Tests werden im Benutzerprofil hinterlegt und dienen der persönlichen Fortschrittskontrolle des Lernenden und geben ihm eine Übersicht über seine individuelle Qualifikationsentwicklung. Ggf. könnten diese Daten (auch anonymisiert) Ausbildern und Personalverantwortlichen einen Einblick in den Stand der Weiterbildung und den Erfolg der Lehrmethoden bieten.

Autoren von Lehrmaterialien sollen von einem solchen Arbeitsplatz aus über die Verwaltungsschnittstelle des Medienservers (Lern-)Medien dem System hinzufügen und diese Medien zu neuen Lehreinheiten zusammenführen können. Dabei werden sie durch die Möglichkeit unterstützt, eine Suche über den gesamten Bestand an Medien durch verschiedene Methoden (Kategorien, Stichwort usw.) durchzuführen.

Die über DCTV ausgestrahlten Sendungen sollen weitgehend automatisiert in den Medienserver als Datenbestand einfließen. Im Gegenzug dazu sollen die durch den Medienserver verwalteten Medienobjekte direkt und indirekt zur Ausstrahlung über die genannten Systeme bereitstehen (Back-End System).

3.3 Umfeld

In der Evaluation befindet sich momentan einerseits ein Lernmanagementsystem (Saba EMS, siehe [SABA00]) zur Verwaltung von Lehrmaterialien (Printmedien, WBTs, CBTs usw.), Ausbildungsressourcen (wie z.B. Seminarräume und deren Ausstattung) und Lernprozessdaten (Benutzerprofile, Lehrpläne und –ziele, Teilnahme an Lehrangeboten, Testergebnisse usw.), in welches ein WBT-Playout-System und virtuelle Klassenraum-Komponenten integriert sind. Andererseits wird ein weiteres Playout- und Authoring-System für WBTs inkl. Benutzermanagement (Lotus LearningSpace Version 4, siehe [Lotus00]) evaluiert. Daneben existiert ein Medienspeicherungs- und zugriffssystem ("Medienserver") zur zentralen Verwaltung, Bearbeitung und Wiedergabe von Medienobjekten und deren Metadaten. Neue CBT-Produktionen werden derzeit im Designprozess "web-fähig" produziert, um in Zukunft als WBT beziehungsweise Bestandteil von DL-Kursen angeboten werden zu können.

Weitere Bemühungen sind auf die Integration der bereits vorhandenen und der sich in Entwicklung befindenden Lehrmethoden gerichtet und sollen in einer Architektur des Gesamtsystems resultieren, welche die Integration aller beteiligten Systeme ermöglicht und spezifischen Anforderungen genügt.

Zur inhaltlichen Integration der Lerninhalte und der Medien ist der Einsatz von Metadaten unerlässlich. Zur Zeit werden hierfür geeignete Metadatenelemente ausgewählt und die Möglichkeiten ihrer automatischen und manuellen Erstellung geprüft.

4. Architektur

Die Metaarchitektur beinhaltet als Richtlinien für das Design vor allem das Drei-Schichten-Modell, d.h. die Trennung in Benutzerschnittstelle, Prozessmanagement und Daten(bank)management [Clements97]. Die Funktionalität des Gesamtsystems wird einzelnen Komponenten durch Verantwortlichkeiten zugeordnet und durch Interaktion dieser Komponenten gewährleistet. Eine Abbildung auf Standards wie z.B. LTSA (Learning Technologies System Architecture, siehe [LTSA99]) wird in einem weiteren Schritt vorgenommen, um die konzeptionelle Architektur vergleichbar mit anderen Systemen zu halten.

Die konzeptionelle Architektur [HP00] beinhaltet als Teilsysteme Komponenten wie Medienserver, WBT-Playout-System, virtuelle Klassenzimmerkomponenten, Kommunikationsdienste und ein Lerner- und Lernmanagement-System, sowie weitere, zur Integration erforderliche Komponenten (siehe Abb. 3).

Die logische Architektur bzw. Ausführungsumgebung enthält die kommerziellen Produkte, die sich parallel zum Architekturprozess in der Komponentenevaluation befinden. Funktionen und Verantwortlichkeiten, die nicht durch diese Produkte abgedeckt werden können, werden neuen, noch zu entwickelnden Komponenten zugeordnet. Diese Komponenten werden zu einem Gesamtsystem zusammengefügt, wobei für die kommerziellen Produkte ggf. Wrapper- und Gluecode zur Anpassung bzw. Austauschbarkeit spezifiziert werden müssen. Die Schnittstellen der einzelnen Komponenten werden definiert sowie das Laufzeitverhalten beschrieben. Ggf. müssen die kommerziellen Komponenten zum Teil erweitert oder angepasst werden. Dies sollte jedoch möglichst vermieden werden, da in der Wartungsphase deren Austausch durch neuere Produktversionen ohne zusätzlichen Aufwand vorzunehmen sein sollte.

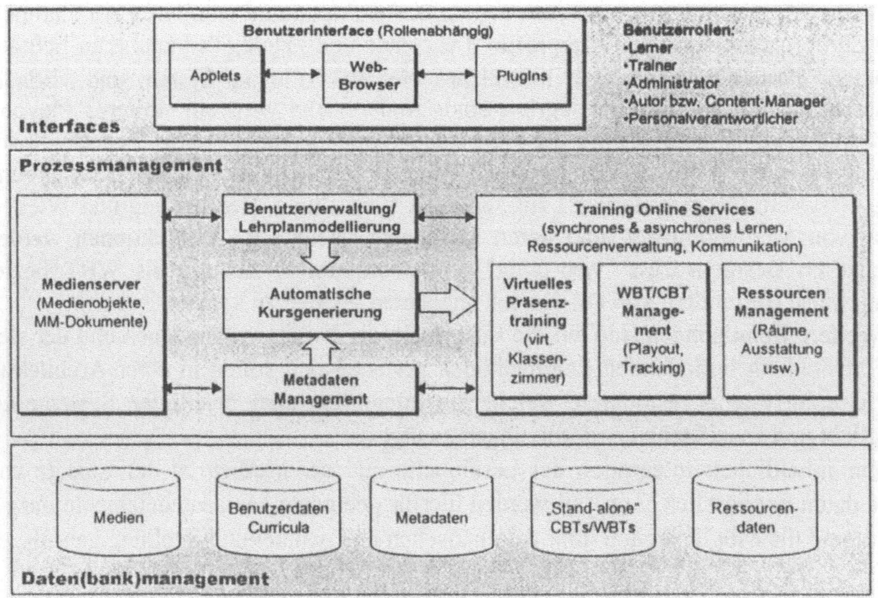

Abbildung. 3. Architektur des integrierten Lernsystems (3-Ebenen-Architektur)

Die inhaltliche Integration der einzelnen Medien wird über geeignete Metadaten vollzogen. Diese Daten über die Mediendaten stellen nicht nur eine Identifikation und weitere Informationen über die Medien zur Verfügung, sondern modellieren ebenfalls die Beziehung zu anderen Medien und erlauben die Einordnung in einen pädagogischen Kontext. Sie stellen daher einen zentralen Ausgangspunkt für Suche, Verwaltung, Komposition und Erstellung von Kursteilen und Komplettkursen dar. Die Eignung von LOM (Learning Objects Metadata, [LOM00]) als Ausgangsbasis für die Auswahl der einzelnen Datenelemente wird momentan untersucht. Zudem sind die verschiedenen Möglichkeiten zur automatischen Generierung von Metadaten für die Lernobjekte sowie die semiautomatische Zuweisung von Metadaten, beispielsweise durch Kategorisierung, von Interesse.

5. Umsetzung

Der Medienserver besteht momentan aus mehreren Informationssystemen (HTTP-Server, Videoserver, RealServer und relationale Datenbank), welche über eine zusätzliche Applikationsschicht auf Basis von Java Enterprice Beans angesprochen wird. Dem Benutzer wird die darüber gebündelte Funktionalität zum einen durch ein Web-Interface unter zu Hilfenahme von Java-Applets zur Verfügung gestellt. Die Funktionalität umfasst das Datenmanagement sowie die Abfrage bzw. Wiedergabe der einzelnen Medien durch die verschiedenen Serversysteme über geeignete, z.B. HTML-Dokumente per http, Video als Ströme per RTSP/RTP usw. Dies erlaubt die Erstellung multimedialer Präsentationen bzw. Schulungsmaterialien, deren gesamter Inhalt durch den Medienserver verwaltet wird. Dadurch wird das zentrale Management der Medien und ihre Wiederverwendbarkeit in verschiedenen Granularitäten ermöglicht. Für die Übertragung multimedialer Lerninhalte , insbesondere von Videoströmen, ist die Berücksichtigung der QoS-Anforderungen durch das System von Bedeutung (siehe [MeEbe99],[EbRu99]).

Neben der graphischen Benutzeroberfläche zum Medienserver ist der Applikationsserver über eine Backend-Schnittstelle mit den restlichen Komponenten der Gesamtarchitektur gekoppelt.

Für das Distance Learning System wurde ein Feldtest durchgeführt, welcher wesentlich durch LearningSpace Version 4 (Lotus) realisiert wurde und Teil der Komponentenevaluation und der Anforderungsanalyse ist. Zur Realisierung der Benutzer- und Ressourcenverwaltung, sowie für das Portal für die Benutzer ist der Einsatz von Saba EMS vorgesehen.

Einer der ersten Schritte wird die Einrichtung eines WBT-Playout- und Managementsystems sowie die Integration des Medienserver darstellen, in welchem der Lehrinhalt der einzelnen Kurse durch den Medienserver verwaltet und zur Verfügung gestellt wird. Das Lernmanagement-System operiert daher als Verwaltungssystem unabhängig von den Inhalten, während die einzelnen Lerninhalte und Medien unabhängig von ihrer Verwendung in verschiedenen Lerneinheiten bearbeitet und verwaltet werden können. Interaktionsdaten wie z.B. Testergebnisse und Fortschrittsindikatoren werden durch Mechanismen des User-Trackings über Standards wie z.B. die der AICC (Aviation Industry CBT Commitee, vgl. [AICC99]) von den Lernobjekten und deren Kompositionen bzw. den Präsentationssystemen an die Benutzerverwaltung kommuniziert.

Die weitere Entwicklung wird sich als Integrationsschritt in Richtung eines Lernportals bewegen, über welches der Benutzer Zugriff auf sämtliche Lehrformen erhält und weitere Informations- und Kommunikationsdienste zur Verfügung stehen. Gemäß den oben vorgestellten Zielen kann er dann beispielsweise nicht nur spezielle WBT- bzw. CBT-Kurse belegen, sondern sich auch für den Besuch von Präsenztrainings anmelden, Printmedien anfordern usw.

In einem weiteren Schritt soll dann über die inhaltliche Integration durch Metadaten die „dynamische" Suche und Zusammenstellung von Kursmaterialien unterstützt werden. Sie soll dem Kursautor bzw. –designer eine Rechercheschnittstelle bereitstellen, über welche er die in Frage kommenden Materialien aus dem Medienpool extrahiert kann.

6. Ausblick

Die hier dargestellten Systeme und Lösungsansätze sind als "work in progress" zu verstehen. Derzeit wird an der konkreten Architektur zur Integration aller Komponenten gearbeitet.

Als Fernziel einer integrierten Architektur ist der Einsatz einer Subkomponente zur (teil-) automatischen Generierung von Kursen geplant. Diese Komponente verwendet zum einen das Benutzerprofil, welches die Präferenzen des Nutzers sowie dessen Vorkenntnisse/Historie beschreibt. Zum anderen werden die Metadaten der Lernmedien und Teilkurse eingesetzt. Für die Generierung der Kurse sind dabei auch die Abhängigkeiten zwischen den Teilkursen/Medien von besonderer Bedeutung. Durch die Nutzer-Präferenzen kann unterschiedlichen Benutzern vergleichbares Wissen in unterschiedlicher Form und Zusammensetzung angeboten werden. Die Präferenzen könnten entweder durch den Benutzer selbst oder einen Trainer manuell in das System eingegeben werden, oder automatisch durch die Erfahrung des Systems mit dem jeweiligen Benutzer und seiner Akzeptanz verschiedener Präsentationsformen oder Lehrmethoden (z.B. messbar durch den Lernerfolg oder die Bearbeitungszeit) generiert werden.

In einer weiteren Ausbaustufe wird die Ablage der DCTV-Sendungen in Verbindung mit der automatischen Generierung von Annotationen und Metadaten durch Sprach- bzw. Sprechererkennung sowie durch Personen- oder Schnitterkennung basierend auf Bildinhaltsanalyse realisiert werden. Durch solche Technologien kann die automatische Generierung von Metadaten wie z.B. Schlagwörter oder Szeneneinteilung für beliebig lange Videosequenzen realisiert werden.

Referenzen

[AICC99] AICC CMI Subcommittee: CMI Guidelines for Interoperability (Document No. CMI001), Sugar City, 1999

[Carney99] David Carney: COTS Product Evaluation and System Design, in The COTS Spot Volume 2 Issue 1, SEI Interactive, Carnegie Mellon Software Engineering Institute, Pittsburgh 1999

[Clements95] Paul C. Clements: From Subroutines to Subsystems: Component-Based Software Development, erschienen in "Component-Based Software Engineering: Selected Papers from the Software Engineering Institute", IEEE Computer Society Press, Los Alamitos, CA 1996 und in "The American Programmer, vol. 8, no. 11", 1995

[Clements97] Paul Clements, Frank Rogers: Three Tier Software Architectures, Carnegie Mellon Software Engineering Institute, 1997

[Dean97] John C. Dean, Mark R. Vigder: System Implementation Using Off-the-shelf Software. In Proceedings of the 9th Annual Software Technology Conference, Department of Defense, 1997

[EbRu99] R. Eberhardt and C. Rueß, "Eine Dienstgüteabbildungs- und –steuerungsarchitektur zur Gewährleistung unterschiedlicher Dienstgüteklassen für Ferntraining und –lernen, Kommunikation in Verteilten Systemen (KiVS '99), TU Darmstadt, 1999.

[ECMA99] ECMA - Standardizing Information and Communication Systems: Standard ECMA-262, Genf 1999

[Glossary00] IEEE LTSC Glossary Working Group P1484.3: Draft Standard for the Learning Technology Glossary, New York 2000

[HP00] Hewlett Packard: Architecting Process Overview, http://www.architecture.external.hp.com/Overview/arch_how_software.htm, 7/2000

[HTML99] W3C: HTML 4.01 Specification, W3C Recommendation, http://www.w3.org/TR/html4/, 1999

[HTTP99] W3C: Hypertext Transfer Protocol -- HTTP/1.1, RFC2616, W3C, http://www.w3.org/Protocols/rfc2616/rfc2616.html, 1999

[Kachmarik] Michael B. Kachmarik: Commercial-off-the-Shelf (COTS) Products -- An Appropriate Strategy for Reuse in the Development of Object Oriented Systems, Endicott Johnson Corporation, Binghamton

[LOM00] Learning Technology Standardization Committee: Draft Standard for Learning Object Metadata, New York 2000

[Lotus00] Lotus: Learning Space 4.0, http://www.lotus.com/home.nsf/welcome/learnspace, 7/2000

[LTSA99] Frank Farance, Joshua Tonkel: Learning Technology Systems Architecture, Draft 5, http://edutool.com/ltsa, 1999

[Man99] Peter Manhart, Johannes Bumiller: Collaborative Web-based Learning in Organizations, WebNet'99, Honolulu, Hawaii, November 1999

[MeEbe99] J. Metzler and R. Eberhardt, "Video Distribution over Intranets in a Telelearning Scenario," Proc. of ICCC'99, Tokyo, Japan, 1999.

[SABA00] SABA: Connecting People to Learning, http://www.saba.com/english/index.htm, 7/2000

[Stavridou] Victoria Stavridou: COTS, Integration and critical systems, Queen Mary and Westfield College, Department of Computer Science, London

[Vigder96] Mark R. Vigder, W. Morven Gentleman, John Dean: COTS Software Integration: State of the art, National Research Council Canada, Institute for Information Technologie, 1996

[Vigder98] Mark R. Vigder: An Architecture for COTS Based Software Systems, NRC Report No. 41603, National Research Council of Canada, 1998

Fehlertolerante Videokommunikation über verlustbehaftete Paketvermittlungsnetze[1]

K. Heidtmann, J. Kerse, T. Suchanek, B. Wolfinger, M. Zaddach

Arbeitsgruppe Telekommunikation und Rechnernetze, Fachbereich Informatik,
Universität Hamburg, Vogt-Kölln-Str. 30, D 22527 Hamburg
heidtmann@informatik.uni-hamburg.de

Kurzfassung Verlustbehaftete Paketvermittlungsnetze besitzen eine Reihe von Unzulänglichkeiten bei der Datenübertragung, deren Folgen für die Videokommunikation gemäß der H.26x- und MPEG-Normen wir aufzeigen. Dabei wird ein Modell entwickelt, das die Fehlerakkumulation reflektiert, die dadurch entsteht, daß Bilder aus Gründen der Datenreduktion lediglich als Differenz zu anderen ähnlichen Bildern codiert werden. Dieses Modell dient als Grundlage für ein neu entwickeltes Fehlertoleranzverfahren, bei dem intracodierte Bildinformationen in gemäß dem Modell berechneten Abständen über mehrere Bilder verteilt gesendet werden. Neben diesem senderseitigen Verfahren werden mehrere vom Empfängerendsystem auszuführende Fehlertoleranzmaßnahmen untersucht. In beiden Fällen werden die erzielten Qualitätsverbesserungen sowohl quantifiziert als auch für eine subjektive Qualitätsbewertung illustriert.

1. Einleitung

Moderne Kommunikationssysteme müssen aufgrund der allgemeinen Digitalisierung und der dadurch möglichen Dienstintegration einem zunehmend breiteren Anforderungsprofil gerecht werden. Insbesondere im multimedialen Kontext müssen neben diskreten auch kontinuierliche Medien unterstützt werden, wobei applikations- und benutzerspezifische Anforderungen in Form von Kriterien zu erfüllen sind, die als Dienstgüte bezeichnet werden. Beispielsweise soll bei einer Sprach- oder Bewegtbildübertragung in Echtzeit der zu übertragende Datenstrom nicht wesentlich verzögert und verformt werden. Verzögerungen, Verzögerungsschwankungen oder Paketverluste in nicht echtzeitorientierten oder entsprechend belasteten Rechnernetzen führen jedoch zu einer unzureichenden Dienstgüte und infolgedessen zu erheblichen Einbußen der Sprach- bzw. Bildqualität beim Empfänger.

Aus Gründen der Komplexitätsreduktion, dem Wunsch nach kostengünstiger Kommunikation oder infolge der Verwendung drahtloser Übertragungswege sind die meisten der gegenwärtig existierenden Kommunikationsnetze (wie das Internet oder Mobilkommunikationsnetze) fehler- und verlustbehaftet und häufig nicht in der Lage, a priori vorgegebene maximale Verzögerungszeiten bei der Übertragung einzuhalten. Man spricht hier von "best-effort"-Netzen, die ihre Kommunikationsdienste so gut

[1] Die Untersuchungen dieses Beitrags wurden auf von der Firma *Sun Microsystems* im Rahmen eines *Academic Eqiupment Grant* (AEG) zur Verfügung gestellten Geräten durchgeführt.

wie gerade möglich realisieren, und dies kann auch sehr schlecht sein. Bei traditioneller Datenkommunikation war die Verwendung dieser Kommunikationsnetze eher unproblematisch, da z.B. bei Datenverlust die Übertragung wiederholt werden konnte. Wiederholungen sind aufgrund der zeitlichen Einschränkungen bei der Echtzeitkommunikation kein geeigneter Mechanismus zum Erhalt der guten Sprach- oder Bildqualität, da die wiederholt übertragenen Dateneinheiten in der Regel zu spät beim Empfänger ankommen würden. Somit ist der einfache "best-effort"-Dienst der meisten paketvermittelten Netze für die neuen multimedialen Anwendungen ungeeignet, solange keine weiteren Verbesserungsmaßnahmen ergriffen werden. Anwendungen mit Audio- bzw. Videoübertragung unter Echtzeitbedingungen sind u.a. IP-(Sprach-) Telefonie, Bildtelefonie, Teleteaching, Telemedizin, Videoconferencing und sonstige verteilte multimediale Anwendungen.

Die Verbesserungsmaßnahmen, die eine ausreichende Qualität entsprechender verteilter Anwendungen mit Echtzeitanforderungen gewährleisten sollen, lassen sich in *netzinterne* und *netzexterne* Maßnahmen klassifizieren. Netzextern soll in diesem Zusammenhang bedeuten, daß man den "best-effort"-Charakter eines Kommunikationsnetzes akzeptiert und versucht, durch zusätzliche Mechanismen in den Endsystemen die durch das Netz realisierte Übertragungsqualität soweit zu verbessern, daß die Anforderungen von Anwendungen mit Echtzeitkommunikation gleichwohl mit hinreichend hoher Wahrscheinlichlichkeit erfüllt werden. Dazu werden Fehlertoleranzverfahren innerhalb der Anwendung oder unmittelbar vor der Übergabe der Nutzdaten an den Transportdienst (z.B. UDP) eingesetzt, um die Kommunikation innerhalb der verteilten Anwendung vor Unzulänglichkeiten der Dienstgüte des Netzes zu schützen. Bei der sogenannten netzinternen Qualitätsverbesserung wird meist durch Eingriffe in die Netzarchitektur versucht, die Dienstgüte des Netzes selbst zu verbessern. Beispiele dafür sind im Kontext des Internet unter den Abkürzungen IntServ und DiffServ bekannt und beruhen im wesentlichen auf Betriebsmittelreservierung, Überdimensionierung ("fat-dumb-pipe") oder Priorisierung des Datenverkehrs bestimmter Anwendungsklassen. Maßnahmen zur netzinternen Qualitätsverbesserung werden im folgenden nicht weiter behandelt. Gegenstand dieses Beitrags sind ausschließlich netzexterne bzw. anwendungsnahe Fehlertoleranzverfahren zur Qualitätsverbesserung bei Videokommunikation. Es handelt sich dabei um die jüngsten Ergebnisse eines seit geraumer Zeit laufenden Forschungsprojekts der Arbeitsgruppe Telekommunikation und Rechnernetze am Fachbereich Informatik der Universität Hamburg ([Koh99, Suc00, Ker00, WoZ00]; zu früher gewonnenen Resultaten vgl. u.a. [BaW97, Wol97, ASW98, Sie98, HeW99, HKZ99, WZB00]).

Das Hauptziel unseres Beitrags besteht in einer detaillierten Bewertung der Effektivität sowohl sender- als auch empfängerbasierter Fehlertoleranzverfahren bei netzexterner Qualitätsverbesserung im Kontext der H.26x- sowie der MPEG-Normen. Bei der Auswahl der von uns bewerteten Fehlertoleranzverfahren haben wir einerseits aus der Literatur bekannte Verfahren herausgegriffen, jedoch überdies auch selbst entwickelte Verfahren beurteilt, und zwar mittels Qualitätsmaßen, die, zumindest partiell, dem subjektiven Qualitätsempfinden menschlicher Betrachter einer Bewegtbildsequenz Rechnung tragen [Roh00].

Um die Anforderungen an Fehlertoleranzverfahren bei Videokommunikation zu motivieren, zeigen wir zunächst in Abschnitt 2 auf, welche Unzulänglichkeiten sich bei der Erbringung von Datenübertragungsdiensten in Kommunikationsnetzen identifizieren lassen und welche Arten von negativen Auswirkungen eine unzureichende Übertragungsqualität haben kann. Die anhand zahlreicher Videosequenzen beurteilten senderbasierten Fehlertoleranzverfahren werden in Abschnitt 3 spezifiziert und die durch sie erzielte Qualitätsverbesserung bewertet. Abschnitt 4 bezieht sich auf die analysierten empfängerbasierten Verfahren.

2. Ein Modell für die Fehlerakkumulation

Wesentlich für die Qualität der vom Empfängerendsystem dargestellten Bewegtbildsequenzen sind zunächst die Datenverluste, die durch die Übertragung verursacht werden. Dazu gehören zunächst die Datenpakete, die bei der Übertragung, z.B. durch Überläufe von Zwischenspeichern, verloren gehen bzw. verfälscht werden. Hierbei ist zu beachten, daß in manchen Netzen gestörte Datenpakete mit Bitfehlern nicht weiter übertragen werden und damit beim Empfänger als Paketverlust erscheinen. Als neuer wesentlicher Aspekt kommen die Echtzeitanforderungen hinzu. Verluste entstehen somit auch durch das zu späte Eintreffen der Datenpakete beim Empfänger, so daß ihr Präsentationszeitpunkt in der zeitlich festgelegten Aufeinanderfolge der Bilder bereits verstrichen ist und sie somit ebenfalls unbrauchbar sind. Die beiden genannten Phänomene werden im folgenden unter dem Begriff *direkter Verlust* subsumiert.

Aber nicht nur direkte Verluste beeinträchtigen die Qualität des decodierten Videostromes. Es bestehen weitgehende Abhängigkeiten innerhalb einzelner Bildrahmen, den Datenstrukturen, welche die Informationen eines Bildes in geeignet codierter und syntaktisch wohldefinierter Form enthalten. Wird ein Bildrahmen in mehrere Datenpakete segmentiert, so kann aufgrund syntaktischer Abhängigkeiten der Verlust einer Dateneinheit dazu führen, daß weitere Dateneinheiten desselben Bildrahmens nicht mehr interpretiert und somit auch nicht decodiert werden können (*indirekter Verlust*). Daher ist ein wesentlicher Punkt zur Erhöhung der Fehlerrobustheit der Übertragung kontinuierlicher Medien die Segmentierung des Datenstromes in für sich getrennt interpretierbare Dateneinheiten (*Application Level Framing* [ClT90]). Geeignete Einheiten stellen aufgrund ihrer syntaktischen Abgeschlossenheit die Blockgruppen (*Group of Blocks, GOB*) bei H.261/H.263 bzw. die Bildscheiben (*Slices*) bei MPEG dar. Indirekte Verluste können nicht nur durch syntaktische Abhängigkeiten induziert werden: Die gängigen blockbasierten Kompressionsverfahren ziehen ihre Effizienz wesentlich aus der Elimination zeitlicher Redundanz unter Ausnutzung hoher Ähnlichkeiten aufeinanderfolgender Bilder, so daß diese meist nur als Differenz zum vorangehenden Bild codiert werden (vgl. [EfS98, Fro97]). Es lassen sich demnach intracodierte Bilder (I-Bilder), welche ohne einen solchen Bezug codiert werden, und referentiell codierte Bilder (P-Bilder) unterscheiden, welche eben diesen zeitlichen Bezug aufweisen, und in ihrer Kompressionseffizienz deutlich besser sind als die I-Bilder. Dieses hat zur Folge, daß ein Verlust eines Bildes oder eines Bildteiles nicht nur das aktuelle, sondern auch alle folgenden P-Bilder betrifft, die dieses Bild direkt oder indirekt referenzieren. Die Verluste äußern sich als negative Auswirkungen in Form verschiedener Artefakte des vom Empfänger dargestellten Videos. Dazu gehören u.a. falsche Farben, unkorrekte Helligkeitsstufen, Unschärfe sowie das Phänomen, daß Teile früherer Bilder an unpassender Stelle im aktuellen Bild erscheinen.

Im allgemeinen hat ein direkter Verlust eines Datenpaketes somit indirekte Verluste aufgrund inhaltlicher Abhängigkeiten bis zum Eintreffen des nächsten intracodierten Bildes zur Folge. Aus dieser Tatsache läßt sich ein Modell zur Bewertung der Schwere von Verlusten hinsichtlich des decodierten Datenstromes entwickeln. Dazu wird angenommen, daß in einem Abstand von (n-1) Bildern jeweils ein intracodierter Bildrahmen zur Elimination von Fehlern codiert wird. Man spricht auch von einer Bildgruppe, die aus einem eröffnenden intracodierten Bild und den bis zum nächsten intracodierten Bild folgenden intercodierten Bildern besteht, und ihrem Codierungsmuster, z.B. $IP^{(n-1)}$ bei einer Bildgruppe aus dem I- und n-1 folgenden P-Bildern. Zu einem logischen Zeitpunkt m wird ein relativer Verlust bezüglich eines Bildrahmens erwartet. Dieser Verlust erstreckt sich aufgrund zeitlicher Abhängigkeiten über (n-m) Bilder und wird in jedem Bild von neuen überlagert. Es ergibt sich stochastisch ein Modell akkumulierter Verluste, wie es in der folgenden Fig. 1 dargestellt ist.

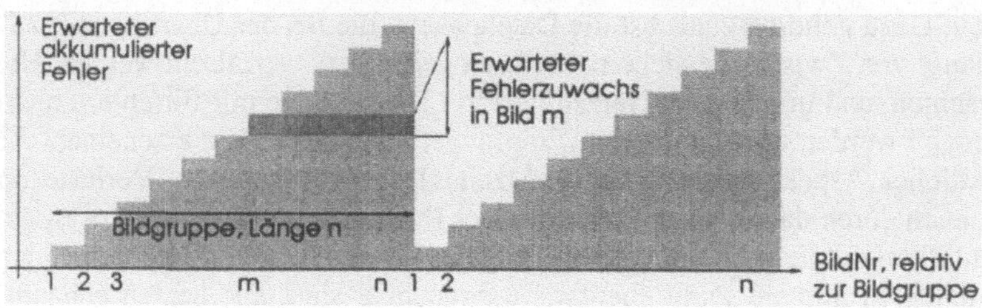

Fig. 1. Modell für den erwarteten akkumulierten Fehler

Hier ist die dunkle Fläche der in Bild m erwartete und sich aufgrund seiner Persistenz bis einschließlich Bild n erstreckende Verlust ε. Die hellgraue Fläche ist die akkumulierte Gesamtstörung in Abhängigkeit von der Sequenznummer des betrachteten Bildes. Es ergibt sich für eine Sequenz der Länge n somit eine erwartete Gesamtbeeinträchtigung von

$$\zeta = \varepsilon \, \frac{n(n+1)}{2} \tag{1}$$

Es bleibt anzumerken, daß die Normen MPEG und H.263 auch bidirektional interpolierte Bildrahmen *(B-Frames)* vorsehen, welche aufgrund ihres zeitlichen Bezuges für Echtzeitkommunikationsbeziehungen nur bedingt geeignet sind. Im wesentlichen bleibt dieses Modell jedoch davon unberührt, da B-Bilder in sich keine weitere Abhängigkeitshierarchie aufbauen, sie selbst also nur von nicht B-Bildern abhängen.

3. Fehlertoleranzmaßnahmen des Senders

Um die Güte der decodierten Bildsequenz hinsichtlich des in Abschnitt 2 vorgestellten Modells auf einem gleichbleibenden Niveau zu halten, wird der Abstand n der intracodierten Bilder innerhalb der Bildsequenz jeweils an den geschätzten momentanen Verlust ε* angepaßt, wobei ζ_{ref} die maximal erduldete Überlagerung von Fehlereinflüssen darstellt. Die Begrenzung ergibt sich aus dem in H.261 und H.263 empfohlenen maximalen I-Bildabstand von 132 Bildern.

$$n = \min\left\{ \left\lfloor \left(\frac{1}{4} + \frac{2\zeta_{ref}}{\epsilon^*} \right)^{0.5} \right\rfloor, 132 \right\},$$ (2)

Als Schätzfunktionen für die augenblickliche Verlustsituation eignen sich sogenannte transiente Schätzer, welche die Einflüsse der Vergangenheit langsam ausblenden und augenblickliche Beobachtung stärker gewichten. Von besonderer praktischer Relevanz ist dabei die geometrische Gewichtungsfunktion, die durch Gewichtung des bisherigen Schätzers mit einer Konstanten α ($0 \le \alpha < 1$) und der augenblicklichen Beobachtung mit Gewichtung ($1-\alpha$) entsteht. Diese Schätzfunktionen haben z.B. im TCP-Protokoll in den letzten 20 Jahren gute Resultate bezüglich der Kalkulation der augenblicklichen Verlustraten und Verzögerungszeiten im Internet gezeitigt. Die Schätzfunktionen werden empfängerseitig ausgeführt, da nur eine dortige Aggregation die Integrität dieses Maßes auch in Anwesenheit von Verlusten übermittelter Kontrollinformationen gewährleistet. Somit ist hierbei zu beachten, daß der Sender jeweils nur mit einem zeitlichen Verzug entsprechend der Paketverzögerung der Kontrollnachrichten den neuesten tatsächlich erhalten Kontrollreport bzgl. des geschätzten Verlustes für seine Kalkulationen heranziehen kann. Es ergibt sich für das hier vorgestellte Verfahren eine Abhängigkeit vom Gütemaß ζ_{ref} und der geometrischen Gewichtung α. In Fig. 2 werden die Einflüsse des Parameters ζ_{ref} anhand einer aufgezeichneten Ereignisspur von an den Sender übermittelten Paketverlustmaßen aufgezeigt.

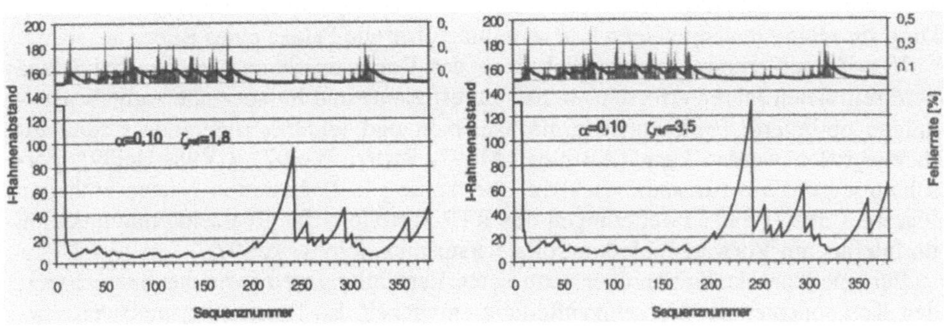

Fig. 2. Ereignisspur der Paketverluste ■ , der transienten Fehler ——— sowie des I-Rahmenabstands —

Es sind durchschnittlich 2.26 % der Pakete von Verlusten betroffen, allerdings mit starken Schwankungen, so daß Spitzenverlustraten von bis zu 30 % zu beobachten sind. Es zeigt sich, daß ζ_{ref} maßgeblich das Niveau des Abstands und der dadurch induzierten Bildgüte bestimmt, während α für die Geschwindigkeit der Reaktionen maßgeblich ist. Ein großes α bewirkt eine starke Gewichtung des augenblicklichen Einflusses und damit eine schnelle Reaktion. Zweifelsohne kann ein zu großes α u.U. schnelle und ungewollte Reaktionen aufgrund von Übergewichtungen nicht repräsentativer Ereignisse nach sich ziehen.

Die Auswirkungen einer Kontrolle der Abstände wird exemplarisch an der Testsequenz der Nachrichtensprecherin Claire (vom FTP-Server dspftp.ece.ubc.ca im Verzeichnis /pub/tmn/qcif_source) demonstriert. Hierzu wurde der Wert von α=0.1 aus den oben aufgeführten Experimenten übernommen, und ζ_{ref} variiert, die linke Graphik in Fig. 3 zeigt ζ_{ref}=1.8, die rechte ζ_{ref}=3.5.

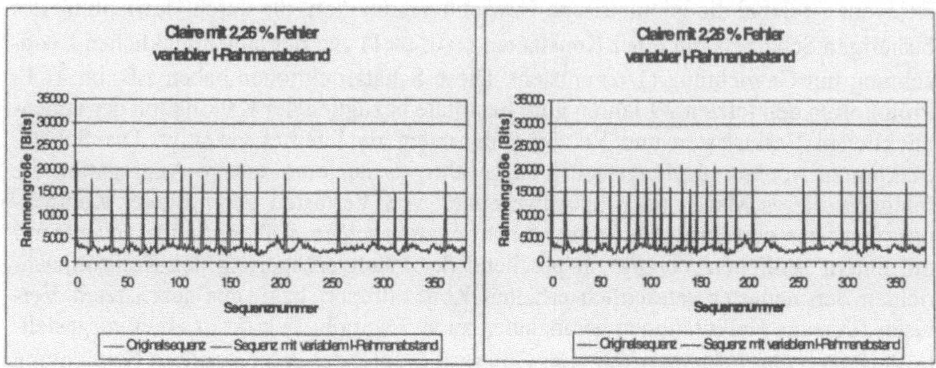

Fig. 3. Ereignisspur der Rahmengröße für die Videoesequenz Claire

Da die intracodierten Bilder massive Lastspitzen erzeugen, sollte man diese Daten auf mehrere aufeinanderfolgende Bilder verteilen, so daß jeweils nur eine Spalte oder Zeile dieser Bilder intracodiert wird. Hierbei bietet sich die spaltenweise Verschränkung zur relativ gleichmäßigen Lastverteilung über alle Pakete eines Bildes an.

Vorwärtsfehlerkorrektur zur Sicherung der Daten durch zusätzliche Redundanz wird seit vielen Jahren erforscht, so daß auf effiziente und für spezielle Aufgabenstellungen optimierte Fehlerkorrekturmechanismen und fehlerkorrigierende Codes zurückgegriffen werden kann [ABE96, LMS97, Riz97, Wol97, RiV98, Hei99]. Forschungsergebnisse zur audiovisuellen Übertragung in IP-basierten Netzen enthalten [Car97, CaB97] und Erweiterungen des RTP-Protokolls für Realzeitkommunikation im Internet um Vorwärtsfehlerkontrollmechanismen liefern [RoS97].

Für eine Kommunikation über vermaschte Vermittlungsnetze wie das Internet wurden Komponenten zur Verkehrsaufteilung entwickelt. Im Internet beispielsweise besteht die Möglichkeit sich bei mehreren Netzdienstanbietern (Providern) gleichzeitig einzuwählen und über diese unterschiedlichen Verbindungen jeweils einen Teil des Datenstromes zu leiten. Die Daten gehen dann u.U. über zumindest teilweise disjunkte Wege durch das Netz. Eine sinnvolle Ergänzung dieses Verfahrens stellt die oben erwähnte Vorwärtsfehlerkontrolle dar, da damit auch der Verlust der Daten über einen der unterschiedlichen Datenpfade kompensiert werden kann. Es wurde bereits eine entsprechende Internettelefonie-Anwendung entwickelt und eingesetzt. Dabei konnte die Wahrscheinlichkeit von Datenverlusten und von inakzeptabel hohen Verzögerungen beträchtlich reduziert und die Qualität einer Echtzeitkommunikation aus der Sicht der Endbenutzer signifikant erhöht werden [Sie98, ASW98].

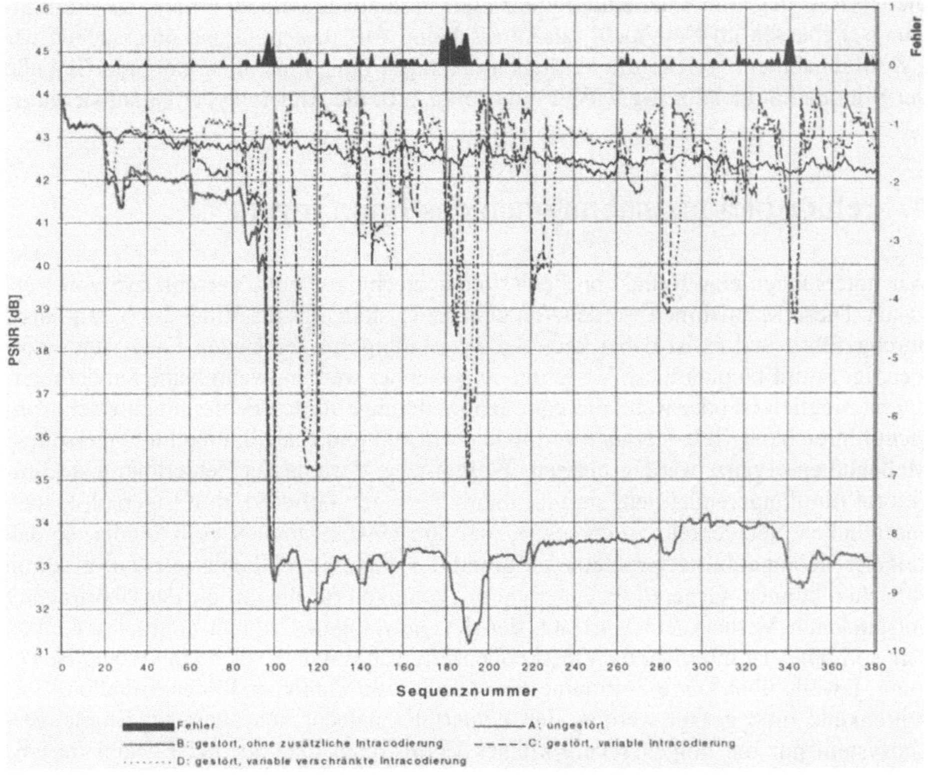

Fig. 4. PSNR der Videoesequenz Claire bei Quantisierung 4

Der PSNR ist ein einfaches objektives Qualitätsmaß und für größere Bildformate
und höhere Bildraten sind unseres Wissens keine besseren Verfahren zur Qualitätsbewertung bekannt [Roh00]. Die Graphik mit den PSNR-Resultaten (Fig. 4) zeigt im
oberen Bereich die Anzahl der zufälligen Verluste. Darunter sind jeweils die entsprechenden Auswirkungen auf die gestörte Bildsequenz zu beobachten, und zwar auf
die ohne Fehlertoleranzmaßnahme in Form zusätzlicher I-Bilder übertragene Videose-
quenz (durchgehende untere Linie B) sowie auf die jeweils in einem Bild (gestrichelt
C) bzw. verschränkt (gepunktet D) gesendeten zusätzlichen I-Bilder. Zum Vergleich
dient die PSNR-Kurve des ungestörten Videos in Form der durchgezogenen Linie A.
Deutlich zu erkennen ist die Qualitätsverbesserung durch die beiden Fehlertoleranzmaßnahmen, deren PSNR-Kurven sich erheblich von der unteren abheben und zwi-
schendurch immer wieder das Niveau derjenigen für das ungestörte Video erreichen,
ja dieses sogar zeitweise übertreffen.

Während Strategien wie Vorwärtsfehlerkorrektur massiv Redundanz auf Paketebe-
ne hinzufügen und somit das Netz in einem nicht zu vernachlässigbaren Maße zusätzlich belasten, erzeugt das oben diskutierte Verfahren, in geeigneten Abständen intracodierte Bildrahmen zu senden, um die Persistenz von Bildfehlern einzugrenzen und
neue Synchronisationspunkte zu schaffen, wesentlich weniger Netzlast. Dennoch wird

die Netzlast gegenüber der Bildsequenz ohne zusätzliche I-Bilder erhöht, was bei Leistungsengpässen im Netz nicht ratsam erscheint. Aus diesem Grund untersuchen wir z.Z. Maßnahmen, welche die zusätzliche Netzlast ohne eine allzu störende Einbuße der Bildqualität gleichzeitig wieder reduzieren, z.B. die Änderung der Quantisierung.

4. Fehlertoleranzmaßnahmen des Empfängers

Wir untersuchen eine Reihe von Fehlertoleranztechniken zum Verschleiern von Verlusten. Diese Maßnahmen werden von dem Endsystem, das die Videodaten empfängt, durchgeführt, und es ist dabei keinerlei Beteiligung des sendenden Endsystems notwendig. Somit können diese Verfahren angewendet werden, wenn keine Senderbeteiligung möglich ist oder wenn die vom Sender durchgeführten Fehlertoleranztechniken nicht hinreichend viele Verluste verhindern können und deshalb um empfängerseitige Maßnahmen ergänzt werden müssen. Wesentliche Vorteile der Fehlertoleranztechniken im Empfängerendsystem sind ihr relativ geringer Aufwand, ihre Eigenart, keinen zusätzlichen Netzverkehr zu erzeugen, und ihre Unabhängigkeit vom Sender, so daß keinerlei Kompatibilitätsprobleme aufgrund der eingesetzten Fehlertoleranzverfahren entstehen können. Generell erzeugen diese Techniken für die infolge der Übertragung entstandenen Verluste einen Ersatz, der dem jeweiligen Original möglichst ähnlich sein soll. Dies ist möglich, da Videosequenzen, insbesondere solche mit wenig Bewegung, jeweils über kurze Zeiträume eine große Zahl ähnlicher Bilder enthalten. Einschränkend muß gesagt werden, daß Fehlertoleranztechniken allein im Empfängerendsystem nur die Folgen relativ kleiner Verlustraten bzw. kleiner Lücken im empfangenen Videostrom verschleiern können. Ohne Fehlertoleranzverfahren hingegen bricht der Decoder beim Auftreten eines Verlustes die Decodierung des Videos ab.

Die meisten Bilder werden als Differenzenbilder (intercodiert) übertragen, d.h. es wird für jeden Bildpunkt die Differenz des Farbwertes aus dem aktuellen Bild zu dem Wert eines korrespondierenden Punktes aus dem vorherigen Bild kodiert. Dadurch entsteht bei einem Verlust im zu dekodierenden Bildstrom der Effekt, daß Artefakte wie gebrochene Kanten oder Unschärfe nicht nur in dem Bild sichtbar sind, in dem der direkte Verlust aufgetreten ist. Vielmehr setzen sich die Artefakte durch die Differenzendekodierung über die Zeit in Form der sogenannten indirekten Verluste fort und bewegen sich durch den Einsatz von Bewegungskompensation auch räumlich über die späteren Bilder. Zwar werden die Artefakte mit der Zeit schwächer, sie können aber für eine kurze Zeit die Bildqualität erheblich senken. Für den Erfolg aller im folgenden genannten Techniken ist ihre Fähigkeit entscheidend, Bewegung aus vorherigen Bildern und der Umgebung des Verlustes gut fortschreiben zu können [Shi00].

Bei der Wiederholung werden verlorene Bildbereiche durch die entsprechenden Bereiche des vorigen Bildes ersetzt. Ist das zu behandelnde Bild das erste Bild, so wird der verlorene Bereich durch korrekt übertragene Bereiche desselben Bildes ersetzt. Diese Technik geht davon aus, daß keine Bewegung im Bild stattfindet, und liefert darum auch gute Ergebnisse für Sequenzen mit wenig Bewegung.

Die mit TCON (Telenor Research's Error Concealment) [Wen99] abgekürzte Fehlertoleranztechnik mindert diesen Nachteil einfacher Wiederholung. Dazu werden die Bewegungsvektoren aus dem jeweils darüberliegenden (korrekt empfangenen) Bildbereich auf den verlorenen Bereich angewendet. Liegt der verlorene Bereich am oberen Bildrand, wird der entsprechende Bereich ohne Bewegungskompensation aus dem vorigen Bild kopiert, d.h. wiederholt. Diese Technik geht davon aus, daß gleichmäßige Bewegung im Bild stattfindet, und liefert darum gute Ergebnisse für Sequenzen mit viel Bewegung. In Sequenzen mit wenig bis mittlerer Bewegungsintensität dagegen sind benachbarte Bewegungsvektoren häufiger einander nicht sehr ähnlich, so daß TCON schlechtere Ergebnisse liefert als Wiederholung.

Werden Mittelwerte der Farbwerte des vorigen und vorvorigen Bereiches für die Fülleinheit verwendet, so stellt sich nicht der erwartete Eindruck einer fortgeschriebenen Bewegung ein, sondern vielmehr ein „Auswaschen" des vorigen Eindrucks. Dasselbe trifft zu, wenn die Fülleinheit gebildet wird durch Addition der Differenzen der Farbwerte aus dem vorigen und dem vorvorigen Bereich auf die Farbwerte des vorigen Bereiches (Differenzenfortschreibung). Durchschnittliche PSNR-Werte von Sequenzen, deren Übertragungsverluste mit diesen Techniken behandelt werden, liegen etwa auf dem Niveau derer, die mit Wiederholung behandelt wurden.

Bei dem von uns entwickelten Verfahren MeBeV (**Me**dian der umgebenden **Bewe**gungsvektoren) werden die korrekt übertragenen Bewegungsvektoren aus der Umgebung des verlorenen Bereiches benutzt, um Bewegungsvektoren für den verlorenen Bereich zu berechnen. Im ersten Schritt werden für jeden Makroblock drei korrekt übertragene Bewegungsvektoren aus dem Bereich über, unter und vor dem verlorenen Bereich identifiziert. Im zweiten Schritt wird der Bewegungsvektor des verlorenen Bereiches gebildet, indem jede Komponente auf den Median der drei Werte gesetzt wird, d.h. jede Komponente wird auf den Wert gesetzt, der nicht der Höchste und nicht der Niedrigste ist. Dabei können in speziellen Situationen dieselben Ergebnisse erzielt werden, wie bei Wiederholung und bei TCON. Fast immer wird durch diese Technik jedoch besserer Qualitätsverlauf erreicht, sofern PSNR als Qualitätsmaß zugrundegelegt wird. Die verwandte Technik MiBeV, bei der ein verlorener Bewegungsvektor gebildet wird als arithmetisches Mittel von drei umgebenden Bewegungsvektoren zeigte dieses Ergebnis nicht. Vielmehr lag der durchschnittliche PSNR zwischen denen von Wiederholung und TCON, weil die Komponenten von Bewegungsvektoren sowohl negative als auch positive Werte annehmen können und der Mittelwert darum tendenziell in der Nähe von Null liegt.

In der Grafik zum PSNR (Fig. 5) werden die Qualitätsverläufe von Wiederholung, TCON und MeBeV bei 5% GOB-Verlusten untereinander sowie mit der ungestörten Bildsequenz Claire bei 15 fps im QCIF-Format bei Quantisierung eins verglichen. Diese Bildsequenz enthält wenig Bewegung. Darum sind benachbarte Bewegungsvektoren selten ähnlich und häufig Null. Bis zum Bild 246 liefert erwartungsgemäß Wiederholung bessere Ergebnisse als TCON. MeBeV wählt in den meisten Fällen die Komponenten der Bewegungsvektoren so, daß die Ergebnisse in der Nähe von Wiederholung liegen bzw. diese übertreffen. Nach Bild 246 wurde die Bildsequenz bei der Kodierung wiederholt, so daß in Bild 247 recht große Differenzen (in 91 P-Makroblöcken und 8 I-Makroblöcken) übertragen werden. Dieses Bild repräsentiert einen Schnitt. In diesem Bild geht GOB 6 verloren. Diese GOB enthielt nur P-Makroblöcke. Alle drei Techniken liefern für diesen Verlust Ergebnisse mit einem starken Qualitätsverlust. Die einzelnen Ergebnisse werden anhand der Bilder im Anhang illustriert. Für diesen Verlust größerer Differenzen zeigt TCON erwartungsgemäß auch im weiteren Zeitverlauf bessere Ergebnisse als die Wiederholung, während MeBeV von allen drei Verfahren bzgl. des PSNR-Verlaufs die besten Ergebnisse liefert.

Die Bildqualität ist kurzfristig abhängig von der empfängerseitig eingesetzten Fehlertoleranztechnik. Untersuchungen mit der vorgestellten und anderen Sequenzen legen den Schluß nahe, daß die Qualität bei Streuverlusten durch die Wahl der Fehlerbehandlung um bis zu 10% (bzgl. PSNR) gesteigert werden kann.

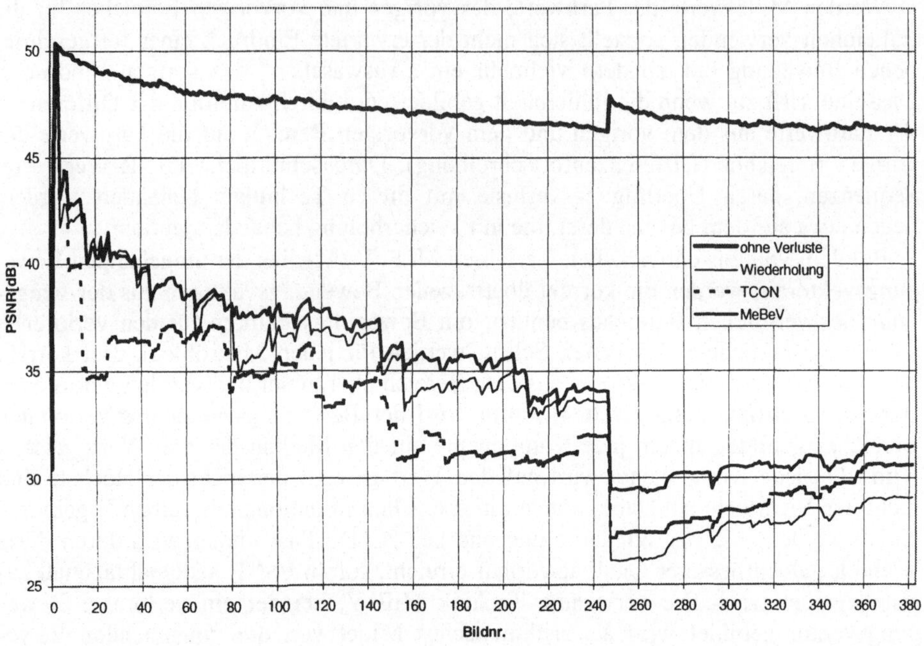

Fig. 5. Vergleich der Fehlertoleranztechniken des Empfängerendsystems

5. Zusammenfassung und Ausblick

Ausgehend von den typischen Unzulänglichkeiten bei der Datenübertragung über verlustbehaftete Paketvermittlungsnetze, der Struktur von Videodaten blockbasierter Kompressions- und Codierungsverfahren und den durch die Verbindung dieser beiden Gegebenheiten hervorgerufenen Folgen für die Bildqualität beim Empfänger, wurde ein Modell zur Bewertung von Verlusten aus Empfängersicht entwickelt. Dieses diente zur Konstruktion eines senderseitigen Fehlertoleranzverfahrens, bei dem, abhängig von den Übertragungsverlusten, intracodierte Bilder zum Ausgleich des Informationsverlustes und als Wiederaufsetzpunkte für die Videodarstellung beim Empfänger gesendet werden. Dieses Verfahren läßt sich modellbasiert durch verschiedene Parameter steuern und liefert sehr gute Qualitätsverbesserungen, die sowohl anhand des PSNR quantifiziert als auch anhand von Beispielbildern illustriert wurden. Die kurzzeitig erhöhte Netzlast durch die größere Datenmenge der intracodierten Bilder wird geglättet durch eine Aufteilung dieser Daten auf mehrere aufeinanderfolgende Bilder.

Ferner wurden verschiedene rein empfängerseitige Fehlertoleranzverfahren miteinander verglichen. Gemäß PSNR wird durch die Berücksichtigung des Medians der den verlorenen Bildbereich umgebenden Bewegungsvektoren (MeBeV) bessere Fehlerverschleierung von direkten Verlusten erreicht als durch bisher bekannte Fehlertoleranztechniken. Die Stärke dieses Verfahrens liegt zum einen darin, daß eine zusätzliche Entscheidung getroffen wird (d.h. höhere Komplexität bei Erzeugung des Schätzers). Zum anderen hat sich gezeigt, daß die Erzeugung von künstlichen Werten durch Mittelwertbildung oder Differenzenfortschreibung keine gute Fehlerbehandlung darstellt. Durchgängig werden bessere Ergebnisse erzielt, wenn aus der korrekt übertragenen Umgebung Werte als Fülleinheiten ausgewählt und unverfälscht eingesetzt werden. Die vorgestellten Techniken wurden im Hinblick auf direkte Verluste entwickelt, d.h. anschaulich, die PSNR-Kurve soll unmittelbar nach einem direkten Verlust möglichst wenig absinken. Weitere Arbeiten sollen zusätzlich auch die zeitliche Entwicklung der indirekten Verluste innerhalb der restlichen Bildsequenz miteinbeziehen, d.h. anschaulich soll die PSNR-Kurve nach einem Verlust für den Rest des Videos auf einem möglichst hohen Niveau gehalten werden.

Die von uns entwickelten und untersuchten sender- und empfängerseitigen Fehlertoleranzverfahren verbessern die Bildqualität bei Videokommunikation über Paketvermittlungsnetze bei Übertragungsunzulänglichkeiten signifikant. Einen Synergieeffekt erhoffen wir uns von der geeigneten und noch zu untersuchenden Kombination beider Vorgehensweisen, wenn unsere modellbasierte Technik von Seiten des Senders größere Paketverluste durch redundante Daten ausgleicht und die Restfehler vom Empfängerendsystem verschleiert werden bzw. erst dann senderseitige Techniken eingesetzt werden müssen, wenn die empfängerseitigen nicht mehr ausreichen.

Literatur

[ABE96] Albanese, A., Blömer J., Edmonds J., Luby M., Sudan M., Priority Encoding Transmission, IEEE Trans. Information Theory 42, 6, Nov. 1996

[ASW98] Albanese A., Siemsglüss S., Wolfinger B., Information Dispersal to Improve QoS on the Internet, Proc. SPIE Intern. Symp. Voice, Video, and Data Comm., Boston, 1998

[BaW97] Bai G., Wolfinger B., Possibilities and Limitations in Smoothing MPEG-coded Video Streams: A Measurement-based Investigation, MMB 97, Freiberg, 1997

[BoT98] Bolot J., Turletti T., Experience with Rate Control Mechanisms for Packet Video in the Internet, ACM SIGCOMM Computer Communication Review 28, 1, pp. 4-15, Jan. 1998

[CaB97] Carle G., Biersack E.W., Survey of Error Recovery Techniques for IP-based Audio-Visual Multicast Applications, IEEE Network Magazine 11, 6, pp. 24-36, Nov./Dec. 1997

[Car97] Carle, G., Error Control for Real-Time Audio-Visual Services, Seminar on High Performance Networks for Multimedia Applications, Dagstuhl, Juni 1997

[ClT90] Clark D.D., Tennenhouse D.L., Architectural Considerations for a New Generation of Protocols, Proc. of SIGCOMM'90, Philadelphia, PA, 1990

[EfS98] Effelsberg W., Steinmetz R., Video Compression Techniques, dpunkt.verlag, Heidelberg, 1998

[Fro97] Froitzheim K., Multimedia-Kommunikation, dpunkt.verlag, Heidelberg, 1997

[Hei99] Heidtmann K., Evaluation of Video Communication over Packet Switching Networks, 3rd European Dependable Computing Conference EDCC-3, Prag, 1999, 24-41

[HeW99] Heidtmann K., Wolfinger B., Analytische Leistungsbewertung von Videokommunikation gemäß H.261 über Paketvermittlungsnetze, MMB 99, Trier, 1999

[HKZ99] Heidtmann K., Kohlhaas C., Zaddach M., Messung der Netzlast und Bewertung der Bildqualität bei Videokommunikation über Paketvermittlungsnetze, 15. GI/ITG-Fachtagung über Architektur von Rechensystemen ARCS'99, Jena, 1999

[ITU00] International Telecommunication Union – Telecommunication Standardization Sector, s. http://www.itu.int

[Ker00] Kerse J., Realisierung von Stabilisierungsmechanismen für H.261/H.263-codierte Videoströme in IP-basierten Rechnernetzen, Diplomarbeit, FB Inform., Univ. Hamburg, 2000

[Koh99] Kohlhaas C., Untersuchung der von Videocodierern erzeugten Verkehrslasten und der durch das Verhalten von Kommunikationssystemen beeinflußten Bildqualität, Diplomarbeit, FB Informatik, Universität Hamburg, 1999

[Roh00] Rohaly A. et al., Final Report from the Video Quality Experts Group (VQEG) on the Validation of objective Models of Video Quality Assessments. Report of the VQEG, VQEG 2000, s. http://www.crc.ca/vqeg

[RoS97] Rosenberg, J., Schulzrinne H., An A/V Profile Extension for Generic Forward Error Correction in RTP, Internet-Draft: draft-ietf-avt-fec, Internet Engineering Task Force, 1997

[Shi00] Shirani S. et al., A Concealment Method for Video Communications in an Error Prone Environment, IEEE J. Selected Areas in Communications 18, 6, 2000

[Sie98] Siemsglüss S., Information Dispersal to Improve QoS on the Internet, Diplomarbeit, FB Informatik, Universität Hamburg, 1998

[Suc00] Suchanek T., Untersuchung der Bildqualität übertragener Videos in Abhängigkeit von Übertragungsverlusten und der Qualitätsverbesserung mit Hilfe von Fehlertoleranzverfahren im Empfängersystem, Diplomarbeit, FB Informatik, Universität Hamburg, 2000

[Wen99] Wenger S. et al, Test model 11. ITU-T SG 16 Contribution (1999)

[Wol97] Wolfinger B., On the Potential of FEC in Building Fault-tolerant Distributed Applications to Support High QoS Video Communication, ACM Symp. Principles of Distributed Computing, PODC97, 1997

[WoZ00] Wolfinger B., Zaddach M., Techniques to improve Quality-of-Service in Video Communications via Best Effort Networks, (zur Veröffentlichung eingereicht)

[WZB00] Wolfinger B, Zaddach M., Bai G., Heidtmann K., Modeling of Primary and Secondary Load in the Internet, Bericht FBI-HH-B-22700, FB Informatik, Universität Hamburg, 2000

Anhang: Exemplarische Veranschaulichung der Verbesserung der Bildqualität anhand des Videos "Claire"

A. Sender- und modellbasierte Fehlertoleranz (4.3% Verluste, $\alpha=0.1$, $\zeta_{ref}=2.3$)

• ohne Fehlertoleranz:

Bild 119

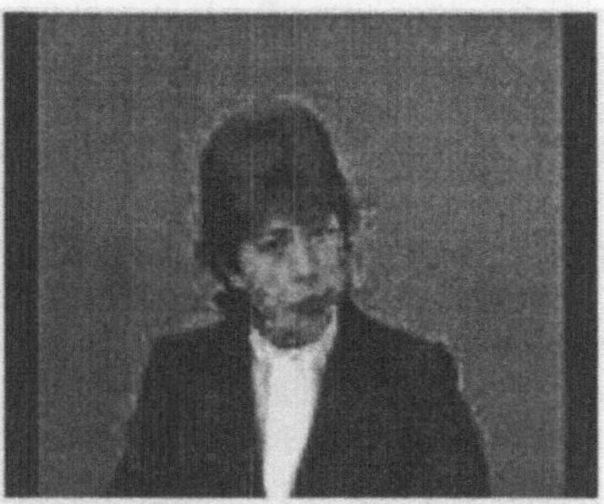

Bild 341

• Nutzung des vorgeschlagenen Fehlertoleranzverfahrens:

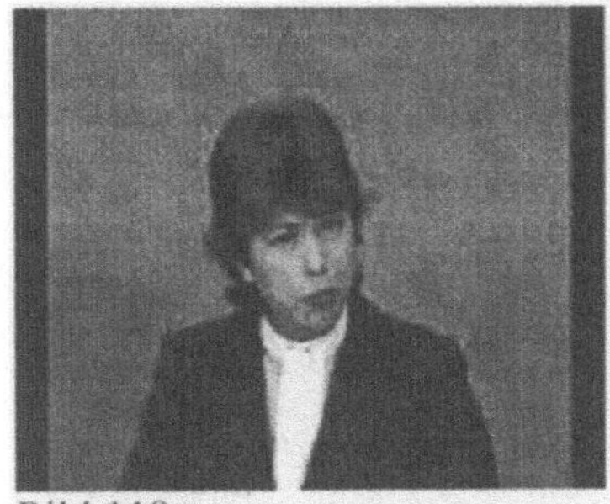

Bild 119

Bild 341

B. Empfängerseitige Fehlertoleranz (5% Verluste, QCIF, Quantisierung 1, 15 fps, Codec: tmn 3.2 (H.263, Version 2)): Bild 247

ohne Fehler
PSNR der Gesamtsequenz: 47,22 dB
PSNR dieses Bildes: 47,98 dB

Wiederholung von GOB 6
PSNR der Gesamtsequenz: 33,5 dB
PSNR dieses Bildes: 26,16 dB

TCON
PSNR der Gesamtsequenz: 32,3 dB
PSNR dieses Bildes: 27,23 dB

MeBeV
PSNR der Gesamtsequenz: 34,91 dB
PSNR dieses Bildes: 29,51 dB

Document Specification and Dissemination with an Extensible Multimedia System

Jürgen Hauser, Kurt Rothermel

University of Stuttgart

Institute of Parallel and Distributed High-Performance Systems (IPVR)

Breitwiesenstr. 20-22

70565 Stuttgart, Germany

e-mail: {hauser, rothermel}@informatik.uni-stuttgart.de

Abstract. The research project MAVA (*Multimedia Document Versatile Archi-tecture*) focuses on simplification of specification and dissemination of multime-dia documents. The problems discussed and solved by the MAVA approach are observed by using existing authoring systems. Application specific multimedia systems provide fixed concepts for only one application area. Generic systems al-low the specification of documents of arbitrary application areas. This leads to complex specifications and the requirement of programming skills for authors.
Goal of the MAVA approach is to simplify authoring of multimedia documents in different application areas by an extensible specification language. This allows to add new language elements for particular application areas to simplify author-ing. While the extension with new media types is addressed by several approach-es the MAVA approach considers also the extension for new particular application areas.
Document dissemination plays also an important role. For the presentation of a document basing on arbitrary language extensions also the presentation system it-self has to be dynamically extended over the Internet.

1. Introduction

There are a lot of different application areas for multimedia documents. Each applica-tion area is characterized by application area specific functionality. Examples for appli-cation areas are computer based trainings (CBT), interactive television (ITV) or games.

The following two examples describe functionality of multimedia documents in two different application areas. The first example is a computer based training (CBT) the second one an interactive television scenario.

A CBT contains multiple choice questions that offer different answers from which the user has to choose the correct one. It offers text fields where users can type in an-swers for questions. The training continues in a different way in case of a correct or false answer. An evaluation of the user's performance is also part of a CBT.

An ITV presentation introduces an alternative interaction mechanism by its remote control. On the remote control there are buttons for simplified navigation in the presen-tation (e.g. a blue button to jump to the main menu).

Document authoring is a time consuming task. It is simplified if authors can use an application area specific language that provides high-level abstractions based on the ap-plication area functionality (e.g. a CBT specification language for the first example or a language for interactive television documents in the second example).

One possibility to support authoring in different application areas is to provide a specific multimedia system for each application area. One example is the usage of Macromedia Authorware for CBTs. This leads to a multitude of different formats, presentations systems and authoring tools that have to be used. And digital libraries for example have to ensure that a user can view all documents what means that besides the document also presentation systems have to be provided.

Another solution to provide application specific functionality is reuse of specifications in generic multimedia systems. A generic multimedia system provides in addition to the original specification model a scripting language (e.g. MHEG [3] or Marcromedia Director [4] and their scripting languages). The application specific functionality is realized using the scripting language. A macro or library concept permits later reuse. These concepts are on programming language level what means that authors still have to have programming knowledge.

Instead of simplifying script programming it would be beneficial to extend the original specification model. Figure 1 shows the specification of an evaluation of a question. If a macro can be used for the evaluation the author must determine where and when the evaluation method is invoked. In contrast, a system based on a high-level language will do this by itself. Additionally, a high level language can be easily graphically visualized.

The same argumentation holds true for example for word processing. Although there is TeX, an author wants to use a high-level "what you see is what you get" application. The introduction of LaTeX macro packages reduces specification complexity but it did not make TeX feasible for everybody.

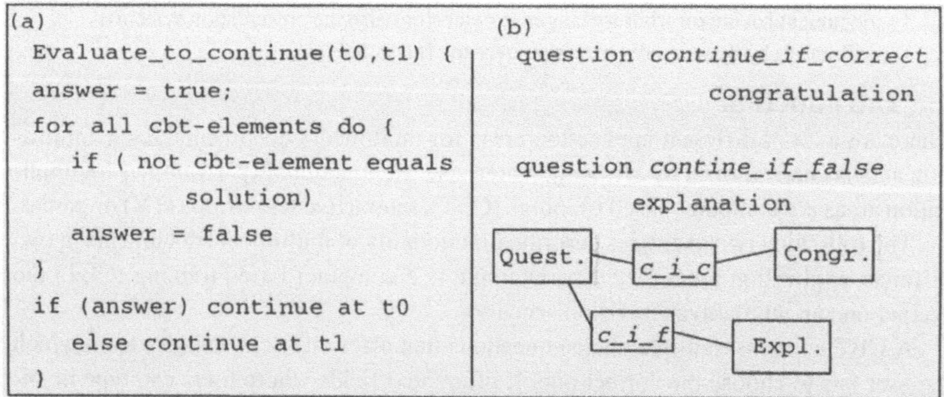

Figure 1 Comparison of (a) a low-level and (b) a high-level specification.

The idea of the MAVA multimedia system is that an author uses a specification language and a document editor that are based on a meta language. The meta language is operator based. An operator is used to specify a relation between media items. Therefore, operators are connected with media items. Authoring of MAVA documents is the direct manipulation of a media item/operator graph what is independent of the application area.

An application specific language extension provides operators and media items that have to be used for the specification of a document in this application area. For the CBT example this means that there is a CBT MAVA extension including for example a check box as media item or operators like *continue_if_false* or *continue_if_correct*.

The semantics of operators are realized in reusable code units called managers. A manager maps the operators used in a document on an internal representation (e.g a scheduling graph). The internal representation is the input for a base manager. A base manager implements the semantics of the internal representation during presentation. The development of managers is simplified by reusing existing base managers.

A manager is a plug-in for the MAVA framework to enable the presentation of a document. Hence, for the document dissemination over a network not only the document itself has to be provided but also required plug-ins. The dissemination process can be optimized by cashing extensions on the client what leads to reduced download times.

Like the presentation system the document editor has to be extended to enable the specification of documents basing on an application area specific language. A document editor extension determins which operators and media items are available in the editor.

The research project MAVA is funded by the German Research Foundation (DFG) in the research initiative "Distributed Processing and Exchange of Digital Documents (V3D2)" [13].

The second section of the paper presents related work. The third section introduces an extensible document specification language to describe multimedia documents. Section four explains the realization of the semantics of a language extension. In section five the component-based architecture of the presentation system is presented. Section six gives some details of a MAVA authoring tool. In section seven the document dissemination is explained. Finally section eight contains a summary.

2. Related Work

Extensibility for multimedia authoring was first mentioned by Drapeau and Greenfiel in 1991 [3]. They consider only extensibility of new media items. Nowadays, regarding object-oriented technology media items are modeled as media classes what allows to add new media items.

Besides extensibility of new media items current research works focuses on the extensibility of the document specification language for new application areas (e.g. for the specification of a computer based training). An extensible system can be used to realize different authoring scenarios.

In [10], Jourdan et. al. present a framework that supports the development of presentation systems for different specification languages for interactive presentations. They do not consider one single system that supports different language extensions. Once they developed a system it can be considered as a system whose specification language cannot be extended. Their approach (providing a framework) simplifies and shortens the development process of new presentation systems (e.g. for a player for Madeus [9] documents or SMIL documents [7]).

In contrast, MAVA provides only one presentation system and one editor that are both extensible. They are extensible by a language for particular application areas for multimedia documents. This leads to a reduced effort compared to the approach of developing proprietary systems for each application area or complex specifications.

For the integration of multimedia into the Internet the W3C recommends the SMIL standard. The specification language of SMIL can be used for interactive presentations but it does not provide language elements for example for a computer based training. Although SMIL is based on XML [1] it is not intended to be extensible by arbitrary language elements. At least a SMIL player will not know how to realize the extension's semantics.

A more general specification language than SMIL is based on XML itself. The specification or realization of semantics of XML-based languages is not part of the standard. Hence, the realization of the semantics is left to applications. The MAVA idea is to use an extensible system whereby the extensions are used to realize the semantics of a particular language. XML will be used as document transfer format because of the similarities of XML and the extensible specification language of MAVA.

3. An Extensible Specification Language

The MAVA approach uses an operator-based meta language. An operator is used to describe a relation between two or more media items. For example "audio *before* animation" means that an audio is played out before an animation.

An operator based approach has been chosen because the adaptability on different application areas requires a model that makes no assumptions about the concepts (i.e. specification languages) that have to be expressed with it. A tree based approach (e.g. SMIL uses such an approach) would be limiting in case of interval operators because the specification is a graph. Other approaches, like Petri nets [12] or the channels of CMIF [5] are limited to their underlying concept. A Petri net can hardly be used to express spatial relations. And the channels of CMIF base on the temporal chronology in a channel.

In MAVA documents are represented as graphs. There are two kinds of nodes, namely media objects and operators. Media objects represent particular media items (e.g. audio or video). All relations or dependencies between media objects are expressed by operators (e.g. that an audio and a video are presented simultaneously). Therefore, edges of the graph are connections between media objects and operators to determine a relation. There is one further document element called container that allows logical grouping of document parts.

Figure 2 shows the graphical notation of the document elements. A graphical notation can be used to visualize attributes of different language elements of the meta language. For example operators have a different representation than media items and hence are easily distinguishable by their graphical representation.

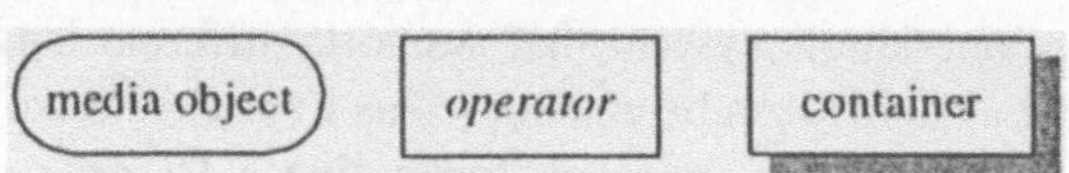

Figure 2 Elements of the MAVA document model.

In the following, the document elements are described in detail:
• *Media objects* represent media items through their attributes. Examples for attributes are the media type (e.g. audio), size of the required presentation area or a

reference (e.g. URL) to media data that has to be presented by the media item during presentation.

- *Operators* are used to specify relations between media objects. For the specification an operator distinguishes between source and destination media objects. The term "text *inFrontOf* image" specifies that the text will be displayed in front of the image and not vice versa. In this example "text" is the source media object and "image" is the destination media object. Operators may have parameters (e.g. the coordinates of a position in the presentation area). To improve readability operators are written in italic letters and source media objects are placed to the left of an operator.

- *Containers* are used to build logical structures in documents. This helps authors to keep track of her document because logical interrelated parts are grouped and replaced by a container. Hence, containers are use to simplify the view on a document and allow the storage of document parts as templates for later reuse.

In the following a special class of operators - the effect operators - are introduced. For their graphical notation see Figure 3.

- *Effect operators* are a special kind of operators. They are used to describe when a particular effect has to take place (e.g. when a media item has to be faded out). Therefore effect operators are always used in conjunction with temporal operators and a media object. An effect operator acts as a destination media of a temporal operator.

Figure 3 Graphical notation of an effect operator.

In Figure 4 a simple computer based training is specified. The document consists of a container representing a question and two further containers one representing a comment after a correct answer and the other one presenting the solution of the question in case of a wrong answer. The different scenes are connect via two operators. The first operator is the correct operator. The operator determines how to continue in case of a correct answer. The false operator determines how to continue in case of a wrong answer. There are also **language** elements to specify questions and their correct solutions.

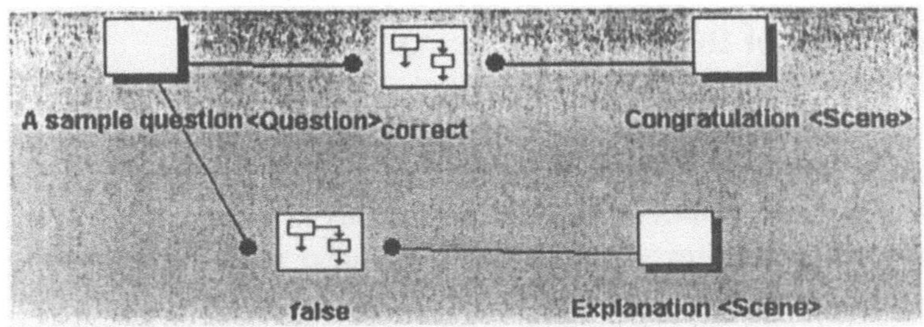

Figure 4 The specification of a simple computer based training.

Figure 5 shows the specification of a simple multimedia document. The document consists of two media items: An image "Bild" which is a picture of a beach and an audio "Musik" representing a title song for the presentation. For the specification of the spatial layout of the document a *center* operator is used to center the image in the presentation area. For the temporal specification a temporal interval operator is used. The *while* operator specifies the parallel presentation of two media items. The *moveTo* effect operator is used to specify the movement of the image media. The destination of the *moveTo* operator is specified by connecting the operator with the image. The *cobegin* operator determines when the movement begins and this happens at the same instant as the play out of the audio starts. The duration and final position of the movement are specified as parameters of the *moveTo* operator. Finally, the semantics of the document are as follows. An image is displayed in the center of the presentation area and during the presentation of the image a title song is played. As the title song starts the image moves out of the presentation area.

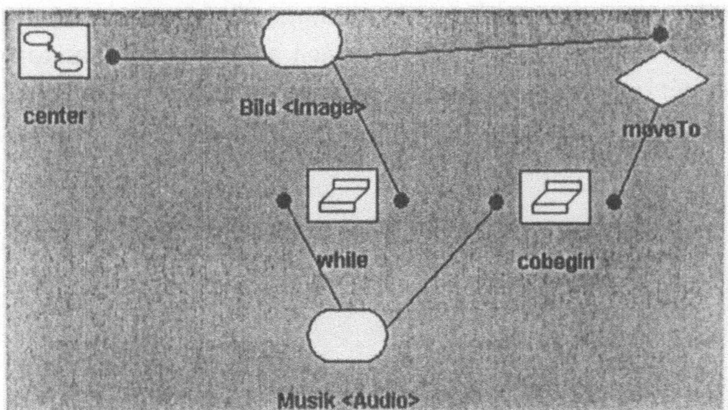

Figure 5 Specification of a simple presentation.

These two examples showed two different specifications supported by the MAVA system. Particular application areas can be supported be extending the system by the definition and realization of new operators and media items. The MAVA approach does not want to specify concepts for application areas. It aims at the integration of existing concepts and the provision of an identical view of the authoring system independently of the application area.

4. Realization of the Language Semantics

The previous section introduced a language extension that was used to specify a simple computer-based training. So far, only language elements have been defined (e.g. the *correct* and *false* operator). They are used during authoring. For the presentation of a document, also the semantics of the operators have to be realized. This means that the presentation system requires an extension corresponding to the language to be capable of presenting a document.

For the realization of the semantics a complete overview of the operators used in a document is needed because in most cases one single operator does not specify the semantics alone. Therefore, operators have only a descriptive meaning and semantics are solely realized in managers.

For the realization of the operators semantics a manager analyzes the document and maps the operators an internal representation that is used as input for a base manager. The MAVA approach makes no assumptions or restrictions for internal representations and base managers. The analysis of the document uses a defined application programming interface (API) for accessing the document model. During play-out of a document a base manager controls the presentation according to its internal representation.

The communication between base managers and media items uses two classes of events. A base manager can register itself at media items for notification events (e.g. button pressed) and send control events (e.g. start or stop presentation) to media items. Both tasks require the definition of particular APIs (e.g. a presentation control API). Whereby each extension may introduce its own API. For the consistent usage of operators in conjunction with media items, it has to be verified that media items support the appropriate APIs. The relation between media items and base managers can be formally specified and verified [6]. The idea is that a media item has to support the event sets that are required for the realization of a concept.

The introduction of a base manager has two advantages for the development of managers. First, the development of managers can be simplified and second reuse of existing base managers for the development of new managers. This will be shown by an example of a manager and a suitable base manager for a temporal concept.

A scheduling graph is a suitable internal representation for a temporal base manager. A detailed discussion about scheduling graphs can be found in [14]. At first a temporal manager will create a scheduling graph according to the operators used in a document. During presentation the temporal base manager uses the scheduling graph to determine when to send control events (e.g. start/stop presentation) to media items.

A base manager acts on an internal representation that differs from the document model. An internal representation is data structure that is suitable for the realization of the semantics of a particular concept. In the case of a temporal manager the document model itself is not a suitable internal representation for the concepts. Using the document model as internal representation leads to a more complex implementation of the base manager. One difference of the scheduling graph compared to the document model is, that the scheduling graph uses a representation with two nodes for each media item and edges to denote a delay. One node for the beginning and one for the end of the presentation interval of a media item. The scheduling graph as a suitable internal representation simplifies the implementation of the scheduling base manager.

The separation of managers and base managers allows reuse of existing base managers for the realization of managers. In the case that an alternative temporal concept has to be realized and integrated the new manager can reuse the scheduling graph. For the new manager only mapping on the scheduling graph has to be realized. Hence, the development of the new managers can be simplified by reuse of existing base managers.

The reuse of base managers was favored because the mapping of new operators on existing operators would be too complex. By considering the *correct* operator it can be shown that the expressiveness of a programming language (e.g. control flow) would be required (e.g. if answer was correct continue at x). Hence, a programming language is used to realize a concept (i.e. a manager).

5. A Presentation System

The concepts introduced with the MAVA system are validated by the design and implementation of a prototype for a document editor and presentation system in Java. With a Java applet the MAVA system can also be embedded into HTML pages.

The specification language is used by authors for the specification of a document. A manager cares for the realization of the semantics of a specification language extension. The presentation system is a framework that allows to plug-in extensions like managers to become capable of presenting a document of a particular application area. Additional extensions of the framework are media items and media viewers. Figure 6 shows the architecture of the MAVA presentation system as it is implemented in the prototype.

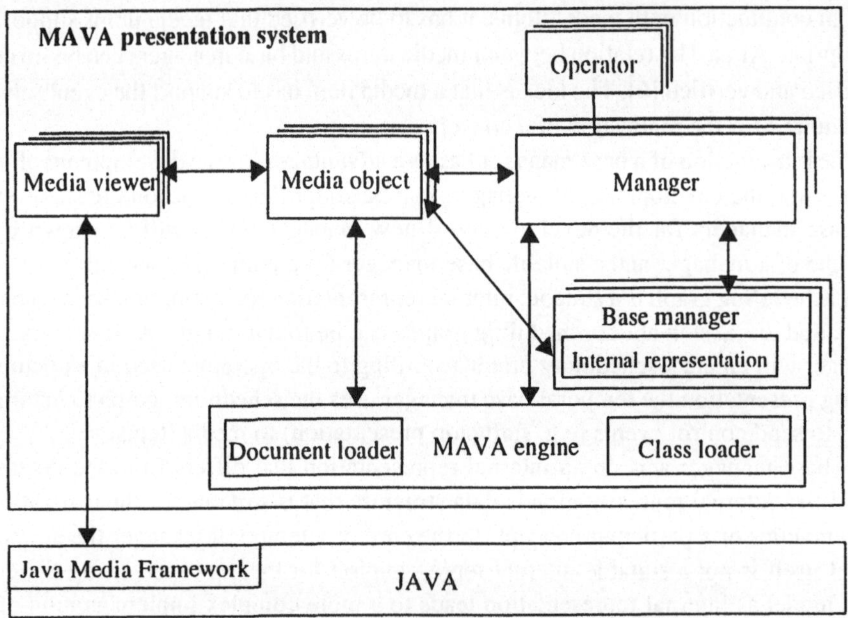

Figure 6 Architecture of the MAVA presentation system.

The MAVA architecture consists of the following components:

- MAVA engine: The MAVA engine is the core of the presentation system. It handles all basic tasks of a presentation system like document loading, class loading and controlling the presentation.
- Class loader: It loads program code like managers, media items and media viewers that are required for the presentation of a particular document.
- Document loader: The document loader is responsible for loading documents from various sources like local disks or network servers. It generates the document model from the storage format of MAVA documents.
- Media objects: A media object is a component of the document model. It is used to realize different types of media items.
- Media viewer: A media viewer is responsible for the visualization of particular media formats (e.g. a mp3 audio).
- Operator: An operator is a component of the document model. It is used to describe relations between media items.

- Manager: Managers are responsible for the realization of the semantics of particular concepts (i.e. a set of operators). Managers map their operators on an internal representation and use a base manager to realize the semantics during presentation.
- Internal representation: Internal representations are models for particular concepts. A manager may create an internal representation and use a base manager to realize the semantics. Internal representations are data structures that are more suitable than the document model itself and therefore simplify the realization of base managers.
- Base manager: Base managers realize a particular model during presentation (e.g. a scheduling graph). The internal representation is used as input for these managers. Hence, base managers simplify the development of managers.

Besides the Java runtime environment, MAVA uses the Java Media Framework [8] to realize media viewers for continuous media items like video or audio media items.

6. A Document Editor

The MAVA document editor (called Med) makes use of the meta language and its application area independence. The design of Med is derived from the meta language. This means that the necessary interactions for authoring is independent of the document's application area. For document authoring in a particular application area an extension for Med is required. The Med extension is a description of available language elements for a particular application area.

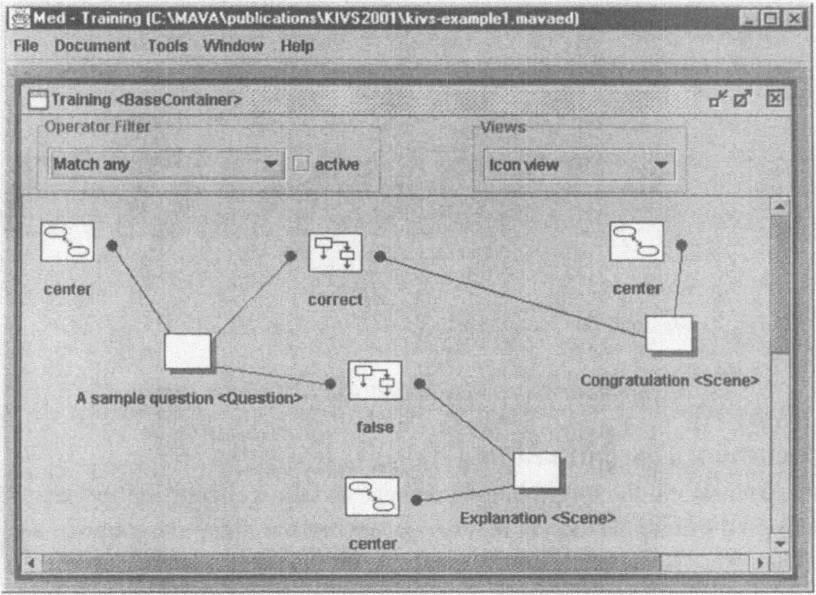

Figure 7 MAVA editor view of a container.

In the user interface Med provides two windows one for available operators and the other one for media items and containers. Each container of a document is visualized using a separate window called container view (e.g. the "Training" window in Figure 7). For the icons in the container view the graphical representation introduced in section 3 is used. For authoring the author drags an operator from the operator selection window and drops it into a container view window. A relation between media items is established by the connection of source and destination media with an operator. To the left and the right of an operator there is a bullet as user interface element to enable the connection of operators and media items. The bullet to the left is used for connections with source media. The author clicks on a bullet and connects a media item to an operator by releasing the mouse button when the mouse is over the media item.

Figure 8 shows the same container as in Figure 7 but with an activated operator filter. The author has activated a filter that masks out all operators that do not belong to a spatial concept. To simplify a container view it is possible to activate different filters. Operators that do not match a certain filtering criteria will be masked out. Hence, an author can concentrate on certain aspects of a document.

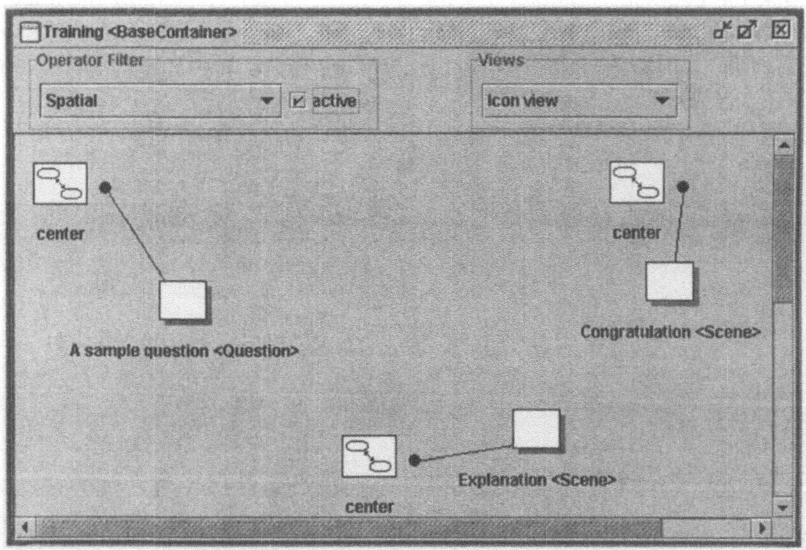

Figure 8 Container view with activated operator filter.

7. Document Dissemination

After the extension of the specification language and the realization of the semantics of the extension the dissemination of MAVA documents has to be considered. If a user selects a document using a specific language (e.g. for a computer based training) his local presentation system is only capable of presenting the document if the required extensions (e.g. manager) are available. Otherwise the presentation system must determine which extensions are requires and where from these extensions can be downloaded.

The dissemination of MAVA documents consists of three steps. At first, the document is loaded from a document storage (Figure 9, step 1). This could be for example a web server. The storage format supports the detection of required extensions. Hence, after an analysis of the document that determines required extensions (step 2) the presentation system will automatically download them (step 3).

The MAVA document transfer format is XML-based. For transfer and storage a document is mapped on an XML representation. The containment relation between containers and operators respectively media items is mapped on nested XML elements. Media items are mapped on empty elements. Each XML element has a fixed attribute that identifies a Java class that is used to build the document model in the presentation system. Attributes of media items and parameters of operators are mapped on XML attributes. The graph structure is modeled by the XML attribute types *ID* and *IDREF*. Hence, operators contain references (*IDREF*) to media items (*ID*).

To specify which extensions are required by a document d, it comprises a sector information SI_d. This sector information describes through URIs which extensions are required for presentation. The MAVA transfer format makes use of the XML names spaces [2] standard. Name spaces are used to identify the required extensions and the uniqueness of the tags for the document elements. The URI of the name space definition identifies a Java jar package.

This approach enables dissemination and presentation of MAVA documents that use a specific language extensions through the Internet. The extension process (step 1 to step 3) is called ad hoc extensibility.

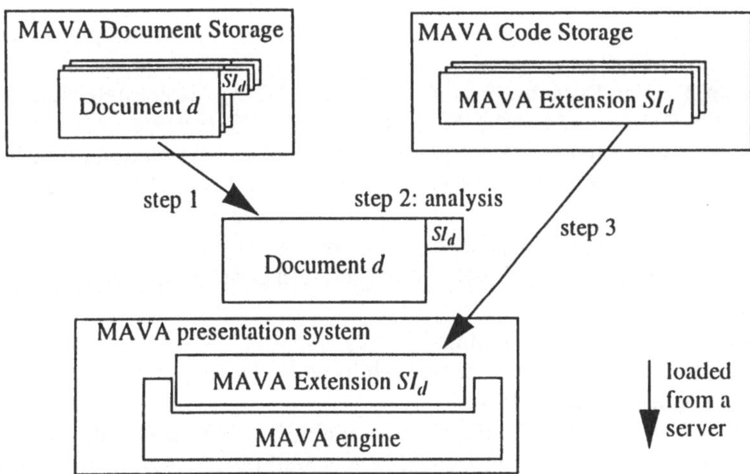

Figure 9 Dissemination of MAVA documents.

8. Summary

An application specific language for multimedia documents cares for simplified document authoring. The presented approach allows the adaption of the specification model for specific applications. This means for authoring that the document specification process will not change independently of the application area the document is specified for. Using different authoring systems for each application area introduces additional effort for authors. This is for example the case if Macromedia Director is used for interactive presentations and Macromedia Authorware for computer-based trainings.

The semantics of a language extension are realized in two steps. The first step is implemented in a manager. A manager maps operators on an internal representation which is the input for a base manager. A base manager controls the presentation of the document according to its internal representation. Base managers and internal representations are reused to simplify the development of new managers.

The MAVA presentation system is a framework that allows to plug-in managers to be capable of presenting documents of a specific application area. Ad hoc extensibility is the automatic download of these extensions before the presentation of a document. Therefore, users need not to bother with updates and configuration tasks of the presentation system.

Future work comprises the integration of application specific views into the MAVA document editor and a feasibility test of the MAVA approach. The test results lead to a detailed usability comparison of the MAVA approach that complements the theoretical results presented in this paper.

References

1. Bray, T., Paoli J., Sperberg-McQueen, C.M. ."Extensible Mark-up Language (XML) 1.0" Working Recommendation. W3C. 1998.
2. Bray, T., Hollander, D. and Layman, A. "Namespaces in XML", Recommendation. W3C. 1999.
3. Drapeau, G.D. and Greenfield, H. "MAEstro - A Distributed Multimedia Authoring Environment". In Proceedings of the Summer 1991 USENIX Conference, 1991.
4. "Director version 8.0". URL: http://www.macromedia.com/products/director. Macromedia. 1999.
5. Hardman, L., Van Rossum, G. and Bulterman, D.C.A. "Structured Multimedia Authoring" In Proceedings of the ACM Multimedia '93. 6/1993.
6. Hauser, J. and Rothermel, K. "Specification and Implementation of an Extensible Multimedia System. In Proceedings of IDMS 2000, LNCS 1905. Springer 2000.
7. Hoschka, P. (Ed.) "Synchronized Multimedia Integration Language (SMIL) 1.0 Specification". W3C Proposed Recommendation. W3C. 4/1998.
8. "Java Media Framework". URL: http://java.sun.com/products/java-media/jmf/index.html.
9. Jourdan, M., Layaida N., Roisin, C., Sabry-ismail, L., Tardif, L. "Madeus, An Authoring Environment for Interactive Multimedia Documents". In Proceedings of the ACM Multimedia 98. 1998.
10. Jourdan, M., Roisin, C., Tardif, L. "A scalable Toolkit for Designing Multimedia Authoring Environments". In special Issue "Multimedia Authoring and Presentation: Strategies, Tools and Experiences" Multimedia Tools and Applications Journal. Kluwer Academic Publishers. 1999.
11. ISO/IEC DIS 13522-5. "Information Technology - Coding of Multimedia and Hypermedia Information - Part 5". 1995.
12. Senac, P., Diaz, M. Leger, A. and de Saqui-Sannes, P. "Modeling Logical and Temporal Synchronization in Hypermedia Systems". IEEE Journal on Selected Areas in Communication, Vol 14, No. 1. 1996.
13. German Research Foundation (DFG). "Distributed Processing and Exchange of Digital Documents (V3D2)". URL: http://www.cg.cs.tu-bs.de/dfgspp.VVVDD.
14. Wirag, S. "Specification and Scheduling of Adaptive Multimedia Documents", Faculty Report 1999/04, University of Stuttgart, 1/1999.

Session 7:

Work in Progress - Anwendungsunterstützung

Eine integrierte Dienstmanagementarchitektur für den qualitätsgesicherten Betrieb von vernetzten Systemen

Sebastian Abeck, Christian Mayerl, Martin Schauer, Dirk Feuerhelm, Lars Dolling

Forschungsgruppe `Cooperation & Management´
Institut für Telematik, Universität Karlsruhe (TH)
Zirkel 2, D-76128 Karlsruhe
[abeck|mayerl|schauer|feuerhelm|dolling]@
cooperation-management.de

Abstract. Der Beitrag beschreibt eine im Rahmen von Forschungs- und Industrieprojekten entstandene Dienstmanagementarchitektur (DMA), durch die bestehende standardisierte Managementarchitekturen erweitert werden. Aufbauend auf den Konzepten zur Überwachung und Steuerung von Netz-, System und Anwendungskomponenten integriert die DMA Werkzeuge, die einen Betreiber bei der Einhaltung von Dienstleistungsvereinbarungen mit Kunden unterstützen.

Einleitung

Die Informationstechnologie (IT) zählt zu den tragenden Säulen einer modernen Industriegesellschaft und wird in Zukunft weiter in den beruflichen und privaten Bereich des Menschen vordringen [CFr99]. Damit die IT eine solche zentrale Rolle übernehmen kann, muss gewährleistet sein, dass die geforderte Funktionalität mit einer vorhersagbaren und garantierten Dienstqualität (Quality of Service, QoS) erbracht wird [WLA98]. Die Soll-Qualität wird durch sog. Dienstleistungsvereinbarungen (DLVs, engl. Service Level Agreements, SLA, [Kar98]) vorgegeben. Durch geeignete Systemarchitekturen wird die Basis geschaffen, dieser Anforderung gerecht zu werden. Hierzu stehen für den Betrieb eines vernetzten Systems Techniken und Werkzeuge des Netz-, System- und Anwendungsmanagements zur Verfügung, die in eine in diesem Beitrag beschriebene Dienstmanagementarchitektur (DMA) zu integrieren sind.

Die in diesem Beitrag vorgestellte Dienstmanagementarchitektur (DMA) zeigt auf, dass nicht nur die Kennzahlen der beteiligten IT-Komponenten sondern auch die den Betrieb der Komponenten sicherstellenden Prozesse notwendig sind [MNM+00]. Die gemessenen Kennzahlen stellen die Ist-Qualität dar, die innerhalb der DMA mit der geforderten Soll-Qualität verglichen werden muss, die ein Kunde bzgl. des von ihm in Anspruch genommenen Dienstes mit dem Betreiber abschließt. Die Überprüfung der Einhaltung der DLVs erfordert eine Abbildung auf die von den Monitorsystemen gelieferten Kennzahlen. Durch einen ständigen Vergleich der (auf der Basis der Kennzahlen beruhenden) Ist-Qualität mit der (auf der Basis der DLVs beruhenden) Soll-Qualität kann durch Priorisierung innerhalb der Abläufe in der

Betreiberorganisation drohenden DLV-Verletzungen vorgebeugt werden. Die DMA ermöglicht dadurch – innerhalb der Grenzen der technischen und organisatorischen Möglichkeiten – eine qualitätsgesicherte Bereitstellung von IT-Diensten.

Integrierte Dienstmanagementarchitektur

Unter dem Begriff der **IT-Managementwerkzeuge** werden in der DMA Werkzeuge zusammengefasst, die unmittelbar die Überwachung und Steuerung des vernetzten Systems und somit der Netz-, System- und Anwendungskomponenten vornehmen. Diese Werkzeuge werden heute auf der Grundlage von standardisierten Managementarchitekturen konzipiert und entwickelt.

Neben den komponentenorientierten („klassischen") Managementwerkzeugen zur Überwachung und Steuerung des vernetzten Systems sind in einer integrierten Managementlösung auch **Prozessmanagementwerkzeuge** zur Unterstützung der Betriebsprozesse vorzusehen.

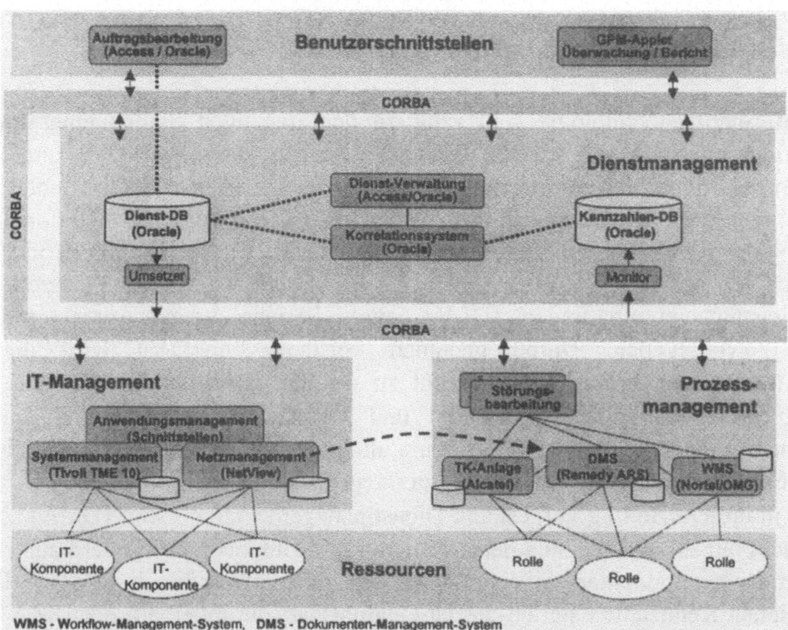

Abbildung 1: Integrierte Dienstmanagementarchitektur

Das bekannteste Prozessmanagementwerkzeug, das bereits heute in komplexen IT-Betrieben zum Einsatz kommt, ist das Trouble Ticket System [Dre97] zur Unterstützung der Störungsbearbeitung.

Die bislang beschriebenen Werkzeuge liefern Komponenten- bzw. Prozess-bezogene Kennzahlen, aus denen der Ist-Wert der gerade erbrachten Qualität ermittelt werden kann. Ein wesentlicher Anteil der gemessenen Kennzahlen wird dazu genutzt, die mit dem Kunden im Rahmen der DLVs vereinbarten Dienstqualitäten zu überprüfen. Die Durchführung des Qualitäts-Soll-Ist-Vergleichs wird in der DMA durch geeignete Dienstmanagementwerkzeuge erbracht.

Dreh- und Angelpunkt der **Dienstmanagementwerkzeuge** als zentraler Bestandteil der DMA ist ein Datenbestand, in dem die mit dem Kunden abgeschlossenen Dienste dokumentiert werden. Der DLV-Datenbestand ist bei Abschluss bzw. Änderung einer DLV geeignet fortzuschreiben und spiegelt den aktuellen Stand abgeschlossener DLVs wider. Neben Informationen über den Dienst und die Kunden werden Informationen über die vereinbarten Qualitätseigenschaften spezifiziert. Die Qualität wird in Form von DLV-Parametern konkretisiert, zu denen jeweils die einzuhaltenden (Qualitäts-Soll-) Werte zugeordnet werden (auch als Qualitätsstufen bzw. Service Levels bezeichnet).

Den DLV-Datenbestand nutzt eine andere Art von Dienstmanagementwerkzeug, der sog. DLV-Umsetzer (vgl. Abbildung 1), dazu, die in der DMA enthaltenen IT-Management- und Prozessmanagementwerkzeuge mit der für diese Werkzeuge jeweils relevanten Qualitäts-Soll-Information zu versorgen. Hierdurch kann die in den IT-Management- und Prozessmanagementwerkzeugen entstehende Qualitäts-Ist-Information (in Form von gemessenen Kennzahlen) mit dem geforderten Soll (in Form der abgeschlossenen DLVs) verglichen werden und ggf. proaktive Maßnahmen zur Sicherstellung der DLVs initiiert werden. Diese Aufgabe wird von einer weiteren Klasse von Dienstmanagementwerkzeugen, den DLV-Monitoren (vgl. Abbildung 1) erbracht. Am Beispiel der Störungsbearbeitung werden Umsetzer und Monitor im folgenden konkretisiert.

Innerhalb der Organisation eines Betreibers nimmt der Störungsbearbeitungs-prozess eine zentrale Stellung hinsichtlich der Durchsetzung vereinbarter DLVs ein. Unter der Annahme beschränkter Kapazitäten in der Störungsbearbeitung sind vorliegende Störungen teilweise sequentiell zu bearbeiten. Ziel ist es, einer Störung eine Priorität zuzuordnen, die möglichst die abgeschlossenen DLVs widerspiegelt.

Umgekehrt müssen für die einzelnen Störungen Messwerte erhoben werden und im Sinne der abgeschlossenen DLVs interpretiert werden, um ein Maß für die Güte der Einhaltung von DLVs zu erhalten.

Die implementierte Lösung benutzt die bereits oben beschriebene DLV-Datenbank und ein auf dem Action Request System (ARS) von Remedy basierendes Störungsbearbeitungswerkzeug. Um Störungen DLV-gerecht behandeln zu können, ist der Zugriff auf die DLV-DB aus der Störungsbearbeitung heraus notwendig. Der Umsetzer ermittelt die zu einem Kunden abgeschlossenen Dienste und die jeweiligen DLVs. Die DLVs dieses Dienstes werden auf die Steuerparameter der Störungsbearbeitung abgebildet, im vorliegenden Fall auf eine Priorität, eine Reaktionszeit und eine Entstörzeit. Jeder Steuerparameter der Störungsbearbeitung ist dabei eine Funktion von den vorhandenen DLVs.

Die ermittelten Parameter werden in die Störungsbearbeitung übernommen und steuern deren weiteren Ablauf. Im vorliegenden Fall geht die Priorität in die Bearbeitungsreihenfolge ein, die Reaktionszeit und die Entstörzeit bestimmen das

Eskalationsverhalten der Störung. Für den umgekehrten Weg, also die Überwachung der Störungsbearbeitung im Sinne der Dienstleistungsvereinbarungen werden wichtige Prozesskennzahlen (Beginn, Ende, Status,...) festgehalten. Diese können mit dem DMA-Werkzeug „Generischer Prozess Monitor" (GPM) ausgelesen und mit den DLV-Werten verglichen werden. Im Unterschied zu vorhandenen Lösungen wird es mit der hier skizzierten Werkzeugumgebung möglich, den Betriebsprozess der Störungsbearbeitung gemäß den abgeschlossenen DLVs durchzuführen.

Zusammenfassung und Ausblick

Mit der in der Informatik deutlich festzustellenden Entwicklung hin zur IT-Dienstleistung mit vertraglich vereinbarten, und juristisch bindenden Qualitätszusicherungen muss sich das IT-Management gleichfalls vom Netz-, System- und Anwendungsmanagement zu einem umfassenden Dienstmanagement entwickeln. Durch diese erweiterte Aufgabenstellung sind neben den "klassischen" IT-Komponentenbezogenen Managementwerkzeugen, die dargestellten Prozess-managementwerkzeuge und die Dienstmanagementwerkzeuge in einer integrierten Dienstmanagementarchitektur (DMA) zu berücksichtigen.

Referenzen

[CFr99] P. Cunningham, F. Fröschl: Electronic Business Revolution – Opportunities and Challenges in the 21st Century, Springer-Verlag, 1999.

[Dre97] G. Dreo Rodosek: A Framework for Supporting Fault Diagnosis in Integrated Network and Systems Management, Dissertation, TU München, 1995.

[Kar98] N. Karten: Establishing Service Level Agreements, www.nkarten.com, 1998

[MNM+00] C. Mayerl, Z. Nochta, M. Müller, M. Schauer, A. Uremovic, S. Abeck: Specification of a Service Management Architecture to Run Distributed and Networked Systems, USM'00, September 2000.

[WLA98] R. Wies, J. Lohrmann, S. Abeck, T. Eckardt: Prozessorientiertes Qualitätsmanagement für IV-Dienstleister – ein Erfahrungsbericht, Wirtschaftsinformatik, Heft 3/98, Vieweg-Verlag, 1998.

A CORBA Domain Management Service

Gerald Brose, Herbert Kiefer, Nicolas Noffke

Institut für Informatik, Freie Universität Berlin,
D–14195 Berlin, Germany
{brose,kiefer,noffke}@inf.fu-berlin.de

Abstract. Policy–based management of large numbers of objects is not adequately supported by current CORBA environments. We discuss and present a policy–neutral Domain Management Service for the grouping of managed objects into domains and the association of policies with these domains. The Domain Service supports domain hierarchies and meta–policies for the resolution of conflicts between policies in overlapping domains.

1   Introduction

In large distributed systems, objects are typically not managed individually but grouped into management domains. This allow managers to structure large systems into manageable subsystems and to model the diverse spheres of management authority and responsibility that are frequently found in large organizations. In the context of policy–based management [Slo94], domains can be regarded as a scoping mechanism for management policies [Hos93, ST94]. To support policy–based management, a number of general–purpose policy languages have been proposed, e.g. [ST94, KKK96, TGML97].

If policy–based management is extended to application management, however, the notion of policies becomes too broad to mandate the definition of a single policy language. We argue that a general management framework must be able to allow the integration of multiple, application–specific policy languages. A modular management infrastructure for CORBA that supports the integration of specific policy languages and mechanisms thus needs a *policy–neutral* domain management service in order to be independent of one particular policy semantics. This paper presents a model for and an implementation of such a service for CORBA that allows the grouping of objects into domains, the construction of domain hierarchies, and the assignment of policies to domains without interpreting the policies. The service can also be used as a generic mechanism to attach arbitrary dynamic properties to CORBA objects and is more flexible than the OMG–specified Property Service [OMG97] because it does not require managed objects to implement service–specific interfaces.

In the remainder of this paper we present our model of policy domains (section 2) and mention implementation aspects (section 3). The paper closes with a summary and an outlook on future work in section 4.

2 A model of CORBA policy domains

The CORBA specification [OMG99] defines interfaces for policies and domains but no service API for managing the life cycle of domain objects, the construction of domain hierarchies, or the membership of objects in domains. An object may be a member in multiple domains, but CORBA requires that every object must be a member of at least one domain. Every domain can have only be associated with one policy of a given type. Individual domains are thus free of conflicts between policies of the same type, such as one access control policy allowing an access and another policy rejecting the same access.

In our model as in [ST94] and [ISO96], a policy domain is basically a relation between a set of member objects and a set of policies. Hierarchical relationships between domains are an important means of expressing delegation of responsibility between authorities and can also model refinement between policies. We model domain hierarchies as acyclic directed graphs where an edge between two domains means that a domain is a child of another domain. The semantics of this relationship is that the parent domain's policies also apply to the members of the child domain. Changes in parent domain policies may affect objects in subdomains whereas policy changes in the child domain only affect the members of that domain and its subdomains. A domain may have multiple parent domains, so the domain graph is not a tree. Allowing multiple parent nodes is useful because it allows to create a union of the parent nodes' policies for the child.

2.1 Meta–Policies

Assuming that policies of different types are entirely orthogonal, there can be no direct policy conflicts within a single domain. Policy conflicts are possible between policies of different domains, however, because objects can be members of more than one domain. Moreover, a domain's policies also apply in its subdomains in a hierarchy. The domain management service should therefore allow the allocation of conflict resolution strategies to potentially conflicting policies. Policy conflicts could, e.g., be resolved by defining a general precedence rule for policies in domains, such as "policies closer to the root of the domain graph take precedence". However, defining a fixed set of general precedence rules will not be appropriate for all policies and applications. We thus call for a *policy type–specific* way of extending the domain service with conflict resolution strategies.

This paper proposes *meta–policies* [Hos93, Küh99, LS99] as a solution. A meta–policy is basically another policy that is associated with a domain and must be interpreted by an enforcement mechanism. We do not attach any more semantics to a meta–policy than that it applies to policies of a given type that in turn apply to the objects in the domain. As with the domain policies, the actual meaning is determined by the mechanism. Meta–policies need not be restricted to conflict resolution as in [Küh99] and [LS99], but can be regarded as general policy operators that are implemented by the individual policy enforcement mechanisms.

2.2   Initial Membership

Because an object must be a member of at least one domain, we must make sure that an object is initially added to a domain on object creation. Otherwise, an object might, e.g., remain unprotected because its creation went unnoticed by an administrator. Object reference creation is performed by CORBA's Portable Object Adapter (POA). A POA can be configured with a set of POA policies, which are not domain–based but simply determine how the POA manages its objects.

To be able to specify the initial domain for newly created objects, the most appropriate approach is to define a new type of POA policy that tells the POA in which domain it should initially place new objects. In our implementation, it is possible to associate a different *InitialMapPolicy* with each POA in a process, either by explicitly creating the POA with this policy in the application code, or by externally specifying the respective system properties. If no such policy has been set, the POA uses a default policy and places all objects in the *ORB domain*, which is an implicit domain for the local process. This implicitly created domain and its rationale are explained in the next section.

3   Implementation Aspects

The implementation of the Domain Management Service uses the JacORB CORBA implementation developed at Freie Universität Berlin. Implementation details can be found in [Kie00]. It provides a GUI management tool called Domain Browser with which domain services can be used centrally by an administrator. The Domain Browser includes an editor for generic policies that can be written as simple lists of name–value pairs and can be conveniently configured to provide different graphical policy editors for different policy types. The access control language VPL [Bro00] that we use to specify object–oriented access control policies requires a different editor, for example.

An important requirement for the implementation is to minimize the performance overhead that is associated with policy lookup operations because this extra cost may render the entire approach infeasible. To enforce access control policies, e.g., every single object access must be checked. It is clearly imperative that remote accesses originating from the enforcement mechanism must be avoided wherever possible. We employ two standard strategies to avoid remote accesses. The first is to use caching of domain state, and the second approach is to exploit locality of domain operations.

To exploit locality, we create a purely local domain graph with its own root. Since this root domain's scope is actually equivalent to the process or ORB boundary, it is called *ORB domain*. Every ORB using our implementation implicitly creates such a domain. In the general case, local objects will need to be part of a larger domain graph. We still create an ORB domain, however, which can then be "mounted" in the global domain graph. In this case, the ORB domain supports locality because it adds local paths between local graph nodes. Without these, even visiting local domains during graph traversal would require remote accesses. Finally, the ORB domain also becomes the demarcation line beyond which caching needs to be employed.

4 Summary and Future Work

The contribution of this paper is a policy–neutral, practically useful domain model for CORBA that supports the definition of meta–policies, which can be used to resolve conflicts between overlapping policy domains. The implementation supports the management of object domains and their related policies and provides a framework for defining policies. Although security policy domains are its prime application area in our project RACCOON, the Domain Service is not limited to security policies. It constitutes a basic management facility that can be used as a building block in a modular, integrated management architecture for CORBA applications. Future work with the Domain Service includes the integration of dedicated VPL support.

Acknowledgments

This work is funded by the German Research Council (DFG).

References

[Bro00]   Gerald Brose. A typed access control model for CORBA. In Frédéric Cuppens, Yves Deswarte, Dieter Gollman, and Michael Weidner, editors, *Proc. ESORICS 2000*, LNCS 1895, pages 88–105. Springer, 2000.

[Hos93]   Hilary H. Hosmer. The multipolicy paradigm for trusted systems. In *Procs. ACM New Security Paradigms Workshop*, pages 19–32, 1993.

[ISO96]   ISO/IEC. *Information Technology — Open Systems Interconnection — Security Frameworks for Open Systems: Overview*. International Standard, ISO/IEC 10181–1:1996(E), 1996.

[Kie00]   Herbert Kiefer. Entwurf und Implementierung eines Domänenverwaltungssystems für CORBA. Master's thesis, Freie Universität Berlin, 2000.

[KKK96]   Thomas Koch, Christoph Krell, and Bernd Krämer. Policy definition language for automated management of distributed systems. 2nd International Workshop on Systems Management, IEEE Computer Society, June 1996.

[Küh99]   Winfried Kühnhauser. *Metapolitiken*. GMD Research Series. GMD, 1999.

[LS99]   Emil C. Lupu and Morris Sloman. Conflicts in policy–based distributed systems management. *IEEE Transactions on Software Engineering*, 25(6):852–896, 1999.

[OMG97]   OMG. *CORBAservices: Common Object Services Specification*, November 1997.

[OMG99]   OMG. *The Common Object Request Broker: Architecture and Specification, Revision 2.3*, June 1999.

[Slo94]   Morris Sloman. Policy driven management for distributed systems. *Journal of Network and Systems Management*, 2(4), 1994.

[ST94]   Morris Sloman and Kevin Twidle. Domains: A framework for structuring management policy. In Morris Sloman, editor, *Network and Distributed Systems Management*, chapter 16. Addison–Wesley, 1994.

[TGML97]   M.T. Tu, F. Griffel, M. Merz, and W. Lamersdorf. Generic policy management for open service markets. In *Proc. International Conference on Distributed Applications and Interoperable Systems (DAIS'97)*, pages 212–222, Cottbus, Germany, September 1997. Chapman & Hall.

An Approach to Reduce Delay and Jitter for Time-Critical Data in IEEE 802.11 Wireless Local Area Networks

Verena Kahmann

Institute of Telematics, University of Karlsruhe, Zirkel 2, 76128 Karlsruhe, Germany

Abstract. Most IEEE 802.11 compliant WLAN products use a contention based medium access protocol, thus quality guarantees for delay can hardly be given. However, applications with needs for small delays should be run in WLANs also. In this short paper, an approach for QoS enhancement with a priority queueing scheme on the link layer is evaluated. This link layer approach has the advantage that existing network adapter products need not be changed. Simulation results show that such a queueing scheme can help to differentiate between several applications at a station and reduce delay and jitter for time-critical data.

1 Introduction

Wireless local area networks (WLANs) have found wide acceptance recently. IEEE 802.11 has emerged as important standard on WLANs with several products on the market. In most of these, the wireless channel is accessed using a contention for the shared medium, so quality guarantees can hardly be given. In this short paper, an approach to reduce delay and jitter for certain applications using a priority queueing scheme on link layer is proposed and evaluated by means of simulation. For implementing this approach, existing products need not be changed. The rest of this short paper is organized as follows. After the IEEE 802.11 standard and Quality of Service (QoS) parameter definitions are summarized in section 2 resp. 3, a priority queueing scheme for enhancing QoS is proposed in section 4, where simulation results show the benefits of such an approach. Related work is discussed in section 5 before we conclude the paper.

2 The IEEE 802.11 standard for wireless LANs

The IEEE 802.11 standard [4] is defined for the physical layer and the MAC layer. The MAC layer comprises the distributed coordination function (DCF) and the optional point coordination function (PCF) which is a polling scheme able to guarantee timely delivery of frames within certain bounds [4, 6].

The key feature of the DCF is a distributed algorithm for gaining access to the radio medium, which relies on carrier sensed multiple access with a backoff algorithm for collision avoidance (CSMA/CA). This algorithm can be used in infrastructure (i.e. with an access point) or ad-hoc mode. Before sending, every station has to sense the medium for a DIFS time interval (DCF interframe space). If the medium is free, a backoff timer is started with an initial value chosen from the contention window (CW) interval [0–CW]. The backoff timer is decreased at fixed time slots within the station, and when zero is reached, the station starts its transmission. Other stations who still have their backoff timer running freeze their timers and defer their transmissions.

Since collisions cannot be detected on the radio link every frame is acknowledged after a short interframe space (SIFS) of time. SIFS is always of shorter length than DIFS. If two stations have chosen the same value from the contention window interval, a collision occurs. The stations double the contention window and restart the distributed algorithm. As the contention window is randomly chosen, transmissions may be deferred and collisions may occur several times. Thus no time guarantees can be given and the DCF is not very well-suited for speech or other real-time data.

3   QoS parameters

Real-time applications put certain requirements on parameters like throughput, delay or jitter. The quantities of those are dependent on the special application. Throughput in our terms is defined as the average number of bits per second passed from the MAC sublayer to higher layers at the destination. Simulations [4] have shown that the throughput in an IEEE 802.11 WLAN is dependent on the amount of data passed down to the MAC sublayer, on the frame length, the channel state and certain MAC layer mechanisms like RTS/CTS. The saturation throughput under ideal channel conditions amounts to around 90 % whereas under bad conditions it can even drop to 20 %. The end-to-end delay is composed by a sum of delays at the single layers. For our analysis we will measure the delay from the time the first bit is sent from the network layer until the time the last bit is passed up to the network layer. We do this to include the queueing delay in the link layer queue as well as the access delay for the medium. As queueing delay and access delay may vary over time, delay jitter occurs, being defined by the maximum difference in the end-to-end delay of any two packets [8].

4   Priority queueing scheme for QoS enhancement

Given the pre-condition of not changing the standard or network adapter products, a reduction of the medium access delay is not easy to achieve if no reduction of the traffic is applied. Therefore we have considered a reduction of the queueing time at the link layer. To achieve this, we apply a priority queueing scheme where the user tags connections with a priority label, e.g. using the scheme of the Differentiated Services architecture. The packets tagged this way are put into one or more separate queues mapped to the priority levels. In our analysis, we have considered one queue for real-time data which is always served first and one for the remaining traffic.

For our simulations, we used the 802.11 model of ns-2 [5] which we extended with the priority queueing scheme. The results presented here are simulations of infrastructure networks (2 Mbit/s bandwidth) with 10 stations. All data traffic is flowing from the access point to the stations, containing one video stream with and one without priority, both taken from traces of H.263 movies with a target bit rate of 64 kbit/s each. The non-real time traffic has been modeled as file transfer connections via TCP from the access point node to other stations in the cell starting at random times. The relative frequency values of the delay for each traffic class are plotted in figure 1.

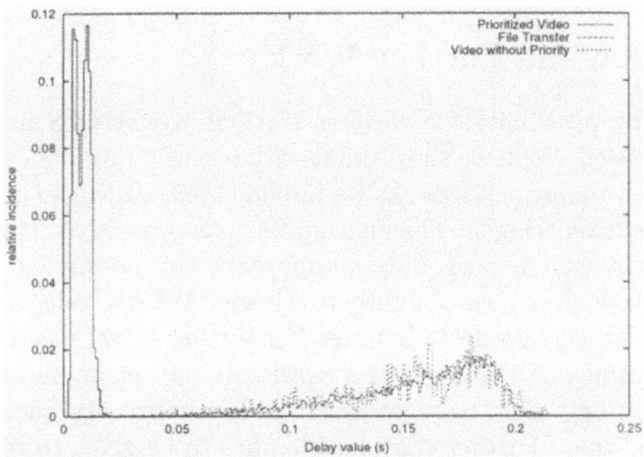

Fig. 1. Relative frequency of delay for different packet classes

The results show that the packets scheduled first experienced much less end-to-end delay and jitter than file transfer and video without priority. Other simulations we performed show that our approach is not as beneficial if there is only video traffic or only UDP connections with medium load. However, the priority queueing performed very well if any file transfer via TCP was started or if UDP traffic load went over 60 % (1.2 Mbit/s). In WLANs with data flows from several stations the jitter values for priority traffic are higher than shown here, because without changing MAC layer parameters priority over other stations cannot be achieved, but the delay is bounded there by applying priority queueing. Thus. if a user has only some applications running with the need for QoS and/or there is TCP traffic in the WLAN, the proposed queueing can help to differentiate between the traffic classes.

5   Related Work

Link layer approaches to enhance QoS on an IEEE 802.11 WLAN have been considered mostly with respect to reduce error probability up to now [1, 2].

Different approaches to improve the behavior of the 802.11 DCF by tuning e.g. contention window sizes have been proposed within the last years [7, 3]. The disadvantage of all these approaches is that the standard has to be changed which might take incalculable time.

In constrast to that, our approach of enhancing the link layer can be implemented at once. A further advantage is that other WLAN stations in the same cell do not suffer from worse quality so our approach is fair in that sense. With approaches changing the standard hardware migration must be done or flows might even be starved. Even if the standard will be changed sometimes, our approach could be implemented and help users to give QoS for their specifically chosen applications.

6 Conclusion and Further Work

In this work, the possibility for wireless stations to get QoS in IEEE 802.11 WLANs is evaluated. We have shown that with existing products where only the DCF is available, timely services can be provided only with the implementation of a priority queueing scheme. The guarantees given are only soft guarantees, as the MAC layer is not changed, but the approach can be implemented quickly. With this approach, even over a slightly overloaded WLAN, selected flows can be transported within certain delay bounds. For further work, measurements with real implementations of Differentiated Services as an example for an Internet QoS architecture and 802.11 are planned. Different priority queueing schemes can be examined then. Further consideration has to be given to roaming within an IEEE 802.11 network. We will include measurements of this into a testbed.

References

[1] B. S. Bakshi et al. Improving Performance of TCP over Wireless Networks. *Computer Communication Review*, 27(4), ACM SIGCOMM, October 1997.

[2] P. Bhagwat et al. Enhancing Throughput over Wireless LANs using Channel State Dependent Packet Scheduling. In *Proceedings of IEEE INFOCOM*, San Francisco, USA, March 1996.

[3] F. Cali et al. IEEE 802.11 Wireless LAN: Capacity Analysis and Protocol Enhancement. In *Proceedings of IEEE INFOCOM*, San Francisco, USA, April 1998.

[4] B. P. Crow et al. IEEE 802.11 Wireless Local Area Networks. *IEEE Communications Magazine*, 35(9), September 1997.

[5] Kevin Fall and Kannan Varadhan. ns Notes and Documentation. The VINT Project, LBNL, http://www.isi.edu/nsnam/ns/, October 2000.

[6] J.-B. Lee and A. Eleftheriadis. A Performance Analysis for the IEEE 802.11 Wireless LAN MAC Protocol. *ACM / IEEE Transactions on Networking*, March 1998.

[7] J. Weinmiller et al. Analyzing and Tuning the Distributed Coordination Function in the IEEE 802.11 DFWMAC Standard. In *International Workshop on Modeling, Analysis and Simulation of Computer and Telecommunication Systems (MASCOTS '96)*, San Jose, California, Februar 1996.

[8] H. Zhang and S. Keshav. Comparison of Rate-Based Service Disciplines. *Computer Communication Review*, 21(4), ACM SIGCOMM, September 1991.

Telekommunikationsnetze in CORBA-basierten Echtzeit-Systemen am Beispiel wirklichkeitsnaher Telepräsenzanwendungen

Guochun Lin, Thomas Unterschütz, Veit Vogel

T-Nova Deutsche Telekom Innovationsgesellschaft mbH
Am Kavalleriesand 3, 64295 Darmstadt
{Guochun.Lin, Thomas.Unterschuetz, Veit.Vogel}@telekom.de

Detlef Reintsema, Ralf Koeppe

Deutsches Zentrum für Luft- und Raumfahrt e.V. (DLR)
Institut für Robotik und Mechatronik
Postfach 1116, D-82230 Weßling
{Detlef.Reintsema, Ralf.Koeppe }@dlr.de

Einführung

In einer typischen Telerobotikanwendung steuert der Mensch (Operator) einen entfernten Roboter (Teleoperator), um verschiedene Manipulationsaktionen durchzuführen. Entsteht dabei unter Verwendung geeigneter Sensordisplays, wie Datenbrille und haptisches Eingabegerät, der subjektive Eindruck in der entfernten oder nicht zugänglichen Umgebung präsent zu sein, spricht man von wirklichkeitsnaher Telepräsenz. Um anspruchsvolle Telemanipulationsaufgaben auszuführen, müssen neben audiovisuellen auch haptische Wahrnehmungen ausgetauscht werden, um das Ertasten von Oberflächen und das Fühlen von Kräften und Bewegungen zu erlauben. Zur Realisierung verteilter Robotikanwendungen wird am Institut für Robotik und Mechatronik des DLR mit CORBA auf eine objektorientierte Middleware-Technologie, offen für verteilte Anwendungen verschiedenster Arten, gesetzt.

Die aktuellen CORBA-Spezifikationen weisen eine Reihe nützlicher Eigenschaften zur Realisierung verteilter Telerobotikanwendungen auf. Dazu zählen neben der Lokationstransparenz, die Unabhängigkeit von der Programmiersprache, der Rechnerarchitektur sowie der Implementation. Diese Eigenschaften stellen die Interoperabilität, die Portabilität und das Interworking verteilter Komponenten sicher. Anwendungen in der Telerobotik stellen allerdings sehr hohe Anforderungen an die zugrundeliegende Netzinfrastruktur bezüglich Echtzeitfähigkeit und Laufzeitverhalten. Bisher versucht die Object Management Group (OMG) mit Real-Time CORBA ein vorhersagbares Laufzeitverhalten von CORBA-Komponenten (mittels Methoden Priorisierung und Scheduling) im Rechner zu unterstützen. Eine Schnittstelle zur Anbindung alternativer echtzeitfähiger Netzarchitekturen ist derzeit jedoch nicht standardisiert, obwohl mit CORBAtelecomms eine Spezifikation existiert, um Dienstgüte im Netz an die speziellen Anforderungen einer Anwendung (Audio/Video Streams) zu binden. Abhilfe können hier leitungsvermittelte Netze wie ISDN, B-ISDN/ATM oder ADSL leisten. Derzeit basiert Nachrichtenkommunikation jedoch einzig auf einer TCP/IP-basierten Transportunterstützung. Aufgrund fehlender Echtzeitunterstützung im TCP/IP-Transportnetz sind über große Distanzen verteilte Echtzeitsysteme für Telepräsenzanwendungen in der Telerobotik oder der Telemedizin kaum realisierbar.

In einer Forschungskooperation zwischen dem DLR (Institut für Robotik und Mechatronik) und der Deutschen Telekom AG wird derzeit eine ATM-basierte CORBA-Plattform für verteilte Telepräsenzanwendungen entwickelt. Dieser Beitrag stellt nachfolgend vor, wie die Integration alternativer Transportnetze über eine offene Transportschnittstelle in CORBA-Plattformen aussehen kann.

Telekommunikationsnetze für verteilte Echtzeitanwendungen

Die Nutzung von Telekommunikationsnetzen für verteilte Echtzeitanwendungen kann auf der Basis offener Standards der OMG und des TINA-C (Telecommunications Information Networking Architecture Consortium) erfolgen. Die OMG stellt mit der Object Management Architecture (OMA) und den zugehörigen CORBA-Spezifikationen ein konsistentes Objektmodell für verteilte Anwendungen zur Verfügung. Das TINA-C hat auf der Basis der ODP-Standards (Open Distributed Processing) Softwarearchitekturen konzipiert, die eine effiziente Integration von Telekommunikationsnetzen, Diensteimplementierung und Dienstebereitstellung unterstützen. Die Objektinteraktion (Interworking) wird hierbei durch eine verteilte Verarbeitungsumgebung (Distributed Processing Environment DPE) sichergestellt. Mit Hilfe der DPE werden die Transportmechanismen einzelner Netze (Internet, ISDN, ATM) vor den Anwendungen verborgen und ein einheitliches Programmiermodell für die Anwendungen verfügbar. Da beide Ansätze eine Reihe von Gemeinsamkeiten aufweisen und einander ergänzen, bieten sich zur Realisierung der DPE CORBA-konforme Produkte an. Auf der Basis des ORB-Produktes ORBacus der Fa. OOC inc. hat die Deutsche Telekom mit dem Open Communication Interface (OCI) einen Protokolladapter für ATM (ATMIOP) implementiert, um B-ISDN/ATM als Transportarchitektur in CORBA-basierten DPE-Realisierungen zu nutzen.

CORBA/ATMIOP: ein ORB-Protokolladapter für ATM

Eine Analyse der Komponentenstruktur des ORBs zeigt, dass eine flexible Anbindung alternativer Transportarchitekturen im Transport Layer, also zwischen Message und Network Layer, erfolgen kann (siehe Fig 1.). Während im CORBA-Standard das General Inter-ORB Protocol (GIOP) die Message-Schicht spezifiziert, beinhaltet die Transport-Schicht Adaptionsfunktionen für das darunterliegende Transportnetz (Network Layer API). In einem TCP/IP-basierten ORB wird die Transport-Schicht durch die Implementierung des Internet Inter-ORB Protocols (IIOP) abgebildet. In einer Zusammenarbeit zwischen der Humboldt-Universität zu Berlin, der Fa. OOC Inc. und der Deutsche Telekom AG wurde ein offenes Schnittstellenkonzept (Open Commucation Interface OCI) erarbeitet, das in einer OCI-IDL-Spezifikation vorliegt. Durch die konkrete Spezialisierung dieser OCI-IDL-Schnittstelle können alternative

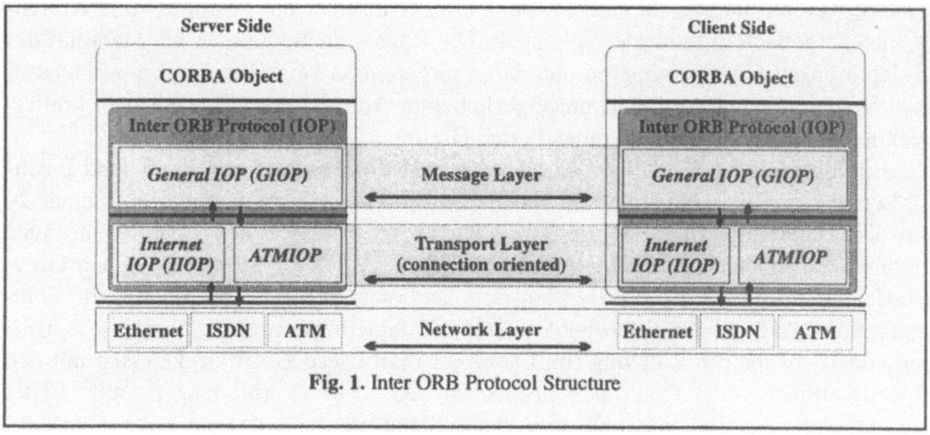

Fig. 1. Inter ORB Protocol Structure

Transportprotokolle, die eine sichere Datenübertragung gewährleisten (z.B. ISDN, B-ISDN/ATM), an den ORB angebunden werden. Eine ausführliche Beschreibung der OCI-IDL-Schnittstelle sowie weiterführende Hinweise sind in den Dokumenten der Firma OOC Inc. zu finden. Nachrichten zwischen verteilten Komponenten (Objekten) werden zwischen ATMIOP-basierten ORBs nun über geeignete ATM-Verbindungen (SVCs oder PVCs) ausgetauscht, wobei die Implementierung des ATMIOP auf das X/Open Transport Interface (XTI) für ATM (Network Layer API, AAL5) zurückgreift.

CORBA/ATMIOP-basierte Telemanipulation

Am Institut für Robotik und Mechatronik werden komplexe Mechatronik- und Antriebssysteme angefangen von multisensoriellen Greifern über künstliche Mehr-Fingerhände bis hin zum Leichtbauroboter entwickelt (siehe Fig. 2). Teleaktionen der künstlichen Hand werden vom Bediener über einen Datenhandschuh kontrolliert (siehe Fig. 3). Die aktuelle Fingerstellung wird hierbei vom Datenhandschuh erfasst und auf der Basis von CORBA/ATMIOP über ATM-Verbindungen an die künstliche Hand weitergeleitet. Kräfte, die während der Handhabungsaufgabe (z.B. beim Greifen) auftreten, werden durch integrierte Sensorik erfasst und über eine weitere CORBA/ATMIOP Verbindung dem Bediener

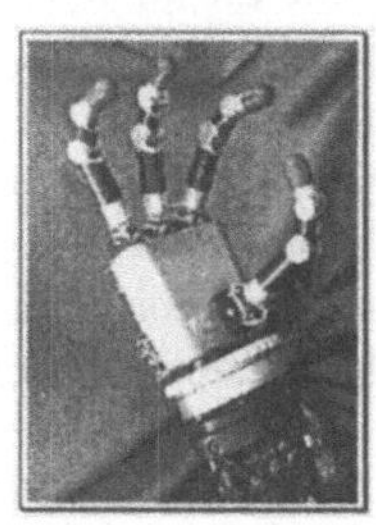

Fig. 3. DLR-4-Fingerhand

auf das Exoskeletton des Datenhandschuhs übertragen. Die Anforderung an den haptischen Kanal, hier beschränken wir uns auf die Übertragung der Wahrnehmung von Kräften und Bewegungen, erfordert eine bidirektionale Datenverbindung. Dabei wird das kraftreflektierende Bediengerät "quasi fest" mit dem Robotersystem gekoppelt.

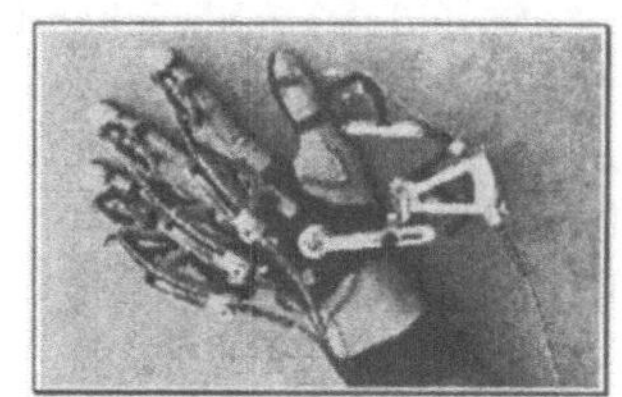

Fig. 2. Datenhandschuh mit Exoskeletton

Hierzu werden die Regelkreise der beiden Systeme über die Positions- und Kraftsignale energetisch miteinander gekoppelt. Die Regelsysteme müssen die Stabilität des Telepräsenzsystems garantieren und dafür sorgen, dass keine Energie im geschlossenen System erzeugt wird, was unweigerlich zum Aufschwingen des mit dem kraftreflektierenden Bediengerät kommandierten Greifers führen würde.

Ein high-fidelity Krafteindruck erfordert eine Übertragung von Kraft- und Positionswerte mit einer Abtastrate von bis zu 1 ms und einer Verzögerungszeit kleiner 20 ms. Die Darstellung dieser Werte erfordert aber nur wenige Bytes. Erste Erfahrungen beruhen auf einer T-Net ATM-Verbindung (PVC, VBR+, 2 Mbit/s) zwischen Oberpfaffenhofen und Darmstadt. Hier hat sich das Potential von ATM für verteilte Echtzeitsysteme (z.B. in der Telerobotik oder der Telemedizin) gezeigt: konstante Totzeiten von 10-12 ms pro Richtung (im Labor < 1 ms). Diese Zeiten decken sich mit den Spezifikationen der Deutschen Telekom AG. Für Verbindungen mit CBR-Vereinbarung werden innerhalb von Deutschland sogar Laufzeiten unter 5 ms pro Richtung garantiert.

Zusammenfassung

Telerobotiksysteme, die einen Eindruck wirklichkeitsnaher Telepräsenz erzeugen, erfordern eine zeitsynchrone Übertragung multimodaler Sinneseindrücke, bestehend aus visuellen, akustischen und haptischen Daten. Neben der Zeitsynchronität, stellt jeder Modalitätenkanal je nach geforderter Qualität sehr spezifische und unterschiedliche Anforderungen an die Übertragungsbandbreite und maximal tolerierbare Verzögerungszeit. Der Austausch multimodaler Daten erfolgt daher über separate Datenverbindungen (Kanäle) für Operationen (Manipulationen), Force-Feedback (Haptik), (Stereo-) Videobilder und Audiodaten, die ganz unterschiedliche Anforderungen an die Dienstgüte (Quality of Service, QoS) der zugrundeliegenden Telekommunikationsnetze stellen.

Auf der Basis von CORBA als Laufzeitumgebung verwirklicht die hier vorgestellte Plug-in-Technik die konsistente Integration geeigneter Informations- und Kommunikationstechnologien, die eine einfache und schnelle Nutzung in der Telerobotik und deren Anwendungsfelder erlaubt. Das CORBA-Paradigma wird damit nicht nur für Anwendungen im Internet, sondern auch für verteilte Echtzeitsysteme und (wirklichkeitsnahe) Telepräsenzanwendungen in anderen populären Telekommunikationsnetzen (B-ISDN, ISDN, ADSL, GSM), insbesondere für sehr spezielle, proprietäre Protokolle, interessant.

Aufgrund der zahlreichen Entwicklungsarbeiten an der Plug-in-Technik im OMG-Memberkreis hat die OMG ein Request for Proposal "Extensible Transport Framework RFP" gestartet. Das Ziel ist ein Standard zur Integration und Anbindung alternativer Transportarchitekturen, um die Portabilität und Interoperabilität in verteilten Umgebungen transportunabhängig zu sichern und letztlich neue Anwendungsgebiete für CORBA zu erschließen. An dieser Stelle möchten wir allen Beteiligten, insbesondere Olaf Kath von der Humboldt-Universität, Marc Laukien von der Fa. OOC Inc. und Rainer Rugggaber von der Universität Karlsruhe für die erfolgreiche Zusammenarbeit danken.

Session 8:

Work in Progress - Anwendungen

Einsatz von LDAP in einer Telekooperationsumgebung

Rasmus Faust, Uwe von Lukas

Zentrum für Graphische Datenverarbeitung e.V.
Joachim-Jungius-Straße 11
D-18059 Rostock
uvl@rostock.zgdv.de

Abstract. Der vorliegende Beitrag behandelt den Einsatz von LDAP als Basisdienst für die unternehmensübergreifende Telekooperation, präsentiert ein Konzept für die Verwaltung konferenzrelevanter Daten unter Einbeziehung statischer und dynamischer Attribute und nimmt eine vergleichende Bewertung verschiedener Implementierungsvarianten vor. Der Schwerpunkt der Ausführungen liegt dabei auf dem applikationsunabhängigen Datenschema, das die Grundlage für die Realisierung der darauf aufbauenden Dienste bildet und maßgeblichen Einfluss auf die Performanz der Gesamtlösung hat.

1 Motivation und Umfeld

Beim computergestützten kooperativen Arbeiten (Computer Supported Cooperative Work, CSCW) ist die Verwaltung von Benutzern, Gruppen und anderen verzeichnisorientierten Daten ein wichtiger Basisdienst [LSG98]. Zum Zugriff darauf wird zunehmend das Lightweight Directory Access Protocol LDAP [HS95] verwendet. Dieses ist heute primär in Intranet-Umgebungen als Verzeichnisdienst weit verbreitet und wird von einer Vielzahl von Produkten (sowohl Clients als auch Servern) unterstützt. Was allerdings noch fehlt, ist einerseits eine Vereinheitlichung eines umfassenden Datenschemas für Konferenzdaten, das von einzelnen Werkzeugen abstrahiert und anderseits eine Untersuchung des Laufzeitverhaltens beim Einsatz eines derartigen Schemas in einer konkreten Systemumgebung. Diese beiden Punkte sollen im Rahmen dieses Beitrags beleuchtet werden.

Das BMBF-Leitprojekt iViP[1], das den Rahmen für die vorgestellten Arbeiten bildet, zielt auf die Konzeption und Realisierung einer umfassenden und flexiblen Arbeitsumgebung für den Ingenieur von morgen, die individuell auf die Erfordernisse der Unternehmen angepasst werden kann [KTA98]. Diese stellt u.a. Systemdienste zur Einbindung und Verwaltung von Applikationen, der Benutzerverwaltung und zur bedarfsgesteuerten Nutzung entfernter Dienste (Software on Demand) zur Verfügung. Aufbauend darauf werden neuartige Werkzeuge zur Spezifikation in frühen Phasen der Produktentwicklung, zum Komplexitätsmanagement oder zur Simulation realisiert und dem iViP-Anwender zusammen mit externen Systemen (CAD, DMU etc.) in einheitlicher Weise verfügbar gemacht. Die vielfältige Unterstützung von unternehmensübergreifenden Kooperationen über den gemeinsamen Zugriff auf Produktdaten, firmenübergreifender Workflows, aber auch die explizite Integration von Werkzeugen für das kooperative Arbeiten ist ein wesentliches Kennzeichen von iViP. Der Einsatz von iViP ist sowohl für kleine und mittlere Unternehmen als auch für Großunternehmen geplant. Die systemtechnische Infrastruktur muss demnach flexibel und skalierbar sein und sich gut in heterogene Umgebungen integrieren lassen.

---

[1] Das Leitprojekt iViP (Innovative Technologien und Systeme für die integrierte Virtuelle Produktentstehung) wird mit Mitteln des BMBF unter Förderkennzeichen 02PL10xxx gefördert und vom Projektträger PFT, Forschungszentrum Karlsruhe betreut.

2 Konzept

Unser Konzept für die LDAP-basierte Verwaltung orientiert sich am allgemeinen Fall einer unternehmensübergreifenden Kooperation, die in Arbeitsgruppen organisiert ist. Individuelle unternehmensinterne Teams oder eine ad-hoc Nutzer-zu-Nutzer-Kommunikation stehen zunächst nicht im Mittelpunkt, können über die entwickelten Konzepte jedoch ebenfalls abgebildet werden.

Die folgende Abbildung gibt einen Überblick über die Architektur der Konferenzkomponente von iViP [LMS00]. Die CSCW Directory Wrapper Komponente dient hierbei als "Protokoll-Brücke" zwischen CORBA und LDAP. Die Komponenten der Architektur (Media Wrapper, Cockpit, Conference Manager und CSCW Directory Wrapper) sind als CORBA-Services in Java implementiert.

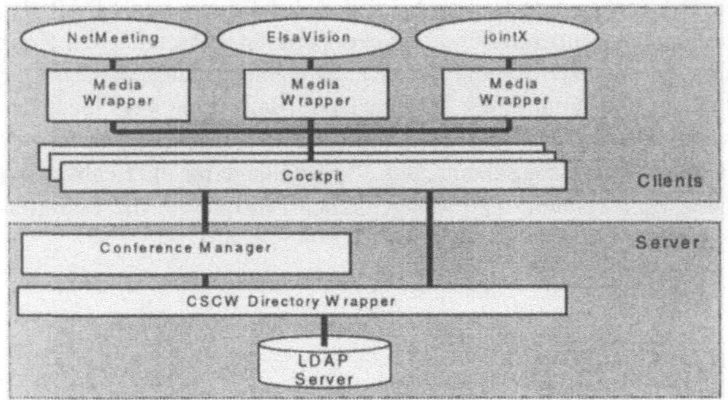

Fig. 1. Architektur der iViP-Konferenzkomponente

Das Cockpit ist die zentrale Benutzungsschnittstellenkomponente für Konferenzen. Es steuert die einzelnen Konferenzmedien, wie beispielsweise NetMeeting, ElsaVision oder jointX über entsprechende Adapter ("Media Wrapper"). Durch die Trennung von Konferenzadministration und Medien wird es auf einfache Weise möglich, zu einer laufenden Konferenz bei Bedarf neue Medien (z.B. Whiteboard) hinzuzunehmen oder nicht mehr benötigte Medien zu deaktivieren, ohne dass die Rollenverteilung neu für dieses Medium konfiguriert werden müsste. Dies stellt einen wesentlichen Vorteil gegenüber den heute bestehenden, nicht integrierten Systemen dar. Auf Serverseite existiert ein Conference Manager, der zur Verwaltung und Steuerung von Konferenzen eingesetzt wird. Diese Komponente ist dafür verantwortlich, konferenzrelevante Daten über den CSCW Directory Wrapper in den LDAP Server zu schreiben.

Für den Anwender erleichtert sich so der Umgang mit parallel eingesetzten Konferenzmedien, die auch auf unterschiedlichen Protokollen basieren können. Zudem kann über die Architektur auch abgefragt werden, welche Konferenzmedien bei anderen Konferenzteilnehmern verfügbar sind und ob diese Kanäle schon belegt sind.

Die Verwendung von LDAP hat den Vorteil, dass sich statische Kontaktinformationen wie E-Mail-Adresse, Postanschrift oder Telefonnummer (die u.a. zum Einberufen von Internetkonferenzen nützlich sind) bereits aus den Angestellten-Verzeichnissen der beteiligten Unternehmen, die heute schon oft in LDAP-Servern abgelegt sind, ermitteln lassen. Dazu kommen dynamische Daten, wie die CORBA-Referenz (IOR) auf das Cockpit des Nutzers, sobald sich dieser einloggt. Damit stehen anderen Nutzern die zum Aufbau einer Kommunikationsverbindung nötigen Daten bereit.

Das Datenschema ist bei LDAP nicht standardisiert (obwohl sich für bestimmte Anwendungen gewisse Schemata etabliert haben). Es kann und muss also für jeden Einsatzzweck festgelegt werden. Durch die Objektklassen und die zugehörigen Attribute wird so spezifiziert, welche Daten verwaltet werden können. Unser Schema entstand nach der Analyse verschiedener Vorarbeiten im Bereich des kooperativen Arbeitens [Böt99, GJ97, NAC97, Smi00], die sich mit LDAP beschäftigten, sowie der Analyse der Datenstrukturen (soweit zugänglich) von verbreiteten Software-Produkten bzw. Protokollen im CSCW-Bereich (Microsoft ILS, ICQ, Netscape Mail, T.120 etc.). Das daraus entwickelte LDAP-Schema bildet damit eine umfassende Grundlage für die einheitliche Verwaltung konferenz-

relevanter Daten über LDAP. Die Skalierbarkeit der Lösung und ein vertretbarer Implementierungsaufwand bei der Einbindung von Software-Werkzeugen waren wesentliche Randbedingungen.

Das Schema speichert folgende Entitäten: *Nutzer* eines CSCW-Systems mit expliziten Kontaktinformationen (E-Mail, Telefon-Nummer etc.) und/oder Verweise auf einen White Pages-Eintrag im
Unternehmen, *Arbeitsgruppen* in Form einer Liste der DNs ihrer Mitglieder, hierarchisch strukturier-
bare *Adressbücher* sowohl für einzelne Nutzer als auch für Arbeitsgruppen sowie öffentliche *Konfe-*
renzen mit Metainformationen und Kontaktpunkt (IOR der Konferenzverwaltung). Die folgende Graphik zeigt ein Beispiel für einen daraus resultierenden Verzeichnisbaum (Directory Information Tree,
DIT) mit dem vorgeschlagenen Schema, wie er sich in einem LDAP-Browser präsentiert:

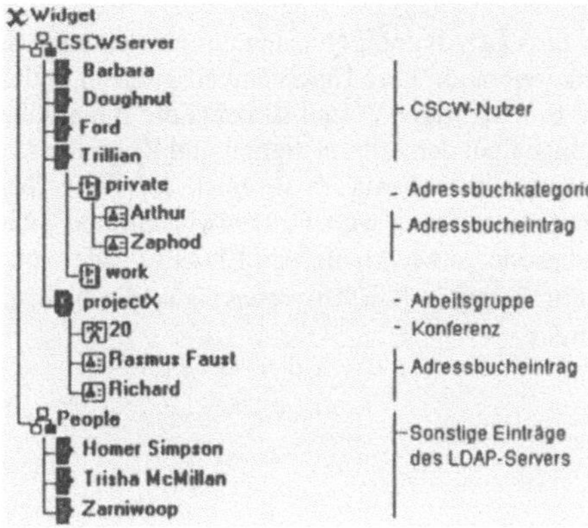

Fig. 2. Beispielhafte Einträge unter Nutzung des CSCW-Schemas

3 Analyse

Da das entwickelte LDAP-Schema in einer interaktiven Umgebung Einsatz finden wird, in der ge-
ringe Verarbeitungszeiten eine wesentliche Rolle spielen, wurden verschiedene Tests durchgeführt
[FL00], um den Einfluss des Schemas auf das Laufzeitverhalten zu ermitteln und Ansatzpunkte für
Optimierungen zu finden.

Ein vergleichender Test unter Nutzung der frei verfügbaren LDAP-Implementierung SLAPD der
University of Michigan [UM96] sollte klären, wie sich die Strukturierung des Verzeichnisbaumes auf
die Komplexität der Anfragen und somit die Verarbeitungsgeschwindigkeit auswirkt. Dabei wurden
ein stark ausdifferenziertes Schema und ein flaches Schema gegenübergestellt und verschiedene
Suchanfragen, wie sie für eine CSCW-Umgebung typisch sind, zum Test verwendet. Beispielsweise
wurden die Mitglieder einer Arbeitsgruppe ermittelt oder nach Adressbucheinträgen, die gewissen
Suchfiltern genügen, gesucht. Unsere Datenbasis bestand dabei aus ca. 550 automatisch generierten
Einträgen. Die Tests fanden lokal statt, d.h. LDAP-Server und Testclient befanden sich auf derselben
Maschine, um Einflüsse des Netzwerks auszuschließen.

Die erste Schema-Variante benutzte eine hohe Zahl von Knoten, d.h. einen stark strukturierten
DIT, während in der zweiten Variante möglichst viel Information in Attributen gespeichert und somit
die Anzahl der Knoten reduziert wurde. Das Schema mit dem stark strukturierten DIT schnitt bei dem
Test (bei fast allen Suchanfragen, eine Ausnahme machte lediglich das Adressbuch, da dieses im
tiefen Schema auch die Arbeitsgruppenmitglieder explizit enthielt) deutlich schlechter als das weniger
stark strukturierte Schema ab – die Ausführung benötigte im Durchschnitt ca. 150% der Zeit, bei
einer einzelnen Operation sogar über 600%. Allerdings konnte im flachen Schema nicht die gesamte
Information des tiefen Schemas abgelegt werden, beispielsweise war es hier nicht mehr möglich,
arbeitsgruppenspezifische Privilegien und Rollen zu einem Nutzer zu speichern.

Ein zweiter Test sollte allgemeine Unterschiede bei verschiedenen Client-Implementationen er-
mitteln. Dem Zugriff über das Java Naming and Directory Interface JNDI [Sun99] wurde dazu eine
CORBA-basierte Lösung gegenübergestellt, bei der der Zugriff auf den LDAP-Server über einen in
Python implementierten CORBA-Wrapper durchgeführt wurde. In dem Test, der sowohl Suchanfra-

gen als auch Modifikationen umfasste, wurden verschiedene Szenarien bezüglich der Verteilung der Komponenten im Netzwerk (Testclient, CORBA-Wrapper und LDAP-Server können jeweils auf verschiedenen Rechnern laufen) durchgespielt. Bei den Messungen wurden nur geringe Vorteile für die JNDI-Variante erkennbar. So sollte die Entscheidung bei der Wahl zwischen JNDI und CORBA-Zugriff stets aufgrund spezieller Randbedingungen im Anwendungsumfeld (beispielsweise konkretes Verteilungsszenario oder notwendige Sprachunabhängigkeit) getroffen werden.

4 Zusammenfassung und Ausblick

Die Arbeiten haben gezeigt, dass LDAP unter Nutzung des entwickelten Schemas flexibel und performant genug ist, um die Telekooperation über Unternehmensgrenzen und unterschiedliche Applikationen hinweg zu unterstützen. Ein wichtiger Vorteil ist dabei die Integration mit bestehenden Datenbeständen, was zu Vereinfachungen bei der Administration und Konsistenzsicherung führt.

Zukünftig gilt es das vorgestellte Schema im Hinblick auf Zeitverhalten sowie weitere Anwendungen (private Internet-Konferenzen etc.) weiter zu entwickeln und Sicherheitsmechanismen einzubauen. Dazu lassen sich insbesondere Merkmale von LDAPv3, wie beispielsweise dynamische Einträge [YWG99] oder signierte Zugriffe [GR99], verwenden, die bislang allerdings noch nicht von allen Servern unterstützt werden.

Literatur

[Böt99] U. Böttge: „Entwicklung eines Konzeptes zur Verwaltung von Informationen für flexible Kommunikationsbeziehungen in der verteilten Produktentwicklung" Diplomarbeit. TU Berlin, April 1999.

[FL00] R. Faust und U. von Lukas: „Using LDAP for cross-enterprise collaboration", Technical Report, Zentrum für Graphische Datenverarbeitung, Rostock, März 2000.

[GJ97] T. Genovese, B. Jennings: „A Common Schema for the Internet White Pages Services", IETF RFC 2218, http://www.rfc-editor.org/rfc/rfc2218.txt, Oktober 1997.

[GR99] B. Greenblatt und P. Richard: „An LDAP Control and Schema for Holding Operation Signatures", http://www.rfc-editor.org/rfc/rfc2649.txt, August 1999.

[HS95] T. Howes, M. Smith: „The LDAP Application Program Interface", IETF RFC 1823, http://www.ietf.org/rfc/rfc1823.txt, August 1995.

[KTA98] F.-L. Krause, T. Tang und U. Ahle: „Virtuelle Produktentstehung" in Proceedings *Prozeßketten für die virtuelle Produktentwicklung in verteilter Umgebung*, VDI-Verlag Düsseldorf, 1998.

[LMS00] U. von Lukas, A. Mähler und E. Scheinhof: „Kommunikation und Kooperation in der integrierten virtuellen Produktentstehung", in A. Iwainsky (Hrsg.) *Tagungsband CAD 2000 – Kommunikation Kooperation Koordination*, Berlin 2000.

[LSG98] J. Likavec, A. Stork und M. Gärtner: „Collaborative Engineering in Heterogeneous Environments", *Journal of Mechanical Engineering, 4th Int. Conference Design to Manufacture in Modern Industry*, Podcetrtek Slovenia, 20-21 September 1999.

[NAC97] Network Application Consortium: „The Lightweight Internet Person Schema", Mai 1997

[RLS99] V. Ryan, R. Lee und S. Seligman: „Schema for Representing CORBA Object References in an LDAP Directory". IETF RFC 2714, http://www.rfc-editor.org/rfc/rfc2714.txt ,Oktober 1999.

[Sea97] A. Sears: „A Scalable Directory Schema in LDAP for Integrated Conferencing Services", Proceedings *INET '97*, http://www.isoc.org/inet97/proceedings, 1997.

[Smi00] M. Smith: „Definition of the inetOrgPerson LDAP Object Class". IETF RFC 2798, http://www.rfc-editor.org/rfc/rfc2798.txt, April 2000.

[Sun99] Sun Microsystems, Inc. „Java Naming and Directory Interface ^{TM} – API" 1999.

[UM96] University of Michigan. „The SLAPD and SLURPD Administrator's Guide". http://www.umich.edu/~dirsvcs/ldap/doc/guides/slapd/guide.pdf, April 1996.

[YWG99] Y. Yaacovi, M. Wahl und T. Genovese: „Lightweight Directory Access Protocol (v3): Extensions for Dynamic Directory Services". IETF RFC 2589 http://www.ietf.org/rfc/rfc2589.txt, Mai 1999.

Sicheres *Nomadic Computing* in Intranet-Umgebungen – Problemstellungen und Lösungskonzepte

Carsten Link, Norbert Luttenberger

Christian-Albrechts-Universität zu Kiel
Institut für Informatik und Praktische Mathematik
`{cli,nl}@informatik.uni-kiel.de`

Abstract. Im vorliegenden Beitrag werden das Anwendungsszenario *nomadic computing* und die sich daraus ergebenden Kommunikationsstrukturen dargestellt. Für die Probleme, die sich einem mobilen Computerbenutzer in fremden Intranets stellen, werden zwei Lösungsansätze vorgestellt, wobei besonders auf Sicherheitsprobleme eingegangen wird.

1 Einführung

Arbeit an wechselnden Aufenthaltsorten ist zu einem Kennzeichen moderner Formen der Arbeitsorganisation geworden. Bezüglich der technischen Arbeitsbedingungen bedeutet der temporäre Aufenthalt bei einer fremden Organisation für die betroffenen Mitarbeiter, die oftmals ihr persönliches und portables Rechensystem (Laptop, Notebook o.ä.) in die neue Umgebung mitbringen, daß sie im gastgebenden Intranet de facto von den Netzwerkdiensten abgeschnitten sind, die im Intranet der eigenen Organisation (dem Heimatnetz) angeboten werden. Aus naheliegenden Gründen werden diese Dienste im Heimatnetz gegen Zugriffe über das Internet abgeschottet. Ausgeschlossen vom Zugriff auf die von diesen Servern vorgehaltenen Informationen und Funktionen kann aber ein Mitarbeiter an seinem neuen Aufenthaltsort viele seiner Aufgaben nur sehr viel umständlicher erfüllen, oder er verliert den Kontakt zu internen Information in nicht akzeptablem Umfang.

Das vorgestellte Szenario fügt sich nahtlos in den Kontext ein, den Kleinrock 1997 unter dem anschaulichen Begriff *nomadic computing* allgemein zusammengefaßt hat [6]. Betont sei hier, daß wir speziell Nomaden betrachten, die sich innerhalb eines fremden Intranets aufhalten.

2 Problemstellung

In diesem Szenario ist es für Nomaden nicht sinnvoll, in einem gastgebenden Intranet die komplette Heimatumgebung wiederherstellen zu wollen; vielmehr ist davon auszugehen, daß der Nomade *dienstespezifisch* auswählen können muß, welche Dienste er aus welchem Netz von welchem Server beziehen will. Beispiel: Ein Nomade möchte unter Beibehaltung seiner e-Mail-Adresse den *mail service* nach wie vor aus seinem Heimatnetz beziehen, während er sicherlich auf einen *print service* im gastgebenden Netz zugreifen will. In Kooperation mit der gastgebenden Organisation müssen also Dienste im gastgebenden Netz identifiziert werden, die möglichst äquivalent zu den „gewohnten" Diensten im Heimatnetz sind. Ein schwierigeres Thema ist der *file service*. Aufgrund der heute meist noch geringeren Datenübertragungsraten und hohen Kosten in Weitverkehrsnetzen kann für den Nomaden eine Mischform sinnvoll sein: Durch das gastgebende Netz wird der Nomade mit Standardapplikationen der jeweiligen Umgebung versorgt, während er ausgewählte Arbeitsdateien z.B. von einem File-Server in seinem Heimatnetz beziehen kann. Um dem Nomaden Zugriff auf Dienste im Heimatnetz zu erlauben, müssen in der Regel zwei Firewall-Systeme durchdrungen werden, nämlich das Firewall-System des gastgebenden Netzes und des Heimatnetzes. Insbesondere das Firewall-System des Heimatnetzes muß dafür Zugriffe zulassen, die „normalerweise" strikt unterbunden werden. Außerdem sollen Dienste benutzer- und dienstespezifisch zur Verfügung gestellt werden. Der Nomade muß gemeinsam mit seinem Gastgeber und dem Administrator des Heimatnetzes verabreden, auf welche Weise ein Zugriff auf welche Dienste erfolgen kann und soll. Die benutzten Sicherheitsparameter (Authentifizierung, Verschlüsselung, ...) hängen vom Benutzer, seinem Aufenthaltsort und dem genutzten Dienst ab. Entsprechende Festlegungen müssen vielmehr kooperativ von den beteiligten Parteien im Sinne der mehrseitigen Sicherheit [7] vorgenommen werden. Nur so können die Sicherheitsinteressen aller beteiligten Parteien durchgesetzt werden. Des weiteren stellen sich mit dem Gastarbeiter-Szenario Managementprobleme, die sich auf das Auffinden von Diensten, der Verwaltung von Zugriffsrechten und auf die Steuerung der anzuwendenden kryptographischen Mechanismen beziehen.

3 Lösungskonzepte

Im Folgenden werden zwei Lösungsansätze untersucht: eine konventionelle Client/Server-Lösung und ein Ansatz, der sich mobile Agenten zu nutze macht.

3.1 Konzept für eine Client/Server-basierte Lösung

Zur Herstellung einer dienstespezifischen Zugangsmöglichkeit für den Nomaden zu Diensten in seinem Heimatnetz werden zum einen die Firewall-Systeme des gastgebenden Netzes und des Heimatnetzes um kryptographische Funktionen zur Erreichung der dargestellten Schutzziele erweitert (*Nomadic Security Gateways*), zum anderen wird in die Kommunikation zwischen Client (im gastgebenden Netz) und Server (im Heimatnetz) ein Paar von zwei weiteren Instanzen eingeschaltet: ein allgemeiner *Proxy*, der auf dem System des Nomaden installiert ist, und ein *Proxy Client* im *Nomadic Security Gateway* des Heimatnetzes. Insgesamt ergibt sich durch diese Anordnung eine Architektur mit drei Schichten. Auf der Diensteschicht befindet sich der für Client/Server-Systeme übliche Austausch zwischen *requests* und *responses*. Auf der darunter liegenden Schicht findet eine Kommunikation zwischen dem Client auf dem Gastarbeitsplatz und dem *Proxy Client* im Heimatnetz des Nomaden statt. Durch die Einführung des *Proxy Client* wird sichergestellt, daß der

Nomade auch solche Server in seinem Heimatnetz erreichen kann, die „von außen" nicht sichtbar sind, also z.B. interne WWW-Server, interne News-Server usw. Der *Proxy Client* agiert als Stellvertreter des Nomaden im Heimatnetz: Da er sich innerhalb des Heimatnetzes befindet, kann er auch interne Server ansprechen. Auf der dritten Schicht findet der eigentliche Nachrichtentransport statt. Der im Gastarbeitsplatz angesiedelte *Proxy* sorgt dafür, daß die ins Heimatnetz gerichteten *requests* mit Authentifizierungsinformation zur Auswertung in den beiden *Nomadic Security Gateways* versehen werden. Zur Erreichung der Schutzziele Vertraulichkeit, Integrität und Authentizität werden *requests* und *responses* im gastgebenden Netz und im Internet über *Security Associations* gemäß IPsec [5] transportiert.

Der Proxy Client, der als integraler Teil dieses *Nomadic Security Gateway* betrachtet wird, hat weiterhin die Aufgabe, die vom Gastarbeitsplatz erzeugte Authentifizierungsinformation auszuwerten und – wie oben dargestellt – einen *request* an den richtigen Server im Heimatnetz weiterzuleiten. Weiterhin werden *responses* vom *Proxy Client* in das gastgebende Netz zurückgeleitet, und zwar an den *Proxy* des Gastarbeitsplatzes. Durch die Einschaltung der Kommunikation über Proxies wird die angestrebte Dienstespezifizität erreicht, obwohl auf der Netzwerkschicht die dienste*unspezifischen* Mechanismen von IPsec verwendet werden. Der Gast muß die Bereitstellung der von ihm jeweils benötigten Dienste mit einer entsprechenden Instanz in seinem Heimatnetz aushandeln. Dazu wird ein zu entwickelnden Management-Protokoll benötigt. Im Zuge der über dieses Protokoll vorzunehmenden Aushandlung werden die genannten Proxies instantiiert. Bei der Entwicklung der Client/Server-basierten Lösungen kann auf eine Vielzahl von Standards zurückgegriffen werden. Die wichtigsten sind IPsec [5] und die damit verbundenen Management-Protokolle.

3.2 Konzept für eine Lösung mit mobilen Agenten

Um mit Hilfe von Agenten [1], [2], [4], [8] die Dienste des Heimatnetzes nutzen zu können, ist es nötig, daß der Nomade eine Agenten-Laufzeitumgebung auf seinem Rechner installiert. Diese Umgebung erlaubt es dem Nomaden, Agenten zu starten, zu konfigurieren, mit einem Auftrag zu versehen und an eine Laufzeitumgebung innerhalb des Heimatnetzes zu schicken. Da das Heimatnetz sowie das gastgebende Netz jeweils über ein Firewall-System mit dem Internet verbunden bzw. von diesem getrennt sind, ist es ohne weiteres nicht möglich, Daten zwischen diesen Netzen zu übertragen. Daher ist es erforderlich, einen Tunnel zwischen den beiden geschützten Netzen herzustellen, um den Agenten-Laufzeitumgebungen die Kommunikation zu gestatten. Dieser Kommunikationskanal wird von den Laufzeitumgebungen benötigt, um Verwaltungsinformationen auszutauschen und den Agenten die Migration zu erlauben. Im Heimatnetz befindet sich wenigstens eine Laufzeitumgebung für Agenten, die den Agenten Zugang zu internen Diensten bietet. Der Einsatz von Agenten erlaubt eine sehr flexible und differenzierte Dienstnutzung. Dies ist einer der großen Vorteile des Agentenparadigmas. Zu den Nachteilen, die der Einsatz von Agenten mit sich bringt, gehören die sich ergebenden Sicherheitsrisiken, da mit Agenten aktive Elemente in den geschützten Bereich des Intranets gelassen werden. Es muß verhindert werden, daß externe Angreifer die Agenten-Laufzeitumgebungen nutzen, um „feindliche" Agenten in ein geschütztes Netz zu schicken und sich damit Möglichkeiten zu erschließen, die bei Beschränkung auf eine Client/Server-Kommunikation durch das Firewall-System verwehrt wären. Im *nomadic computing-*

Szenario kann man diese Gefahren dadurch ausschließen, daß zwischen den beteiligten Netzen nur gegenseitig zertifizierte Agenten zugelassen werden. Weiterhin wird durch Authentifizierung sichergestellt, daß Verbindungen nur zwischen autorisierten Laufzeitumgebungen aufgebaut werden. Digitale Signaturen machen Manipulation von Agenten erkennbar und erlauben es, vertrauenswürdige Agenten zu kennzeichnen. Des weiteren schützt Verschlüsselung den Kommunikationskanal zwischen den Laufzeitumgebungen vor dem Einblick oder der Manipulation durch Angreifer aus dem Internet als auch aus dem gastgebenden Netz.

4 Fazit

In diesem Artikel wurden verschiedene Lösungsansätze vorgestellt, die jeweils Vor- und Nachteile aufweisen. Beiden Lösungen ist gemein, daß ein Mechanismus geschaffen werden muß, der autorisierten Benutzern das Überwinden von mehreren Firewall-Systemen gestattet. Ebenso ist bei beiden Lösungen ein administratives Regelwerk und Software zu dessen Durchsetzung nötig, welche den Umfang der Ressourcennutzung und deren Sicherheitsparameter benutzer- und dienstspezifisch festlegen. Die hier vorgestellten technischen Konzepte sollen in einem *nomadic computing*-Testbed praktisch realisiert werden, das für Demonstrationen und Evaluierungen zur Verfügung steht. Dabei soll vor allem ein Management von Zugriffsmöglichkeiten für beide Lösungsansätze unter den Prämissen der mehrseitigen Sicherheit geschaffen werden.

Literatur

[1] Bradshaw, J.M.: *Software Agents*. Cambridge (Mass.) u.a. (MIT Press) 1997, ISBN 0-262-52234-9.
[2] Franklin, S., Graesser, A.: Is it an Agent or just a Program?: A Taxonomy for Autonomous Agents. In: *Proceedings of the Third International Workshop on Agent Theories, Architectures, and Languages*. Springer 1996.
[3] Hagen, L., Breugst, M., Magedanz, Th.: *Impacts of Mobile Agent Technology on Mobile Communication System Evolution*. IEEE Personal Communications, vol. 5, no. 4 (August 1998), pp. 56–69.
[4] Jennings, N.R., Wooldridge, M.J.: *Agent Technology*. Berlin u.a. (Springer) 1998, ISBN 3-540-63591-2.
[5] Kent, S., Atkinson, R.: *Security Architecture for the Internet Protocol*. RFC-2401, 1998.
[6] Kleinrock, L.: Nomadic Computing and Communications. elektronisch: http://bob.nap.edu/readingroom/books/whitepapers/
[7] Müller, G., Rannenberg, K. (Eds.): *Multilateral Security in Communications (Vol. 3) – Technology, Infrastructure, Economy*. München u.a. (Addison-Wesley-Longman) 1999, ISBN 3-8273-1360-0.
[8] Vigna, G. (Ed.): *Mobile Agents and Security*. (Springer) 1998, ISBN 3-540-64792-9.

My Home is my Network or how to HAVi

Reinhard Baier, Christian Gran, Andreas Zisowsky

GMD FOKUS, Kaiserin–Augusta–Allee 31, D–10589 Berlin, Germany
{baier, gran, zisowsky}@fokus.gmd.de

Abstract. HAVi is a new standard which aims to handle the communication between many different kinds of home devices. This paper briefly introduces the HAVi specification and describes how HAVi can be positioned among other standards, like MHP, OSGi and Jini. It gives an overview of the implementation effort at GMD FOKUS in this area and concludes with suggestions for enhancements of HAVi.

1. Introduction

A number of new standards related to the home environment pop up: The Multimedia Home Platform (MHP) from the Digital Video Broadcast (DVB, http://www.dvb.org) consortium with a powerful TV or STB as the central unit to control the home and retrieve and present multimedia data – delivered via broadcast mechanisms. The Open Service Gateway initiative (OSGi, http://www.osgi.org) industry group defines an open standard for connecting the home network and its applications with commercial Internet services. In the home there are at least two alternatives to get the home network up and running: Jini (http://www.sun.com/jini) and HAVi (http://www.havi.org). Jini is a Java-based standard from Sun Microsystems, which enables a plug and play network based on TCP/IP. HAVi is an abbreviation for "Home Audio Video interoperability". The HAVi organization was founded by Grundig, Hitachi, Matsushita Electric Industrial (Panasonic), Philips, Sharp, Sony, Thomson, and Toshiba. It has defined a system architecture where audio and video equipment from different vendors can be easily connected to an in–home audio/video network and interoperate with each other.

MHP and OSGi are complementary to HAVi, because they have a different focus. MHP defines mainly the connection to the broadcast stream and the platform to present the incoming multimedia data. OSGi deals with a gateway which allows to download applications from the Internet. It focuses on a platform and high level applications for e–commerce solutions.

Jini is a direct competitor to HAVi, as it also defines a protocol for a plug and play network. But while HAVi defines in detail all interfaces which may be used for multimedia equipment – Jini defines only how to define an interface. As long as Jini does not define specific interfaces for devices it cannot support interworking between devices from different vendors. However, Sun Microsystems and Sony have announced a HAVi/Jini bridge to connect both network topologies. So, if we have a running HAVi network, in the future we may even have the chance to connect to a Jini device.

The remainder of this paper will focus on HAVi. The following sections will show some possible scenarios, give an overview of the HAVi base architecture and the user interface and will describe the implementation efforts at GMD FOKUS.

2. Scenarios

Consumer electronics, white goods, and other home appliances should be able to communicate with each other within an in-home network. A VCR or a HiFi amplifier for example which are able to present their user interface on a TV screen will allow to control that device with a more sophisticated user interface than the device could present with its own buttons and small LCD.

For audio/video equipment HAVi defines the necessary APIs to fulfill this task. Future VCRs will have a built–in user interface (a so-called havlet), which can be displayed by TV sets. The user can then control the VCR through this havlet by means of the remote control of the TV or it can be directly controlled by applications such as an Electronic Program Guide. In the case of HAVi the IEEE 1394 network is used for video streaming as well as for device control.

A more complex scenario is shown in fig. 1. Connected to the home network are a washing machine, a water sensor, and a camera - all located in the cellar – as well as a TV set and an ISDN/Internet gateway. The washing machine is running and due to a failure some water flows into the cellar. The water sensor stops the washing machine and turns off the water. Now the users need to be informed. If someone is watching TV, a small on–screen text message might be appropriate, but if nobody is at home, an SMS could be delivered to a mobile phone, or an e–mail with an attached picture taken from the camera could be generated to inform the user that there is a problem.

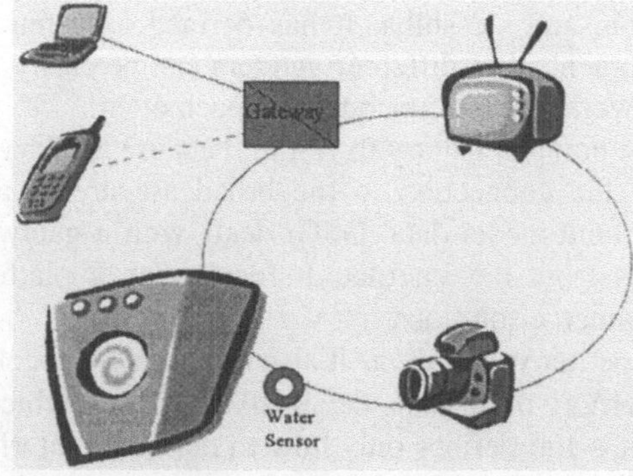

Fig. 1. A possible scenario: This example shows the combination of consumer electronics and household appliances through the in–home network.

3. Home Audio Video Interoperability Architecture

The HAVi architecture specifies a set of application programming interfaces (APIs) allowing consumer electronic manufacturers and third parties to develop devices and applications for the home network. The architecture assures that products from different vendors can cooperate to perform complex value-added services.
Applications and user interfaces (havlets) are written in Java. HAVi differentiates between *devices* and *functional components*. A typical consumer electronics device encompasses more than one functional component. A normal TV set, for example, is generally one physical device, but it contains several distinct controllable entities: tuner, display, audio amplifier, etc. HAVi defines a fixed set of APIs, which describe the methods provided by the functional component modules (FCMs). These methods are sent from an application to the FCMs, and translated into a native language there. The native language command is then sent from the FCM to the appropriate target device. HAVi defines FCMs for a tuner, a VCR, a clock, a camera, an AV disc, an amplifier, a display, an AV display, a modem and a web proxy.

Services are modeled in self–contained entities (software elements), accessible through a well–defined interface. The software elements of the HAVi architecture support the basic notion of network management, device abstraction, inter–device communication, and user interface management. Collectively, these software elements expose a set of services for building portable distributed applications on the home network.

4. HAVi User Interface

The HAVi User Interface (HAVi UI) consists of a collection of Java classes. It can be used by havlets to allow user interaction with specific functional component modules (FCMs) within the HAVi network or to access Application Modules to provide services to the user. Additionally it may be used by proprietary applications on the device that provides the Java virtual machine. HAVi UI is an environment that permits the creation of complex interactive applications that go far beyond the simple control of devices.

Havlets are usually not executed on the same device, where their Java bytecode is stored. A TV set for example may provide the necessary environment including the HAVi UI classes and download the havlet from a distant VCR. So the user can control the VCR from the TV.

5. Implementation

GMD FOKUS is implementing a full HAVi platform including the HAVi stack, HAVi UI, a PC-based full audio-video device and an interface builder.

- HAVi Stack

The basic communication between software elements is achieved through the Messaging System which is based on a network-dependent entity, the Communication Media Manager. Although the HAVi standard describes that layer based on IEEE 1394 only, other communication media may also be used. Currently, there are only a few devices available in the market that support IEEE 1394. Therefore, we decided to add a communication layer for testing and demonstration purposes on top of UDP/IP. The physical features of IEEE 1394, such as networking with auto–detection of plugging and unplugging of devices, are simulated in this case.

- HAVi UI

The implementation of HAVi UI by GMD FOKUS is kept generic and flexible. Thus, it supports different types of devices with diverse capabilities. It is conformant to the HAVi specification with some extensions to maintain compliance with MHP as well.
To increase flexibility, a pre–processing mechanism was developed. All platform–dependent defaults – looks, layout and background – can be defined at compile–time. That allows manufacturers to configure their user interface for multiple platforms easily.

- Interface Builder

The Interface Builder developed by GMD FOKUS is a graphical tool which allows to develop the user interfaces of havlets. The goal is to make HAVi UI accessible to non–programmers. It completely hides the Java source code and allows the user to build havlets without programming a single line of code. The Interface Builder creates full HAVi–compliant Java source code. The Interface Builder implements a complete edit-compile-test cycle, so that user interfaces can be tested without leaving the tool. The user interface of the tool itself is configurable and it saves project and window layout between sessions.

6. Future Extensions

The HAVi definition is quite detailed and this will help different manufactures to build devices which can communicate with each other. Currently, HAVi does not address devices outside the home audio/video area, like kitchenware, washing machines, PC equipment and so on.
There are two alternatives to make these devices available in a HAVi network:

- Define each new device as a HAVi device. This ensures interoperability, but it would make a HAVi extension quite large and difficult to manage.
- Define one HAVi device for every new kind of subnetwork. For each kind of network there can be one HAVi device which acts like a bridge to all devices in the new network. The bridge should allow to address a specific device in the non-Havi network and to perform some standardized simple methods.

Verteilte Kommunikation in der Praxis: Ein neuer Verkehrstelematik-Dienst „Parken & Leiten"

Ralf Hinz

DaimlerChrysler Forschung und Technologie
Wilhelm-Runge-Str. 11
D - 89081 Ulm
ralf.hinz@daimlerchrysler.com

Abstract. Im Rahmen des BMBF-geförderten Projekts MoTiV[1] sowie damit zusammenhängenden DaimlerChrysler-internen Projekten wurden Prototypen realisiert, die zeigen, wie durch die gemeinsame Nutzung eines Parkleitsystems und eines fahrzeugautonomen Zielführungssystems ein neuer Dienst für Autofahrer geschaffen werden kann: "Parken & Leiten".
Da am Ende einer jeden Autofahrt der Bedarf nach Parkraum steht, liegt es nahe, die Funktionalität von heute angebotenen Navigationssystemen derart zu erweitern, dass sie den Autofahrer nicht nur zu seinem Zielort leiten, sondern ihn zu einem seinen Bedürfnissen entsprechenden Parkplatz lotsen. Die wesentlichen Vorteile, die durch diesen Dienst entstehen, sind erhöhter Komfort für den Fahrer, höhere Sicherheit durch weniger Ablenkung des Fahrers, verringerter Parkraumsuchverkehr, sowie bessere Nutzung von Parkraum

Einführung

„Am Ende einer jeden Autofahrt steht der Bedarf nach freiem Parkraum." Dies und die Tatsachen, dass bereits in vielen Städten hohe Summen in die Infrastruktur für Parkleitsysteme geflossen sind und immer mehr Fahrzeuge mit (dynamischen) Navigationssystemen ausgestattet werden, hat unser Projektteam zu dem Entschluss geführt, einen Demonstrator zu realisieren, in dem alle diese Komponenten zu einem verteilten System zusammengeführt werden.

Ziel war es, einen Autofahrer nicht einfach zu einer bestimmten Straße zu führen oder ihm eine lange Liste von im Navigationssystem hinterlegten Parkplätzen anzubieten, sondern ihn <u>direkt zu dem für ihn am besten geeigneten Platz</u> zu lotsen.

Der Ablauf einer Parkraumsuche sollte sich in etwa so abspielen: Der Fahrer spricht seinen Parkwunsch in ein Mikrofon (entweder in der einfachen Form *„ich möchte in Ulm parken"* oder auch komplexer, z. B. *„ich möchte von elf bis 18 Uhr in Stuttgart in der Nähe des Hauptbahnhofes parken"*), der Fahrzeug-Rechner sendet den Parkwunsch (z. B. über GSM-SMS[23] an die Parkleitzentrale, diese gleicht den

---

[1] Mobilität und Transport im intermodalen Verkehr
[2] Global System for Mobile Communications
[3] Short Message Service

Wunsch mit den freien Plätzen (die Informationen holt sie zyklisch oder bei Bedarf von den lokalen Parkleitsystemen) ab und sendet eine Empfehlung an das Fahrzeug. Hier stellt der Fahrzeug-Rechner die Information optisch und / oder akustisch dar und programmiert das Zielführungssystem.

Anforderungen

Zu den wesentlichen Anforderungen an das System gehören neben der Tatsache, dass das Navigationssystem selbstverständlich zur Einfahrt zu einem nicht vollständig belegten Parkhaus oder Parkplatz führt, eine Benutzeradaptierbarkeit (*soll die Auswahl des Parkplatzes nach Preis, Nähe zum Ziel, Service-Leistungen etc. erfolgen; von wann bis wann will der Fahrer parken, ...*), eine geeignete Mensch-Maschine-Schnittstelle (*die im Idealfall auch während der Fahrt bedient werden können sollte*) und die Unabhängigkeit von speziellen Geräten und Kommunikationsnetzen. Ferner sollten Standardisierungsbestrebungen, z. B. der GATS[4] hinreichend berücksichtigt werden. Selbstverständlich soll das System skalierbar (*an unterschiedlich große Mengen von Benutzern und an eine hoffentlich wachsende Zahl von Ballungsräumen*) und erweiterbar (*z. B. um neue Funktionen, wie Buchung / Reservierung*) sein.

Komponenten des Gesamtsystems

Das Gesamtsystem wurde zunächst in drei Teilsysteme gegliedert: Das **mobile System** (Fahrer, Fahrzeug mit Navigations-System und Rechner), eine **Parkleitzentrale**, die den Dienst „Parken & Leiten" anbietet, und **lokale Parkleitsysteme**, die Informationen über freie Parkräume liefern können.

Als mobiles System wird ein Serienfahrzeug genutzt, das mit einem Navigationssystem, einem Industrie-PC[5] und verschiedenen Ein- / Ausgabegeräten ausgestattet wurde. Zusätzlich sind Kommunikations-Endgeräte zur Nutzung von GSM und DAB (Digital Audio Broadcast) eingebaut.

Die Parkleitzentrale ist ebenfalls ein handelsüblicher Rechner mit Modem (*zur Kommunikation mit dem Ulmer Parkleitsystem*) und GSM-Modul (*zur Kommunikation mit den mobilen Systemen*). Außerdem kann dieser Rechner eine Verbindung zu einem Internet bekommen (*um z. B. Parkrauminformationen im WWW[6] darzustellen*), und per ISDN[7] kann er mit dem DAB-Multimediaserver der Telekom kommunizieren.

---

[4] Global Automotive Telematics Standard
[5] Personal Computer
[6] World Wide Web
[7] Integrated Services Digital Network

Schnittstellen

Die Schnittstellen zwischen den Teilsystemen sind eine Grundlage für eine potenzielle Erweiterbarkeit und eine Anbindung an Systeme, die andere Telematik-Dienste zur Verfügung stellen.

Bereits vor dem ersten Schritt der Umsetzung wurde deutlich, dass praktisch jedes Parkleitsystem ein Unikat mit entweder proprietären oder aber ohne Schnittstellen an die Außenwelt ist. Aus diesem Grund wurde darauf verzichtet, Vorschläge für eine Standardisierung zu machen. Für den ersten Ulmer Prototypen konnte eine Schnittstelle, über die die aktuellen Belegungsdaten der an das System angeschlossenen Parkhäuser und Tiefgaragen durch die „Parkleitzentrale" abgeholt werden können, nach wenigen kurzen Telefonaten realisiert werden.

Anders die Schnittstelle zwischen Fahrzeug und Parkleitzentrale. Da die Anzahl der Benutzer in Zukunft hoffentlich deutlich größer ist als die Anzahl von an das System angebundenen Parkleitsystemen, ist ein Einsatz von Standards unabdingbar. Als Kommunikationsnetze werden derzeit GSM (speziell der Kurznachrichtendienst SMS) und DAB eingesetzt. Die darauf aufsetzenden Protokolle sind bei DAB das MOT-Protokoll[8], bei GSM wird entweder ein auf dem GATS Auskunftsdienst aufsetzender Dienst genutzt, alternativ wird nach wie vor ein proprietäres Protokoll genutzt, mit dem sich neue Anwendungen oder Ausprägungen zu Testzwecken schneller realisieren lassen.

Die Daten, die mit Hilfe dieser Protokolle über GSM übertragen werden, sind Parkwünsche (*dies schließt Angaben über den aktuellen Aufenthaltsort, den Zielort und sämtliche weiteren Spezifikationen ein*) und Informationen über den empfohlenen Parkraum (*Koordinaten für das Navigationssystem, Name des Parkhauses, Preis-Informationen, etc.*). Bei DAB werden zyklisch Parkrauminformationen gesendet, die vom Fahrzeug-Rechner ausgewertet werden können.

Das Projekt im Umfeld von MoTiV

Im Rahmen des BMBF-geförderten Projekts "MoTiV" trugen andere Projektpartner dazu bei, das Angebot von Parkraummanagementdiensten zu vergrößern.

Dies geschah einerseits durch die Umsetzung von anderen Ausprägungen von Parkraummanagementdiensten, andererseits durch eine räumliche Ausweitung: Park-Dienste waren zum Ende der MoTiV-Laufzeit verfügbar in Ulm (DaimlerChrysler), Berlin (VW / Gedas), Braunschweig (Bosch), Köln (BMW), Frankfurt (Opel) und Stuttgart (debis Systemhaus). Darüber hinaus sind statische Parkdaten, d. h. Informationen über Parkräume, allerdings ohne aktuelle Belegungsdaten, für ganz Deutschland verfügbar (debis Systemhaus).

---

[8] Multimedia Object Transfer

Ausblick

Die zunehmende Verbreitung von Navigationssystemen lässt hoffen, dass diese auch Zusatzfunktionalitäten bereit stellen, zu denen z. B. die verbesserte Parkraumsuche gehören kann. Außer einer Verfügbarkeit von Endgeräten ist es allerdings erforderlich, dass ein „Dienste-Anbieter" einen neuen Dienst wie „Parken & Leiten" anbietet.

Über den Prototyp hinaus sind noch weitere Funktionen denkbar, z. B. eine Monitoring-Komponente: Diese sorgt dafür, dass der Fahrer „umgeleitet" wird, wenn „sein" Parkplatz während der Anfahrt belegt wird.

Auch das Buchen von Parkraum in Verbindung mit einer eventuellen Reservierung bietet interessante Perspektiven. Diese Funktion konnte aus zwei Gründen noch nicht realisiert werden: Einerseits gibt es in der Regel bauliche Einschränkungen (*wenn es eine Schlange vor einer Parkhauseinfahrt gibt, nützt auch ein gebuchter Platz wenig. Eine zweite Zufahrt ist nicht in allen Parkhäusern vorhanden*), andererseits stellt sich die Frage nach dem Beginn der Zahlungspflicht (*wurde ein Parkplatz in einem bei Ankunft gefüllten Parkhaus gebucht, so müsste ein Fahrzeug entfernt werden, um den gebuchten Platz frei zu machen. Da dies in der Praxis kaum möglich ist, müsste der Parkplatz ab der Buchung frei gehalten werden. Das bedeutet aber, dass er auch ab dann zu zahlen ist. Dieses Konzept lässt sich zumindest im schwäbischen Raum vermutlich nicht durchsetzen*). Festzustellen ist allerdings, dass die Möglichkeit der Buchung eines Parkplatzes so häufig nachgefragt wird, dass es interessant sein könnte, weitere Alternativen zu entwickeln

Session 9:

Mobile Kommunikationsnetze

Lokalisierung mobiler Teilnehmer unter Berücksichtigung regelmäßigen Verhaltens

Thomas Ziegert

Technische Universität Dresden, Fakultät Informatik, Institut für Systemarchitektur,
Mommsenstr. 13, 01062 Dresden,
`ziegert@rn.inf.tu-dresden.de`

Zusammenfassung Das Verhalten mobiler Teilnehmer hinsichtlich der Veränderung ihres Standortes wird immer durch eine mehr oder weniger stark ausgeprägte Determiniertheit gekennzeichnet sein. Ein mobiler Teilnehmer kann einige Standorte im Vergleich zu anderen besonders häufig oder bevorzugt zu einer bestimmten Zeit aufsuchen. Weiterhin lassen sich Abhängigkeiten in der Abfolge, mit der bestimmte Standorte frequentiert werden, feststellen. Ebenso existiert häufig eine stärkere Beziehung zu einer eingeschränkten Gruppe von Kommunikationspartnern. Zusammenfassend kann man von zeitlichen und räumlichen Abhängigkeiten sprechen. In diesem Beitrag wird eine alternative Methode zur Lokalisierung mobiler Teilnehmer bei hierarchischer Organisation des Lokalisierungssystems vorgestellt, die wiederkehrende Verhaltensweisen der Teilnehmer berücksichtigt. Sie wurde unter dem Gesichtspunkt entwickelt, die Ausdehnung der Hierarchie objektbezogen bzw. verhaltensabhängig zu erweitern oder einzuschränken, um so einen Kompromiß zwischen zentraler und verteilter Verwaltung zu erreichen, der im jeweiligen Fall die besten Ergebnisse liefert. Weiterhin werden die Ergebnisse einer simulativen Untersuchung der vorgestellten Methode präsentiert.

1 Motivation

Lokalisierungsmechanismen arbeiten i. d. R. auf einer zentralen Datenbank oder einer Hierarchie von Datenbanken, welche Standortinformationen über mobile Teilnehmer enthalten. Die Lokalisierungsmechanismen konventioneller Mobilfunksysteme, wie z. B. die des GSM (Global System for Mobile Communications, [16]) oder mobiler Netzwerkprotokolle, wie Mobile IP [18], verwenden global gültige und relativ statische Methoden, sowohl zur Aktualisierung der Information bezüglich des aktuellen Aufenthaltsortes als auch zur Suche mobiler Teilnehmer. Weiterhin berücksichtigte man bei ihrer Entwicklung stark die Annahme, daß sich mobile Teilnehmer größtenteils in der Nähe ihres Heimatstandortes aufhalten und hauptsächlich mit lokalen Partnern kommunizieren (siehe auch [2]). Man spricht hierbei von *locality of reference* und *locality of movement*. Von diesen Annahmen abweichendes Verhalten führt bei Anwendung der darauf abgestimmten Lokalisierungsmechanismen zu Leistungseinbußen ([16, 7]).

Die Forderung nach lebenslang gültigen Rufnummern bzw. Identifikatoren für mobile Teilnehmer, wie sie zukünftige Systeme bieten sollen [17], kann durch

Methoden, die einen Heimatbereich voraussetzen, nur mit zusätzlichem Aufwand gelöst werden, da es sich hier verbietet, aus dem Identifikator direkt das Heimatregister abzuleiten. Eine Reihe von Forschungsarbeiten (z. B. [2, 3, 13]) und auch die UMTS-Standardentwürfe [23, 14] schlagen deshalb die verteilte Anordnung der Knoten in einer Hierarchie in der Form eines Baumes vor. Eine Abbildung des Teilnehmeridentifikators auf eine Heimatdatenbank ist hier i. d. R. nicht notwendig. Lokale Rufe an Teilnehmer, die sich in der Nähe der Ortes aufhalten, aus dem der Ruf stammt, können immer lokal vermittelt werden. Probleme ergeben sich bei dieser Methode, wenn sich Ortswechsel und Rufe häufen, die nicht in das einmal gewählte Hierarchieschema „passen". In solchen Fällen werden viele Hierarchieebenen involviert, und es muß eine Vielzahl von Nachrichten versendet werden, bevor die Aktualisierung der Verweise auf den aktuellen Standort abgeschlossen oder eine Rufanforderung aufgelöst werden kann.

2 Verwandte Arbeiten

In [12] wird eine Methode beschrieben, die sich überlappende Aktualisierungsregionen (Location Areas) benutzt, um das Problem der häufigen Aktualisierung bei Bewegungen im Randbereich von Aktualisierungsregionen zu lösen. Aufenthaltsbereiche bzw. Zellen am Rande einer Aktualisierungsregion werden hier auch den jeweils benachbarten Aktualisierungsregionen zugewiesen. Auf diese Weise führen Teilnehmerbewegungen innerhalb des „Randstreifens" nicht zu einer ständigen Aktualisierung der benachbarten Blattknoten und hierarchisch höher gelegener Knoten. Nimmt man an, daß die Verteilung der Nutzer über alle Aktualisierungsregionen gleich bleibt, so werden durch diese Methode im Vergleich zur Ausgangskonfiguration die Signalisierungskanäle der in den Randstreifen gelegenen Aufenthaltsbereiche stärker belastet. D. h., die Reduzierung der Aktualisierungskosten hat hier unter Umständen die Erhöhung der Belastung der Signalisierungskanäle der Funkschnittstelle zur Folge. Setzt man eine entsprechende Rufanzahl voraus, erzielt diese Methode nicht den gewünschten Effekt. Ein weiteres Problem ergibt sich aus der Tatsache, daß die Überlappung der Aktualisierungsregionen nicht objekt- bzw. gruppenbezogen sondern global erfolgt. Objekte, die sich über die durch benachbarte Aktualisierungsregionen gemeinsam verwaltete Aufenthaltsbereiche hinaus bewegen, sorgen dafür, daß das Problem weiterhin besteht. Abhilfe kann hier die objektbezogene bzw. verhaltensabhängige Erweiterung oder Einschränkung der Ausdehnung der Hierarchie schaffen, da hier ein Kompromiß zwischen zentraler und verteilter Verwaltung erreicht werden kann, der im jeweiligen Fall die besten Ergebnisse liefert. Im folgenden werden vorhandene Lokalisierungsmethoden vorgestellt und einer Wertung unterzogen, die der Klasse der hierarchisch organisierten Lokalisierungssysteme mit Einbeziehung der Verhaltensmuster mobiler Teilnehmer zuzuordnen sind. Ein ausführlicher Überblick zu weiteren Lokalisierungsmechanismen ist z. B. in [1] zu finden. In [3] wird eine Lokalisierungsmethode vorgestellt, die Aktualisierungsregionen nutzerbezogenen zu sogenannten *Partitionen* zusammenfaßt. Eine Partition vereint mehrere Blattknoten des Baumes. Zu jeder Partition wird ein *repräsentativer* Knoten innerhalb der Hierarchie bestimmt, der aktualisiert wird, wenn ein mobiles Objekt die Partition betritt oder verläßt. Der repräsentative Knoten ist der erste Knoten in der Hierarchie, der alle Knoten der Partition überspannt. Durch die Bildung von Partitionen wird die Suche nach dem entsprechenden Objekt abgekürzt, da der repräsentative Knoten nach Erhalt einer Anfrage sofort die in der Partition enthaltenen Blattknoten befragt. Weiterhin erlaubt die Methode die Reduzierung der Anzahl der Aktualisierungsoperationen für Objekte, die sich häufig innerhalb ihrer Partitionen bewegen. Wird sie in Mobilfunksystemen eingesetzt, kann sie eine erhebliche Belastung der Broadcast-Kanäle der den Blattknoten zugeordneten Aufenthaltsbereiche bzw. Zell-Cluster hervorrufen. Ein Ansatz zur Lokalisierung mobiler Objekte in großen vernetzten Systemen wird in [24] beschrieben. Dabei werden innerhalb der Hierarchie für jedes mobile Objekt Verweise gespeichert, die vom Wurzelknoten zum aktuellen Blattknoten führen. Suche und Aktualisierung finden entsprechend der konventionellen hierarchischen Methode[1] statt. Zusätzlich wird eine *dynamische Optimierung* eingeführt. Dabei werden Blattknoten zusammengefaßt, die Aktualisierungsregionen verwalten, zwischen denen Objekte regelmäßig migrieren. Bewegt sich ein Objekt nun innerhalb des Gebietes, daß durch die zu einer *Subregion* zusammengefaßten Blattknoten abgedeckt wird, erfolgt nur eine Aktualisierung des ersten gemeinsamen Knotens der Subregion. Dadurch nimmt die Anzahl der zur Aktualisierung notwendigen Nachrichten und Datenbankoperationen ab. Weiterhin wird eine Optimierung der Suche vorgenommen. Dazu werden infolge einer Suchanfrage an den für die Subregion verantwortlichen Knoten Verweise entlang des Suchpfades, der vom die Suche auslösenden Blattknoten zum verantwortlichen Knoten führt, hinterlegt[2]. So können nachfolgende Suchanfragen schneller beantwortet werden. Der Einsatz der Methode in Mobilfunksystemen kann wiederum zu einer erhöhten Belastung der Broadcast-Kanäle führen, da die Blattknoten selbst keine Informationen zu den Objekten speichern, die sich in den ihnen zugeordneten Aufenthaltsbereichen befinden.

Eine flexible Gestaltung der Hierarchie kann durch gezielte Plazierung der Verweise auf die Datenbanken in der Blattebene des Baumes erreicht werden. Die grundlegende Anordnung der Knoten im Baum nach der konventionellen hierarchischen Methode bleibt dabei erhalten. Die im weiteren vorgestellte Methode verfolgt diese Überlegung.

3 Eine alternative Lokalisierungsmethode

3.1 Vorbetrachtungen

Regelmäßiges Bewegungsverhalten erzeugt eine relativ konstante Menge von Aufenthaltsbereichen l_n, welche ein mobiles Objekt mit hoher Wahrscheinlich-

---

[1] D. h. Suche und Aktualisierung werden hier entlang der Verweiskette über den Wurzelknoten des Unterbaumes mit der geringsten Anzahl an Hierarchieniveaus durchgeführt, der die beiden beteiligten Blattknoten (Datenbanken) enthält.

[2] Eine ähnliche Verfahrensweise im Kontext mobiler Internet-Protokolle wird in [25] vorgeschlagen.

keit aufsucht. Diese häufig frequentierten Aufenthaltsbereiche bilden eine Teilmenge der Menge der Aufenthaltsbereiche $\mathbf{L} = \{l_n \mid n \in \mathbb{N}\}$ des Systems. Diese Teilmenge soll im folgenden als *Bewegungsmuster* M_B bezeichnet werden. Bewegungsmuster werden abhängig vom jeweiligen Objekt $o_i \in \mathbf{O}$ gebildet ($\mathbf{O} = \{o_i \mid i \in \mathbb{N}\}$ sei dabei die Menge aller kommunizierenden Objekte). Sie sind in einem vorgegebenen Zeitraum, im folgenden als Gültigkeitszeitraum $\Delta_m; m \in \mathbb{N}$ bezeichnet, definiert.

Definition 1 *Ein Bewegungsmuster $M_B(o_i, \Delta_m)$ ist die Menge der Aufenthaltsbereiche $l_n \in \mathbf{L}$, deren Attraktivität $a(l_n, o_i)$ hinsichtlich der Standortwahl für ein bestimmtes mobiles Objekt o_i innerhalb des Gültigkeitszeitraumes Δ_m einen bestimmten Schwellwert τ_B überschreitet.*

Für den Gültigkeitszeitraum Δ_m gilt: $\Delta_m \leq \mathbf{T}$. $\mathbf{T}$ bezeichnet den *Beobachtungszeitraum*. Der Beobachtungszeitraum kennzeichnet einen Zeitabschnitt in der Vergangenheit, in dem Regelmäßigkeiten im Verhalten mobiler Objekte vom System festgestellt wurden. Es ist jedoch auch möglich, daß ein Nutzer bzw. ein Objekt im System Vorgaben hinsichtlich seines zukünftigen Verhaltens hinterlegt. Muster im Verhalten sollten eine gewisse Periodizität aufweisen, so daß ihre Hinterlegung im System als Hinweis auf das zukünftige Verhalten des betreffenden Objektes dienen kann. Gültigkeitszeiträume treten innerhalb des Beobachtungszeitraumes i. d. R. periodisch auf. Ein Bewegungsmuster kann z. B. jeden Tag von 9.00 bis 11.00 Uhr gültig sein. Ein mobiles Objekt o_i kann mehrere Bewegungsmuster besitzen, z. B. über einen Tag verteilt.

Das Kommunikationsverhalten bestimmt, ob und wie häufig mit bevorzugten Kommunikationspartnern Informationen ausgetauscht werden. Bevorzugte Kommunikationspartner sind potentielle Interessenten für aktuelle Standortinformationen bezüglich des betreffenden mobilen Objektes. Bei bidirektionaler Kommunikation und beidseitiger Mobilität beruht dieses Interesse auf Gegenseitigkeit. Regelmäßiges Kommunikationsverhalten erzeugt eine wenig veränderliche Menge von bevorzugten Kommunikationspartnern (Objekten) aus der Menge der mobilen Objekte. Diese Menge erhält hier die Bezeichnung Kommunikationsmuster M_K. Für ein Kommunikationsmuster gilt: $M_K \subseteq \mathbf{O}$.

Definition 2 *Ein Kommunikationsmuster $M_K(o_i, \Delta_m)$ beinhaltet Objekte $o_j \in \mathbf{O}$, für die die Attraktivität $a(o_j, o_i)$ hinsichtlich der Kommunikation mit dem mobilen Objekt $o_i \in \mathbf{O}$ innerhalb des Gültigkeitszeitraumes Δ_m einen bestimmten Schwellwert τ_K überschreitet.*

D. h., o_i wird innerhalb von Δ_m mit großer Wahrscheinlichkeit von Objekten aus der Menge M_K gerufen. Für die Lokalisierung eines mobilen Objektes o_i sind nur die an dieses Objekt gerichteten Kommunikationsanforderungen relevant, da vom Objekt ausgehende Rufe keine Lokalisierung desselben nach sich ziehen. Kommunikationsmuster können im zeitlichen Verlauf variieren. Für den Gültigkeitszeitraum Δ_m gelten die bereits für Bewegungsmuster getroffenen Aussagen.

3.2 Das Verfahren

Den Ausgangspunkt bilden die im letzten Abschnitt beschriebenen Kommunikations- und Bewegungsmuster mobiler Objekte, die das individuelle Objektverhalten widerspiegeln. Dabei wird davon ausgegangen, daß Informationen zum Kommunikations- und Bewegungsverhalten der Teilnehmer im System vorliegen bzw. gewonnen werden können. Strategien zur automatischen Gewinnung und Verteilung dieses Wissens wurden im Rahmen der hier beschriebenen Arbeiten bisher nicht entwickelt, und die Abschätzung des dafür notwendigen Aufwandes erfolgte bisher ebenfalls noch nicht. Diese Punkte bleiben Untersuchungsgegenstand weiterführender Arbeiten.

Die Blattknoten des Baumes werden objektabhängig zu *Aktivitätszentren (AZ)* zusammengefaßt. Aktivitätszentren enthalten die Blattknoten, die die Aufenthaltsbereiche verwalten, welche ein mobiles Objekt über einen endlichen Zeitraum aufsucht und zwischen denen es häufig migriert. Sie werden direkt aus den für das jeweilige Objekt gültigen Bewegungssmustern abgeleitet. Ein Bewegungsmuster unterscheidet sich von einem Aktivitätszentrum nur durch die Art der enthaltenen Objekte. Es enthält Aufenthaltsbereiche im Gegensatz zu Blattknoten[3]. Innerhalb ihres Gültigkeitszeitraumes besitzen Aktivitätszentren den Zustand *aktiv*, zu jedem anderen Zeitpunkt den Zustand *inaktiv*.

Definition 3 *Ein Aktivitätszentrum* $\mathbf{AZ}_{i,m}$ *eines mobilen Objektes* o_i *enthält Blattknoten* k_B*, welche die Aufenthaltsbereiche* l_n *verwalten, die im Bewegungsmuster* $M_B(o_i, \Delta_m)$ *des Objektes enthalten sind.*

Informationen zum aktuellen Aufenthaltsort eines mobilen Objektes sollten möglichst an dem Ort gespeichert werden, an dem sie häufig benötigt werden, um eine schnelle Beantwortung von Suchanfragen zu ermöglichen. Für die hier besprochene Methode bedeutet das, daß die Informationen zu vorhandenen Aktivitätszentren an mögliche Kommunikationspartner aus dem Kommunikationsmuster des jeweiligen Objektes $M_K(o_i, \Delta_m)$ bzw. an die Knoten in der Hierarchie des Lokalisierungssystems, welche sich in der Nähe des aktuellen Aufenthaltsbereiches dieser Partnerobjekte befinden, zu verteilen sind. Die Menge der Blattknoten k_B, die diese Informationen erhalten, wird im folgenden als *Verteilungsmenge* bezeichnet.

Definition 4 *Die Verteilungsmenge* $\mathbf{V}_{i,m}$ *für ein Aktivitätszentrum* $\mathbf{AZ}_{i,m}$ *ergibt sich aus:*

- *den im Aktivitätszentrum enthaltenen Knoten,*
- *dem ersten Knoten innerhalb der Hierarchie* $k_{i,m}$*, der die Menge der im AZ enthaltenen Blattknoten überspannt und*
- *der Menge der Blattknoten* k_B*, die die über den Zeitraum* Δ_m *gültigen Aufenthaltsbereiche der im Kommunikationsmuster* $M_K(o_i, \Delta_m)$ *des betreffenden Objektes enthaltenen Kommunikationspartner verwalten.*

---

[3] Einem Blattknoten können auch mehrere Aufenthaltsbereiche zugeordnet sein.

Das bedeutet, daß jeder Knoten, der in der Verteilungsmenge $\mathbf{V}_{i,m}$ enthalten ist, eine Kopie, der in $\mathbf{AZ}_{i,m}$ enthaltenen Informationen besitzt. Dadurch kann eine an einen Knoten aus dieser Menge gerichtete Lokalisierungsanfrage bezüglich des mobilen Objektes o_i während des Gültigkeitszeitraumes Δ_m sofort durch eine Anfrage an die in $\mathbf{AZ}_{i,m}$ enthaltenen Knoten beantwortet werden. Der das jeweilige Aktivitätszentrum überspannende Knoten $k_{i,m}$ enthält Verweise auf alle Knoten der Verteilungsmenge $\mathbf{V}_{i,m}$. Das versetzt ihn in die Lage, das betreffende Aktivitätszentrum jederzeit zu aktivieren bzw. zu deaktivieren.

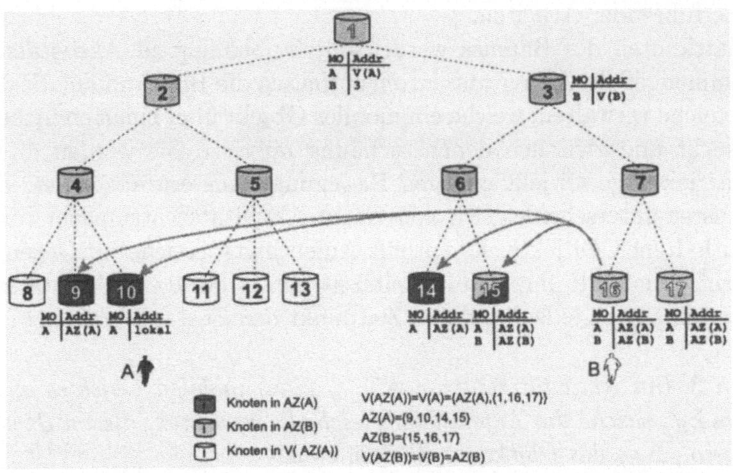

Abbildung 1. Beispiel für den Ablauf eines Rufaufbaus über ein Aktivitätszentrum

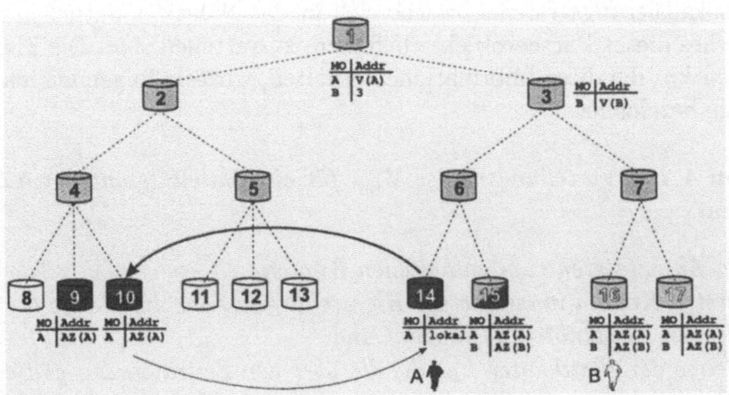

Abbildung 2. Aktualisierung bei Bewegung innerhalb eines Aktivitätszentrums

Abbildung 1 zeigt das Aktivitätszentrum für die Objekte A mit $AZ = \{9, 10, 14, 15\}$ und B mit $AZ = \{15, 16, 17\}$. Suchanfragen werden durch eine Multicast-Nachricht an alle im Aktivitätszentrum enthaltenen Blattknoten aufgelöst. Abbildung 1 zeigt den Ablauf eines Rufaufbaus für den Fall, daß Objekt B mit Objekt A kommunizieren möchte. Die Verteilungsmenge für das Aktivitätszentrum des Objektes A in Abbildung 1 ergibt sich zu $V = \{1, 9, 10, 14, 15, 16, 17\}$, wenn sich nur Objekt B im Kommunikationsmuster des Objektes A befindet. Befindet sich ein Kommunikationspartner nicht im Verwaltungsbereich eines Blattknotens der Verteilungsmenge, d. h., trifft eine Suchanfrage eines Partners ein, der sich nicht im Kommunikationsmuster des gerufenen Objektes befindet, so wird diese über den das AZ überspannenden Knoten $k_{i,m}$ aufgelöst. Solange sich ein mobiles Objekt innerhalb eines gültigen Aktivitätszentrums bewegt, findet eine Aktualisierung ausschließlich auf der Ebene der Blattknoten statt (siehe Abbildung 2). Bei Betreten oder Verlassen eines Aktivitätszentrums werden die konventionellen, der Hierarchie entsprechenden Operationen zur Aktualisierung der Standortdaten im Lokalisierungssystem ausgeführt und eine Aktivierung bzw. Deaktivierung der Verweise auf das entsprechende Aktivitätszentrum ausgelöst. Für die Bildung der Aktivitätszentren kommen nur mobile Objekte in Frage, die ein sehr regelmäßiges Verhalten bzgl. Bewegung und Kommunikation zeigen. Abweichungen vom ermittelten Verhalten sollten selten auftreten, wobei kurze Abweichungen tolerierbar sind. Das bedeutet für das Schema, daß ein Objekt o_i sein Aktivitätszentrum innerhalb des Gültigkeitszeitraums Δ_m nicht oder nur sehr selten und nur für einen kurzen Zeitraum verläßt. Die Verweise auf Aktivitätszentren werden in den betreffenden Blattknoten der Verteilungsmenge gesichert. Diese entscheiden dann autonom über die Gültigkeit der einzelnen Aktivitätszentren (Zustandswechsel der AZ auf aktiv bzw. inaktiv). Die Möglichkeit, Aktivitätszentren außerplanmäßig zu deaktivieren, falls starke Abweichungen vom festgestellten regelmäßigen Verhalten erkannt werden, ist vorgesehen. Kann von einem Knoten der Verteilungsmenge innerhalb des Gültigkeitszeitraumes eines Aktivitätszentrums für das betreffende Objekt eine Anfrage nicht aufgelöst werden, wird eine Suche nach dem konventionellen Schema durchgeführt. Der Knoten aus der Verteilungsmenge, der die Anfrage auslöst, teilt über diese gleichzeitig mit, daß ein Fehlerfall auftrat. Im Objektprofil, welches der Blattknoten des derzeitigen Aufenthaltsbereiches speichert, wird dadurch ein Zähler für Fehlschläge erhöht. Überschreitet dieser Zähler die festzulegende Schwelle für fehlgeschlagene Lokalisierungsversuche über die Menge der Knoten im AZ, so wird eine Multicast-Nachricht an alle Mitglieder der Verteilungsmenge $V_{i,m}$ geliefert, was in einer außerplanmäßigen Deaktivierung des betreffenden AZ resultiert.

4 Simulationsmodell

Im Rahmen von [20, 26] entstand eine Umgebung zur Simulation von Mobilitätsmanagementmethoden. Sie gestattet die Nachbildung wesentlicher Aspekte verschiedener Lokalisierungskonzepte und deren quantitative Analyse. Sie besteht aus zwei Modulen: dem *Verkehrsgenerator* und dem *Analysemodul*. Der Verkehrsgenerator erzeugt anhand der vorgegebenen Parameter einen Ereignisstrom, der die Ereignisse *Bewegung des mobilen Objektes X von Aktualisierungsregion A nach Aktualisierungsregion B* und *Kommunikationsanforderung des mobilen Objektes X an das mobile Objekt Y* enthält. Dieser Ereignisstrom wird dem Analysemodul übergeben, welches die zu simulierende Mobilitätsmanagementmethode nachbildet und die Analyseergebnisse liefert. Die Unterteilung erwies sich als sinnvoll, da sie es ermöglicht, verschieden parametrisierte bzw. unterschiedliche Lokalisierungsalgorithmen mit bereits erzeugten Ereignisströmen zu untersuchen. Der Verkehrsgenerator wurde in C++ unter Zuhilfenahme der Container-Bibliothek *Standard Template Library (STL)* [9] und des *SimPack C++ Simulation Toolkit* [8], das die grundlegende Funktionalität zur Implementierung von Simulationswerkzeugen für die diskrete, ereignisorientierte Simulation zur Verfügung stellt, implementiert. Das Analysemodul besteht aus einem C++ Rahmen, der allgemeine Klassen enthält, die allen Lokalisierungssystemen eigen sind und solche, die eine Spezialisierung dieser in Bezug auf eine bestimmte Lokalisierungsmethode darstellen. Durch die Wiederverwendbarkeit lassen sich weitere Lokalisierungsmethoden mit geringem Aufwand implementieren. Das Analysemodul wird mit Informationen zur jeweiligen Struktur des Lokalisierungssystems, d. h. Abhängigkeiten zwischen den Knoten und dem auszuführenden Lokalisierungskonzept und weiteren methodenspezifischen Angaben parameterisiert. Die Analyse erfolgt anhand des vorgegebenen Ereignisstromes durch Abarbeitung der entsprechenden methodenspezifischen Algorithmen zur Suche und Aktualisierung. Die Entscheidung für die Entwicklung eines eigenen Simulationswerkzeuges fiel, nachdem eine Untersuchung vorhandener Werkzeuge ergab, daß diese die Untersuchung größerer Systeme (Anzahl der Teilnehmer, Aufenthaltsbereiche > 100) schlecht oder nicht unterstüzen.

Im folgenden soll das Simulationsmodell, welches die Grundlage der durchgeführten Experimente und der im nächsten Abschnitt präsentierten Ergebnisse bildet, näher erläutert werden. Für die betrachtete geographische Region wurde eine Zellenanzahl von 12288 gewählt. Jeweils 12 Zellen[4] des Modells bildeten eine Aktualisierungsregion. Das Modell besitzt 1024 quadratisch angeordnete Aktualisierungsregionen. Bei einem Zellradius von im Durchschnitt $500\,\mathrm{m}$ (Fläche $\approx 0,65\,\mathrm{km}^2$, bei hexagonalen Zellen) ergibt das eine Fläche von $7987,2\,\mathrm{km}^2$ (zum Vergleich: Das Bundesland Sachsen umfaßt eine Fläche von ca. $18341\,\mathrm{km}^2$). Das Modell besitzt 6 Hierarchieniveaus, d. h. eine Baumhöhe von $h(k_w) = 5$. Die Knoten der Niveaus eins bis fünf besitzen jeweils 4 Kindknoten. Die Anzahl der Teilnehmer wurde auf 20.000 festgelegt. Größere Konfigurationen hätten die Simulationszeit sehr ausgedehnt und der Speicherbedarf hätte die zur Verfügung stehenden Ressourcen der verwendeten Hardware überschritten[5]. Im folgenden

---

[4] Eine Anzahl von 12 Zellen pro Aktualisierungsregion bzw. *Location Area* stellt nach [15] einen für zukünftige Mobilfunksysteme möglichen Wert dar.

[5] Es wurden verschiedene Pentium II PCs mit 128 und 256 MByte Hauptspeicher (Betriebssystem: WindowsNT 4.0) verwendet.

Abschnitt werden die Ergebnisse beschrieben, die für die 3 in Tabelle 1 dargestellten Untermodelle ermittelt wurden.

Parameter	Modell (a)	Modell (b)	Modell (c)
Rufrate in h^{-1}	\multicolumn{3}{c}{$3,0$}		
Rufdauer in min	$2,5^c$		
Bewegungsrate[a] in h^{-1}	$\{3; 6; 15; 36\}$		
Distanz d der Kommunikationspartner	$d = 10$	$d = 6$	$d = 2$
$h(k_{i,m})$	$0\ldots5$	$0\ldots3$	$0\ldots2$
Anzahl der Elemente im Aktivitätszentrum[b]	$0\ldots15$	$0\ldots10$	$0\ldots5$
Anzahl bevorzugter Kommunikationspartner[b]	$1\ldots10$		$1\ldots5$
Wahrscheinlichkeit dafür, daß ein bevorzugter Partner gewählt wird	$0,9$	$0,6$	$0,3$

[a] Die durchschnittliche Anzahl von Ortswechseln je Zeiteinheit ist ein Maß
für die Geschwindigkeit, mit der sich das betreffende Objekt bewegt.

[b] Bei rein zufälligem Verhalten haben diese Parameter einen Wert von null.

[c] Laut [15] beträgt derzeit die durchschnittliche Rufdauer 100 s, gemessen in
einem GSM1800 Netz, es wird jedoch eine deutliche Steigerung erwartet
und deshalb wurde hier ein Wert von 150 s angenommen.

Tabelle 1. Parameter des Simulationsmodells

Die Belegung der Parameter Rufrate, durchschnittliche Rufdauer und Bewegungsrate wurde für alle Untermodelle identisch gewählt, da diese Parameter den
gleichen Einfluß auf alle zu untersuchenden Lokalisierungsmethoden ausüben.
Die in Tabelle 1 enthaltenen Werte für die Ruf- und die Bewegungsrate beschreiben den Mittelwert. Für die Verteilung der Zwischenankunftszeit der Bewegungen und Rufe sowie für die Rufdauer wurde eine Exponentialverteilung
angenommen, was nach [19] eine durch Untersuchungen an realen Systemen ge-
rechtfertigte Annahme darstellt (siehe auch [6,5]). Die verschiedenen Bewegungsraten sollen jeweils einen Fußgänger (ca. 6 km/h), einen Radfahrer (ca. 15 km/h),
ein KFZ in der Innenstadt (ca. 40 km/h) und ein KFZ auf der Autobahn (ca.
100 km/h) modellieren. Die Werte für die „Entfernung" zwischen zwei Kommunikationspartnern beschreiben die Länge des Weges bzw. den Abstand zwischen
den beiden Blattknoten, an denen die jeweiligen Objekte zum Zeitpunkt des Ru-
fes registriert sind. Die drei Modelle sollten eine von (a) nach (c) abnehmende
Eignung des Verhaltens der betrachteten Objekte für die Anwendung der alternativen Methode modellieren. D. h., Modell (a) sollte sehr gute und Modell (c)
eher negative Resultate bei Anwendung der alternativen Methode hervorrufen,
wobei jedoch zu beachten ist, daß für die jeweiligen Modelle eine relativ hohe

maximale Anzahl an Knoten im Aktivitätszentrum gewählt wurde. Die Simulationszeit für alle Modelle betrug 8 h. Ziel der Simulation war es, Werte (mittlere Anzahl der Datenbankanfragen/-aktualisierungen je Operation usw.) für die sogenannte *busy hour* zu gewinnen. Die Werte wurden für ein Konfidenzniveau von 99% bestimmt. Die genauen Angaben zu den Konfidenzintervallen der in Abbildung 3 dargestellten Werte können [26] entnommen werden. Zur Bestimmung der Dauer der transienten Phase und der Konfidenzintervalle wurde ein frei verfügbares Statistikmodul der Politecnico di Torino [10], welches nach dem *sequentiellen Batch-Means-Verfahren* (siehe [22]) arbeitet, in das Analysemodul integriert.

5 Auswertung

In diesem Abschnitt sollen die betreiberbezogenen und die nutzerbezogenen Kosten der konventionellen und alternativen Methode verglichen werden. Die jeweiligen Werte für die betreiber- und nutzerbezogenen Kosten ergeben sich durch die Addition der mittleren Anzahl der pro Operation notwendigen Nachrichten und Datenbankoperationen (Anfrage und Aktualisierung). In die nutzerbezogenen Kosten gehen Nachrichten und Datenbankoperationen, die parallel ablaufen, nur einmal ein, da durch die parallele Ausführung von Operationen nur einmalig Kosten (Verzögerung) für den Nutzer entstehen. Die Datenbankoperationen Anfrage und Aktualisierung wurden gleich bewertet. D. h., es floß ausschließlich die nicht gewichtete, je Operation (Suche und Aktualisierung) notwendige, mittlere Anzahl in die Berechnung ein, da keine Werte z. B. für den zeitlichen Aufwand der jeweiligen Datenbankoperation vorlagen. Es ist jedoch davon auszugehen, daß der zeitliche Aufwand für eine Aktualisierung höher ausfällt als der für eine Abfrage.

Die Abbildungen 3(a) und 3(b) zeigen jeweils den Quotienten aus den durch die alternative Methode verursachten Kosten je Operation und den durch die konventionelle Methode verursachten Kosten je Operation C'/C bzw. $\hat{C}'/\hat{C}$ in Abhängigkeit von der Bewegungsrate. Dabei gilt für die Bezeichner:

C: betreiberbezogene Kosten je Operation, konventionelle Methode,
C': betreiberbezogene Kosten je Operation, alternative Methode,
$\hat{C}$: nutzerbezogene Kosten je Operation, konventionelle Methode,
$\hat{C}'$: nutzerbezogene Kosten je Operation, alternative Methode.

Die in Abbildung 3 dargestellten Ergebnisse bestätigen die von Modell (a) nach (c) abnehmende Eignung des Verhaltens der betrachteten Objekte für die Anwendung der alternativen Methode. Die Ergebnisse für Modell (c) in Abbildung 3 zeigen, daß eine Objektpopulation, die regelmäßiges Ruf- und Bewegungsverhalten aufweist, welches pro Operation nur eine relativ geringe Anzahl von Knoten innerhalb der Hierarchie einbezieht, gut durch die konventionelle Methode behandelt wird. Die durch die alternative Methode möglichen Einsparungen fallen deutlich geringer aus als in den Modellen (a) und (b). Je höher die Anzahl der einbezogenen Knoten bzw. Hierarchieebenen wird, desto günstiger wirkt

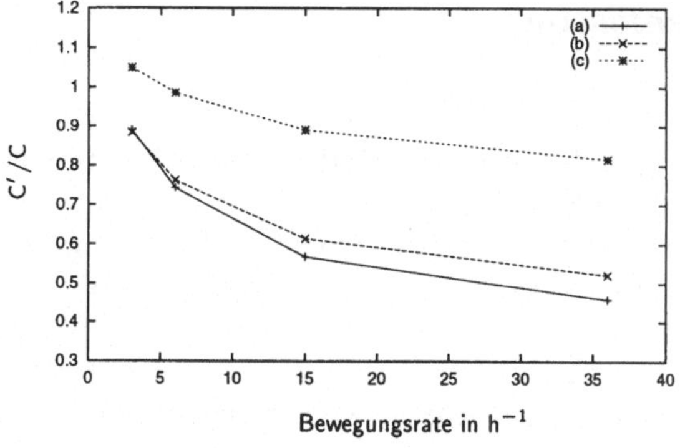

(a) betreiberbezogen

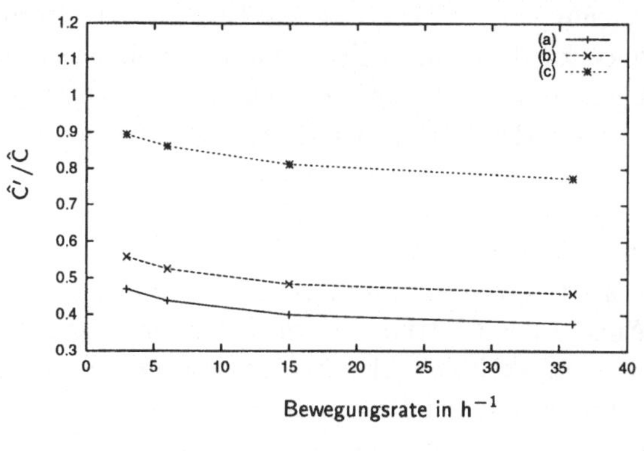

(b) nutzerbezogen

Abbildung 3. Kosten pro Operation, Modelle (a-c)

sich der Einsatz der alternativen Methode sowohl auf die betreiber- als auch auf die nutzerbezogenen Kosten aus. Die nutzerbezogenen Kosten der alternativen Methode in den Modellen (a) und (b) betragen nur noch nahezu die Hälfte der Kosten der konventionellen Methode (siehe Abbildung 3(b)). Die Abhängigkeit der Kosten von der Bewegungsrate wird in beiden beschriebenen Abbildungen deutlich. Eine höhere Bewegungsrate hat einen Anstieg der Aktualisierungsrate zur Folge. Die Aktualisierungskosten gewinnen bei höheren Bewegungsraten einen stärkeren Einfluß auf die operationsbezogenen Kosten. Dadurch kommen die geringeren Werte für die Kosten der alternativen Methode zustande. Die Ergebnisse und der Vergleich einzelner Parameter kann [26] entnommen werden.

6 Zusammenfassung

Die im diesem Beitrag beschriebene Methode der Aktivitätszentren faßt Blattknoten des Lokalisierungssystems objektbezogen, abhängig vom Bewegungs- und
Kommunikationsverhalten der betrachteten Objekte zusammen und definiert so
objektbezogene Aktualisierungsregionen. Aktivitätszentren durchbrechen somit
die statisch auferlegte Hierarchie und rekonfigurieren die Menge der Knoten im
Lokalisierungsnetzwerk zu einer an das jeweilige Objekt angepaßten Hierarchie.
Mobile Objekte, die ein der Hierarchie entsprechendes Verhalten zeigen, werden
auch weiterhin über die konventionellen Verfahren lokalisiert. Die objektspezifi-
schen Methoden werden als zusätzliche Eigenschaft eingeführt. Mit Hilfe eines im
Rahmen der beschriebenen Arbeiten enstandenen Simulationswerkzeuges wurde
die entwickelte Lokalisierungsmethode anhand eines komplexen Szenarios untersucht. Die Untersuchungen ergaben, daß der Einsatz der alternativen Methode
in einer im Vergleich zur konventionellen Methode hohen Kostenersparnis (Anzahl der notwendigen Datenbankoperationen und Nachrichten je Operation bzw.
Zeitschritt) führt, wenn die Anzahl der Blattknoten im Aktivitätszentrum den
maximalen Abstand zwischen zwei Blattknoten im Baum nicht übersteigt. Dieser Wert übt einen entscheidenden Einfluß auf die erreichbare Kostenersparnis
aus, weil er den für die Suche notwendigen Aufwand bestimmt. Die betreiberbezogenen Gesamtkosten, die die Methode hervorruft, werden besonders dann
stark durch die Anzahl der Blattknoten im Aktivitätszentrum bestimmt, wenn
die Kommunikation im Verhalten der betrachteten Objekte dominiert. Durch
den Einsatz effizienter Multicast-Protokolle (bei einer entsprechenden physikalischen Struktur des Signalisierungsnetzwerkes) sollte sich diese Abhängigkeit
verringern. Geht man weiterhin davon aus, daß die Abfrage der Datenbank eines Blattknotens (bei entsprechender Dimensionierung) durch die Abfrage einer
Datenstruktur, die vollständig im Hauptspeicher liegt, realisiert werden kann,
ist eine weitere Senkung des Aufwandes möglich. Weiterhin hängt der mögliche Optimierungsgrad von der Lage des das Aktivitätszentrum überspannenden
Knotens ab. Befindet sich dieser auf einem der oberen Hierarchiniveaus[6] fällt die
durch die alternative Methode mögliche Kostersparnis höher aus.

Die in diesem Beitrag vorgestellten Untersuchungen haben gezeigt, daß es
bei Vorhandensein von Regelmäßigkeiten im Mobilitäts- und Kommunikationsverhalten mobiler Objekte möglich ist, den Aufwand zu reduzieren, der zu ihrer
Lokalisierung notwendig ist. Die vorgestellte Lokalisierungsmethode könnte z. B.
in zukünftigen Mobilfunksystemen der vierten Generation zum Einsatz kommen.
Ebenso ist eine Optimierung hierarchischer Verfahren zum Mobilitätsmanagement in MobileIPv4 bzw. MobileIPv6- Protokollen [11, 21] sowie in CellularIP
möglich, z. B. in Kombination mit den in [4] vorgestellten Routing- bzw. Paging
Caches.

---

[6] Dabei wird das Vorhandensein einer entsprechenden Anzahl von Hierarchieniveaus
vorausgesetzt.

Literatur

1. I. F. Akyildiz und J. S. M. Ho. On Location Management for Personal Communications Networks. *IEEE Communications Magazine*, 34(9):138–145, Sept. 1997.

2. B. Awerbuch und D. Peleg. Concurrent Online Tracking of Mobile Users. In *Proceedings of SIGCOMM'91*, S. 221–233. ACM, Sept. 1991.

3. B. R. Badrinath, T. Imielinski und A. Virmani. Locating Strategies for Personal Communication Networks. In *Proceedings of IEEE Globecom 92 Workshop on Networking for Personal Communications Applications*, Dez. 1992.

4. A. T. Campbell, J. Gomez und A. G. Valko. An Overview of Cellular IP. In *Proceedings of IEEE Wireless Communications and Networking Conference (WCNC'99)*, Sep. 1999.

5. C. D. Carothers und R. M. Fujimoto. Distributed Simulation: An Effective Modeling Tool for Large-Scale PCS Networks. Technical report, College of Computing, Georgia Institute of Technology, Atlanta, Georgia 30332, 1996.

6. C. D. Carothers, R. M. Fujimoto und Y.-B. Lin. Distributed Simulation of Large-Scale PCS Networks. In *Proceedings of the 2nd International Workshop on Modeling, Analysis and Simulation of Computer and Telecommunications (MASCOTS '94)*, S. 2–6, Feb. 1994.

7. Y.-J. Cho, Y.-B. Lin und H. C.-H. Rao. Reducing the Network Cost of Call Delivery to GSM Roamers. *IEEE Network*, 11(5):19–25, Sept. 1997.

8. P. A. Fishwick. *Simulation Model Design and Execution: Building Digital Worlds*. Prentice-Hall International Series in Industrial and Systems Engineering, 1. Auflage, 1995. ISBN 0130986097.

9. B. Fomitchev. STLport Projekt, 1998. http://www.stlport.org/index.shtml.

10. A. Francini. *Statistics User Manual*, 1994. http://www1.tlc.polito.it/ancles/statistics.ps.gz.

11. E. Gustafsson, A. Jonsson und C. E. Perkins. Mobile IP Regional Registration draft-ietf-mobileip-reg-tunnel-03.txt, Juli 2000.

12. J. S. M. Ho. *Mobility Management for Personal Communication Networks*. Dissertation, School of Electrical and Computer Engineering, Georgia Institute of Technology, Mai 1996.

13. J. Jannink, D. Lam, N. Shivakumar, J. Widom und D. C. Cox. Efficient and Flexible Location Management Techniques for Wireless Communication Systems. In *Proceedings of the Second ACM International Conference on Mobile Computing and Networking MobiCom '96*, Nov. 1996.

14. Implementation Aspects of the UMTS Database, Mai 1994. R2066/PTTNL/MF1/DS/P/061/b1.

15. NESSY3, Simulation Results, Dez. 1994. R2066/SEL/NESSY3/DS/P/084/b1.

16. M. Mouly und M.-B. Pautet. *The GSM System for Mobile Communications*. Cell & Sys, 1992. ISBN 2-9507190-0-7.

17. R. Pandya. Numbers and Identities for Emerging Wireless/PCS Networks. *IEEE Personal Communications*, 4(3):8–14, Juni 1997.

18. C. Perkins. IP mobility support, Okt. 1996. RFC 2002.

19. C. Rose und R. Yates. Mobility Analysis of Call Records in a Cellular Switch. Technical report, WINLAB, Rutgers University, Sept. 1995.

20. C. Sieber. System zur Validierung von Lokalisierungsmethoden für mobile Objekte. In *Kommunikation in Verteilten Systemen (KiVS), 11. ITG/GI-Fachtagung, Darmstadt, 2.-5. März 1999*, S. 528–533, März 1999.

21. H. Soliman, C. Castelluccia, K. El-Malki und L. Bellier. Hierarchical MIPv6 mobility management draft-ietf-mobileip-hmipv6-00.txt, Oktober 2000.

22. O. Spaniol und S. Hoff. *Ereignisorientierte Simulation: Konzepte und Systemrealisierung*. International Thomson Publishing GmbH, 1. Auflage, 1995. ISBN 3-8266-0122-X, Thomson's Aktuelle Tutorien Nr. 7.

23. UMTS System Structure Document (Revised), Dec. 1995. R2066/BT/PM2/DS/P/113/b1.

24. M. Steen, F. J. Hauck, P. Homburg und A. S. Tanenbaum. Locating Objects in Wide-Area Systems. *IEEE Communications Magazine*, S. 104–109, Jan. 1998.

25. F. Teraoka, K. Claffy und M. Tokoro. Design, Implementation, and Evaluation of Virtual Internet Protocol. In *12th International Conference on Distributed Computing Systems*, S. 170–177, Washington, D.C., USA, Juni 1992. IEEE Computer Society Press.

26. T. Ziegert. *Nutzung von Verhaltensmustern zur Lokalisierung mobiler Objekte*. Dissertation, Technische Universität Dresden, Mommsenstr. 13, 01062 Dresden, April 2000.

High Quality Mobile Communication

H. Hartenstein*, A. Schrader*, A. Kassler•, M. Krautgärtner[†], C. Niedermeier[†]

* Computer & Communication Research Laboratories Heidelberg, NEC Europe Ltd
email: {Hannes.Hartenstein|Andreas.Schrader}@ccrle.nec.de

• University of Ulm
email: {Andreas.Kassler}@informatik.uni-ulm.de

[†] Siemens AG Munich
email: {Michael.Krautgaertner|Christoph.Niedermeier}@mchp.siemens.de

Abstract. Future communication environments have to support mobility at various levels ranging from device and personal to session and service mobility. Much effort is currently beeing spent in the areas of cellular access technology, wireless LAN technology and mobility support in IP (Mobile IP). There is a clear trend that the IP protocol is becoming the dominant networking protocol. Since standard IP networks do not provide any guarantees for the transmission quality parameters, there is a clear demand for a comprehensive QoS mechanism, which allows for adaptation in a mobile environment using heterogeneous devices with heterogeneous access networks.

In this paper we present a project on defining and implementing a comprehensive QoS framework for 'Mobility and Service Adaptation in Heterogeneous Mobile Communication Networks' (MASA). Our thesis is that, in order to provide high quality communication for mobile users, media processing facilities as well as mobility handling and handoff decision mechanisms should be closely integrated into a QoS framework. This allows, e.g., to base handoff decisions on *all* available QoS elements such as availability of transcoding units or local resource management. The *MASA* framework is able to release applications of QoS-related work as much as possible and, in addition, hides the complexity of network QoS mechanisms from the applications. The MASA QoS framework is able to support users with the ability to continue ongoing sessions even during handoffs and device changes (session mobility).

We present an outline of the general *MASA* architecture, consisting of distributed autonomous QoS Brokers that can be placed on the (potentially mobile) end-system, on intermediate network nodes (e.g. router, switches) and on transcoding units (gateways). The Brokers are supported by Managers and Controllers responsible for different tasks like resource, network, media, policy and mobility management. As an example, we describe the internal structure of the MASA *Mobility* Manager.

Keywords: *QoS, Mobility Management, Seamless Handover, Wireless Networks*

1 Introduction

The Internet offers challenging new opportunities for the development of communication applications such as video conferencing, multimedia distance learning, virtual reality group chatting, secure online shopping and banking, distributed games and many more. Some applications like IP telephony (or sometimes simplified VoIP) [7] have already become one of the most challenging business areas in the communication industry. In order to develop the Internet to be a widely deployed, commonly accepted communication medium allowing everywhere usage by everybody anytime, three major problems have to be solved.

First of all, the most well-known problem lies in the fact that today's Internet does not support any kind of guarantees for real-time multimedia streaming with adequate qualities. Therefore, effective methods for providing *Quality of Service* (QoS) are needed. Secondly, a less recognized problem is that among all of the above mentioned applications capturing, processing, transmitting, receiving and presenting media information are the crucial elements and have to be re-implemented within every application again. This results in an enormous waste of implementation resources and in a heterogeneous collection of incompatible applications. Thus, from our perspective there is a need for a *media architecture* that supports applications with multimedia streaming and processing facilities. Such an architecture eases the development of new challenging applications which can be implemented merely as a collection of graphical user interfaces using the architecture interfaces to realize the media processing. Last but not least, since more and more devices will be mobile, many multimedia applications should also be able to run in mobile environments. However, mobile environments are characterized by low bandwidth (compared to wired networks), quickly changing link qualities, as well as a wide variety of different access technologies. Therefore, taking also the mobility-specific needs into account we propose a comprehensive *media-centric QoS architecture with mobility support*. With this architecture a mobile user will be supported to get the highest possible quality according to some user criterion wherever she is located. The decision of the actual transmission parameters should be based on monitoring information about the status of the network as well as the local end-system resources and has to provide a tradeoff between the user's QoS policy settings and the network operators service level agreements.

The rest of the paper is organized as follows. In section 2 we review some related works. Section 3 introduces the *MASA* QoS framework. Whereas subsection 3.1 outlines the general design of the *MASA* system, subsection 3.2 describes the typical structure of *MASA* on end-systems. It is out of the scope of this paper to give detailed descriptions of all the broker's manager components. Instead we will restrict ourselves to a discussion on mobility management aspects in section 4. Section 5 summarizes the concept and gives some ideas for future extensions.

2   Related Works

In recent years, a number of approaches have been proposed to enhance the Internet with different Classes of Services (CoS). Most of them concentrate only on certain aspects of the overall QoS problem, like media filtering [16] or resource reservation [5]. Others only operate on certain layers of the communication model, like the network layer (e.g. DiffServ [2], IntServ [12]) or the application layer [11]. Some architectures only cover certain entities of the end-to-end transmission path, like the end-system [10]. Some architectures are integral, but some key features are missing, like inter-session relationships [3], or load-balancing and fast handover [9]. None of the approaches provide separation of the actual media processing activities from the application and the combination with QoS issues. For further references and comparisons of QoS architectures, see [1, 9]. On the other hand, frameworks have been developed to provide applications with media processing facilities, for example the Java Media Framework (JMF)[14]. However, these frameworks do not provide any kind of QoS mechanisms.

Although all mentioned approaches provide important mechanisms for parts of the QoS problem, an overall optimal solution can only be achieved, if all mechanisms are handled within an integrated comprehensive end-to-end management system. In the following we introduce the *MASA* QoS framework as such an integrated architecture.

3   The MASA QoS Framework

The *MASA* QoS Framework (Mobility and Service Adaptation in Heterogeneous Mobile Networks) is a joint project of NEC Europe Ltd. Heidelberg, Siemens AG Munich and the University of Ulm. The *MASA* framework was designed to fulfill the requirements of a *comprehensive integrated end-to-end QoS multimedia management system*, invoking all entities on the transmission path, like sender, network nodes, transcoding nodes, switches, routers, filter nodes, gateways and receivers. *MASA* allows the usage of underlying network layer QoS technologies (e.g. DiffServ, IntServ, MPLS, etc.), and also hides the complexity of these mechanisms from the applications. By controlling the complete communication infrastructure *MASA* is able to support QoS in a way which can neither be realized inside the applications nor with the underlying network QoS technologies alone.

The framework follows an object-oriented design and most of the components (except some operating system specific tasks) are implemented in Java. This allows for downloading plugable components from different parties. Through the usage of open interfaces we can reach a high flexibility. The design also fulfils other important rules like separation of media processing and control or separation of tasks with different timing constraints etc (see also [3]). Since not all of the possible components have to be used on all locations, our design also provides scalability which is extremely important if we consider the usage of *MASA* on terminals with limited facilities, e.g., future UMTS devices.

3.1 Architectural Overview

The *MASA* QoS architecture consists of a distributed set of autonomous QoS Brokers (fig. 1) which can be placed on the (potentially mobile) end-system, on intermediate network nodes (e.g. router, switches) and on transcoding units (gateways). Each Broker is responsible for the brokerage between managers with very different tasks, like resource, network, media, monitoring, policy and mobility management.

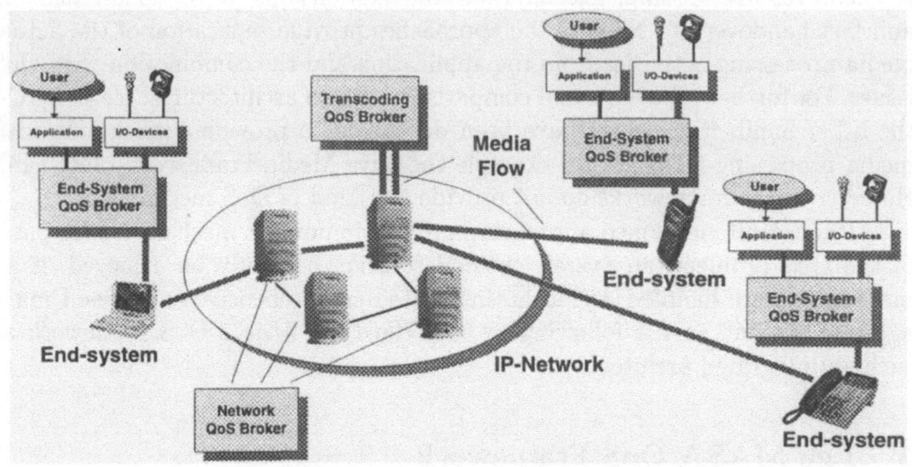

Fig. 1. Distributed set of autonomous QoS Brokers.

The main task of the *End-System QoS Broker* is to coordinate, orchestrate and manage local and remote resources for multimedia streaming and service quality, to map the user's QoS wishes to appropriate QoS parameters and to support mobility with the use of different access networks (e.g. GSM, Wireless-LAN, UMTS, etc.) We will describe the *MASA* end-system QoS Broker in detail in section 3.2.

Network QoS Brokers can be regarded as centralised QoS management units which support the end-system QoS Brokers and organise the orchestration of all streams in the respective network domain according to the network management policy. The network QoS Broker monitors network resources, decides admission in cooperation with other admission controlling entities (e.g. H.323 Gatekeepers) and realises load balancing and fairness concepts for all participating systems. The actual behaviour of the network QoS Broker depends on the location of the respective network node, e.g. core network router, access network router, media gateway, LAN switch etc.

The *Transcoding QoS Broker* can be instantiated if heterogeneous clients must be supported in a multi-party conference scenario or if special network characteristics on certain network links have to be supported with mechanisms like adaptive Forward Error Correction (FEC), appropriate transmission protocols (e.g. wireless-TCP), etc. Transcoding QoS Brokers can also realize simple filter mechanisms. In our framework we use filter routers to realize priority filtering based on priority settings within the RTP header. This allows for very fast and fine-grained adaptation schemes which are combined with coarse-grained sender rate adaptation schemes in the end-systems.

Communication between this distributed collection of QoS Brokers is realized via appropriate interfaces. Main communication issues are capability exchange methods, QoS routing mechanisms, admission and authorization requests, and the management of media channels.

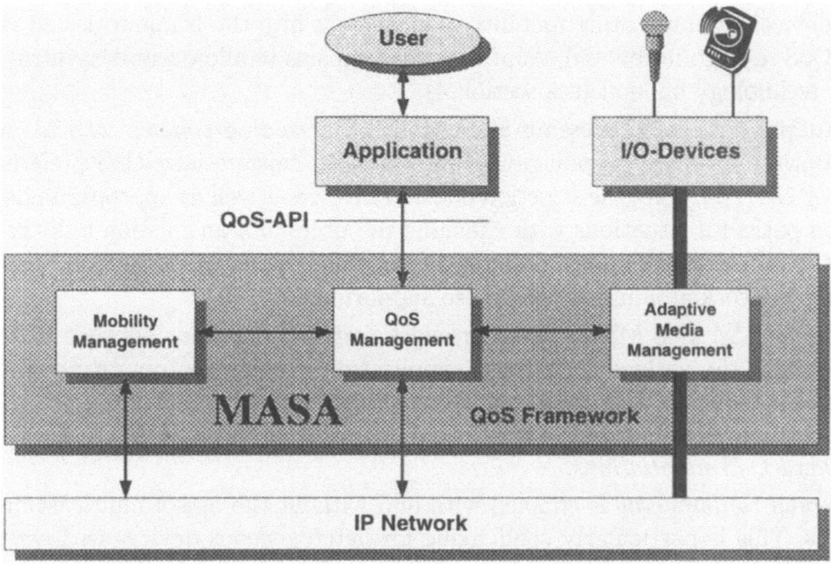

Fig. 2. General Structure of *MASA* on end-systems.

Fig. 2 outlines the general concept of *MASA* on end-systems. As a major feature, *MASA* separates the adaptive media management from the applications. The media management is controlled by the QoS management which is closely coupled with the integrated mobility management.

MASA presents applications with mechanisms for the processing and transmission of 'high quality' multimedia streams, i.e. adapted to the user's QoS wishes and the available infrastructure. Applications subscribe to the system and use the provided facilities via a respective QoS-API. This API can be used to instantiate multimedia sessions. Within the *MASA* QoS management, the hierarchical concept of participants, session, streams and flows is used. Each participant can have several media sessions with other participants (at remote machines) at the same time. The sessions consists of an arbitrary number of streams with one or more actual media flows. This allows for the usage of layered coding.

The set-up of a complete chain of media processors, consisting of capture devices, codecs, effect processors, etc., can be controlled via this API. Appropriate graphical user interfaces are provided to present media information (e.g. video panel). Since *MASA* provides a flexible mechanism to *plug-in* arbitrary components to capture, process, code, transmit, receive, decode and display any kind of media, the applications are shielded from that low-level complexity. Adaptive and layered coding can be used seamlessly by any application to allow for scaleable media transmission.

With respect to mobility, efficient handoff algorithms are a cost-effective way of enhancing the capacity and QoS of cellular systems [15]. *MASA* supports mobile devices by integrating mobility management into the framework and using fast QoS re-negotiation and adaptation mechanisms to allow seamless intra- and inter-technology handoff (see section 4).

Adaptive media processing is controlled via *trading policies*. *MASA* offers appropriate intuitive graphical user interfaces to capture user QoS preferences (policy GUI) allowing the selection of a certain CoS as well as appropriate degradation paths for situations with changing resources or transmission link characteristics. On network nodes, preference-controlled management of QoS capabilities for network administration is also supported.

The *MASA* QoS Management provides *mapping functions* between QoS parameters at the various levels (user, application, framework, operating system, network sub-system and network layer), to hide underlying QoS parameters from users and applications and support applications with mechanisms to allow *soft* and *hard QoS negotiations*.

Group conferencing is enabled with and without the use of multicast mechanisms. This is particularly challenging for heterogeneous devices with varying capabilities, like resources, media processing mechanisms, etc. Clients are supported with *capability exchange* mechanisms in order to agree on a certain service quality and to dynamically join and leave ongoing sessions. To support different service levels for group communication *audio and video filtering* is used on network level (packet-based) as well as on application level (content-based). To support heterogeneous devices with incompatible communication mechanisms, appropriately placed *transcoding units* can be used. These units allow for downloading codecs on demand. The placement and optimization of transcoding and filter units can follow intelligent algorithms to optimize network load and processing requirements.

The provision of differentiated CoS demands for the introduction of charging and billing mechanisms. The *MASA* architecture supports control of media quality in relation to a cost-over-quality function which is part of the user's QoS preferences GUI.

In the following subsection we outline one possible structure of *MASA* components on end-systems.

3.2   The End-System QoS Broker

Fig. 3 outlines a typical structure of *MASA* on end-systems, like multimedia
terminals. The *End-System QoS Broker* is the central intelligence unit which is
supported by a set of QoS Managers which in turn are supported by appropriate
QoS Controllers. With this hierarchy of Manager/Controller structures, the QoS
Broker can delegate separate tasks for controlling and processing media streams
and therefore provides a clear separation of tasks with different time constraints.

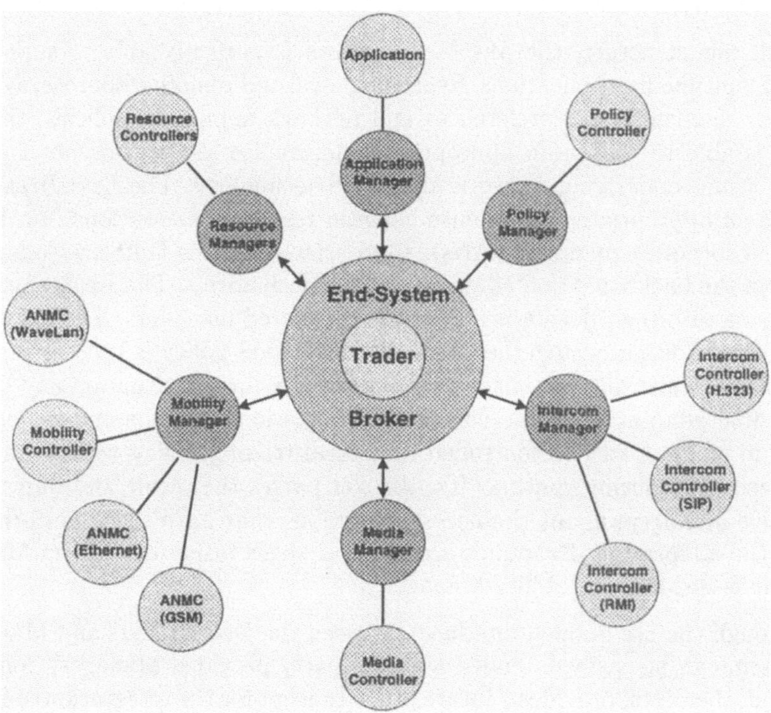

Fig. 3. Hierarchical structure of *MASA* on end-systems.

The *Policy Manager*, e.g., is responsible for the storage and retrieval of QoS
preferences within a user profile and for presenting an appropriate policy GUI to
the user. The Policy Controller enables the access to a policy database (in accor-
dance with the IETF QoS Policy Framework [6]) for storing the profiles as well
as QoS trading policies used inside the QoS Brokers. The *Resource Managers*
are responsible for controlling the available resources (like CPU, memory, network, etc.) via the respective Resource Controllers. This is of special importance
for real-time communication with limited tolerance against delay and jitter. The
Media Manager is responsible for the provision and orchestration of actual media
processing entities, like codecs, packetizers, etc., inside the Media Controller. It

also monitors the transmission parameters and reports aggregated statistic information to the Broker. The *Intercom Manager* is used to allow inter-Broker communication. The *Application Manager* provides applications with their specific needs. This allows to support different categories of applications, like VoD or IP-Telephony. The Application Manager maps typical requests from applications (e.g. SIP protocol sequences) to the Broker QoS API. With this mechanism we achieve a better flexibility and also support legacy code. The *Mobility Management* is responsible for the support of device mobility and enables the usage of different access devices. The Mobility Manager will be explained in detail in the next section.

With this structure, the *MASA* framework is perfectly able to support all kinds of multimedia applications. Regarding local and remote resources, available media mechanisms, user preferences and network admission policies, the QoS Broker is able to choose an appropriate compromise and to provide a certain CoS by using underlying network layer QoS technology. The QoS Broker can produce an appropriate compromise between resource reservations (via RSVP; mainly in corporate managed LANs), appropriate CoS (via DiffServ Codepoints; mainly in the backbone) and adaptive scaling mechanisms. The Broker regularly requests monitoring information from the connected managers. The aggregated monitoring information together with the user's QoS policy is used as input for the included trader mechanims which analysis the current situation and decides for possible adaptation of the current active sessions. On the end-system, the algorithm of the trader is controlled by a local trading policy which can easily exchanged even during runtime. The Broker parses the result and informs the respective managers about the necessary actions that have to be performed to realize the adaptation. Examples are codec changes inside the Media Manager or handoffs inside the Mobility Manager.

Through the use of open interfaces between the QoS Brokers and Managers, the system can be easily extended with 3rd party provided Manager/Controller pairs and, therefore, provides a future proof-concept for the integration of further mechanisms (e.g. Managers for location awareness using GPS Controllers). We use a combination of a generic interface description which must be implemented by all involved managers and more specific interfaces for each manager. The generic interface allows for basic control of participants, sessions, streams, and flows, whereas the specific interfaces can offer methods which are only important for the specific manager, e.g. defining a thread priority via the CPU Resource Manager. This plug-in mechanism can be explicitly used to support any (future) underlying network technology (e.g. wired or wireless access networks). For example, within the *MASA* project, different realisations of the Media Manager are provided by the project partners. The NEC *AQUARIUS* (Adaptive Quality of Service Architecture of Intelligent Universal Services) Media Manager is built in Java. Through the usage of JMF [14] as a Media Controller *AQUARIUS* is able to download, install and maintain a broad range of audio/video codecs to filter and transmit media, ranging from low bandwidth speech codecs (e.g. GSM) to high quality video streaming (e.g. H.261/H.263, MPEG-1/2/4).

4   The MASA Mobility Manager

In order to allow a mobile user to roam between various operators, between public and private networks, between wired and wireless networks, and between different access technologies, the mobility management within the *MASA* framework is based on Mobile IP (for an introduction cf., e.g., [13]). As a layer 3 approach, Mobile IP provides a more generic mobility management than any L2 mechanism and at the same time releases applications of any mobility concerns. In our current implementation Mobile IPv4 is used but could be substituted by a Mobile IPv6 implementation because of the modularity of the architecture.

Mobile IP can be conceptually split up into the following three parts: *i)* signalling and configuration, *ii)* data transport, and *iii)* movement detection plus handoff decision. The movement detection mechanisms specified in Mobile IP are based on whether a mobile node is able to hear some agent advertisements that are periodically sent by home or foreign agents. Since these advertisements are usually sent only once per several seconds, no fast handoffs can be achieved with these mechanisms. Therefore, we use (downlink) signal quality measurements to achieve faster movement detection and focus on mobile node initiated handoffs.

The mobility management part on a *MASA* end-system has been structured as illustrated in figure 3. The *Mobility Controller* is a standard Mobile IP daemon with the difference that it does not implement any handoff decision mechanism. Thus, the Mobility Controller is able to send/receive and process Mobile IP signalling messages like registration requests/replies, but performs any action only when told so by the Mobility Manager. For each network interface an *Access Network Monitor Controller* (ANMC) measures link quality parameters and reports them to the Mobility Manager. The quality parameter might be a boolean value like link integrity in the case of Ethernet or some real value for example measuring signal-to-noise ratio in the case of a wireless LAN. The *Mobility Manager* processes the information of the ANMCs and either directly forces a handoff or informs the QoS Broker of available access options. In the case when no foreign agents are present in a access network, the mobile node has to operate in co-located care-of-address mode and, therefore, has to be able to acquire a topologically correct IP address by means of DHCP. For this purpose, an *IP Address Controller* might be needed in addition.

The purpose of the tight integration of mobility management and handoff control with the QoS architecture is to support seamless handoffs for realtime communications. The QoS Broker has a more complete knowledge -compared to the Mobility Manager- a handoff decision can be based on. While the Mobility Manager deals with IP connectivity, the QoS Broker can also take into account issues related to service mobility and admission control. For example, when the Mobility Manager advertises a new access network, the QoS Broker (with the help of all managers) can base the decision whether to handoff to the new network on cost policies, available codecs in the Media Manager, required resources at the processor, the current location, and so on. Thus, a handoff is only initiated when a successful completion of the handoff can be expected. This aspect is particularly important for future scenarios with a wide range of wireless access alternatives.

The interface between Mobility Manager and QoS Broker essentially consists of methods *new_network* and *removed_network* that announce the addition/removal of an access option to the QoS Broker as well as methods *request_handoff* (QoS Broker requests a handoff to a specific network) and *get_parameters* (QoS Broker requests some quality parameters). In addition, a method *set_threshold* allows the QoS Broker to register an event filter at the Mobility Manager in order to avoid excessive polling of quality parameters.

We achieve seamless handoffs by following the *make before break* philosophy, i.e., all negotiation for registering in a new network are done while the mobile node is still able to send/receive packets over the old network. In the case of an inter-technology (vertical) handoff this can be easily achieved: when for each access technology the mobile node is equipped with a specific interface, the mobile node is able to listen to one interface while registering with a new network over a different interface. Thus, the handoff problem is basically a *multi-homing* problem. The new registration is done via the new network (called a *forward handoff*). In the case of an intra-technology (horizontal) handoff the interface can usually only communicate on IP level with one base station at a time (for example, in IEEE 802.11 a mobile node is associated with a single access point when using infrastructure mode). Thus, a typical handoff procedure will first break the old *mobility binding* before establishing the new one via the new access network. In order to be able to benefit from the "make before break" approach even in the case of an intra-technology handoff, we have developed a method where the new mobility binding is established via the old network (i.e. a *backward handoff*) and *simultaneous bindings* are used [8]. Thus, packets destined for the mobile node will be delivered to the old and new base stations, and the mobile node only has to reconfigure its interface in order to complete the handoff.

In our current testbed, the mobile node is equipped with Ethernet, Wave-LAN, and GSM cards. The Mobility Controller is running Dynamics Mobile IP [4] in co-located care-of-address mode. The interface between Mobility Controller and Mobility Manager is based on the Dynamics API. The interface for the WLAN ANMC is based on the Linux Wireless Extension. The Ethernet ANMC currently checks only the link integrity flag. The 'make-before-break' approach leads to times for physical interruption of about 5 msec, i.e., seamless handoffs can be performed.

5 Conclusion and Future Work

We have presented the *MASA* Framework as a comprehensive integrated end-to-end QoS multimedia management system with mobility support for heterogeneous wireless environments. A distributed set of autonomous, flexible QoS Brokers, located on end-systems, network nodes and transcoding entities can be easily extended with new Manager/Controller pairs through the usage of open interfaces. By using exchangeable trading policies, all aspects of mobile multimedia communication can be organised and managed by a de-centralised intelligence mechanism. As an example, we demonstrated the interworking of the QoS and mobility management systems for seamless handoffs of mobile devices. The framework has been implemented and the interworking of the various components of the different project partners has been tested. As example applications, we have realized small prototypes for Video on Demand, Video Conferencing, Audio Broadcasting and IP-Telephony.

Currently we are integrating DiffServ routers in our testbed and develop mapping functions between QoS policies and DiffServ classes for the above mentioned application scenarios. Future work will concentrate on appropriate trading policies and the provision of new management components, for example location awareness for improved handoff detection.

References

1. C. Aurrecoechea, A. Campbell, and L. Hauw. A Survey of QoS Architectures. *Multimedia Systems Journal*, 6(3):138–151, May 1998.
2. A. Blake, D. Black, M. Carlson, E. Davies, Z. Wang, and W. Weiss. *RFC2475: An Architecture for Differentiated Services.* IETF.
3. A. Campbell, G. Coulson, and D. Hutchinson. A Quality of Service Architecture. *ACM Computer Communication Review*, April 1994.
4. Dynamics. *Mobile IPv4 implementation.* http://www.cs.hut.fi/Research/Dynamics/.
5. L. Zhang et. al. RSVP: A new Resource ReSerVation Protocol. *IEEE Network*, (9):8–18, 1993.
6. S. Gai, J. Strassner, D. Durham, S. Herzog, H. Mahon, and F. Reichmeyer. *Internet Draft: QoS Policy Framework Architecture.* IETF, February 1999.
7. S. Gessler, O. Haase, and A. Schrader. A Service Platform for Intelligent Internet Telephony. In *The 1st IP Telephony Workshop (GI)*, April 2000.
8. H. Hartenstein, K. Jonas, and R. Schmitz. Seamless Inter-Domain Handoffs via Simultaneous Bindings. *Proc. European Wireless 2000, Dresden, Germany*, September 2000.
9. A. Kassler and P. Schulthess. An End-to-End Quality of Service Management Architecture for Wireless ATM Networks. In *Proc. HICSS'32*, Hawaii, Jan 1999.
10. K. Lakshman and R. Yavatkar. AQUA: An Adaptive End-System Quality of Service Architecture. In *High Speed for Multimedia Applications*, pages 155–177. Kluwer Academic Publishers, 1996.
11. K. Nahrstedt. *An Architecture for End-to-End Quality of Service Provision and its Experimental Validation.* PhD thesis, Department of Computer and Information Science, University of Pennsylvania, August 1995.
12. D. Clark R. Braden and S. Shenker. *RFC1633: Integrated Services in the Internet Architecture: An Overview.* IETF, June 1994.
13. J. D. Solomon. *Mobile IP.* Prentice Hall, 1998.
14. Sun. *The Java Media Framework Version 2.0 API.* http://java.sun.com/products/java-media/jmf.
15. N. Tripathi, J. Reed, and H. VanLandingham. Handoff in cellular systems. *IEEE Personal Communications*, Dec. 1998.
16. N. Yeadon, F. Garcia, D. Hutchinson, and D. Shepherd. Filters: QoS Support Mechanisms for Multipeer Communications. *IEEE Journal on Selected Areas in Communications*, 14(7), September 1993.

Evaluating the GPRS Radio Interface for Different Quality of Service Profiles

Christoph Lindemann and Axel Thümmler

University of Dortmund
Department of Computer Science
August-Schmidt-Str. 12
44227 Dortmund, Germany
http://www4.cs.uni-dortmund.de/~Lindemann/

Abstract. This paper presents a discrete-event simulator for the General Packet Radio Service (GPRS) on the IP level. GPRS is a standard on packet data in GSM systems that will become commercially available by the end of this year. The simulator focuses on the communication over the radio interface, because it is one of the central aspects of GPRS. We study the correlation of GSM and GPRS users by a static and dynamic channel allocation scheme. In contrast to previous work, our approach represents the mobility of users through arrival rates of new GSM and GPRS users as well as handover rates of GSM and GPRS users from neighboring cells. Furthermore, we consider users with different QoS profiles modeled by a weighted fair queueing scheme. The simulator considers a cell cluster comprising seven hexagonal cells. We provide curves for average carried traffic and packet loss probabilities for different channel allocation schemes and packet priorities as well as curves for average throughput per GPRS user. A detailed comparison between static and dynamic channel allocation schemes is provided.

Keywords: Wireless and mobile communication networks, performance evaluation, IP networks, discrete-event simulation.

1 Introduction

The *General Packet Radio Service (GPRS)* is a standard from the *European Telecommunications Standards Institute (ETSI)* on packet data in GSM systems [6], [14]. By adding GPRS functionality to the existing GSM network, operators can give their subscribers resource-efficient wireless access to external Internet protocol-based networks, such as the Internet and corporate intranets. The basic idea of GPRS is to provide a packet-switched bearer service in a GSM network. As impressively demonstrated by the Internet, packet-switched networks make more efficient use of the resources for bursty data applications and provide more flexibility in general.

In previous work, several analytical models have been developed to study data services in a GSM network. Ajmone Marsan et al. studied multimedia services in a GSM network by providing more than one channel for data services [1]. Boucherie and Litjens developed an analytical model based on Markov chain analysis to study the performance of GPRS under a given GSM call characteristic [4]. For analytical tractability, they assumed exponentially distributed arrival times for packets and exponential packet transfer times, respectively. On the other hand, discrete-event simulation based studies of GPRS were conducted. Meyer et al. focused on the performance of TCP over GPRS under several carrier to interference conditions and coding schemes of data [10]. Furthermore, they provided a detailed implementation of the GPRS protocol stack [11]. Malomsoky et al. developed a simulation based GPRS network dimensioning tool [9]. Stuckmann et al. studied the correlation of GSM and GPRS users with the simulator GPRSim [13].

This paper describes a discrete-event simulator for GPRS on the IP level. The simulator is developed using the simulation package CSIM [12] and considers a cell cluster comprising of seven hexagonal cells. The presented performance studies were conducted for the innermost cell of the seven cell cluster. The simulator focuses on the communication over the radio interface, because this is one of the central aspects of GPRS. In fact, the air interface mainly determines the performance of GPRS. We studied the correlation of GSM and GPRS users by a static and dynamic channel allocation scheme. A first approach of modeling dynamic channel allocation was introduced by Bianchi et al. and is known as *Dynamic Channel Stealing (DCS)* [3]. The basic DCS concept is to temporarily assign the traffic channels dedicated to circuit-switched connections but unused because statistical traffic fluctuations. This can be done at no expense in terms of radio resource, and with no impact on circuit-switched services performance if the channel allocation to packet-switched services is permitted only for idle traffic channels, and the stolen channels are immediately released when requested by the circuit-switched service.

In contrast to the models developed in [4], [9], [10], and [11], our approach additionally represents the mobility of users through arrival rates of new GSM and GPRS users as well as handover rates of GSM and GPRS users from neighboring cells. Furthermore, we consider users with different QoS profiles modeled by a weighted fair queueing scheme according to [5].

The remainder of the paper is organized as follows. Section 2 describes the basic GPRS network architecture, the radio interface, and different QoS profiles, which will be considered in the simulator. In Section 3 we describe the software architecture of the GPRS simulator, details about the mobility of GSM and GPRS users, the way we modeled quality of service profiles, and the workload model we used. Results of the simulation studies are presented in Section 4. We provide curves for average carried traffic and packet loss probabilities for different channel allocation schemes and packet priorities as well as curves for average throughput per GPRS user.

2 General Packet Radio Service

On the physical layer, GSM uses a combination of *Frequency Division Multiple Access (FDMA)* and *Time Division Multiple Access (TDMA)* for multiple access. Two frequency bands are reserved for GSM operation, one for transmission from the mobile station to the *Base Transceiver Station (BTS)* (uplink) and one for transmission form the BTS to the mobile station (downlink). Each of these bands is divided into 124 single carrier channels of 200 kHz width. A certain number of these frequency channels is allocated to a BTS, i.e., to a cell. Each of the 200 kHz frequency channels is divided into eight time slots that form a TDMA frame. A time slot lasts for a duration of 0.577 ms and carries 114 bits of information. The recurrence of one particular time slot defines a physical channel. A GSM channel is called *Traffic Channel (TCH)* and a channel allocated for GPRS is called *Packet Data Channel (PDCH)*.

In conventional GSM, a physical channel is permanently allocated for a particular user during the entire call period (whether data is transmitted or not). In contrast, GPRS allocates channels only when data packets are sent or received, and they are released after the transmission. For bursty traffic this results in a much more efficient usage of the scarce radio resource. With this principle, multiple users can share one physical channel. GPRS allows a single mobile station to transmit on multiple time slots of the same TDMA frame. This results in a very flexible channel allocation: one to eight time slots per TDMA frame can be allocated to one mobile station. On the other hand a time slot can be assigned temporarily to a mobile station, so that one to eight mobile stations can use one time slot. GPRS includes the functionality to increase or decrease the amount of radio resources allocated to GPRS on a dynamic basis. The PDCHs are taken from the common pool of all channels available in the cell. The mapping of physical channels to either packet-switched (GPRS) or circuit-switched (conventional GSM) services can be performed statically or dynamically ("capacity on demand"), depending on the current traffic load. A load supervision procedure monitors the load of the PDCHs in the cell. According to the current demand, the number of channels allocated for GPRS can be changed. Physical channels not currently in use by conventional GSM can be allocated as PDCHs to increase the quality of service for GPRS. When there is a resource demand for services with higher priority, e.g. GSM voice calls, PDCHs can be de-allocated.

Because of the scarcity of wireless channel capacity, aggressive admission control will likely be employed to fully utilize the wireless link. Therefore GPRS subscribers can choose their own QoS profile consisting of *precedence class*, *delay class*, *reliability class*, *peak throughput class* and *mean throughput class*. For a detailed description of the GPRS network architecture we refer to [14], the GPRS Radio Interface to [8], and for QoS profiles proposed by the ETSI to [6].

3   The Simulation Model

We consider a cluster comprising of sever hexadiagonal cells in an integrated GSM/GPRS network, serving circuit-switched voice and packet-switched data calls. The performance studies presented in Section 4 were conducted for the innermost cell of the seven cell cluster. We assume that GSM and GPRS calls arrive in each cell according to two mutually independent Poisson processes, with arrival rates λ_{GSM} and λ_{GPRS}, respectively. GSM calls are handled circuit-switched, so that one physical channel is exclusively dedicated to the corresponding mobile station. After the arrival of a GPRS call, a *GPRS session* begins. During this time a GPRS user allocates no physical channel exclusively. Instead the radio interface is scheduled among different GPRS users by the *Base Station Controller (BSC)*. Every GPRS user receives packets according to a specified workload model. The amount of time that a mobile station with an ongoing call remains within the area covered by the same BSC is called *dwell time*. If the call is still active after the dwell time, a handover toward an adjacent cell takes place. The *call duration* is defined as the amount of time that the call will be active, assuming it completes without being forced to terminate due to handover failure. We assume the dwell time to be an exponentially distributed random variable with mean $1/\mu_{h,GSM}$ for GSM calls and $1/\mu_{h,GPRS}$ for GPRS calls. The call durations are also exponentially distributed with mean values $1/\mu_{GSM}$ and $1/\mu_{GPRS}$ for GSM and GPRS calls, respectively.

To exactly model the user behavior in the seven cell cluster, we have to consider the handover flow of GSM and GPRS users from adjacent cells. At the boundary cells of the seven cell cluster, the intensity of the incoming handover flow cannot be specified in advance. This is due to the handover rate out of a cell depends on the number of active customers within the cell. On the other hand, the handover rate into the cell depends on the number of customers in the neighboring cells. Thus, the iterative procedure introduced in [2] is used to balance the incoming and outgoing handover rates, assuming that the incoming handover rate $\lambda_{h,GSM}^{(in)}(i)$ of GSM calls and $\lambda_{h,GPRS}^{(in)}(i)$ of GPRS calls at step i is equal to the outgoing handover rate $\lambda_{h,GSM}^{(out)}(i-1)$ and $\lambda_{h,GPRS}^{(out)}(i-1)$ computed at step i-1.

Since in the end-to-end path, the wireless link is typically the bottleneck, and given the anticipated traffic asymmetry, the simulator focuses on resource contention in the downlink (i.e., the path BSC $\rightarrow$ BTS $\rightarrow$ MS) of the radio interface. Because of the anticipated traffic asymmetry the amount of uplink traffic, e.g. induced by acknowledgments, is assumed to be negligible. In the study we focus on the radio interface. The functionality of the GPRS core network is not included. The arrival stream of packets is modeled at the IP layer. Let N be the number of physical channels available in the cell. We evaluate the performance of two types of radio resource sharing schemes, which specify how the cell capacity is shared by GSM and GPRS users:

- the *static scheme*; that is the cell capacity of N physical channels is split into N_{GPRS} channels reserved for GPRS data transfer and $N_{GSM} = N - N_{GPRS}$ channels reserved for GSM circuit-switched connections.

- the *dynamic scheme*; that is the N physical channels are shared by GSM and GPRS services, with priority for GSM calls; given n voice calls, the remaining N-n channels are fairly shared by all packets in transfer.

In both schemes, the PDCHs are fairly shared by all packets in transfer up to a maximum of 8 PDCHs per IP packet ("multislot mode") and a maximum of 8 packets per PDCH [6].

The software architecture of the simulator follows the network architecture of the GPRS Network [14]. To accurately model the communication over the radio interface, we include the functionality of a BSC and a BTS. IP packets that arrive at the BSC are logically organized in two distinct queues. The transfer queue can hold up to $Q = 8 \cdot n$ packets that are served according to a processor sharing service discipline, with n the number of physical channels that are potentially available for data transfer, i.e. $n = N_{GPRS}$ under the static scheme and $n = N$ under the dynamic scheme. The processor sharing service discipline fairly shares the available channel capacity over the packets in the transfer queue. An arriving IP packet that cannot enter the transfer queue immediately is held in a first-come first-served (in case of one priority) access queue that can store up to K packets. The access queue models the BSC buffer in the GPRS network. Upon termination of a packet transfer, the IP packet at the head of the access queue is polled into the transfer queue, where it immediately shares in the assignment of available PDCHs. For this study, we fix the modulation and coding scheme to CS-2 [14]. It allows a data transfer rate of 13,4 kbit/sec on one PDCH. Figure 1 depicts the software architecture of the simulator.

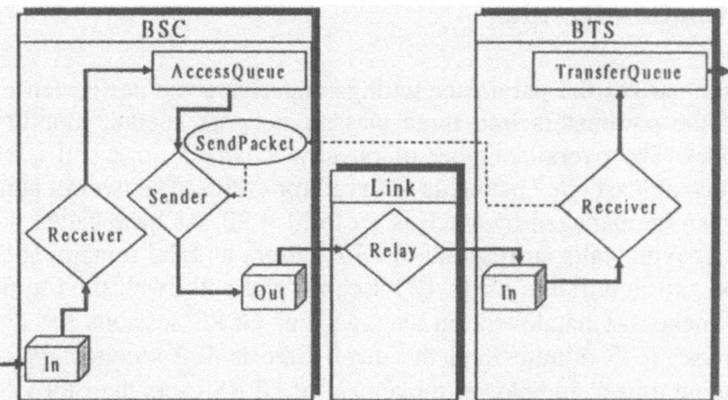

Figure 1. Software Architecture of GSM/GPRS Simulator

To model the different quality of service profiles GPRS provides, the simulator implemented a *Weighted Fair Queueing (WFQ)* strategy. The WFQ scheduling algorithm can easily be adopted to provide multiple data service classes by assigning each traffic source a weight determined by its class. The weight controls the amount of traffic a source may deliver relative to other active sources during some period of time. From the scheduling algorithm's point of view, a source is considered to be active if it has data queued at the BSC. For an active packet transfer with weight w_i the portion of the bandwidth $B_i(t)$ allocated at time t to this transfer should be

$$B_i(t) = \frac{w_i}{\sum_j w_j} \cdot B(t)$$

where the sum over all active packet transfers at time t. The overall bandwidth at time t is denoted by $B(t)$ which is independent of t in the static channel allocation scheme.

The workload model used in the GPRS simulator is a *Markov-modulated Poisson Process (MMPP)* [7]. It is used to generate the IP traffic for each individual user in the system. The MMPP has been extensively used for modeling arrival processes, because it qualitatively models the time-varying arrival rate and captures some of the important correlations between the interarrival times. It is shown to be an accurate model for Internet traffic which usually shows self-similarity among different time scales. For our purpose the MMPP is parameterized by the two-state continuous-time Markov chain with infinitesimal generator matrix Q and rate matrix Λ:

$$Q = \begin{pmatrix} -\alpha & \alpha \\ \beta & -\beta \end{pmatrix}, \qquad \Lambda = \begin{pmatrix} \lambda_1 & 0 \\ 0 & \lambda_2 \end{pmatrix}$$

The two states represent bursty mode and non-bursty mode of the arrival process. The process resides in bursty mode for a mean time of $1/\alpha$ and in non-bursty mode for a mean time of $1/\beta$ respectively. Such an MMPP is characterized by the *average arrival rate* of packets, λ_{avg} and the *degree of burstiness,* B. The former is given by:

$$\lambda_{avg} = \frac{\beta \cdot \lambda_1 + \alpha \cdot \lambda_2}{\alpha + \beta}$$

The *degree of burstiness* is computed by the ratio between the bursty arrival rate and the average arrival rate, i.e., $B = \lambda_1/\lambda_{avg}$.

4   Simulation Results

Table 1 summarizes the parameter settings underlying the performance experiments. We group the parameters into three classes: network model, mobility model, and traffic model. The overall number of physical channels in a cell is set to $N = 20$ among which at least one channel is reserved for GPRS. The overall number of GPRS users that can be managed by a cell is set to $M = 20$. As base value, we assume that 5% of the arriving calls correspond to GPRS users and the remaining 95% are GSM calls. GSM call duration is set to 120 seconds and call dwell time to 60 seconds, so that users make 1-2 handovers on average. For GPRS sessions the average session duration is set to 5 minutes and the dwell time is 120 seconds. Thus, we assume longer "online times" and slower movement of GPRS users than for GSM users. The average arrival rate of data is set to 6 Kbit/sec per GPRS user corresponding to 0.73 IP packets per second of size 1 Kbyte.

Model Typ		Parameter	Base Value
Network Model		Number of physical channels, N	20
		Number of fixed PDCHs, N_{GPRS}	1, 2, 4
		Maximum number of GPRS users, M	20
		BSC buffer size, K	1000 IP-packets
		Transfer rate for one PDCH (CS-2), $\mu_{service}$	13.4 Kbit/sec
Mobility Model		GSM handover arrival rate, $\lambda_{h,GSM}$	0.3/sec
		GPRS handover arrival rate, $\lambda_{h,GPRS}$	0.075/sec
		Average GSM voice call duration, $1/\mu_{GSM}$	120 sec
		Average GSM voice call dwell time, $1/\mu_{h,GSM}$	60 sec
		Average GPRS session duration, $1/\mu_{GPRS}$	300 sec
		Average GPRS session dwell time, $1/\mu_{h,GPRS}$	120 sec
Traffic Model	Users	GSM/GPRS call arrival rate, $\lambda = \lambda_{GSM} + \lambda_{GPRS}$	1.0/sec
		Percentage of GSM users	95%
		Percentage of GPRS users	5%
		Percentages of customers with paket priority 1, 2, 3	10%, 30%, 60%
		Weights for packet priorities 1, 2, 3	4/7, 2/7, 1/7
	Packet Data	Average arrival rate of data, λ_{avg}	6 Kbit/sec
		Degree of burstiness, B	5
		Average duration of bursty phase, $1/\alpha$	2 sec
		Average duration of non-bursty phase, $1/\beta$	20 sec

Table 1. Base parameter setting of the simulation model

The simulation experiments consisted of two phases. First the incoming handover flow of GSM and GPRS users must be computed iteratively from the outgoing handover flow. This phase takes 4-6 short (6 seconds) and 3-4 longer (2 minutes) iterations to get an accurate balance between the handover flows. The second phase consists of the main simulation run. It takes a duration of about 30 minutes to achieve a confidence level of 95%. The curves presented show the confidence intervals as dashed lines and the mean values in solid lines. In all curves the arrival rate of GSM and GPRS users is varied to study the cell under increasing load conditions.

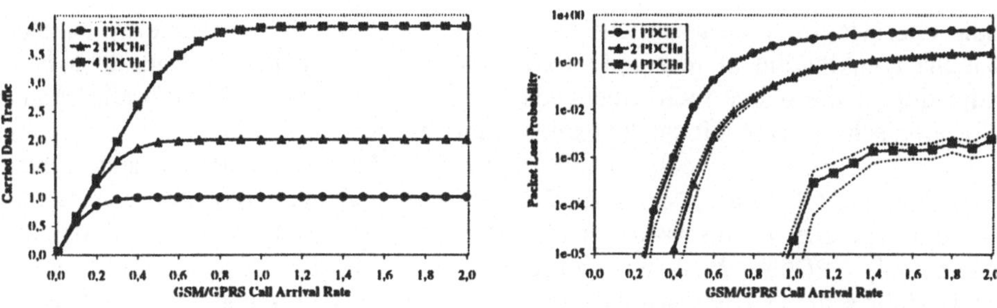

Figure 2. Carried data traffic and packet loss probability for static channel allocation

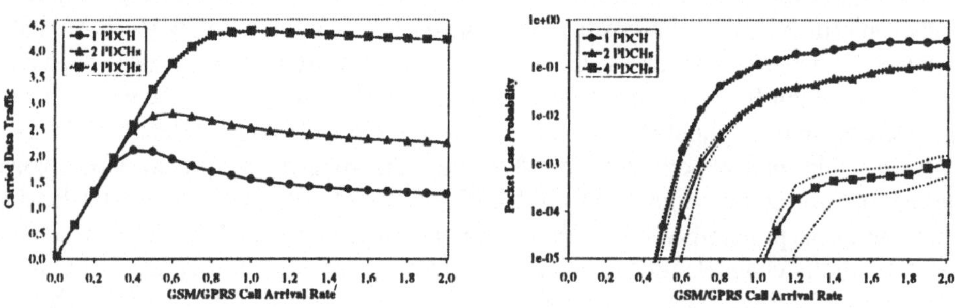

Figure 3. Carried data traffic and packet loss probability for dynamic channel allocation

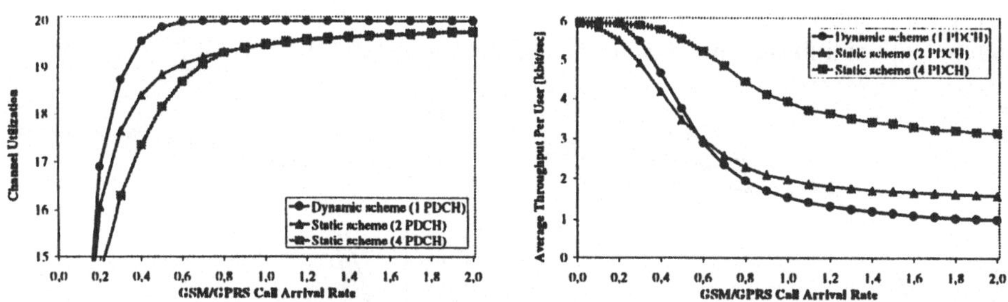

Figure 4. Channel utilization and throughput per user for static and dynamic channel allocation

Figure 2 presents curves for carried data traffic and packet loss probabilities due to buffer overflow in the BSC for the static channel allocation scheme and one packet priority. For GPRS 1, 2, and 4 PDCHs are reserved, respectively. The remaining channels can be used by GSM calls. With 4 PDCHs the system overloads at an arrival rate of 0.8 GSM/GPRS users per second. This corresponds to an average of 12 GPRS users in the cell (see Figure 7). In Figure 3 we present corresponding curves for the dynamic channel allocation scheme. For GPRS 1, 2, and 4 PDCHs are reserved, respectively but more PDCHs can be reserved "on demand". That means that additional PDCHs can be reserved if they are not used for GSM voice service. From Figure 3 we observe that for low traffic in the considered cell GPRS makes effectively use of the on demand PDCHs. For example if 1 PDCH is reserved GPRS utilizes up to 2 PDCHs at an arrival rate of 0.4 GSM/GPRS users per second. But with increasing load the overall performance of GPRS decreases because of concurrency among GPRS users, and more important, priority of GSM users over the radio interface. In comparison with the static channel allocation scheme we conclude that the combination of reserved PDCHs and on demand PDCH leads to a better utilization of the scarce radio frequencies. The only advantage of the static channel allocation scheme is that it can be realized more easily.

Figure 4 presents a comparison of overall channel utilization and average throughput per GPRS user for the static and dynamic channel allocation scheme. For the static scheme we reserved 2 and 4 PDCHs respectively and for the dynamic scheme only 1 PDCH. We observe a higher overall utilization of physical channels by the dynamic scheme. Comparing the dynamic with the static scheme for 2 PDCHs we detect a slightly higher throughput for low traffic load for dynamic channel allocation. This results from the high radio channel capacity available to GPRS users in this case. They can utilize up to 8 PDCHs for their transfer (in contrast to 2 PDCHs in the static scheme). When load increases, GSM calls allocate most of the physical channels. Thus, throughput for GPRS users decreases very fast. In the static scheme (4 PDCHs) the decrease in throughput is not so fast, because GSM calls do not effect the PDCHs.

In an additional experiment, we study the performance loss in the GSM voice service due to the introduction of GPRS. Figure 5 plots the carried voice traffic and voice blocking probability for different numbers of reserved PDCHs. The results are valid for both channel allocation schemes because of the priority of GSM voice service over GPRS. The presented curves indicate that the decrease in channel capacity and, thus, the increase of the blocking probability of the GSM voice service is negligible compared to the benefit of reserving additional PDCHs for GPRS users.

Figure 6 shows carried data traffic and packet loss probabilities for the dynamic channel allocation scheme and different packet priorities. For GPRS 1 PDCH is

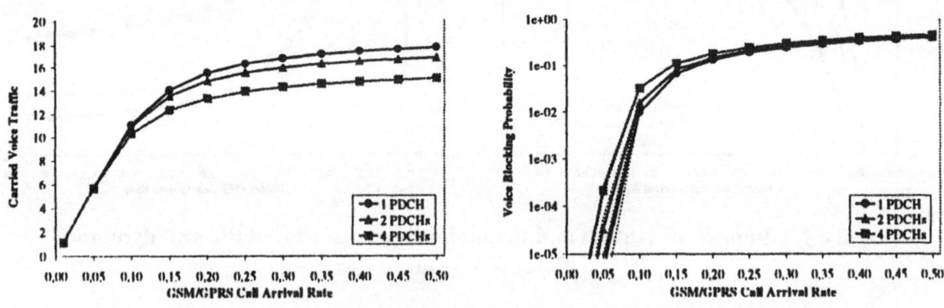

Figure 5. Impact of GPRS on GSM voice service: carried voice traffic and voice blocking probability

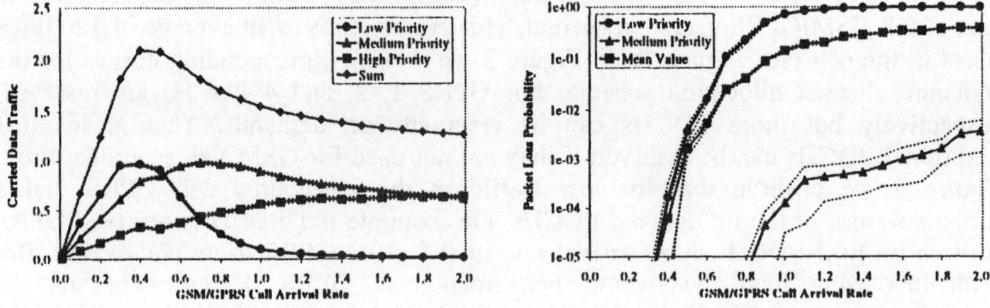

Figure 6. Carried data traffic and packet loss probability for different packet priorities

reserved. Weights for packets with priority 1 (high), 2 (medium), and 3 (low) and percentages of GPRS users utilizing these priorities are given in Table 1. We observe that for low traffic in the considered cell most channels are covered by packets of low priority. This is due to the high portion of low priority packets (60%) among all packets sharing the radio interface. With increasing load medium priority packets and at last high priority packets suppress packets of lower priority and therefore the utilization of PDCHs for low and medium priority packets decreases. For a call arrival rate of up to 2 calls per second the loss probability of high priority packets is still less than 10^{-5} and therefore the corresponding curve is omitted in Figure 6.

Figure 7 presents curves for average number of GPRS users in the cell and blocking probabilities of GPRS session requests due to reaching the limit of M active GPRS sessions. We observe that for 2% GPRS users the maximum number of 20 active GPRS sessions is not reached. Therefore, the blocking probability remains very low. For 10% GPRS users and increasing call arrival rate, the average number of sessions approaches its maximum. Thus, some GPRS users will be rejected. It is important to note that the curves of Figure 7 can be utilized for determining the average number of GPRS users in the cell for a given call arrival rate. In fact, together with the curves of Figure 2 and 3, we can provide estimates for the maximum number of GPRS users that can be managed by the cell without degradation of quality of service. For example, for 5% GPRS users and 1 PDCHs reserved, in the static allocation scheme a packet loss probability of 10^{-3} can be guarantied until the call arrival rate exceeds 0.4 calls per second, i.e., until there are on the average 6 active GPRS users in the cell. For the dynamic allocation scheme a packet loss probability of 10^{-3} can be guarantied until the call arrival rate exceeds 0.6 calls per second corresponding to 9 active GPRS users in the cell on average.

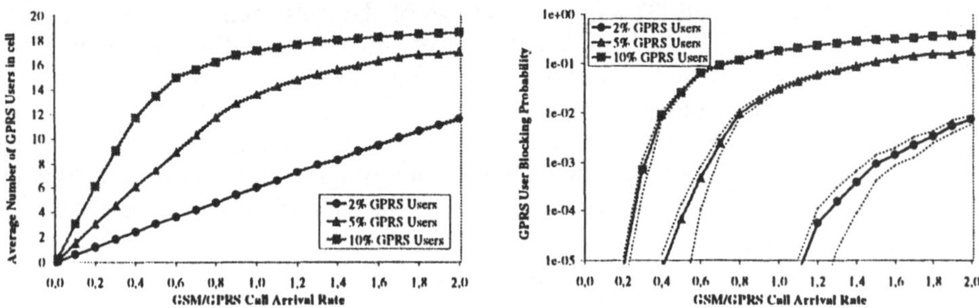

Figure 7. Average number of GPRS users in the cell and GPRS user blocking probability

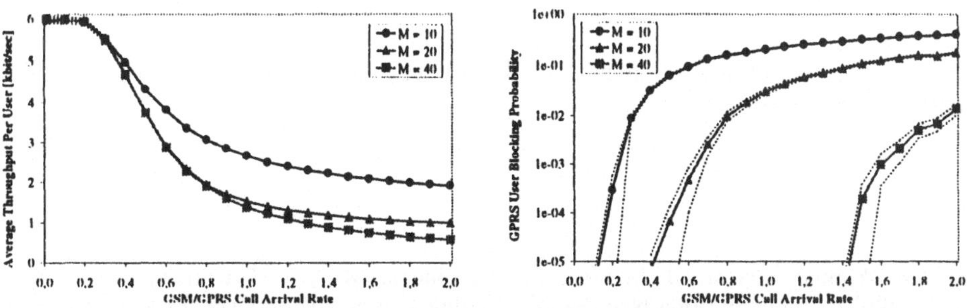

Figure 8. Average throughput per user and GPRS user blocking probability for different maximum numbers of GPRS users

Figure 8 investigates the impact of the maximum number of GPRS user per cell to the performance of GPRS for the dynamic channel allocation scheme with 1 PDCH reserved. Of course, the expected number of GPRS users should be less than the maximum number in order to avoid the rejection of new GPRS sessions. On the other hand, the maximum number of active GPRS sessions must be limited for guaranteeing quality of service for every active GPRS session even under high traffic. The tradeoff between increasing performance for allowing more active GPRS sessions and the increasing blocking probability for GPRS users is illustrated by the curves of Figure 8.

Conclusions

This paper presented a discrete-event simulator on the IP level for the General Packet Radio Service (GPRS). With the simulator, we provided a comprehensive performance study of the radio resource sharing by circuit switched GSM connections and packet switched GPRS sessions under a static and a dynamic channel allocation scheme. In the dynamic scheme we assumed a reserved number of physical channels permanently allocated to GPRS and the remaining channels to be on-demand channels that can be used by GSM voice service and GPRS packets. In the static scheme no on-demand channels exist. We investigated the impact of the number of packet data channels reserved for GPRS users on the performance of the cellular network. Furthermore, three different QoS profiles modeled by a weighted fair queueing scheme were considered.

Comparing both channel allocation schemes, we concluded that the dynamic scheme is preferable at all. The only advantage of the static scheme lies in its easy implementation. Next, we studied the impact of introducing GPRS on GSM voice service and observed that the decrease in channel capacity for GSM is negligible compared to the benefit of reserving additional packet data channels for GPRS. With the curves presented we provide estimates for the maximum number of GPRS users that can be managed by the cell without degradation of quality of service. Such results give valuable hints for network designers on how many packet data channels should be allocated for GPRS and how many GPRS session should be allowed for a given amount of traffic in order to guarantee appropriate quality of service.

Acknowledgements

The authors would like to thank Joachim Przybilke for implementing the GPRS simulation environment.

References

[1]   M. Ajmone Marsan, S. Marano, C. Mastroianni, M. Meo, Performance Analysis of Cellular Communication Networks Supporting Multimedia Services, *Proc. 6th Int. Symp. on Modeling, Analysis and Simulation of Computer and Telecommunication Systems, Montreal, Canada*, 274-281, 1998.

[2] M. Ajmone Marsan, G. De Carolis, E. Leonardi, R. Lo Cigno, M. Meo, How Many Cells Should Be Considered to Accurately Predict the Performance of Cellular Networks?, *Proc. European Wireless, Munich, Germany*, 1999.

[3] G. Bianchi, A. Capone, L. Fratta, L. Musumeci, Dynamic Channel Allocation Procedures for Packet Data Services over GSM Networks, *Proc. ISS'95, Berlin, Germany*, 246-250, 1995.

[4] R.J. Boucherie, R. Litjens, Radio Resource Sharing in a GSM/GPRS Network, *Proc. 12th ITC Specialist Seminar on Mobile Systems and Mobility, Lillehammer, Norway*, 2000.

[5] L.F. Chang, Z. Jiang, N.K. Shankaranarayanan, Providing Multiple Service Classes for Bursty Data Traffic in Cellular Networks, *Proc. 19th Conf. on Computer Communications (IEEE Infocom), Tel-Aviv, Israel*, 2000.

[6] ETSI, Digital cellular telecommunications system (Phase 2+); General Packet Radio Service (GPRS); Service description; Stage 2, *GSM recommendation 03.60*, 1999.

[7] W. Fischer, K. Meier-Hellstern, The Markov-modulated Poisson process (MMPP) cookbook, *Performance Evaluation* **18**, 149-171, 1993.

[8] R. Kalden, I. Meirick, M. Meyer, Wireless Internet Access Based on GPRS, *IEEE Personal Comm.* **7**, 8-18, Apr. 2000.

[9] Sz. Malomsoky, Sz. Nádas, G. Tóth, P. Zarándy, Simulation based GPRS Network Dimensioning, *Proc. 12th ITC Specialist Seminar on Mobile Systems and Mobility, Lillehammer, Norway*, 2000.

[10] M. Meyer, TCP Performance over GPRS, *Proc. 1st Wireless Communications and Networking Conference (WCNC), New Orleans*, 1999.

[11] M. Meyer, S. Hoff, A. Schieder, A Performance Evaluation of Internet Access via the General Packet Radio Service of GSM, *Proc. 48th Vehicular Technology Conference (VTC), Ottawa, Canada*, 1760-1764, 1998.

[12] H. Schwetman, Object-oriented Simulation Modeling with C++/CSIM17, *Proc. of the 1995 Winter Simulation Conference*, Eds. C. Alexopoulos, K. Kang, W. Lilegdon, D. Goldsman, 529-533, 1995.

[13] P. Stuckmann, F. Müller, GPRS Radio Network Capacity and Quality of Service using Fixed and On-Demand Channel Allocation Techniques, *Proc. 51th Vehicular Technology Conference (VTC), Tokyo, Japan*, 2000.

[14] B.Walke, Mobilfunknetze und ihre Protokolle 1/2, B.G. Teubner, 2000.

Session 10:

Softwaretechnologien für Verteilte Systeme

Sicherheitsdienste für mobile Agentenanwendungen

Jürgen Bohn[1] und Günter Karjoth[2]

[1] ETH Zürich, Haldeneggsteig 4, IFW,
CH-8092 Zürich, Schweiz
bohn@inf.ethz.ch
[2] IBM Forschungslabor Zürich, Säumerstrasse 4,
CH-8803 Rüschlikon, Schweiz
gka@zurich.ibm.com

Zusammenfassung Mobile Agenten ermöglichen eine flexible Ausführung von verteilten Anwendungen, was sie attraktiv macht für den Einsatz im Bereich des elektronischen Handels, Netzwerkmanagements und der Groupware. Der erfolgreiche Einsatz mobiler Agenten hängt aber auch davon ab, in wieweit der Schutz von Agenten gewährleistet ist. Wir identifizieren generische Sicherheitsdienste zum Schutz mobiler Agenten, welche obige Anwendungsszenarien abdecken, und stellen diese in einem Rahmenwerk dem Anwendungsentwickler bereit. In einer prototypischen Implementierung bieten wir unterschiedliche Realisierungen des gleichen Dienstes an, um gegebenenfalls von der Verfügbarkeit sicherer Hardware zu profitieren. Eine mobile Agentenanwendung benutzt diese Dienste, um eine sichere Produktrecherche zu realisieren.

1 Motivation

Die Attraktivität der mobilen Agententechnologie [11] beruht insbesondere auf möglichen Anwendungsszenarien aus den Bereichen elektronischer Handel, Netzwerkmanagement und Groupware. Eine Stärke des Paradigmas mobiler Agenten liegt darin, dass es den Entwurf, die Implementierung und die Wartung verteilter Anwendungen wesentlich einfacher und intuitiver gestaltet. In verteilten Systemen lassen sich die autonomen, miteinander kooperierenden Parteien in natürlicher und verständlicher Weise als mobile Agenten modellieren. Während für viele Einzelfälle herkömmliche Lösungsansätze ohne den Gebrauch mobiler Agenten existieren, so stellt das Paradigma mobiler Agenten ein Rahmenwerk zu Verfügung, welches all diese Fälle gleichzeitig abdeckt und behandelt [3].

Trotz der anfänglichen Euphorie hat sich die Technologie nur zögerlich verbreitet. Dies liegt nicht zuletzt daran, dass ein Grundproblem der mobilen Agenten, die Frage nach der Sicherheit, noch nicht zufriedenstellend gelöst ist. Während der Schutz des Wirtssystems vor böswilligen Agenten bereits relativ gut verstanden ist, besteht noch Forschungsbedarf beim *Schutz des Agenten* vor zufälliger oder böswilliger Manipulation [15,16]. Für den Nutzer von mobilen Agentenanwendungen ist dieser Sicherheitsaspekt von besonderer Bedeutung. Mag der Ausfall einer Plattform im Gesamtsystem geduldet werden, die fehlende Zuverlässigkeit und der mangelnde Integritätsschutz der eigenen mobilen Agenten wird jedoch kaum toleriert. Die Sicherheitseigenschaften mobiler Agenten sind deshalb für die Akzeptanz und Verbreitung von Agentenanwendungen ein kritischer Faktor.

Heutige Wirtssysteme schützten Agenten vor Manipulationsversuchen durch andere Agenten, in dem diese in isolierten Adressräumen ausgeführt werden. Dabei erlauben proxy-basierte Zugriffsmechanismen den Austausch von Agentenobjekten. Die Ausführungsplattform selber hat aber Zugriff auf alle unverschlüsselten Daten des Agenten und kann daher den internen Kontrollfluss ausspionieren und zum eigenen Vorteil manipulieren. Es stellt sich damit die Frage nach der Verlässlichkeit der ausführenden Plattform, und wie man sich gegen betrügerische Manipulationen schützen oder diese zumindest zuverlässig erkennen kann.

Einen ersten Ansatz von allgemeinen Sicherheitsdiensten für mobile Agenten findet man bei Karnik [9], der drei konkrete Mechanismen für Containerklassen zum Schutz der Daten mobiler Agenten beinhaltet. Wir erweitern diese Dienste hin zu einem ersten Rahmenwerk von generischen Sicherheitsdiensten, bei dem von der konkreten Realisierung abstrahiert wird und verschiedene Implementierungen der gleichen Dienstschnittstelle, z.B. mit oder ohne Verwendung sicherer Hardware, bereitgestellt werden können. Als Anwendungsszenario zur Veranschaulichung dient die preisvergleichende Produktrecherche (*comparison shopping*): Der mobile Agent eines Kunden besucht eine Reihe von elektronischen Marktplätzen (Agentenplattformen), auf denen er von den jeweils vorhandenen Händleragenten ein Produktangebot einholt. Nachdem der mobile Agent eine gewisse Anzahl solcher Angebote gesammelt hat, kehrt er zum Ursprungsort zurück und übergibt seinem Auftraggeber das beste gefundene Angebot.

2 Ansätze zum Schutz mobiler Agenten

Die größte zu bewältigende Gefahr für mobile Agenten bleiben betrügerische Rechnerplattformen, von denen eine Vielzahl möglicher Angriffe ausgehen können, wie zum Beispiel das Auspionieren oder Manipulieren von Daten, Code oder Kontrollfluss [7,17]. Existierende Lösungen zum Schutz des Agenten vor unbefugten Dritten können danach unterschieden werden, ob sie aktiven oder passiven Schutz gewähren. Während die Verwendung von Kryptographie es erlaubt, Daten innerhalb des Agenten zu verbergen und deren Integrität zu überprüfen, scheint heute nur die Verwendung spezieller, vertrauenswürdiger Hardware in der Lage zu sein, die Manipulation von Agenten zu verhindern. Es gibt zwar bereits mehrere Lösungsansätze zum Schutz mobiler Agenten, die nur auf Software beruhen (u.a. verschlüsselte Funktionen [13], Detektionsobjekte [12], Agenten als zeitweilige Software-Blackbox [5], oder redundante Ausführung und Replikation von Agenten [14]), ihre praktische Einsatzfähigkeit ist jedoch begrenzt [7].

Sichere, vertrauenswürdige Geräte erscheinen bezüglich ihrer Funktionsweise nach außen hin als eine Blackbox. Kritische Operationen des Agenten werden so ausgelegt, dass sie nur innerhalb dieser sicheren Geräte ausführbar sind und sich somit dem Einfluss des zugehörigen Rechners entziehen. Die Bandbreite derartiger Geräte reicht von nur kreditkartengroßen Chipkarten über komplette geschützte Rechner bis hin zur teuren Spezialhardware.

Auf Grund dieser Sachlage muss aber ein Rahmen von Sicherheitsdiensten gewährleisten, dass der Schutz der Ausführung mobiler Agenten gegen Manipulation und Ausspionieren sowohl durch existierende Lösungen, wie die Verwendung von sicheren, vertrauenswürdigen Geräten, als auch durch noch zu entwickelnde Verfahren realisiert werden kann.

Interoperable und sichere mobile Agentenanwendungen erfordern offene Agentensysteme, welche einen Rahmen von Sicherheitsdiensten besitzen, deren Schnittstellen bekannt sind und allen Teilnehmern zur Verfügung stehen. Neben den kryptographischen Dienstprimitiven, wie z.B. Methoden zur Verschlüsselung, digitale Signaturverfahren oder kryptographische Hashfunktionen, und den darauf aufbauenden bereits vorgestellten elementaren Sicherheitsdiensten, treten mit zunehmender Nähe zur Anwendung weitergehende Sicherheitsbedürfnisse und Forderungen auf. Um den zusätzlichen Anforderungen Rechnung zu tragen, werden problemspezifische Sicherheitsmechanismen und -protokolle erforderlich.

3   Klassifikation der zu schützenden Daten

Die Sicherheit mobiler Agenten erfordert den Schutz des Zustandes des Agenten und deren Ausführung auf unsicheren Plattformen. Der Zustand eines Agenten ist dabei durch das auszuführende Programm und die mitgeführten Daten bestimmt. Sicherheitsdienste gewähren den Schutz der Integrität und Vertraulichkeit der mitgeführten Daten bzw. ihrer Auswertung.

Besitzt das auszuführende Programm eines Agenten zur Laufzeit einen statischen Charakter, kann dessen Integrität zum Zeitpunkt der Ankunft bei einer Plattform anhand von digitalen Signaturen bzw. Zertifikaten (einer bekannten vertrauenswürdigen Instanz) überprüft werden. Im Fall eines dynamischen Nachladens von Programmcode während der Ausführung auf fremden Plattformen, wie es zum Beispiel Java ermöglicht, muß zudem noch dessen Kompatibilität überprüft werden. Diese Überprüfungen dienen jedoch vorrangig dem Schutz der Plattform vor bösartigen Agenten und nicht dem Schutz des Agenten selbst vor Manipulationen während dessen Ausführung.

Auch wenn die Integrität des Programms gewährleistet ist, kann der Ausführungszustand des Agenten, definiert durch seinen Variablenzustand und dem Ausführungskontext (Befehlszähler, Aufrufverschachtelung, etc.), von der auszuführenden Plattform (leicht) manipuliert werden. Bis heute sind aber keine wirkungsvollen Verfahren zum Schutze der sicheren Ausführung eines Agenten bekannt, abgesehen von der bereits erwähnten Ausführung (von zumindest sicherheitskritischen Kompoenenten) in einer sicheren vertrauenswürdigen Hardware oder in Form von verschlüsselten Programmen.

Die anwendungsspezifischen Daten eines mobilen Agenten klassifizieren wir – im Hinblick auf deren Persistenz – ebenfalls als statisch oder dynamisch. Eine weitere Untergliederung des Datenanteils ist nach semantischen Gesichtspunkten in Nutzdaten, Metadaten und Prüfdaten möglich. Als Nutzdaten bezeichnen wir all jene Daten und Informationen, die zur Erledigung der primären Aufgaben des Agenten benötigt bzw. gesammelt werden, z.B. die gesammelten Angebote in der Produktrecherche. Die Metadaten seien diejenigen Daten, die nur indirekt zur Lösung der durch den Agenten zu bearbeitenden Aufgabenstellung beitragen, etwa Auftragsparameter oder die Liste der zu besuchenden Händler. Die Prüfdaten tragen nicht zur Erfüllung der eigentlichen Agententätigkeit bei, sondern dienen ausschließlich dem Schutz der Integrität und Vertraulichkeit der Nutzdaten, Metadaten oder gar des Codes selbst.

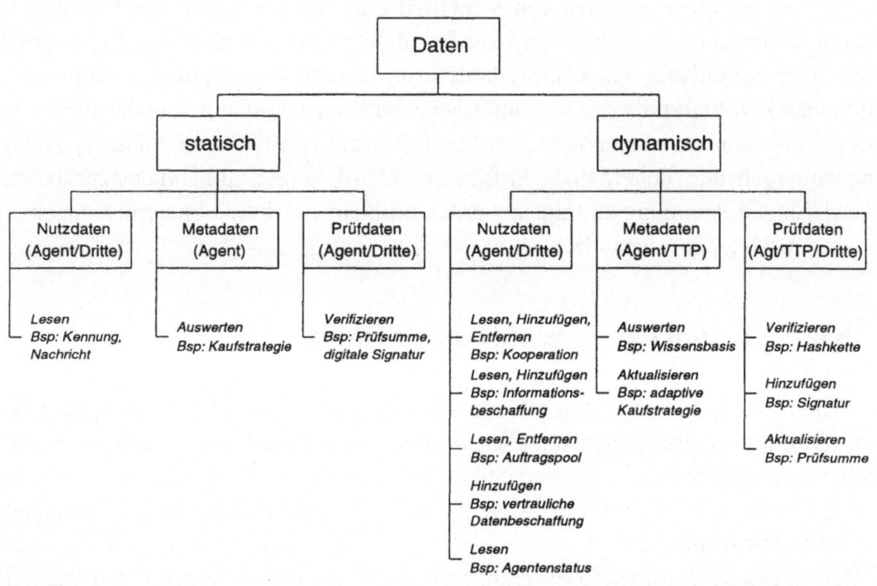

Abbildung 1: Klassifikation der Daten mobiler Agenten und Identifikation der darauf operierenden Dienstprimitiven.

Die auf den verschiedenen Datenarten operierenden Parteien lassen sich in die folgenden drei Gruppen einteilen: Der mobile Agent selbst, eine von allen teilnehmenden Parteien als vertrauenswürdig anerkannte Instanz (Trusted Third Party, TTP), sowie alle anderen am System beteiligten Parteien (Dritte). Abbildung 1 zeigt eine baumartige Klassifikation der Datenarten mobiler Agenten. Die Begriffe in den Blättern nennen die Parteien, die i.a. auf den jeweiligen Datentyp zugreifen. Darunter werden in einer Liste die anfallenden Primitiven identifiziert, die typischerweise auf den entsprechenden Daten operieren, zusammen mit einem kurzen praktischen Beispiel. Bei den dynamischen Nutzdaten werden die Primitiven darüber hinaus gemäß ihrem möglichen Auftreten gruppiert.

Anhand dieser Gliederung lassen sich nun grundlegende Datentypen und Sicherheitsdienste für mobile Agentenanwendungen ableiten, wie in Tabelle 1 dargestellt. Es zeigt sich, dass viele elementare sichere Dienste sich durch verschiedene Ausprägungen von sicheren Containerklassen bereitstellen lassen. Als Container bezeichnen wir dabei – in der allgemeinsten Ausprägung – einen Behälter, dem Objekte beliebigen Typs hinzugefügt und entnommen werden können. Die Containerklasse stellt entsprechende Methoden bereit. Spezialisierungen sind beispielsweise möglich durch Einschränkung der zugelassenen Objektklassen (Typisierung) oder der Zugriffsmethoden (z.B. nur lesenden Zugriff gestatten).

Derartige Containerklassen haben zwei Hauptvorteile: Erstens sind sie für den Entwickler einfach zu benutzen und leicht in Anwendungen zu integrieren, weil sie sich in Bezug auf die Funktionalität nur unwesentlich von herkömmlichen Containerklassen unterscheiden. Zweitens lässt sich so leicht die Trennung von Schnittstelle und Implementierung realisieren, so dass die tatsächlich verwendeten Sicherheitsmechanismen transparent zur Anwendungsentwicklung und zur Laufzeit gewählt werden können. Mit der gewählten Modellierung in Java wird diese Trennung analog zum SPI-Konzept aus `Java 2` gelöst, durch Definition von sogenannten Diensterbringer-Schnittstellen (*Service Provider Interfaces*, SPI).

Tabelle 1: Grundlegende Sicherheitsdienste für mobile Agentenanwendungen.

Datenart	Operation	sicherer Dienst	Java Dienstklasse
statisch			
Nutzdaten	Lesen	ausschließlich lesen	`ReadOnlyContainer`
Metadaten	Auswerten	sichere Berechnung	`SecureComputation`
Prüfdaten	Auswerten	kryptograph. Primitive	`java.security.*`
dynamisch			
Nutzdaten	Lesen, Hinzufügen, Entfernen	integritätsgeschützt abschließbar	`IntegrityStack,` `LockableContainer`
	Lesen, Hinzufügen	integritätsgeschützt und kein entfernen	`PushOnlyIntegrityStack,` `AppendOnlyContainer`
	Lesen, Entfernen	kein hinzufügen	`RemoveOnlyContainer`
	Hinzufügen	ausschließlich hinzufügen	`SecretAppendOnlyContainer`
	Lesen	ausschl. lesen, dyn. Inhalt	`DynamicReadOnlyContainer`
Metadaten	Auswerten	sichere Berechnung	`SecureComputation`
	Aktualisieren	sichere Berechnung	`SecureComputation`
		kryptograph. Primitive	`java.security.*`
Prüfdaten	Verifizieren	kryptograph. Primitive	`java.security.*`
	Auswerten	sichere Berechnung	`SecureComputation`
	Aktualisieren	kryptograph. Primitive sichere Berechnung	`java.security.*` bzw. `SecureComputation`

4 Rahmen von Sicherheitsdiensten

Die Sicherheitsdienste aus Tabelle 1 fassen wir zu einen (Software-)Rahmen zusammen, der prototypisch als Java-Bibliothek realisert wurde [2]. Die einzelnen Dienste können durch unterschiedliche Mechanismen realisiert werden, so dass mobile Agentenanwendungen flexibel gestaltet werden können.

`SecureComputation` ist eine abstrakte Dienstschnittstelle und steht für die sichere Ausführung von Operationen, z.B. die Aktualisierung von Prüfdaten oder die Auswertung eines Angebotes. Konkrete Realisierungen, zum Beispiel in dedizierter

Hardware oder als verschlüsseltes Programm, garantieren die Integrität und/oder Geheimhaltung der Ablauflogik.

Die nutzdatenbezogenen Containerdienstklassen können jeweils auf einen bestimmten Kreis von Benutzern eingeschränkt werden. Daraus ergeben sich dann entsprechende Gruppencontainerdienste, wie z.B. `GroupLockableContainer` oder `GroupAppendOnlyContainer`, bei denen etwa ein bei der Benutzung erforderlicher geheimer Containerschlüssel mit den öffentlichen Public-Key Schlüsseln der ausgewählten Gruppenmitglieder verschlüsselt wird.

Der `AppendOnlyContainer` erlaubt nur das Anhängen von Daten an den bereits vorhandenen Datenbestand sowie das Lesen der vorhandenen Daten. Der davon abgeleitete `SecretAppendOnlyContainer` verschlüsselt zusätzlich die abgelegten Daten mit dem öffentlichen Schlüssel des Empfängers, um die Vertraulichkeit der Daten zu gewährleisten. Ihre Realisierung erfolgt mit Hilfe des `PushOnlyIntegrityStack`-Dienstes, bei dem Objekte auf den Stack abgelegt, nicht aber entnommen werden dürfen. Die unerlaubte Entnahme oder Veränderung von Objekten wird je nach Implementierung entweder durch einen Software-Mechanismus erkannt oder durch entsprechende Prüfmaßnahmen innerhalb einer sicheren Hardware unterbunden.

Der `PushOnlyIntegrityStack` ist eine Spezialisierung von `IntegrityStack`, dessen Implementierung in zwei Abstraktionsschritten erfolgt. In der ersten Stufe fußen die abstrakten Stackklassen auf einer generischen Diensterbringer-Schnittstelle nach dem SPI-Konzept, dem Interface `StackCryptoServices`, das allgemeine Methoden zur Bereitstellung der Stackfunktionalität definiert. Die zweite Stufe stellen Implementierungen dieser SPI-Schnittstelle dar, wie z.B. die Klasse `IntegrityStack`. Hier werden die sicherheitskritischen Funktionen verborgen und realisiert. Dabei findet die Abbildung der allgemeinen Stackprimitiven auf konkrete kryptographische Softwarebibliotheken oder sichere Hardware statt.

Dieser Rahmen von elementaren Sicherheitsdiensten stellt Bausteine für den Entwurf sicherer Agentensysteme auf anwendungsnaher Ebene dar. Er dient als Grundlage für die Erstellung problemspezifischer, komplexerer Sicherheitsdienste. Eine prototypische Implementierung und Anwendung der beschriebenen Sicherheitsdienste erfolgte auf dem Aglets Agentensystem [10]. Der realisierte Rahmen mit den beschriebenen (und ggf. noch weitere zu identifizierende, applikationsspezifischere) Dienste lässt dem Anwender die freie Wahl der Implementierung (z.B. mit Trusted Hardware oder ohne).

5 Anwendungsszenario: Sichere Produktrecherche

Um die Einsetzbarkeit der vorgestellten Sicherheitsdienste zu prüfen, implementierten wir eine mobile Agentenanwendung zur preisvergleichenden Produktrecherche [2]. Dies ist eine der am häufigsten zitierten Anwendungen von mobilen Agenten im elektronischem Handel. Ein *preisvergleichender Agent* macht im Auftrag seines Besitzers (dem Kunden) selbständig aus einer an sich unüberschaubaren Anzahl von Händlern und Angeboten die in Frage kommenden (hier: günstigsten) Angebote ausfindig.

Die Grundzüge einer agentenbasierten preisvergleichenden Produktrecherche umfassen dabei im Wesentlichen zwei Arten von Agenten: Den vom Kunden beauftragten Suchagenten (oder Einkaufsagenten, falls der Agent mit der entsprechenden Befugnis ausgestattet ist) sowie eine Anzahl von Verkaufsagenten, die auf Anfrage Auskünfte über aktuelle Händlerangebote geben. Der realisierte Ablauf der Produktrecherche ergibt sich wie folgt:

1. Der Kunde instruiert (auf der Heimatplattform) den mobilen Agenten mit der Beschreibung der zum Kauf gewünschten Ware und gibt mit Hilfe eines Adressbuches die Liste der zu besuchenden elektronischen Marktplätze an (Wegbeschreibung).
2. Anschließend migriert der Agent vom Rechner des Kunden zum ersten elektronischen Marktplatz. Dort angekommen stellt der Agent eine Produktanfrage an alle vorhandenen Händleragenten. Nach Erhalt der Preisangebote werden diese gespeichert, und der Agent setzt seine Reise fort zum nächsten Marktplatz, wo er dieselbe Anfrage wieder stellt.
3. Nachdem der Agent alle Marktplätze besucht und eine gewisse Menge von Angeboten eingeholt hat, kehrt er zurück zur Heimatplattform. Hier werden dem Auftraggeber alle gesammelten Angebote präsentiert und das preisgünstigste Angebot zum Kauf vorgeschlagen.

Die Beschreibung der Route des Agenten ist statisch, da sie in diesem Fall zu Beginn festgelegt wird, und kann deshalb kryptographisch mit Hilfe der Dienstklasse `Read-OnlyContainer` gesichert werden. Die Routenplanung kann aber alternativ auch dynamisch erfolgen, etwa durch den Einsatz von Verzeichnisagenten, die dem mobilen Agenten unterwegs die Verfügbarkeit weiterer Marktplätze und Händleragenten mitteilen. Darüber hinaus können Marktplätze in unserem Modell einen oder mehrere Händleragenten beherbergen. Dies hat den Vorteil, dass bei der Verwendung von sicherer Hardware diese nur einmal für jeden Marktplatz zur Verfügung gestellt werden muss, und nicht für jeden Händler einzeln.

Um die Integrität und Vertraulichkeit der gesammelten Daten zu gewährleisten, verwendet der mobile Agent den Dienst `SecretAppendOnlyContainer`. Dabei kann man unter zwei Varianten auswählen, um mit oder ohne Einbezug von Chipkarten die gesammelten Daten sicher zu verknüpfen. Für die chipkartenlose Variante implementierten wir ein Protokoll von Karjoth *et al.* [6], in der die kryptographischen Operationen auf dem Wirtssystem ausgeführt werden. Die andere Variante setzt auf den händlerseitigen Einsatz von Chipkarten, die wir hier näher beschreiben. Durch Verwendung der entsprechenden SPI-Implementierungen können beide Protokolle in einfacher Weise in die Anwendung integriert werden.

5.1 Protokoll

Die chipkartenbasierte Implementierung des `SecretAppendOnlyContainer` beruht auf einer Spezialisierung eines Protokolls von Devanbu und Stubblebine, in dem sichere, aber resourcenlimitierte Hardware Stacks und Queues auf unsicheren Rechnern speichern können, während nur eine konstante Speichermenge innerhalb der sicheren Hardware benötigt wird [4].

Der sparsame Umgang mit Speicher auf der Chipkarte ist für mobile Agenten sehr wichtig, da nur einzelne Elemente des Stacks und die Kontrollinformationen in der sicheren Hardware für Prüfzwecke bearbeitet werden müssen, während die unter Umständen sehr umfangreichen restlichen Daten im externen Speicher gehalten werden können. Die sicherheitskritische Datenstruktur enthält dabei nur den geheimen Anker und den zuletzt berechneten Wert der Hashkette, mit deren Hilfe sich die Integrität der externen Daten überprüfen lässt, wie in Abbildung 2 gezeigt.

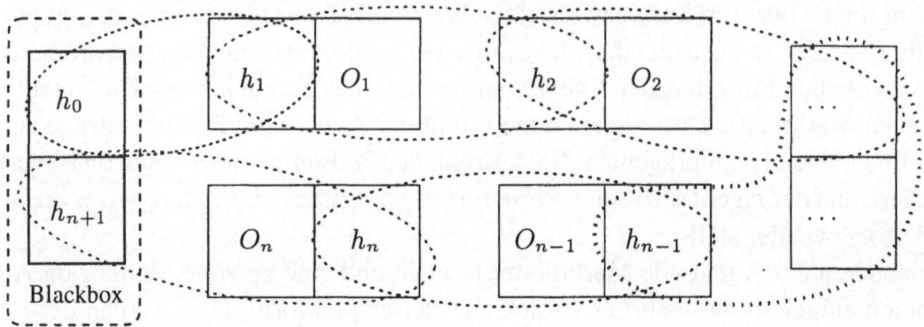

Abbildung 2: Aufbau der integritätsschützenden Hashkette: h_0 ist der geheime Startwert, h_{n+1} der (offengelegte) Abschluss. Die rekursive Berechnung der Hashwerte h_i erfolgt über den durch die gestrichelten Ellipsen umfassten Daten. Das Datentupel $\langle h_0, h_{n+1}\rangle$ erlaubt die Überprüfung der Hashkette und wird nur innerhalb der sicheren Hardware ausgewertet und aktualisiert.

Die Sicherheit der Hashkette beruht auf dem strikten Schutz der kritischen Protokolldaten, repräsentiert durch das Tupel $\langle h_0, h_{n+1}\rangle$, die immer nur innerhalb der Blackbox entschlüsselt, ausgewertet und aktualisiert werden. Der vorgehaltene Abschluss h_{n+1} verhindert die unentdeckte Manipulation (Entfernen, Hinzufügen, Verändern) von Datenobjekten: Die Neuberechnung der Hashkette ergibt im Falle eines verändernden Eingriffes aufgrund der Kollisionsfreiheit der kryptographischen Hashfunktion einen von h_{n+1} verschiedenen Endwert $\widehat{h_{n+1}}$, so dass die Veränderung erkannt wird. Als eindeutiger Identifikator der Hashkette dient der Hashwert $h_1 = \mathrm{Hash}(h_0)$, der öffentlich bekanntgemacht wird. Die nur dem Erzeuger der Dateninstanz bekannte geheime Verankerung h_0 verhindert, dass die Hashkette unbemerkt durch eine andere in sich konsistente Hashkette ersetzt werden kann, die über andere Daten berechnet wurde.

Wie wir festgestellt haben, sind aber beide Angriffe in Karnik's Realisierung des `AppendOnlyContainer` möglich, ohne das diese später erkannt werden können [2]. Daten können hinzugefügt oder entfernt, weil der Abschluss der Hashkette nicht geheimgehalten wird, und die Verankerung kann ersetzt werden, weil diese nur durch eine Verschlüsselung mit dem öffentlichen Schlüssel des Erzeugers geschützt ist.

5.2 Implementierung

Unsere Implementierung der Containerklasse benutzt eine JavaCard [1], deren Leistungsfähigkeit und Speicherplatz groß genug ist, die Angebote der einzelnen Händler sicher in die Angebotsliste einzufügen. Immer wenn der mobile Agent auf einer unsicheren Plattform ein neues Angebot im `SecretAppendOnlyContainer` ablegt, wird innerhalb der JavaCard die integritätsschützende Kontrolldateneinheit des unterliegenden `PushOnlyIntegrityStacks` entsprechend aktualisiert. Unerlaubte Operationen wie etwa das Entfernen von Objekten aus dem Container werden von der sicheren Hardware blockiert; Manipulationen an der Datenstruktur unter Umgehung der Blackbox können stets nachgewiesen werden (mit Ausnahme von Replay-Attacken). Alle JavaCards teilen sich dabei ein Public-Key-Schlüsselpaar. Zum Zeitpunkt der Initialisierung des Container werden die Kontrolldaten mit dem öffentlichen Blackbox-Schlüssel versiegelt und können fortan nur noch innerhalb der JavaCards entschlüsselt und modifiziert werden; sie entziehen sich somit dem Wirkungskreis der Händlerplattformen.

Zur Ausgabe und Verwaltung der JavaCards wird eine vertrauenswürdige *Blackbox–Behörde* (Trusted Third Party) benötigt, die sich z.B. aus dem Zusammenschluss der beteiligten Händler zu einem Händlerring ergeben könnte. Zu deren denkbaren Aufgaben zählen u.a. die Verwaltung und Verteilung des Blackbox-Schlüssels und dessen Erneuerung in regelmäßigen Zeitintervallen. Eine gelegentliche Überprüfung der SmartCards kann zudem Manipulationsversuche der am Händlerring teilnehmenden Händler aufdecken, um ggf. rechtliche Schritte einzuleiten.

6 Ausblick

Ein Rahmen von Sicherheitsdiensten erlaubt die Erstellung sicherer, mobiler Agentenanwendungen in offenen Agentensystemen. Generische Basisdienste, wie etwa die Containerklassen, wie auch komplexere, anwendungsorientierte Sicherheitsdienste verringern den Entwicklungsaufwand. Am Beispiel der Produktrecherche wurde die Realisierung und der Einsatz exemplarischer Sicherheitsdienste des Rahmens demonstriert. Eine Implementierung in Java mit dem Aglets Agentensystem liegt vor [2].

Die Konfigurierbarkeit des Software-Rahmens schafft Spielraum für die Befriedigung individueller Sicherheitsbedürfnisse von mobilen Agentenanwendungen. So erlaubt der Rahmen die transparente Ersetzung einzelner Module, wenn zum Beispiel höhere Sicherheitsanforderungen gestellt werden oder sich herausstellt, dass ein konkreter Mechanismus nicht die Eigenschaften des Dienstes, welchen er realisieren soll, erfüllt. Die im vorherigen Kapitel beschriebene Realisierung des `AppendOnlyContainers` beruht auf einem Protokoll, in dem sich alle JavaCards ein Public-Key-Schlüsselpaar teilen. Dies erleichtert zwar die Verwaltung des Systems, kann aber für Anwendungen mit höheren Sicherheitsanforderungen nicht genügen. Es ist aber jederzeit möglich, dieses Modul durch eine Implementierung eines Protokolls aus [8] zu ersetzen, in dem jede JavaCard ein eigenes Public-Key-Schlüsselpaar besitzt.

Da es zahlreiche Anwendungsgebiete und Einsatzszenarien für mobile Agenten gibt, stellt sich die Frage, ob ein Sicherheitsrahmen wie vorgestellt neben Basisdiensten auch anwendungsspezifische Sicherheitsdienste bereitstellen kann. Dazu untersuchen wir gegenwärtig verschiedene Anwendungskategorien, wie etwa E-Commerce (Comparison Shopping, Auktionen, Börsenmakler), Netzwerk- und Systemmanagement (Routing, Konfiguration, Wartung, Überwachung), Störungsmanagement (Unterstützung für fehlertolerante, robuste Dienste), und Workflow-Management.

Die Auseinandersetzung mit dem Paradigma mobiler Agenten zeigt, dass diese Technologie ein großes Potential für zukünftige Entwicklungen und Einsatzszenarien bietet, nicht nur im elektronischen Handel. Die Frage der Sicherheit und des Schutzes mobiler Agenten ist und bleibt jedoch *das* Kernproblem. Der vorgestellte Rahmen von Sicherheitsdiensten bringt die mobilen Agenten dem praktikablen Einsatz einen Schritt näher. Dennoch ist das Grundproblem, der Schutz der Ausführung von Agenten auf nicht vertrauenswürdigen Plattformen, nicht grundsätzlich gelöst, da der Einsatz sicherer Hardware die Einbeziehung einer dritten, vertrauenswürdigen Partei erfordert.

Literatur

1. M. Baentsch, P. Buhler, T. Eirich, F. Höring, and M. Oestreicher. JavaCard – from hype to reality. *IEEE Concurrency*, 7(4):36–43, Dez. 1999.
2. J. Bohn. Sicherheitsdienste für Mobile-Agenten-Anwendungen in elektronischen Märkten. Diplomarbeit, Universität Karlsruhe, Feb. 2000.
3. D. Chess, C. Harrison, and A. Kershenbaum. Mobile agents: Are they a good idea? In J. Vitek and C. Tschudin (Hsg.), *Mobile Object Systems - Towards the Programmable Internet*, Lecture Notes in Computer Science 1222, S. 25–47. Springer-Verlag, 1997.
4. P. T. Devanbu and S. G. Stubblebine. Stack and queue integrity on hostile platforms. In *IEEE Symposium on Research in Security and Privacy*, S. 198–206. IEEE Press, 1998.
5. F. Hohl. Time limited blackbox security: Protecting mobile agents from malicious hosts. Lecture Notes in Computer Science 1419, S. 92–113. Springer-Verlag, 1998.
6. G. Karjoth, N. Asokan, and C. Gülcü. Protecting the computation results of free-roaming agents. In K. Rothermel and F. Hohl (Hsg.), *Mobile Agents (MA'98)*, Lecture Notes in Computer Science 1477, S. 195–207. Springer-Verlag, 1998.
7. G. Karjoth and J. Posegga. Mobile agents and Telcos' nightmares. *Annales des Télécommunications*, 55(7/8):29–41, 2000.
8. G. Karjoth. Secure mobile agent-based merchant brokering in distributed marketplaces. In *Agent Systems, Mobile Agents, and Applications*, Lecture Notes in Computer Science 1882, S. 44–56. Springer-Verlag, 2000.
9. N. M. Karnik und A.R. Tripathi. *A security architecture for mobile agents in Ajanta*. In *20th International Conference on Distributed Computing Systems*, S. 402–409. 2000.
10. D. Lange and M. Oshima. *Programming and Deploying Java Mobile Agents with Aglets*. Addison Wesley Longman, 1998.
11. F. Mattern. Mobile Agenten. *it+ti – Informationstechnik und Technische Informatik*, (4): 12–17, 1998.
12. C. Meadows. Detecting attacks on mobile agents. In *Workshop on Foundations for Secure Mobile Code*. Position Statement. Washington, DC, 1997. `http://www.cs.nps.navy.mil/research/languages/statements/meadows.ps`
13. T. Sander and C. F. Tschudin. Towards mobile cryptography. In *IEEE Symposium on Research in Security & Privacy*. S. 215–224. IEEE Press, 1998.
14. F. B. Schneider. Towards fault-tolerant and secure agentry. In M. Mavronicolas und P. Tsigas (Hsg.), *Distributed Algorithms*. Lecture Notes in Computer Science 1320, S. 1–14. Springer-Verlag, 1997.
15. G. Vigna (Hsg.). *Mobile Agents and Security*. Lecture Notes in Computer Science 1419. Springer-Verlag, 1998.
16. J. Vitek and C. Jensen (Hsg.). *Secure Internet Programming: Security Issues for Mobile and Distributed Objects*, Lecture Notes in Computer Science 1603. Springer-Verlag, 1999.
17. B. Yee. A sanctuary for mobile agents. In Vitek und Jensen [16], S. 261–273.

Performance Evaluation of Various Migration Strategies for Mobile Agents

Peter Braun, Christian Erfurth, and Wilhelm Rossak

Computer Science Department
Friedrich Schiller University Jena
D-07740 Jena, Germany
`Peter.Braun@informatik.uni-jena.de`
`http://tracy.informatik.uni-jena.de`

Abstract. In the last years several prototypes of mobile agent systems were developed. Based on the programming language and available transmission techniques, several ways of migrating a mobile agent has been implemented. We can divide pull and push strategies. A strategy in the first class uses dynamic download techniques to transmit only necessary code, whereas a strategy in the second class always transmits all agent's code to the next platform. In this paper we give an overview of state-of-the-art migration strategies for mobile agents and compare them with regard to network load and transmission time. We propose a simple mathematical model to show the influence of various network parameters, and present results of first measurements to point out that there is no strategy that in all cases leads to a minimum transmission time.

1 Introduction

In the last years, research and development of mobile agents made a great leap forward. Along with the wide spread of Java based applications, mobile agents became extensively popular not only in research, but also in industrial projects. Some of the mobile agent systems developed in the last years are Aglets [8] by IBM, Voyager [11, 12] by ObjectSpace, Concordia [10] by Mitsubishi. Systems developed through university research are for example Mole [20], Discovery [9], Ara [13], and MAP [17]. Research in the area of mobile agents is looking at languages that are suitable for mobile agent programming [3,6], and languages for agent communication [1]. Very much effort is put into security issues [21], control issues [2,19], and design issues [5]. Several prototypes of real-world applications in the area of information retrieval, management of distributed systems, and mobile computing are in development [15,18].

The performance aspect of Java-based mobile agents has not been considered in literature, so far. In our opinion, as mobile agents are disseminated in wider application areas their performance is of increasing importance. Within the life-cycle of a typical mobile agent we find several points at which performance can be improved. We can divide these points into two classes according to *transmission aspects* and *runtime aspects*. In the first class, all techniques are summarized that influence network load and transmission time during agent migration. After an agent has declared it's intention to migrate, all data and state information must be serialized by the underlying mobile agent system. Then, the agent is transmitted to the destination platform via a network connection. Transmission time is influenced by network bandwidth and network latency and can be reduced by code compression techniques and by restricting the number of class files and data items that must be transmitted. After the agent has been received at the destination platform data and state information must be deserialized to start execution. In the second class we place techniques by which an agent's execution time can be improved, e.g. by using a sophisticated Java Virtual Machine with dynamic code optimization. Some work has been done in the above mentioned areas, however, not with regard to mobile agents. Philippsen and Haumacher [14] present new efficient object serialization techniques for Java, Krintz et al. [7] deal with optimizing mobile code by reducing the transfer delay by splitting class files and Java archives into smaller transmission units. Other work that deals with reducing the number of bytes to transmit by using extensive compression techniques shall only be mentioned here [4, 16].

In this paper we only deal with transmission aspects. Especially, we are interested in performance effects that result from the *migration strategy*, i.e. the way how code and data are transmitted during migrations. An agent typically consists of several class files and a lot of data and state information. For example, one migration strategy defines that all class files are transmitted as one *package* along with the agent's data, whereas in another strategy only the agent's data are transmitted, and all classes are downloaded dynamically on demand. In this paper we will show results of a performance evaluation of state-of-the-art migration strategies. We will show that the migration strategy can influence performance in a non-neglectable way. By a simple mathematical model we will point out differences between various migration strategies for a specific mobile agent domain with regard to different types of network. First experiments indicate that dynamic class loading and code size influence the agent's performance, too.

The rest of this paper is structured as follows: In Sect. 2 we give a brief overview of the state-of-the-art migration strategies. In Sect. 3 we introduce our model for network load and transmission time, and in Sect. 4 we present results of our first experiments. In the last section we draw conclusions of our work and give an outlook to further development.

2 Migration Strategies

In this section we will have a look at the way code and data can be transmitted to the destination platform. Concerning code transmission, we can distinguish three strategies: Some systems offer a migration strategy that we call *push-all-to-next strategy*. The code of the agent (together with the code of all referenced objects) and the serialized agent, are transmitted at once. The strategy is fast, because only one transmission is necessary for the complete agent, and it corresponds to one of the main characteristics of mobile agents, that is autonomy. The agent needs no connection to the home platform, from which it was started. The drawback of this method is that code is transmitted to the destination site that is probably never used. The second approach does not transmit any code along with the data transmission. We call this *pull strategy*. After receiving and unmarshaling the agent's data, the mobile agent system on the destination site tries to invoke the given method and then starts loading the corresponding class file dynamically. Pull strategy can be further divided in *pull-per-unit* and *pull-all-units*. The first strategy dynamically loads code on a per-class policy, whereas the second strategy loads all class files immediately if one class file must be loaded. This strategy can be slower than the active one, because several network connections may be necessary to load all required class files. When you delegate this task to the Java Virtual Machine, one network connection per class is needed (pull-per-unit), unless you have combined several class files in one Java archive (pull-all-units). The major drawback of this migration strategy is that there must be an open network connection, or at least a fast way to reconnect, either to the home platform or to the last platform the agent came from. If it is impossible to connect to one of these platforms the agent can not be executed.

The third migration strategy is *push-all-to-all* strategy. As in the active one the complete code of an agent is transmitted, but not only to the next destination, but to all destination platforms the agent is going to visit. Of course, this requires that the agent knows all it's destinations in advance, e.g. by a given itinerary. When an agent arrives on a destination platform the execution can start immediately without any further code downloading.

3   Performance Model and Evaluation

In this section we model network load and transmission time for an agent's round-trip to an ordered set of platforms $\mathcal{L} = \{L_1, \ldots, L_m\}$. The agent consists of some class files, which can be dynamically loaded during execution from the agent's home platform. The decision on which class files must be loaded is influenced by the communication of the agent to the local agent server. To model network load, we assume that an agent consists of n units (classes) of code, each of length $B_c^k, k = 1, \ldots, n$, some data of length B_d, and state information of length B_s. A request to load a specific code unit has length B_r. The probability of dynamically loading code unit k on platform L_i is $P_{L_i}^k$. By this we can model two aspects. First, it expresses the probability that a specific code sequence is to be executed. Second, we can also model the fact that a code is already in a local code cache. On platform L_i the agent's data increases by d_{L_i} bytes.

The migration process consists of marshalling data and state, transmitting data, state, and code to the destination platform, and unmarshalling of data and state information. To model the round-trip time, we make the following simplifications. Marshalling and unmarshalling of data is linear in time and modeled by $\mu : \mathbb{N} \to \mathbb{R}$. For each pair of platforms we know throughput $\tau : \mathcal{L} \times \mathcal{L} \to \mathbb{R}$

and delay $\delta : \mathcal{L} \times \mathcal{L} \to \mathbb{R}$ in advance. We divide the migration process in three steps. First, the agent migrates from it's home platform L_h to the first platform L_1 of the given itinerary. Second, the agent migrates from platform L_i to platform L_{i+1}, where $i = 1, \ldots, m - 1$. Last, the agent migrates back to it's home platform.

3.1 Network Load

For the following we assume that $L_\mathrm{h} \neq L_i, i = 1, \ldots, m$. We define $B_\mathrm{c} = \sum_{k=1,\ldots,n} B_\mathrm{c}^k$. $S \in \{\mathrm{pushnext}, \mathrm{pushall}, \mathrm{pullunit}, \mathrm{pullall}\}$ stands for a migration strategy. The network load for the migration from the agent's home platform is calculated by

$$
B_\mathrm{lve}(\mathcal{L}, S) = \begin{cases}
B_\mathrm{c} + B_\mathrm{d} + B_\mathrm{s} & \text{if } S = \mathrm{pushnext} \\
|\mathcal{L}| B_\mathrm{c} + B_\mathrm{d} + B_\mathrm{s} & \text{if } S = \mathrm{pushall} \\
B_\mathrm{d} + B_\mathrm{s} + \sum_{k=1,\ldots,n} P_{L_1}^k (B_\mathrm{r} + B_\mathrm{c}^k) & \text{if } S = \mathrm{pullunit} \\
B_\mathrm{d} + B_\mathrm{s} + B_\mathrm{r} + B_\mathrm{c} & \text{if } S = \mathrm{pullall}
\end{cases}
$$

A migration from L_a to L_{a+1}, with $a = 1, \ldots, m - 1$ has network load of $B_\mathrm{mig}(\mathcal{L}, a, S) =$

$$
\begin{cases}
B_\mathrm{c} + B_\mathrm{d} + \sum_{l=1,\ldots,a} d_{L_l} + B_\mathrm{s} & \text{if } S = \mathrm{pushnext} \\
B_\mathrm{d} + \sum_{l=1,\ldots,a} d_{L_l} + B_\mathrm{s} & \text{if } S = \mathrm{pushall} \\
B_\mathrm{d} + \sum_{l=1,\ldots,a} d_{L_l} + B_\mathrm{s} + \sum_{k=1,\ldots,n} P_{L_{a+1}}^k (B_\mathrm{r} + B_\mathrm{c}^k) & \text{if } S = \mathrm{pullunit} \\
B_\mathrm{d} + \sum_{l=1,\ldots,a} d_{L_l} + B_\mathrm{s} + B_\mathrm{r} + B_\mathrm{c} & \text{if } S = \mathrm{pullall}
\end{cases}
$$

When the agent migrates to it's home platform, the network load amounts to

$$
B_\mathrm{home}(\mathcal{L}, S) = B_\mathrm{d} + \sum_{i=1,\ldots,m} d_{L_i} + B_\mathrm{s}
$$

3.2 Execution Time

The time to load all necessary code units dynamically on platform L_s is

$$
\phi_s = \sum_{k=1,\ldots,n} P_{L_s}^k \left(\delta(L_s, L_\mathrm{h}) + \frac{B_\mathrm{r} + B_\mathrm{c}^k}{\tau(L_s, L_\mathrm{h})} \right) .
$$

The corresponding execution time for migrating an agent from the home platform is

$$T_{\mathrm{lve}}(\mathcal{L}, S) =$$

$$
\begin{cases}
2\mu(B_{\mathrm{d}} + B_{\mathrm{s}}) + \delta(L_{\mathrm{h}}, L_1) + \frac{B_{\mathrm{lve}}(\mathcal{L},S)}{\tau(L_{\mathrm{h}},L_1)} & \text{if } S = \text{pushnext} \\[2mm]
2\mu(B_{\mathrm{d}} + B_{\mathrm{s}}) + \sum_{l=1,\dots,m} \left(\delta(L_{\mathrm{h}}, L_l) + \frac{B_c}{\tau(L_{\mathrm{h}},L_l)} \right) + \frac{B_{\mathrm{d}}+B_{\mathrm{s}}}{\tau(L_{\mathrm{h}},L_1)} & \text{if } S = \text{pushall} \\[2mm]
2\mu(B_{\mathrm{d}} + B_{\mathrm{s}}) + \delta(L_{\mathrm{h}}, L_1) + \frac{B_{\mathrm{d}}+B_{\mathrm{s}}}{\tau(L_{\mathrm{h}},L_1)} + \phi_1 & \text{if } S = \text{pullunit} \\[2mm]
2\mu(B_{\mathrm{d}} + B_{\mathrm{s}}) + \delta(L_{\mathrm{h}}, L_1) + \frac{B_{\mathrm{d}}+B_{\mathrm{s}}}{\tau(L_{\mathrm{h}},L_1)} + \delta(L_1, L_{\mathrm{h}}) + \frac{B_r+B_c}{\tau(L_1,L_{\mathrm{h}})} & \text{if } S = \text{pullall}
\end{cases}
$$

Note, that marshalling and unmarshalling of date and state information each takes $\mu(B_{\mathrm{d}} + B_{\mathrm{s}})$ of time. We define $B_{\mathrm{d,s}}^a = B_{\mathrm{d}} + \sum_{l=1,\dots,a} d_{L_l} + B_{\mathrm{s}}$, which is the amount of accumulated data and state information at platform L_a . The time to migrate from L_a to L_{a+1}, with $a = 1, \dots, m-1$ is

$$T_{\mathrm{mig}}(\mathcal{L}, a, S) =$$

$$
\begin{cases}
2\mu(B_{\mathrm{d,s}}^a) + \delta(L_a, L_{a+1}) + \frac{B_{\mathrm{mig}}(\mathcal{L},a,S)}{\tau(L_a,L_{a+1})} & \text{if } S = \text{pushnext} \\[2mm]
2\mu(B_{\mathrm{mig}}(\mathcal{L}, a, S)) + \delta(L_a, L_{a+1}) + \frac{B_{\mathrm{mig}}(\mathcal{L},a,S)}{\tau(L_a,L_{a+1})} & \text{if } S = \text{pushall} \\[2mm]
2\mu(B_{\mathrm{d,s}}^a) + \delta(L_a, L_{a+1}) + \frac{B_{\mathrm{d,s}}^a}{\tau(L_a,L_{a+1})} + \phi_{a+1} & \text{if } S = \text{pullunit} \\[2mm]
2\mu(B_{\mathrm{d,s}}^a) + \delta(L_a, L_{a+1}) + \frac{B_{\mathrm{d,s}}^a}{\tau(L_a,L_{a+1})} + \delta(L_{a+1}, L_{\mathrm{h}}) + \frac{B_r+B_c}{\tau(L_{a+1},L_{\mathrm{h}})} & \text{if } S = \text{pullall}
\end{cases}
$$

The time to migrate to the home platform is

$$T_{\mathrm{home}}(\mathcal{L}, S) = 2\mu(B_{\mathrm{home}}(\mathcal{L}, S)) + \delta(L_m, L_{\mathrm{h}}) + \frac{B_{\mathrm{home}}(\mathcal{L}, S)}{\tau(L_m, L_{\mathrm{h}})}$$

3.3 Evaluation

To evaluate an agent's round-trip based on this simple model, we consider the following scenarios. An agent consists of five classes, the code size of each class can be seen in Table 1. The initial data size of the agent is 5 kByte and the initial state size is 3 kByte. The agent has to migrate to four platforms, on each platform it has to communicate to the local agent server. As a result, the agent's data increases by 5 kByte on each platform. Fig. 1 (left) compares round-trip times in a homogeneous network of four different mobile agents, each using one specific migration strategy, while varying the class download probabilities in four scenarios. The homogeneous network is modeled by a throughput $\tau = 100$ kByte/sec and delay $\delta = 5$ ms. The four scenarios of class download probabilities can be seen in Table 1. In the first scenario only one class is downloaded, whereas in the last scenario all classes must be downloaded. The second and third scenario model that only few resp. many classes must be downloaded. In contrast, Fig. 1 (right) compares round-trip times in a heterogeneous network of four different mobile agents and different class downloading probability scenarios. The heterogeneous network is modeled with a ring topology, in which transmission time is small for connections between adjacent platforms, but high for downloading data from the home platform.

Table 1. Code size and download probabilities in four different scenarios.

class number	size in kByte	class download probability			
		scenario 1	scenario 2	scenario 3	scenario 4
1	10	1	1	1	1
2	15	0	0,5	1	1
3	15	0	0,2	0,8	1
4	15	0	0	0,5	1
5	15	0	0	0,2	1

As can be seen from the model, network load using strategies push-all-to-next, push-all-to-all, and pull-all-units are almost equal. The only difference are code requests that must be sent to the home platform in strategy pull-all-units. Strategy pull-per-unit has only in case of downloading all classes a higher network load than the other strategies, because one code request must be sent for each class file. In the best case, this strategy leads to a large reduction of network load, which can be up to 80%.

As shown in Fig. 1 in a homogeneous network the mobile agent's transmission time using strategies push-all-to-next, push-all-to-all, and pull-all-units are almost the same. The additional time to open a network connection and transmit the code request to the home platform takes only a few milliseconds. Strategy pull-per-unit is faster than all other strategies in a homogeneous network, even if more classes must be downloaded. As already mentioned above, only in the case of downloading all class files, this strategy leads to a higher transmission time, because of several code requests that must be sent to the home platform. As can be seen in Fig. 1 (right) in a heterogeneous network, strategies push-all-to-all and pull-all-units take the same time, again. However, transmission time is higher than in strategy push-all-to-next, because in these strategies all class files must be transmitted using slow network connections, whereas in strategy push-all-to-next, code and data is sent via very fast network connections. The diagram shows that in a heterogeneous network strategy pull-per-unit is slower than push-all-to-next even if not all classes must be downloaded. Again, this is because code must be download from the home platform via slow network connections.

4   Experimental Validation

In this section we show first results of experiments that we are performing using our mobile agent system TRACY. TRACY is a general purpose mobile agent system, implemented on top of the Java 2 platform. TRACY was designed to provide basic services for stationary and mobile agents, like communication and migration. The main difference of TRACY as compared to other mobile agent systems is that it provides a migration model that offers a flexible alternative to a

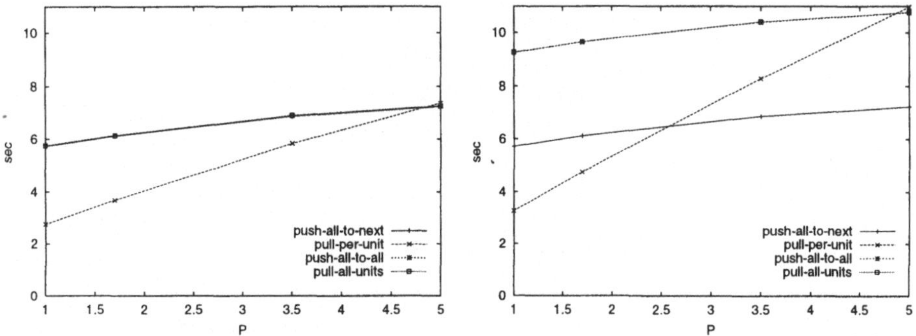

Fig. 1. Round-trip time for four different migration strategies in a homogeneous (left) and heterogeneous (right) network.

pure agent model and a pure network transmission model. From the agent's view it means that the agent server offers a multitude of different migration strategies the agent can choose from. Currently, we have have already implemented all migration strategies mentioned in Sec. 2. From the researcher's point of view it means that the complete process of migrating an agent is accessible to the programmer and can be adapted, so that new migration techniques can be easily implemented.

To perform the experiments we chose an application from the information retrieval domain. Each platform has a database with documents of different types, e.g. simple text file, structured text files in XML or HTML, and images. Each document is characterized by a set of keywords. The agent has to visit each platform. First, it filters all documents according to a given set of keywords. The result is a set of *interesting* documents. Second, all these documents are examined in detail, which results in the set of all *significant* documents from which the agent takes a copy before migrating to the next platform. To examine an interesting document, a specific class file for the given document type is necessary on the current platform. Therefore, an agent consists of one class file for the agent itself, which contains code to perform the first step and all auxiliary tasks, like communication and route managing. Additionally, there are five other class files, each for one document type, which contain special code for the second step. If the agent finds a document of a specific type, the corresponding class file must be downloaded dynamically, if it is not already on the current platform.

The experimental setup consists of a cluster of five agent systems connected via a local area network which can be classified as a homogeneous network. On each platform we can change the number of document types that the agent will find interesting. By this we can directly influence the number of classes that will be downloaded. In the first experiment, the agent class files are very small. The main class is about 12 kByte, and each of the additional class files is about 2 kByte. In Fig. 2 (left diagram) the results can be seen for various numbers of document types found interesting and various migration strategies. It can be seen that the execution time increases for all migration strategies with

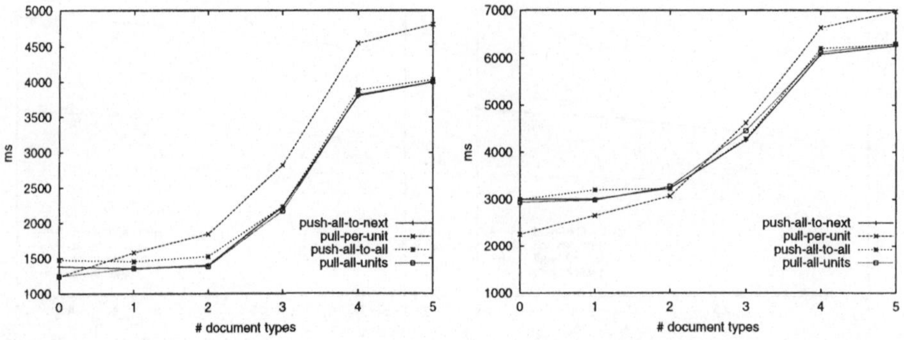

Fig. 2. Round-trip times for various migration strategies using small (left) classes and big (right) classes.

the number of interesting document types. This is, because the agent's data increases as more interesting and significant documents are found. As could be expected from the model, strategies push-all-to-next, push-all-to-all, and pull-all-units are almost equal in time. The pull-per-unit strategy is faster in case of no interesting documents than all other methods because only the agent class itself must be transmitted. However, even if only one additional class file must be loaded (of size 2 kByte) strategy push-per-unit is about 17% slower than the push-all-to-next strategy. With increasing number of document types the pull-per-unit strategy is in average more than 23% slower than the push-all-to-next strategy. This performance difference only results from the fact that code must be downloaded dynamically.

In the second experiment we artificially blew up class files to lengthen transmission times. The agent class file is about 12 kByte, again, the additional class files are about 25 kByte, now. The results can be seen in Fig. 2 (right diagram). If no or only few additional class files must be downloaded, pull-per-unit strategy is up to 33% faster than the other strategies. If more than two additional class files must be downloaded then this strategy is slower than all other strategies for the same reason mentioned above. In the case that all classes must be downloaded, this strategy is about 12% slower as compared to the other strategies. The reason that with longer class files the pull-per-unit strategy is faster even for more document types is because of the overall difference of the network load. For example, if only one additional class file must be downloaded, an agent with pull-per-unit strategy produces an overall network load of at least 148 kByte (only code), whereas an agent with push-all-to-next strategy produces a network load of 548 kByte (only code).

5 Conclusions

In this paper we gave an overview of state-of-the-art migration strategies and compared them with regard to network load and transmission time. We proposed a simple mathematical model and presented results of first experiments. It could be seen that very different migration strategies (push-all-to-next, pull-all-units, push-all-to-all) lead to almost the same execution time. In contrast, from the experiments can be concluded that the pull-per-unit strategy, which is used in several mobile agent systems today, is a bad choice in some cases. This result is contradictory to our model predicting this strategy will always be faster than the other strategies in homogeneous networks. At this point we have to admit that we likely made too naive assumptions about network latency in our model. The experiments indicated that latency must be set about ten times higher than we did. Notwithstanding, we were able to show that there is no migration strategy that is best in every situation. Additionally, on basis of our results it can be inferred that mobile agents' performance depends on several factors, like network parameters, code size, and not at least the dynamic behavior of the agent which influences class file downloading. Most of these parameters are inherent dynamical, i.e. they can not be predicted in advance. In conclusion we may say that our results indicate that it is worthwhile to decide which migration strategy a mobile agent should use. However, this decision process must be based on parameters that can not be known by the programmer in advance. Our future work will be directed in developing a new migration strategy, which combines both strategies push-all-to-next and pull-per-unit. This new strategy should be aware of some of the above mentioned parameters, so that it can decide which strategy will be applied best in a given situation. We hope, that we will be able to supplement our mobile agent system by some kind of net-awareness to monitor throughput and latency to neighbor platforms.

References

1. J. Baumann, F. Hohl, N. Radouniklis, K. Rothermel, and M. Straßer. Communication concepts for mobile agent systems. In Rothermel [18], pages 123–135.
2. J. Baumann and K. Rothermel. The shadow approach: An orphan detection protocol for mobile agents. Technical Report 1998/08, Universität Stuttgart, Fakultät für Informatik, 1998.
3. G. Cugola, C. Ghezzi, G. P. Picco, and G. Vigna. Analyzing mobile code languages. In J. Vitek and C. Tschudin, editors, *Mobile Object Systems: Towards the Programmable Internet (MOS'96), Linz, July 1996*, volume 1222 of *Lecture Notes in Computer Science*, pages 93–110, Berlin, 1997. Springer Verlag.
4. M. Franz and T. Kistler. Slim Binaries. *Communications of the ACM*, 40(12):87–94, 1997.
5. D. K. Hammer and A. T. M. Aerts. Mobile Agent Architectures: What are the Design Issues? In *Proceedings International Conference and Workshop on Engineering of Computer-Based Systems (ECBS'98), Jerusalem, March/April 1998*, pages 272–280. IEEE Computer Society Press, 1998.
6. F. C. Knabe. *Language Support for Mobile Agents*. PhD thesis, Carnegie Mellon University, Paittsburgh, Pa., Dec. 1995.
7. C. Krintz, B. Calder, and U. Hölzle. Reducing Transfer Delay Using Java Class File Splitting and Prefetching. In L. Meissner, editor, *Proceedings of the 1999 ACM SIG-PLAN Conference on Object-Oriented Programming, Systems, Languages & Ap-*

plications (OOPSLA'99), November 1999, pages 276–291, New York, 1999. ACM Press.

8. D. B. Lange and M. Ishima. *Programming and Deploying Java Mobile Agents with Aglets*. Addison-Wesley, Reading, MA, 1998.
9. S. Lazar and D. Sidhu. Discovery: A Mobile Agent Framework for Distributed Applications. Technical report, Maryland Center for Telecommunications Research, Department of Computer Science and Electrical Engineering, University of Maryland Baltimore County, 1998.
10. Mitsubishi Electric ITA. *Mobile Agent Computing – A White Paper*, 19 Jan. 1998.
11. ObjectSpace Inc. *ObjectSpace Voyager Core Package Technical Overview: The Agent ORB for Java*, Dec. 1997. http://www.objectspace.com/voyager.
12. ObjectSpace Inc. *ObjectSpace Voyager Core Package Version 2.0: Technical Overview*, 1998. http://www.objectspace.com/voyager.
13. H. Peine. An introduction to mobile agent programming and the Ara system. Technical Report ZRI-Report 1/97, Department of Computer Science, University of Kaiserslautern, Germany, 1997.
14. M. Philippsen and B. Haumacher. More efficient object serialization. In *Proc. of the 11th IPPS/SPDP'99 Workshops Held in Conjunction with the 13th International Parallel Processing Symposium and 10th Symposium on Parallel and Distributed Processing, San Juan, Puerto Rico, USA, April 1999*, volume 1586 of *Lecture Notes in Computer Science*, 1999.
15. E. D. Pietro, O. Tomarchio, G. Iannizzotto, and M. Villari. Experiences in the use of Mobile Agents for developing distributed applications. In *Workshop su Sistemi Distribuiti: Algoritmi, Architetture e Linguaggi (WSDAAL'99), L'Aquila (Italy), September 1999*, 1999.
16. W. Pugh. Compressing Java class files. *ACM SIGPLAN Notices*, 34(5):247–258, May 1999.
17. A. Puliafito, O. Tomarchio, and L. Vita. MAP: Design and Implementation of a Mobile Agents Platform. Technical Report TR-CT-9712, University of Catania, 1997.
18. K. Rothermel, editor. *Proceedings of the First International Workshop on Mobile Agents (MA'97), Berlin, April 1997*, volume 1219 of *Lecture Notes in Computer Science*, Berlin, 1997. Springer Verlag.
19. K. Rothermel and M. Straßer. A protocol for preserving the exactly-once property of mobile agents. Technical Report 1997/18, Universität Stuttgart, Fakultät für Informatik, 1997.
20. M. Straßer, J. Baumann, and F. Hohl. Mole – a Java based mobile agent system. In M. Mühlhäuser, editor, *Proceedings of the 2nd ECOOP Workshop on Mobile Object Systems: Agents on the Move, Linz, July 1996*, pages 28–35. dpunkt Verlag, 1997.
21. G. Vigna. *Mobile Agents and Securtiy*, volume 1419 of *Lecture Notes in Computer Science*. Springer Verlag, New York, 1998.

Generative Softwarekonstruktion auf Basis typisierter Komponenten

Frank Griffel, Christian Zirpins und Stefan Müller-Wilken

Arbeitsgruppe Verteilte Systeme – Fachbereich Informatik
Universität Hamburg
Vogt-Kölln-Str. 30, D-22527 Hamburg
{griffel|zirpins|smueller}@informatik.uni-hamburg.de

Zusammenfassung Die komponentenbasierte Entwicklungssicht erhält zunehmend Aufmerksamkeit, insbesondere auf Grund der von ihr in Aussicht gestellten vielversprechenden Vorteile wie besserer Produktivität, Test- und Wartbarkeit, Wiederverwendung und Qualität. Andererseits fehlt immer noch ein solides Fundament, auf dem sich solche Erwartungen gründen können. Zumindest bildet jedoch ein kompositorisches Vorgehen zweifellos den Kern kompentenbasierter Entwicklung. Dieser Beitrag stellt daher einen als *Generative Softwarekonstruktion* bezeichneten Entwicklungsprozess vor, der auf Basis eines *interaktionsorientierten* Typmodells eine hochgradig automatisierte Komposition verteilter Anwendungssysteme erlaubt. Das semantisch reiche Typmodell wird dabei als Erweiterung des aktuellen CORBA Component Model vorgestellt, unterstützt eine typkorrekte und bei Bedarf automatisch adaptierende Komposition und wird anhand seiner Anwendung in der Finananzdienstleistungsdomäne illustriert.

1 Generative Softwarekonstruktion

Das Komponentenparadigma ist vielleicht der aussichtsreichste Kandidat auf dem Weg zu einer industriellen Softwareproduktion. Von deren typischen Merkmalen (nach [14]) wie

- Fertigung auf Abruf / bei Bedarf aus vordefinierten Produktbestandteilen
- Auftreten von Drittanbietern die nach gemeinsamen Spezifikationen arbeiten
- Produktpflege/-wartung durch Teile-Austausch
- Unterstützung kompletter Lieferketten von der Fertigung bis zur Auslieferung

ist jedoch auch die heutige Komponentendiskussion noch weit entfernt und vielfach von Wunschdenken geprägt. Um diese Erwartungen erfüllen zu können, reicht eben nicht allein die Betonung des Bausteinaspekts in der Softwareentwicklung, sondern der gesamte Entwicklungsprozess muss überdacht werden. Die Programmierung „Zeile-für-Zeile" ist für die heute rasch und in guter Qualität zu liefernden, zunehmend komplexeren Anwendungen nicht mehr adäquat. Ein Zusammensetzen aus vorgefertigten Bausteinen erscheint deutlich angemessener. Je stärker eine solche Komposition durch entsprechende Entwicklungsumgebungen unterstützt und automatisiert werden kann, um so leichter können robuste und fehlerfreie Lösungen produziert werden. Daher werden Softwareentwicklungsumgebungen und -werkzeuge zukünftig immer stärker von *generierenden* Konzepten durchdrungen werden, die ausgehend von überschaubaren und anwendungsnahen (problembezogenen) Architekturbeschreibungen komplexe technische Anwendungssysteme erstellen zu können.

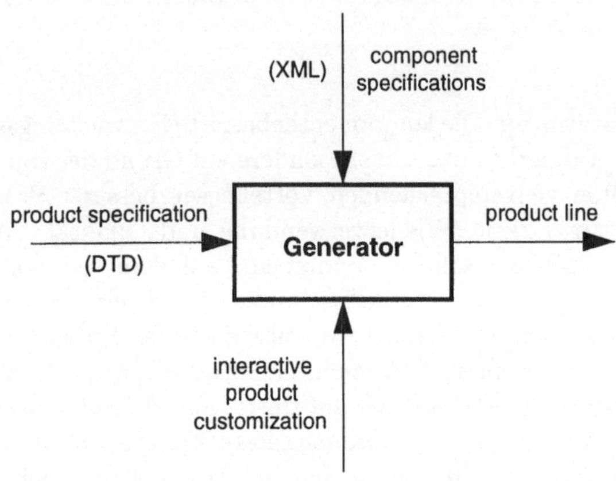

Abbildung 1. Grundkonzeption einer generativen Systemerstellung

Abbildung 1 illustriert das Prinzip einer Generator-basierten Anwendungserstellung aus bereitstehenden Komponenten. Grundidee ist die Parametrisirung des Generators mit einer Spezifikation der gewünschten Anwendung. Die Analyse dieser Architekturspezifikation erlaubt dem Generator dann die Auswahl passender Komponenten. Deren individuelle Konfigurationen sind zum Teil durch die gewählte Kombination mit anderen Komponenten festgelegt, zum Teil kann jedoch noch eine manuelle Einstellung erwünschter Eigenschaften durch den Entwickler erfolgen. Ergebnis der Generierung ist dann eine konkrete, ausführbare Applikation. Genau genommen kann der Output des Generators als *Produktlinie* bezeichnet werden, da eine ganze Reihe von ähnlichen Anwendungen erzeugt werden kann, die sich in wesentlichen Elementen oder Eigenschaften gleichen und ein identisches Anwendungsproblem adressieren. Wird der Generator mit unterschiedlichen, aber einer gemeinsamen Domäne zugehörigen Architekturspezifikationen parametrisiert, kann insbesondere auch von einer entstehenden *Produktfamilie* gesprochen werden, innerhalb derer beispielsweise ein hoher Wiederverwendungsgrad einzelner Komponenten möglich wird.

Der Beitrag gliedert sich im Weiteren wie folgt. Abschnitt 2 führt den zu Grunde gelegten Entwicklungsprozess ein und stellt die Arbeitsweise des entwickelten Generators vor. Im Abschnitt 3 werden aktuelle verwandte Ansätze diskutiert. Abschnitt 4 gibt einen Überblick über das konzipierte Typmodell und stellt seine Verwendung vor. Der zusammenfassende Ausblick in Abschnitt 5 schließt den Artikel ab.

2   Der Entwicklungsprozess

Der Erfolg und die Mächtigkeit des beabsichtigten generativen Szenarios steht und fällt mit der Exaktheit und den Ausdrucksmöglichkeiten der Eingabespezifikationen - und hier zunächst der Architekturspezifikation. Diese basiert ihrerseits wiederum auf einer sorgfältigen und vollständigen Analyse der zu unterstützenden Anwendungsdomäne. Wichtigste Voraussetzung ist also die Domänenanalyse (bzw. ein „domain engineering"), die damit auch den ersten Schritt im gesamten Entwicklungsprozess darstellt. Methoden der Domänenanalyse sind ein rasch an Bedeutung gewinnendes Forschungsfeld (vgl. etwa [1]) und leisten einen erheblichen Beitrag zu einer problem- bzw. anwendungsnahen Softwareentwicklung, indem sie Fachkonzepte bereitstellen, die unabhängig von konkreten technologischen Aspekten sind. Insbesondere verlagern sich Betrachtungen, wie sie sich meist in einer Modellierungsphase finden, dabei zum Teil in die Aufbereitung eines Anwendungsbereichs, etwa die Gruppierung oder Zuordnung einzelner Merkmale zu Entitäten der Domäne.

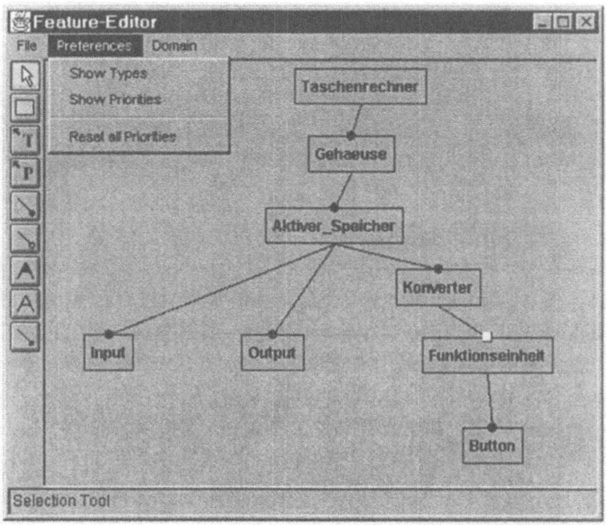

Abbildung 2. FeatureEditor zur Architekturspezifikation

Dies funktioniert allerdings erst dann zufriedenstellend, wenn eine entsprechende Formalisierung der Ergebnisse der Domänenanalyse erreicht werden kann. Hinsichtlich des Ziels einer generativen Konstruktion ist dabei zugleich das Zusammenspiel der Architektur mit den Spezifikationen bereitstehender Komponenten zu beachten. Der hier vorgestellte Ansatz setzt dabei nach erfolgter

Domänenanalyse ein und überlappt erst mit dem sich anschließenden Formalisierungsprozess und zwar in Form eines Werkzeugs zur Erstellung sogenannter *Merkmalsdiagramme* wie sie aus der „Feature-Oriented Domain Analysis" [2] bekannt sind. Dieses in Abbildung 2 illustrierte Werkzeug erlaubt zum einen die interaktive Erstellung von Merkmalsstrukturen („feature structures") [5], zum anderen die Erstellung der architekturellen Struktur einer zu entwickelnden Applikation. Die Entscheidung zugunsten solcher Merkmalsdiagramme anstelle von UML fiel hier aufgrund der wesentlich einfacheren und weniger mit technischen Details überfrachteten Darstellung, die damit die fachorientierte Kommunikation mit dem späteren Anwender / Kunden erleichtert. Andererseits verfolgt unser Ansatz ja gerade die Abstraktion von der Programmierebene, so dass viele Details gar nicht in Erscheinung treten müssen und die auftretenden Merkmale einer Anwendung eine direkte Zuordnung vorhandener Komponenten erlauben. Insbesondere entfällt damit die frühe Einschränkung des Variabilitätsgrades durch entsprechende UML-Konstrukte (vgl. [10]), so dass variantenreichere Produktlinien generiert werden können.

Der Diagrammeditor liefert die grafisch erstellten Spezifikationen in Form von DTD-Dateien sowie Merkmalsstrukturen in Form von Klassenspezifikationen. Während erstere die eigentliche Eingabe für den Generator darstellen, tragen letztere zur Typrepräsentation innerhalb des Typmanagers bei (vgl. Abschnitt 4). Die DTD-Dateien folgen dabei einem erweiterten CORBA Component Metamodell (CCM) [3], da eine konkrete Festlegung auf eine Implementationstechnik bzw. ein konkretes (programmiersprachliches) Komponentenmodell vermieden werden soll. Auf diese Weise erschließt sich dem Generator ein maximaler Pool von Komponenten. Abbildung 3 zeigt das resultierende Zusammenspiel der einzelnen Werkzeuge innerhalb der implementierten Entwicklungsumgebung.

2.1 Phasen der Generierung

Die Auswertung des Metamodells durch den Generator führt in einer ersten Phase (Spezifikationsphase) zur Auswahl passender Komponenten, die die Architekturspezifikation korrekt zu erfüllen vermögen. Die Spezifikationen der Komponenten bedienen sich dabei einer erweiterten Instanziierung des CCM-Metamodells in Form des in Abschnitt 4 vorgestellten Typmodells bzw. dessen XML-Deskriptoren. Auf diese Weise stellt sich das „Ausfüllen" der Architekturspezifikation für den Generator als ein konstruktives Parsing der XML-Spezifikationen dar, indem ein schrittweiser Test gegen die zugehörige DTD erfolgt[1].

Die zweite Arbeitsphase des Generators umfasst die Konfiguration der ausgewählten Komponenten, wobei diese Phase zeitlich mit der ersten verwoben ist, da die schrittweise Komponentenauswahl möglicherweise bereits von bestimmten Konfigurationen abhängt oder umgekehrt diese erfordert. Verbleibende Freiheitsgrade werden dem Anwendungsentwickler in Form einer angeleiteten Konfiguration („Wizard") angeboten.

---

[1] Dies stellt eine Umkehrung des üblichen Verhältnisses zwischen DTD und XML-Datei dar und erfordert einen speziellen Parser!

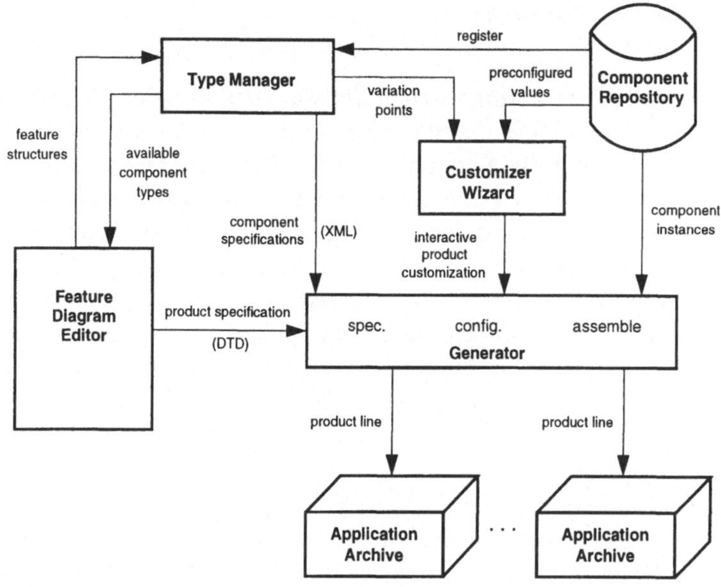

Abbildung 3. Prinzipsicht der generativen Entwicklungsumgebung

Ist dieses Customizing abgeschlossen (das unter Umständen auch zur Auswahl zusätzlicher Komponenten durch den Generator geführt hat), erstellt der Generator ein Anwendungsskelett zur Verknüpfung aller ausgewählten Komponenten gemäß den Architekturvorgaben. Die zur Verknüpfung benötigten Informationen können dabei vollständig den eingelesenen Komponentenspezifikationen entnommen werden, da diese alle Verbindungspunkte explizit beschreiben. Wurde bisher von „Komponentenauswahl" gesprochen handelte es sich genau genommen um die Auswahl von Komponententypen.

Erst in der dritten Phase - der Konstruktionsphase - selektiert der Generator konkrete Komponenteninstanzen gemäß den im Skelett angegebenen Typen und setzt entsprechende Variationspunkte gemäß seinen Konfigurationsvorgaben. Die Konstruktion schließt mit dem „Verpacken" aller Anwendungsbestandteile zu einem Anwendungsarchiv ab, um für die anschließenden Deployment- und Installationsphasen eine handhabbare Einheit bereitzustellen.

Die ebenfalls zum Komponentenmodell der OMG gehörenden Deployment- und Assembly-Deskriptoren erlauben die Festlegung bzw. automatisierte Unterstützung der Einsatzkonfiguration („deployment") bzw. der Auslieferung und Installation der Anwendungsbestandteile in der Zielsystemumgebung. Die Einsatzkonfiguration kann dabei beispielsweise die Auswahl von Transaktionsmodi oder Sicherheitsattributen umfassen, während die Installation z.B. Informationen benötigt, welche programmiersprachlichen Klassen auf welchen Rechnerknoten vorliegen müssen. Unser Ansatz erlaubt somit nicht nur die server-zentrierte Komponentensicht, die das unterliegende CCM nahe legt, sondern auch die erwünschte „freie" Komposition von Anwendungsbausteinen.

3 Verwandte Ansätze

Der Wunsch nach einer automatischen Softwareerstellung im Sinne einer Generierung ist nicht neu, sondern besitzt seine Anfänge spätestens in den Bemühungen der frühen KI, die die Vorstellung sich selbst programmierender Systeme u.Ä. hervorbrachte, diese visionären Ideen jedoch nicht umzusetzen vermochte. Weit pragmatischerer sind die neueren Ansätze, die etwa im Rahmen der Generischen (GP), der Adaptiven (AP) [12] und der Aspekt-orientierten (AOP) [11] sowie der Subjekt-orientierten Programmierung (SOP) [9] betrachtet werden. Gemeinsam ist solchen Ansätzen die Betonung der Entkopplung von strukturellen („funktionsblinde" Architektur) und verhaltensbezogenen („strukturblinder" Code) Systemeigenschaften, die getrennte Bearbeitung einzelner Systemaspekte („separation of concerns" [10]) und die fachliche Anwendungsnähe durch Betonung der Domänenanalyse.

Den Leitlinien „Trennung" und „Entkopplung" stehen dann automatische Mechanismen zur Rekombination der zunächst separat modellierten und eventuell programmierten Systemaspekte gegenüber. Diese Mechanismen haben dann einen entsprechenden transformativen oder generativen Charakter, um ein reales System zu produzieren. Ansätze wie GenVoca bzw. Jakarta [6] zielen dann explizit auf die Erzeugung eines problemspezifischen Generators, der dann wiederum das gewünschte Endprodukt erstellen kann.

Überhaupt sind diese Ansätze geprägt von der Vorstellung aus einer domänenspezifischen „Eingabesprache" - eventuell unter Kombination mit einer Konfigurationssprache - eine problembezogene Zielsprache zu erzeugen, in der dann die eigentliche Anwendung formuliert wird. Microsofts „Intentionelles Programmieren" (IP) [10] verdeutlicht diesen Trend besonders markant, indem die eigentlichen Ausdrucksmöglichkeiten der Sprache zur Systemprogrammierung (eigentlich besser: „-formulierung") völlig frei definierbar und damit beliebig problemnah werden. Alle Ansätze sind jedoch nach wie vor den „lines-of-code" sehr nahe und ihre Endprodukte besitzen wiederum keinen kompositorischen Charakter.

Die Komponentensicht stellt nun eine ideale Kombination mit den grundlegenden Ideen der angeführten Ansätze dar, indem sie klar abgegrenzte Bausteine bereitstellt, die zum einen direkt die Rolle einzelner Systemaspekte übernehmen können, zum anderen die notwendigen Mechanismen zur Verknüpfung und Konfiguration vereinfachen, da sie per se von der Codezeilenebene abstrahieren. Ein „Verweben" systemdurchdringender („horizontaler") Aspekte (z.B. Sicherheit) wie sie die AOP vorsieht, ist in der Praxis komplexer Anwendungssysteme beispielsweise schwierig zu automatisieren.

Nehmen wir jedoch eine Dienstleistungssicht ein, d.h. eine Komponente ist für genau diesen Aspekt „zuständig" und stellt ihn entsprechend den anderen Systembestandteilen bereit, kann die wünschenswerte Trennung der Belange aufrechterhalten werden bei gleichzeitiger Vereinfachung der Systemerstellung. Letztlich liegt diese Sicht Buskonzepten wie dem CORBA ORB mit angegliederten Diensten oder einem EJB-Container mit den Dienstfunktionen für die in ihm enthaltenen Komponenten ohnehin zugrunde.

Unser hier vorgestellter Ansatz ist also klar als ein Komponenten-basierter Generator positioniert, d.h. geht von der Zusammensetzung einer Softwareapplikation aus bereits vorhandenen Komponenten aus. Es steht weder die Erweiterbarkeit noch die Spezialisierung sprachlicher Ausdruckmittel im Vordergrund, sondern die automatisierte Konstruktion (in Abgrenzung zum Begriff der Programmierung) des gewünschten Endprodukts. Dann müssen allerdings an die Beschreibungen bzw. Spezifikationen der vorhandenen Bausteine hohe Ansprüche gestellt werden, um einem Generator ausreichende Informationen zur korrekten Anwendungserstellung bereitzustellen. Ferner sollte der Generator nicht auf einem bestimmten Komponentenmodell basieren, um möglichst flexibel und technologieunabhängig einsetzbar zu sein. Stattdessen liegt es nahe von entsprechenden Meta-Modellen für Komponenten auszugehen. Unser zugehöriges Typmodell wird im Folgenden vorgestellt.

4 Klassifikation von Komponenten

Komponenten-Metamodelle wie das der CORBA Components führen eine ganze Reihe von abstrakten Konstrukten und Informationen ein, die eine sinnvolle Obermenge zu den Eigenschaften konkreter Komponententechnologien bieten und somit die Definition von Komponententypen erlauben. Eine Klassifikation von Komponenten ist für den oben beschriebenen generativen Konstruktionsprozess unabdingbar, da nur sie Entscheidungskriterien während der Komponentenauswahl bzw. -suche des Generators bereitstellen kann. Eine Klassifikation durch Typisierung ist naheliegend, allerdings nicht unproblematisch: Der Generator muss sich auf (mindestens) zwei Aussagen beziehen können. Zum einen wann „passt" ein Komponententyp in einen „Slot" der Architekturspezifikation - wir bezeichnen dies als die Frage nach der *Konformität*, zum anderen wann kann eine Komponente mit einer anderen kombiniert werden - wir bezeichnen dies als die Frage nach der *Kompatibilität*. Modelle wie das CCM sehen zwar explizit einen „componenttype" (in Form einer XML-Beschreibung) vor, beantworten jedoch nicht die Fragen nach potentieller Konformität bzw. Kompatibilität - diese beschränkt sich auf die Überprüfung der Namensgleichheit entsprechender XML-Elemente. Wir haben daher zum einen zunächst Mechanismen zur praktischen Verarbeitung des CCM-Metamodells in Form eines Typmanagements geschaffen, zum anderen das Modell erweitert, um eine flexible Klassifikation und zugehörige Vergleichsmöglichkeiten bereitstellen zu können.

Abbildung 4 zeigt zur Illustration Ausschnitte aus den ensprechenden XML-Repräsentationen einer Hexidezimal-Koverter-Komponente für einen Taschenrechner. Gezeigt sind Teile der Komponentenspezifikation selbst, ein Ereignis auf semantischer Ebene (Business Event) sowie eine Nachricht auf syntaktischer Ebene. Die Komponente selbst wird im gezeigten Fall lose und verteilt über das Java Message Queue System (JMS) an andere Bausteine gekoppelt. Die Modellbeschreibung und der Generator erlauben die Einbeziehung weitgehend beliebiger Technologien, insbesondere lokale wie verteilte.

```
<gencomponent>
<classname name="HexConverter"/>
<description>converts from hexadecimal to decimal</description>
<feature name="number system" value="hexadecimal"/>
</gencomponent>
<componentfeatures>
<corbacomponent>
  <repositoryid/>
  <transaction use="not-supported"/>
  <threading policy="serialize"/>
  <configurationcomplete set="true"/>
  <componentfeatures name="" repid= "F1">
    <ports>
      <emits emitsname="NumberCalculated" eventtype="JMS Event"
        eventname="NumberCalculated"/>
      <emits emitsname="NumberChanged" eventtype="JMS Event"
        eventname="NumberChanged"/>
      <consumes consumesname="NumberCalculated" eventtype="JMS Event"
        eventname="NumberCalculated"/>
      <consumes consumesname="NumberChanged" eventtype="JMS Event"
        eventname="NumberChanged"/>
    </ports>
  </componentfeatures>
</corbacomponent>
</componentfeatures>

<semBEType typename = "NumberChanged">
  <feature name = "NUMBER_CHANGED" datatype = "tuple_of_1" >
    <feature name = "NUMBER" datatype = "String" />
  </feature>
</semBEType>

<syntMessageType typename="NumberChanged">
  <OperationTypes>
    <OperationType typename="numberChanged">
      <parameter>
        <datatype type="NumberChangedEvent"></datatype>
      </parameter>
      <returnvalue></returnvalue>
    </OperationType>
  </OperationTypes>
  <CommunicationType value="Synchron"></CommunicationType>
  <CommunicationModelType value="MessageQueueModel">
  </CommunicationModelType>
</syntMessageType>
```

Abbildung 4. Illustration der XML-Repräsentationen des Typmodells

Die exakt definierte Typisierung von Komponenten stellt zudem eine ausgezeichnete Grundlage zur zukünftigen Realisierung von Qualitäts- und Verifikationskriterien dar, da gegen die entsprechenden Typspezifikationen *getestet* werden kann.

4.1 Konzeption des Typmodells

Das Typmodell ist ebenfalls ein Metamodell, um eine Vielzahl konkreter Typsysteme für Komponenten abbilden zu können. Der Typ einer Komponente ist dabei als eine in drei Ebenen untergliederte Baumstruktur repräsentiert (vgl. Abb. 5). Er ist definiert über eine Anzahl von Mengen sogenannter „Business Events" (BEs). Die Wahl dieser Bezeichnung rührt aus der gewünschten Anwendungsnähe der Komponentensicht her und stellt keine Einschränkung der Allgemeinheit des Typmodells dar.

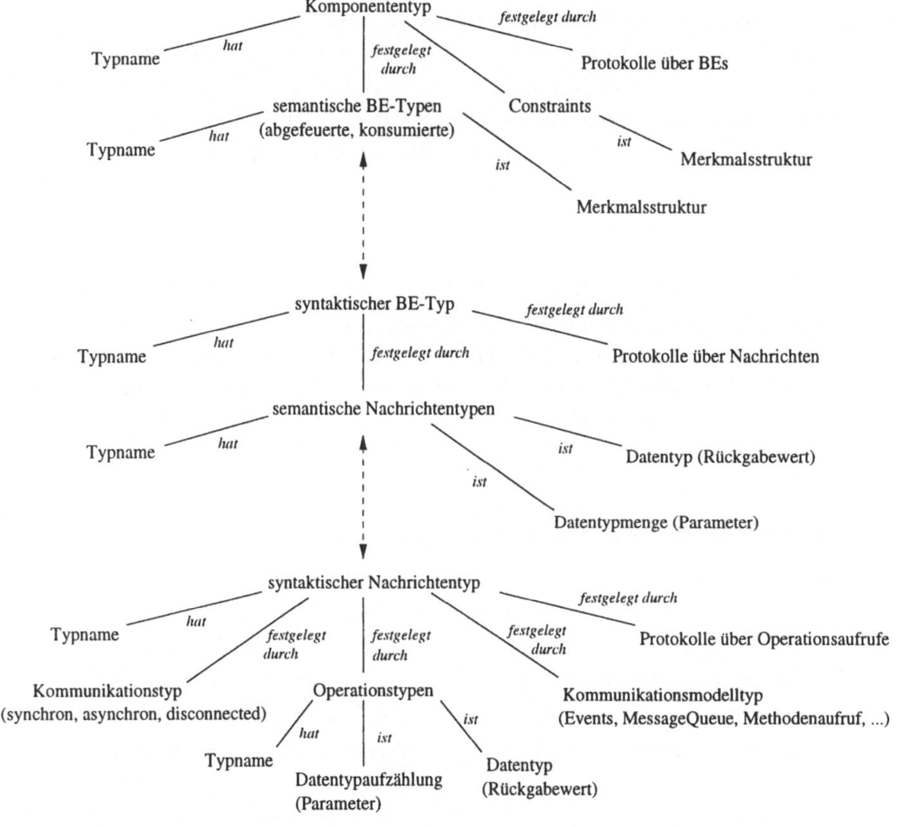

Abbildung 5. 3-stufiges Typmodell

Das Typmodell ist damit *interaktionsorientiert*, d.h. wir gehen davon aus, dass die an der Oberfläche einer Komponente beobachtbaren Vorgänge, die Komponente vollständig definieren und im Rahmen einer Anwendungsdomäne Klassen von Komponenten gebildet werden können, die alle eben jene Vorgänge unterstützen. Wir bezeichnen daher diese Ebene des Typmodells auch als *semantische* Ebene. Diese Business Event Sicht korrespondiert zugleich mit den UML (2.0) Konzepten „Kollaboration" und „Aktivität" und ist in der Vorgehensweise z.B auch vergleichbar mit der „Typbildung" in Smalltalk in Form sogenannter Nachrichtenprotokolle. Ebenso geht sie auf natürliche Weise konform zu „Business Component" -Konzepten [14].

Die BEs selbst drücken also zunächst nur eine Semantik im Sinne einer gewählten Anwendungsdomäne aus, bedürfen zu ihrer Materialisation jedoch einer Syntax, die in Form der zweiten Ebene - der Nachrichtenebene - definiert ist. Jedes Business Event setzt sich aus einer Menge von Nachrichten zusammen, deren Austausch zwischen Kollaborationspartnern zur Realisierung der gewünschten Anwendungssemantik führt. Die Konkretisierung der Nachrichten erfolgt dann in Ebene drei in Form von Operationstypen, die letztlich der klassischen signaturbasierten Schnittstellenbeschreibung gleicht, allerdings nicht auf ein spezifisches Kommunikations- oder Technologiemodell festgelegt ist.

Alle drei Ebenen spezifizieren ihre jeweiligen Konstrukte zum einen strukturell über Merkmalsstrukturen, zum anderen verhaltensmäßig über als deterministische endliche Automaten (DEAs) repräsentierte Protokolle, um ein semantisch reiches Modell zu erhalten. Die Repräsentation als DEAs ist ausreichend ausdrucksstark, da das zu Grunde gelegte Komponentenmodell Nebenläufigkeit *innerhalb einer* Schnittstelle ausschliesst. Die Merkmalsstrukturen selbst können dabei auch Richtlinien in Form sogenannter Policies repräsentieren, die dann Randbedingungen über die Eigenschaften bzw. das Verhalten festlegen können. Wir verwenden hier nicht die Object Constraint Language (OCL) wie sie etwa die Catalysis-Notation zur semantischen Absicherung von Komponenten vorsieht, da unser eigener Policy-Formalismus [15] eine leichtere automatische Verarbeitung und insbesondere die Unifikation mehrerer Randbedingungen erlaubt, was wir für eine konsistenzerhaltende Komposition während der Generierung ausnutzen.

4.2 Typarten und -beziehungen

Die Einteilung der Typrepräsentation in mehrere Ebenen erlaubt zum einen getrennte Vergleiche syntaktischer und semantischer Natur und damit jeweils die Betrachtung nur einer problembezogenen Informationsmenge („Tun zwei Komponenten das gleiche?", „Passen ihre Kommunikationsmodelle zueinander?", etc.), zum anderen bildet sie die Grundlage für die Definition flexibler Typrelationen, indem alle drei Ebenen jeweils mehr oder weniger vollständig berücksichtigt werden.

So sprechen wir zunächst von verschiedenen Typarten. Typart-1 kennzeichnet dabei zunächst Typen für die der klassische Subtypbegriff einhergeht mit der Substitutionsfähigkeit des Supertypen durch den Subtyp. Zur Vermeidung von Vererbungsanomalien modellieren wir allerdings dabei explizit getrennt reduzierte Subtypen und erweiterte Subtypen - erweiterte Subtypen tragen im Falle der Substitution das Risiko semantischer Unverträglichkeiten und das Typmanagement generiert entsprechende Hinweise (vgl. etwa auch „join" vs. „subtype" in [7]).

Typart-2 bezeichnen wir als Verhaltenstyp. Er erlaubt eine (Unter-) Klassifikation von Komponenten die in einer Typart-1 Beziehung stehen durch Kennzeichnung unterschiedlichen Verhaltens. Hierzu wird auf die abgelegten Protokollspezifikationen und Constraints zurückgegriffen. Die Typart-3 schließlich wird als technischer Typ bezeichnet und kennzeichnet ansonsten gleiche Typen durch Unterscheidung ihrer Operationstypen und Kommunikationsmodelle. Diese Typarten können dann in verschiedene Beziehungen zueinander stehen, die jeweils das Auswertungsergebnis bei einer Kompatibilitäts- oder einer Konformitätsprüfung bestimmen.

Abbildung 6 zeigt exemplarisch das sich ergebende Assoziationsgeflecht[2] des Typmanagers am Beispiel einer ableitbaren Subtypbeziehung zwischen einer „Sparkassen" - und einer „Bank" -Komponente.

4.3 Typmanagement

Der praktische Einsatz des Typmodells erfolgt über eine als Typmanager bezeichnete Komponente, die die Registrierung entsprechender Komponententypen erlaubt. Die vom Typmanager bereitgestellten Funktionen gliedern sich dabei grob in vier Kategorien: Die eigentlichen Typvergleiche, das Anzeigen der Wissensbasis (z.B. manuelle Suche, Browsing), die (automatische) Suche nach bestimmten Komponententypen, sowie die Verwaltung von Domänen, da die Wissenbasis selbst (hierarchisch) in Domänen separiert ist gemäß der Gültigkeit (Sinnhaftigkeit) einzelner Komponententypen für bestimmte Anwendungsdomänen. Abbildung 7 illustriert die als Typexplorer bezeichnete Benutzeroberfläche des Typmanagers während eines Vergleichs der schon oben dargestellten Bank-, Sparkassen- und Kundentypen.

Adaption und Rollen Eine bemerkenswerte Eigenschaft des Typmanagers ist die Fähigkeit zur Bereitstellung von Komponentenadaptern, im Falle der Kopplung zunächst inkompatibler Komponenten. Hierzu können einerseits explizit als Adapter gekennzeichnete manuell erstellte Komponenten registriert werden, die dann bei Bedarf automatisch korrekt zugeordnet und verwendet werden. Andererseits ist der Typmanager in der Lage automatisch Adapter für alle syntaktischen Ebenen der Typhierarchie zu generieren. Hierfür haben wir einen Adaptionsalgorithmus in Anlehnung an [16] implementiert. Die für diesen notwendigen Äquivalenzregeln leitet der Typmanager aus dem Assoziationsgeflecht der zu adaptierenden Komponenten ab. Die resultierenden Adaptertypen sind konzeptuell zunächst technologieunabhängig; ihre konkreten Instanzen sind dann allerdings jeweils spezifisch für eine konkrete Komponententechnologie (z.Z. für JavaBean- und COM-Komponenten).

Der Einsatz solcher Adapter geht auf unsere Arbeiten [8] zurück (dort als Interzeptoren bezeichnet) und harmoniert mit der heutigen Forderung der Komponentendiskussion nach aktiven Konnektoren [7,12] und subjektivistischen -

---

[2] Die entsprechende Struktur ist analog zu den *TopicMaps* des Standard ISO/IEC 13250:1999.

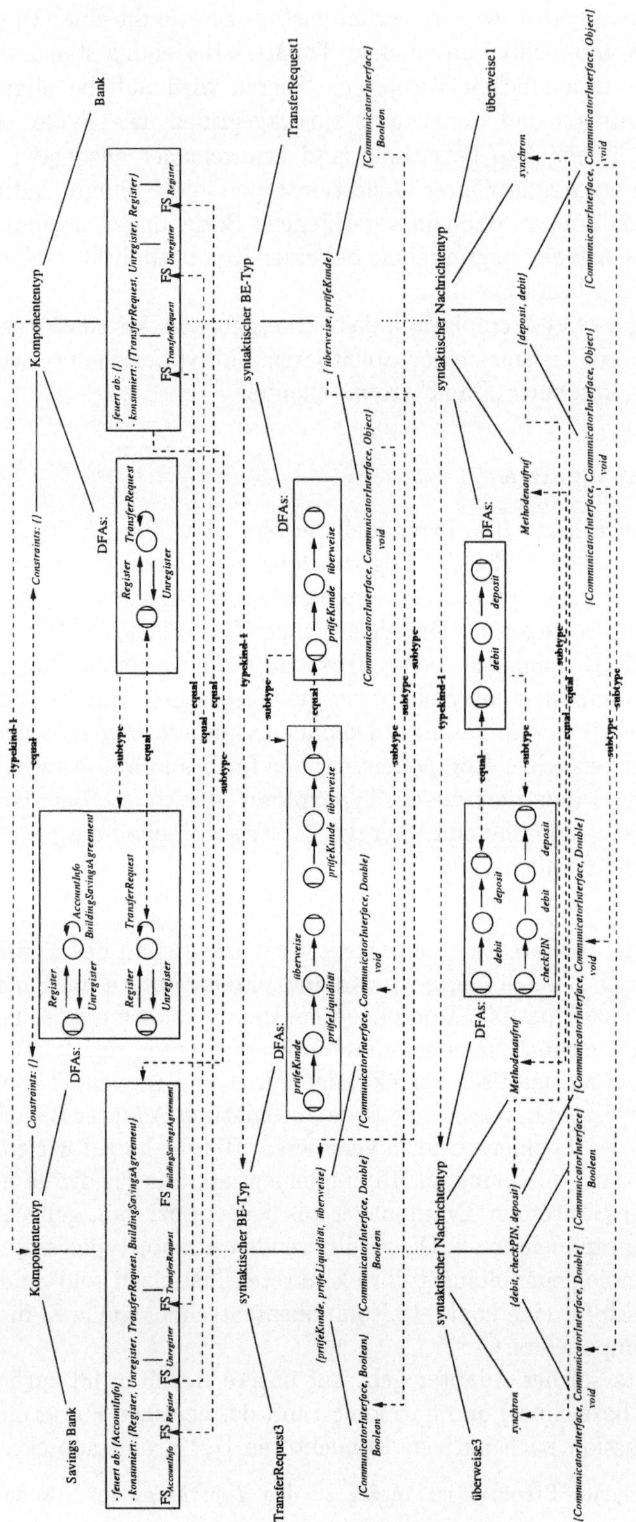

Abbildung 6. Assoziationsgeflecht einer Subtypbeziehung im Typmanager

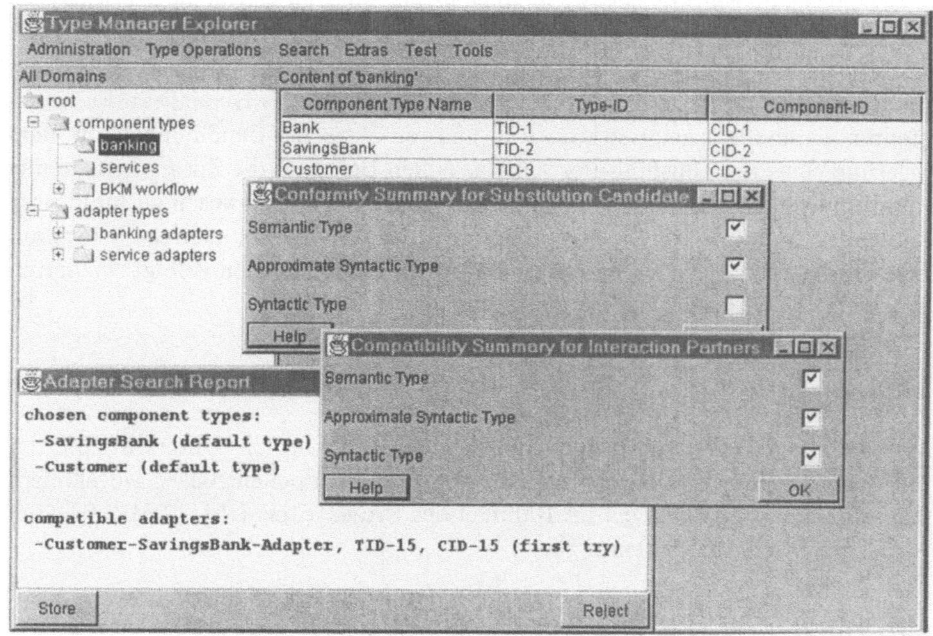

Abbildung 7. Interaktive Benutzung des Typmanagers

d.h. rollen- und situationsbezogen dynamisch generierten - Schnittstellen [6].
Der Bedeutung bzw. Mächtigkeit von Rollen- bzw. Personality-Konzepten [4]
für die Modellierung wird zunehmend Aufmerksamkeit zuteil, da sie zu kompakteren, flexibleren und wiederverwendbareren Modellen führen. Wir tragen diesem
Umstand in unserem Typmodell durch die explizite Definition von Rollen Rechnung: Die oberste Ebene des Typmodells kann mehr als eine semantische Spezifikation umfassen. Im Ergebnis kann eine Komponente eines solches Typ dann
verschiedene Rollen durch die Kennzeichnung der jeweils gültigen semantischen
Spezifikation annehmen bzw. in ihnen in der Anwendungsdomäne auftreten.

5 Resümee und Ausblick

Wir haben in diesem Beitrag einige Aspekte der Konzeption und Implementation einer Umgebung zur Etablierung einer Generativen Softwarekonstruktion
aus vorgefertigten Softwarekomponenten vorgestellt. Herzstück des generativen
Prozesses ist dabei der - konstruktive - Test der Modelle zur Verfügung stehender Einzelbausteine gegen ein zugehöriges Architekurmodell, dessen Ausdrucksmittel direkt zur Spezifikation einer Anwendungsarchitektur verwendet werden.
Das dabei verwendete Typ-Metamodell setzt auf den MOF-Beschreibungen des
„CORBA Component Models" auf, erweitert dieses jedoch um exakt definierte,
semantisch reiche Typbeziehungen, um den Anforderungen einer automatischen
Verarbeitung durch einen Generator gerecht zu werden.

Neben dem Einsatz des Typmanagements im Rahmen einer Softwarekonstruktion, arbeiten wir derzeit an dessen Integration mit einem erweiterten JINI-Lookup-Service (LUS), um auch auf der Ebene systemnaher Dienste komplexere Such- und Auswahlstrategien realisieren zu können. Die Universialität des vorgestellten Typmodells zeigt sich auch in unseren aktuellen Bemühungen zur Realisierung eines E-Publishing-Portals, das einem Benutzer die Zusammenstellung unterschiedlicher Anwendungsdienste aus dem Publikationswesen zu funktionalen Ketten im Sinne von Gesamtprozessen unter Beteiligung mehrerer Dienstanbieter ermöglicht. Die dafür notwendige Dienstklassifikation erfolgt wiederum mit Hilfe des vorgestellten Typmanagements.

Danksagung

Wir danken der Deutschen Forschungsgemeinschaft für die Unterstützung der hier vorgestellten Arbeiten zum „Basic Research Component-based Develoment Environment" (BARCODE) im Rahmen des Projekttitels DFG 1061-2 („Dynamically Configurable Software").

Literatur

1. http://www.sei.cmu.edu/domain-engineering.
2. http://www.sei.cmu.edu/domain-engineering/FODA_bib_ref.html.
3. http://www.omg.org: Dokument orbos/99-07-01.
4. http://www.ccs.neu.edu/home/lblando/personalities.
5. B. Carpenter. *The logic of typed feature structures*. Cambridge Univ. Press, 1992.
6. D. Batory. http://www.cs.utexas.edu/users/schwartz.
7. D.F. D'Souza and A.C. Wills. *Objects, Components, and Frameworks with UML*. Addison Wesley, 1999.
8. F. Griffel, K. Müller–Jones, and W. Lamersdorf. Komponentenbasierte Entwicklung interoperabler Software auf heterogenen Middleware–Plattformen. In H. C. Mayr, editor, *Beherrschung von Informationssystemen, Tagungsband der Informatik'96*, number 88 in Schriftenreihe der Österreichischen Computer Gesellschaft, pages 327–342. R. Oldenbourg, 1996.
9. W. Harrison and H. Ossher. http://www.research.ibm.com/sop.
10. K. Czarnecki and U.W. Eisenecker. *Generative Programming – Methods, Tools, and Applications*. Addison Wesley, 2000.
11. G. Kiczales. http://www.parc.xerox.com/csl/projects/aop.
12. K. Lieberherr. http://www.ccs.neu.edu/research/demeter.
13. O. Nierstrasz and D. Tsichritzis, editors. *Object–Oriented Software Composition*. The Object–Oriented Series. Prentice–Hall International Ltd., 1995.
14. P. Herzum and O. Sims. *Business Component Factory*. Wiley, 2000.
15. M. T. Tu, F. Griffel, M. Merz, and W. Lamersdorf. Generic Policy Management for Open Service Markets. In H. König, K. Geihs, and T. Preuß, editors, *Distributed Applications and Interoperable Systems, DAIS'97 Cottbus, Germany*, pages 211–222. IFIP, Chapman & Hall, Oktober 1997.
16. D. M. Yellin and R. E. Strom. Collaboration Specifications and Component Adaptors. Forschungsbericht RC 20054 (88710) 5/4/97, T.J. Watson Research Center, Mai 1995.

Eingeladener Vortrag III:

M. Lübbehusen; smapCo GmbH

Der Wireless Application Service Provider: „Chance im m-commerce"

Dr. Michael Lübbehusen

smapCo - smart mobile applications Company GmbH
✉ Harburger Schloßstrasse 6-12, 21079 Hamburg,
☎ 040/766 29-3003, 💻 040/76629-3033
www.smapco.com

Die Anzahl der Mobilfunkteilnehmer wird allein in Deutschland auf 40 Millionen Teilnehmer bis Ende 2000 steigen.. Die Penetration mit WAP-fähigen Handys wird aufgrund der dynamischen Marktentwicklung und der hohen Ersatzbeschaffungsrate (alle zwei Jahre ein neues Handy) schnell auf ca. 80% anwachsen: Das sind 35 Millionen WAP-Handys Ende 2003 in Deutschland bzw. weit über 100 Millionen in Europa.

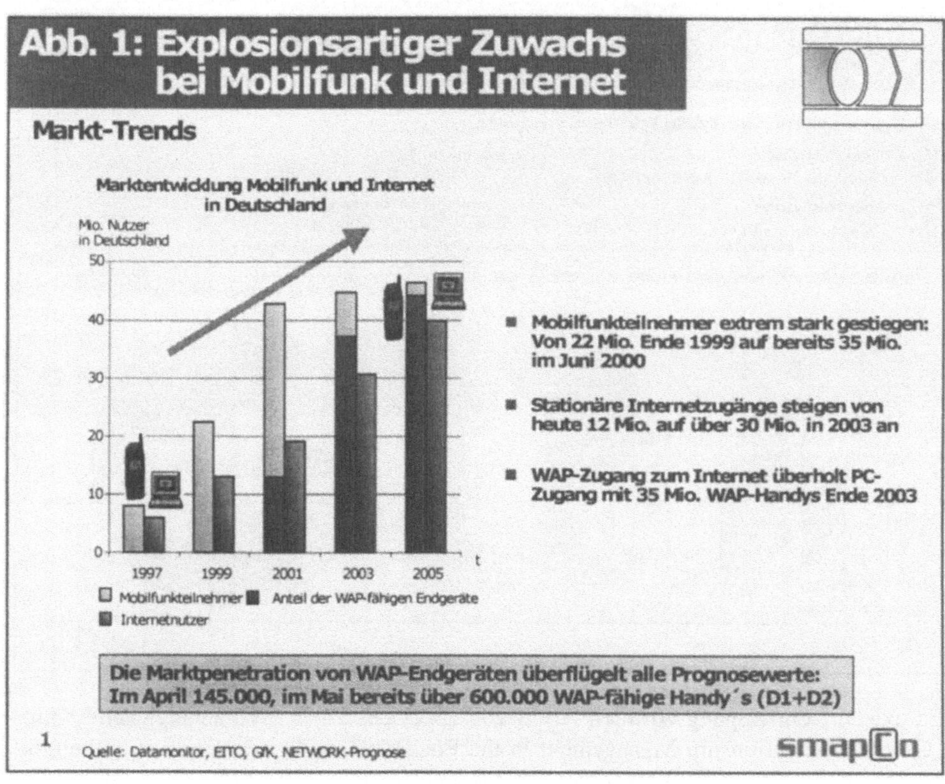

Aktuelle Studien zeigen:

Die Marktpenetration von WAP-Endgeräten überflügelt bereits heute alle Prognosewerte: Im April 145.000, im Mai bereits über 600.000 WAP-fähige Handys und 2,8 Millionen im September 2000 (D1+D2) [Abb.1].

Die aktuellen Nutzungszahlen bleiben noch etwas hinter den Erwartungen zurück. Viele Services entsprechen hinsichtlich Nutzen und Bedienung noch nicht den Erwartungen der Nutzer - doch das ist eine lösbare Aufgabe.

Der stationäre Internetzugang über den PC wird im selben Zeitraum von 12 Millionen auf ungefähr 30 Millionen steigen (Deutschland). Dabei werden Internet und Mobilfunk zum „mobilen Internet" zusammenwachsen.

Die Wachstumsdynamik beider Märkte ist hoch, damit entsteht eine gegenseitige Stimulation, die Technologie wird zum Standard im Massenmarkt. Erfahrung und Akzeptanz des Internets sind bereits vorhanden, das fördert die schnelle Penetration von mobilen Services.

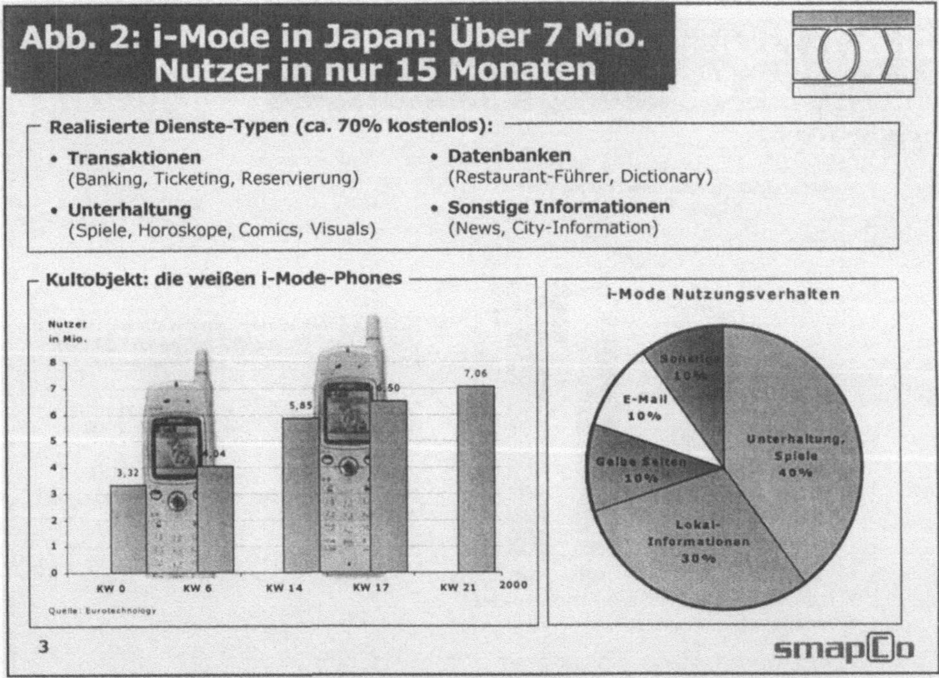

Es existiert ein Zugang zu allen Arten von „Services 24 h anytime/anywhere", d.h. „Customer-Relationship Management in the Pocket". Der digitale Content ist bereits vorhanden. Das Mobile Internet baut auf ein umfassendes Internet-Angebot auf.

Der Blick nach Japan verdeutlicht das Potential und die Dynamik von mobilen Services:

I-Mode in Japan (technisch verwandt mit GPRS) konnte über 7 Millionen Nutzer in nur 15 Monaten gewinnen [Abb. 2].

Schwerpunkt der Dienstenutzung sind Unterhaltung/Spiele und lokale Informations- und Transaktionsdienste.

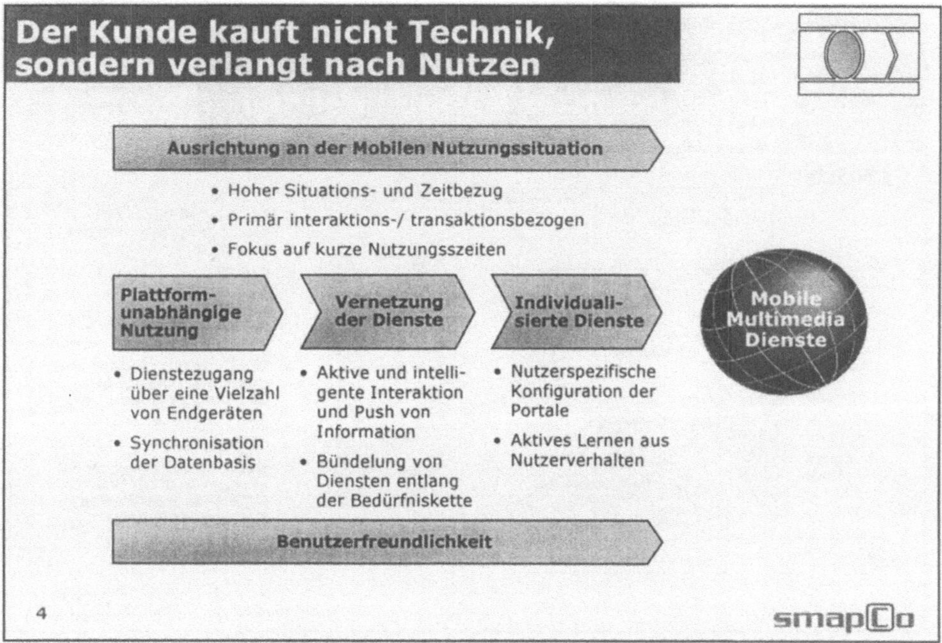

Der Schlüssel zum Erfolg von mobilen Services liegt in einem Dienstkonzept - welches sich an den Kundenbedürfnissen in der mobilen Nutzungssituation ausrichtet, d.h. neben der allgemeinen „Benutzerfreundlichkeit", d.h. zum Beispiel auch schneller Zugang zu den Services, fordern mobile Nutzer:

<u>Einen hohen Situations- und Zeitbezug der Applikation</u>

„Location based Services", also Serviceangebote rund um einen bestimmten Standort (Restaurantfinder, Sonderangebote etc.) haben einen hohen Situationsbezug - sie sind nur an diesem Standort relevant.

Andererseits die aktive Benachrichtigung, z.B. wenn eine Aktie unter einen bestimmten Kurs fällt oder Situations- und Zeitbezug bestimmen den primären Nutzen eines mobilen Serviceangebotes.

<u>Interaktions- bzw. transaktionsbezogene Dienste</u>

Die reine Information genügt nicht - erst Interaktion und Transaktion lösen ein Problem.

<u>Kurze Nutzungszeiten und schnellen Zugang,</u> um schnell und einfach zum gewünschten Ergebnis zu kommen - schon allein um Gebühren zu sparen.

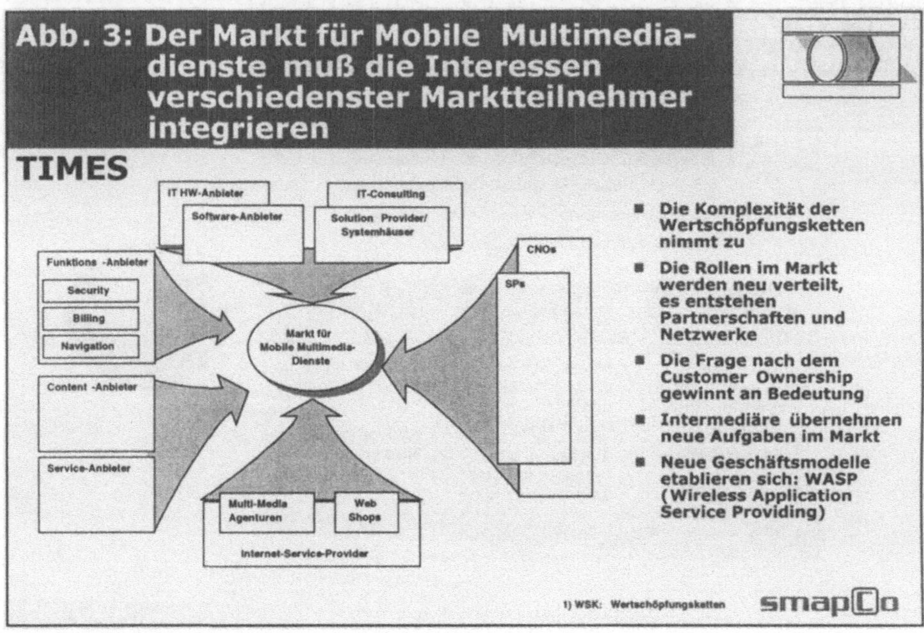

Die Entwicklung von mobilen Multimedia Services wird dazu führen, daß Grenzen zwischen Märkten weiter verwischen und sich Wettbewerbsumfeld und Wertschöpfungsketten entscheidend verändern.

Die Komplexität der Leistungserstellung nimmt dramatisch zu und erfordert neue Kompetenzen. Zur erfolgreichen Vermarktung von mobilen Services müssen die Leistungen verschiedenster Marktteilnehmer mit unterschiedlichen Interessen integriert werden: Content, Funktionalität, Betrieb und Distribution über alle Netze. Interessenskonflikte bestehen primär zwischen Content-/Serviceanbieter und Netzbetreibern. Die Content-/Serviceanbieter streben nach universeller Verfügbarkeit über alle Netze, in gleicher Qualität und zu gleichen Nutzungsbedingungen. Die Netzbetreiber streben nach Exklusivität und Neukunden im Rennen um die Marktführerschaft [Abb.3].

Intermediäre - also Vermittler können hier neue Aufgaben übernehmen und Interessen bündeln. Ein neues Geschäftsmodell mit großem Erfolgspotential ist „Wireless Application Service Providing" (WASP) [Abb.4].

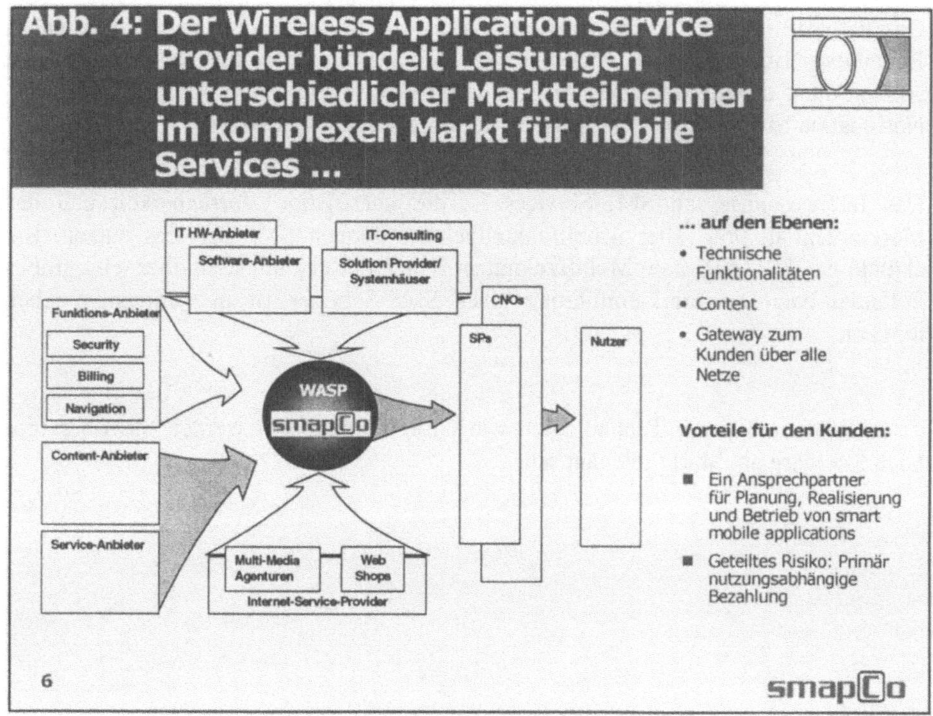

WASP's bündeln die Leistungen untschiedlicher Marktteilnehmer im komplexen Markt für mobile Services und bieten:

- Outsourcing von komplexer und teurer Technologie

- hochperformanten 24 Stunden x 7 Tage Betrieb

- skalierbare „State-of-the-Art" Technologie und Know-how

- ein „Gateway" für Kunden über alle Mobilfunknetze

- kalkulierbare Kosten ohne Kapitalbindung

- komplementäre Dienste und Services

- „One-step-shopping" für Planung, Realisierung und Betrieb

Mit SMS und WAP beginnt der m-commerce schon heute:

Über eine Milliarde versendete SMS/Monat und mehr als 3.000 WAP Dienste (Deutschland) sprechen für sich.

Noch überwiegt die „Mail-Funktionalität" mit 90% aller SMS-Nachrichten - also der Versand einer Kurznachricht (max. 160 Zeichen) an einen Freund oder Geschäftspartner. Doch automatisierte Informationsdienste gewinnen schneller an Bedeutung. Bereits in den nächsten 6-12 Monaten rechnen die Netzbetreiber mit einem Anteil an alle SMS-Nachrichten von ca. 30%. Beispiele hierfür sind „SMS-Notification bzw. Information Services" für e-mail oder Börsenkurse.

Das Interessanteste an SMS-Services ist die kurzfristige Verfügbarkeit und das Marktpotential: 96% aller Mobilfunkteilnehmer können SMS-Services nutzen. Bei aktuell ca. 35 Millionen Mobilfunknutzern in Deutschland stellt dies ein großes Potential dar. Die Markteinführung eines SMS-Services ist in wenigen Wochen möglich.

Trotz WAP und neuer Technologien wie GPRS und UMTS werden SMS-Services noch 3-5 Jahre am Markt relevant sein.

Session 11:

Dienstgüte

Layer4+ Supported Class of Service

Till Harbaum[1], Heinrich J. Stüttgen[2], and Martina Zitterbart[1]

[1] Institute of Operating Systems and Computer Networks
Technical University of Braunschweig, Germany
[2] Network Product Development Laboratories Heidelberg
NEC Europe Ltd.

Abstract. Class of Service (CoS) support within the Internet is currently discussed and may become reality in the near future. Current applications usually lack the ability to articulate their service demands in order to make use these new services. Integrating support for such applications into the network is desirable and would allow these applications to coexist with future service-aware applications.

The router based Layer 4+ (L4+) approach for flow detection and classification presented in this paper addresses this issue. Together with DiffServ capable routers, seamless Class of Service integration for existing applications (L4+ CoS) can be achieved without the introduction of new end-to-end signaling protocols.

1 Introduction

The increasing popularity of the Internet during the last years is largely due to one single application, namely the World Wide Web. Among other effects, it has introduced the Internet into everyday's life. This led to a dramatic growth in the number of users in the Internet. Additionally, it is expected that many devices (e.g., cameras and refrigerators) will be Internet-capable in the near future and, thus, billions of users/devices will need to be served on the Internet [1]. This also affects the diversity of networked applications with all kinds of different requirements, for example, considering bandwidth, delay or delay jitter experienced in the network.

Due to the current dominance of the World Wide Web, HTTP traffic plays a dominant role in today's Internet. For applications, such as real-time audio and video, Class of Service (CoS) [2] support within the network is needed. The current Internet and the majority of applications based on it do not provide any significant support of Class of Service. In order to improve this situation, several recent developments focus on the integration of CoS on the existing Internet (e.g., RSVP [3], DiffServ [4]). However, this implies, that either the application communicate their CoS requirements to the network or the network discovers the requirements itself. The latter has the advantage that no changes to the applications are required. Layer 4+ Classification presented in this paper is an example for such an approach.

Typically, CoS support requires the extension of existing applications [5] or the development of new applications [6] to take advantage of the new services.

A video conferencing tool, for example, may wish to receive a specific service for each one of the involved data streams (e.g., audio, audio, chat, whiteboard).

The approach of Layer 4+ (L4+) Classification presented in this paper migrates the responsibility to articulate serivice demands from end systems and applications to the edge devices connecting them to the wide area network (cf., Figure 1).

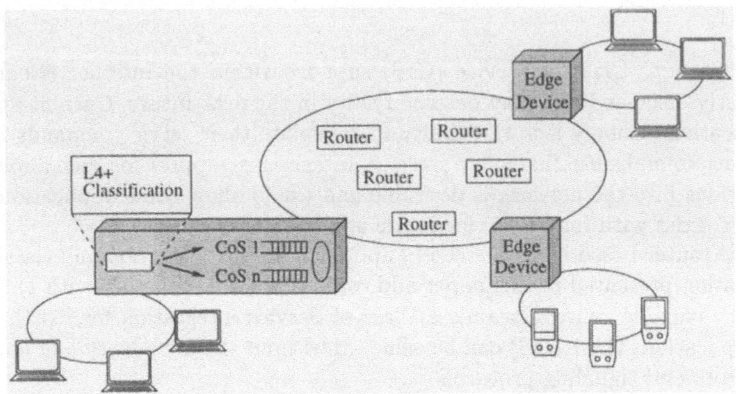

Fig. 1. Edge devices with Layer 4+ Classification

In opposite to similar approaches, which are limited to transport layer information [7], the presented L4+ Classification makes use of all layers including the application layer, i.e., multiple fields are considered for classification. This allows for flexible integration of existing applications (e.g., conferencing tools like the MBone tools, as well as popular web browsers etc.) into a CoS supporting network. Unlike proprietary solutions [8], this approach can be seamlessly integrated into DiffServ networks that are currently under development. The approach, however, is not limited to DiffServ networks. It could also be used in conjunction with ATM, Integrated Services, MPLS and the like.

1.1 Related Work

A very simple and straight forward usage of information derived from the transport layer is the establishment of firewalls on a per application basis. Based on the UDP/TCP port numbers forwarding of specific data streams is blocked [9].

More advanced examples of the usage of layer 4 information within routers are load balancing in server farms [10] and automatic redirection in order to access server mirrors or data caches [11]. The basic idea behind these applications is to allow the router to detect specific application requests and to ignore or modify the real destination address in order to redirect the request to some other machine. The goal is to redirect the access to a server with lower load or a server that is located closer to the client or that provides faster access than the server originally addressed.

1.2   Outline

The reminder of this paper is structured as follows. Section 2 outlines L4+ CoS support, the HTTP and RTP flow detection algorithms are presented in section 3. Results with a prototype implementation based on DiffServ are presented in section 4. Section 5 concludes the paper.

2   Layer 4+ Class of Service

Within this section, the main structure of our L4+ Class of Service (L4+ CoS) is outlined. Subsequent sections focus in detail on some selected issues.

L4+ CoS is, for example, placed on the edge device between the LAN and the DiffServ-based backbone network. It is part of the performance critical forwarding engine of an IP router, i.e., it is involved in the data path through the router and, thus, has to be executed on a per packet basis. L4+ CoS can be subdivided into three components (cf., Figure 2): the L4+ Classifier, the CoS mapper and the CoS (Differentiated Services).

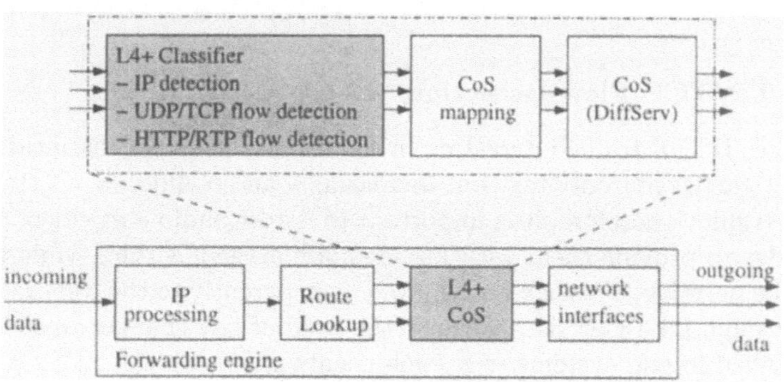

Fig. 2. L4+ Class of Service

The L4+ Classifier analyzes the traffic flowing through the edge device and extracts information from the transport and application layer. This is translated by the CoS mapper into classifications used by the CoS. In order to do so, the L4+ Classifier evaluates the payload fields of the IP packets (layer 4 and above), detects the payload type carried in transport layer packets (e.g., H.261 encoded RTP video or MPEG-based HTTP video) and extracts relevant information from these data (including protocol headers). This way, UDP and TCP flows as well as HTTP and RTP flows can be detected. Once a flow has been detected, the corresponding information is introduced in the classification table and can be used for subsequent packets flowing through the L4+ Classifier. This reduces the amount of L4+ Classification needed for packets belonging to already detected flows. Moreover, since edge devices typically handle a moderate number of data streams this does not lead to very high storage requirements.

The CoS mapper follows the L4+ Classifier. Based on the data provided by the L4+ Classifier, it initiates the setup of proper CoS for the corresponding data stream. The CoS mapper translates the information received from the classifier to the parameters needed by the CoS. The CoS mapper implements an interface between the content specific output of the L4+ Classifier and the CoS specific input to the CoS.

The CoS is independent from the L4+ Classifier and may, e.g., be a DiffServ implementation.

3 Flow Detection

As depicted in figure 2, the major task of the L4+ Classifier is the detection of different types of data flows. This subsection outlines two different types of L4+ flow detection that have been investigated in our approach: HTTP/TCP flow detection and RTP/UDP flow detection. These two examples are somewhat representative for the problems involved in application layer flow detection because they are connection-oriented and connectionless. Moreover, the way information is made available to the L4+ Classifier differs significantly in both cases.

3.1 HTTP/TCP Flow Detection

What makes HTTP traffic interesting in the context of L4+ Classification is the fact that it carries not only text but increasingly audio and video is transmitted as HTTP traffic. Therefore, it is important to detect audio and video, for example, in order to provide them with an adequate class of service while travelling through the network. This can be achieved transparently to the web-based applications through L4+ CoS, i.e., without the need of any changes to the software being installed in end systems (e.g., web clients and servers).

TCP Flow Detection Although the interest is on the detection and classification of HTTP flows, TCP flow detection requires some attention in this context as well. The basic question that needs to be raised is: how exact does the classification need to be? Our approach is to correctly detect most of the HTTP flows, but to accept that some of them may not be detected. The reasons for this decision will be explained in the following.

The first issue that needs to be considered here is the precise detection of a TCP connection. In order to support the re-establishment of TCP connections and the re-usage of port numbers additional fields in the TCP header are analysed. This way information about changes in the connection state (e.g., SYN, FIN) is extracted and, e.g., if a connection is terminated, the corresponding entry can be removed from the classification table. The additional overhead involved is neglectable.

The second issue of interest relates to segmentation and reassembly being part of TCP as well as of IP. Basically, IP reassembly would be needed as well as TCP data buffering of up to 64 kBytes per data flow. Since the overhead of such a "perfect" detection is considered as being very high, it was not decided to be used in our L4+ Classifier. Measurements have shown, that without reassembly, a detection probability of over 99% was achieved.

HTTP Flow Detection Once a TCP flow is detected with one of the above mentioned alternatives and the payload is extracted, the edge device will scan the TCP payload for HTTP header fields. The HTTP header is based on human readable text and contains fields with fixed length and position as well as optional tags with variable length and positions. The string search used in the L4+ Classifier is based on the Boyer-Moore algorithm [15].

The information about the length of the HTTP payload derived from the header (Content-Length) is used to skip the HTTP payload. Because HTTP 1.1 allows several subsequent HTTP transfers within one TCP connection and a detected HTTP flow may still be analyzed to detect additional HTTP headers of subsequent HTTP connections on the same port. If an HTTP content-length field was detected within the HTTP header analysis, the value is extracted and used to skip the analysis of the subsequent payload and to restart the flow detection after the complete HTTP payload has been transferred.

Once a flow is known to not contain HTTP information, the connection will be marked as non-HTTP-traffic and TCP payload classification for the according TCP address/port pair will be suspended until the connection has been closed and/or re-opened. Once a connection is established, it is used by the same application as long as the connection exists. At the time an application is closed, all its connections are closed, too.

The classification table holds the entries that provide the information about detected flows and their CoS provision. Entries are removed whenever the end of a transmission is detected (e.g., end of TCP transmission was detected by a set FIN bit in the TCP header). If a TCP connection breaks or if a UDP data transfer ends, this is not explicitly indicated at transport level. Therefore, a timeout mechanism in the classifier removes unused entries after a pre-defined time interval (currently two minutes) in order to keep the table size small. Timeouts on data flows that are still used are not critical, since the arrival of further data will automatically cause a new entry to be created. In summary, a mixture of soft-state and hard-state concepts is applied for classification table management.

3.2 RTP/UDP Flow Detection

While HTTP is an example for a currently very popular request/response protocol, with upcoming real time video and audio applications connectionless streaming protocols may become increasingly important. Currently, RTP is typically used for audio and video transmission on the Internet, for example, for audio and video transport with the MBone tools [16]. RTP is based on the connectionless transport protocol UDP. L4+ Classification of RTP flows is somewhat troublesome. RTP does not use a standardized protocol type nor does it use well-known ports. Therefore, it is not sufficient to investigate UDP information only in order to detect an RTP flow. The payload needs to be analyzed as well. RTP flow detection is based on the algorithm published in [17].

A single RTP header does not provide enough information for a successful classification. Basically, the version field (must be set to 2), the payload field (a limited number of valid entries) and the sequence number can be used at RTP level. Therefore, a number of subsequent UDP packets need to be considered. The sequence number of the RTP header is included into the classification for proper flow detection. The probability of correctly detecting such a flow depends on the number of packets checked.

Since RTP is connectionless, no connection setup messages or termination messages are sent. Therefore, it is impossible for the L4+ Classifier to precisely detect the termination and re-establishment of subsequent application level flows that use the same UDP port. However, RTP content is also checked for the purpose of flow detection. Thus, if a terminated RTP flow is instantly replaced by a different RTP stream carrying the same type of content, the L4+ Classifier can not recognize this. It will simply resynchronize on the new sequence numbers and serve the new RTP stream with the same class of service as the previous one. Typically, this would also happen, if the change in flows could be detected and, thus, is not considered as drawback since both are carrying the same type of content. In case the type of content of the new RTP flow differs from that of the old RTP flow, this will be detected by the L4+ Classifier and a re-classification regarding CoS will take place.

4   Experimental Results

Based on the prototype implementation, a testbed has been established in our network laboratory and various experiments and measurements have been conducted. One scenario that has been setup in the testbed is depicted in figure 3. A 2 Mbit/s WaveLAN [19] was integrated as bottleneck link between two Ethernet networks. Edge devices that are enhanced with L4+ CoS were placed at the border of the wireless network. An HTTP server (apache) and an RTP server (rtpplay) were further integrated into the testbed in order to provide real life traffic patterns. Servers and receivers were separated by the wireless network.

4.1   L4+ CoS Operation

An interesting application for L4+ CoS is the problem of UDP/TCP suppression. This problem exists due to TCPs ability to adopt to network congestion and the possibility to flood the net with UDP data. The following example will show how

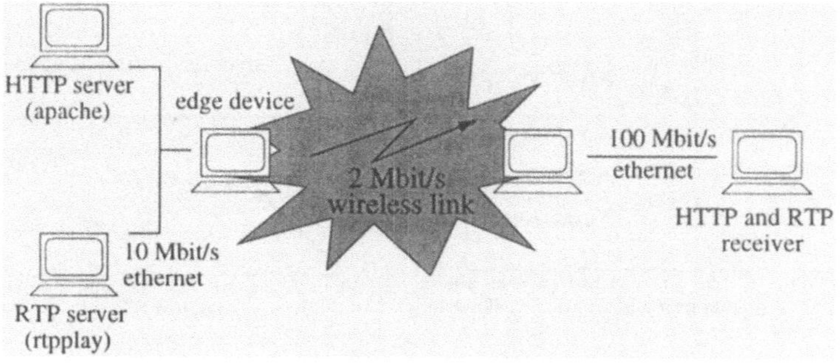

Fig. 3. DiffServ-based testbed with L4+ CoS

L4+ CoS can be used to circumvent these problems and to avoid problems while using high bandwidth UDP transmissions together with TCP transmissions.

The transmission rates depicted in figure 4(a) show the impact of a UDP based RTP video transmission on TCP based HTTP transfers. The measurements show the throughput of HTTP and RTP traffic in subjection to the aspired RTP video rate (0 to 2000 kbit/s). The measurements were done in five minute intervals using a HTTP file download and a adjustable RTP video transmission. The accuracy of the UDP and TCP rates were verified using artifical UDP and TCP data sources (a modified version of the tcpblast application) over the same five minutes interval with similar results.

Without L4+ based CoS, the HTTP stream uses the full bandwidth, if available (cf., figure 4(a)). The increasing RTP traffic supersedes the HTTP traffic. As long as the full physical bandwidth of 2 Mbit/s is available to the HTTP traffic, the HTTP bandwidth reaches 1.2 Mbit/s (effective maximum data rate on the wireless media). But, with increasing RTP rate, the HTTP traffic is reduced to 250 kbit/s and the RTP traffic uses more than 1 Mbit/s of the available bandwidth. This is caused by the fact that HTTP is a TCP based protocol which tries to adopt to bandwidth limitations by reducing the transfer speed (slow start mechanism). The UDP based RTP traffic does not use such mechanisms and, therefore, uses the full bandwidth and causes the TCP based traffic to slow down. Since often multimedia streams (video and audio) are transferred via HTTP, too, a degradation of HTTP traffic in this way may be unacceptable.

Figure 4(b) shows the same scenario, but with L4+ CoS and DiffServ support. In this case the edge device is configured to reserve 800 kbit/s for differentiated services premium service. The L4+ Classifier is configured to classify selected HTTP traffic (a video transmission) as premium service. The graph shows that the HTTP traffic classified uses this reserved 800 kbit/s premium service and is not affected by the RTP. The transmission of an MPEG video used in the example was still running at satisfying speed.

These measurements were performed with unmodified real-life-applications (applications used for HTTP analysis were the Netscape Navigator (web browser)

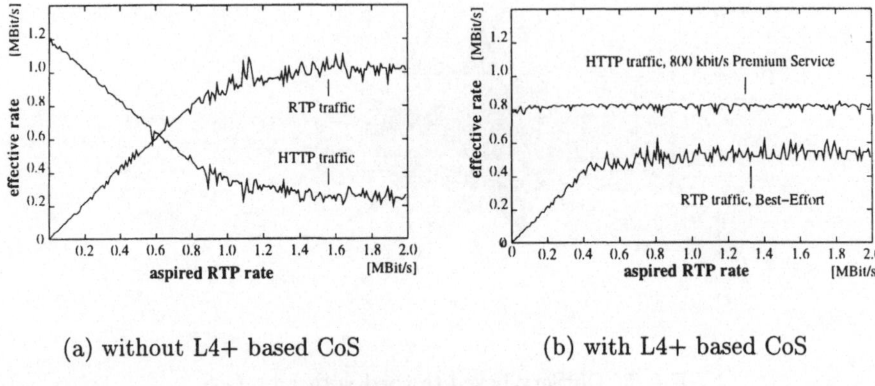

(a) without L4+ based CoS   (b) with L4+ based CoS

Fig. 4. HTTP/RTP tests

with an MPEG player, the wget-tool (command line HTTP client) and the
Apache server (HTTP server)). Applications used for RTP analysis were the
MBone tools vic (video sender and receiver), vat and rat (audio sender and re-
ceiver) and the RTP-tools for capturing and playback of RTP sessions. Without
L4+ CoS these application cannot profit from any class of service provided by
the communication system.

4.2 Performance Results

It is important, to consider the performance impact of L4+ CoS on edge devices.
Since the different ways of flow detection and classification, for example of HTTP
and RTP, have a different performance impact on the router CPU, they were
discussed separately with respect to performance.

The measurements were done in user space, with the classifier running as a
separate program on the router. This way, measurements with real life traffic as
well as with program generated traffic were possible. Furthermore, measurements
on other unix platforms were possible as well, since the classification routines
themselves are independent from the underlying host operating system.

The analysis of the HTTP header within the TCP payload requires complex
string search routines, since HTTP uses an ASCII header with varying offsets to
the different header fields. The current implementation uses a modified Boyer-
Moore string search algorithm to find the required entries in the HTTP header
(e.g., the content type and content length fields). The measurements have shown,
that the proposed algorithm needs in average 6.5 μs to find the interesting header
fields within one packet on a Pentium-200. Additional caching routines can increase the speed by about 10%. These caching routines make use of the fact,
that consecutive HTTP packets often have the same HTTP header fields starting at the same offset. Further measurements included the post-processing of
the detected header fields. E.g., the extraction of a numerical value from the
ASCII header as needed to extract the value stored in the content length entry

required one additional microsecond. The overall processing time of the HTTP classifier for an HTTP packet is in average $10\mu s$ for finding content type and content length field and extracting the values stored in both fields.

Additional measurements on real life traffic investigating 100.000 HTTP packets have shown, that about 17% of all observed packets were HTTP header packets, which means that one sixth of all packets processed by the observed router will have to be processed by the HTTP classifier in order to provide Layer 4+ supported class of Service support. The observed packets had an average length of 932 bytes. Therefore, the HTTP classifier became active every 44kbit. A Pentium-200 is, therefore, able to process about 4.4 Gbit/s incoming network traffic. Tests with a Pentium-III-600 showed, that this machine processes about three times the data of the Pentium-200.

The RTP classifier has less impact on the router performance than the HTTP classifier. The detection of valid RTP headers together with the sequence number analysis requires about 400 ms for 1.000.000 packets (400 ns per packet). With an average packet length of 932 bytes, this leads to an overall processing rate of 20 Gbit/s on a Pentium-200 CPU.

5   Conclusions

The inclusion of information derived from the transport layer up to the application layer into the forwarding process is currently discussed with respect to e.g. IP firewalls, server load balancing and implicit redirection of network traffic. It seems very feasible, to include this information into CoS class mapping as well in order to provide an implicit per application CoS support for todays applications.

We investigated the possibilities to use information derived from the transport layer up to the application layer in detail on two very different protocols, the currently very popular TCP based HTTP protocol and the UDP based RTP protocol as an example for upcoming real time protocols for audio and video applications.

Experiments have shown, that both protocols could be integrated into the layer 4+ supported CoS and remarkable service improvements were possible for existing non-CoS-aware applications. Furthermore, these tests have shown, that the performance impact of layer 4+ Classification on the router is manageable.

We consider Layer 4+ CoS to be an intermediate step in the seamless migration from the current Internet without CoS/QoS support to a QoS/CoS supporting Internet used by CoS/QoS aware applications.

References

1. Communications of the ACM - Feature topic "Embedding the Internet"; Volume 43, Number 5, May 2000
2. C. Metz; IP QoS: Traveling in First Class on the Internet; IEEE Internet Computing, Volume 3, Number 2, March/April 1999

3. R. Braden, L. Zhang, D. Estrin, S. Herzog, and S. Jamin; Resource Reservation Protcol (RSVP) - Version 1, Functional Specification; July 1995

4. S. Blake, D. Black, M. Carlson, E. Davies, Z. Wang, W. Weiss; An Architecture for Differentiated Services; Request for Comments 2475, IETF Network Working Group, December 1998

5. L. Perrinjaquet; SRP-ENABLED VIC; http://icawww1.epfl.ch/ĺperrinj, EPFL Lausanne, 1999

6. M. Ott, G. Michelitsch, D. Reininger, G. Welling; An Architecture for Adaptive QoS and its Application to Multimedia Systems Design; Computer Communications special issue on Guiding Quality of Service into Distributed Systems; NEC CCRLE Publications, May 1997

7. Layer 4 QoS Now Supported on All SmartSwitches; Cabletron Networks 'Hot Sheet' Press Release; http://www.cabletron.com/switching/layer4qos.pdf

8. VIPswitch Introduces 36 Port, Layer 5 Ethernet Switch; http://www.netcorp.qc.ca/news/pr13.html; VIPswitch Press Release, April 1999

9. William R. Cheswick and Steven M. Bellovin; Firewalls and Internet Security; Addison Wesley; 1994

10. S. Sathaye; The Ins and Outs of Layer 4+ Switching; NANOG meeting; Denver, USA, Jan 1999

11. M .Hofmann and K. Sabnani; Streaming Broadcasting over the Internet; Proc. of the ATM2000, Heidelberg, Germany, June 2000

12. Layer 4 QoS Now Supported on All SmartSwitches; http://www.enterasys.com/technologies/switching/layer4qos.html

13. K. Thompson, G. J. Miller, and R. Wilder; Wide-Area Internet Traffic Patterns and Characteristics; IEEE Network Magazine, vol. 11, no.6, December 1997

14. G. Seres et al; Measurement-Based Simulation Model for TCP over ATM; ICATM'99 Conference Proceedings, June 99

15. M. Crochemore and W. Rytter; Text Algorithms; Oxford University Press, New York; 1994

16. R. Wittmann and M. Zitterbart; Multicast - Protocols and Applications; Morgan Kaufmann Publishers; May 2000

17. H. Schulzrinne et al; RTP: A Transport Protocol for Real-Time Applications; Request for Comments 1889, IETF, January 1996

18. T. Harbaum, M. Zitterbart, F. Griffoul (NEC), J. Rötig (NEC), S. Schaller (NEC), H. J. Stüttgen (NEC); Layer 4+ Switching with QoS supprt for RTP and HTTP; Globecom '99, Rio, Brasil, December '99

19. http://www.wavelan.com

Active QoS Routing

Michael Welzl[1], Alfred Cihal[1] und Max Mühlhäuser[2]

[1] Johannes Kepler Universität Linz, Telekooperation
Altenberger Straße 69, A-4040 Linz, Österreich;
`michael@tk.uni-linz.ac.at`,
`http://www.tk.uni-linz.ac.at/~michael`
[2] Technische Universität Darmstadt, Telekooperation
Karolinenplatz 5, D-64289 Darmstadt, Deutschland

Zusammenfassung In Active Networks (AN) kann an jeden Netzknoten Code verschickt werden, der auf ausgewählte Pakete angewendet wird. So wird u.a. die Einführung neuer Protokollmechanismen wesentlich vereinfacht. Wir stellen für solche AN ein neues Verfahren namens Active-QoS-Routing (AQR) vor. Damit wird es ohne Änderung der verwendeten Routingprotokolle und ohne Erweiterung von deren Metriken möglich, QoS-basiertes Routing zu betreiben. Zusätzlich schlagen wir eine Erweiterung der Node-OS-Spezifikation innerhalb von AN vor, die es erlaubt, aus in Routern bereits vorhandenen Werten QoS-Parameter zu berechnen. Mittels Simulation konnten wir eine signifikant bessere Performance von AQR gegnüber Shortest Path Routing nachweisen.

1 Einleitung

Active Networks (AN) zeichnen sich dadurch aus, dass Knoten dieser Netzwerke Pakete nicht nur weiterleiten, sondern den Inhalt untersuchen und geforderte Berechnungen durchführen [1]. Eine der Zielsetzungen dabei ist es, den für normale Netzwerke üblichen langwierigen Normungsprozess zu umgehen. An die Stelle einer Einigung über verwendete Protokolle soll eine Abstimmung der verwendeten Modelle und Methoden treten [2].

Charakteristisch für AN ist die Unterteilung in drei Schichten: Aktive Anwendungen (AA), das sogenannte Execution Environment (EE) und, auf unterster Ebene, das Knoten-Betriebssystem (Node-OS). Entsprechend der Spezifikation der Node-OS Schnittstelle [3] stellt dieses Flows, einen Thread-Pool, einen Memory-Pool und Channels zur Verfügung. Gemäß den in der Litaratur eingeführten Definitionen von AN ist es jedoch den aktiven Anwendungen nicht möglich, auf untere Schichten der Protokollhierarchie zuzugreifen. Mit Spawning Networks und dem Genesis Kernel [4] wurde ein alternatives Konzept vorgestellt, das stattdessen auf einem sogenannten virtuellen Overlay-Netzwerk beruht. Da aber eine Implementierung zur Zeit nicht verfügbar ist und auch einen tiefen Eingriff in bestehende Strukturen bedeuten würde, scheint dieses Konzept für das geplante Einsatzgebiet ungeeignet zu sein.

Diese Arbeit soll zeigen, dass mit einer geringen Änderung der Architektur von Active Networks ein aktives QoS Routing ohne Eingriff in bestehende Routing-Protokolle und ohne Erweiterung von Routing-Metriken möglich wird.

2 Vorgeschlagene Änderungen zur Node-OS-Spezifikation

Wir schlagen wie erwähnt vor, in Active Networks lesenden Zugriff auf untere Protokollschichten zu erlauben. Hierfür bietet sich aufgrund der Aufgabenteilung in der Hierarchie nur das Node-OS an, wenn auf eine saubere Implementierung geachtet werden soll.

Die erwähnten Channels sind Teil der Schnittstelle zwischen Node-OS und Execution Environment. Sie stellen eine Abstraktion von Netzwerkverbindungen für Execution Enviroments dar. Laut derzeit gültiger Spezifikation stellt ein Node-OS lediglich Funktionen für den Auf- und Abbau solcher Channels und zum Senden und Empfangen von Paketen zur Verfügung [3]. Es ist kein Mechanismus vorgesehen, um Eigenschaften eines Channels abzufragen.

Wir schlagen vor, eine Erweiterung der Spezifikation vorzunehmen:

1. Jedem Channel werden bei Erzeugung die Eigenschaften der zu Grunde liegenden physischen Netzwerkverbindung zugewiesen.

2. Es werden Funktionen zum Auslesen derjenigen Parameter bereitgestellt, die entsprechend den Eigenschaften der Netzwerkverbindung relevant sind.

Wichtig ist anzumerken, dass es sich bei diesen Parametern nicht um sogenannte QoS-Parameter handelt (wie z.B.: aktuell verfügbare Bandbreite, zu erwartende Paket-Verlust-Rate), die in verbreiteten Rechnernetzen neu zu ermitteln wären. Stattdessen sind die relevanten Werte - im Falle IP-basierter Netzwerke - bereits in der Managment Information Base (MIB) des Routers vorhanden. Beispiele dafür sind MTU und die Zähler für ifIn- und ifOutOctets, aus denen sich Dienstgütespezifikationen errechnen lassen.

Es wurden sogar schon EEs entwickelt, die einen Zugriff auf diese Werte erlauben. Bekanntes Beispiel hierfür ist das System „Smartpackets", bei dem die MIB direkt ausgelesen werden kann. Dieses EE ist allerdings speziell für Netzwerk-Management-Aufgaben entwickelt worden und erlaubt MIB-Zugriffe nur für entsprechend autorisierte Netzwerk-Administratoren [5].

Nachfolgend wird skizziert, wie die Implementierung der vorgeschlagenen Erweiterung den in diesem Artikel vorgestellten neuen Ansatz für QoS-Routing ermöglicht. Durch Auswertung ausgewählter MIB-Parameter entlang eines Netzwerkpfades kann dieses QoS-Routing ohne Veränderung bestehender Routing-Mechanismen verwirklicht werden. Es sind auch keine Eingriffe in die derzeit gebräuchlichen Routing-Metriken notwendig.

3 Vorteile von Active Routing gegenüber klassischen Ansätzen

Für QoS-basiertes Routing werden im Allgemeinen zwei Methoden beschrieben: Die Erweiterung bzw. Änderung der verwendeten Routing Metriken und die Verwendung von Source Routing [6].

Die Mehrzahl der QoS-basierten Routing-Methoden benutzen die erforderlichen Dienstgüteparameter in Routing-Protokollen als link- oder verbindungsspezifische Werte zusätzlich zu den Link-Kosten. Dies bedarf einer netzwerkübergreifenden Normung; im Zuge dieser Normung müssen die Dienstgüteparameter sowie deren Berechnung festgelegt werden. In der Praxis lassen sich jedoch Eigenschaften wie die durchschnittlich verfügbare Bandbreite schwer allgemein definieren; die Funktion zu deren Berechnung hängt typischerweise sowohl vom zugrundeliegenden Netzwerk als auch von den Erfordernissen der Anwendung ab.

Source Routing als Basis für Dienstgüteunterstützung, wird beispielsweise in [6] oder in [7] an Hand einer Erweiterung des in OSPF verwendeten Dijkstra-Algorithmus beschrieben. Da AQR auf Source Routing basiert, wird auf die spezielle Problematik dieser Methode in einem späteren Kapitel eingegangen.

Mit unserem Ansatz auf der Basis von Active Networks können Dienstgüteparameter flexibel (z.B. anwendungsabhängig) definiert und berechnet werden. Eine Festlegung auf allgemein spezifizierte Dienstgüteparameter und deren Berechnung innerhalb des Node-OS ist nicht erforderlich. Das Node-OS stellt lediglich in Routern bereits vorhandene Werte zur weiteren Verarbeitung durch eine AA zur Verfügung. Dies schafft eine weitgehende Unabhängigkeit von der Art des zugrundeliegenden Netzwerkes. Es ist Aufgabe der AA, die gelieferten Werte entsprechend ihres Verwendungszweckes zu verarbeiten und zu interpretieren.

Wichtig ist also festzuhalten, dass Active-QoS-Routing nicht primär darauf abzielt, gegenüber bekannten Verfahren qualitative Verbesserungen im Mittel über alle Anwendungen zu erzielen. Vielmehr steht die Abkehr von in Routern fest implementierten Mechanismen zur Berechnung und Bereitstellung von QoS-Parametern im Vordergrund; aus Sicht spezifischer Anwendungsklassen und deren Interpretation bestimmter QoS-Parameter ist allerdings sehr wohl auch eine qualitative Verbesserung zu erwarten. Entsprechend dem Stand unserer Forschung beschränken wir uns nachfolgend allerdings darauf, den generellen Machbarkeitsnachweis zu liefern und die signifikante Verbesserung gegenüber klassischen IP-Routing aufzuzeigen.

4 Mechanismus

Active-QoS-Routing basiert auf der Annahme, dass im AN eine Link-State-Tabelle vorliegt wie von OSPF oder einem vergleichbaren Routing-Algorithmus generiert. Weiters müssen die zur Berechnung der Dienstgüte erforderlichen Informationen zur Verfügung stehen; dafür ist wie erwähnt lesender Zugriff auf untere Schichten normalerweise notwendig und hinreichend. Für den speziellen

Fall der Übertragungsverzögerung (Delay) kann dieser Lesezugriff sogar entfallen, da diese (zumindest bei über Timeserver synchronisierten Knoten) direkt aus der Systemzeit berechnet werden kann.

Eine Anwendung, die eine bestimmte QoS-Anforderung stellt, löst folgenden Prozess aus:

- Aus der Routing-Tabelle werden alle nicht-zyklischen Pfade zum Ziel berechnet.
- Entlang aller festgestellten Pfade werden Messpakete unter Verwendung von Multicast auf AN-Ebene verschickt.
- Jeder Knoten prüft eine im Messpaket enthaltene QoS-Mindestanforderung. Kann diese nicht erfüllt werden, wird das Paket verworfen.
- Der QoS-Parameter wird mit dem für den Knoten gültigen Wert verglichen und bei Bedarf korrigiert.
- Der Empfängerknoten erhält die Pakete, die die QoS-Mindestanforderung erfüllen und erstellt daraus bis zum Ablauf einer den Anforderungen entsprechend festzulegenden Zeitspanne eine Liste aller gültigen Pfade.
- Der Empfängerknoten wählt aus dieser Liste den Pfad mit dem besten QoS-Parameter aus und sendet diesen in einem Antwortpaket an den Ausgangsknoten zurück.

Dieser Prozess wird in bestimmten zeitlichen Abständen wiederholt, um auf geänderte Netzwerkzustände reagieren zu können.

5 Kritische Betrachtung und Fragestellungen

Offensichtlich ist bei der hier beschriebenen Methode im Besonderen, wie bei Verwendung von Source Routing im Allgemeinen, die Frage der Skalierbarkeit kritisch zu betrachten. Der Einsatz von AQR durch eine große Anzahl von Anwendungen kann die Begrenzung der Netzwerk- und Router-Belastung durch untere Schranken für die Aktualisierungsabstände erfordern. Eine andere Möglichkeit stellt die Beschränkung der Benutzung von AQR auf bestimmte Flows, z.B. solche mit langer Ausführungszeit, wie in [8] in anderem Zusammenhang beschrieben, dar. Im Vergleich mit QoS-Routing-Verfahren aus der Literatur ist allerdings anzumerken, dass auch diese — insbesondere aufgrund der erweiterten Metriken — zu einer Router-Mehrbelastung führen, deren Skalierbarkeit typischerweise noch nicht hinreichend gesichert ist; dasselbe gilt für die Netzwerkbelastung, da üblicherweise Daten über veränderte QoS-Parameter ausgetauscht werden.

Andererseits hat sich mit Link-State-Routing schon in klassischen IP-Netzen ein schlecht skalierbarer Routing-Ansatz (im Vergleich zu Distance-Vector-Routing) durchgesetzt, was bereits zu erheblichen Beschränkungen der Größe von Routing-Domänen führt. Es ist daher zu erwarten, dass ein pragmatischer Ansatz für die Randbedingungen des Einsatzes von AQR im Internet gefunden werden kann. Unsere bisherigen Simulationen bestärken diese Annahme. Numerische Werte zu Parameterschranken und Netz- bzw. Router-Belastungen können in diesem Artikel allerdings noch nicht angegeben werden, da die hierfür erforderlichen umfangreiche Untersuchungen noch nicht abgeschlossen sind. In diese fließen u.a. folgende Fragestellungen zur Parametrisierung von AQR ein:

- In welchen Zeitabständen sollen die Messungen durchgeführt werden?
- Wann soll vom empfangenden Knoten das Antwortpaket gesendet werden?
- Sollen Messpakete über verbindungsorientierte oder -lose Protokolle versendet werden?

Die bisherigen Ergebnisse unserer Simulations-Testreihen zeigen, dass diese Fragen nicht leicht einheitlich beantwortet werden können. Vielmehr hängen auch diese Werte und Methoden von den Dienstgüteparametern und deren anwendungsabhängiger Spezifikation ab. Gerade diese Beobachtung unterstreicht andererseits die Sinnhaftigkeit unseres Ansatzes: sie zeigt die Notwendigkeit einer flexiblen QoS-Berechnung und rechtfertigt den Einsatz einer Lösung, die auf AN basiert.

6   Simulation von Active QoS Routing

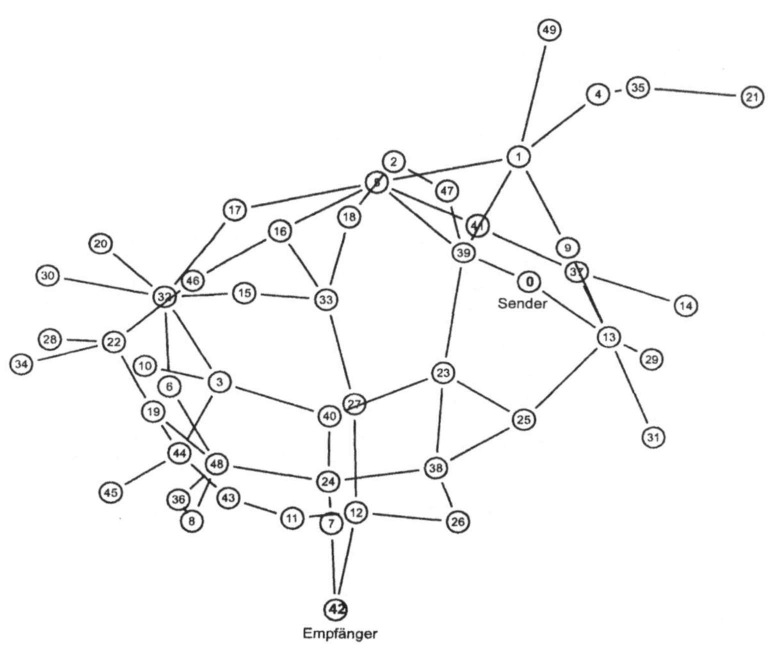

Abbildung 1. Verwendete Topologie

6.1 Verwendete Werkzeuge

Unsere Simulationen basieren auf dem Network-Simulator "ns" in Version 2.1b6. Die erforderlichen Änderungen und Erweiterungen werden als Quellcode auf [9] dokumentiert.

6.2 Netzwerktopologie

Für die hier diskutierte Testreihe wurde die in Abbildung 1 dargestellte Topologie mit 50 Knoten verwendet.

6.3 Der Algorithmus

Wir verzichten vorerst auf die Verwendung eine optimierten Algorithmus, um zu zeigen, dass auch mit einer sehr simplen Lösung ein entscheidender Vorteil gegenüber Shortest-Path-Routing erzielt werden kann.

Dabei wird kein Multicast verwendet, auf die Aufteilung des constant-bit-flows auf mehrere Pfade wird verzichtet. Für die Pfadsuche wird eine Erweiterung der Tiefensuche nach Sedgewick [10] eingesetzt.

Zum besseren Verständnis folgt eine Darstellung des Algorithmus in Pseudo-Code.

```
/*----------------------*/
/*   Initialisierung   */
/*----------------------*/

  for(i=0; i<maxV; i++)    // initialisieren der Adjazenzmatrix
    for(j=0; j<maxV; j++)
      if(link_exists_in_OSPF_table(i, j))
        a[i][j]=1;
      else
        a[i][j]=0;

  waveid = 0;                 // Nummer der Paket-Welle
  *bestPath = [Quelle, Ziel];  // Knoten haben eindeutige Nummern
  *bestPathCopy = [Quelle, Ziel];
  smallestDelay = GROESSTER MOEGLICHER WERT;
  max_delay = WERT;           // WERT wird von Anwendung uebergeben;


/*-------------------------------------------*/
/*   Versenden einer Messpaket-Welle   */
/*-------------------------------------------*/

void visit(int k, char path[], int val[]) {

  VERLAENGERE path UM k;

  if(k == destination) {
    send_packet(path);
    return;
  }

  int t;
  val[k] = 1;
  for(t=0; t<maxV; t++)
    if(a[k][t] != 0)
      if(val[t] == 0)
```

```
            visit(t, path, val);
}


send_packet(path) {

   new packet(pkt);
   pkt->time = NOW;              // Absendezeitpunkt
   pkt->path = path;             // der Strict-Source-Routing-Pfad
   pkt->pathcopy = path;         // Kopie des vollstaendigen Pfads fuer Empfaenger
   pkt->waveid = waveid;         // fortlaufende Nummer der Paket-"Welle"
   pkt->code = {                 // Der Active-Code
      if(NOW - pkt->time < max_delay) {
         ENTFERNE ERSTEN EINTRAG IN path;
         send(pkt, dest=erster path-eintrag);
      }
      else
         drop(pkt);

   send(pkt, dest=ERSTER EINTRAG IN path);
}


KOPIERE bestPath NACH bestPathCopy;
smallestDelay = GROESSTER MOEGLICHER WERT;      // Reinitialisierung

int val[maxV];
for(i=0; i<maxV; i++) val[i]=0;
char path[maxPath] = "";
visit(atoi(argv[2]), path, val);
waveid++;

/*-------------------------------------*/
/*    Herstellung des Antwortpaketes   */
/*-------------------------------------*/

recv(pkt) {

        new packet(replypkt);
        replypkt->delay = NOW-pkt->time;      // berechnetes Gesamtdelay
        replypkt->path = pkt->pathcopy;       // vollstaendiger Pfad
        replypkt->waveid = pkt->waveid;       // Paket-Welle
        send(replypkt, dest = source of pkt);
}


/*-------------------------------------*/
/*   Sender verarbeitet Antwortpaket   */
/*-------------------------------------*/

recv(replypkt) {

        if( (replypkt->delay < smallestDelay) && (replypkt->waveid == waveid) ) {
           smallestDelay = replypkt->delay;
           KOPIERE replypkt->path NACH bestpath;
        }
}
```

6.4   Ergebnis

Trotz des Verzichts auf optimierende Maßnahmen konnte ein gegenüber Shortest-Path-Routing um durchschnittlich 20 % kürzeres Delay erreicht werden. Für die in Abbildung 2 dargestellten Simulationsergebnisse wurden folgende Einstellungen verwendet:

- Zeit zwischen den Messpaketwellen: 3,5 Sekunden
- Störverkehr: durchschnittlicher TCP-Verkehr

- nominelle Bandbreite: 1 Mb im gesammten Netzwerk
- Senderknoten: 0
- Empfängerknoten 42

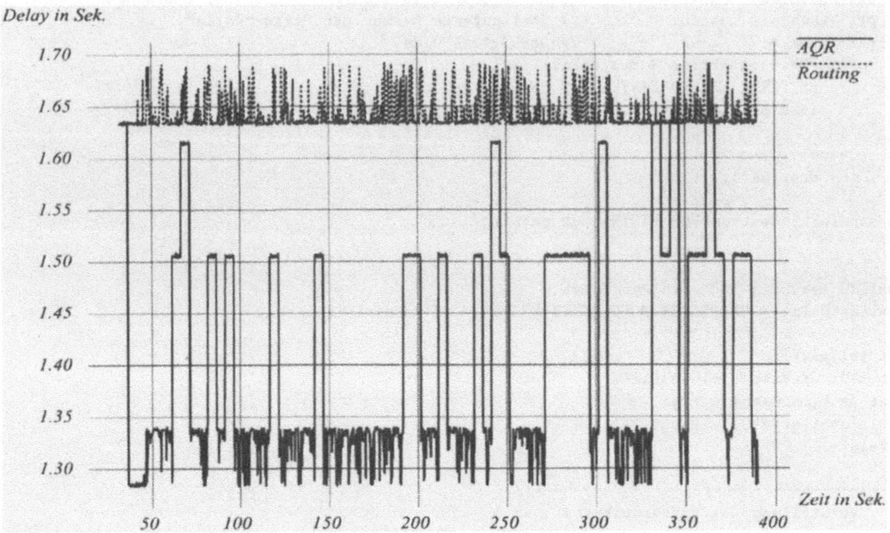

Abbildung 2. AQR versus Shortest-Path-Routing

6.5 Der erweiterte Algorithmus

Wir haben folgende Änderungen am Algorithmus durchgeführt:

- Verwendung von Multicast für Messpakete zur Reduktion der Netzwerkbelastung
- Möglichkeit der Aufteilung des Nutzverkehrs auf mehrere Pfade

Von der Aufteilung des Nutzverkehrs erwarten wir geringere Schwankungen in der erzielten Dienstgüte, eine bessere Auslastung des Netzwerks und eine Verhinderung einer durch den Flow selbst ausgelösten Oszillation zwischen mehreren Pfaden. Die Aufteilung erfolgt durch Festlegen eines Toleranzwertes, um den der jeweilige QoS-Parameter über- bzw. unterschritten werden darf. Als erstes Ergebnis zeigt Abbildung 3 die Abhängigkeit des gemessenen durchschnittlichen Delays von der Wahl dieses Wertes. Es zeigte sich dabei ein deutlicher Anstieg des durchschnittlichen Delays bei Überschreitung von 8% Toleranz.

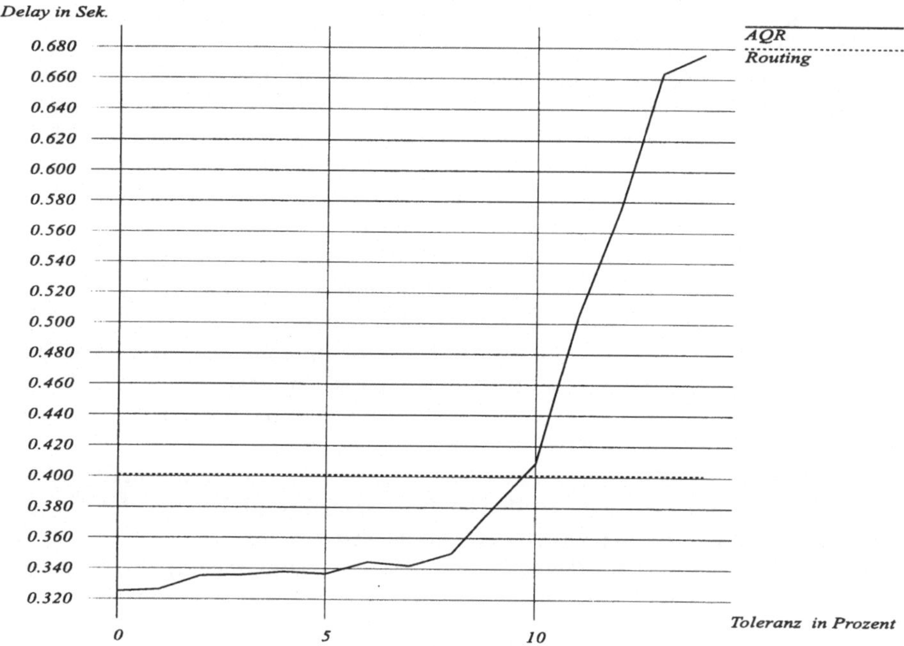

Abbildung 3. Delay bei verschiedenen Toleranzwerten

7   Schlussbemerkungen

Wir haben eine Möglichkeit vorgestellt, mittels Active Networks eine Form des
QoS-basierten Routing zu verwirklichen. Die verwendete Methode hat wesentliche Vorteile gegenüber herkömmlichen Ansätzen: sie kommt ohne Änderung
bestehender Routing-Protokolle und ohne zusätzliche Routing-Metriken aus; Als
Voraussetzung für den breiten und allgemeinen Einsatz schlagen wir eine Änderung der Node-OS-Spezifikation vor, da für die Berechnung von QoS-Parametern
typischerweise ein Zugriff auf verschiedene Kenngrößen des zugrundeliegenden
Netzwerks notwendig ist.

Die diskutierten Simulationen bezüglich des QoS-Parameters „Delay", welche wir durchführten, zeigten eine signifikant bessere Performance von AQR
gegenüber Shortest-Path-Routing. Weitere Simulationen unter Verwendung des
erweiterten Algorithmus und von weiteren QoS-Parametern sind durchzuführen.
Diese sollen auch Aufschluß über Ausmaß und Randbedingungen der Skalierbarkeit bringen, ein für QoS-Routing allgemein noch nicht hinreichend untersuchtes
Problem. Einige Antworten hierzu sind bis zur KIVS bereits zu erwarten.

Literatur

1. David L. Tennenhouse, Jonathan M. Smith, W. David Sincoskie, David J. Wetherall
   and Gary J. Minden: *A Survey of Active Network Research* . IEEE Communications
   Magazine, Vol. 35, No. 1, pp80-86. January 1997

2. John Guttag: *Report on Active Network Activity.* Active Nets Workshop, March 1997, Baltimore, MD.
3. AN Node OS Working Group: *Node OS Interface Specification*, Edited by Larry Peterson, 24 Jänner 2000
4. A. Campbell, M. Kounavis, D. Villela, H. De Meer, K. Miki, J. Vicente: *The Genesis Kernel: A Virtual Network Operating System for Spawning Network Architectures*, Second IEEE Conference on Open Architectures and Network Programming, OPENARCH '99, New York, March 26-27, 1999.
5. B. Schwartz, A.W. Jackson, T. Strayer, W. Zhou, R.D. Rockwell and C.Partridge: *Smart Packets for Active Networks*, Second IEEE Conference on Open Architectures and Network Programming, OPENARCH '99, New York, March 26-27, 1999.
6. Z. Wang and J. Crowcroft. *Quality-of-Service Routing for Supporting Multimedia Applications.* IEEE JSAC, 14(7):1288–1234, September 1996.
7. R. Guerin and A. Orda and D. Williams. *QoS Routing Mechanisms and OSPF Extensions* IETF Internet Draft , November 1996.
8. Anees Shaikh, Jennifer Rexford, and Kang G. Shin. *Load-sensitive routing of long-lived ip flows.* In Proceedings of SIGCOMM, September 1999.
9. http://www.tk.uni-linz.ac.at/~micky/AQR.html
10. Robert Sedgewick: *Algorithmen*, Addison-Wessley (Deutschland) GmbH, 2. korrigierter Nachdruck 1995.

Real-Time Support on Top of Ethernet

Rainer Koster and Thorsten Kramp

Distributed Systems Group, Dept. of Computer Science
University of Kaiserslautern, P.O. Box 3049, 67653 Kaiserslautern, Germany
{koster,kramp}@informatik.uni-kl.de

Abstract Ethernet is a widely used low-cost networking technology. It however lacks the determinism and resource management features needed to meet real-time requirements of multimedia applications, for instance. This paper presents the $B_{E}A_{T}$ communication service that adds basic real-time mechanisms on top of Ethernet to the Linux operating system while supporting the use of conventional applications and protocols such as TCP and UDP.

To avoid the indeterminism of the CSMA/CD network access control a token mechanism has been employed. Priorities can be attached to packets and are taken into account in allocating bandwidth locally, for the messages on the node, as well as globally, among the nodes on the network. Moreover, shares of network bandwidth can be reserved by tasks, controlled by a utilization-based admission test. In addition, a global notion of time is needed for time constraints to be meaningful in a distributed real-time system. $B_{E}A_{T}$ therefore integrates a clock synchronization algorithm with the communication mechanisms. By directly accessing low-level packet transmission an accuracy in the order of $10\,\mu s$ is achieved. The overhead introduced by the $B_{E}A_{T}$ communication service is about 10% for processing time as well as for network bandwidth.

1   Introduction

Programs with soft real-time requirements are more and more commonly used, particularly for multimedia applications. These programs are run on off-the-shelf computers which are often connected by bus-based Ethernet [2]. This networking infrastructure, however, does not provide support for timing constraints on messages. In this paper, we present an approach for providing network-wide message priorities, bandwidth reservation, and clock synchronization on low-cost hardware.

In a real-time system, resource allocation needs to be tied to timing constraints. For process scheduling, general-purpose operating systems commonly support priorities according to the POSIX.4 standard [1] for controlling the precedence among tasks competing for processing time. Based on this mechanism, more sophisticated scheduling algorithms can be employed — for instance, by a high-priority resource-management process that assigns the priorities of the other tasks appropriately. While many systems provide this basic real-time support for the management of processing time, usually there is nothing equivalent for the management of network bandwidth.

Widely used low-cost networks employ a *carrier sense multiple access* (CSMA) medium access control scheme. With this technology, however, message transmission times are not predictable, because network access is controlled in a statistical way. Several nodes may try to send at the same time, which causes message transmission to fail and to be repeated later. There is no way to determine for sure which node will send next. Moreover, bandwidth is assigned to all nodes according to a statistically fair policy and not based on priorities. Both of these properties are not acceptable for real-time systems.

The possibility for tasks to reserve network bandwidth is another feature that should be added to the communication service. Reservations must be taken into account in sending messages on each node as well as in assigning shares of bandwidth to each node on the network.

To address these problems we have built a communication service called $B_{E\!A\!T}$ for the Linux operating system [4]. In designing the protocol we have pursued following goals:

- Transmission time should be predictable. Unbounded message latencies are not acceptable for hard real time. As basis for providing soft guarantees a bound also simplifies the design of higher layers and facilitates statistical statements.
- Communication should be reliable. If messages can be lost they possibly must be resent, effectively introducing unbounded latencies.
- Network access must be granted according to message priorities. Usually packets are queued for sending in a FIFO order by the kernel and bandwidth of a shared network is allocated according to some kind of fair scheduling among nodes. Both of these policies, however, cause priority inversion and unpredictable message latencies.
- TCP and UDP must still be available together with the new service allowing real-time and non real-time applications to coexist. Disabling standard protocols would preclude many programs and make it hard to use the system not only for testing but also as a development platform.
- To preserve hardware independence, device drivers should not be modified. Otherwise, the service would rely on a particular type of Ethernet card, or require porting changes to a variety of drivers.

Section 2 presents the $B_{E\!A\!T}$ protocol. The integration of clock synchronization is described in Section 3. Section 4 discusses related work and Section 5 outlines conclusions and future work.

2   The Protocol

First of all, deterministic medium access control is needed, because in case of a collision CSMA/CD backs off for a random time introducing unpredictable behavior. Since this scheme is implemented on the Ethernet card itself, we cannot directly access the network, but can only build on top of this medium access scheme. Hence, many of the protocols that have been proposed for time-constraint communication [6] are not applicable in this case. For instance, virtual time CSMA (VTCSMA) [9] cannot be used, because there is no way to check whether the network is busy at a given time.

To achieve deterministic network access, a token passing mechanism has been chosen, because it can easily be added to the kernel and be built on top of an Ethernet. If a node does not have the token, no more packets are passed on from the kernel send queue to the device driver. When the token arrives, the send queue is unblocked and waiting packets are released. After a given time the token itself is sent to the next node in a virtual ring. This approach requires all nodes on the LAN to cooperatively run this protocol, which at least should not be a problem in a centrally administered local network.

To schedule the sending of packets based on priorities, the regular kernel FIFO send queue is replaced by a priority queue. The token itself must be assigned the highest priority to make sure it is sent regardless of waiting packets.

Moreover, priorities should be enforced also globally, that is, messages should not wait for other nodes sending lower-priority messages. Hence, each node attaches the priority of its most waiting message to the token, somewhat similarly to the approach defined in ISO 8802/5 for the token ring [3].[1] When a token is received indicating that somewhere in the network a message is waiting with a higher priority than any message on the current node, the token is passed on immediately. Still there may be priority inversion for a bounded time: A message priority is taken into account only after the token has visited the sending node, that is, between the message becoming ready and its node receiving the token, other nodes may send lower priority data.

On our system without message collisions, packet loss has been experienced only in case of a buffer overflow. Choosing large enough buffer sizes for kernel send and receive queues can avoid packet loss here, too, provided the system is not continuously overloaded. Then, it seems to be reasonable to assume this layer of the network stack to be reliable. However, messages still can be lost, if a buffer on a higher layer overflows, in Linux that is a socket receive buffer. This problem, however, can be avoided only by the application itself, because messages are necessarily lost, if data is sent faster than it is received and buffers of the communication system are bounded.

Token processing consumes resources for itself and, hence, reduces the amount of CPU time as well as network bandwidth that is available for user programs. The more often a token needs to be processed by a node, the higher the overhead. This relation, on the one hand, suggests long token holding times. Short holding times, on the other hand, reduce the waiting time before accessing the network. Measurements have shown an overhead in CPU capacity of about 10% for a token holding time of 1 ms on an otherwise idle network [4]. The results for network bandwidth are shown in Figure 1 and discussed below.

Experiments have been run for token holding times of 1 ms, 3 ms, 10 ms, and 100 ms. Additionally, in the mode labeled "fast" the token is always passed on

---

[1] There are only eight priority levels defined in the token ring standard, which is insufficient for real-time scheduling [7].

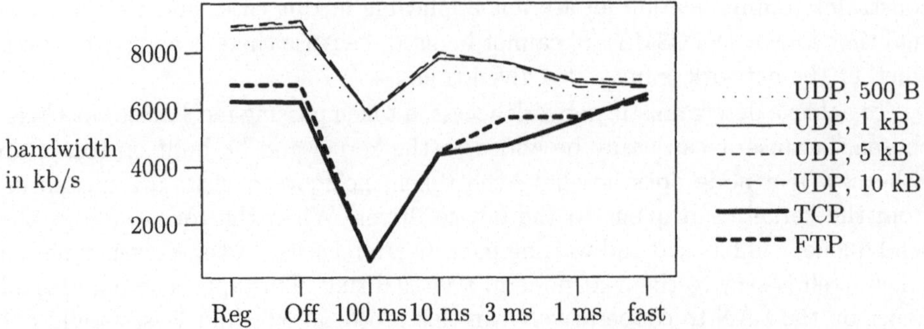

Fig. 1. Usable bandwidth

immediately, if there is nothing to be sent. For comparison, a regular Linux 2.0.30 kernel has been used ("Reg") as well as the modified kernel with the token mechanism deactivated ("Off"). The network is a 10base2 Ethernet with three computers connected to it.

For each configuration 1 MB of data have been sent with several protocols. For UDP, different packet sizes have been used. The UDP graph drops monotonously for holding times larger than 10 ms. The reason is the overhead caused by the token. The shorter the token holding time, the more frequently the token is sent leaving fewer resources for user data. A second performance drawback is caused by the time the sender needs to wait for the token. All nodes keep the token for the token holding time when the network is idle, but pass it on quickly, if there is nothing to send on the local node but somewhere else. With this scheme and three nodes, a node starting to send may have to wait up to three times the holding time before transmitting the first packet. The graphs for 1 kB, 5 kB, and 10 kB packets differ slightly, because large packets are fragmented by the IP layer. The bandwidth achieved for 500 byte packets, however, is a few hundred kb/s lower, because twice as many packets need to be processed.

Performance of TCP is very low for 100 ms, monotonously increasing for shorter holding times. This behavior probably is caused partly by the flow control mechanism of this protocol, which is not designed for sending in bursts whenever a token is present. With decreasing holding times the granularity of time slots with and without send permission becomes finer, providing a better approximation of a regular network to the TCP flow control mechanism. The ftp program uses TCP to copy file from one machine to another. Hence, its performance graph mostly agrees with that of TCP.

Based on the global priorities, resource reservation has been implemented according to following rules:

- Packets with reservation have higher priority than packets without.
- Regular priorities control precedence among packets with reservation as well as among packets without reservation.

– Packets exceeding a reserved bandwidth a processed like packets without reservation, implementing a policing mechanism.

An admission test must check whether a reservation request can be granted or not. Since the network is shared among nodes not more than the total available bandwidth may be reserved by the sockets on the network altogether. The information what share of the bandwidth is still available is attached to the token. When the token arrives at a node, the available bandwidth is increased by the amount of the reservations that have been cancelled during the last token circulation. Then, pending requests are processed. They are accepted if there are sufficient resources and rejected otherwise. The token is sent on with updated information about the currently available bandwidth.

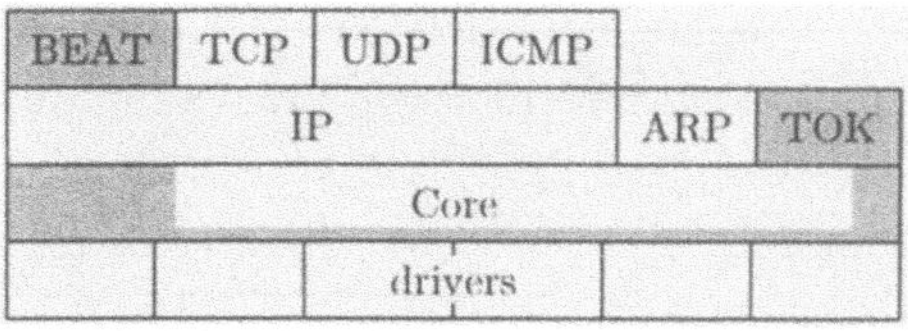

Fig. 2. Modified Linux Networking Modules

Figure 2 shows how B_{EAT} is built into the Linux 2.0 networking code. Tokens are a special type of Ethernet packets in addition to ARP and IP packets. On top of the IP layer there are modules for TCP, UDP and ICMP. B_{EAT} has been added here as is described above. Of course, the core layer had to be modified in order to block the sending of packets if the token is not present. Since kernel version 2.2, Linux provides extensive support for scheduling network packets. A newer version of B_{EAT} has been implemented as a kernel module instantiating a particular packet scheduler. The transport-level part of B_{EAT} is mainly an extention of UDP. Priorities and reservations are set for each socket via *socket options* and are then attached to each packet send through the socket. Figure 3 demonstrates how the communication service works. Task characteristics are given in the following table.

Task	Start	Sender	Amount	Protocol	Priority	Reservation
1	0 s	node 3	10 MB	UDP	–	–
2	1.1 s	node 2	3 MB	UDP	–	–
3	9.1 s	node 3	6 MB	B_{EAT}	med	–
4	10.9 s	node 2	1 MB	B_{EAT}	high	–
5	13.9 s	node 2	3 MB	B_{EAT}	low	3 Mb/s

3 Clock Synchronization

In a distributed real-time system, time constraints need to be communicated from one node to another. The differences of the system clocks on different

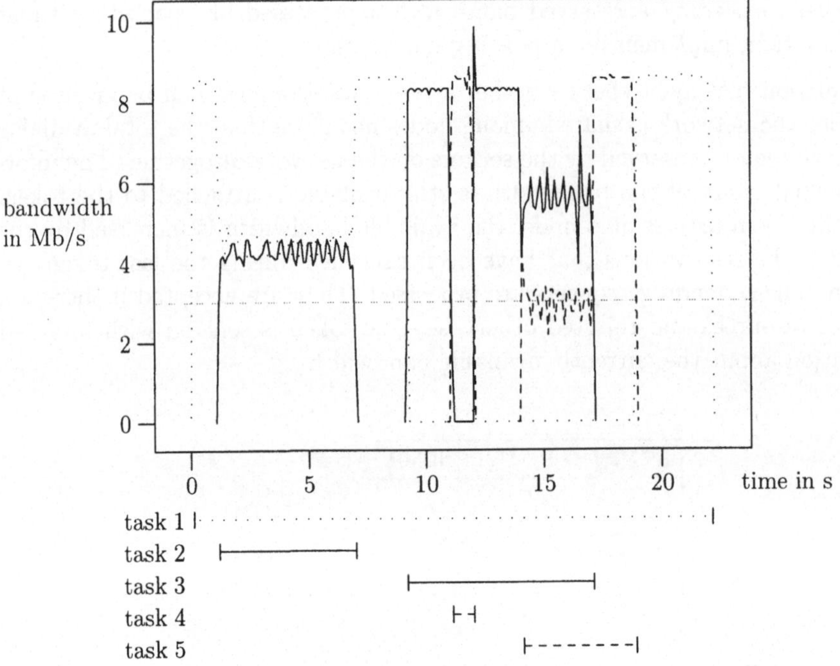

Fig. 3. The $B_{\!E\!A\!T}$ communication service

nodes, however, cannot be neglected, because the frequencies of the underlying hardware oscillators do not match exactly and even fluctuate over time. Hence, there needs to be a way of synchronizing the clocks. Integrating synchronization in the basic communication service allows measuring the transmission time very precisely and achieves a higher accuracy and a lower overhead than implementing this feature on a higher layer.

The easiest way of adding time stamps for measuring transmission times is doing so when the kernel queues a packet for sending, or receives one, respectively. In this case however, transmission time heavily depends on the time it takes to traverse the buffers, that is on their fill level. On a loaded network much longer transmission times would be observed than on an unloaded one. While the dependency on the send queue fill level can be removed by measuring the send time just before the packet is released to the Ethernet card, the variable delays caused by buffers on the card still impede time measuring. Ideally, the send time stamp would be added just before the token is put on the network and the receive time stamp immediately after reception. However, both events happen inside the Ethernet card and cannot be logged by the kernel.

The token mechanism, however can make sure the network is unloaded and buffers are empty when the transmission time is measured. In regular intervals a measuring circulation is scheduled. After receiving a token it is sent again immediately, with a send time stamp attached. The host could not be sending before, because it did not have the token and, hence, no permission to sent. In this kind of situation, the send buffer of the card is guaranteed to be empty, and data packets may be waiting in the kernel queue. Due to its higher priority the token bypasses the kernel queue and is sent to the next machine. By then, the receiving host should have emptied the receive buffer of its network card allowing the token to be delivered immediately to the kernel, which adds the receive time stamp.

Experiments show that times observed in this way are stable enough to use them as a basis for clock synchronization. Only occasionally, there are significant deviations, which are probably caused by delayed receive interrupts on a heavily loaded system. To reduce the impact of such effects, outliers are filtered and the transmission time is averaged over several measurements. These averaged values show derivations of mostly less than 10 μs.

4 Related Work

The RETHER protocol is most related to B_{EAT} also providing bandwidth reservations on top of Ethernet hardware [8]. RETHER uses a fixed token rotation time for one circulation, which nodes can reserve shares of. In one cycle, the token is first passed between nodes with real-time traffic, which may send according to their reserved shares before passing on the token. After that, the token is circulated among all nodes for sending non real-time traffic for the remaining time of this circulation. The use of a fixed circulation time provides more predictable latencies than B_{EAT}, if all real-time traffic is periodic and has the same period, which can be configured as token rotation time. Priorities could be applied only among messages on one node. B_{EAT} in contrast, is based on global message priorities and, hence, provides a lot more flexibility, allowing the priorities to be set for instance, according to an earliest deadline first or rate monotonic algorithm.

Some variants of the CSMA protocol based on a virtual time (VTCSMA) have been proposed to provide deterministic medium access [9]. Scheduling policies such as earliest deadline first, can be implemented by such an algorithm. Messages are sent according their deadline with respect to a virtual clock on each node. This approach, however, cannot be built on top of regular Ethernet hardware, because it needs direct control over the shared medium.

5 Conclusions

Applications with soft real-time requirements and dynamic resource needs are becoming more common, for instance in the field of multimedia. Real-time operating systems and networks, however, are not widely used yet in this domain, partly due to higher cost, partly due to the lack of conventional applications. This paper has proposed an Ethernet-based communication service that adds basic real-time support to the widely used Linux system. B_{EAT} allows priorities to be attached to packets. These priorities are considered locally by ordering the kernel send queue as well as globally by granting network access to the node with the highest priority message waiting. A token mechanism allows to access the network in a deterministic way. Tasks can also reserve shares of network bandwidth. Moreover, a clock synchronization algorithm has been integrated with the communication service.

B_{EAT} can be easily deployed to provide resource management support without requiring particular networking hardware. It has been a valuable tool for providing the infrastructure for experimental setups involving applications with timing constraints [5].

In contrast to the shared bus, switched topologies are becoming more common for Ethernet networks. In this case, the proposed token mechanism is overly restrictive, because two pairs of nodes can communicate via the switch without interfering with each other. If full-duplex mode is used, each node has the full bandwidth to the switch and contention can only occur if several senders overload the line from the switch to one node. Future versions of B_{EAT} should address this scenario.

References

1. Bill O. Gallmeister. *POSIX.4: Programming for the Real World*. O'Reilly & Associates, January 1995.
2. International Organization for Standardization. *ISO 8802-3; Information processing systems — Local area networks — Part 3: Carrier sense multiple access with collision detection (CSMA/CD) access method and physical layer specifications*, 1989.
3. International Organization for Standardization. *ISO/IEC 8802-5; Information technology — Telecommunications and information exchange between systems — Local and Metropolitan area networks — Specific requirements — Part 5: Token ring access method and physical layer specifications*, 1995.
4. R. Koster. Design of a real-time communication service for local-area networks. Diplom thesis, Department of Computer Science, University of Kaiserslautern, May 1998.
5. R. Koster and T. Kramp. Smart proxies for end-to-end QoS control. In *Proceedings of Middleware 2000 (International Conference on Distributed Systems Platforms and Open Distributed Processing)*. IFIP/ACM, April 2000.
6. James F. Kurose, Mischa Schwarz, and Yechiam Yemini. Multiple-access protocols and time-constraint communication. *Computing Surveys*, 16(1), March 1984.
7. K. W. Tindell, A. Burns, and A. J. Wellings. Guaranteeing hard real-time end-to-end communications deadlines. Technical Report RTRG/91/107, University of York, UK, December 1991.
8. C. Venkatramani and T. Chiueh. Design, implementation, and evaluation of a software-based real-time ethernet protocol. In *Proceedings of ACM SIGCOMM '95*, 1995.
9. Wei Zhao and Krithi Ramamritham. Virtual time CSMA protocols for hard real-time communication. *IEEE Transactions on Software Engineering*, 13(8):938–952, August 1987.

Fun Factor Characterization of User Perceived Quality of Service for Elastic Internet Traffic

Joachim Charzinski

Siemens Information and Communication Networks,
Hofmannstr. 51, D-81359 Munich, Germany,
`j.charzinski@ieee.org`

Abstract. Classical quality of service (QoS) measures such as packet loss probability, delay or delay variation are available for non-elastic network traffic. However, most of today's data traffic is transported over the Transmission Control Protocol (TCP) in the Internet, and TCP uses a flow control mechanism to adapt a connection's bit rate to the resources available in the network in order to get the same "fair share" of bandwidth as the other TCP connections sharing the same bottleneck link. Recent efforts in describing elastic traffic have recalled Processor Sharing models and tried to establish bandwidth related QoS measures such as "delay factors" or "fun factors" to describe the user perceived quality of service for elastic traffic applications. In this paper we discuss possible definitions of fun factors as well as DNS and TCP properties that influence the bit rates achievable with elastic traffic. Measurement results give an indication of the rates occurring in the Internet. They also reveal the delays and success rates to be expected from DNS requests, which can be a major cause of delay in HTTP retrievals.
Keywords: Internet Traffic; TCP; User Perceived QoS; Fun Factor; Elastic Traffic; HTTP Traffic; DNS Latency; Measurement

1 Introduction

Traditional quality of service (QoS) measures like mean delay, delay quantiles, delay variation or packet loss probability miss the point when they are employed with elastic traffic. The traffic patterns observed in today's Internet exhibit fractal characteristics due to long-range dependence introduced by heavy-tailed distributions of transmitted file sizes [9, 5]. Although it is still possible to estimate packet loss probabilities for the long-range dependent traffic ([1] and references therein), there are two problems associated with using packet loss as a QoS measure for elastic traffic: On the one hand, TCP is well able to adapt its transmission rate to bandwidth bottlenecks, so that the packet loss probability is kept at a certain low level, which is also evaluated by TCP for rate feedback information. The packet loss rate computed from traffic models for unelastic traffic is therefore only related to real network performance as long as this computed loss rate is low enough not to influence TCP [6, 10, 3]. On the other hand, a low bandwidth can have a significant impact on the perceived QoS of a connection as the main use of most TCP connections is to transport a given traffic volume from one host to another. A good QoS measure should therefore consider the achievable bandwidth as a relevant parameter for elastic traffic.

In order to offer a QoS measure which has more relation to user perceived performance than per-packet delay or loss figures, the author proposed to use a "fun factor" [3] as a normalized quantity to describe the impact that a shared trunk line has on the bandwidth available to a user's elastic traffic. Other authors have used delay factors [6, 10, 14] to describe the relative increase in transfer time in a connection due to the presence of competing elastic traffic in a network element.

In order to obtain figures for the performance metrics to be expected in the real Internet, active measurement studies have been carried out. Krishnamurthy and Wills [8] analyzed the influence of HTTP protocol options on HTTP performance by actively testing downloading times from selected sites using different combinations of options. Similarly, Huitema and Weerahandi [7] investigated the performance of DNS servers by actively requesting name resolution and comparing the performance of different servers and the evolution of loss rates and response times over a period of six months. In contrast, the performance evaluation approach in this paper is purely passive as it is based on an analysis of real user traffic packet traces captured before for other purposes [4].

In Sec. 2, fun and delay factors are put into relation and some possible alternative definitions for fun factors are given. Sec. 3 shows a very coarse structure of a download using HTTP/TCP and explains effects limiting the throughput or increasing the delay of a download. Finally, in Sec. 4 measurement based evidence for the mean and distribution of fun factors as well as the effects discussed before is given.

2 Fun Factors

In [3], an *access fun factor* Φ was introduced as the ratio between ideal and real download time in a TCP connection.

$$\Phi_{Access} = \frac{t_{ideal}}{t_{real}} \tag{1}$$

This definition provides a simple way of determining which proportion of the access line capacity c_{AL} could be utilized by a connection with a value of 100 % being the optimum case corresponding to 100 % fun (relative to this specific access line). An average value $\varphi = E[\Phi]$ was defined with respect to per connection averaging.

On the other hand, the delay factors $F_R = 1/\Phi$ occurring in other analyses [6, 10, 14] are supposed to be averaged into a mean value of f_R as time averages. Apart from the general difference between $E[1/X]$ and $1/E[X]$, there is a major difference between the two averaging methods: Averaging over time emphasizes the influence of the quality found in long lasting connections whereas averaging per connection gives short connections a higher weight.

The above definitions of Φ and F_R are both useful per se only if the target of interest is a single TCP connection. As current Web browsers use multiple parallel connections to reduce the downloading time for small icons on a page, a good QoS measure should be able to cope with multiple parallel connections of interest. In addition, there can be pauses between successive downloads within the same HTTP/TCP connection, leading to very low fun factor values if Φ is determined according to (1). Another case is clients running elastic and stream applications in parallel, in this way reducing the bit rate available to elastic traffic on the individual access link, which should be reflected in a change of the reference capacity in (1).

There are several further options which could also make up good components of a "fun factor" measure. One idea is to include an absolute delay component, i.e. defining downloads of a whole page taking less than one or two seconds to have a fun factor of One. On the other side of the scale, one could consider an absolute reaction time component limiting the fun factor to something like 0.9 if there was a delay of more than two seconds before any download was started. The reason for this proposal is found in DNS lookup times as discussed in sections 3.2 and 4.3.

Yet another proposal for defining a fun factor is to use a "state-of-the-art" standard reference rate representing the rates to be expected from the current Internet. The influence of round trip times on TCP performance as discussed in sections 3.1 and 4.4 could be included in such a reference rate. Another advantage of this approach in comparison to (1) is that Φ would allow the comparison of QoS between different access media.

In [3, 14], φ or f_R is used to dimension an access trunk in order to allow the individual access lines to have a high utilization when needed. A reverse application of fun factors is also to consider a high starting value of c_{AL} and to reduce c_{AL} until fun factors of around 0.2–0.5 are reached, in this way searching for the right access line rate to offer to the market at a given time.

3 Limiting Effects

Apart from congestion in the network, there are other limiting effects on HTTP and TCP performance [13, 12] such as the round trip time, TCP dynamics of short connections or DNS reaction times.

3.1 TCP Effects

As shown e.g. in [12], the sustained throughput B of a TCP connection is limited by the round-trip time t_{RT} between transmitter and receiver under the condition of a constant random packet loss probability p inside the network as long as the throughput is limited by independent packet losses in the network.

$$B \approx \frac{1}{t_{RT}} \sqrt{\frac{3}{2 \cdot b \cdot p}} \tag{2}$$

If there is no loss in the network, the throughput achievable by TCP in the steady state is of course limited by other factors, e.g. limited bandwidth on access links. The parameter b is the number of packets acknowledged with each received acknowledgment. According to [2], there must be an acknowledgment at least for every second data packet, leading to $b \in [1, 2]$. Observing 2 million HTTP/TCP connections, the author has found an average of 0.75 acknowledgments per data packet [4], corresponding to $b \approx 1.3$.

TCP connections used for HTTP can have a very short duration and consist of only a few packets [4], preventing the connection from reaching a steady state. Therefore, the throughput of HTTP/TCP connections may be determined by further influencing factors beside the ones included in (2):

- If a TCP segment is lost while the window size is still at its initial value of 1, a fast retransmit is not possible and instead the sender waits until a predefined timeout occurs. Therefore a packet loss in a short TCP connection can introduce a considerable amount of additional delay of around three seconds.

- A new TCP connection starts increasing its transmission window roughly exponentially over time according to the *slow start* rules.[1] Depending on the congestion situation in the network, short connections can either benefit or suffer from this fact. If competing longer connections have small congestion window sizes and threshold values, the exponential increase will help the short connections in gaining an advantage over the longer connections. If in contrast the other connections have large congestion window sizes, a short connection will get a considerably lower rate as it will end before its window has reached a comparable size.

3.2 DNS Response Time

Whenever a user or an embedded element on a Web page selects a new server to retrieve a page or image from, the domain name of this server has to be translated into an IP (Internet Protocol) address. Using the Domain Name System (DNS) protocol, the host requests an address lookup from a DNS server sending a UDP packet to port 53. The result is returned from port 53 of the server to the same port that the client sent the request from.

Most browsers show the user if they are currently resolving the server's IP address or if they are receiving data. Therefore, the user's situation can be described as depicted in Fig. 1: After requesting a new page by clicking at a link, the user observes a phase of inactivity when the browser waits for the DNS response. After the browser got the response, – in the case of a successful connection set-up – a phase of activity follows where the requested items are downloaded. Of course there are many more variations on this theme as there can be TCP timeouts, unreachable networks or servers etc. or a Web page can consist of many elements coming from different servers, thus each requiring a separate DNS lookup. The important point here is to see that the DNS lookup time can have a significant impact on the duration of a download, which will be quantified using measurement results in Sec. 4.3.

4 Measurement Results

In this section, measurement results are presented which show the achievable rates in real-world Internet access. Additional evaluations are used to show the impact of TCP effects and DNS latency on the duration of HTTP/TCP connections. The packet traces have originally been recorded to analyze user and application traffic characteristics but are also useful for the network performance evaluation scope of this paper.

---

[1] The phase is called *slow start* because the transmitter starts sending data packets at a low ("slow") rate, not because it would increase the speed slow*ly*, which is definitely not the case.

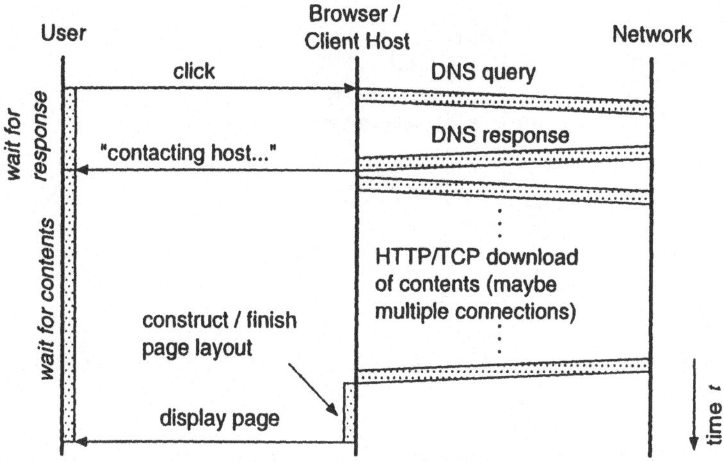

Fig. 1. Reaction and download times for Web access, relation between user and network communication.

4.1 Measurement Setup

The results given in this section have been obtained from two different measurements, which will be referred to as "Trace A" and "Trace B" in the following. Both traces were recorded at Ethernet segments that were close enough to the client computers to allow observation of the *complete* traffic to and from users' computers. The same traces have been used in an evaluation of HTTP traffic characteristics in [4].

Trace A was collected from May to December 1998, when in an ADSL field trial 100 students' PCs were connected to their university's backbone network in Münster, Germany. A sketch of the network and measurement layout is depicted in Fig. 2. The ADSL lines were configured to 2.5 Mbit/s downstream (from the network to the user) and 384 kbit/s upstream (from the user to the network). 15 concentrators serving six to seven users each were connected with 10 Mbit/s Ethernet links to an Ethernet switch. The backbone connection to the University's campus network was a 100 Mbit/s optical Ethernet line. Using the packet duplication feature of the Ethernet switch, the packets exchanged with one of the concentrators could be observed by a traffic monitor running a modified version of tcpdump [11] and the port to be observed could be changed via remote management on a weekly basis. In total, during the six months of monitoring, 14 million IP packet headers belonging to HTTP were collected, covering around 480,000 TCP connections.

Trace B was recorded during five weeks in March and April 1999, when the traffic at a local Internet Service Provider (ISP) called "Bürgernetz Fünfseenland" close to Munich, Germany, was monitored using the same software as with Trace A. The network and measurement setup is sketched in Fig. 3. Around 300 mostly residential subscribers shared 30 dial-up lines allowing modem, single or double ISDN line access plus compression. The traffic monitor was attached to the Ethernet segment connecting the access server to the Internet access router, which provided a 128 kbit/s link to the In-

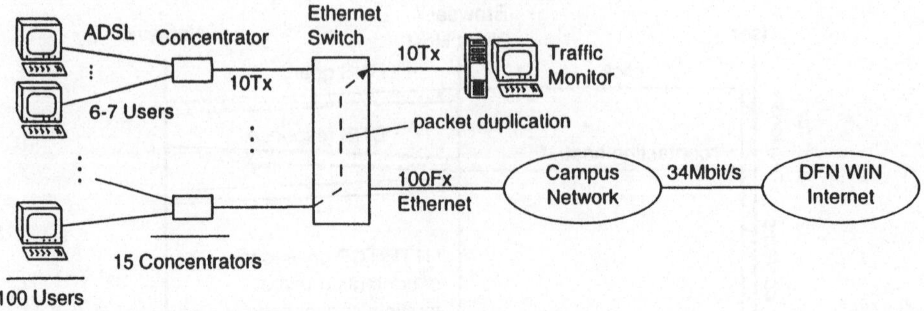

Fig. 2. Measurement setup to collect Trace A in the ADSL Münster field trial.

ternet. Here, 43 million IP packet headers belonging to HTTP were collected, covering around 1.6 million TCP connections.

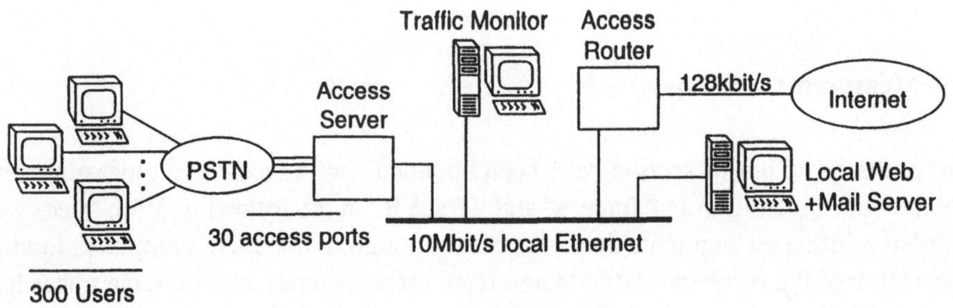

Fig. 3. Measurement setup to collect Trace B at Bürgernetz Fünfseenland, a local ISP offering modem and ISDN access.

Most of the following evaluations will be based on two "flow" classifications extracted from the packet traces. TCP connections were reconstructed as the packets bearing the same pair of IP addresses and TCP port numbers, starting with a SYN (TCP "synchronize", i.e. connection set-up) packet and being complete if at least one FIN (TCP "final", i.e. connection release) or RST (TCP "reset", i.e. connection abort) packet has been observed. Client sessions on the other hand were isolated by aggregating all packets carrying the same client IP address and belonging to the specified service (HTTP). A timeout value of 600 seconds (ten minutes) was used to determine the end of a client session. The timeout period itself was not counted as part of the client session. The numbers of HTTP/TCP connections and client sessions observed in traces A and B is summarized in Tab. 1.

4.2 Rate Distributions

As discussed in Sec. 2, there are two ways of averaging the rates obtained in a TCP connection in order to derive an average fun factor. Here, both averaging methods are used

Table 1. Number of connections and client sessions observed in Traces A and B.

Trace	HTTP/TCP Connections	Client Sessions
A	480794	2260
B	1576151	9253

on measured data. Fig. 4 depicts the distribution of per-connection mean downstream rates. Every connection has the same weight in this distribution, leading to short connections being over-emphasized in the result. In order to remove the impact of pauses between successive HTTP GET requests sharing the same TCP connection, a curve has been added to the plot which is restricted to those connections in which exactly one HTTP GET request was observed. This restriction has very little impact on the resulting connection bit rates. An additional curve has been added evaluating only connections to partner hosts inside the high-speed German research network (DFN WiN), showing an increase of the average bit rates by approximately a factor of somewhat less than two. As one would expect, the rates achievable with modem or ISDN access (Trace B) are less than those that can be obtained over ADSL lines (Trace A).

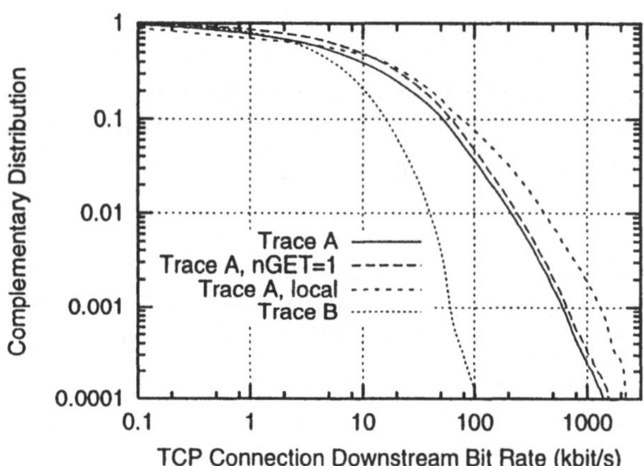

Fig. 4. Complementary distribution of mean downstream HTTP/TCP connection bit rates, determined as the ratio of total downstream traffic volume in a connection to the duration of the connection. Trace A results have been further restricted to connections with only one GET request (nGET=1) or connections to hosts within the DFN WiN (local).

If one were to convert the distributions from Fig. 4 into access fun factor distributions, $\Phi = 1$ would correspond to 2.5 Mbit/s for Trace A and to around 64 kbit/s (depending on the actual access speed) for Trace B.

The corresponding mean and median bit rate and access fun factor values are summarized in Tab. 2. The mean fun factor is in the one percent range for the ADSL lines and around ten percent for the modem/ISDN lines. Due to the high variance of rates obtained from the Internet, the median values are even lower than the averages: There are a few very good (high rate) connections but also a lot with a very low rate.

Table 2. Per-connection downstream bit rates and access fun factor values derived from packet traces A and B. Fun factors Φ have been determined with respect to the respective access line capacity c_{AL}.

Trace	c_{AL} in kbit/s	mean rate in kbit/s	median rate in kbit/s	Φ average	Φ median
A	2500	20.6	6.0	0.8 %	0.24 %
A (nGET=1)	2500	25.7	9.7	1.0 %	0.39 %
A (local)	2500	34.7	8.5	1.4 %	0.34 %
B	(64)	6.7	3.9	10.5 %	6.09 %

The other fun factor averaging strategy – time based averages – is pursued in Fig. 5. Here, one of the problems of the per-connection analysis above could be resolved: Instead of looking at single TCP connections, the aggregated bit rate of all parallel connections can be considered. The curves in Fig. 5 give the complementary distribution of short-time (1 s) average bit rates conditioned on the bit rate being greater than zero. Consequently, time intervals with zero bit rate are not considered and during activity intervals, the aggregated bit rate of all parallel TCP connections is evaluated. The choice of using averaging intervals of 1 s is a compromise between a short averaging time giving a high time resolution but being affected by queueing effects leading to artificially high rates on the one hand and long averaging time intervals reducing the effect of packet queueing but also reducing the time resolution. One second is also an appropriate time scale for evaluating user perceived QoS for elastic services as this time may be regarded as the border between "always fast enough" and "noticeably slowed down".

The average and median results summarized in Tab. 3 show that – as expected – the per time averages of aggregated traffic are higher than the per connection averages given above. The ADSL fun factors are still very low, which is due to the individual access lines being drastically over-dimensioned for the existing Internet of the time of measurement. The modem/ISDN fun factors are in a region where it would be interesting to analyze if it was "the Internet" backbones or the access link to the local ISP that limited the achievable rates due to congestion.

Table 3. Per-client average downstream bit rates and access fun factor values Φ for HTTP traffic derived from packet traces A and B. Values of Φ have been determined relative to access line capacity c_{AL}. Averaging was performed with respect to the one second intervals in which the clients received traffic, i.e. on a time basis, in contrast to the per-connection basis used in Tab. 2.

Trace	c_{AL} in kbit/s	mean rate in kbit/s	median rate in kbit/s	Φ average	Φ median
A	2500	54.7	15.5	2.2 %	0.62 %
B	(64)	23.8	18.0	37.2 %	28.13 %

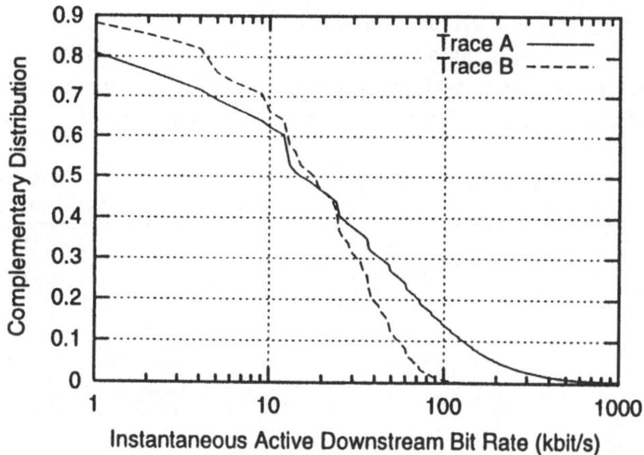

Fig. 5. Complementary distribution of instantaneous bit rates, determined as one second averages of the downstream bit rate within HTTP client sessions under the condition that the client received HTTP traffic during that second.

The results in this section indicate that (a) a simple definition of the access fun factor based on the access line capacity c_{AL} is misleading for high values of c_{AL} and that (b) it may be interesting to use available rates from up-to-date Internet measurements as a reference for Φ. Another approach may be to use the Φ results in order to find an appropriate access line rate c_{AL} for a given backbone network and its rate distribution. Judging from the 95th percentile of rates in Fig. 5, a value of c_{AL} between 200 and 300 kbit/s might have been appropriate at the time of the measurement of Trace A.

4.3 DNS Responses

In Fig. 1, the influence of the DNS lookup latency on browser reaction times was sketched. It is clear that even with an infinitely fast transmission in the subsequent HTTP/TCP connection, a long DNS lookup time cannot be compensated. Therefore, in order to provide a high user perceived quality, DNS lookups must be fast enough not to be disturbing, e.g. the reaction time should be below something like 300 ms. Also the success rate of DNS lookups should of course be high enough for DNS failures not to be perceived as a frequent problem.

The mean and variance of DNS reaction times as well as the success rate observed in traces A and B is summarized in Tab. 4. The success rate observed in Trace B is much lower than that in Trace A. In both traces, the mean reaction time is extremely high. This mean does not reflect the typical reaction time, as can be seen in the complementary distributions plotted in Fig. 6: 90 % of all requests are answered within 175 ms in Trace A and within 1.8 s in Trace B. Considering a typical client timeout of 15 s, another 1–2 % of DNS failures will have been observed due to timeouts.

From these response time distributions, it is obvious that DNS latency can be a major problem for the QoS perceived with Web access. However, an ISP has little influence on the DNS performance when remote DNS servers are unreachable or unavailable.

Table 4. DNS latency and success rate with 95 % confidence intervals from Student-t tests. The success rate was determined using a very high timeout value of one day in order to capture if a reply was eventually received. Additional shorter timeout limits significantly reduce the mean latency that is observed in practice while increasing the failure rate.

Trace	Number of Samples	Success Rate	Mean Latency in seconds	Coeff. of Variation of Latency
A	273000	99.5 % ±0.1 %	10.2±7	7.9±0.5
B	262000	96.3 % ±0.6 %	10.3±3.5	6.7±0.7

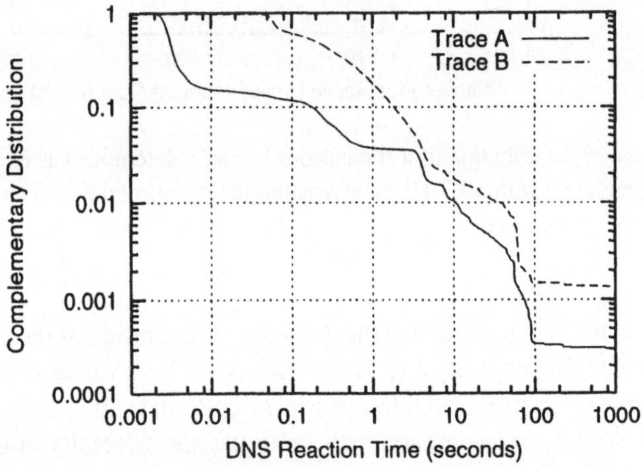

Fig. 6. Complementary distribution of DNS reaction times observed in Trace A (ADSL Münster) and Trace B (Modem or ISDN access to Bürgernetz Fünfseenland).

4.4 Correlations

Fig. 7 depicts the correlation between the downstream volume and the mean downstream rate of an HTTP/TCP connection. Each observed connection is represented by a black dot. The grey value is changed towards lighter values on a logarithmic scale to indicate a higher number of connections with the same combination of volume and rate. A closer look at the upper bounds of the dot clouds in Fig. 7 reveals that the achievable downstream rate in a connection increases approximately with the square root of the downstream connection data volume in both traces, leading to the conclusion that from the two adverse effects determining the rate of short TCP connections discussed in Sec. 3.1, the small window size in short TCP connections has a greater influence on the overall performance than the chance to increase the window size exponentially instead of linearly when other (longer) connections operate in the congestion avoidance region.

According to (2), the achievable throughput between a client and a server is expected to be roughly inversely proportional to the round trip time t_{RT}. This prediction can be confirmed by evaluating the correlation between round trip times and downstream rates in TCP connections. As the round trip time could not be determined directly from the traces, the time between the client-to-server and the server-to-client SYN (TCP connection set-up) packets was used as a simple approximation for the round-trip time.

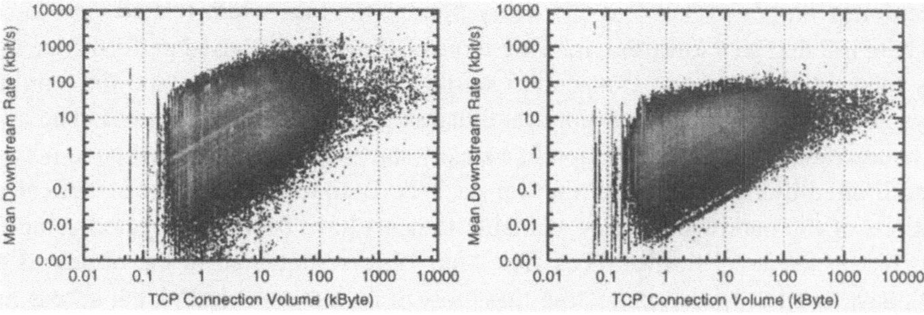

Fig. 7. Correlation between downstream volume and mean downstream bit rate in HTTP/TCP connections. Left: Trace A, right: Trace B. One dot is plotted for each observed connection. The brighter areas in the middle indicate more connections with the same parameter combination.

This time obviously includes additional delay due to the servers' reaction times but the inverse proportionality predicted by (2) is clearly visible in Fig. 8.

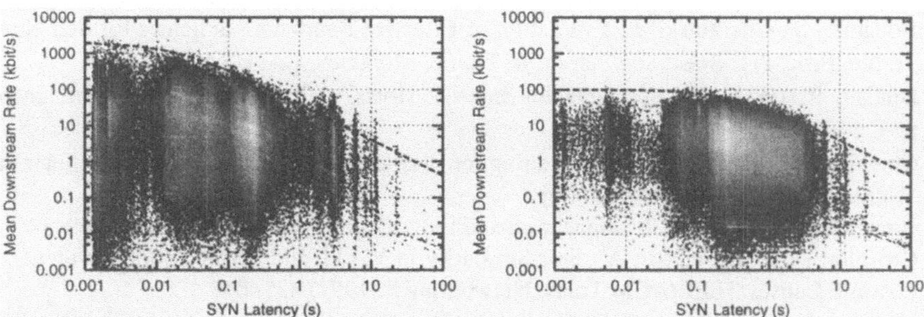

Fig. 8. Correlation between SYN round-trip time and mean downstream bit rate in HTTP/TCP connections. Dashed lines indicate functions $y=\frac{a}{x+b}$. Left: Trace A, $a=40$ kbit, $b=20$ ms. Right: Trace B, $a=40$ kbit, $b=400$ ms. One dot is plotted for each observed connection. The brighter areas in the middle indicate more connections with the same parameter combination.

As the traffic monitor was positioned at a certain distance from the clients, the round trip time measured between the monitor and the server is less than the total round trip time between client and server. This and the limited access line bit rates cause the saturation observed in Fig. 8 at very short round trip times.

5   Conclusions

Different factors determine connection set-up delays and bit rates achieved in a TCP connection over the Internet, which are an important aspects in the users' perception of Web performance. Whereas in the past, most Internet performance evaluations have concentrated on per-packet loss and delay figures, the bandwidth related "fun factor" used here is a first step towards capturing more of the message based performance measures relevant to the users. Connection set-up delays are not only due to round-trip delays and Web server reaction times but also due to DNS response times. The available bandwidth of a TCP connection in a steady state in a congested backbone network is also limited by the round-trip time for packets. Both aspects and the statistical distributions of the bandwidth really available to users have been investigated using two extensive packet level traffic traces. The "fun factors" obtained in the observed networks have been very low, indicating that most of the time, the individual access lines were overdimensioned with respect to the bit rate available from the Internet. Larger downloads have obtained higher average bit rates than lower downloads, which is due to TCP's startup behavior. Starting a TCP connection to a new host that the client computer previously had no communication with can take a significant amount of time due to the very long DNS latency observed in many cases. This is the main reason why a future version of "fun factor" definitions for perceived Web performance should include a combination of latency and rate based components.

References

[1] Bodamer, S., Charzinski, J.: Evaluation of Effective Bandwidth Schemes for Self-Similar Traffic. Proc. ITC Spec. Seminar on IP Traffic, Monterey, CA, USA (2000)

[2] Braden, R. (Ed.): Requirements for Internet Hosts – Communication Layers. Internet RFC 1122 (1989)

[3] Charzinski, J.: Fun Factor Dimensioning for Elastic Traffic. Proc. ITC Spec. Seminar on IP Traffic, Monterey, CA, USA (2000)

[4] Charzinski, J.: HTTP/TCP Connection and Flow Char. Perf. Eval. **42** (2000) 149–162

[5] Crovella, M.E., Bestavros, A.: Self-Similarity in World Wide Web Traffic: Evidence and Possible Causes. IEEE/ACM Trans. Networking **5** (1997) 835–846

[6] Heyman, D.P., Lakshman, T.V., Neidhardt, A.L.: A New Method for Analysing Feedback-Based Protocols with Applications to Engineering Web Traffic over the Internet. Proc. ACM Sigmetrics'97, Seattle, WA, USA; ACM Perf. Eval. Review **25** 24–38

[7] Huitema, C., Weerahandi, S.: Internet measurements: the rising tide and the DNS snag. Proc. ITC Spec. Seminar on IP Traffic, Monterey, CA, USA (2000)

[8] Krishnamurthy, B., Wills, C.E.: Analyzing factors that influence end-to-end Web performance. Computer Networks **33** (2000) 17–32.

[9] Leland, W.E., Taqqu, M.S., Willinger, W., Wilson, D.V.: On the Self-Similar Nature of Ethernet Traffic. Proc. ACM Sigcomm'93, San Francisco, CA, USA (1993) 183–193

[10] Lindberger, K.: Balancing Quality of Service, Pricing and Utilization in Multiservice Networks with Stream and Elastic Traffic. Proc. ITC 16, Edinburgh, UK (1999) 1127–1136

[11] McCanne, S., Leres, C., Jacobson, V.: tcpdump. LBNL Network Research Group, ftp://ftp.ee.lbl.gov/tcpdump.tar.Z

[12] Padhye, J., Firoiu, V., Towsley, D., Kurose, J.: Modeling TCP Throughput: A Simple Model and its Empirical Validation. Proc. ACM Sigcomm'98, Vancouver, Canada (1998)

[13] Padmanabhan, V.N. Mogul, J.C.: Improving HTTP Latency. Comp. Netw. and ISDN Systems **28** (1995) 24–35

[14] Riedl, A., Perske, M., Bauschert, T., Probst, A.: Dimensioning of IP Access Networks with Elastic Traffic. Proc. Networks 2000, Toronto, Canada (2000)

Session 12:

Dienstmanagement

Signalisierungsplattform zur netzübergreifenden Dienststeuerung in heterogener TIME Infrastruktur

Wolfgang Kellerer, Peter Sties

Technische Universität München (TUM)
Lehrstuhl für Kommunikationsnetze (LKN)
Arcisstraße 21, 80333 München, Germany
{kellerer, sties}@ei.tum.de, http://www.ei.tum.de/

Zusammenfassung. Die heutige Kommunikationsinfrastruktur ist geprägt von einer wachsenden Heterogenität von Fest- und Mobilfunknetzen, sowie einer Vielzahl unterschiedlicher Endgeräte aus den Bereichen Telekommunikation, Information und Medien / Entertainment (TIME). Eine weitreichende Nutzbarkeit von Informations- und Kommunikationsdiensten setzt daher einen Zugang zu diesen Diensten unabhängig von der Netzinfrastruktur voraus. Darüberhinaus müssen diese Dienste über bislang getrennte Netze übergreifend arbeiten können. Um eine derartige Konvergenz heterogener Netze auf Dienstebene zu erreichen, wurde am Lehrstuhl für Kommunikationsnetze der Technischen Universität München eine Signalisierungsplattform für die netzunabhängige Dienststeuerung entwickelt. Unsere Architektur beschreibt ein komponentenorientiertes Serversystem, das übergeordnet zu den Netzen angeordnet ist.

In der vorliegenden Arbeit geben wir einen Überblick über das Gesamtkonzept und beschreiben die Komponenten der Plattform, die die Netzunabhängigkeit realisieren: Die Netzadaptoren. Neben Netzadaptoren, welche die Architektur-interne Signalisierung auf Netz-API umsetzen, gibt es spezielle Adaptoren für den Teilnehmerzugang, für den Zugang zu Content Ressourcen und für Spezialressourcen. Ein Lookup-Server zur dynamischen Registrierung der Adaptoren vervollständigt die Architektur. Die Kommunikation zwischen den verteilten Komponenten der Architektur erfolgt über ein Signalisierungsprotokoll, das in Anlehnung an das Session Initiation Protocol (SIP) der IETF definiert wurde.

1 Einführung

Die derzeitige Kommunikationslandschaft ist geprägt von verschiedenen Kommunikationssystemen, die als verteilte Systeme unterschiedliche Anforderungen erfüllen. Gerade in der heutigen Zeit, die von der Konvergenz bisher getrennter Informations-, Kommunikations- und Verteildienste geprägt ist, reicht ein System alleine nicht aus, um alle Teilnehmeranforderungen (Qualität, Bandbreite, Dienstvielfalt) zu erfüllen. Vielmehr sind an der Erbringung von Teilnehmerdiensten viele Instanzen in unterschiedlichen Protokollebenen und an verschiedenen Stellen in den Netzen (z.B. Server, Netz, Endgerät) beteiligt. Eine Vielzahl konkurrierender oder sich ergänzender Kommunikationssysteme bildet eine stark heterogene Landschaft aus Standards und Systemen in den TIME Bereichen Telekommunikation (z.B. ISDN, GSM), Information (z.B. Internet, WAP) und Medien / Entertainment (z.B. CATV, DVB). In allen Bereichen ist neben den Bestrebungen zur Vereinheitlichung z.B. mit B-ISDN/ATM oder UMTS/IMT2000 derzeit eher eine starke Tendenz zur weiteren Diversifikation zu beobachten. Bestehende Systeme werden weitergenutzt, um den steigenden Bandbreitenbedarf zu decken, bzw. bisher unbeachtete Systeme erfahren einen neuen Nutzen (z.B. Data Broadcasting, Powerline Communication). Daher ist es auch in Zukunft äußerst unwahrscheinlich, daß eine einzige, einheitliche Netzinfrastruktur vorherrschen wird.

Der laufende Wettbewerb unter den Anbietern von Informations- und Kommunikationsdiensten für die Endteilnehmer, der durch die jüngste Deregulierung auf dem Telekommunikations- und Informationsmarkt noch weiter verschärft wird, trägt darüberhinaus dazu bei, daß der Bedarf wächst, verschiedene Netze zu kombinieren, um auf diese Weise mehr Teilnehmer ansprechen zu können. Es sind die Dienste, die die verschiedenen Anbieter untereinander auszeichnen. Diese Dienste müssen schnell über unterschiedliche Netze an die Teilnehmer gebracht werden, um einen möglichst großen Marktanteil zu erzielen. Die Einbeziehung neuer, bisher anders genutzter Netze, wie z.B. Verteilnetze für Kommunikationsdienste, bringt dabei weitere Vorteile, um sich von der Konkurrenz abzuheben und eine größere Zahl von Teilnehmern zu erreichen.

Dienste sind einem schnellen Lebenszyklus unterworfen. Um die zügige Einrichtung und Erbringung von Diensten auf unterschiedlichen Netzen zu ermöglichen, sind neue Lösungen gefordert, die eine netzunabhängige Beschreibung und Steuerung der Dienste unterstützen und zusätzlich von den verschiedenen Endgeräten der Teilnehmer abstrahieren.

Um diesen Anforderungen Rechnung zu tragen wurde am Lehrstuhl für Kommunikationsnetze der Technischen Universität München eine Architektur für eine netzunabhängige Dienststeuerung entwickelt, die eine Steuerung von Diensten auf heterogenen Netzen realisiert. Dabei sind folgende Anforderungen berücksichtigt:

- Heterogenität der Netze und unterschiedliche Endgeräte für die Dienststeuerung transparent machen

- Unabhängigkeit der Dienststeuerung von netzspezifischen Steuerungsdetails

- Ausnutzung von vorhandenen netzspezifischen Diensten über bestehende APIs

- Kombination von Netzen zur übergreifenden Dienststeuerung

- Schnelle und einfache Dienstentwicklung und Erweiterbarkeit

- Adaptivität bezüglich sich ändernder Infrastruktureigenschaften

- Einfache Zugangsmöglichkeit für Teilnehmer über unterschiedliche Netze/Kommunikationstechnologien

In der vorliegenden Arbeit werden nach einem Überblick über das Gesamtkonzept die Mechanismen unserer Plattform beschrieben, welche die Unabhängigkeit der Steuerung von den spezifischen Eigenschaften und den eigenen Signalisierungsprotokollen der Netze realisieren. Das ist neben den unterschiedlichen Adaptorkomponenten für Teilnehmerzugang und Netzsteuerung insbesondere das neu entwickelte

Signalisierungsprotokoll *SesCP*, das die asynchrone Kommunikation zwischen den Steuerungskomponenten und den Adaptorkomponenten sicherstellt.

Die weitere Arbeit gliedert sich wie folgt. Zunächst verdeutlichen in Abschnitt 2 einige Dienstszenarien das Ziel unseres Ansatzes. Ein Überblick über die netzunabhängige Dienststeuerplattform und die grundlegenden Konzepte wird in Abschnitt 3 gegeben. Abschnitt 4 geht näher auf die Netz-Adaptor-Komponenten ein, die die Netzunabhängigkeit realisieren. Das Signalisierungsprotokoll, über das die verteilten Komponenten der Architektur kommunizieren wird anschließend in Abschnitt 5 beschrieben. Zusammenfassung und Ausblick schließen die Arbeit ab.

2 Dienste und Dienstszenarien

Die Dienststeuerplattform ist zu den heterogenen Netzen und den Netzen unterschiedlicher Betreiber übergeordnet angesiedelt. Sie stellt allen Teilnehmern in den angeschlossenen Netzen ihre Dienste bereit. Es ist insbesondere Aufgabe der Dienststeuerung *höhere Dienste* zu erbringen, die über die Funktionalität der einzelnen Netze hinausgehen. Dies umfaßt zum einen die Funktionalität, Dienste übergreifend in heterogenen Netzen zu steuern. Zugangsnetz und Ausführungsnetz können dabei vollständig getrennt verwaltet werden. Zum anderen ermöglicht die Plattform eine Kombination von bisher getrennten Kommunikationsdiensten, um auf diese Weise neue Dienste zu schaffen (z.B. Konferenz plus Video Abruf). Darüberhinaus erlaubt die Programmierbarkeit der Dienststeuerung die Entwicklung neuer, teilnehmerspezifischer Dienste.

Die folgenden Beispiele zeigen mögliche Szenarien zukünftiger netztransparenter Dienstnutzung.

- Während einer Telefonkonferenz zwischen einem H.323 Multimedia PC und einem GSM Telefon beschießen die Teilnehmer eine Multimediapräsentation aus dem Internet zu Rate zu ziehen. Während der H.323 Teilnehmer diese direkt empfangen kann, erhält der mobile Teilnehmer die Präsentation auf seinem ebenfalls mitgeführten Laptop über ein terrestrisches digitales Rundfunknetz.

- Ein Unternehmensberater mit wechselnden Aufenthaltsorten greift auf seine Intranet-Informations-Dienste über Internet-Browser, WAP-Handy oder per Sprachzugang in seinem Dienstwagen zu.

- Während einer ISDN basierten Multimedia-Konferenz wird ein Teilnehmer über das Internet und ein weiterer über UMTS zugeschaltet, ohne daß die Netze explizit von den Teilnehmern angewählt werden.

- Über seinen zentralen Kalender kann ein Geschäftsmann seine globale Erreichbarkeit automatisch konfigurieren. Dabei kann er nicht nur seine persönlichen Einstellungen über unterschiedliche Netze/Dienste vornehmen (WWW, Email, Voice), sondern diese gelten auch für alle Kommunikationssysteme, die er benutzt.

3 Netzunabhängige Signalisierungsplattform

Um die oben beschriebenen und illustrierten Anforderungen zu erfüllen, wurde eine neuartige Dienstarchitektur definiert, die sich insbesondere durch eine Strukturierung in funktionale Module auszeichnet. Bild 1, rechts, zeigt das zugrundeliegende Referenzmodell, in dem die unabhängigen Funktionen unterschieden werden.

Anwendungen (Applications) werden hier von der reinen Dienststeuerung (Service Control) getrennt. Die Dienststeuerung verwaltet nur die Dienstparameter und steuert den Dienstablauf. Teilnehmerdatenverwaltung und Teilnehmerzugang (User Control), sowie die Steuerung der Kommunikationsbeziehungen (Communication Control) und die Verwaltung der Netzressourcen (Resource Control) erfolgen in getrennten Modulen. Aber auch hier ist die Steuerung unabhängig von spezifischen Netzparametern. Adaptoren (Mediation) übernehmen den Zugang zu den unterschiedlichen Kommunikationsnetzen und realisieren die völlige Unabhängigkeit der Steuerplattform von den Netzen und den darin befindlichen Netzressourcen (Networks, Resources). Transparent für die Steuerplattform ist ebenfalls die Ansteuerung von Endgeräten oder Serverelementen.

3.1 Komponenten der Dienstarchitektur

Die Realisierung der oben skizzierten Funktionen in konkreten Komponenten der Dienstarchitektur erfolgt in Anlehnung an Prinzipien der verteilten Systeme. Dabei wird insbesondere auf die TINA Session Konzepte zurückgegriffen [2] (siehe Bild 1, links). In der Teilnehmersteuerung (User Control) vertritt ein User Proxy als Stellvertreter den Teilnehmer in der Zugangs-Session (Access Session). Der Access Session obliegt auch die Verwaltung aller Teilnehmer-spezifischen Daten. Unabhängig von Teilnehmer- und Netz-spezifischen Daten steuert ein Service Session Manager (SSM) einen instanzierten Dienst. Der Communication Session Manager (CSM) wählt je nach Teilnehmerdaten und den Anforderungen des SSM aus der Registry geeignete Adaptoren aus und steuert darüber die für die Dienstausführung erforderlichen Kommunikationsbeziehungen.

Die eben skizzierte Dienstarchitektur beschreibt eine Serverstruktur aus asynchron kommunizierenden Komponenten, die über Adaptoren Zugang zu unterschiedlichen Kommunikationsnetzen hat, generell aber unabhängig von einer Netzinfrastruktur ist. Sie beschreibt somit einen unabhängigen Dienstanbieter, der auf verschiedene, ihm in der Regel nicht gehörende, Infrastrukturen für die Erbringung seiner Dienste zugreift. Das Serversystem ist somit nicht in einem Endgerät (Intelligent Terminals) oder in bestimmten netzspezifischen Ressourcen (Intelligent Networks) sondern vielmehr auf einer unabhängigen Dienstebene über den Netzen angeordnet: "Intelligence on Top of the Networks".

Weitere Details zur Steuerung von Diensten und zum Zusammenspiel der Komponenten können [1] entnommen werden. Der Schwerpunkt der vorliegenden Arbeit liegt auf der Realisierung der Netzunabhängigkeit.

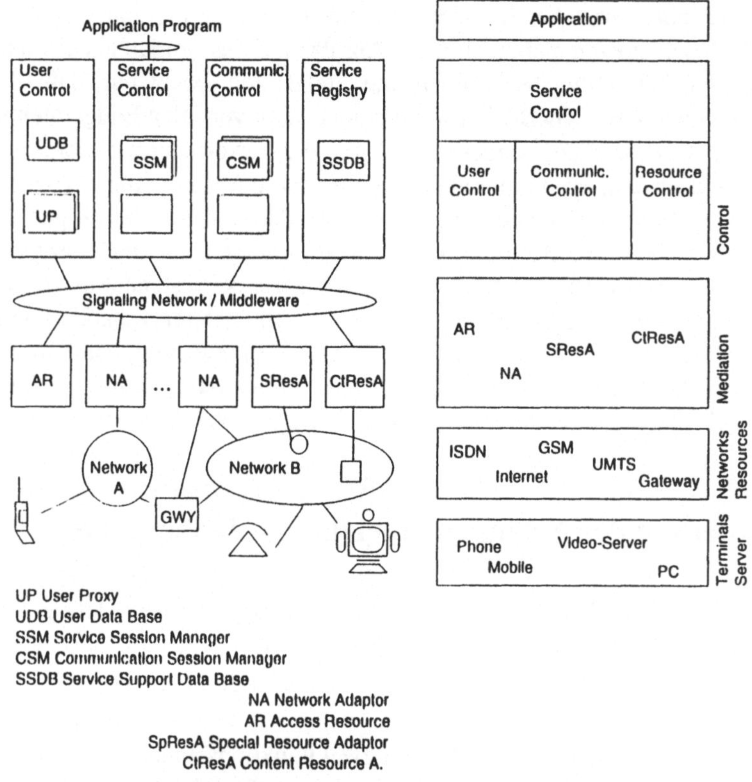

UP User Proxy
UDB User Data Base
SSM Service Session Manager
CSM Communication Session Manager
SSDB Service Support Data Base

NA Network Adaptor
AR Access Resource
SpResA Special Resource Adaptor
CtResA Content Resource A.

Bild 1: Architektur der netzunabhängigen Dienststeuerung

3.2 Diskussion alternativer Ansätze

Im folgenden Abschnitt werden alternative Ansätze diskutiert, die generell für eine netzunabhängige Dienststeuerung in Frage kommen, und es wird ihr Zusammenhang mit der vorliegenden Arbeit dargestellt.

Das Internet Protokoll (IP) an sich stellt durch seine netzverbindende Eigenschaft eine Plattform für eine Infrastruktur-unabhängige Dienststeuerung dar. Doch zum einen entspricht die endgerätebasierte Realisierung von Diensten nicht unserem Ansatz der Unabhängigkeit von den Endgeräten, zum anderen fehlen notwendige Eigenschaften für Telekommunikationsdienste wie QoS und Vergebührung im IP Transportdienst. Selbst wenn in erweiterten Protokollgenerationen (IPv6) viele Probleme gelöst werden, so gibt es auch dort keine Funktion, die Diensteigenschaften adaptiv auf die Transportnetze abbildet, um deren Eigenschaften auszunutzen.

Middleware-basierte Ansätze wie z.B. die Telecommunications Information Networking Architecture (TINA) [2] sind vielversprechend hinsichtlich der Erbringung komplexer Dienste und erlauben eine Ansteuerung und Auswahl von Netzelementen auf höherer Ebene als beim IP. Während die TINA Kern-Architektur auf eine B-ISDN/ATM Infrastruktur abzielt, werden in weiterführenden Projekten Konzepte für andere

Netze insbesondere bestehende Telekommunikationsnetze [3] und IP basierte Netze entwickelt. Doch stützen sich auch diese Ansätze auf das Vorhandensein der Middleware auf allen beteiligten Netzknoten und Endgeräten. Nicht nur, daß Middleware Technologien wie z.B. CORBA bei weitem noch nicht von allen Endgeräten und Netzknoten unterstützt werden, sondern auch, daß die Performanceprobleme noch nicht endgültig geklärt sind, macht diese Ansätze für unsere Anforderungen ungeeignet. Die abstrakte Modellierung von Diensten in TINA wiederum läßt sich sehr gut übertragen.

Ähnlich wie bei den Middleware-Systemen fordern auch die Ansätze der Programmable Networks, z.B. [4], und der Active Networks [5] standardisierte Interfaces, die in allen beteiligten Netzknoten und teilweise in Endgeräten vohanden sein müssen. Dies ist bei unserem hier beschriebenen Ansatz nicht notwendig, bei dem die Netzinfrastruktur nicht modifiziert werden muß. Unser Ansatz basiert auf den derzeit entstehenden hochstehenden Steuerungsschnittstellen für Kommunikationsnetze wie z.B. PARLAY [6].

4 Realisierung der Netzunabhängigkeit: Adaptor Units

Die Unabhängigkeit der Dienststeuerung von netzspezifischen Details wird durch Adaptoren erreicht, die als intelligente Signalisierungs-Gateways das Serversystem an Netzelemente koppeln. Wir unterscheiden generell drei Typen von Adaptoren: Network Adaptors (NA), Content Resource Adaptors (CtResA) und Special Resource Adaptors (SpResA). Daneben rechnen wir zwei Funktionseinheiten des Serversystems ebenfalls zur Adaptorebene, die keine echte Gatewayfunktion haben, aber die Adaptivität unterstützen: die Access Resource (AR) für einen Teilnehmerzugang, der unabhängig von der Form der Informationsdarstellung beim Teilnehmer ist, und die Service Registry (SR) zum dynamischen Anbinden von Netzressourcen (= Lookup Service). Im folgenden wird auf die Funktion und die Realisierung der Adaptor-Units näher eingegangen.

4.1 Adaptoren für Kommunikationsnetze und -ressourcen

Die Network Adaptors (NA) stellen einen Zugang zu Kommunikationsnetzen bereit und ermöglichen die Einrichtung von Kommunikationsbeziehungen in denselben. Dabei können die NAs auf hochstehende, mächtige 3rd Party Interfaces zugreifen wie z.B. PARLAY [6], oder die architektureinheitliche Signalisierung wird auf einfache UNI Schnittstellen umgesetzt. Für Kommunikationsbeziehungen die nicht stellvertretend (3rd Party) aufgebaut oder über sequentiell gekoppelte UNIs gesteuert werden können, sind NAs vorgesehen, die über Gateways Kommunikationsbeziehungen vom Netzrand her einrichten (Network Edge Initiated, z.B. Internet Gateways, DVB-T Kopfstation). Um die Funktionalität mächtiger Schnittstellen auszunutzen, werden Kommunikationsbeziehungen möglichst abstrakt auf ein Netz abgebildet. Beispiel: Falls ein Interface bereits die Einrichtung von Videokonferenzen erlaubt, wird dies ausgenutzt und es entfällt die komplexe Aufteilung in und Koordinierung voneinzelnen Point-to-Point Verbindungen.

Neben den NA bieten die SpResA Schnittstellen zu Ressourcen in den Netzen wie z.B. Konvertern, Mischern, etc. CtResA bieten ergänzend Schnittstellen zu Servern in den Netzen, die Inhalte bereitstellen, z.B. Ansageeinheiten, Videoserver, Game Server. Die Signalisierungsplattform bleibt damit unabhängig von Informationsinhalten (Content).

Jeder Adaptor bildet die architektureinheitliche Signalisierung auf die jeweilige, netzspezifische Signalisierung ab und kontrolliert eine Kommunikationsbeziehung in seinem Netz. Dafür besteht er aus einer generischen Einheit zum Protokollhandling (Protocol Agent), einer spezifischen Komponente und einer Abbildungseinheit dazwischen. Mögliche standardisierte oder proprietäre Netz-APIs oder Netz-Komponenten, auf denen die Adaptoren aufsetzen, sind: UNI (ISDN), INAP (IN), PINT (IN-SCP), PARLAY, JTAPI, JAIN (ISDN), Gatekeeper (H.323), Proxy Server (SIP). Daneben können auch beliebige neue Adaptoren entwickelt werden, um neue Netze anzubinden, insbesondere auch Broadcast-Netze.

Die Verwendung der Datenübertragungseigenschaften von terrestrischen Broadcast-netzen wie z.B. DVB-T und DAB verspricht eine verbesserte Unterstützung für breitbandige, mobile Dienste. Zur Datenübertragung über DVB-T wurde im Rahmen der Dienstarchitektur ein System entwickelt und realisiert, das sowohl die unidirektionale Datenübertragung im Broadcast oder Multicastbetrieb als auch eine Kombination mit schmalbandigen Rückkanälen erlaubt [7]. Die Ansteuerung dieses Brodacast Netz Adaptors verspricht für die vorgestellte Dienststeuerung neue Möglichkeiten zur Dienstrealisierung.

4.2 Service Mobility: Flexibler Dienstzugang mit XML

Die Signalisierung zwischen den Teilnehmern und dem Serversystem ist bei den oben vorgestellten Adaptoren beschränkt auf die Möglichkeiten, die die netzspezifische Signalisierung bietet. Gerade neue Dienste können aber damit nicht oder nur sehr umständlich angeboten werden. Darüberhinaus erlaubt ein signalisierungstransparenter Zugang einen Netz- und Endgeräte-unabhängigen Dienstzugriff (Service Mobilty). Unser Konzept sieht daher die Verwendung eines zusätzlichen Adaptors vor, der die Darstellung der dienstspezifischen Signalisierung für den Teilnehmer übernimmt: die Access Resource (AR).

Wir verwenden dabei eine flexible Hypertext-basierte Lösung. Der Inhalt des Hypertextservers, der je nach Signalisierung des Serversystems dem Teilnehmer angezeigt wird, ist in XML gespeichert bzw. es werden über Servlets dynamisch XML Seiten aus einer LDAP Teilnehmerdatenbank erzeugt. Durch die Verwendung von XML wird eine darstellungsunabhängige Beschreibung des anzuzeigenden Inhalts erreicht. Diese kann adaptiv je nach Fähigkeiten des Teilnehmerendgerätes z.B. in HTML für Multimedia Endgeräte, in WML für WAP Handys oder in VoxML für die Sprachausgabe auf Telefonen ausgegeben werden. Das Darstellungsformat wird in Style Files (XSL) festgelegt. Diese bestimmen auch, welche Inhalte in der jeweiligen Darstellung sinnvoll angezeigt werden. Abbildung 2 gibt einen Überblick über die prototypische Implementierung der AR. Für die Realisierung wird unter Linux ein Apache Web-Server mit dem COCOON Plug-In für die Verarbeitung von XML eingesetzt.

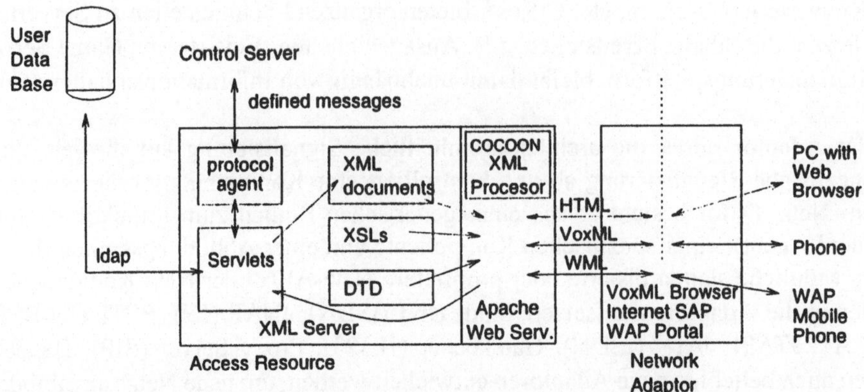

Bild 2: Darstellungsunabhängiger Dienstzugang

4.3 Service Discovery: Adaptive Auswahl von Netzressourcen

Um zur Laufzeit auf Änderungen in der Dienstarchitekturumgebung reagieren zu können, beinhaltet das Serversystem eine sogenannte Service Registry als weitere Adaptorkomponente. Diese unterstützt die Kommunikationssteuerung (Communication Control) in der Auswahl geeigneter Netz- und Ressourcenadaptoren. Dabei erlaubt ein Mechanismus aus den bekannten Service Discovery Ansätzen die Registrierung der Kommunikationsdienste der Adaptoren in der Registry (siehe Bild 3). In der Registry können neben der (internen) Adresse und der angebotenen Netz-Dienstparametern auch weitere Parameter, wie z.B. Preise abgespeichert werden. Darüberhinaus ist es angedacht auch dynamische Parameter wie z.B. die momentane Auslastung oder die Verfügbarkeit (bei Mobilnetzen) zu speichern. Die Realisierung der Service Discovery Komponenten in unserem Prototypen basiert auf SUN's JINI Technologie.

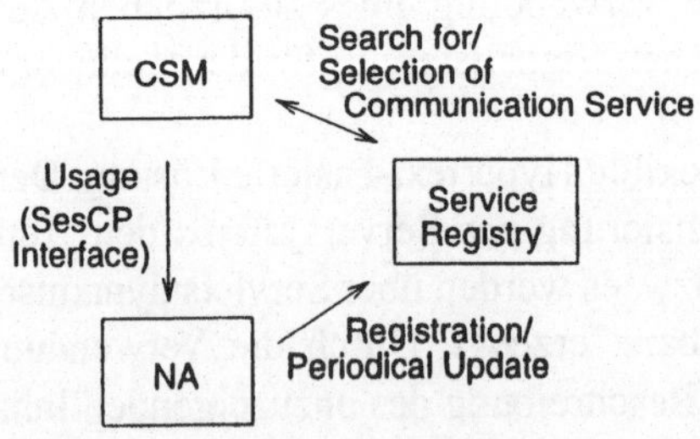

Bild 3: Service Discovery für die Ressourcenverwaltung

5 Server Middleware: SIP basierte Signalisierung

Durch die strenge Separierung in getrennte Funktionseinheiten für Teilnehmerdaten, Dienststeuerung und Kommunikationssteuerung wird die Komplexität für die Steuerung von Diensten reduziert. Darüberhinaus können die verschiedenen Komponenten der Dienststeuerung verteilt angeordnet werden. Dies wird insbesondere durch die gewählten Schnittstellen und den darauf definierten Meldungssatz unterstützt über den die verteilten Komponenten asynchron Nachrichten austauschen. Der Meldungssatz ist dabei möglichst einfach gehalten, um zum einen eine unkomplizierte Realisierung zu ermöglichen und um zum anderen Flexibilität zu schaffen, d.h. unabhängig zu sein von der Implementierung bestimmter Dienstklassen.

Das Session Initiation Protocol (SIP) der IETF [8] bietet die hierfür geforderte Einfachheit in Kombination mit Flexibilität d.h. Offenheit zur Unterstützung verschiedener Dienste. Wir haben auf Basis von SIP das *Session Control Protocol* (SesCP) für die Signalisierungsplattform entwickelt. Tabelle 1 gibt einen Überblick über die verwendeten Meldungen und stellt den Bezug zu SIP dar.

Tabelle 1

Meldung	Kurzbeschreibung	Bezug zu SIP
ACCESS	Teilnehmerzugang zur Dienststeuerung und Management des Teilnehmerprofils	REGISTER
INVITE	Anforderung eines Dienstes und Änderung der Dienstkonfiguration (Einladen eines Tln., etc.)	INVITE
SETUP	Anforderung der Einrichtung von Kommunikationsbeziehungen	INVITE
OK	Antwort auf INVITE / SETUP	OK (1xx)
ACK	Bestätigung von OK und Ausführungsaufforderung	ACK
INFO, STATUS	Abfrage / Mitteilung von Informationen (z.B. Teilnehmerprofil)	-
END, BYE	Beendigung der Teilnahme (BYE) oder des ganzen Dienstes (END)	BYE
CANCEL	Vorzeitiger Abbruch einer Dienstanforderung	CANCEL

Im Session Control Protocol wird auch die aus TINA abgeleitete Separierung in die drei Steuerungsbereiche User, Service und Communication Control (siehe Abschnitt 3) unterstützt. Jeder Steuerungsbereich verwaltet, wie bereits beschrieben, seine eigene Sicht auf den Dienst (Dienstbeschreibung). Die SesCP Meldungen kommunizieren diese Bereichs-spezifischen Dienstbeschreibungen oder Teile davon zwischen den Architekturkomponenten, um die verschiedenen Sichten auszutauschen. Dabei wird die Dienstbeschreibung beginnend von einem abstrakten Modell (Teilnehmersicht: Dienstname und Teilnehmer) schrittweise detailliert, bis schließlich konkrete Kommunikationsbeziehungen in den Netzadaptoren eingerichtet werden (QoS Parameter, Verbindungsgraph). Die Hauptkomponenten der drei Steuerungsbereiche (UP, SSM, CSM) wirken dabei als (SIP-) Proxy Server zur Verarbeitung und Weiterleitung der Dienstbeschreibung.

Abbildung 4 zeigt einen typischen Meldungsaustausch zur Einrichtung von Kommunikationsbeziehungen zwischen der Dienststeuereinheit (SSM) und der Kommunikationssteuerung (CSM). Dabei wird zum einen der Einsatz des dreischrittigen Meldungsablaufes (INVITE, OK, ACK) nach dem Atomic Action Prinzip deutlich [9]. Das dreischrittige Protokoll erlaubt das Zusammenfügen verschiedener Steuereinheiten (NA, SpResA) zu einem Verbindungsgraphen und dessen Aushandlung. Durchgeschalten wird erst, wenn alle Einheiten positiv geantwortet haben (OK).

Zum anderen kommt die strikte Trennung von Dienst und Teilnehmerdaten zum Ausdruck. Erst der CSM fordert Teilnehmerdaten wie aktueller Netzzugang an (INFO). Die initiale SETUP Meldung des SSM enthält nur abstrakte Parameter, auf

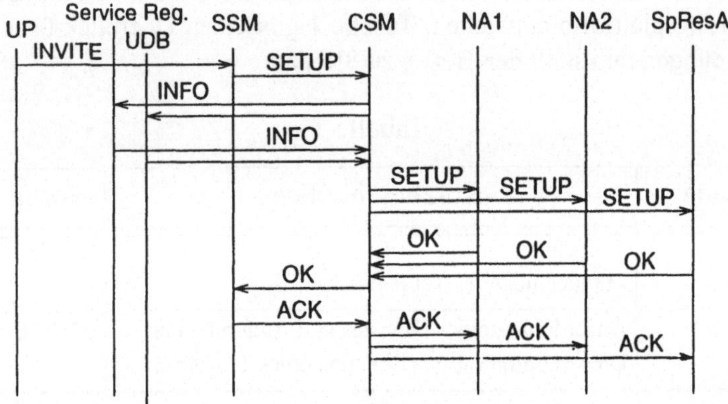

Bild 4: Anforderung von Kommunikationsbeziehungen

deren Basis der CSM die Netze bzw. deren Adaptoren auswählt.

Eine prototypische Realisierung der Signalisierungsarchitektur erfolgt derzeit mit der formalen Beschreibungssprache SDL.

6 Zusammenfassung und Ausblick

In der vorliegenden Arbeit wird eine neuartige Architektur zur netzübergreifenden Steuerung von Informations- und Kommunikationsdiensten unabhängig von Netzen und Endgeräten vorgestellt. Auf diese Weise wird der zunehmenden Heterogenität einerseits und dem Verlangen nach personalisierten, netzunabhängigen Diensten andererseits Rechnung getragen. Der Schwerpunkt der Ausführungen liegt auf den Komponenten, die im Sinne einer auf asynchronem Nachrichtenaustausch basierenden Middleware die Netzunabhängigkeit realisieren. Neben Adaptor-Komponenten für die Anpassung von Signalisierungsnachrichten werden Komponenten für einen darstellungsunabhängigen Dienstzugang beschrieben. Adaptivität bezüglich sich ändernder Netzinfrastruktur wird durch Service Discovery Mechanismen unterstützt.

Die vorgestellte Architektur ermöglicht es in Weiterführung des Abstraktionsgedankens, der mit der Einführung von mächtigen APIs wie z.B. dem PARLAY API aufgekommen ist, Dienste netzübergreifend zu steuern. Damit haben auch reine Dienstanbieter die Möglichkeit, neue Dienste schnell, Netz- und Endgeräte-übergreifend anzubieten. Durch die Verwendung eines Signalisierungsprotokolls, das auf dem

IETF Protokoll SIP basiert, wird der Übergang auf ein IP basiertes Next Generation Network vereinfacht, indem die Einbeziehung von vorhandener Infrastruktur in zukünftige IP basierte Netze über die vorgestellte Signalisierungsplattform erreicht werden kann.

7 Literatur

[1] W. Kellerer. *A Versatile Network Independent Server Architecture for Multimedia Information and Communication Services.* In: H. van As (Editor) Telecommunication Network Intelligence, Kluwer, 2000. Proceedings of SmartNet 2000, Vienna, September 2000, pp. 331-350.

[2] *TINA Service Architecture*, Telecommunications Information Networking Architecture Consortium, Http://www.tinac.com, 1997.

[3] E. Holz, O. Kath, M. Geipl, G. Lin, and V. Vogel. *The CAMOUFLAGE Project: Introduction of TINA into Telecommunication Legacy Systems.* In Proceedings of TINA'97, November 1997, pp. 206-215.

[4] C. Gbgaguidi, J.-P. Hubaux, M. Hamdi, and A. Tantawi. *A Programmable Architecture for the Provision of Hybrid Services.* IEEE Communications Magazine, Vol. 37, No.7, July 1999, pp. 110-116.

[5] K. L. Calvert, S. Bhattacharjee, E. Zegura, G. Tech, J. Sterbenz. *Directions in Active Networks.* IEEE Communications Magazine, October 1998, pp. 72-78.

[6] F.-K. Bruhns. *Parlay - the API for Secure and Open Access to Networking Functionality for Third Party Applications outside the Network.* In Proceedings of: ICIN'2000, Bordeaux, January, 2000, pp. 17 - 21.

[7] W. Kellerer, P. Sties and J. Eberspächer. *IP Based Enhanced Data Casting Services over Radio Broadcast Networks.* In Proceedings of IEEE ECUMN'00, Colmar, France, October 2000, pp. 195-203.

[8] M. Handley, H. Schulzrinne, E. Schooler, and J. Rosenberg. *SIP: Session Initiation Protocol.* IETF Request for Comments, RFC 2543, March 1999.

[9] ITU-T Recommendations X.851/2. *Information Technology Open Systems Interconnection - Protocol For The Commitment, Concurrency And Recovery Service Element.* ITU-T, 1993.

Management-Aufgaben bei komponentenbasierten verteilten Systemen im Fahrzeug-Telematikbereich

Volker Feil[1] und Matthias Stümpfle[2]

[1] Universität Stuttgart, Institut für Nachrichtenvermittlung und Datenverarbeitung,
Pfaffenwaldring 47, 70569 Stuttgart, Germany
`feil@ind.uni-stuttgart.de`

[2] DaimlerChrysler AG, Research and Technology 3, Vehicle IT-Architecture, HPC T728,
70546 Stuttgart, Germany
`matthias.stuempfle@daimlerchrysler.com`

Kurzfassung Der Beitrag beschreibt die Software-Architektur DANA (*Distributed Systems Architecture for Networks in Automotive Environments*), mit der komponentenbasierte verteilte Systeme für die Fahrzeugtelematik dynamisch zusammengebaut werden können. Im Gegensatz zu den verbreiteten Technologien, die ein Zusammenbau von „Off-The-Shelf"-Komponenten mit Hilfe von Tools erlauben, werden Komponenten bei DANA durch eine im System verteilte Management-Software zur Laufzeit ins System aufgenommen bzw. wieder entfernt. Hierzu muss dieses Management folgende Grundaufgaben bearbeiten: Die Anordnung von Komponenten im verteilten System, die Bereitstellung einer Funktionalität zur Komponenten-Entdeckung und die Verwaltung der Kommunikationsbeziehungen zwischen Komponenten. In diesem Beitrag wird auf Mechanismen zur Bearbeitung dieser Aufgaben eingegangen und Implementierungsaspekte, die insbesondere Ergebnisse bei einer prototypischen Realisierung einschliessen, vorgestellt.

1 Einleitung

Immer mehr Software-Dienste und -Anwendungen halten Einzug ins Fahrzeug. So gehören beispielsweise im Bereich der Fahrzeugtelematik der digitale Rundfunk, Navigation, Notruf, Verkehrsinformationsdienste, Fahrzeug-Diagnose aber auch Internet-Dienste wie E-Mail und WWW [4] entweder schon zur Standard-Ausstattung oder stehen kurz vor der Einführung.

Im nächsten Abschnitt wird die Entwicklung der für solche Anwendungen und Dienste notwendigen Software-Systeme im Telematikbereich für Fahrzeuge aufgezeigt. Die Realisierung solcher Systeme durch Software-Komponenten ist ein vielversprechender Ansatz. Durch Management-Software können Komponenten dynamisch und ohne manuelle Eingriffe zu einem System zusammengesetzt werden. In den darauf folgenden Abschnitten wird auf die wesentlichen Aufgaben dieses Komponenten-Managements eingegangen.

Komponenten müssen angeordnet, d. h. einem Gerät zugeordnet werden (Abschnitt drei). Ihnen muss es möglich gemacht werden, andere Komponenten, die gesuchte Dienste anbieten, zu entdecken (Abschnitt vier). Möchte eine Komponente den Dienst einer anderen Komponente nutzen, so muss das Einrichten einer Kommunikationsbeziehung zwischen diesen Komponenten ermöglicht werden (Abschnitt fünf).

Im sechsten Abschnitt werden schließlich relevante Arbeiten zur dynamischen Komponentenanordnung vorgestellt und mit dieser Arbeit verglichen.

2 Software-Systeme im Bereich der Fahrzeugtelematik

Schon heute ist die Software im Fahrzeug auf Rechner verteilt, die im Motor- und Komfortbereich z. B. über den CAN-Bus und im Telematikbereich über den optischen D2B-Ring [2] zur Übertragung von Audio-Daten miteinander gekoppelt sind. In Zukunft werden noch breitbandigere Übertragungsmedien eingesetzt werden. Um auch Video-Bilder darstellen zu können, wird eine Vernetzung des Fahrzeug-Telematikbereichs durch einen optischen MOST-Ring [7] oder einen IEEE 1394-Bus [14] angestrebt. Beide Übertragungsmedien erlauben es, Daten sowohl asynchron (z. B. Internet-Daten) als auch synchron/isochron (z. B. Video-Ströme) auszutauschen. Im Fahrzeug der Zukunft werden eine Vielzahl von Anwendungen, die unterschiedliche Dienstgüten (QoS, Quality of Service) erfordern, innerhalb eines heterogenen verteilten Systems koexistieren.

2.1 Evolution der Software-Systeme im Fahrzeug-Telematikbereich

Die Innovationszyklen im IT-Bereich sind so kurz, dass Anwendungen und Dienste in der Regel während der Lebensdauer eines Fahrzeuges (ca. 10 Jahre) veralten und ersetzbar werden bzw. ergänzt werden müssen. Aus diesem Grund muss die Austauschbarkeit von Diensten und Anwendungen während der Fahrzeug-Lebensdauer gewährleistet sein. Wegen dieser Hauptanforderung wird eine Entwicklung im Fahrzeug-Telematikbereich hin zu komponentenbasierten verteilten Systemen erwartet:

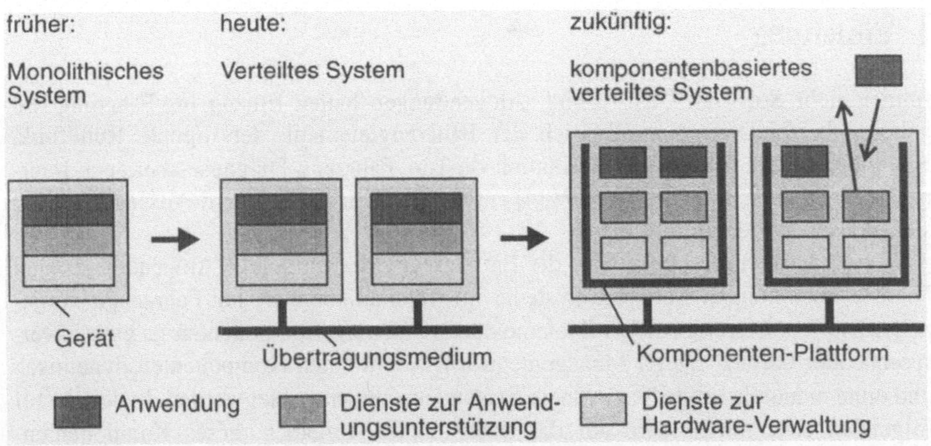

Bild 1: Entwicklung von monolithischen zu komponentenbasierten verteilten Systemen

Bild 1 zeigt, dass früher Anwendungen (und Dienste) durch ins Fahrzeug eingebaute „Stand-Alone"-Geräte realisiert wurden. Heutzutage sind Anwendungen auf mehrere Geräte verteilt, die über ein Bussystem gekoppelt sind. Die Software ist hierbei noch statisch an die Hardware gebunden. Erst durch einen nächsten Entwicklungsschritt, bei dem die Software in einzelne Komponenten aufgeteilt wird, wird die starre Beziehung zwischen Hard- und Software aufgehoben. Somit können Software-Komponenten an die Fahrzeug-Hardware zur Systemlaufzeit gebunden werden. Das Aufnehmen (bzw. auch Entfernen) von Software-Komponenten geschieht transparent für Nutzer (Fahrer und Passagiere) durch die Existenz einer Management-Software. Im Gegensatz zu manuellen Software-Updates (z. B in der Werkstatt) ist hierbei eine Möglichkeit gegeben, das System während der Fahrzeug-Lebensdauer mit neuer Funktionalität an neue Gegebenheiten anzupassen oder zu erweitern.

2.2 Komponentenbasierte Systeme

In diesem Beitrag wird unter dem Begriff Software-Komponente binärer Code [12] verstanden, der in ein System während dessen Laufzeit aufgenommen werden kann. Die rasche Verbreitung neuer Technologien wie z. B. dem *Enterprise Java Beans*-Konzept [17] oder dem *CORBA Component Model* [8] zeigen den wachsenden Erfolg der Komponenten-Software. Solche Technologien erlauben es, komplexe Systeme aus „Off-The-Shelf"-Komponenten zusammenzubauen. Sie ermöglichen diesen Zusammenbau z. B. durch visuell unterstützende Werkzeuge und durch die genaue Spezifikation von Schnittstellen. Darüber hinausgehend soll nun durch DANA der Zusammenbau des Systems dynamisch während der Systemlaufzeit durch eine Management-Software ermöglicht werden.

Bild 2 zeigt, mit welchen Funktionalitäten Komponenten im Telematikbereich des Fahrzeugs versehen sein können.

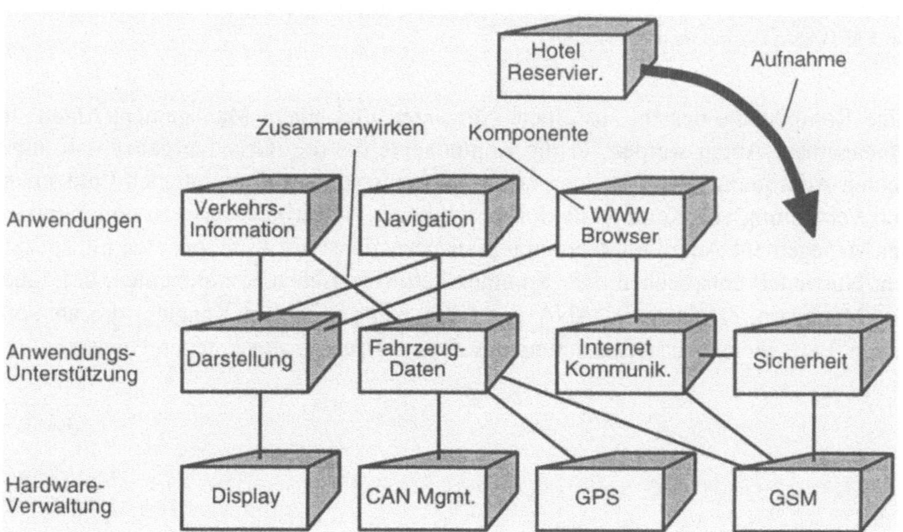

Bild 2: Software-Komponenten im Telematikbereich des Fahrzeugs

Die Komponenten, die im System verteilt sind, wirken hierbei zusammen. Beispielsweise bereitet die Navigations-Komponente in Bild 2 Fahrzeug-Daten auf, die wiederum vom Motorbereich (CAN-Bus) oder einem GPS-Empfänger stammen können. Die aufbereiteten Daten, werden dann an eine Komponente weitergereicht, die für die Darstellung der Daten verantwortlich ist. Diese Komponente sorgt dann z. B. dafür, dass die Daten auf dem richtigen Bildschirm dargestellt werden, falls mehrere Bildschirme im Fahrzeug installiert sind.

2.3 DANA – Eine Architektur für komponentenbasierte verteilte Systeme

Bild 3 zeigt das bei DANA [3] (*Distributed Systems Architecture for Networks in Automotive Environments*) entwickelte Komponenten-Modell.

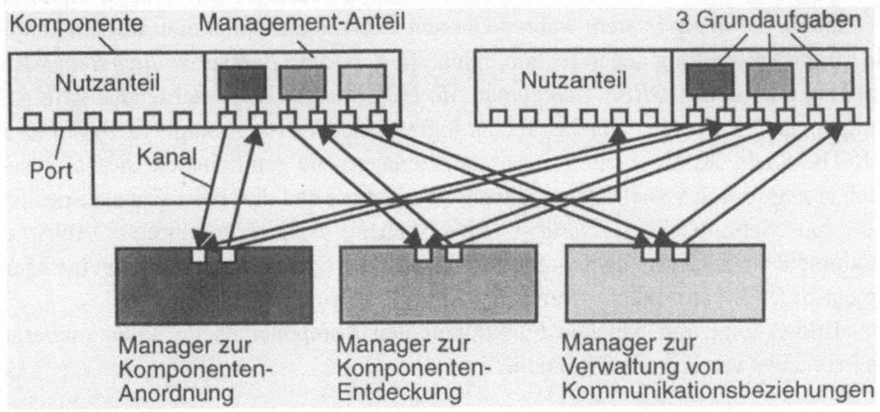

Bild 3: DANA-Komponenten-Modell

Eine Komponente besteht aus einem Nutzanteil und einem Management-Anteil. Im Management-Anteil werden für die Komponente die drei Grundaufgaben – Komponenten-Anordnung, Bereitstellung eines Mechanismus zur Komponenten-Entdeckung und Verwaltung von Kommunikationsbeziehungen – bearbeitet. Hierzu kommuniziert der Management-Anteil mit mehreren Managern, die selbst Komponenten mit speziellem Nutzanteil entsprechen. Die Kommunikation zwischen Komponenten, d. h. auch mit Managern, erfolgt bei DANA mit Hilfe von gerichteten Kanälen, die an Ports enden. Ports dienen zur Bezeichnung des Zugangs zu den angebotenen Diensten.

3 Anordnung von Komponenten

Eine Hauptaufgabe des Managements ist es, die dynamische Aufnahme neuer Komponenten ins System zu ermöglichen. In diesem Abschnitt wird diese Anordnungs-Aufgabe feiner untergliedert.

3.1 Mechanismen für die Anordnung von Komponenten

Dabei sind mehrere Aspekte zu beachten:

Speicherung. Es muss entschieden werden, ob Komponenten durch einen nicht-flüchtigen Speicher persistent auch während einer Systeminaktivität im System gehalten werden (*Caching*).

(Re-)Konfiguration. Weiter ist zu klären, welchem Gerät eine Komponente bei einem aktiven System zugeordnet werden kann, damit sie ihren Teil zur Systemfunktionalität beiträgt. Wichtige Parameter bei der Zuordnung einer Komponente zu einem Gerät sind die von der Komponente zur Laufzeit benötigten Hardware-Ressourcen, die durch andere Software-Komponenten erbrachten Dienste sowie Dienstgüteanforderungen, die bei der Ressourcenzuteilung berücksichtigt werden müssen.

Die Konfigurationsaufgabe wird immer zuerst bei der System-Initialisierung gelöst. Sie wird jedoch, während das System aktiv ist, fortlaufend neu gestellt. So erfordert ein i. a. unvorhersehbares Laufzeitverhalten der Kontrollflüsse von Komponenten ein dynamisches Balancieren der Last. Zudem müssen zur Laufzeit durch vom System (z. B. durch Komponentenabhängigkeiten oder durch Benutzer-Initiative) oder von außerhalb (z. B. durch Einspielen von Software-Aktualisierungen, *Updates*) kommende Initiativen neue Komponenten aufgenommen werden. Unter dem Begriff *Komponentenabhängigkeit* (siehe auch [6]) wird hierbei verstanden, dass aktive Komponenten im System angebotene Dienste benötigen, und deshalb die Existenz weiterer, diesen Dienst erbringende Komponenten gewährleistet sein muss.

Weiter kann sich durch die Mobilität des Fahrzeugs die drahtlose Zugangstechnologie so ändern kann, dass temporär für das Fahrzeug ein kostengünstiger Zugang zur externen Infrastruktur zur Verfügung steht. Es kann deshalb durchaus sinnvoll sein, Komponenten auf bereitstehende Rechner in der Infrastruktur auszulagern, um so die Erweiterung der Systemfunktionalität während des kostengünstigen Zugangs zu ermöglichen [9].

Sicherheit. Natürlich muss bei der Anreicherung des Telematiksystems um neue Funktionalität die Erfüllung der gegebenen Sicherheitsanforderungen gewährleistet sein. So ist bei der Aufnahme von Komponenten in bestimmte Systembereiche deren Echtheit (Authentizität) nachzuweisen. Die Verifikation der Authentizität kann prinzipiell durch einen Signierungsmechanismus für Komponenten ermöglicht werden. Die zur Überprüfung der Signatur benötigten öffentlichen Schlüssel können dann durch eine Zertifizierungs-Infrastruktur ins Fahrzeug gelangen.

3.2 Implementierungsaspekte

Java besitzt mit seinen Eigenschaften der Objekt-Serialisierung und des Klassen-Ladens das Potenzial, als einheitliche Grundlage für Komponenten-Plattformen eingesetzt zu werden. Eine solche Vereinheitlichung ist erstrebenswert, wenn Komponenten zu einem erst zur Laufzeit bestimmten Gerät zugeordnet werden sollen.

Neue Tendenzen im Umfeld der eingebetteten Systeme zeigen, dass Java durchaus skalierbar im Verbrauch von Speicher- und Rechenleistung sein kann. So ist der minimale Speicherbedarf einer JBED-Maschine 10 kByte [13]. Deshalb ist es denkbar, dass Java im bezüglich des Verbrauchs von Speicher und Rechenleistung konservativen Fahrzeugumfeld durchaus eine wichtige Rolle übernehmen kann.

Beim realisierten Prototypen wird momentan eine auf Linux laufende JVM als Komponentenplattform verwendet. Linux ist hierbei vor allem wegen seines frei verfügbaren Quell-Codes als Entwicklungsplattform sehr attraktiv. So konnte z. B. eine bestehende Treiber-Entwicklung für den IEEE 1394-Bus [1] für den prototypischen Einsatz u. a. um einen isochronen Übertragungsdienst erweitert und modifiziert werden. Das prototypische System soll nun in einem nächsten Schritt um Plattformen erweitert werden, die voraussichtlich im Fahrzeug-Telematikbereich in Zukunft eine Rolle spielen können. So sind hier eingebettete Systeme zu nennen, die je Rechner nur eine JVM als Plattform zur Ausführung von Java Byte Code (z. B. JBED) beinhalten. Solche JVMs setzen direkt auf die Hardware ohne Unterstützung eines zusätzlichen Betriebssystems auf. Komponenten-Plattform und Betriebssystem sind zu einer Einheit verschmolzen.

4 Entdeckung von Komponenten

Um einen Dienst nutzen zu können, muss eine Komponente eine andere, diesen Dienst bereitstellende Komponente innerhalb des Systems finden.

4.1 Mechanismen für die Entdeckung von Komponenten

Eine bekannte Möglichkeit, Diensterbringer zu entdecken, besteht darin, dass diese Diensterbringer sich bei einer zentralen Stelle im verteilten System registrieren, damit eine suchende Instanz bei dieser Registratur nach einem Dienst nachfragen kann. Ein bekannter Vertreter für diesen Mechanismus ist z. B. der *Naming Service* von CORBA [15]. Bei lokal begrenzten Netzen, insbesondere wenn solche Netze auf Broadcasting-Medien (z. B. Ethernet oder IEEE 1394) beruhen, kann zudem vorteilhaft die Kommunikationsart des Broadcastings eingesetzt werden. So ermöglicht Jini [18], dass durch Broadcasting-Nachrichten nach Registraturen (*Lookup Services*) gesucht wird oder im umgekehrten Fall, dass sich die Registratur per Broadcasting bekannt macht. Auch bei UPnP [16] werden durch Broadcasting *Announce*-Pakete mit Dienst-Informationen verbreitet bzw. mit *Discovery*-Paketen nach dem Ort bestimmter Dienste gefragt.

Bei DANA tauschen spezielle Manager, sogenannte LSM (*Local Service Manager*) Dienst-Informationen per Broadcasting aus (siehe Bild 4). Diese LSM sind für die Komponenten ihres Gerätes verantwortlich. Komponenten müssen deshalb beim lokalen LSM registriert werden bzw. können bei ihm diensterbringende Komponenten erfragen.

Es gilt immer, dass der Ort der diensterbringenden Komponente im heterogenen Verteilten System durch ein einheitliches Adressierungsformat beschrieben werden muss. Folglich wird auch im DANA-Management eine von den Hardware-Adressen losgelöste, logische Adressierung verwendet.

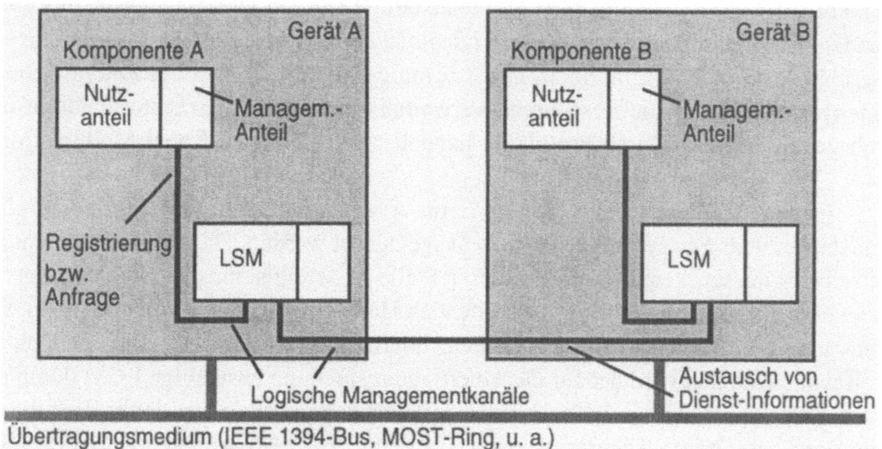

Bild 4: Austausch von Dienst-Informationen

4.2 Implementierungsaspekte

Ein Problem beim Einsatz universeller Technologien wie Jini und UPnP im Fahrzeugbereich ist, dass durch ihre Universalität nicht die im Fahrzeug häufig vorkommenden leistungsschwachen Geräte miteinbezogen werden können. Das einheitliche Adressierungsformat wird z. B. bei diesen universellen Technologien durch die Existenz der IP-Schicht erreicht, damit jedes Gerät, das dann zumindest IP-Funktionalität bereitstellen muss, durch eine IP-Adresse adressierbar ist. Bei der Realisierung des Broadcasting-Mechanismus muss, wie auch die prototypische Implementierung zeigt, jedoch lediglich auf ein einheitliches Format der Broadcasting-Nachrichten geachtet werden, so dass auf sehr einfache Weise bei der Implementierung der Management-Software auch leistungsschwache Geräte berücksichtigt werden können. Zwischen Geräten mit verschiedenen Plattformen kann durchaus ein Austausch dieser Broadcasting-Nachrichten stattfinden. So können auch Dienste im System berücksichtigt werden, die nicht von Komponenten auf den in Abschnitt 3 geforderten einheitlichen Komponenten-Plattformen angeboten, sondern durch Software bzw. Hardware auf sehr einfachen Geräten bereitgestellt werden.

5 Verwaltung von Kommunikationsbeziehungen

Damit ins System geladene Komponenten mit anderen Komponenten unter Gewährleistung einer gewünschten Dienstgüte kommunizieren können, muss eine Verwaltung von Kommunikationsbeziehungen vorgesehen werden.

5.1 Mechanismen zum Verwalten von Kommunikationsbeziehungen

Bei DANA werden Kommunikationsbeziehungen zwischen Komponenten durch logische Kanäle dargestellt. Kanäle können eingerichtet, zu Punkt-zu-Mehrpunkt-Kanäle erweitert, reduziert und wieder abgebaut werden. Das hierfür benötigte Kanal-Management wird durch mehrere Manager realisiert. Wenn ein Übertragungsmedium vorhanden ist, müssen die betroffenen *Local Channel Manager* (LCM), die für die Ressourcen-Verwaltung in einem Gerät verantwortlich sind, und ein *Range Channel Manager* (RCM) für die Ressourcen-Verwaltung auf dem Übertragungsmedium miteinbezogen werden. Durch Protokolle handeln zwei LCM die Kanal-Modifikationen aus.

In Bild 5 initiiert der LCM in Gerät A einen Vorgang zum Einrichten eines Kanals, bei dem *Establish*-Nachrichten ausgetauscht werden. Da das Management nur logische Adressen kennt, muss an dieser Stelle im Treiber für das Übertragungsmedium eine Umsetzung auf die entsprechenden Hardware-Adressen vorgenommen werden, um die Management-Nachrichten übertragen zu können. Bei geräteübergreifenden Kanälen wird der für das Übertragungsmedium zuständige RCM durch den Austausch von *MediaAlloc*-Nachrichten miteingebunden. Er sorgt dafür, dass die für den Kanal geforderte Dienstgüte auch auf dem Übertragungsmedium gewährleistet wird, falls dies möglich ist.

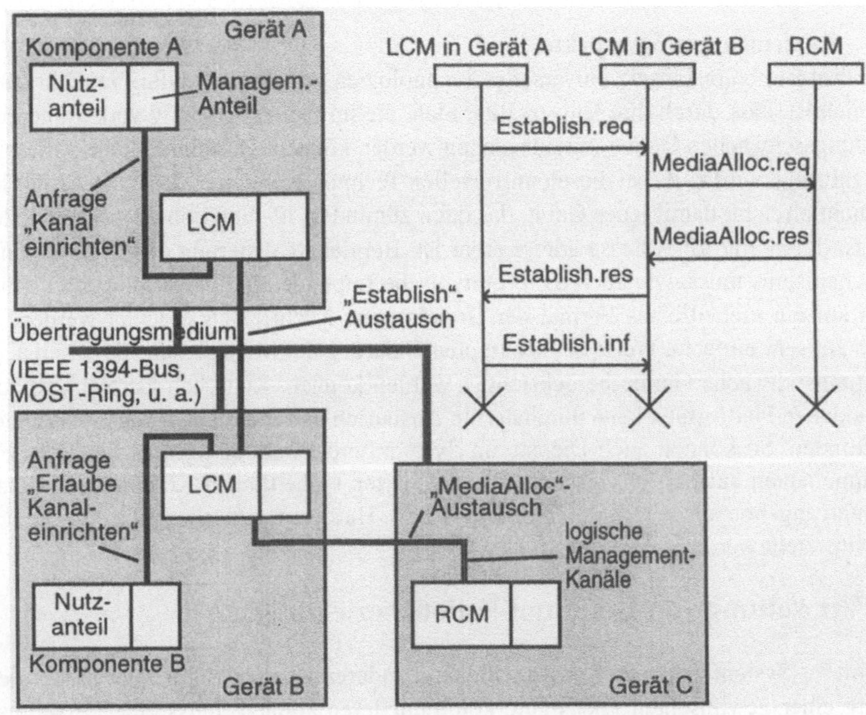

Bild 5: Kanal Einrichten

5.2 Implementierungsaspekte

Der bei der prototypischen Implementierung verwendete, getaktete IEEE 1394-Bus erlaubt es, Daten asynchron bzw. isochron in Form von Rahmen zu übertragen. Bei DANA sorgt ein RCM für die Verwaltung isochroner Ressourcen. Über ihn kann ein Knoten Bandbreite reservieren. Wenn keine Überreservierung vorliegt, wird eine erfolgreiche Bus-Arbitrierung zur Übertragung von Daten innerhalb eines Zyklusses (ca. 125µs) gewährleistet. Ein IEEE 1394-Knoten entspricht beim Prototypen einer handelsüblichen PCI-Host-Adapter-Karte.

Für die Ressourcen-Verwaltung bei der prototypischen Implementierung werden folgende Schritte beachtet:

Ressourcen-Reservierung im Initiator-Gerät. Nach der Initiierung einer Kanal-Modifikation durch eine Komponente (Initiierung „Kanal einrichten" in Bild 5), versucht der zuständige LCM, die lokal im Gerät für diesen Kanal benötigten Ressourcen zu reservieren (bzw. freizugeben). Falls beispielsweise ein Kanal zum Senden von Daten mit einer garantierten Datenrate von mindestens 8 MBit/s eingerichtet werden soll, muss der LCM ein spezielles Bandbreitenregister im IEEE 1394-Knoten auf einen entsprechenden Wert setzen. So muss eingetragen werden, dass ein 128 Byte großer isochroner Rahmen je Zyklus versendet wird (128Byte/125µs>8MBit/s). Nach der Reservierung dieser Ressource gibt der LCM durch das Versenden einer *EstablishReq*-Nachricht die Inititative an den LCM im empfangenden Gerät weiter.

Ressourcen-Reservierung für den Bus. Der beauftragte LCM erkennt, dass die *EstablishReq*-Nachricht aus einem anderen Gerät stammt, und dass deshalb ein geräteübergreifender Kanal eingerichtet werden muss. Er leitet deshalb die Initiative unmittelbar an den für das Übertragungsmedium zuständigen RCM durch eine *MediaAllocReq*-Nachricht weiter. Bei der prototypischen Implementierung stehen RCM für Ethernet und IEEE 1394 zur Verfügung. Während der RCM für Ethernet jeden Versuch zur Bandbreitenreservierung durch eine Fehlernachricht zurückweist, sorgt der RCM für IEEE 1394 durch Verwaltung aller Bandbreite-Reservierungen dafür, dass keine Überreservierung an Bandbreite stattfindet. Danach wird die Initiative wieder an den LCM im beauftragten Gerät zurückgegeben.

Ressourcen-Reservierung im beauftragten Gerät. Da der LCM im beauftragten Gerät für das Einrichten eines Endpunktes eines empfangenden Kanals zuständig ist, muss er seinem IEEE 1394-Knoten mitteilen, welcher isochrone Kanal abgehört werden soll.

Nach dem Einrichten eines Kanals kann innerhalb jeder Komponente über einen eindeutigen Bezeichner für das Kanalende (CEI, *Channel Endpoint Identifier*) auf den an einem Port endenden Kanal zugegriffen werden. Dies bedeutet, dass eine ortstransparente Kommunikation ermöglicht wird, bei der keiner Komponente der Ort des Kommunikationspartners in Form einer Adresse bekannt sein muss. Durch die den Kanal realisierende Software, zu der auch der Treiber für das Übertragungsmedium gehört, können dann vom sendenden Kanalende aus alle empfangenden Kanalenden adressiert werden. Prinzipiell ist bei Punkt-zu-Mehrpunkt-Kanälen die Verwendung von Mulicast-Hardware-Adressen möglich.

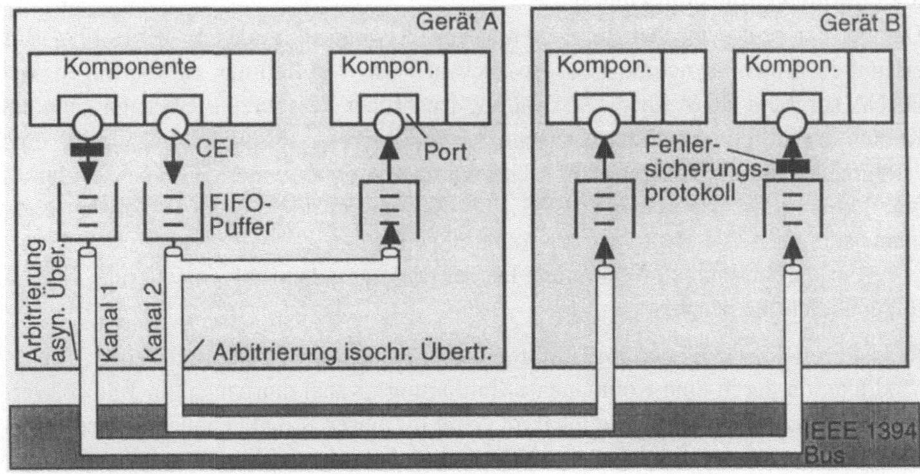

Bild 6: Realisierung von Kanälen

Bild 6 zeigt exemplarisch die Realisierung von zwei Kanälen. Über Kanal 1 können Daten ohne Bandbreitegarantie (asynchrone Übertragung) zuverlässig mit Hilfe eines Fehlersicherungsprotokolls zwischen zwei Komponenten ausgetauscht werden. Über Kanal 2 empfangen zwei Komponenten Daten von einer sendenden Komponente. Für die Übertragung der Daten auf dem IEEE 1394-Bus steht eine garantierte Bandbreite zur Verfügung.

6 Verwandte Arbeiten

In diesem Abschnitt werden relevante Arbeiten, die sich mit der dynamischen Aufnahme von Komponenten beschäftigen, vorgestellt. Zudem findet eine Abgrenzung zwischen DANA und diesen Arbeiten statt.

In [9] wird eine Internet basierte Komponentenarchitektur für Fahrzeug Client- und Serversysteme vorgestellt, die zu COSIMA [10] weiterentwickelt wurde. DANA setzt prinzipiell ebenfalls auf die Arbeiten zu dieser Architektur auf, wobei der Schwerpunkt auf die Dienst-Entdeckung und Kommunikations-Verwaltung in verteilten Systemen mit leistungsschwachen Endgeräten gelegt wird. Während die Architektur von [9] und COSIMA als eine auf das Internet aufsetzende Middleware betrachtet werden kann, greift DANA durch spezielle Treiber direkt auf das jeweilige Übertragungssystem (z. B. IEEE 1394) zu. Internet-Pakete werden folglich über einen eingerichteten DANA-Kanal ausgetauscht.

Weiter gibt es Arbeiten, die das Laden von Komponenten zu einem Client untersuchen. So bestehen bei [11] die Komponenten aus Java Beans [17], die durch ein XML-Format beschrieben werden, damit sie auf einen Ziel-Rechner geladen werden können. Im Unterschied hierzu werden Komponenten bei DANA nicht auf einen einzigen Ziel-Rechner sondern in ein verteiltes System eines Fahrzeuges geladen. Während einige Mechanismen z. B. zur Erfüllung der Sicherheitsanforderungen (Zertifizierung von Komponenten bzw. Einführung von *Trusted Third Parties*) sich ähnlich sind, existieren bei DANA noch weitere Mechanismen hinsichtlich der Komponenten-Anordnung, Dienst-Entdeckung und Kommunikationsverwaltung im Verteilten System.

In [5] wird eine Architektur zur automatischen Konfiguration von komponentenbasierten verteilten Systemen erläutert. Das Ziel, gemäß dem sogenannten *WYNIWYG*-Paradigma (*What You Need Is What You Get*) nur den minimal notwendigen Satz von Komponenten ins System zu laden, ist auch bei DANA vorhanden. Zudem werden Grundvoraussetzungen für das Laden von Komponenten benannt, die auch für DANA gelten: Die von der Komponente benötigten Hardware-Ressourcen (Beschaffenheit und Kapazität) und die zu nutzenden Dienste, die durch Software erbracht werden, müssen vorhanden sein. Hierbei wird die Reservierung lokaler Hardware-Ressourcen (CPU, Speicher) bei der Komponenten-Anordnung berücksichtigt. Im Unterschied dazu billigt man bei DANA jedoch auch dem Kommunikationsmedium reservierbare Ressourcen zu. Man geht also keineswegs von einem „Best Effort"-Netz (z. B. Internet) aus. Die Folge davon ist, dass bei DANA eine Kommunikationsbeziehung zwischen dynamisch angeordneten Komponenten zuerst erfolgreich eingerichtet werden muss. Weiter bildet in [5] CORBA mit seinen Diensten (z. B. *Naming Service*) die Grundlage sowohl für die Architektur als auch für die Implementierung im verteilten System. Bei DANA werden hingegen nur grundlegende Mechanismen und Austauschformate von Management-Nachrichten spezifiziert. Die Implementierung selbst kann für jedes Gerät optimiert werden.

7 Zusammenfassung und Ausblick

In diesem Beitrag wurde die komponentenbasierte Architektur für verteilte Systeme im Fahrzeug DANA vorgestellt. Es wurde ein Komponentenmodell eingeführt, das auf der Bearbeitung von Grundaufgaben zur Komponenten-Anordnung und -Entdeckung und zur Verwaltung von Kommunikationsbeziehungen zwischen Komponenten durch ein Management beruht.
In einem nächsten Schritt soll die Architektur anhand der Einbeziehung von eingebetteten Systemen bei der prototypischen Implementierung weiter validiert und hinsichtlich der Berücksichtigung der dort vorherrschenden Randbedingungen überprüft werden. Während die Mechanismen zur Komponenten-Entdeckung und Kommunikationsverwaltung durch DANA genau spezifiziert sind, ist die Spezifikation der Mechanismen zur Komponenten-Anordnung Gegenstand der aktuellen Forschung bei DANA. Ziel ist es, eine umfassende Architektur für komponentenbasierte verteilte Systeme für den Fahrzeug-Telematikbereich zu erhalten.

8 Literatur

1. A. Bombe, S. Rougeaux, E. Pirker: The Linux 1394 project, http://linux1394.sourceforge.net/

2. C. Ciocan: The Domestic Digital Bus System (D2B). IEEE Transactions on Consumer Electronics, vol. 36, no. 3, (1990) 619-622

3. V. Feil, U. Gemkow, M. Stümpfle: A Vehicular Software Architecture Enabling Dynamic Alterability of Services Sets, In: C. Linnhoff-Popien, H.-G. Hegering (ed.): USM 2000, LNCS 1890, München (2000) 68-80

4. A. Jameel, M. Stümpfle, D. Jiang, A. Fuchs: Web on Wheels: Toward Internet-Enabled Cars. IEEE Computer, vol. 31 (1998) 69-71

5. F. Kon: Automatic Configuration of Component-based Distributed Systems. PHD Thesis, University of Illinois at Urbana-Champaign (2000)

6. F. Kon, R. H. Campbell: Dependence Management in Component-Based Distributed Systems. IEEE Concurrency, 8(1), (2000) 26-36

7. P. König, C. Thiel: Media Oriented Systems Transport. it + ti – Informationstechnik und Technische Informatik, vol. 5 (1999) 36-42

8. J. Mischkinsky (ed.): CORBA 3.0 New Components Chapters. OMG, CORBA Component Model FTF Draft (1999)

9. M. Stümpfle, A. Jameel: Eine Inernet basierte Komponentenarchitektur für Fahrzeug Client- und Serversystemes. In: R. Steinmetz (ed.): Kommunikation in Verteilten Systemen (KiVS), 11. ITG/GI-Fachtagung (1999) 6 - 19

10. M. Stümpfle, et. al.: COSIMA – A Component System Information and Management Architecture. IEEE Intelligent Vehicles Symposium 2000, Dearborn, USA (2000)

11. S. Rudkin, A. Smith: A Scheme for Component Based Service Deployment. In: C. Linnhoff-Popien, H.-G. Hegering (ed.): USM 2000, LNCS 1890, (2000) 68-80

12. C. Szyperski: Component-Software. Addison-Wesley, New York (1997)

13. J. Tryggvesson, T. Mattson, H. Heeb: JBED: Java for Real-Time Systems. Dr. Dobb's Journal, Miller Freemann (1999)

14. IEEE: Standard for a High Performance Serial Bus. IEEE Std. 1394-1995 (1996)

15. OMG: Naming Service Specification. CORBA Services V. 1.0 (2000)

16. UPnP Forum: www.upnp.org

17. Sun Microsystems, Inc.: Java Beans Specification, V. 1.01 (1997)

18. Sun Microsystems. Inc.: Jini Architecture Specification, V 1. 01 (1999)

Reduzierung der Anzahl von Übertragungen in „Floating Car Data" – Diensten

Walter J. Franz

DaimlerChrysler AG
Forschung und Technologie 3, FT3/KK
Tel.: 0731 505 2125
walter.franz@daimlerchrysler.com

Abstract. *Unter „Floating Car Data"-Diensten werden Verfahren verstanden, welche Daten aus Fahrzeugen an eine Dienstezentrale übertragen. Diese verknüpft die Daten aus vielen Fahrzeugen und sendet die Ergebnisse an die Dienstteilnehmer zurück. Typische FCD-Dienste sind Stau- bzw. Stauende-Detektion oder die Erfassung von Wetterbedingungen. Werden nun FCD-Dienste für die breite Masse von Fahrzeugen verfügbar, so senden bei Auftreten eines Ereignisses unter Umständen sehr viele Fahrzeuge Daten an die Zentrale, was den Dienst verteuert. Die hier beschriebenen Verfahren lösen das Problem, indem sie statistisch die Sendezeitpunkte der einzelnen Fahrzeuge derart verzögern, daß dienstespezifische Randbedingungen trotzdem erfüllt werden. Dabei wird auch berücksichtigt, daß die Fahrzeuge im allgemeinen ein Ereignis nicht gleichzeitig, sondern zu unterschiedlichen Zeitpunkten detektieren. Durch das vorgeschlagene Verfahren läßt sich die Anzahl der Übertragungen zur Dienstezentrale maßgeblich reduzieren. Zudem wird im Vergleich zu heutigen Lösungen der Aufwand zur Verwaltung von Fahrzeugen durch die Dienstezentrale wesentlich verringert. Die Leistungsfähigkeit der Algorithmen wird durch statistische Analyse anhand von Beispielsrechnungen nachgewiesen.*

Problemstellung

Unter „Floating Car Data"-Diensten versteht man Dienstleistungen, die darauf basieren, daß Daten, die im Fahrzeug erfaßt werden und die bisher nur lokal im Fahrzeug verwendet werden, zu einer Dienstezentrale übertragen werden. Dort werden diese Daten mit den Daten aus einer Vielzahl anderer Fahrzeuge verknüpft und Schlußfolgerungen abgeleitet. Beispiele für solche Dienste sind: Staudetektion, Unfalldetektion oder Wettererkennung, z.B. Detektion von starkem Regen [1], [2].
Die Aussagesicherheit der von der Zentrale gezogenen Schlußfolgerungen läßt sich steigern, wenn man eine genügend große Anzahl von Fahrzeugen einbeziehen kann. Andererseits ist dies problematisch, da teure zellulare Mobilfunknetze zur Datenübertragung verwendet werden müssen. Es ist daher ein Kompromiß zwischen der Anzahl der Übertragungen und der Aussagesicherheit notwendig.
Zur Kommunikation der Fahrzeuge zur Zentrale („Uplink") setzt man in den heutigen noch prototypischen Systemen den SMS-Nachrichtendienst der GSM-Netze ein. Die

Übertragung der Ergebnisse der Auswertungen der Zentrale zu den Fahrzeugen („Downlink") kann z.B. über einen Broadcastkanal (DAB, GSM-SMS-CB) durchgeführt werden.

Das letztendliche Ziel für Floating Car Data-Anwendungen ist deren Einführung für die breite Masse der Fahrzeuge. Dann tritt das Problem auf, daß im Falle des Eintretens eines Ereignisses unter Umständen viele Fahrzeuge innerhalb einer sehr kurzen Zeit Uplink-Meldungen senden. Dadurch wird erstens der Dienst verteuert und zweitens wird das Kommunikationssystem kurzzeitig stark belastet.

Es ist daher notwendig, die Übertragungen im Uplink derart zu kontrollieren, daß nur soviele Übertragungen wie notwendig durchgeführt werden. Diese sollten zudem zeitlich derart entkoppelt sein, daß die Zeitspanne, die der FCD-Dienst bis zu einer Detektion eines Ereignisses zuläßt, möglichst gleichmäßig für die Übertragungen genutzt wird. Selbstverständlich muß die Koordination der Kommunikationsvorgänge ohne direkte Kommunikation zwischen den Fahrzeugen selbst und mit minimalem Aufwand durch die Zentrale verbunden sein.

Lösungsansätze

Die im folgenden beschriebenen Algorithmen basieren auf einer statistischen Verzögerung der Sendezeitpunkte im Uplink. Dies bedeutet: Erkennt ein Fahrzeug ein Ereignis, das eine Datenübertragung zur Dienstezentrale erfordert, so sendet es nicht sofort, sondern generiert eine Pseudozufallszahl, anhand derer die Wartezeit bis zur Initiierung des Sendevorgangs bestimmt wird.

Nach Eintritt eines Ereignisses wird die Zentrale so viele Nachrichten abwarten, wie sie benötigt, um auf das Ereignis schließen zu können. Dabei erwartet die Zentrale diese Meldungen innerhalb einer Zeitspanne, welche von der Art des FCD-Dienstes abhängt. Beispiel: Eine Zentrale benötigt zum Erkennen der Position eines Staubeginns 10 Meldungen innerhalb von drei Minuten. 100 Fahrzeuge fahren während dieser Zeit an das Stauende heran. Ziel ist es, die Sendevorgänge der Fahrzeuge derart zu verzögern, daß während der drei Minuten mindestens zehn Fahrzeuge und möglichst wenig mehr als zehn Fahrzeuge senden.

Da in dieser Arbeit statistische Verfahren als Lösungsansatz vorgeschlagen werden, besteht eine Restwahrscheinlichkeit, daß weniger Fahrzeuge innerhalb der gewünschten Zeit senden. Diese Wahrscheinlichkeit muß von der Zentrale kalkulierbar sein. Die komplementäre Wahrscheinlichkeit dazu wird im folgenden als statistische Sicherheit der Zentrale (σ) bezeichnet.

Eine weitere Randbedingung ist, daß im allgemeinen die Fahrzeuge ein Ereignis nicht gleichzeitig sondern individuell zu verschiedenen Zeitpunkten detektieren. Die Streuung dieser Detektionszeitpunkte hängt vom Anwendungsfall ab. Starker Regen in einem Gebiet z.B. kann an verschiedenen Stellen zu verschiedenen Zeitpunkten auftreten. Ein falsche Downlinkmeldung durch die Zentrale andererseits wird von sehr vielen Fahrzeugen nahezu gleichzeitig als Ereignis detektiert.

Heutige Strategien zur Verringerung der Anzahl der Uplink-Übertragung sehen eine deterministische Lösung vor, indem den Fahrzeugen Rollen zugeteilt werden. Aktive Fahrzeuge übertragen die Nachrichten, Fahrzeuge in passiven Rollen hingegen nicht.

Diese Strategien erfordern einen hohen Verwaltungsaufwand in der Dienstezentrale, da die Fahrzeuge einzeln behandelt werden müssen [3]. Für die hier vorgeschlagenen Verfahren werden Parameter von der Dienstezentrale nicht fahrzeugindividuell, sondern an die Gesamtmenge der Fahrzeuge im FCD-Dienst übertragen.

Obige Aussagen lassen sich als *Bedingung 1* wie folgt formulieren:

Die Zentrale steuert die Berechnung der Wartezeiten der Fahrzeuge derart, daß innerhalb einer dienstespezifischen, vorgegebenen Zeit t_d mit der Wahrscheinlichkeit σ mindestens a Fahrzeuge aus der Menge der teilnehmenden Fahrzeuge (Anzahl N) die Nachrichten gesendet haben.

Nach der Zeit t_d hat die Zentrale mit der Wahrscheinlichkeit σ mindestens die notwendigen a Übertragungen von den N Fahrzeugen empfangen. Sie erkennt das Ereignis und sendet im Downlink die Zustandsmeldung an die Fahrzeuge. Die Fahrzeuge empfangen diese Meldung. Alle Fahrzeuge, die bis dahin noch nicht gesendet haben, senden nicht. Die Gesamtzahl der Übertragungen wird somit verringert.

Wie eingangs dargestellt, berechnen die Fahrzeuge die Sendeverzögerungen anhand einer Zufallsverteilung, die sowohl den Fahrzeugen, als auch der Zentrale bekannt ist. Nicht beschrieben wurde bisher, wie diese Zufallsverteilung parametrisiert wird. Ausgehend von den Werten von N, a, t_d und σ kann die Zentrale einen freien Parameter der Verteilungsfunktion derart berechnen, daß die Bedingung 1 erfüllt ist. Dieser Parameter wird den Fahrzeugen übermittelt. Der zusätzliche Downlink-Kommunikationsaufwand dieses Verfahrens beschränkt sich demnach auf die Übermittlung dieses einen Parameters pro FCD-Dienst.

Modell

In diesem Abschnitt wird der Ablauf der hier vorgeschlagenen Algorithmen zusammengefaßt und weitere zur Berechnung notwendige Größen (**Tabelle 1**) definiert.

1. Eine Menge bestehend aus N Fahrzeugen nimmt an einem FCD-Dienst teil.

2. Die Zentrale berechnet aus N und den dienstespezifischen Größen t_d, σ und a einen freien Parameter der verwendeten Verteilungsfunktion und übermittelt diesen an die Fahrzeuge.

3. Ein Ereignis, das eine Meldung von den Fahrzeugen an die Zentrale erfordert, tritt ein. Die Fahrzeuge generieren eine Pseudozufallszahl entsprechend der Verteilungsfunktion und Parametrisierung. Sie verzögern ihren Übertragungszeitpunkt entsprechend (Zufallsvariable T_x). Die Fahrzeuge detektieren das Ereignis im allgemeinen nicht gleichzeitig, sondern statistisch verteilt zu verschiedenen Zeitpunkten. Die Zeitverzögerungen bis zur Detektion werden durch die Zufallsvariable T_e beschrieben. Die Verteilung von T_e ist vom jeweiligen FCD-Dienst abhängig und wird z.B. aus empirischen Daten gewonnen.

4. Die Zentrale empfängt die Nachrichten und wartet, bis eine genügend große Anzahl (a) von Nachrichten empfangen wurde, um das Ereignis mit ausreichender statistischer Sicherheit (σ) zu detektieren. Sie sendet dann die Zustandsänderungsmeldung an die Fahrzeuge zurück.

5. Alle N Fahrzeuge empfangen die Nachricht zur Zeit t_f. Hat ein Fahrzeug die Meldung über das eingetretene Ereignis bis dahin noch nicht gesendet, so sendet das Fahrzeug nicht.

Zielgrößen zur Bewertung des Verfahrens

1. Mittlere Zeit t_a zwischen Auftreten des Ereignisses und der Übertragung von genau a Nachrichten an die Zentrale (gesucht Minimum).
2. Mittlere Anzahl der an die Zentrale übertragenen Meldungen (gesucht Minimum).

Param.	Beschreibung
N	Anzahl der betroffenen Fahrzeuge
a	Notwendige Anzahl von Meldungen
σ	Wahrscheinlichkeit mit der ein Ereignis innerhalb t_d detektiert wird
T_e	Zufallsvariable der Zeit, bis zu der die Fahrzeuge ein Ereignis detektieren.
t_d	Detektionszeit für Ereignisse durch die Zentrale
t_a	Zeit, bis genau a Uplink-Übertragungen
t_f	Zeit bis zur Rückmeldung des Ergebnisses im Downlink

Tabelle 1. Übersicht über die verwendeten Parameter

Analyse

Ausgangspunkt der Analyse sind die Verteilungsfunktionen der Verzögerung der Sendezeitpunkte der Fahrzeuge (T_x) und der Detektionszeitpunkte der Fahrzeuge (T_e). Die Summe dieser Zufallsvariablen ergibt die Zeit zwischen Auftreten eines Ereignisses und dem Sendezeitpunkt eines Fahrzeugs ($T = T_x + T_e$). (1) beschreibt die Verteilungsfunktion der Verzögerungszeit des Sendevorgangs im Fahrzeug.

$$P(T \leq t) = F_T(t) \tag{1}$$

Für die Verteilungsdichtefunktion $f_T(t)$ der Zuvallsvariable T gilt

$$f_T(t) = \int_0^t f_e(t_e) \cdot f_x(t - t_e) \cdot dt_e \tag{2}$$

Die Zufallsvariable X beschreibe die Anzahl der Fahrzeuge, die eine Nachricht an die Zentrale senden. Betrachtet man N Fahrzeuge und sucht man die Wahrscheinlichkeit $P(T \leq t, X \geq a)$, daß mindestens a Fahrzeuge aus N innerhalb von t senden, so gilt (3). Gleichung (3) wird von der Zentrale zur Berechnung der Parameter der Verteilung nach (1) verwendet. Die Zentrale geht von aus Bedingung 1 aus. Es gilt daher (4):

$$P(T \leq t, X \geq a) = \sum_{n=a}^{N} \binom{N}{n} \cdot P(T \leq t)^n \cdot (1 - P(T \leq t))^{N-n} \tag{3}$$

$$P(T \le t_d, X \ge a) = \sigma \quad \text{oder} \quad \sigma = \sum_{n=a}^{N} \binom{N}{n} \cdot P(T \le t_d)^n \cdot (1 - P(T \le t_d))^{N-n} \qquad (4)$$

Mit (4) kann man einen freien Parameter der Wahrscheinlichkeitsverteilung $F_T(t)$ z.B. mit numerischen Methoden bestimmen.

Der Erwartungswert der Anzahl der Übertragungen ($E[X(t)]$) in Abhängigkeit von der Zeit errechnet sich wie folgt:

$$E[X(t)] = \sum_{n=1}^{N} n \cdot P(T \le t \mid X = n) \qquad (5)$$

Es sei T_a die Zufallsvariable, die die Zeitspanne beschreibt, bis genau a Übertragungen an die Zentrale erfolgt sind. Durch Einsetzen der noch zu berechnenden Zeit t_a in (5) erhält man die Zielgröße 2. T_a ergibt sich aus dem Umstand, daß genau a-1 Fahrzeuge bereits gesendet haben und der Wahrscheinlichkeit, daß just in $T_a = t_a$ das a-te Fahrzeug sendet. Die gesuchte Wahrscheinlichkeit ergibt sich also aus dem Produkt der Wahrscheinlichkeit, daß genau a-1 Fahrzeuge innerhalb von t_a gesendet haben und der Verteilungsdichtefunktion für das a-te Fahrzeug. Hierbei muß berücksichtigt werden, daß jedes der N Fahrzeuge dasjenige sein kann, das als a-tes sendet. Die hierdurch erhaltene Funktion beschreibt die Verteilungsdichtefunktion $f_a(t)$ von T_a. Den Erwartungswert erhält man aus dem Integral dieser Funktion multipliziert mit der Zeit:

$$E[T_a] = \int_0^{\infty} t \cdot P(X(t) = a - 1 \mid N^* = N - 1) \cdot f_T(t) \cdot N \; dt \quad \text{mit} \quad f_T(t) = \frac{\partial F_T(t)}{\partial t} \qquad (6)$$

Hat man den Erwartungswert von T_a berechnet (Zielgröße 1), so ergibt sich die Zielgröße 2 durch den Erwartungswert der Anzahl der Übertragungen der Zeit ($t_a + t_f - t_d$), da nach dem Erkennen des Ereignisses durch die Zentrale noch die Zeit, bis die Rückmeldung an die Fahrzeuge erfolgt ist ($t_f - t_d$), berücksichtigt werden muß.

Beispielsrechnung

In diesem Abschnitt werden oben beschriebene Formeln angewendet und die Werte für die Zielgrößen berechnet. Dabei wird von folgendem Szenario ausgegangen:
Die Anzahl der Fahrzeuge sei $N = 100$. Zur Detektion des Ereignisses sind $a = 10$ Meldungen notwendig. σ sei $0,99$. Die maximale Dauer für die Detektion t_d sei 10 Zeiteinheiten (z.B. Sekunden). Die maximale Zeit bis zur erfolgten Rückmeldung im Downlink betrage $t_f = 15$.

Negativ exponentiell verteilte Verteilungsfunktion für T

In diesem Beispiel wird eine negativ exponentiell verteilte Verteilungsfunktion mit Parameter λ für T verwendet. In den Berechnungen in diesem Abschnitt detektieren alle Fahrzeuge das Ereignis zur gleichen Zeit. Diese Einschränkung wird im nächsten Abschnitt aufgehoben. Für die Berechnung des Parameters λ nach (4) ergibt sich daher folgende Gleichung.

$$\sigma = \sum_{n=a}^{N} \binom{N}{n} \cdot \left(1 - e^{-\lambda \cdot t_d}\right)^{n} \cdot \left(e^{-\lambda \cdot t_d}\right)^{N-n} \tag{7}$$

Durch numerisches Lösen dieser Gleichung ergibt sich für λ ein Wert von: $\lambda_l = 0{,}0196$. Als Erwartungswerte für die Anzahl der Übertragungen während den Zeiten t_d und t_f ergeben sich: $E[X(t_d)] = 17{,}84$ und $E[X(t_f)] = 25{,}53$.

Der Erwartungswert der Zeit, bis genau $a = 10$ Fahrzeuge gesendet haben, ergibt sich zu $E[T_d|X=a] = 5{,}33$.

Da die Zentrale im Schnitt bereits nach $E[T_d]$ das Ereignis detektiert und $(t_f - t_d) = 5$ Zeiteinheiten für den Downlink benötigt werden, werden im Schnitt $E[X(E[T_d] + t_f - t_d)] = 18{,}38$ Übertragungen zur Zentrale gesendet.

Beispiel mit verschiedenen Detektionszeitpunkten

In diesem Abschnitt wird davon ausgegangen, daß die Fahrzeuge zu verschiedenen Zeiten ein Ereignis detektieren. Die Verteilung der Zufallsvariable T_e sei durch Auswerten von empirischen Werten gewonnen und bekannt. Intuitiv erwartet man, daß der Verlauf der Verteilungsdichtefunktion eine Art „Glockenkurve" ergibt, bei der unmittelbar nach der Zeit $t_0 = 0$ zuerst nur wenige Fahrzeuge das Ereignis detektieren, dann ein Maximum erreicht wird und die Wahrscheinlichkeit danach wieder stark abnimmt. Die Gamma-Verteilung erfüllt ein solches Verhalten. Für die beispielhaften Berechnungen wird T_e als Gamma-verteilt (8) angenommen, der Parameter α wird zu $\alpha=2$ gesetzt (9). Diese Verteilung besitzt den Wertebereich $[0,\infty]$ und die gewünschte Glockenform.

$$f_{\chi}(t) = \frac{\zeta \cdot (\zeta \cdot t)^{\alpha-1} \cdot e^{-\zeta \cdot t}}{\Gamma(\alpha)} \quad \text{mit } t > 0 \text{ und } \alpha > 0,\ \zeta > 0 \tag{8}$$

$$f_{\theta}(t_{\theta}) = \zeta^2 \cdot t_{\theta} \cdot e^{-\zeta \cdot t_{\theta}} \quad \text{mit } \Gamma(2) = 1 \tag{9}$$

Für die Wartezeit bis zum Sendebeginn (T_x) wird auch hier eine negativ exponentielle Verteilung verwendet. Das Integral aus (2), das die Verteilungsdichte für $T = T_e + T_x$ berechnet, ergibt sich zu (10), die Verteilungsfunktion zu (11). Die Verteilung der Detektionszeitpunkte der Fahrzeuge ist wie eingangs beschrieben dienstespezifisch, aus empirischen Werten gewonnen und somit bekannt. Für dieses Beispiel wird die Gammaverteilungsfunktion nach (9) mit $\zeta = 1$ angenommen.

$$f_T(t) = \int_0^t f_{\theta}(t_{\theta}) \cdot f_x(t - t_{\theta}) \cdot dt_{\theta} = \int_0^t \lambda \cdot \zeta^2 \cdot t_{\theta} \cdot e^{((\lambda-\zeta)t_{\theta} - \lambda \cdot t)} \cdot dt_{\theta} = \lambda \cdot \zeta^2 \cdot \frac{e^{-\lambda \cdot t} - e^{-t \cdot \zeta} \cdot (1 + (\zeta - \lambda) \cdot t)}{(\zeta - \lambda)^2} \tag{10}$$

$$F_T(t) = 1 + e^{-(\lambda+\zeta)t} \cdot \frac{\left(\lambda \cdot \zeta^2 \cdot t + 2 \cdot \lambda \cdot \zeta - \lambda^2 \cdot \zeta \cdot t - \lambda^2\right) \cdot e^{\lambda \cdot t} - \zeta^2 \cdot e^{\zeta \cdot t}}{(\zeta - \lambda)^2} \tag{11}$$

Setzt man diese Formeln in die oben beschriebenen Gleichungen ein und berechnet man die Zielfunktionen mit den gegebenen Werten, so ergeben sich die in Tabelle 2 dargestellten Ergebnisse.

	λ	$E[X(t_d)]$	$E[X(t_f)]$	$E[X(E[T_a]+t_f-t_d)]$	$E[T_a\|X=a]$
T_e berücksichtigt	0,0247	17,87	27,41	20,35	6,24
T_e nicht berückstgt.	0,0196	17,84	25,53	18,38	5,33

Tabelle 2. Ergebnisse mit und ohne gleichzeitiger Detektion des Ereignisses.

Vergleicht man die Ergebnisse mit und ohne gleichzeitiger Detektion, so stellt man folgendes Verhalten des Systems fest. Die Zentrale berechnet auch bei verschiedenen Detektionszeitpunkten den Parameter der Verteilungsfunktion von T_X derart, daß weiterhin innerhalb von t_d mit der Wahrscheinlichkeit σ mindestens a Fahrzeuge senden. Da aber nun die effektive Zeit, zwischen Auftreten des Ereignisses und Ablauf von t_d geringer ist, es vergeht die Zeit T_e bis die Fahrzeuge das Ereignis detektieren, erhöht die Zentrale den Parameter λ. Dies bedeutet eine höhere Senderate.

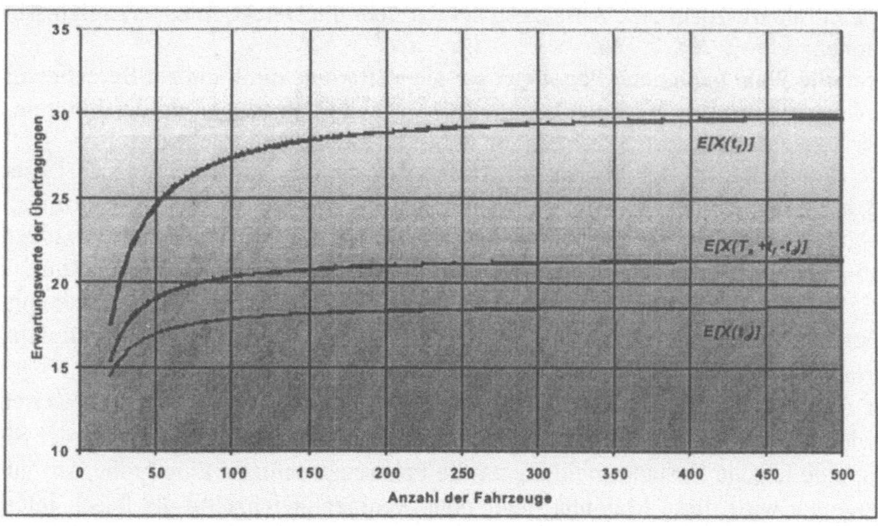

Bild 1. Anzahl Übertragungen bei variabler Anzahl von Fahrzeugen

Eine erhöhte Senderate führt zu einer höheren Belastung des Mobilfunksystems. Dies äußert sich dadurch, daß in der Zeit zwischen Erkennen des Ereignisses durch die Zentrale und Rücksenden des Ereignisses im Downlink (Zentrale zu Fahrzeugen) mehr Fahrzeuge senden. Dies erklärt die erhöhten Erwartungswerte der Anzahl der Übertragungen im Uplink von $X(t_f)$ und $X(t_a + t_f - t_d)$.

Wie aus Tabelle 2 entnommen werden kann, konnte die Gesamtzahl der potentiellen 100 Übertragungen rund um den Faktor 5 verringert werden.

In Bild 1 wird die Anzahl der Fahrzeuge zwischen 20 und 500 variiert. Es zeigt sich, daß sich die Erwartungswerte der Anzahl der Übertragungen bei hohen Teilnehmerzahlen Grenzwerten nähern. Somit wird das gewünschte Verhalten erzielt, daß auch bei sehr großen Teilnehmerzahlen die Anzahl der Übertragungen gering gehalten und durch die Zentrale einfach gesteuert werden kann.

Verzichtet man auf die Verzögerung der Sendezeitpunkte, so liegen die Erwartungswerte der Anzahl der innerhalb von t_d und t_f sendenden Fahrzeuge in diesem Beispiel sehr nahe bei der jeweiligen Anzahl der Fahrzeuge N.

Möglichkeiten und Grenzen des Verfahrens

Das in dieser Arbeit beschriebene Verfahren verfolgt das Ziel, die Anzahl der Übertragungen bei der Detektion eines neuen Ereignis im Uplink zu reduzieren, indem die Fahrzeuge nicht sofort, sondern statistisch verzögert senden. Dieses Vorgehen ist sinnvoll, um die teure Kommunikation über Mobilfunksysteme zu reduzieren und um der Zentrale trotzdem eine Aussagesicherheit über die Detektion eines Ereignisses zu erlauben.

Durch die Wahl geeigneter Parameter für die Verteilungsfunktion zur Berechnung der Sendeverzögerungen, genügen wenige übertragende Fahrzeuge, um der Zentrale mit einer hohen statistischen Sicherheit ein aufgetretenes Ereignis anzuzeigen.

Eine Einschränkung der Einsetzbarkeit des Verfahrens ergibt sich aus der Tatsache, daß bei einer Reihe von FCD-Anwendungen die Fahrzeuge nicht gleichzeitig ein Ereignis detektieren, sondern zeitlich verzögert. Ist diese „natürliche" Verzögerung groß gegenüber den Zielgrößen, so ist eine zusätzliche künstliche Verzögerung nicht nötig. Liegen die Detektionszeiten der Fahrzeuge jedoch in der Größenordnung der angestrebten Zugriffsverzögerungen oder sind sie gar kleiner, so werden durch das Verfahren wesentliche Verbesserungen erzielt.

Ein Anwendungsfall, bei dem das vorgestellte Vorgehen besonders gut verwendet werden kann, ist, wenn die Zentrale aufgrund einer falschen Einschätzung der Situation, eine falsche Zustandsmeldung an die Fahrzeuge schickt. Eine große Anzahl der Fahrzeuge wird diese Meldung mehr oder weniger gleichzeitig als falsch interpretieren und daraufhin den Sendevorgang einleiten. In diesem Fall wird die Anzahl der sendenden Fahrzeuge durch das vorgestellte Verfahren drastisch reduziert.

Ein weiteres Beispiel ist, wenn die Zentrale einen Zustand bei den Fahrzeugen abfrägt („Polling"). Das beschriebene Verfahren eröffnet die Möglichkeit, auf sehr einfache Art einen Abfragemodus zu realisieren. Die Zentrale übermittelt nur einen Parameter und kann aus der Menge der Fahrzeuge die gewünschte Anzahl von Stichprobenwerten ermitteln und dann mittels Hypothesentests mit der gewünschten statistischen

Sicherheit Schlußfolgerungen ziehen. Der Aufwand in der Zentrale im Vergleich zu einer fahrzeugindividuellen Abfragetechnik ist um ein Vielfaches geringer.

Als Einschränkung kann empfunden werden, daß die Zentrale die Anzahl der am Dienst teilnehmenden Fahrzeuge kennen muß. Erste Untersuchungen hierzu haben gezeigt, daß es genügt, wenn die Zentrale nur einen Schätzwert der Fahrzeuge kennt. Abweichungen um +- 20% können als unkritisch angesehen werden.

Der Schätzwert von N kann dadurch gewonnen werden, indem man das Verfahren nicht nur für spontane Ereignisse einsetzt, sondern auch für die Erfassung von kontinuierlichen Daten zur Übersicht über die Verkehrssituation. Hierzu wird den Fahrzeugen wie gehabt ein Parameter von der Zentrale übermittelt, der eine Zufallsverteilung dimensioniert. Mit deren Hilfe wird der folgende Zeitpunkt einer Uplink-Datenübertragung bestimmt. Die zeitliche Verzögerung bezieht sich jetzt jedoch nicht auf den Eintritt eines vordefinierten Ereignisses, sondern vielmehr auf die letzte Datenübertragung. Jedes Fahrzeug sendet somit zeitlich statistisch verteilt eine Folge von Datensätzen an die Zentrale. Die Zentrale empfängt mit diesem Verfahren eine Folge von Übertragungen von der Menge aller am FCD-Dienst teilnehmender Fahrzeuge, deren Rate sie durch den Parameter λ steuern kann. Dadurch erhält die Zentrale die notwendige Grundversorgung mit Verkehrsinformationen. Durch Messen der Rate der Übertragungen kann die Zentrale unter Berücksichtigung von λ und der verwendeten Verteilungsfunktion einen Schätzwert für N ermitteln. Insbesondere durch den kombinierten Einsatz der vorgeschlagenen Verfahren für spontane Ereignisse, für Abfragen durch die Zentrale (Polling) und zur Steuerung der kontinuierlichen Grundversorgunge der Zentrale läßt sich N abschätzen.

Detaillierte Untersuchungen zu diesen Strategien zur Abschätzung von N und zur notwendigen Genauigkeit sind geplant.

Zusammenfassung

Das in diesem Beitrag beschriebene Verfahren hat zum Ziel, die Anzahl der Übertragungen im Rahmen von FCD-Diensten auf das notwendige Minimum zu reduzieren. Dies geschieht, indem man die Zeitspanne nutzt, die die Zentrale zum Erkennen eines Ereignisses zuläßt, um mit statistischen Verfahren die Uplink-Übertragungen der Fahrzeuge geeignet in dieses Zeitintervall abzubilden.

Dabei gibt die Zentrale eine genügend kleine Wahrscheinlichkeit vor, mit der der statistisch mögliche Fall eines Fehlers beschrieben werden kann. Anhand von Beispielrechnungen wurde gezeigt, daß eine starke Reduzierung der Übertragungen mit den vorgeschlagenen Verfahren erreicht werden kann, auch wenn man berücksichtigt, daß die Fahrzeuge ein Ereignis in der Regel nicht gleichzeitig, sondern statistisch verteilt detektieren.

Die vorgestellten Verfahren erlauben zudem im Vergleich zu einem deterministischen Vorgehen einen verringerten Verwaltungs-, Kommunikations- und Rechenaufwand in der Zentrale.

Literatur

1 Mannesmann AG: Process and Device for obtaining Traffic Situation Data, Patentschrift WO 97/29471, 1997
2 Huber, W.; Lädke, M.; Ogger, R.: Extended Floating-Car Data for the Aquisition of Traffic Information, Proceedings 6th World Congress on Intelligent Transport Systems (ITS 99), Toronto, November 8-12, 1999
3 Global Automotive Telematics Standards; CEN TC 278: Road Traffic and Transport Telematics.

CIM/CORBA-basiertes Management verteilter kooperierender Managementsysteme

Alexander Keller

IBM Research Division, T.J. Watson Research Center
P.O. Box 704, Yorktown Heights, NY, USA
Telephone: (914) 784 7593, Telefax: (914) 784 6183
`alexk@us.ibm.com`

Zusammenfassung Web-basierte Technologien wie Portale und e-business Applikationen ermöglichen Unternehmen in zunehmendem Umfang das Outsourcing von IT-Diensten an sog. Application Service Provider (ASP), die ihrerseits Netzdienste von Internet Service Providern (ISP) in Anspruch nehmen. Die daraus resultierende Schichtung von Diensterbringer/Dienstnutzer-Beziehungen bei der Bereitstellung komplexer Anwendungsdienste erschwert jedoch die Lokalisierung und Identifikation der Ursache beim Auftreten von Fehlern. Dies liegt nicht zuletzt daran, daß der Austausch von Managementinformation zwischen den Managementsystemen der Diensterbringer gegenwärtig nur unzureichend funktioniert. Der Kern dieses Problems ist, daß derzeit keine offengelegten Schnittstellen existieren, die einem Dienstnutzer Zugriff auf die Managementsysteme eines Diensterbringers gestatten. Naturgemäß handelt es sich bei solchen *kooperierenden Managementsystemen* um verteilte Anwendungen, die wiederum ihrerseits administriert werden müssen. Es ist daher notwendig, geeignete Managementinformation und -dienste zu definieren, um Managementsysteme in heterogener Umgebung überwachen und steuern zu können.

Der vorliegende Beitrag stellt einen neuen Ansatz zur Lösung dieser Problematik vor, der auf einem Objektmodell zur Instrumentierung verteilter kooperierender Managementsysteme beruht. Dieses Objektmodell wurde unter Berücksichtigung existierender Standards für den Entwurf verteilter Anwendungen (*Reference Model of Open Distributed Processing, RM-ODP*) sowie deren Management (*Common Information Model, CIM*) erstellt und erweitert diese um die spezifischen Eigenschaften von Managementsystemen. Eine CORBA/Java-basierte Implementierung weist die praktische Anwendbarkeit der vorgestellten Konzepte nach.

1 Einführung und Motivation

Die Frage "Was sind die Charakteristiken verteilter Anwendungen aus Sicht des integrierten Managements?" ist derzeit Gegenstand mehrerer Untersuchungen [18, 4, 3]. Im Vergleich zu anderen Managementbereichen (wie zum Beispiel dem Netz- und Systemmanagement) besteht jedoch beim sog. Anwendungsmanagement Unklarheit, wie ein geeignetes Managementmodell der statischen und dynamischen Aspekte verteilter Anwendungen auszusehen hat.

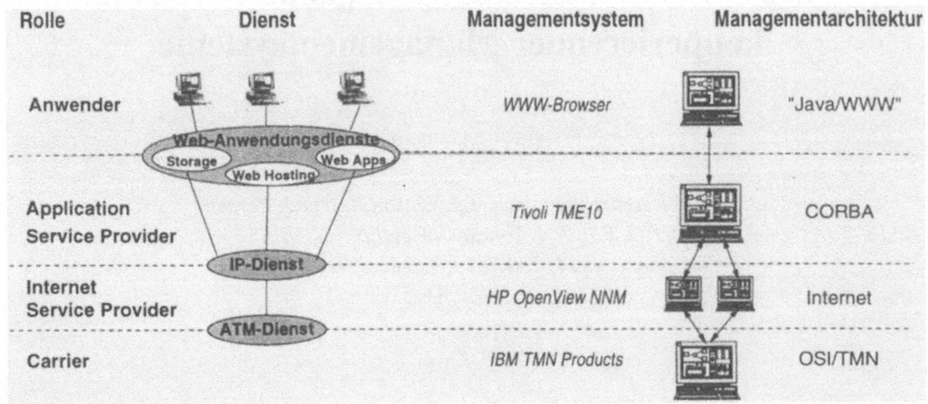

Abbildung 1. Outsourcing von IT-Diensten erfordert die Kooperation von Managementsystemen

Diese Problematik wird durch neuartige web-basierte Technologien wie e-business Applikationen und Portale verschärft, da diese eine wesentlich höhere Flexibilität und Dynamik als traditionelle Client/Server-Architekturen besitzen: Neben technischen Vorteilen wie dem lastabhängigen Zuschalten weiterer Serverknoten in Spitzenzeiten bietet sich Unternehmen insbesondere die Möglichkeit, weitreichendes Outsourcing von IT-Diensten an sog. *Application Service Provider (ASP)* vorzunehmen, um Kostensenkungspotentiale auszuschöpfen. Demgegenüber hat ein ASP (hierzu zählen ebenfalls *Storage Service Provider*, die Speicherkapazität bereitstellen) die Möglichkeit, dieselbe Systeminfrastruktur für zahlreiche Kunden zu verwenden und nutzt seinerseits die entstehenden Synergieeffekte. Insbesondere vollzieht sich Outsourcing von IT-Diensten auf weiteren Ebenen, wie Abbildung 1 verdeutlicht: Ein ASP macht von einem ISP Gebrauch, um IP-Konnektivität zu erhalten, während dieser die Leitungen (bzw. Netzdienste wie ATM oder Frame Relay) eines Telekom-Carriers anmietet. Man erhält somit geschichtete Diensterbringer/Dienstnutzerbeziehungen, an deren Schnittstellen jeweils Dienstgütevereinbarungen (*Service-level Agreements, SLA*) [20] getroffen werden.

Um SLAs jedoch überwachen und durchsetzen zu können, ist es notwendig, daß die Managementsysteme der beteiligten Provider in der Lage sind, Informationen auszutauschen. Wie der rechte Teil von Abbildung 1 verdeutlicht, ist dies jedoch keineswegs selbstverständlich: Neben dem Problem, daß das Zusammenwirken der Managementsysteme unterschiedlicher Hersteller dadurch erschwert wird, daß diese in der Regel auf verschiedenen Management*architekturen* basieren[1], existieren insbesondere keinerlei Festlegungen, welche Art von Information Managementsysteme bereitstellen bzw. welche Dienste diese anbieten sollen. Der vorliegende Beitrag behandelt diese Fragestellung und stellt ein Objektmodell für verteilte kooperierende Managementsysteme vor. Es spezifiziert einen Mindestumfang an Instrumentierung,

---

[1] Aus Platzgründen ist in diesem Beitrag eine eingehende Behandlung der Problematik einer *Integration von Managementarchitekturen* mittels Management-Gateways nicht möglich; wir verweisen hierzu auf [15, 17, 13], die sich dieser Thematik eingehend widmen.

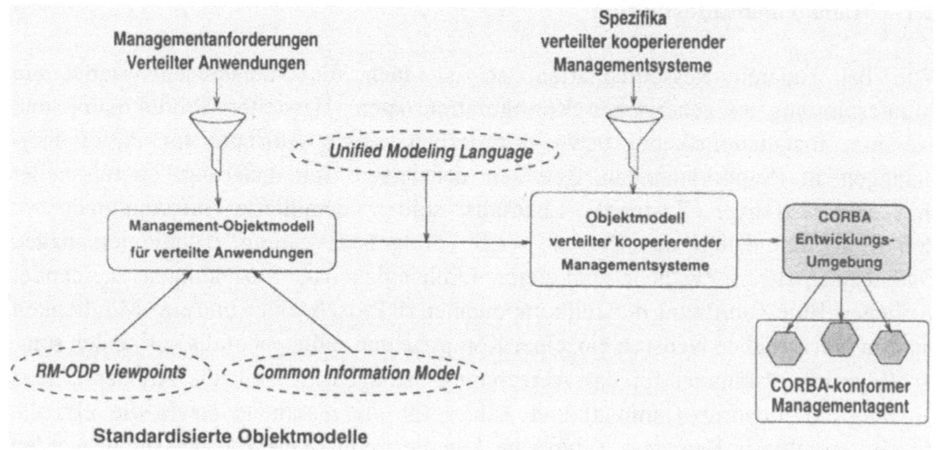

Abbildung 2. Überblick über das Vorgehensmodell des Beitrags

der für die Überwachung und Steuerung von Managementsystemen erforderlich ist. Dies schließt sowohl das Managementsystem selbst (als administrierte Ressource) ein, als auch den einheitlichen Zugriff auf in der Datenbank des Managementsystems gespeicherte Information über von ihm verwaltete Ressourcen (wie z.B. Systeme, Netzkomponenten oder Applikationen) ein.

Das Vorgehensmodell dieses Beitrags ist in Abbildung 2 dargestellt: Wir werden zunächst in Abschnitt 2 die Anforderungen an das Management verteilter kooperierender Managementsysteme vorstellen, die wir anhand mehrerer Szenarien in der Praxis gewonnen haben. Diese Analyse wird uns in Abschnitt 3 helfen, existierende Ansätze im Bereich des Anwendungsmanagements kritisch zu bewerten; besonderes Augenmerk widmen wir hierbei dem ODP-Referenzmodell der ISO sowie dem *Common Information Model (CIM)* der DMTF, da sich diese beiden Ansätze besonders gut für unsere Aufgabenstellung eignen. Wir haben diese beiden Standards als Grundlage unseres Modells gewählt und um die Spezifika verteilter kooperierender Managementsysteme erweitert. Das auf CIM und ODP basierende Modell wird in Abschnitt 4 vorgestellt, wobei wir insbesondere auf die neu definierten Objektklassen und Assoziationen eingehen. Anschließend stellen wir unsere CORBA/Java-basierte prototypische Implementierung vor. Der Beitrag schließt mit einer Zusammenfassung unserer Erfahrungen und zeigt gegenwärtig untersuchte Folgefragestellungen auf.

2 Anforderungsanalyse

Wir befassen uns in diesem Abschnitt mit der Analyse der Spezifika verteilter kooperierender Managementsysteme und leiten daraus die Anforderungen an das in Abschnitt 4 beschriebene Objektmodell ab. Hierbei unterscheiden wir zwischen der Managementinformation d.h. der Datenmenge zur umfassenden Beschreibung eines Systems (Abschnitt 2.1), sowie den Managementdiensten, also dem Funktionsumfang, der für dessen Management erforderlich ist (Abschnitt 2.2).

2.1 Managementinformation

Wie bei anderen Ressourcenarten, so ist auch für Managementsysteme ein Mindestumfang an generischen Konfigurationsdaten (Hersteller, Produktname und -version, Installationsdatum usw.) erforderlich, sowie Attribute für das Fehlermanagement (Supportangaben, Zeit seit der letzten Initialisierung, operationeller und administrativer Zustand). Ebenfalls sollten detaillierte Informationen zu den Teilkomponenten des Systems (z.B. Ereignisverwaltung, Topologiemanager, Datenbank), deren Zustände und deren (Abhängigkeits-) Beziehungen zueinander vorliegen. Eine Zuordnung der Teilkomponenten zu Prozeßnamen und eine Möglichkeit für den individuellen Neustart einzelner Komponenten sollte ebenfalls vorhanden sein.

Relevante Parameter für das Abrechnungsmanagement sind: die Art der Lizenz (nodelocked, floating, Campus) und Zähler für die maximale sowie die aktuelle Anzahl simultaner Benutzer. Zahlreiche kommerzielle Managementsysteme werden mit Lizenzservern ausgeliefert, die diese Informationen bereitstellen. Für den Betrieb des Managementsystems ist die Funktionsfähigkeit seines Lizenzservers maßgeblich.

Das Sicherheitsmanagement spielt eine wesentliche Rolle in verteilten Umgebungen, da Managementsysteme verschiedener Dienstleister kooperieren müssen: Jedes Managementsystem muß Auskunft über seine administrative Domäne sowie die von ihm verwalteten Agenten, untergeordneten Managementsysteme und Gateways geben können. Ferner müssen geeignete Mechanismen zum Schutz gegen unbefugten Zugriff sowie eine Administrationsmöglichkeit für autorisierte Interaktionen mit Partnersystemen vorhanden sein.

Informationen für das Leistungsmanagement beinhalten Parameter zur Konfiguration von Caching-Mechanismen für häufig benötigte Managementdaten (wie z.B. die Cachegröße oder die Gültigkeitszeiträume von Ressourcendaten). Zähler zur Messung der Bearbeitungs- und Antwortzeiten sowie zur Ermittlung der Auslastung oder der Anzahl der Anfragen über benutzerdefinierte Zeiträume liefern gute Hinweise über vorhandene Engpässe.

2.2 Managementdienste

Dienste für das Konfigurationsmanagement haben zum Ziel, neue Systeme problemlos in eine bestehende Managementinfrastruktur einzubringen, indem diesen Konfigurationsprofile anhand ihrer Domänenzugehörigkeit bzw. Funktionsumfang dynamisch zugewiesen werden. Hierzu muß ein Managementsystem die Definition von Konfigurationsprofilen gestatten, die u.U. an untergeordnete Systeme verteilt werden. Es muß außerdem in der Lage sein, selbst solche Profile zu erhalten und zu verarbeiten.

Große praktische Relevanz für das Fehlermanagement haben Operationen zur Überprüfung des Zustands einzelner Komponenten eines Managementsystems sowie Dienste zum Starten, Stoppen und Wiederaufsetzen nach Auftreten eines Fehlers. Maßnahmen zur Überprüfung der Ressourcendatenbank auf Konsistenz sowie das Ausführen diverser Administrations- und Diagnoseprozeduren sollten in regelmäßigen Intervallen erfolgen. Beim Auftreten von schweren Fehlern sind die Ereignis- und Fehlerlogs eines Managementsystems eine wichtige Informationsquelle;

einheitliche Mechanismen zum Betrachten, Auswerten und Durchsuchen hinsichtlich frei definierbarer Kriterien sind ebenfalls von hoher Bedeutung.

Die Konfiguration von Diensten zur Ereignismeldung, die Initiierung von Managementoperationen auf Partnersystemen und die Registrierung für spezielle Ereignistypen erfordert das Vorhandensein geeigneter Sicherheitsdienste und -policies.

Leistungs- und Abrechnungsdienste wie z.B. das Generieren von Berichten über die Nutzung von Ressourcen (Statistiken, Trends, nach diversen Kriterien wie z.B. Durchsatz, Verzögerung oder Last aufbereitete Systemdaten) stellen eine wesentliche Planungsgrundlage dar. Die Identifikation relevanter Systeme und Parameter sowie die Kombination der obengenannten Basisgrößen werden aus den spezifischen Gegebenheiten und Zielvorgaben einer Unternehmung abgeleitet. Folglich müssen Mechanismen bereitgestellt werden, die eine flexible Kombination der Meßgrößen sicherstellen, um aus Ressourcendaten aussagekräftige Managementinformation zu gewinnen.

3   Existierende Ansätze für das Anwendungsmanagement

Die ersten Ansätze für das Management verteilter Anwendungen stammen von der Internet Engineering Task Force: Die Spezifikationen der IETF Application MIBs (*applMib* [11] und *sysApplMib* [14]) sind jedoch auf die Gegebenheiten eines speziellen Betriebssystems zugeschnitten[2] und die Problematik des objektbasierten IETF-Ansatzes beeinträchtigen deren Anwendbarkeit: Ein beträchtlicher Anteil der in der Application MIB definierten Tabellen dient lediglich dazu, die Managementinformation nach unterschiedlichen Kriterien zu indizieren. Ferner ist anzumerken, daß sich beide MIBs ausschließlich auf die passive Überwachung (Monitoring) von lokal installierten Anwendungen beschränken. Weitere Ansätze für das Management verteilter Anwendungen sind:

Der IEEE 1387.2 *POSIX Software Administration Standard* [7] definiert Managementinformation, die auf Softwareverteilung und -installation zugeschnitten ist. Es handelt sich hierbei um statische Information, die die Struktur von Softwarepaketen (in einem UNIX-Umfeld) beschreibt.

Die *Distributed Software Administration (XDSA)* Spezifikation der Open Group [21] erweitert IEEE 1387.2 und verfügt daher ebenfalls über keinerlei Managementinformation, die sich etwa mit den dynamischen bzw. Laufzeitaspekten einer Anwendung befaßt. Vielmehr bestehen die Erweiterungen hauptsächlich darin, diverse Befehle (swinstall, swlist, swmodify etc.) sowie ein Format für Installations-Images festzulegen.

Die Tivoli *Application Management Specification (AMS)* [1] definiert allgemein-gültige Objektklassen für das Management verteilter Anwendungen sowie deren Beziehungen zur Systeminfrastruktur und kann als Vorläufer von CIM (siehe unten) angesehen werden.

Das *Application Response Measurement (ARM) API* [2] und seine Erweiterungen [10] haben zum Ziel, Antwortzeitmessungen von Transaktionen durchzuführen, um

---

[2] die Übersicht der laufenden Anwendungen entspricht der UNIX-Prozeßtabelle und die darin enthaltenen Informationen können somit nicht auf jeder Systemplattform ermittelt werden.

Aussagen über die Bearbeitungszeit von Aufträgen (und damit das Leistungsvermögen der Anwendungen) zu treffen. Grundlage hierfür ist, daß die betreffende Anwendung eine ARM-Schnittstelle anbietet, was jedoch in der Praxis nur selten der Fall ist.

Es ist festzuhalten, daß die existierenden Ansätze hauptsächlich auf die statischen Aspekte verteilter Anwendungen abstellen und hier einige Überschneidungen bezüglich der bereitgestellten Informationsmenge bestehen. Demgegenüber wird dem *dynamischen* Verhalten verteilter Anwendungen kaum Aufmerksamkeit gewidmet, obwohl dies – wie die Ausführungen in Abschnitt 1 gezeigt haben – von ausschlaggebender Bedeutung ist.

3.1 Das ISO Reference Model of Open Distributed Processing (RM-ODP)

RM-ODP [8] definiert generische Begriffe, Konzepte und Regeln zur Beschreibung verteilter Anwendungen. Obwohl RM-ODP nicht explizit auf das Management dieser Anwendungen eingeht, so werden doch Aussagen bezüglich der allgemeingültigen Eigenschaften verteilter Anwendungen getroffen; man kann davon ausgehen, daß die Struktur beliebiger verteilter Anwendungen den Festlegungen des RM-ODP folgt und ODP somit einen generischen Minimalumfang an Informationen über verteilte Anwendungen bereitstellt, der auch für deren Management genutzt werden kann.

Unsere Analyse der ODP-Konzepte nach Managementgesichtspunkten ergibt, daß 2 der insgesamt 5 in ODP definierten sog. *Viewpoint Languages* – nämlich die *Computational* und *Engineering Viewpoint Languages* – wichtig sind, da sie diejenigen Gegebenheiten verteilter Anwendungen beschreiben, die besondere Relevanz für das Management besitzen. Konzepte, die in der *Information Language* festgelegt werden, beziehen sich auf semantische Eigenschaften des Informationsaustauschs und sind nicht unmittelbar für (technisches) Management relevant. Da eines der Ziele integrierten Managements darin besteht, von den implementierungstechnischen Spezifika einer Ressource zu abstrahieren, ist auch die *Technology Language* für unsere Zwecke schlecht geeignet. Die Verwendung der *Enterprise Language* gestattet die Definition von unternehmensbezogenen Kriterien wie Rollen, Aufgaben und Zuständigkeiten, die jedoch für die hier untersuchte Fragestellung zu abstrakt sind.

Die Konzepte der **Computational Language** gestatten die funktionale Zerlegung eines Systems in interagierende Objekte. Management-Objektklassen wie *operation, signal* oder *binding* sind wichtig, um Beziehungen zwischen Managementobjekten zu beschreiben. Es sei an dieser Stelle festgehalten, daß keine andere (Management) Architektur ähnliche Konzepte anbietet, obwohl diese essentiell zur Ermittlung dynamischer Beziehungen zwischen verteilten Anwendungen sind. Die in der *Computational Language* definierten Objektklassen sind in Abbildung 3 dargestellt.

Die **Engineering Language** definiert Mechanismen und Komponenten für die Interaktion zwischen Objekten in einem verteilten System. Beispiele für aus dieser Sprache abgeleitete Objektklassen sind *node, capsule, cluster, channel*, die für dynamische Aspekte des Anwendungsmanagements hilfreich sind. Die Definition des *capsule*-Konzepts aus [9] verdeutlicht dies: "A configuration of engineering objects forming a single unit for the purpose of encapsulation of processing and storage"; *capsule* entspricht daher einem Prozeß, der innerhalb eines Betriebssystems abläuft.

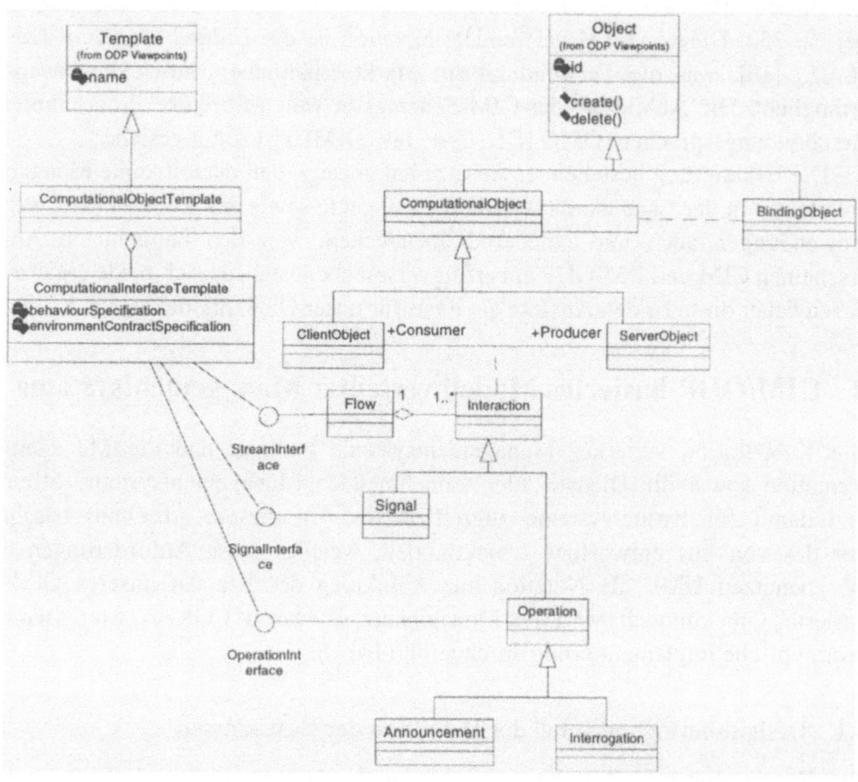

Abbildung 3. Die Objektklassen des RM-ODP Computational Viewpoint

3.2 Das Common Information Model der Distributed Management Task Force

CIM [6] ist ein objektorientierter Ansatz zur Definition von Managementobjekten für beliebige Ressourcen sowie deren Beziehungen zueinander. Zur Vermeidung von Mehrfachvererbung macht CIM weitreichenden Gebrauch von Assoziations- bzw. Aggregationsbeziehungen: Diese Beziehungen werden als Assoziationsklassen modelliert. Das *Core Schema* definiert grundlegende abstrakte Ressourcenklassen wie z.B. *service access point, service, product, system, logical device* sowie einen Mechanismus, um einen oder mehrere Parameter einer Ressource zu modifizieren (*setting*). Ferner sind mehrere *Common* Schemas definiert [5]: Das *System Schema* erweitert das Core Schema um Objektklassen für Aufträge, Betriebssysteme, Prozesse, Threads, Dateisysteme, Endsysteme und Cluster. Das *Application Schema* behandelt das Management verteilter Anwendungen und ist für die in diesem Beitrag behandelte Problemstellung besonders relevant: Es definiert Managementobjekte für verteilte Anwendungen (*application system*), deren logische (*software feature*) und physische Komponenten (*software element*). Zusätzlich werden diverse Prüfverfahren (Kompatibilität bzgl. Betriebssystemversion, verfügbarem Speicherplatz usw.) sowie Aktionen (*reboot, execute program*) festgelegt. Die Summe der in den insgesamt 14 CIM Schemas definierten Objektklassen liegt gegenwärtig bei ca. 250. Die von CIM verwendete Notation ist die *Unified Modeling Language (UML)* [19], was die Verwendung am Markt erhältlicher Entwicklungswerkzeuge ermöglicht. Die Abbildung der CIM-Schemas in weit verbreitete Programmier- und Beschreibungssprachen (OMG IDL, C++, Java, XML) ist somit gesichert.

Die Evaluierung bestehender Ansätze hat gezeigt, daß derzeit keine Managementarchitektur in der Lage ist, die vielfältigen Aspekte sowie den Lebenszyklus verteilter Anwendungen auch nur annähernd abzudecken. Von den betrachteten Ansätzen erscheinen CIM und RM-ODP am erfolgversprechendsten, da sich beide ergänzen; wir haben daher diese beiden Ansätze als Basis für unser Objektmodell gewählt.

4   CIM/ODP-basiertes Modell verteilter Managementsysteme

Die Kooperation verteilter Managementsysteme bedingt, daß die Managementinformation sowie die Dienste aller teilnehmenden Managementsysteme offengelegt und damit für Partnersysteme zugreifbar sind. In diesem Abschnitt beschreiben wir das von uns entworfene Objektmodell, welches diese Anforderungen erfüllt. Wir benutzen UML als Notation zur Abbildung der Klassen unseres CIM/ODP-basierten Objektmodells verteilter Managementsysteme auf CORBA, womit wir unsere prototypische Implementierung durchgeführt haben.

4.1   Designüberlegungen bei der Definition der Basisklassen

Die Beschreibung in Abschnitt 3.2 hat verdeutlicht, daß der Umfang an bereits definierter Managementinformation CIM zu einer soliden Grundlage für die Modellierung verteilter Systeme und Anwendungen macht. Problematisch ist jedoch, daß gegenwärtig der Laufzeitaspekt nur unzureichend abgedeckt wird: Dynamische Bindungen, Warteschlangen, Anfragen oder Signale sind noch nicht in CIM enthalten.

Die ODP *Computational Language* hilft, diese Lücke zu füllen, da in ihr exakt diese Begriffe definiert sind (vgl. Abbildung 3). Die ODP *Engineering Language* bietet jedoch keinen Mehrwert gegenüber CIM, da beide Standards sowohl die Bestandteile, als auch die Ausführungsumgebung einer verteilten Anwendung beschreiben (z.B. Threads, Prozesse, Betriebssystem, Endbenutzersystem).

Wir haben daher die Konzepte der ODP Computational Language mit den CIM *Core*, *System* und *Application Schemas* kombiniert, um die Basisklassen unseres Objektmodells zu erhalten, die wir anschließend um die Spezifika verteilter kooperierender Managementsysteme erweitern. Somit ist bereits ein beträchtlicher Umfang an wichtiger Information für das Anwendungsmanagement nahe an der Wurzel der Vererbungshierarchie vorhanden: Beschreibungen von Applikationen, deren Diensten und Komponenten sowie ihre Beziehungen zu Betriebssystemprozessen sind bereits an dieser Stelle spezifiziert. Die Tatsache, daß einzelne Komponenten (sowie die gesamte Anwendung) gestartet, angehalten und wiederaufgesetzt werden können findet man hier ebenso wieder, wie Hinweise auf Bindungen zur Laufzeit. Hierbei handelt es sich um Managementinformation, die in traditionellen Managementarchitekturen (wie z.B. dem SNMP-basierten Management) lediglich in Ressourcen-spezifischen Beschreibungen festgelegt ist und somit für jede Anwendung eigens neu definiert werden muß.

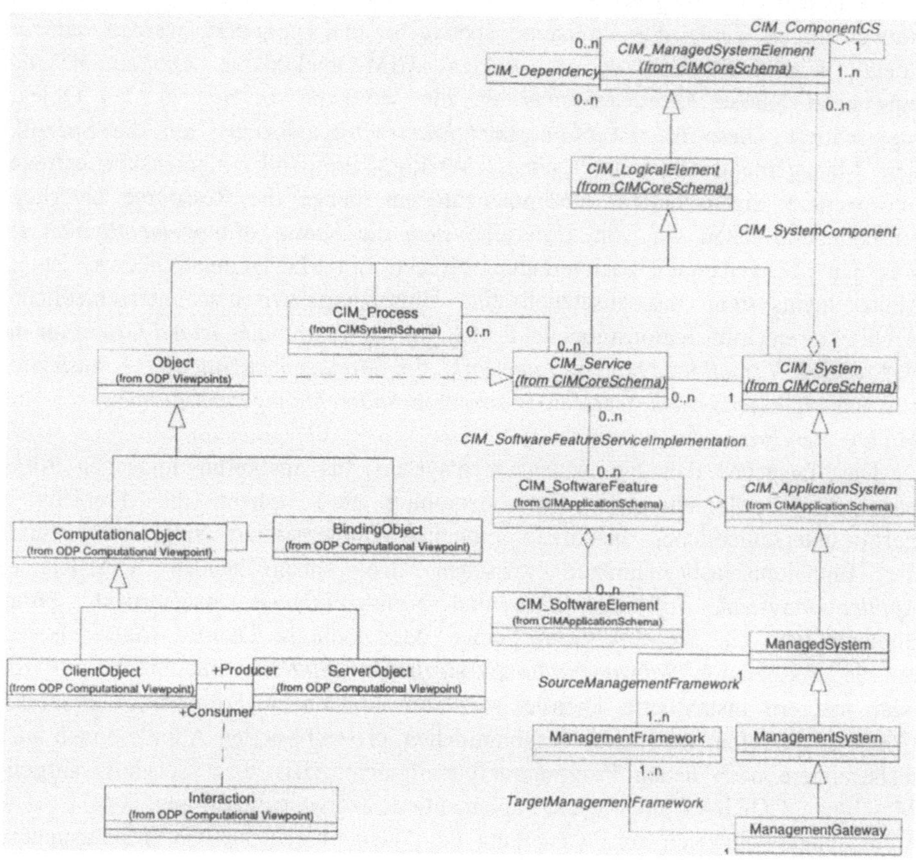

Abbildung 4. CIM/ODP–basiertes Objektmodell verteilter Managementsysteme (Ausschnitt)

4.2 Managementsystem-spezifische Objektklassen

Die 3 relevanten CIM Schemata (Core, System, Application) enthalten ca. 75 Objektklassen und ebensoviele Assoziationen; von ca. einem Drittel dieser Objektklassen haben wir zusätzliche Klassen abgeleitet, um die spezifischen Aspekte von Managementsystemen zu berücksichtigen. Die graphische Darstellung des gesamten Objektmodells ist in diesem Beitrag nicht möglich, weshalb wir in dem in Abbildung 4 dargestellten Klassendiagramm auf folgende Managementinformation verzichten müssen: Die Objektklassen für Ereignis- und Fehlerlogs sowie die von den CIM-Klassen *Check* und *Action* abgeleiteten Objekte, z.B. zur Überprüfung der Systemgegebenheiten. Außerdem entfallen sämtliche Objektklassen mit Bezug zu Produkt- und Bestellinformationen. Ferner konnten wir Attributdefinitionen (Name, Datentyp, Default-Wert, Flags für schreib-/lesbare Attribute, CIM Qualifiers) sowie Methodensignaturen (Argumente, Rückgabewerte) nicht übernehmen, da diese die Lesbarkeit der Abbildung stark beeinträchtigt hätten. Der in Abbildung 4 dargestellte Ausschnitt des Objektmodells illustriert jedoch die wesentlichen Überlegungen.

Zunächst muß ausgedrückt werden, daß Managementsysteme selbst verteilte Anwendungen sind, die ihrerseits überwacht und gesteuert werden müssen. Hierzu leiten wir von der (abstrakten) CIM-Objektklasse *ApplicationSystem* eine neue Klasse *ManagedSystem* ab, die sämtliche zu managenden Objekte repräsentiert. Diese ist mit *ManagementFramework* assoziiert, um die Spezifika der Managementarchitektur (Name, Version, Protokoll, Namenskonventionen und weitere Eigenschaften) zusammenzufassen, denen die Ressource unterliegt. Anschließend leiten wir von *ManagedSystem* die Klasse *ManagementSystem* ab, was den obengenannten Sachverhalt ausdrückt. Ein Management-Gateway ist ein Managementsystem, das zusätzlich eine Umsetzung zwischen unterschiedlichen Architekturen (Informationsmodelle, Protokolle) vornimmt; dies ist der Grund für die Assoziation *TargetManagementFramework*, die *ManagementGateway* – zusätzlich zur von *ManagedSystem* geerbten Assoziation *SourceManagementFramework* – mit *ManagementFramework* verbindet.

Die Tatsache, daß ein Managementsystem aus mehreren logischen Komponenten (Topologiemanager, Zustandsmonitor etc.) besteht, die ihrerseits in Form unterschiedlicher Installationseinheiten implementiert sind, wird durch die Enthaltenseinsbeziehungen zwischen den entsprechenden CIM-Klassen *ApplicationSystem*, *SoftwareFeature* und *SoftwareElement* ausgedrückt. Ferner implementiert ein *SoftwareFeature* einen oder mehrere Dienste (*Service*), was mit der Assoziation *SoftwareFeatureServiceImplementation* verdeutlicht wird. Ein oder mehrere instantiierte Dienste wiederum können in Form eines Prozesses (*Process*) ablaufen, was neben herkömmlichen, prozeßbasierten Applikationen auch insbesondere nach neuen Programmierparadigmen (EJBs, Java Servlets, virtuelle Maschinen, CORBA Components) implementierte Software einschließt.

Besonders hilfreich zur Darstellung des Sachverhalts, daß ein (Management-) System eine beliebige Anzahl unterschiedlicher Managementobjekte beinhalten kann, ist das *Composite* Design Pattern, das *System* mit *ManagedSystemElement* sowie dessen Subklassen verbindet. Es bildet in unserem Fall die Grundvoraussetzung dafür, daß wir sowohl die softwaretechnischen Bestandteile des Managementsystems selbst modellieren können (rechter Teil der Grafik), als auch die von ihm verwalteten Ressourcen, deren zugehörige Managementobjekte üblicherweise in dessen Datenbank abgespeichert sind (linker Teil). Diese Managementobjekte sind Instanzen der ODP-Objektklassen, welche Client- und Server-Objekte (sowie deren Interaktionen und Bindungen) darstellen. Ein Partnersystem ist somit in der Lage, das instrumentierte Managementsystem selbst sowie die von ihm verwalteten Ressourcen zu administrieren.

4.3 Prototypische Implementierung

Wir haben die kommerzielle Managementplattform *Tivoli NetView* sowie ein von uns entwickeltes CMIP/SNMP Management-Gateway [12] instrumentiert und die CORBA-basierten Managementagenten in Java implementiert. Die C-APIs des Managementsystems wurden von uns mit IDL-Kapseln versehen, was uns die Möglichkeit bietet, über CORBA darauf zuzugreifen. Client-seitig haben wir einerseits eine web-basierte Benutzerschnittstelle auf der Basis des JavaORBs *VisiBroker for*

Java realisiert, sowie ebenfalls einen Zugang für ein weiteres Managementsystem geschaffen, was uns den Zugriff auf den Agenten auf zweierlei Arten gestattet.

Die Wiederverwendung von CORBA-Diensten war ebenfalls ein Ziel unserer Arbeit. Insbesondere das Navigieren durch die zahlreichen Assoziationen sowie das Aufzählen der Objekte am jeweils anderen Ende einer Assoziation sollte durch die CORBA-Dienste *Query* sowie *Relationship* geleistet werden. Bedauerlicherweise war die uns zur Verfügung stehende Implementierung dazu nicht in der Lage, weshalb wir die entsprechende Funktionalität innerhalb der Objekte zeitaufwendig selbst implementieren mußten. Zukünftig verfügbare CIM Object Manager werden dies jedoch leisten können, was den Implementierungsaufwand deutlich verringern wird.

Als problematisch erwies sich ebenfalls die Implementierung eines hinreichend feingranularen Sicherheitskonzeptes zum Zugriff auf die in den Systemen gespeicherte Ressourceninformation. Schließlich wird ein Provider nur diejenige Informationsmenge offenlegen, die ein Dienstnutzer unbedingt benötigt. Ein auf Zielvorgaben basierendes Viewkonzept könnte dies leisten, jedoch befinden sich die Arbeiten der IETF/DMTF *Policy*-Arbeitsgruppen noch in einem frühen Stadium; insbesondere sind gegenwärtig keine *Policy Engines* verfügbar, die eine flexible und einheitliche Vergabe und Überprüfung von Zugriffsrechten gestatten. Unser Prototyp stützt sich daher auf die (proprietären) Mittel von *NetView* zur View-Definition ab.

5   Zusammenfassung und Ausblick

Wir haben in diesem Beitrag einen neuen Ansatz für CIM/CORBA-basiertes Management verteilter kooperierender Managementsysteme vorgestellt. Die Notwendigkeit hierfür ergibt sich aus der Tatsache, daß das stark zunehmende Outsourcing von IT-Dienstleistungen die Kooperation der Managementsysteme aller beteiligten Partner erfordert, um eine schnelle Ermittlung von Fehlern über Providergrenzen hinweg zu gewährleisten. Dies erfordert die Offenlegung eines Mindestumfangs an Managementinformation und -diensten. Einige charakteristische Beispiele hierfür wurden vorgestellt. Die zentrale Fragestellung des Beitrags ist, wie Managementsysteme – als ein Spezialfall verteilter Anwendungen – modelliert werden können, um eine möglichst große Menge an Managementinformation und -diensten von generischen Modellen für das Anwendungsmanagement zu übernehmen. Wir haben bestehende Ansätze eingehend untersucht und die Kombination von ODP und CIM gewählt, da sich diese Modelle gut ergänzen und eine Vielfalt an wichtiger Information beinhalten. Darauf aufbauend, haben wir ein Objektmodell entworfen und implementiert, das sowohl die Steuerung eines Managementsystems selbst ermöglicht, als auch den Zugriff auf die Daten der von ihm verwalteten Ressourcen gestattet. Eine prototypische Implementierung weist die praktische Anwendbarkeit unseres Ansatzes nach.

Unsere gegenwärtigen Arbeiten befassen sich mit der Migration der Implementierung in die von der DMTF gegenwärtig entwickelte *Web-based Enterprise Management (WBEM)* Infrastruktur. Die dabei aufgeworfenen Fragestellungen hinsichtlich der Filterung und Übermittlung von Ereignismeldungen sowie der Sicherheit und Skalierbarkeit in großen Umgebungen werden es uns ermöglichen, die praktische Anwendbarkeit dieser Architektur zu beurteilen.

Literatur

[1] Application Management Specification. Version 2.0. Tivoli Systems. (November 1997)

[2] Application Response Management. Version 2.0. Tivoli Systems. (November 1997)

[3] Bauer, M., Bunt, R. et al.: Services Supporting Management of Distributed Applications and Services. IBM Systems Journal *36*(4), 508 – 526 (1997)

[4] Brusil, P., Hellerstein, J., Lutfiyya, H.: Applications Management – Current Practices, Research Results, and Future Directions. Journal of Network and Systems Management *6*(3), 361 – 366 (September 1998)

[5] Bumpus, W., Sweitzer, J., Thompson, P., Westerinen, A., Williams, R.: Common Information Model: Implementing the Object Model for Enterprise Management. J. Wiley & Sons 2000

[6] Common Information Model (CIM) Version 2.2. Specification. Distributed Management Task Force. (Juni 1999)

[7] IEEE Standard for Information Technology - Portable Operating System Interface (POSIX) - System Administration - Part 2: Software Administration. IEEE Standard 1387.2. The Institute of Electrical and Electronics Engineers. (1995)

[8] Open Distributed Processing – Reference Model. IS 10746. International Organization for Standardization and International Electrotechnical Committee. (1995)

[9] Open Distributed Processing – Reference Model – Part 3: Architecture. IS 10746-3. International Organization for Standardization and International Electrotechnical Committee. (1995)

[10] Johnson, M. W., Smead, S.: Beyond ARM 2.0 - API Extensions that enable pervasive Service Level Instrumentation. Computer Measurement Working Group. Dezember 1998

[11] Kalbfleisch, C., Krupczak, C., Presuhn, R., Saperia, J.: Application Management MIB. RFC 2564. IETF. (Mai 1999)

[12] Keller, A.: Tool-based Implementation of a Q-Adapter Function for the seamless Integration of SNMP-managed Devices in TMN. In: *Proceedings of the IEEE/IFIP Network Operations and Management Symposium (NOMS 98)*. IEEE Press. New Orleans, USA, Februar 1998, pp.400–411

[13] Keller, A., Neumair, B.: Interoperable Architekturen als Basis eines integrierten Managements. In Zitterbart, M. (Hrsg.): *GI/ITG–Fachtagung Kommunikation in Verteilten Systemen*. Springer Verlag, Februar 1997

[14] Krupczak, C., Saperia, J.: Definitions of System-Level Managed Objects for Applications. RFC 2287. IETF. (Februar 1998)

[15] Pavlou, G.: A Novel Approach for Mapping the OSI-SM/TMN Model to ODP/OMG CORBA. In Sloman, M., Mazumdar, S., Lupu, E. (Hrsg.): *Proceedings of the 6th IFIP/IEEE International Symposium on Integrated Network Management*. IEEE Publishing, Mai 1999

[16] Rational Rose 98i: Using Rational Rose. Rational Software Corporation. Februar 1998

[17] Soukouti, N., Hollberg, U.: Joint Inter-Domain Management: CORBA, CMIP and SNMP. In Lazar, A. A., Saracco, R., Stadler, R. (Hrsg.): *Proceedings of the 5th IFIP/IEEE International Symposium on Integrated Network Management*. Chapman and Hall, Mai 1997

[18] Sturm, R., Bumpus, W.: Foundations of Application Management. J. Wiley & Sons 1998

[19] OMG Unified Modeling Language Specification. Version 1.3 ad/99-06-08. Object Management Group. (Juni 1999)

[20] Verma, D.: Supporting Service Level Agreements on IP Networks. Macmillan Technical Publishing 1999

[21] Systems Management: Distributed Software Administration. CAE Specification C701. The Open Group. (Januar 1998)

Preisträger

1999/2000

Entwicklung und Leistungsbewertung einer ATM-Funkschnittstelle

Dr. Dietmar Petras

Lehrstuhl für Kommunikationsnetze, RWTH Aachen
petras@comnets.rwth-aachen.de
http://www.comnets.rwth-aachen.de/~petras

Zusammenfassung Im April 1997 wurde beim ETSI das Projekt BRAN (Broadband Radio Access Networks) eingerichtet [2], um breitbandig übertragende Drahtlossysteme wie ATM-LAN und RLL zu standardisieren. Die Dissertation [4], deren Ergebnisse in diesem Papier zusammengefaßt werden, hat wesentliche Grundlagen dafür gelegt, indem Techniken für die Funkschnittstelle entworfen, analysiert und allgemeinverständlich in die Fachdiskussion eingeführt worden sind. Sie sind heute Bestandteil der Konzepte für drahtlose ATM-Systeme der verschiedenen an der ETSI-Standardisierung beteiligten Hersteller.
Der Autor schlägt vor, die in Einführung befindlichen, auf dem ATM-Verfahren beruhenden Festnetze durch drahtlose Zugangsnetze zu ergänzen, um feste, bewegliche und mobile Endgeräte mit einer Multiplexübertragungsrate von ca. 20 Mbit/s über Funk anzuschließen. Die Kommunikationsdienste benötigen unterschiedlichen Durchsatz, Verzögerung und Bitfehlerhäufigkeit. Dementsprechend arbeitet der Autor zunächst die Unterschiede kabelgebundener und funkbasierter Multiplexer heraus und entwickelt dann einen zugehörigen Funkprotokollstapel, der die dienstgütespezifische Zuteilung von Übertragungskapazität an Terminals steuert.
Neben Funktionen zur adaptiven Kapazitätszuweisung des Mediums über Zeitschlitze zur Übertragung von ATM-Zellen werden Zugriffsprotokolle und ein fehlerbehandelndes Sicherungsprotokoll entwickelt. Kollisionsauflösungsalgorithmen und ihre Leistungsparameter werden sorgfältig analytisch und simulativ verglichen und ein blockierungsfreies Verfahren ausgewählt. Für repräsentative Verkehrslastszenarien kann simulativ gezeigt werden, daß die Leistungsparameter der ATM-Funkschnittstelle trotz funkbedingter Übertragungsfehler denen eines kabelgebundenen Multiplexers nahekommen.

1 Asynchroner Transfermodus, ATM

Bei dem asynchronen Transfermodus (ATM) handelt es sich um ein verbindungsorientiertes Paketvermittlungsverfahren basierend auf virtuellen Verbindungen [8]. Von den Anwendungen resultierende Datenströme oder Datenpakete werden am Netzrand von der ATM-Anpassungsschicht (ATM Adaptation Layer, AAL) in ATM-Zellen konstanter Länge segmentiert. Eine ATM-Zelle besteht aus einem 5 Byte langen Kopf mit Informationen für die Vermittlungssteuerung sowie einem 48 Byte langen Körper mit Benutzerdaten. Das für diese Arbeit wesentliche Merkmal des asynchronen Transfermodus ist das in Abb. 1 veranschaulichte Multiplexen von ATM-Zellen in Netzknoten, das nach dem asynchronen Zeitmultiplex erfolgt. Dabei werden Zellen gegebenenfalls gepuffert, so daß sie zufällige Verzögerungen erfahren.

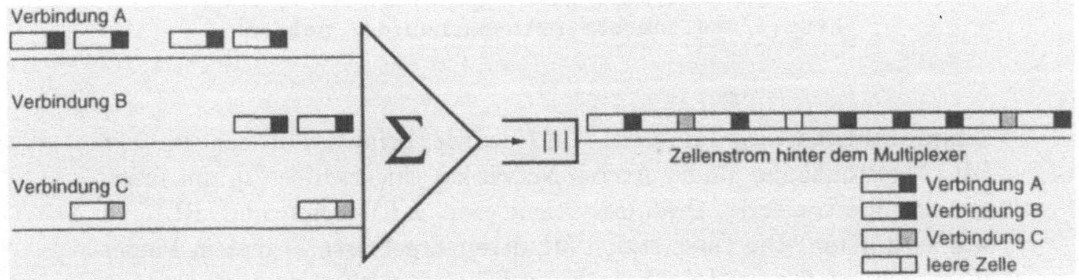

Abbildung 1. Asynchrones Zeitmultiplex von ATM-Zellen in Netzknoten

2 Dienstgüte in ATM-Netzen

ATM-Netze sind diensteintegrierende Netze. Daher ist die Fähigkeit zur Garantie von Dienstgüte zwingend, um Echtzeitdienste unterstützen zu können. Dienstgüte muß beim Verbindungsaufbau vereinbart werden und wird während des Betriebs einer Verbindung überwacht und gesteuert. Dies erfolgt unter anderem durch folgende Maßnahmen:

Verkehrsvertrag wird zwischen Netz und Anwendung ausgehandelt und beschreibt pro ATM-Verbindung vereinbarte Verkehrs- und Dienstgüteparameter, z. B.

- mittlere Datenrate λ
- mittlere/maximale Zellverzögerung $\overline{\tau}_d/\tau_{d\,max}$
- maximale Zellverlusthäufigkeit CLR_{max}

Dienstgütesteuerung in Netzknoten steuert mittels Zellenscheduler das asynchrone Multiplexen von ATM-Zellen unter Verwendung der ATM-Dienste, z. B.:

ATM-Dienst		Echtzeitgarantie	typische Anwendung
Constant Bit Rate	CBR	ja	Sprache
Variable Bit Rate	VBR	ja	Video-Codec, z. B. MPEG
Unspecified Bit Rate	UBR	nein	Daten

Überlastabwehr verwirft zur Entlastung von Netzknoten gezielt ATM-Zellen

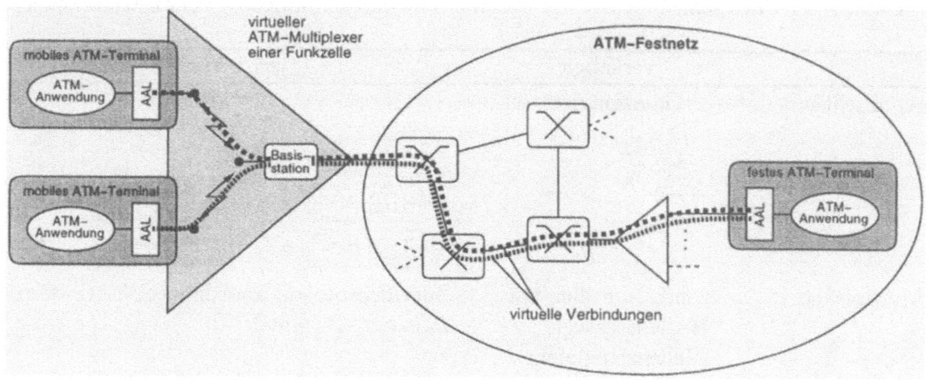

Abbildung 2. Eine Funkzelle entspricht einem verteilten ATM-Multiplexer

3 Architektur und Protokolle einer ATM-Funkschnittstelle

Diese Arbeit fokussiert auf die Architektur und die Protokolle einer ATM-Funkschnittstelle. Sie beschränkt sich dabei auf die isolierte Analyse einer einzelnen Funkzelle und vernachlässigt die Wirkungen zwischen Nachbarzellen wie Gleichkanalinterferenzen, dynamische Kanalvergabe oder Handover.

Aufgrund dieser Vereinfachung läßt sich eine Funkzelle (Abb. 2) mit der zentralen Basisstation (BS), die an ein ATM-Netz angeschlossen ist, und den ATM-Terminals (wireless Terminal, WT) als ein verteilter ATM-Multiplexer interpretieren. In den Terminals segmentiert die ATM-Anpassungsschicht jeglichen Verkehr in ATM-Zellen, so daß auf dem Funkmedium das asynchrone Multiplexen von ATM-Zellen erfolgt.

Für die Entwicklung des Protokollstapels der Funkschnittstelle kann man aus der Implementierung von verkabelten ATM-Multiplexern lernen. Dazu werden in Tab. 1 die Unterschiede zwischen einem verkabelten und einem schnurlosen Multiplexer gegenübergestellt.

Ein verkabelter Multiplexer enthält üblicherweise kurze Eingangspuffer sowie einen zentralen Ausgangspuffer. Das Beschreiben des Ausgangspuffers wird durch den Zellenscheduler entsprechend einer bestimmten Bedienstrategie gesteuert. Im verteilten schnurlosen Multiplexer stellt sich jedoch auf dem Uplink das Problem, daß die Eingangspuffer über die Terminals verteilt sind. Es wird ein Zugriffsprotokoll benötigt (Medium Access Control, MAC), das den Wettbewerb zwischen den Terminals koordiniert. Dieses Protokoll muß die Funktion des Schedulers übernehmen. Desweiteren erfordert die Funkübertragung ein flexibles Fehlersicherungsverfahren, das von der logischen Verbindungssteuerung (Logical Link Control, LLC) ausgeführt wird.

Ein weiterer wesentlicher Unterschied besteht in der üblichen Multiplexrate. Multiplexer des Festnetzes haben mindestens eine Multiplexrate von

Tabelle 1. Unterschiede zwischen verkabeltem und schnurlosem ATM-Multiplexer

	verkabelt	schnurlos
Architektur	konzentriert 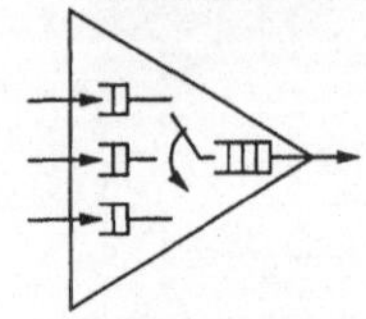	verteilt 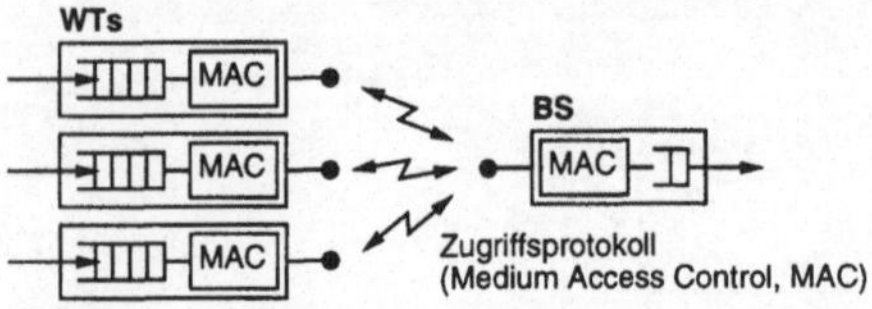
Multiplexen	zentrale Puffer mit Bedienstrategie (Zellenscheduler)	Zugriffsprotokoll koordiniert Wettbewerb zwischen Terminals
Fehlersicherung	undefiniert	Funkübertragung erfordert flexibles Fehlersicherungsverfahren
Multiplexrate	$\gg 155\,\mathrm{Mbit/s}$	typisch $20\,\mathrm{Mbit/s}$
Ursache für Zellverluste	Pufferüberläufe	Verspätungen bei Echtzeitdiensten Pufferüberläufe bei Datendiensten

$155\,\mathrm{Mbit/s}$. Bei dessen hohen Raten liegt die Ursache von Zellverlusten im wesentlichen im Überlauf von Puffern. Demgegenüber wird im Funksystem die Rate durch die Verfügbarkeit von Funkressourcen begrenzt und liegt typischerweise bei $20\,\mathrm{Mbit/s}$. Dadurch entstehen bei Echtzeitdiensten Zellverluste nicht mehr durch Pufferüberläufe, sondern durch Verspätungen, weil Zellen nach Überschreiten ihrer maximalen Verzögerung vom Empfänger verworfen werden.

4 Dienstgütesteuerung an der ATM-Funkschnittstelle

Das Problem der Dienstgütesteuerung an der ATM-Funkschnittstelle läßt sich folgendermaßen formulieren:

Wie muß das Multiplexen von ATM-Zellen gesteuert werden, um

- für jede Echtzeitverbindung (CBR, VBR)
- unter Wahrung der erlaubten Zellverlusthäufigkeit CLR_{max}
- die zulässige maximale Zellverzögerung $\tau_{d\,max}$ zu garantieren?

Es wird dabei angenommen, daß wegen der Fehlersicherung Zellverluste nur bei Zeitüberschreitungen auftreten, wenn also die Verzögerung τ_d einer ATM-Zelle die maximale Verzögerung $\tau_{d\,max}$ überschreitet.

Der Lösungsansatz orientiert sich an den Lösungen für verkabelte Multiplexer [8]. Dabei wird ein Scheduler mit statischen Prioritäten zwischen ATM-Diensten verwendet, wobei CBR-Dienste mit höchster Priorität bedient werden, vor VBR und UBR. Innerhalb einer Prioritätsstufe wird jeweils eine dienstspezifische Bedienstrategie ausgeführt. Die Bedienstrategien für die Echtzeitdienste müssen dabei insbesondere die Wartezeiten steuern.

5   Optimale Bedienstrategie für VBR-Dienste

Im Folgenden wird eine optimale Bedienstrategie für Echtzeitdienste hergeleitet, wobei insbesondere auf VBR-Dienste fokussiert wird.

Zur Herleitung wird ein Wartemodell betrachtet, das die Aspekte der Funkübertragung auf die Multiplexrate reduziert und somit den Einfluß von Zugriffsprotokoll und Übertragungsfehlern vernachlässigt. Das Modell verwendet unbegrenzte Puffer und beschränkt sich auf Markovquellen. Es resultiert der M/D/1-∞ Warteraum in Abb. 3. Dieses Modell hat den Vorteil, daß es analytische Lösungen ermöglicht.

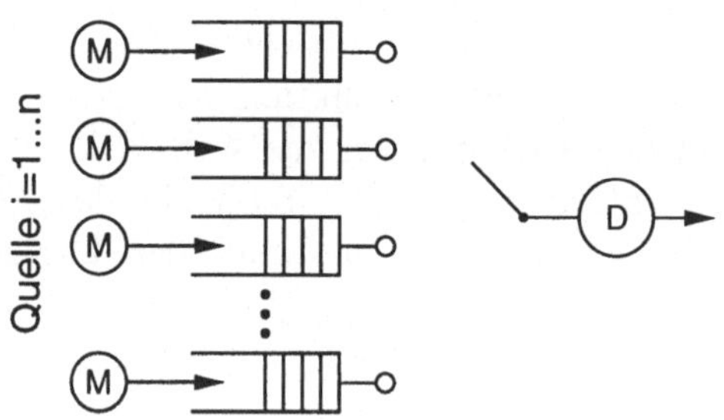

Abbildung 3. M/D/1-∞ Warteraum

Es läßt sich nun das folgende Optimierungsproblem formulieren:

- Minimierung der Summe von Zellverlusten (durch Zeitüberschreitung)
- unter Wahrung der verbindungsspezifischen CLR_{max}

Zur Berechnung der Zellverlusthäufigkeit muß die Verteilungsfunktion der Wartezeiten bekannt sein. Für M/D/1-∞ Warteräume kann die Wartezeitverteilung $P(\leq \tau_d)$ approximiert werden, wenn die ersten beiden Momente der Wartezeit W, $W^{(2)}$ bekannt sind. Dies erfolgt durch eine entartete negative Exponentialverteilung nach (1).

$$P(\leq \tau_d) = 1 - (1-p)e^{-\mu\tau_d} \qquad \text{mit} \quad p = 1 - \frac{2W^2}{W^{(2)}} \quad \text{und} \quad \mu = \frac{2W}{W^{(2)}} \qquad (1)$$

Die Approximation hat sich insbesondere für die hier interessierenden hohen Wartezeiten für hinreichend exakt erwiesen.

Für die Bewertung von Bedienstrategien wird im Folgenden ein beispielhaftes Verkehrsszenario mit drei Verbindungen verwendet. Tabelle 2 enthält die Parametrierung für Ankunftsrate, maximale Verzögerung und maximale Zellverlusthäufigkeit. Dabei erfolgt eine Normierung auf die deterministische Bediendauer.

Das Szenario ermöglicht statistisch gesicherte Ergebnisse innerhalb vertretbarer Simulationsdauern (< 24 h). Alle folgenden Ergebnisse haben einen relativen LRE-Fehler [9] von weniger als 5 %.

444

Tabelle 2. Verkehrsszenario zur Leistungsbewertung

i	λ_i	$\tau_{d\,max,i}/\tau_{slot}$	$CLR_{max,i}$
1	0.2	10	10^{-4}
2	0.45	22	10^{-2}
3	0.2	32	10^{-4}

5.1 Bewertung und Vergleich der Strategien: FCFS, ORU

Es werden die beiden Bedienstrategien First-Come-First-Serve (FCFS) und Optimized-Relative-Urgency (ORU) betrachtet. Die Bewertung erfolgt anhand der komplementären Verteilungsfunktion der Übertragungsverzögerungen $P(> \tau_d)$. Diese ist in den Diagrammen aus Abb. 4 halblogarithmisch aufgetragen. Die Dienstgüteanforderungen der drei Verbindungen sind durch Kreise angedeutet. Die maximale Verzögerung bestimmt den Abszissenwert des Kreises und die maximale Zellverlusthäufigkeit den Ordinatenwert. Die Dienstgüte einer Verbindungen wird eingehalten, wenn die Kurve der Übertragungsverzögerungen unterhalb des Kreises verläuft.

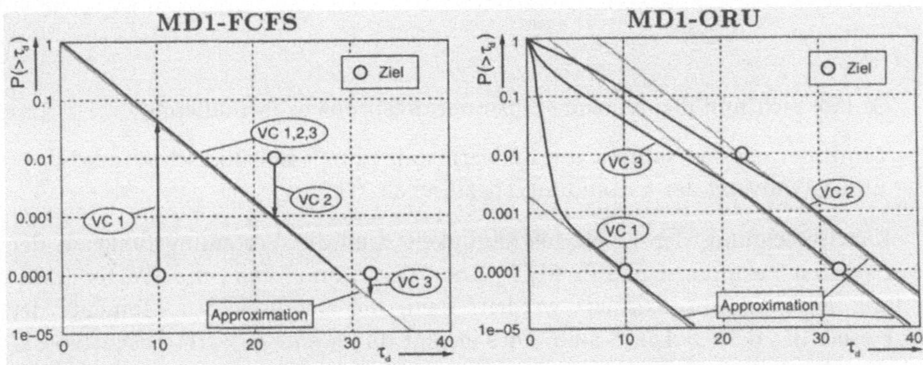

Abbildung 4. Komplementäre Wartezeitverteilung $P(> \tau_d)$ als Ergebnis von Approximation und Simulation des MD1 Modells. Die Kreise zeigen die jeweils geforderte maximale Zellverlusthäufigkeit.

Bei der FCFS Strategie wird jeweils die Zelle mit niedrigstem Ankunftszeitpunkt als nächste übertragen. Das Diagramm aus Abb. 4 links enthält $P(> \tau_d)$ als Ergebnis von Approximation und Simulation des MD1 Modells. Man erkennt, daß die Approximation die tatsächlichen Verzögerungen sehr gut annähert.

Die FCFS Strategie behandelt alle Verbindungen gleich. Dabei werden die Verbindungen 2 und 3 zu gut behandelt, während die Dienstgüte der Verbindung 1 nicht eingehalten wird. Man erkennt, daß die FCFS-Strategie für Echtzeitdienste nicht geeignet ist.

Als günstigste Bedienstrategie hat sich die Relative-Urgency Strategie erwiesen. Dabei wird jeweils die Zelle mit höchster Dringlichkeit als nächste übertragen. Die Dringlichkeit wird durch den Wert U_{RU} ausgedrückt, mit kleineren Werten für höhere Dringlichkeit. Der Wert $U_{RU\,i}$ für die i-te Verbindung berechnet sich nach (2) mit dem verbindungsspezifisches Offset $\Delta\tau_{d\,max,i}$.

$$U_{RU\,i} = t_0 + \tau_{d\,max,i} + \Delta\tau_{d\,max,i} \tag{2}$$

Die Literatur [10] liefert Formeln für die Berechnung der ersten beiden Momente der Wartezeit, so daß die Approximation möglich ist. Man findet, daß die Kurven im Schwanzteil parallel verlaufen und daß das Verhältnis der Offsetwerte $\Delta\tau_{d\,max,i}$ untereinander den Abstand der Kurven bestimmt.

Damit die Dienstgüte aller Verbindungen gleich fair erfüllt wird, müssen die Offsetwerte $\Delta\tau_{d\,max,i}$ so gewählt werden, daß alle Kurven denselben Abstand zu ihren Kreisen haben. Dazu werden die $\Delta\tau_{d\,max,i}$ nach (3) gewählt.

$$\Delta\tau_{d\,max,i} = \frac{1}{\mu}\ln\left(CLR_j\right) \quad \text{mit } \mu \text{ aus Approximation für FCFS} \tag{3}$$

Diese Parametrierung wird als *Optimized Relative Urgency* (ORU) bezeichnet und wurde im rechten Diagramm der Abb. 4 angewendet. Die Simulation stimmt erneut sehr gut mit der Approximation überein, und die Dienstgüte aller Verbindungen wird wie erwartet gleich fair erfüllt.

5.2 Selektives Verwerfen verspäteter ATM-Zellen

Bisher wurden alle verspäteten Zellen dennoch übertragen, obwohl sie wahrscheinlich von der empfangenden Applikation verworfen werden. Es wurde daher untersucht, wie sich das Verwerfen verspäteter Zellen vor der Übertragung auswirkt.

Die Bewertung erfolgt anhand des Verkehrsszenarios aus Tab. 3. Im Diagramm der Abb. 5 sind die Kurven für die Optimized-Relative-Urgency Strategie aufgetragen, und zwar mit und ohne Verwerfen. Die Ergebnisse ohne Verwerfen sind zum Vergleich grau aufgetragen. Durch das Verwerfen treten keine Zellverluste durch Zeitüberschreitung mehr auf. Die Anzahl verworfener Zellen je Verbindung ist durch die Raute dargestellt, wobei der Wert an der Ordinate abzulesen ist. Man erkennt, daß die Anzahl verworfenen Zellen deutlich niedriger ist, als die Anzahl von Verspätungen ohne Verwerfen. Dadurch wird deutlich, daß das Verwerfen verspäteter Zellen Überlastsituationen vermeidet und auflöst.

6 Verteilter Scheduler am Uplink der Funkschnittstelle

Die bisherigen Untersuchungen stellen klare Anforderungen an den Scheduler der Funkschnittstelle. Es stellt sich jetzt das Problem der Realisierung des verteilten Schedulers am Uplink. Das Verfahren, das vom hier entwickelten Protokollstapel angewendet wird, wird in Abb. 6 erläutert.

Tabelle 3. Verkehrsszenario zur Bewertung des Verwerfens verspäteter Zellen

VC	λ	$\tau_{d\,max}$	ORU	CLR gefordert	CLR ohne Verw.	CLR mit Verw.
1	0.15	20	27.3	10^{-2}	$6.5 \cdot 10^{-3}$	$2.0 \cdot 10^{-3}$
2	0.2	25	32.3	10^{-2}	$6.5 \cdot 10^{-3}$	$2.0 \cdot 10^{-3}$
3	0.1	10	2.7	10^{-4}	$9.0 \cdot 10^{-5}$	$< 10^{-6}$
4	0.1	15	7.7	10^{-4}	$8.9 \cdot 10^{-5}$	$< 10^{-6}$
5	0.1	12	4.7	10^{-4}	$9.2 \cdot 10^{-5}$	$< 10^{-6}$
6	0.05	40	32.7	10^{-4}	$9.0 \cdot 10^{-5}$	$< 10^{-6}$
7	0.15	35	35	10^{-3}	$9.2 \cdot 10^{-4}$	$1.9 \cdot 10^{-6}$

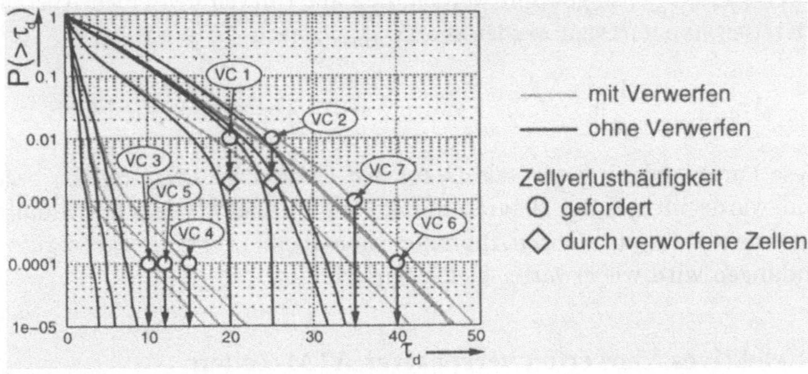

Abbildung 5. Verwerfen verspäteter Zellen vermeidet und löst Überlastsituationen

Auf der linken Seite von Abb. 6 befinden sich die Protokollinstanzen eines Terminals und auf der rechten Seite die der Basisstation. Die Verkehrsquellen im Terminal modellieren die virtuellen Verbindungen der ATM-Schicht. Die ATM-Zellen müssen in der Basisstation an die ATM-Schicht ausgeliefert werden.

Neuankünfte werden im Terminal in den Sendepuffern gespeichert. Der LLC-Scheduler selektiert nicht nur die dringendste Zelle zur Übertragung, sondern liefert zusätzlich eine Aussage über den derzeitigen Kapazitätsbedarf des Terminals. Dieser wird als ca. 3 byte große Kapazitätsanforderung mit Hilfe des *Request-Channel*-Protokolls an die Basisstation signalisiert. Die Basisstation speichert diese Nachricht pro registriertem Terminal. Damit ist der MAC-Scheduler in der Lage, das Terminal mit der dringendsten ATM-Zelle zu bestimmen. Der MAC-Scheduler legt damit die Übertragungsreihenfolge für Terminals fest. Das Zugriffsprotokoll (MAC-Protokoll) realisiert diese Übertragungsreihenfolge auf dem physikalischen Kanal, indem es die Zeitschlitzreservierungen aller Terminals mitteilt. Wenn ein Terminal erfährt, daß es in einem Zeitschlitz senden darf, dann selektiert der LLC-Scheduler die

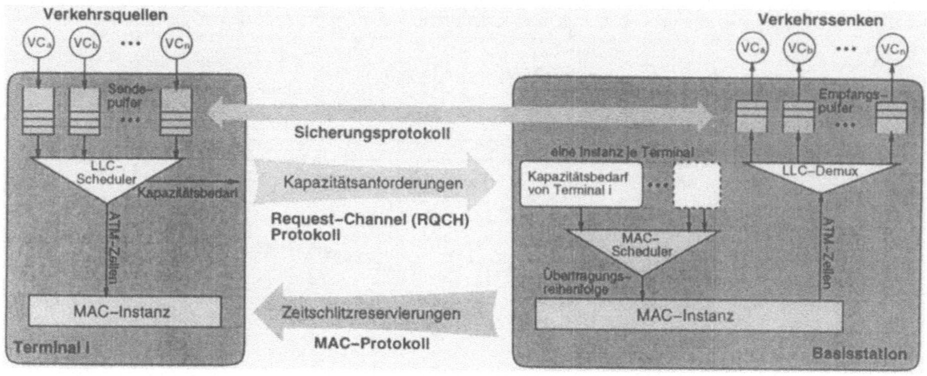

Abbildung 6. Verteilter Scheduler am Uplink der Funkschnittstelle

dringendste ATM-Zelle zur Übertragung. Nach der Übertragung muß die Zelle gegebenenfalls im Empfangspuffer gespeichert werden, um die Neuübertragung einen verlorenen vorherigen Zelle abzuwarten. Derartige Wiederholungsübertragungen werden durch das Sicherungsprotokoll gesteuert, das zwischen Sende- und Empfangspuffer ausgeführt wird.

Zusammenfassend lassen sich also folgende Funktionsgruppen identifizieren:

- *Request-Channel (RQCH) Protokoll* signalisiert Pufferbelegung der Terminals
- *MAC-Scheduler* berechnet Zeitschlitzreservierungen für Terminals
- *MAC-Protokoll* signalisiert Zeitschlitzreservierungen
- *LLC-Scheduler* selektiert ATM-Zelle zur Übertragung
- *Sicherungsprotokoll* steuert Wiederholungsübertragungen

7 *Dynamic Slot Assignment* (DSA++) MAC-Protokoll

Bekannte Zugriffsprotokolle basieren zumeist auf einer TDM-Rahmenstruktur und stellen Terminals synchrone Kanäle zur Verfügung [11]. Diese Protokolle ermöglichen jedoch kein asynchrones Multiplexen auf Ebene von ATM-Zellen. Das läßt sich andererseits mit ALOHA-artigen Zugriffsprotokollen realisieren [1], die jedoch zufälligen Charakter besitzen und nicht die Umsetzung der geforderten Bedienstrategien ermöglichen.

Es ist daher ein neuer Ansatz nötig, der die durch den MAC-Scheduler vorgegebene Übertragungsreihenfolge konsequent umsetzt. Dieses neue Protokoll wird *Dynamic-Slot-Assignment*-Protokoll (DSA++) genannt [7]. In Abbildung 7 wird beispielhaft seine Realisierung auf einem Zeitduplexkanal betrachtet. Es handelt sich um ein periodenorganisiertes Protokoll, wobei jede sogenannte *Signalisierungsperiode* aus einer Downlinkphase und einer Uplinkphase besteht. Die Periodenlänge ist variabel und wird dem Verkehr angepaßt.

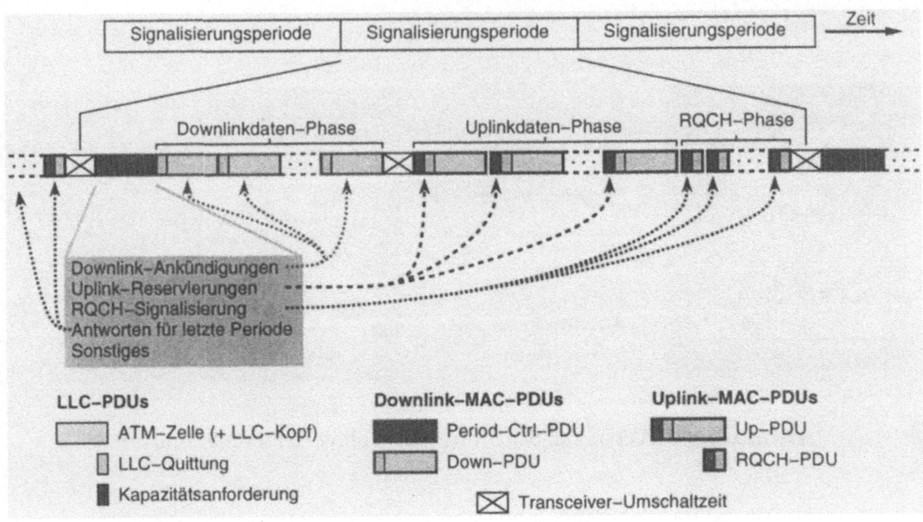

Abbildung 7. Dynamic Slot Assignment (DSA++) MAC-Protokoll

Im unteren Teil von Abb. 7 sind die Protokolldateneinheiten (PDU) zusammengestellt. Die LLC-Protokolle (Sicherungsprotokoll und RQCH-Protokoll) übertragen ATM-Zellen, Quittungen und Kapazitätsanforderungen. Die PDU des MAC-Protokolls auf dem Downlink bestehen aus einer ATM-Zelle und einer Quittung. Zusätzlich gibt es eine spezielle *Period-Control-PDU* zur Signalisierung der Zeitschlitzreservierungen. Auf dem Uplink wird analog je eine ATM-Zelle zusammen mit einer Quittung übertragen. Zusätzlich wird jedoch huckepack noch eine Kapazitätsanforderung übertragen. Terminals mit Neuankünften von ATM-Zellen dürfen desweiteren sogenannte *Request-Channel-PDUs* benutzen, die nur eine Quittung und eine Kapazitätsanforderung enthalten.

Zu Beginn einer Signalisierungsperiode berechnet der MAC-Scheduler die Übertragungsreihenfolge für diese Periode. Die Zeitschlitzreservierungen werden dann am Anfang der Periode mit einer *Period-Control-PDU* an die Terminals signalisiert, und zwar nach Downlink und Uplink sortiert. Am Ende der Periode stehen zusätzliche kurze Zeitschlitze für *Request-Channel-PDUs* zur Verfügung.

Terminals mit Neuankünften können ihre Kapazitätsanforderung nicht huckepack zu einer ATM-Zelle übertragen. Stattdessen müssen sie in den kurzen Zeitschlitzen senden. Der Zugriff erfolgt durch Zufallszugriff. Es ist leicht einsichtig, daß der Algorithmus zur Auflösung von Kollisionen beim Zufallszugriff einen enormen Einfluß auf die Verzögerungen von ATM-Zellen hat. In der Literatur finden man jedoch nur Algorithmen, die auf Stabilität und Effizienz optimiert wurden [1]. Hier ist jedoch ein Verfahren erforderlich, das auf Geschwindigkeit optimiert ist oder sogar eine maximale Verzögerung garantieren kann und dabei gleichzeitig effizient ist. In der Dissertation [4]

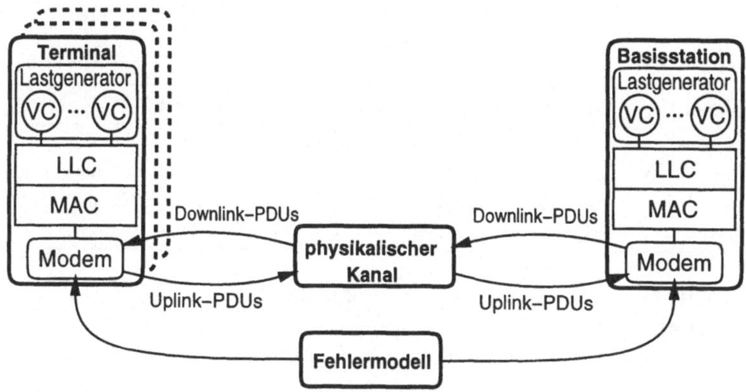

Abbildung 8. Integriertes stochastisches Simulationsmodell zur Systemanalyse und Leistungsbewertung

werden derartiger Kollisionsauflösungsalgorithmen sorgfältig untersucht und ein neuartiger Gruppentestalgorithmus entwickelt und analysiert, der genau diese Anforderungen erfüllt [6].

Neben dem Zufallszugriff hat auch die Übertragung von Quittungen einen sehr großen Einfluß auf die Systemperformance, da bei Echtzeitdiensten Quittungen zumeist nicht huckepack übertragen werden können. Zu detaillierten Untersuchungen wird auf [5] verwiesen.

8 Integriertes stochastisches Simulationsmodell

Die Leistungsbewertung des hier vorgestellten Protokollstapels erfolgt mit einem integrierten stochastischen Simulationsmodell. Es beruht auf einer ereignisgesteuerte Simulation in C++.

In Abbildung 8 sind die Blöcke des Simulators dargestellt. Links befinden sich die Terminals und rechts die Basisstation. Der Simulator enthält eine detaillierte Implementierung der Protokolle. Die Protokolle kommunizieren über ein Modell des physikalischen Kanals, das mit der Granularität von Zeitschlitzen arbeitet. Übertragungsfehler werden durch statistische Fehlermodelle des Funkkanals auf der Ebene von Paketfehlern modelliert. Der zu tragende Verkehr resultiert aus stochastischen Modellen realer Applikationen.

9 Simulationsszenario zur Leistungsbewertung

Die im Folgenden präsentierten Simulationsergebnisse beruhen auf dem Verkehrsszenario in Tab. 4. Das Szenario verwendet mehrere ATM-Verbindungen verschiedener Dienste, nämlich vier Spracheverbindungen, einen ISDN-Primärmultiplexanschluß, zwei MPEG-Videoverbindungen und vier Datenverbindungen.

Tabelle 4. Simulationsszenario zur Leistungsbewertung

#	Dienst	Modell	ATM-Dienst	λ	$\sum$Last	τ_{dmax}	τ_{dmax}/τ_{slot}
4	Sprache	CBR	CBR	64 kbps	3%	2 ms	100
1	ISDN-P.MUX	CBR	VBR	2 Mbps	22%	5 ms	250
2	MPEG-Video	autoreg.	VBR	1 Mbps	22%	30 ms	1500
4	Daten	Poisson	UBR	460 kbps	20%	undef.	undef.

Kanalkapazität: 50.000 ATM-Zellen/s ($\widehat{\approx}$ 20 Mbit/s) $\Rightarrow$ $\tau_{slot} = 20\,\mu$s

Kanalmodelle: 1. fehlerfreie Übertragung
2. unkorrelierte Paketfehler mit $P_e = 2.5 \cdot 10^{-2}$
3. korrelierte Paketfehler mit $P_e = 2.5 \cdot 10^{-2}$ nach Gilbert-Modell

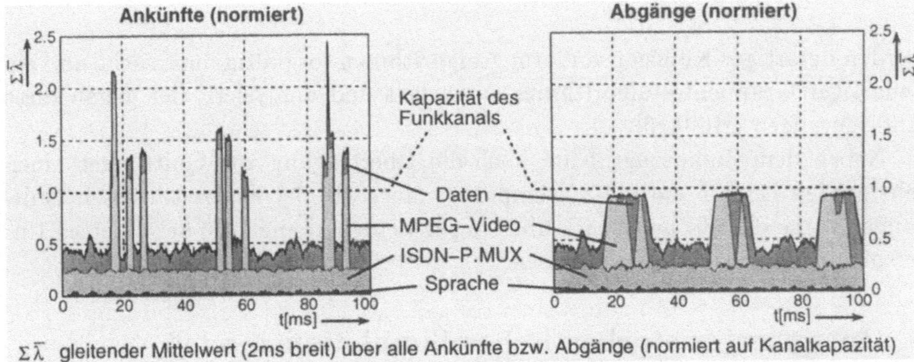

Abbildung 9. Gleitender Mittelwert $\sum \bar{\lambda}$ (2ms breit) über alle Ankünfte bzw. Abgänge (normiert auf Kanalkapazität) im Szenario aus Tab. 4.

Zur Veranschaulichung des Verkehrsverhaltens ist in Abb. 9 der 2 ms breiter gleitender Mittelwert über alle Ankünfte über ein Zeitfenster von 100 ms aufgetragen, und zwar normiert auf die Kanalkapazität. Der Anteil der Dienste am Verkehr ist durch verschiedene Grautöne gekennzeichnet. Als erstes quantitatives Ergebnis der Systemanalyse sind auf die gleiche Weise auch die Abgänge des Systems aufgetragen, die der Bedienung auf dem Kanal entsprechen. Man erkennt an dieser Darstellung, wie die Stapelankünfte der Videoverbindungen durch Puffern verbreitert werden. Desweiteren erkennt man die priorisierte Bedienung, da etwa Daten erst bedient werden, nachdem die Videostapel abgearbeitet worden sind.

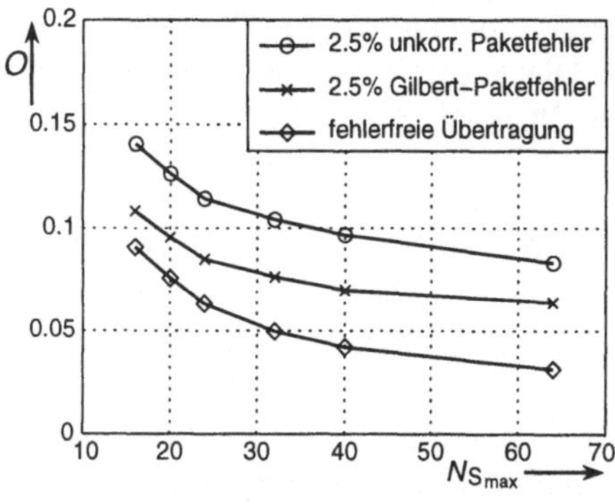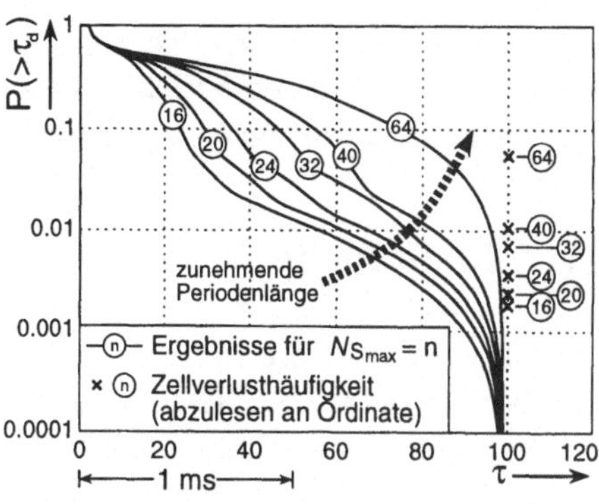

Abbildung 10. Links, Signalisierverkehr O versus Periodenlänge $N_{S\,max}$ und rechts, komplementäre Wartezeitverteilung $P(> \tau_d)$ des Sprachdienstes am Uplink (2.5% unkorr. Paketfehler)

10 Optimierung der Periodenlänge

In diesem Abschnitt wird der Einfluß der maximalen Periodenlänge auf die Systemperformance bewertet. Auf der einen Seite reduzieren lange Perioden den Signalisierverkehr, da je Periode einmal die Downlinksignalisierung erfolgt. Auf der anderen Seite erhöhen kurze Perioden die Dynamik des Protokolls und reduzieren die Verzögerungen von Echtzeitdiensten.

Dies ist in den Diagrammen der Abb. 10 gegenübergestellt. Im linken Diagramm ist der auf die Kanalkapazität normierte MAC/LLC-Signalisierverkehr O gegen die maximale Periodenlänge $N_{S\,max}$ aufgetragen. Der Signalisierverkehr beinhaltet Downlinksignalisierung, Zufallszugriff, Quittierung aber auch Übertragungsfehler, weil so die Auswirkung von Übertragungsfehlern auf die Signalisierung berücksichtigt wird.

Es werden dabei drei verschiedene Kanalmodelle betrachtet, und zwar fehlerfreie Übertragung, 2.5 % unkorrelierte Paketfehler und 2.5 % Büschelfehler, die durch ein Gilbertmodell generiert werden [3].

Man erkennt zum einen, daß der Signalisierverkehr recht niedrig ist, im fehlerfreien Fall unter 10 %. Mit zunehmender Periodenlänge nimmt er wie erwartet ab. Ab 30 Zeitschlitzen Periodenlänge ist der weitere Gewinn nur noch 2 %. Desweiteren erkennt man, daß unkorrelierte Fehler destruktiver auf die Signalisierung wirken als korrelierte Fehler.

Im rechten Diagramm ist für den ungünstigen Fall der unkorrelierten Fehler die komplementäre Wartezeitverteilung $P(> \tau_d)$ der Sprachverbindungen aufgetragen. Die Kurven sind über die maximale Periodenlänge $N_{S\,max}$ parametriert. Man erkennt deutlich die zunehmenden Verzögerungen und Zellverluste bei zunehmender Periodenlänge. Mit langen Perioden läßt sich die Dienstgüte des Sprachdienstes nicht garantieren.

Daher wird im Folgenden eine maximale Periodenlänge von 20 Zeitschlitzen gewählt, was $400\,\mu s$ entspricht. Die bessere Dienstgüte für Echtzeitdienste wird dabei allerdings mit einer 2-3 % niedrigeren Effizienz erkauft.

11 Zusätzliche Verzögerung durch RQCH-Signalisierung

Als nächstes wird die Performance des Zufallszugriffs bewertet. Dazu wird ein simulationstechnischer Trick angewendet, der den Anteil des Zufallszugriffs an den Verzögerungen eliminiert, indem die Basisstation direkt per Funktionsaufruf in die Terminals hineinschaut. Alle neuen Uplink-Kapazitätsanforderungen werden somit unmittelbar vom Scheduler der Basisstation berücksichtigt. Dies wird in Abb. 11 als *perferkter Uplink* bezeichnet. Die Bewertung erfolgt wieder anhand der komplementären Wartezeitverteilung. Die Kurven sind für die beiden Fehlermodelle aufgetragen und dem fehlerfreien Fall gegenübergestellt.

Man erkennt, daß selbst beim Sprachdienst mit sehr kurzen geforderten maximalen Verzögerungen von $2\,ms$ der Zufallszugriff den kleineren Anteil der Verzögerungen hervorruft. Bei den Stapelankünften der Videoquellen verschwindet der Einfluß des Zufallszugriffs fast vollständig.

12 Zusammenfassung

In der Arbeit wurde ein Protokollstapel für die Funkschnittstelle eines drahtlosen ATM-Systems vorgestellt. Die Anforderungen an die Protokolle wurden mit Hilfe verkehrstheoretischer Betrachtungen hergeleitet und die Notwendigkeit für eine Dienstgütesteuerung mit einem verteilten ATM-Zellenscheduler gezeigt. Für Echtzeitdienste wurde der Vorteil von terminorientierter Bedienung und von Verwerfen verspäteter ATM-Zellen nachgewiesen.

Es erfolgte eine Leistungsbewertung mit Hilfe eines integrierten stochastischen Simulationsmodells. Die Simulationsergebnisse lassen sich folgendermaßen zusammenfassen:

- Schnurlose ATM-Übertragung mit Dienstgütegarantie über einen Mobilfunkkanal, wie er hier modelliert wurde, ist realisierbar.
- Dabei ermöglicht der Protokollstapel einen hohen Durchsatz mit weniger als 10 % Signalisierverkehr.
- Die Verzögerungen, die dabei entstehen, entsprechen denen eines verkabelten ATM-Multiplexers mit derselben Multiplexrate, also 50.000 ATM-Zellen/s.

Literatur

[1] D. Bertsekas and R. Gallager. *Data Networks*. Prentice-Hall, Englewood Cliffs, NJ, 1987.

[2] BRAN Project. Broadband Radio Access Networks (BRAN): Terms of References. Technical report, ETSI, 1997.

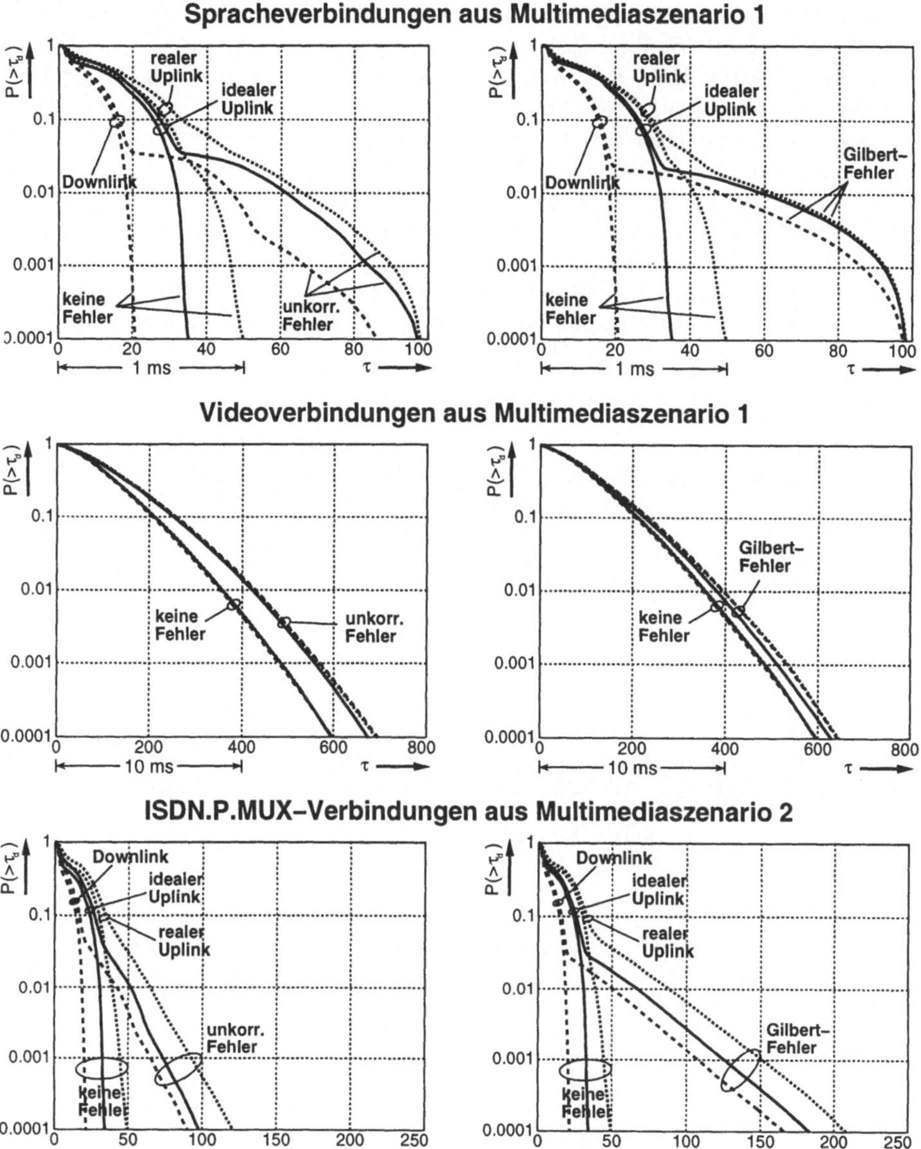

Abbildung 11. Zusätzliche Verzögerung durch RQCH-Signalisierung

[3] E. N. Gilbert. Capacity of a burst-noise channel. *Bell System Techn. Journal*, 39:1253–1266, September 1960.

[4] D. Petras. *Entwicklung und Leistungsbewertung einer ATM-Funkschnittstelle.* Dissertation, Kommunikationsnetze, RWTH Aachen, 1998.

[5] D. Petras and A. Hettich. Performance Evaluation of a Logical Link Control Protocol for an ATM Air Interface. *Int. J. of Wireless Information Networks*, 4(4):225–232, October 1997.

[6] D. Petras and A. Krämling. Fast Collision Resolution in Wireless ATM Networks. In *2nd MATHMOD*, Vienna, Austria, February 1997.

[7] D. Petras and A. Krämling. Wireless ATM: Performance Evaluation of a DSA++ MAC Protocol with Fast Collision Resolution by a Probing Algorithm. *Int. J. of Wireless Information Networks*, 4(4):215–223, October 1997.

[8] E. Rathgeb and E. Wallmeier. *ATM – Infrastructur für die Hochleistungskommunikation*. Springer, Berlin Heidelberg New York, 1997.

[9] F. Schreiber and C. Görg. Stochastic Simulation: A Simplified LRE-Algorithm for Discrete Random Seqeunces. *AEÜ*, 50(4):233–239, 1996.

[10] B. Walke. *Realzeitrechner-Modelle*. Oldenbourg Verlag, 1978.

[11] B. Walke. *Mobilfunknetze und ihre Protokolle*. B.G. Teubner, Stuttgart, 1998.

Konzeption und Bewertung einer TINA-konformen Architektur für das Mobilitätsmanagement von UMTS

Frank Imhoff

Rheinisch-Westfälische Technische Hochschule Aachen
Lehrstuhl für Informatik 4, Kommunikation und Verteilte Systeme
Ahornstraße 55, 52056 Aachen
imhoff@informatik.rwth-aachen.de

Abstract. Diese Arbeit analysiert verschiedene agentenbasierte Ansätze eines Mobilitätsmanagements für künftige Mobilfunknetze wie UMTS. Dazu werden zunächst die Vorschläge des TINA-Konsortiums aufgegriffen, um auf der Basis eines objektbasierten verteilten Systems die Voraussetzungen dafür zu schaffen. Die vorgestellten Ansätze erlauben eine Vielzahl örtlich parallel existierender Dienstanbieter, Dienstvermittler und Netzbetreiber sowie eine hierarchielose Adressierung der Benutzer über die Grenzen von Netzbetreibern und Dienstanbietern hinweg. Besonderes Augenmerk wird bei der analytischen Gegenüberstellung der Ansätze auf die Minimierung der Belastung der Luftschnittstelle und auf die Reduzierung des Signalisierungsverkehrs gelegt. Gleichzeitig werden die Verzögerungszeiten beim Aufbau einer Verbindung und beim Handover berücksichtigt.

1. Einleitung

Mit der Einführung des Universal Mobile Telecommunication System (UMTS) soll die Funktionalität bestehender festnetzgebundener und mobiler Telekommunikationssysteme, Satellitenkommunikationssysteme sowie weltweite Ortungs- und Navigationssysteme integriert und neueste Technologien einbezogen werden. Dazu sind Übertragungskapazitäten von bis zu 2 Mbit/s geplant. Besondere Beachtung finden darüber hinaus die Einführung von *Universal Personal Telecommunication* (UPT) sowie neuartige, individualisierte Telekommunikationsdienste (Tailored Services), da in diesem Sektor mit dem größten Wachstum gerechnet werden muss. Diese Dienste müssen zu diesem Zweck vom Dienstanbieter selbst kurzfristig, hoch flexibel und kostengünstig generiert werden können, ohne dass wesentliche Änderungen oder der Neuaufbau bestehender Netzstrukturen erforderlich werden. Damit kommt man dem Wunsch nach, jeden beliebigen Dienst unabhängig vom verwendeten Netz, Netzbetreiber und Endgerät zur Verfügung stellen zu können.

Dieser Wunsch stellt jedoch erheblich höhere Ansprüche an das Location Management und macht umfangreichere Handover-Prozeduren erforderlich als bei anderen zellularen Netzen wie beispielsweise GSM. Unter anderem wird eine dynamische Aufteilung der Location Areas und eine verteilte Datenbankstruktur diskutiert [TA 97]. Die meisten Ansätze lassen aber außer Acht, dass ein Kunde aufgrund einer weitreichenden Konkurrenz der Anbieter von Diensten in UMTS sehr häufig den Dienstanbieter wechseln oder sogar Verträge mit mehreren Dienstanbietern über den gleichen Dienst abschließen könnte. Aufgrund des ständigen Wechsels zwischen Dienstanbietern und einer zunehmenden Mobilität der Benutzer, ist es sinnvoll, von einem anbieter- oder wohnortbezogenen Nummernschema abzusehen und eine völlig hierarchielose Adressierung zu verwenden. Daraus ergibt sich im Vergleich zu den heutigen GSM-Netzen jedoch wiederum ein erheblicher Mehraufwand für das Mobilitätsmanagement, da u.a. auf ein zentrales *Home Location Register* verzichtet werden muss. Anders als bei GSM-Netzen wird daher die Datenhaltung nicht nur auf die verschiedenen Domänen des UMTS-Netzwerks verteilt, sondern auch innerhalb der Domänen ist eine weitreichende Verteilung vorgesehen. Diese Struktur bietet den Vorteil, dass benutzerspezifische Daten sehr nah an dem jeweiligen Aufenthaltsbereich des Benutzers gespeichert werden können. Jedoch ist im Vergleich zu zentralisierten Varianten der Datenhaltung ggf. mit einem erheblichen Mehraufwand für die Suche und die Erhaltung der Konsistenz der Daten zu rechnen. Deshalb beschäftigen sich eine Reihe von Forschungsarbeiten mit der Datenhaltung im Hinblick auf die Verteilung der Daten und die Optimierung der Suchverfahren. Exemplarisch sei hier auf [Ho 97] und [La 95] verwiesen.

Zur Steuerung von Telekommunikationsmehrwertdiensten ist darüber hinaus die weitgehende Nutzung der aus bestehenden Festnetzen bekannten Technologie der *Intelligenten Netze* (IN) vorgesehen. Jedoch weisen bisherige IN-Konzepte eine Reihe von Nachteilen auf. Insbesondere handelt es sich um nahezu proprietäre Systeme, es ist nur eine sehr geringe Objektorientierung bei der Software vorgesehen und es existiert nur eine unzureichende Trennung zwischen den Dienstanbietern und Netzbetreibern [Ma+ 96]. Gerade letzteres ist aber sehr wünschenswert, um eine Vielzahl konkurrierender Dienstanbieter zu etablieren, ohne dass diese gezwungen sind, in teure Infrastruktur zu investieren.

2. Telecommunication Information Network Architecture

Im TINA-Konsortium haben sich eine Reihe von Hardwareherstellern, Netzbetreibern und Dienstanbietern zusammengeschlossen, um Vorschläge für ein herstellerunabhängiges System zu entwickeln. Neben der Unterstützung einer breiten Palette von Telekommunikationsdiensten aller Art und deren schneller und kostengünstiger Einführung soll gewährleistet werden, dass z.B. Tailored Services kostengünstig erzeugt werden können [Um 97]. Diese Realisierung findet objektorientiert auf der Grundlage offener verteilter Systeme statt. Objekte kapseln Daten sowie Programme, stellen definierte Schnittstellen zur Verfügung und werden unabhängig von ihrer späteren Positionierung im Netz entwickelt. Diese Positionierung erfolgt in einem *Distributed Processing Environment* (DPE-Knoten) unabhängig von zugrundeliegender Hardware. Bei diesen DPE-Knoten kann es sich um leistungsfähige Großrechner, Cluster und auch um tragbare Endgeräte handeln.

Die spezifischen Daten eines Benutzers, wie Profile, Berechtigungen, Abrechnungsdaten usw. werden im Rahmen der TINA-Spezifikationen in einem speziellen Objekt zusammengefasst. Hinzu könnten beispielsweise Bewegungsprofile und besondere Anforderungen des Benutzers kommen. Dementsprechend kommt diesem als "User Agent" bezeichneten Objekt zentrale Bedeutung beim Mobilitätsmanagement zu. Der User Agent repräsentiert einen Benutzer innerhalb einer Domäne. Alle Anfragen an den Benutzer gehen zuerst an den User Agent. Diesem ist die Position des Endgerätes im Netz bekannt, genauer gesagt: Der User Agent kennt die Netzwerkadressen der Schnittstellen der Objekte, die auf dem DPE-Knoten des Endgerätes positioniert sind. Besondere Probleme treten jedoch bei mobilen Endgeräten auf, da hier die besonders übertragungsfehleranfälligen Luftschnittstelle überwunden werden muss. In diesem Zusammenhang sei auf [Ma+ 96] und [Br+ 96] verwiesen, die durch Einführung einer separaten *Mobilitätsschicht* Ansätze zur Lösung dieses Problems bieten.

Auf die Abläufe, die einem Verbindungsaufbau zugrunde liegen, soll hier nicht genauer eingegangen werden, diese sind u.a. in [Im 98] nachzulesen. Es zeigt sich dabei sehr schnell, dass die weitreichende Verwendung des User Agent sinnvoll ist, um den für die Lokalisierung und den Verbindungsaufbau erforderlichen Signalisierungsverkehr über die Luftschnittstelle möglichst gering zu halten, da dieses Objekt den Benutzer mit seinem Endgerät in der Domäne des Retailers repräsentiert. Alle Anfragen an einen Benutzer laufen zunächst beim zugeordneten User Agent ein. Eine Reihe dieser Anfragen kann der User Agent aufgrund der dort gespeicherten Präferenzen und der verfügbaren Dienstmerkmale des Benutzers auch dann beantworten, wenn augenblicklich keine Verbindung zum Endgerät besteht.

In dieser Arbeit wird eine ähnliche Baumstruktur zur Datenhaltung vorgeschlagen wie sie bisher für UMTS vorgesehen ist. Die Knoten des Baums werden jedoch auf jeder Ebene durch DPE-Knoten realisiert, so dass im Unterschied zu UMTS ggf. auf jedem Knoten Softwareobjekte positioniert und Operationen mit diesen Softwareobjekten ausgeführt werden können. Den Blattknoten sind wie bei UMTS eine Anzahl von nebeneinander liegenden Location Areas zugeordnet. Dabei bleibt es dem Netzbetreiber und damit den vorherrschenden Gegebenheiten, z.B. dem Benutzeraufkommen, dem Verkehrsaufkommen, den geographischen Besonderheiten etc., überlassen, wie diese Struktur im Hinblick auf die Anzahl der Ebenen und des Verzweigungsgrads sowie der Anzahl der Location Areas pro Blattknoten realisiert wird.

Es stellt sich nun die Frage, wie die Softwareobjekte so auf den verschiedenen DPE-Knoten positioniert werden können, dass ein möglichst geringer Signalisierungsverkehr sowie kurze Verzögerungen bei Verbindungsaufbau und Handover erreicht werden können. Einzelheiten über die Abläufe dieser Operationen sowie das zugrundeliegende Business-Modell können ebenfalls in [Im 98] nachgelesen werden.

3. Verschiedene Konzepte zur Datenhaltung

Voraussetzung für eine Bewertung der folgenden Vorschläge zur Positionierung stationärer und mobiler Agenten ist die mathematische Modellierung der vorgeschlagenen Baumstruktur eines Retailers sowie ein Modell des Benutzerverhaltens. Dazu wird ein saturierter Baum vom Grad g und der Tiefe d herangezogen. Jedem Blattknoten dieses Baums sind g Location Areas zugeordnet. Insgesamt werden also g^d Location Areas abgedeckt, deren Flächen aufgrund der dazu besonders geeigneten Symmetrieeigenschaften als benachbarte Hexagone gleicher Größe angenommen werden [Ho 97].

Zur Analyse der Leistungsfähigkeit sind im wesentlichen zwei Faktoren von Bedeutung: Zum einen muss die Belastung des Netzes berücksichtigt werden, die durch Bewegungen der Benutzer und die daraus folgenden Location-Update-Operationen sowie durch verbindungsbezogene Operationen verursacht werden. Insbesondere muss auf das Verhältnis zwischen der Anzahl durchzuführender Location Updates und der Anzahl durchzuführender Operationen zum Verbindungsaufbau (*Call-Operationen*) ein besonderes Augenmerk gelegt werden. Zum anderen muss die Entfernung modelliert werden, die zwischen den beteiligten Knoten einer Location-Update-Operation oder einer Call-Operation liegen. Dazu wird zunächst ein Modell entworfen, welches das Bewegungs- und Anrufverhalten der Benutzer in einem Mobilkommunikationsnetz im Hinblick auf die Entfernung zwischen dem alten und dem neuen Aufenthaltsgebiet bzw. zwischen dem Anrufer und dem Angerufenen widerspiegelt.

Es ist davon auszugehen, dass die von einer Location-Update-Operation betroffenen Gebiete ebenso wie die von einem Anruf betroffenen Gebiete nicht allzu weit auseinander liegen, also in der Regel zwischen benachbarten Location Areas stattfinden. Für ein solches lokal konzentriertes Szenario wird angenommen, dass die Wahrscheinlichkeit für notwendige Operationen auf einer Ebene (Levelwahrscheinlichkeit) von den Blattknoten in Richtung des Wurzelknotens exponentiell abnimmt. Für die Richtigkeit dieser Annahme spricht, dass Location Updates in der Regel zwischen benachbarten Location Areas stattfinden und die von einem Knoten abgedeckte Fläche dem Erreichen höherer Knoten exponentiell zunimmt (siehe [Ho 97]).

Mit Hilfe des Parameters α lassen sich nun verschiedene Szenarien in bezug auf das Bewegungs- und Anrufverhalten der Benutzer analysieren. Dabei steht ein zunehmendes α für eine zunehmende lokale Konzentration der durchschnittlichen Bewegungen der Benutzer. Auf Grund der Korrelation zwischen α und der durchschnittlichen Ausdehnung des Bewegungs- und Anrufverhaltens wird im folgenden von der Lokalität eines Szenarios gesprochen und der Parameter α als Lokalitätsparameter bezeichnet. Eine ausführlichere Einführung des Lokalitätsparameters ist in [Kü+ 98] zu finden. Um die Lokalitätsparameter für den Verbindungsaufbau zwischen den Teilnehmern und für die Bewegung der Teilnehmer unterscheiden und beliebige Szenarien berechnen zu können, wird zwischen α_{Call} für den Verbindungsaufbau sowie α_{LU} für die Location Updates unterschieden. Weiterhin steht λ_{LU} für die Anzahl der an das Netz herangetragenen Location Updates und λ_{Call} für die Anzahl der herangetragenen Calls.

Der Ankunftsprozess dieser Location Updates und Calls kann als Poissonprozess mit der Ankunftsrate $\lambda_{Gesamt} = \lambda_{LU} + \lambda_{Call}$ modelliert werden. Die Wahrscheinlichkeit für die Ankunft eines Location Updates kann durch $p_{LU} = \lambda_{LU} / \lambda_{Gesamt}$ und die Wahrscheinlichkeit für die Ankunft eines Calls durch $p_{Call} = \lambda_{Call} / \lambda_{Gesamt}$ bestimmt werden. $\lambda_{LU} / \lambda_{Call}$ wird als Call-to-Mobility-Rate (C/M) bezeichnet. Mit diesem Mobilitätsmodell können nun die Verkehrsgleichungen erster Ordnung, d.h. die Berechnung der Ankunftsraten an einem Knoten des Baums, aufgestellt werden. Diese Berechnung wurde für die verschieden vorgeschlagenen Varianten zur Verwaltung der stationären bzw. der mobilen Agenten durchgeführt, um mit Hilfe des in der Warteschlangentheorie sehr häufig verwendeten BCMP-Theorems [Ba+ 75] die mittleren Ausführungszeiten für Location Updates und Calls zu berechnen.

3.1 Stationäre Datenhaltung

Für die Beurteilung des Verkehrsaufkommens innerhalb des Baums wird zunächst festgelegt, welche Operationen und Weiterleitungen stattfinden müssen. Die folgende Analyse beschränkt sich jedoch auf die bei Location Updates und Call-Operationen stattfindenden Prozesse. Durch andere Operationen verursachter Signalisierungsverkehr kann aufgrund des zu erwartenden Aufkommens gegenüber dem normalen Verbindungsaufbau vernachlässigt werden. Außerdem entsprechend diese Operationen in der Regel entweder dem Ablauf der Call- oder dem der Location-Update-Operation, so dass für eine Einbeziehung lediglich der Parameter für die jeweilige Ankunftsrate variiert werden müsste.

Voraussetzung für die exakte Ermittlung der stationären Zustandswahrscheinlichkeiten der Knoten des Baums ist die Annahme, dass die Bedienzeiten der verschiedenen Benutzerklassen in den Knoten stark differieren. Demnach muss angenommen werden, dass es sich bei der Bedienstrategie in den Knoten des Baums um *Processor Sharing* (PS) handelt, obwohl in der Realität eine *First-Come-First-Served-Strategie* (FCFS) zu erwarten ist. Es hat sich aber gezeigt, dass PS bei der Benutzung des BCMP-Theorems eine hinreichend gute Approximation von FCFS erlaubt [De 95]. PS ermöglicht darüber hinaus eine beliebige Bedienzeitverteilung der Knoten und damit eine unterschiedliche mittlere Bedienzeit für Aufträge verschiedener Klassen.

Die Aufträge an das Netz bestehen aus zwei unabhängigen Poisson-Ankunftsströmen (Location Updates und Calls) und die mittlere Ankunftsrate λ_x, $x \in \{LU, Call\}$, darf zunächst lastabhängig sein. Diese Annahmen führen zu einem Knoten vom Typ M/G/1-PS, während für die Übertragungsstrecken zwischen den einzelnen Knoten ein D/∞-Knoten angenommen wird. D.h. die Verzögerung beim Empfang der Aufträge an den einzelnen Knoten richtet sich im wesentlichen nach einem konstanten, von der mittleren Größe der Aufträge und der Länge der Übertragungsstrecken abhängigen Wert.

Für die verschiedenen Bedienraten wurden Werte angenommen, die mit Hilfe von Simulationen ermittelt wurden. Die simulativ ermittelten Werte wurden entsprechend der zu erwartenden Steigerung der Rechenleistungen innerhalb der nächsten zehn Jahre skaliert wurden. Dieser Zeitraum scheint angemessen, da vorher nicht mit der Einführung eines auf der Basis von Softwareobjekten verwalteten Telekommunikationssystems zu rechnen ist.

Die berechneten Werte für Location-Updates und Call-Operationen einer stationären Datenhaltung mit Softwareobjekten sind in [Kü+ 98] bereits veröffentlicht worden. Es zeigt sich, dass es offenbar nur dann ist sinnvoll ist, wenn die Mobilität und das Anrufverhalten der Teilnehmer eher lokal beschränkt sind. Weiterhin sind hohe Call-to-Mobility-Raten (C/M) bei dieser Art der Datenhaltung nicht möglich, da sowohl die Gesamtantwortzeiten für Location Updates als auch die für den Verbindungsaufbau erforderlichen Zeiten sehr schnell steil ansteigen. Um diesen schon bei relativ geringen C/M auftretenden Instabilitäten infolge überlasteter Knoten entgegenzuwirken und für kürzere Zeiten beim Verbindungsaufbau zu sorgen, muss nach einer anderen Strategie zur Verteilung der Daten gesucht werden. So wurde im folgenden untersucht, ob sich Verbesserungen im Hinblick auf die Antwortzeiten und die Stabilität erzielen lassen, wenn die User Agents zu dem Knoten migrieren, denen das jeweilige Terminal augenblicklich zugeordnet ist.

3.2 Datenhaltung mittels migrierender Agenten auf den Blattknoten

Eine Location-Update-Operation bei migrierenden Agenten ist nicht zuletzt aus Sicherheitsgründen vergleichsweise kompliziert (siehe [KI 98]). Es zeigt sich, dass die Wartezeiten bei zunehmenden Call-Operationen und bei zunehmenden α_{LU} sinken, während sie bei zunehmenden α_{Call} ansteigen. Grund dafür ist, dass bei einer Zunahme der α_{LU} mehr Migrationen stattfinden müssen als bei kleinen α_{LU}, so dass die Blattknoten nicht nur mit zeitaufwendigen Location-Update-Operationen belastet sind, sondern auch einfache Dereferenzierungs- und Rückkehroperationen durchführen müssen. Dabei sinkt bei Berücksichtigung aller Operationen die durchschnittliche Belastung der Knoten und folglich auch die durchschnittliche Wartezeit.

Im Gegensatz dazu führt eine Vergrößerung der Werte für α_{Call} nur zu zusätzlichen Weiterleitungsoperationen an den Blattknoten. Die sehr niedrigen Werte für die Wartezeiten an den Blattknoten dürfen jedoch nicht über die stark ansteigenden Werte für Knoten höherer Ebenen hinweg täuschen. Für höhere Knoten, insbesondere für den Wurzelknoten, steigen die Wartezeiten schon bei sehr hohen C/M und kleinen Werten für α extrem an.

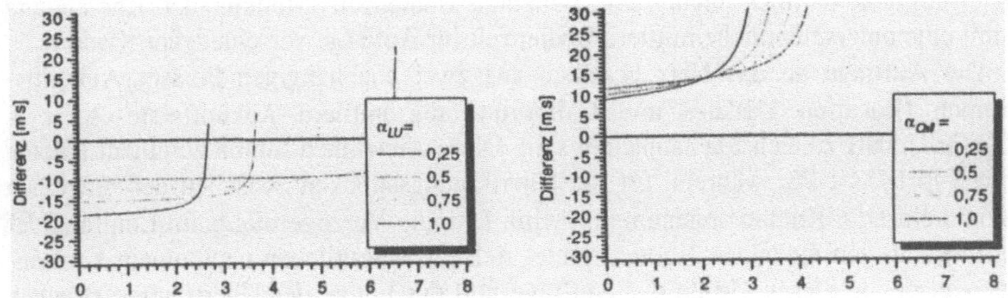

Fig. 1. Differenz zwischen den Gesamtantwortzeiten für Location-Update-Operationen Δt_{LU} (links) und Call-Operationen Δt_{Call} (rechts) der statischen Datenhaltung und der Datenhaltung mittels migrierender Agenten in Abhängigkeit von C/M

Im Vergleich zur statischen Datenhaltung in den Blattknoten, wie sie für UMTS bisher vorgesehen ist, ergibt sich bei der Datenhaltung mittels migrierender Agenten eine deutliche Verbesserung der Antwortzeiten für Call-Operationen. Jedoch sind die Antwortzeiten für Location Updates, bedingt durch die erforderlicher Migrationen der User Agents, auch unter Berücksichtigung der Vermaschung aller Knoten der zweiten Ebene, erheblich schlechter (siehe Fig. 1). Der Vorteil der Datenhaltung mittels zwischen den Blattknoten migrierender Agenten besteht also nicht nur in einer erheblichen Verkürzung der Antwortzeiten für Call-Operationen, sondern vor allem auch in der Verbesserung der Stabilität des Gesamtsystems. Fig. 2 zeigt die Gesamtdifferenz der Antwortzeiten.

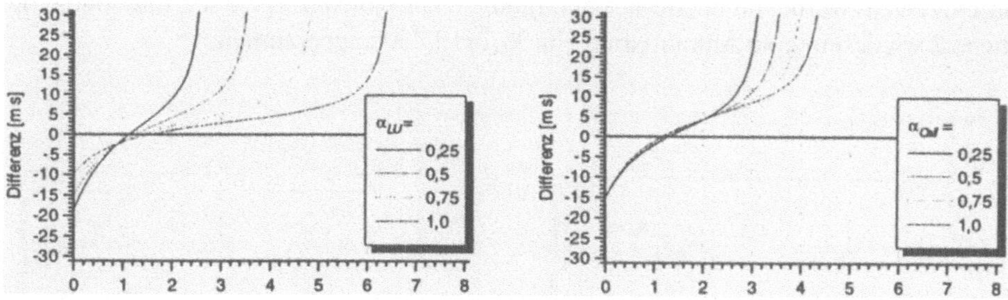

Fig. 2. Gesamtdifferenz der Antwortzeiten bei statischer Datenhaltung und Datenhaltung mittels migrierender Agenten über C/M mit α_{Call}=0.5 und verschiedenen α_{LU} (links) sowie α_{LU}=0.5 und verschiedenen α_{Call} (rechts)

Dabei zeigt sich, dass die Überlegenheit einer Datenhaltung mit zwischen den Blattknoten migrierenden Agenten gegenüber einer statischen Datenhaltung nur bei größeren C/M zum Tragen kommt, nämlich dann, wenn die Einsparungen durch die verkürzten Antwortzeiten bei Call-Operationen die Verschlechterungen bei Location-Update-Operationen aufwiegen. Jedoch wird durch die extrem anwachsenden positiven Zeitdifferenzen deutlich, dass durch das Migrationsverfahren eine erheblich größere Stabilität des Systems gewährleistet ist. Darüber hinaus ist zu erkennen, dass der Einfluss des Lokalitätsparameters α_{LU} auf die Gesamtdifferenz der Antwortzeiten einen größeren Einfluss besitzt als α_{Call}.

Um den gegenüber der statischen Datenhaltung durch verlängerte Antwortzeiten bei Location Updates entstehenden Nachteil möglichst weitgehend zu kompensieren, liegt es nahe, die User Agents nicht nur zwischen den Blattknoten, sondern auf eine höhere Ebene des Baums zu migrieren.

3.3 Datenhaltung mittels migrierender Agenten auf einer höheren Ebene

Bei dieser Variante ist eine Migration aller User Agents auf einer Ebene $k < d$ des Baums vorgesehen. Vorteilhaft ist dabei die mit steigender Höhe der Ebene abnehmende Wahrscheinlichkeit, bei Location Updates eine Migration der User Agents durchführen zu müssen, da von den Knoten höherer Ebenen eine zunehmende Anzahl von Location Areas abgedeckt wird. Nachteilig wirkt sich die zunehmende Belastung der Knoten des Baums durch die mit dem Grad g anwachsende Anzahl der User Agents pro Knoten sowie eine Verlängerung der Wege zwischen den Objekten des Terminals und den im Festnetz angesiedelten Objekten aus.

Es stellt sich heraus, dass die Belastung des Wurzelknotens und der Knoten der Ebene 2 bei kleinen Werten für die Lokalitätsparameter bereits sehr früh zunimmt. Eine zusätzliche Belastung durch die Platzierung der User Agents scheidet daher für diese beiden Ebenen aus. Bei einem Baum der Tiefe $d = 4$ bleiben lediglich die beiden unteren Ebenen zur Platzierung der Objekte übrig, so dass für diese Variante der Datenhaltung ausschließlich Ebene 3 zur Verfügung steht. Insgesamt ergibt sich die in Fig. 3 dargestellte Gesamtdifferenz zwischen den bisher untersuchten Migrationsverfahren. Dazu wurde unter Berücksichtigung einer vollständigen Vermaschung der Ebene 2 wiederum eine Ankunftsrate von $\lambda_{LU}=10.000$ angenommen.

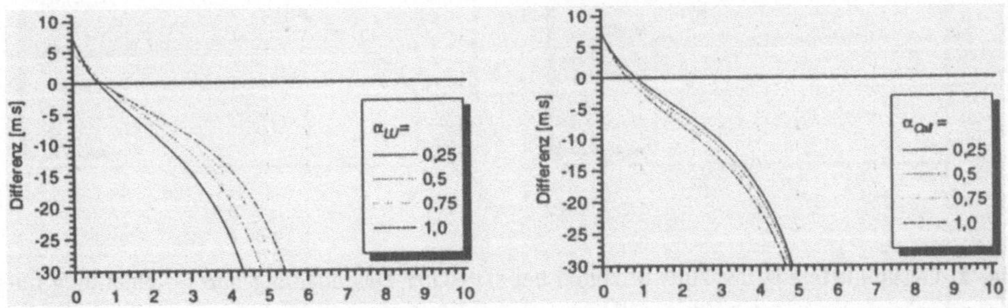

Fig. 3. Gesamtdifferenz der Antwortzeiten auf Grundlage der Datenhaltung ausschließlich auf den Blattknoten und ausschließlich auf Ebene k=3 mit $\alpha_{Call}=0.5$ (links) sowie $\alpha_{LU}=0.5$ (rechts)

Es zeigt sich, dass die Datenhaltung mittels migrierender Agenten auf der Ebene $k = 3$ nur bei C/M < 1 kürzere Gesamtantwortzeiten zu erzielen sind. Die Stabilität des Gesamtsystems ist durch die zu erwartende Überlastung der Knoten der Ebene $k = 3$ bei C/M $\approx$ 5 deutlich früher als beim Migrationsverfahren zwischen den Blattknoten nicht mehr gegeben. Um eine Verbesserung der Stabilität und ggf. gleichzeitig eine Verbesserung der Antwortzeiten zu erzielen, soll daher im folgenden eine Verteilung der User Agents über *mehrere* Ebenen des Baums analysiert werden.

3.4 Datenhaltung auf mehreren Ebenen des Baums

Grundgedanke dieser Verteilung ist das unterschiedliche Mobilitäts- und Anrufverhalten der Benutzer. So könnten die User Agents von sehr mobilen Benutzern mit einer eher geringen C/M zwischen höheren Knoten des Baums migriert werden. Hingegen werden Benutzer, die sich in der Regel sehr wenig bewegen, auf den unteren Ebenen des Baums platziert. Damit kann man sich die Verbesserung der Antwortzeiten von Location Updates auf höheren Knoten zunutze machen, während die Antwortzeiten eines Verbindungsaufbaus bei den Benutzern, deren User Agents auf Knoten niedrigerer Ebenen migrieren, weiterhin möglichst kurz sind. Hinzu kommt, dass durch die Auswahl einer geeigneten Verteilung der User Agents auf die Knoten eine gleichmäßige Auslastung der verschiedenen Ebenen und dadurch eine möglichst große Stabilität des Gesamtsystems erreicht werden kann.

Zunächst soll von einer festen Verteilung der User Agents auf die unterschiedlichen Ebenen ausgegangen werden. Migrationen eines User Agents, der einer Ebene k zugeordnet ist, sind dann nur zwischen den Knoten der Ebene k möglich. Der Netzbetreiber müsste bei der Realisierung eines solchen Konzepts die Einteilung der Benutzer, z.B. nach dem Mobilitätsverhalten der vergangenen Tage, vornehmen oder aber – je nach den Präferenzen des Benutzers bzgl. der Verzögerungen beim Verbindungsaufbau – eine feste Einteilung von vornherein vorsehen.

Die Modellierung einer solchen Variante der Datenhaltung unterscheidet sich vom vorangegangenen Konzept nur durch die notwendige Überlagerung der Auslastungen und Besuchshäufigkeiten für die einzelnen Benutzerklassen. Gegenüber der Datenhaltung ausschließlich auf den Blattknoten ergeben sich bei der Datenhaltung auf mehrere Ebenen des Baums durch die abnehmende Anzahl der erforderlichen Migrationen erhebliche Unterschiede bei den Antwortzeiten für Location Updates. Fig. 4 zeigt die Differenz Δt_{LU} der Antwortzeiten von Location Updates gegenüber der Datenhaltung auf den Blattknoten in Abhängigkeit von der anteilsmäßigen Verteilung der User Agents auf die verschiedenen Ebenen und der Call-to-Mobility-Rate. Dazu wird der Anteil der User Agents auf Ebene 2 auf 5% festgelegt. Die Anteile der Ebenen 3 und 4 werden jeweils variiert.

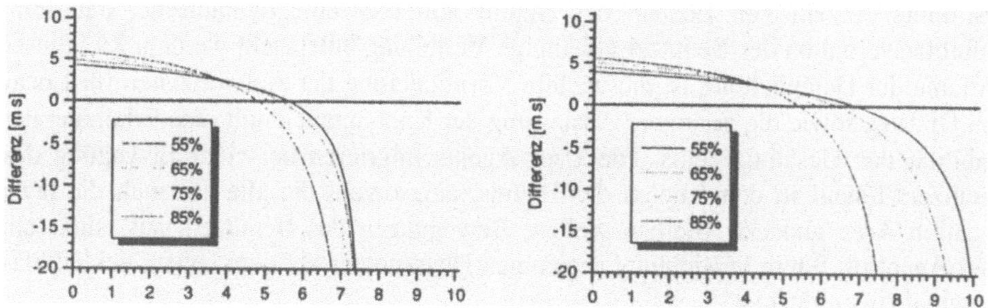

Fig. 4. Differenz der Antwortzeiten von Location Updates in Abhängigkeit von der Verteilung (angegeben ist der Anteil der dritten Ebene) der User Agents auf den verschiedenen Ebenen mit $\alpha_{LU}=\alpha_{Call}=0{,}5$ (links) sowie $\alpha_{LU}=\alpha_{Call}=0{,}75$ (rechts)

Es ist deutlich zu sehen, dass bei der Positionierung der User Agents auf mehreren Ebenen schon bei kleinen C/M eine Überlastung des Gesamtsystems früher herbeigeführt wird, als es bei der Speicherung auf nur einer Ebene. Jedoch sind die Antwortzeiten für Location-Update-Operation bei kleineren C/M deutlich besser, je größer der Anteil der User Agents auf Ebene 3 ist.

Hingegen verursachen die aufgrund der z.T. höheren Positionierung der User-Agents verlängerten Wege für Call-Operationen eine deutliche Verschlechterung der Antwortzeiten. Damit ergibt sich insgesamt ebenfalls kaum eine Verbesserung gegenüber der Datenhaltung auf den Blattknoten. Ausschließlich bei sehr kleinen C/M sind bei den durchschnittlichen Gesamtantwortzeiten Δt_{Gesamt} bessere Werte zu erzielen. Zur genaueren Betrachtung der Ergebnisse muss neben der Call-to-Mobility-Rate auch der Fall berücksichtigt werden, dass weit mehr Location-Update-Operationen als Operationen zum Verbindungsaufbau durchgeführt werden müssen.

Bei allen bisherigen Betrachtungen der Datenhaltung auf mehreren Ebenen wurde von denselben Lokalitätsparametern und Ankunftsraten für alle Klassen von Benutzern ausgegangen. Damit bleibt eine u.U. sinnvolle Verteilung von Agenten besonders mobiler Benutzer auf die höheren Ebenen sowie eine bevorzugte Positionierung auf den unteren Ebenen für Benutzer, die sehr häufig Call-Operationen ausführen, unberücksichtigt. Diese Möglichkeit ist hier jedoch nicht ohne weiteres zu analysieren, da das verwendete Modell keine Angaben über das Verhalten einzelne Benutzer oder Gruppen von Benutzern macht. Es besteht lediglich die Möglichkeit, eine Variation der Werte für die einzelnen Ebenen vorzunehmen, um festzustellen, ob sich dadurch eine Verbesserung der Antwortzeiten ergibt. Trotzdem bleibt bei dieser Art der

Datenhaltung das Problem, dass eine feste Verteilung der User Agents existiert. Insofern berücksichtigt diese Datenhaltung keine aktuellen Bewegungsmuster. Daher wird abschließend untersucht, ob mit Hilfe einer dynamischen Verteilung der User Agents in Abhängigkeit von der Bewegung der Benutzer insgesamt kürzere Antwortzeiten erreicht werden können.

3.5 Datenhaltung durch dynamische Migration auf allen Ebenen des Baums

Im Gegensatz zu der zuvor analysierten Verteilung der User Agents auf eine bestimmte Anzahl von Ebenen des Baums soll hier eine dynamische, d.h. vom Mobilitätsverhalten der Benutzer abhängige Verteilung untersucht werden. Ziel dieser Variante der Datenhaltung ist die weitere Verminderung der Antwortzeiten für Location Updates sowie die geringere Auslastung der Knoten und damit eine Erhöhung der Stabilität des Gesamtsystems. Die User Agents migrieren bei einer Bewegung des Benutzers hinauf in den Knoten des Baums, der sowohl die alte als auch die neue Location Area abdeckt. Bleiben weitere Bewegungen des Benutzers aus, sinkt ein User Agent im Baum in Richtung desjenigen Blattknotens ab, dem augenblicklich das Terminal zugeordnet ist.

Nach welcher Wartezeit dieses Absinken stattfindet, hängt von der erreichten Ebene, von der augenblicklichen Auslastung des betroffenen Knotens und von den Vorgaben des Netzbetreibers oder Benutzers ab. Insbesondere Knoten höherer Ebenen erreichen aufgrund der Baumstruktur deutlich früher sehr hohe Auslastungen, so dass hier von einer kurzen Wartezeit ausgegangen werden muss. Da Operationen, die der Initialisierung einer Migration dienen oder die nach dem Beenden der Migration eines User Agents ausgeführt werden, deutlich höhere Auslastungen hervorrufen als etwa Migrationen oder Dereferenzierungen, muss ggf. für höhere Knoten ganz auf die Möglichkeit einer Positionierung von User Agents verzichtet werden. In diesem Fall sinkt ein aufgestiegener User Agent gleich wieder bis zur höchsten Ebene, der User Agents aufnehmen kann, ab. Höher im Baum angesiedelte Knoten bleiben dadurch ohne zusätzliche Belastung durch beginnende oder abgeschlossene Migrationen.

Das Absinken der User Agents von einer einmal erreichten höheren Position erfolgt nach Möglichkeit in Zeiträumen mit geringer Auslastung der Knoten. Dadurch können kumulative Belastungen der Knoten durch sinkende Migrationen vermieden werden. Steigt die Auslastung bestimmter Knoten dennoch über ein gewisses Maß an, muss es von dort vermehrt zum Absinken von User Agents kommen. Es ist daher geboten, wie bei der vorangegangen Variante zunächst den maximalen Anteil der User Agents auf einer Ebene zu ermitteln, um einen allzu frühen Verlust der Stabilität des Gesamtsystems zu verhindern. Abschließend zeigt sich an der in Fig. 5 dargestellten Gesamtdifferenz Δt_{Gesamt}, dass lediglich bei einer C/M $\leq$ 0,5 ein Vorteil gegenüber der Datenhaltung auf den Blattknoten zu erzielen ist. Jedoch wird dieser Vorteil auf Kosten einer stark verminderten Stabilität des Systems erzielt, die sich aus einer frühzeitigeren Überlastung der Ebene 3 ergibt.

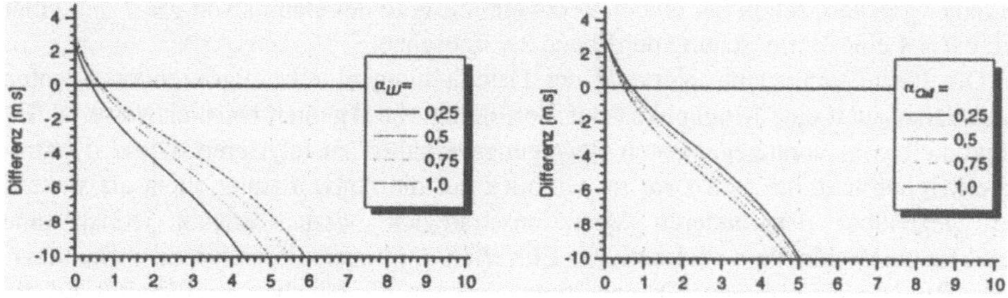

Fig. 5. Differenz der Gesamtantwortzeiten Δt_{Gesamt} für alle Operationen mit α_{Call}=0,5 (links) und α_{LU}=0,5 (rechts) sowie einem Anteil von 65% der User Agents auf Ebene 3

Zusammenfassung und Ausblick

Bei der Gegenüberstellung der Ergebnisse der fünf in dieser Arbeit analysierten Konzepte zur Datenhaltung mittels sogenannter *Agenten* stellte sich eine deutliche Überlegenheit der Verfahren heraus, die eine Migration der Agenten in Abhängigkeit von der Bewegung der Benutzer vorsehen. Stationäre Agenten führen zwar in der Regel zu kürzeren Antwortzeiten bei Location Updates, jedoch werden diese durch eine erheblich Zunahme der Antwortzeiten für Call-Operationen ausgeglichen. Dieses dem augenblicklich für UMTS vorgesehenen statischen Ansatz zur Datenhaltung sehr ähnliche Konzept führt darüber hinaus aufgrund durchschnittlich deutlich längerer Verbindungswege zu einer frühzeitigeren Überlastung der Knoten des Netzes.

Beim Vergleich der übrigen vier Konzepte zur Datenhaltung durch migrierende Agenten stellte sich eine Migration zwischen den Blattknoten des baumförmig aufgebauten Netzes zunächst als die vorteilhafteste Methode heraus. Zwar sind hierbei die Antwortzeiten für Location Updates länger als bei allen anderen Ansätzen, jedoch sind die Verbindungswege für Call-Operationen minimal, so dass die entsprechenden Antwortzeiten sehr kurz ausfallen. Die Stabilität des Gesamtsystems ist ebenfalls den anderen Verfahren gegenüber am höchsten, da die im Baum höher liegenden Knoten am wenigsten durch aufwendige Operationen belastet werden. Alle anderen Migrationsverfahren gehen hingegen von einer Migration zwischen den Knoten höherer Ebenen aus. Folge dieser Variante ist zwar eine Verkürzung der Antwortzeiten für Location Updates, jedoch ergeben sich neben der herabgesetzten Stabilität des Gesamtsystems längere Antwortzeiten für Call-Operationen. In Abhängigkeit vom Verhältnis der Call-Operationen gegenüber den Location-Update-Operationen, also bei einer Zunahme der Call-to-Mobility-Rate, führt dieses zu einer Verschlechterung der gesamten Leistungsfähigkeit.

Um eine frühzeitige Überlastung des Gesamtsystems zu verhindern, muss eine weitreichende Entlastung der höheren Knoten erreicht werden. Insbesondere der Wurzelknoten des baumförmigen Netzwerkes wird bei einer zunehmenden Mobilität der Teilnehmer so stark in Anspruch genommen, dass dieser zuerst überlastet wird. Es ist daher geboten, schon bei einem Verzweigungsgrad des Baums von $g = 7$ und einer Tiefe $d = 4$ eine Vermaschung der Ebene 2 vorzusehen.

Die fünfte untersuchte Variante der Datenhaltung mittels migrierender Agenten stellt daher auch eine Möglichkeit zur Verfügung, die Agenten beispielsweise in Abhängigkeit vom vorangegangenen Bewegungsverhalten zu migrieren. Diese dynamische Migration stellte sich zwar im Hinblick auf die Antwortzeiten nicht als vorteilhaft gegenüber den anderen Migrationsstrategien heraus, erlaubt jedoch eine flexiblere, individuellere und evtl. im Einzelfall – je nach Diensttyp oder Benutzerverhalten - besser geeignete Datenhaltung. So kann der Netzbetreiber Einfuß auf die Verteilung der Daten durch Anpassung des Migrationsverhaltens nehmen, beispielsweise um bestimmte Knoten weniger zu belasten. Dadurch können diese Knoten weniger leistungsfähig ausgebaut und Investitionen eingespart werden. Wie ein solcher spezifischer Sink-Algorithmus aussehen muss und welche Vorteile sich aus der Verwendung im einzelnen ergeben, bleibt weiterreichenden Forschungen vorbehalten.

Literatur

[Ba+ 75] F. Basket, K. M. Chandy, R. R. Muntz, F. G. Palacoise: *Open, Closed and Mixed Networks of Queues with Different Classes of Customers*. Journal of the ACM, Vol. 22, No. 2, pp. 248-260, April 1975

[Br+ 96] W. v. d. Broek, H. Korte, W. Levelt: *The impact of Terminal Mobility on TINA*, Proceedings of TINA '96 Conference, VDE-Verlag, 1996, pp. 75-89

[De 95] P. Depuis: *An European View on the Transition Path Towards Advanced Mobile Systems*; IEEE Personal Communications, Februar 1995, pp. 60-63

[Ho 97] S. Hoff: *Mobilitätsmanagement in offenen Systemen – Leistungsbewertung von Verzeichnisdiensten*. Dissertation, RWTH Aachen, 1997

[Im 98] F. Imhoff: *Konzeption und Bewertung einer TINA-konformen Architektur für das Mobilitätsmanagement von UMTS*, Diplomarbeit RWTH-Aachen 1998

[KI 98] A. Küpper, F. Imhoff: *TINA-Compliant Service Provision and Numbering in UMTS*. Proceedings of 6th International Conference on Telecommunications, Edinburgh, März/April 1998.

[Kü+ 98] A. Küpper, F. Imhoff, S. Hoff: *Evaluation of Agent Concepts for 3rd Generation Mobile Networks*. Proceedings of 3rd Workshop on Personal Wireless Communications (PWC '98), Tokyo, April 1998.

[La 95] D. R. Lawniczak: *Modellierung und Bewertung der Datenverwaltungskonzepte in UMTS*, Aachener Beiträge zur Mobil- und Telekommunikation, Bd. 2, Augustinus Buchhandlung 1995

[Ma+ 96] Th. Magedanz, R. Popescu-Zeletin: *Intelligent Networks: Basic Technology, Standards and Evolution*. International Thomson Computer Press, London, 1996

[Ta 97] S. Tabbane: *Location Management Methods for Third-Generation Mobile Systems*. In: IEEE Communications Magazine, August 97, pp. 72-84

[Um 97] UMTS-Task Force: *UMTS Task Force Report*, 1997

Spezifikations- und Meßmethodik für ein adaptives Dienstgütemanagement[1]

Jan-Peter Richter

sd&m AG, Lübecker Straße 1, 22087 Hamburg
`Jan-Peter.Richter@sdm.de`

Abstract. Die Beherrschbarkeit einer so komplexen Aufgabe, wie die Verwendung adaptiver Fehlertoleranzverfahren zum Zwecke der Dienstgüteregelung, ist nur möglich, wenn die grundlegenden Konzepte eindeutig definiert und die verwendeten Methoden wohlverstanden sind. Der Artikel beschreibt die Inhalte der Dissertationsschrift [1], in der dieses Problemfeld wie folgt behandelt wird: Um die in der Literatur beschriebenen Konzepte zu präzisieren und weiterzuentwickeln, wird ein Rahmenwerk allgemeingültiger Dienstgütebegriffe vorgestellt, das unabhängig vom spezifischen Problemfeld der paketorientierten Datenübertragungsdienste ist und es daher erlaubt, Managementprobleme auf allen Ebenen einer komplexen Anwendung in einer einheitlichen, abstrakten Sichtweise zu betrachten. Das Rahmenwerk erlaubt die formale Definition von Fehlertypen sowie die formale Spezifikation der Dienstgüteeigenschaften von Diensterbringer-/Dienstbenutzersystemen. Vor dem Hintergrund des formalen Rahmenwerkes werden eine Reihe grundsätzlicher Fragen der Dienstgüteunterstützung durch ein adaptives Management näher beleuchtet. Die Ergebnisse dieser theoretischen Vorarbeiten werden benutzt, um Fragen der Meßmethodik für ein adaptives Dienstgütemanagement zu klären. Um die dargestellten Zusammenhänge zu illustrieren, wird das Flexible Continuous Media Transfer System (FCMTS) vorgestellt, dessen umfassende prototypische Realisierung erstmals eine weitgehende Parametrisierung der Dienstgüteordnung erlaubt sowie ein neuartiges Verfahren zur Auswahl und Veränderung der Protokollmechanismen zur Laufzeit enthält. Die Dienstgüteeigenschaften des FCMT-Diensterbringers werden formal spezifiziert, und es wird in einer Reihe von Meßversuchen die Leistungsfähigkeit der Meßinfrastruktur sowie die Wirkungsweise eines adaptiven Dienstgütemanagements mittels Auswahl und Parametrisierung von Mikroprotokollmaschinen dokumentiert.

1   Einleitung

Mit den besonderen Anforderungen, die die Übertragung von kontinuierlichen Mediendatenströmen stellen, ist die Aufgabe der Dienstgüteunterstützung in digitalen Kommunikationsnetzen in das Zentrum vieler Forschungsaktivitäten getreten.

In den meisten Szenarien multimedialer Anwendungen stellt eine vollständige Datenintegrität sowie die vollständige Einhaltung der Zeiteigenschaften der Medienda-

---

[1] Die Arbeit wurde in der Arbeitsgruppe Telekommunikation und Rechnernetze des Fachbereichs Informatik der Universität Hamburg durchgeführt.

teneinheiten zwar eine wünschenswerte Eigenschaft jedoch keine absolute Bedingung für die Nutzbarkeit des Transportdienstes für die Anwendung dar. Dieser Umstand ist dadurch zu begründen, daß die audiovisuelle Kommunikation an der Mensch/Maschine-Schnittstelle eine so hohe natürliche Redundanz besitzt, daß Abweichungen zwischen versendeten und empfangenen Mediendaten in beschränktem Maß toleriert werden können. Im Gegensatz zur verteilten Datenverarbeitung in der Vergangenheit öffnet sich so ein breites Spektrum zwischen dem optimalen und dem inakzeptablen Systemverhalten. Da mit einem immer besseren Systemverhalten in der Regel auch ein gesteigerter Aufwand und damit höhere Kosten verbunden sind, ist es auch im Interesse des Dienstbenutzers, wenn es zulässig ist, daß das System in gewissen Grenzen suboptimal arbeitet.

Für eine geregelte Interaktion zwischen Diensterbringern und Dienstbenutzern ist es bezüglich dieses Möglichkeitsspektrums notwendig, Konzepte der Dienstgüte bzw. der Dienstgüteunterstützung einzuführen. Die zu bewältigenden Probleme können durch folgende Fragestellungen charakterisiert werden:

- Nach welchen Kriterien kann die Güte eines Übertragungsdienstes bewertet werden?
- Wie können die Anforderungen im Rahmen einer Dienstgüteverhandlung im Zuge des Verbindungsaufbaus charakterisiert werden?
- Was kann der Diensterbringer bezüglich seines Verhaltens zusichern?
- Welche Mechanismen und Strategien können eingesetzt werden, um die Einhaltung der Dienstgüteanforderungen ausreichend sicherzustellen und wie können Anwendung und Transportdiensterbringer reagieren, falls die Dienstgüteanforderungen nicht erfüllt werden (können)?

1.1 Prinzipien der Dienstgüteunterstützung

Die in der umfangreichen Literatur dokumentierte Diskussion zum Thema Dienstgüteunterstützung ist bezüglich der letzten Frage am weitesten vorangeschritten.

Im Falle der Leitungsvermittlung, wie sie in den klassischen analogen und digitalen Telefonienetzen verwendet wird, ist es typischerweise nur möglich, den Bedarf an Übertragungskapazität pessimistisch abzuschätzen und eine entsprechende durchgeschaltete Verbindung exklusiv zu reservieren. Das Verfahren der Leitungsvermittlung ist daher für dienstintegrierende digitale Netze unökonomisch und soll deshalb hier nicht weiter betrachtet werden.

Für Paket- oder zellvermittelte Netze wird in der Literatur für verschiedene Ebenen ein breites Spektrum von Mechanismen zur Einhaltung der Dienstgüteanforderungen diskutiert [2, 3]: Zugangskontrolle (call admission control, CAC), Ressourcenreservierung, dienstgütebasierte Wegeermittlung (QoS routing), Verkehrsglättung (traffic shaping), Staukontrolle (congestion control), Lastüberwachung (policing), dienstgütebasierte Ablaufplanung (scheduling) im Netz und in den Endsystemen, dienstgüteabhängige Wahl der Protokollmechanismen, Dienstgüteüberwachung (QoS monitoring), Dienstgütedegradation, Medienskalierung (media scaling), Dienstgüteneuverhandlung sowie weitere spezielle Mechanismen. Diesen Mechanismen ist gemein, daß sie von einem Dienstgütemanagement eingesetzt werden können, um das Verhalten des Übertragungssystems, wie es von einem isoliert betrachteten Dienstbenutzer wahrgenommen wird, positiv zu beeinflussen. Diese Beeinflussung hat zum Ziel, negative Einflüsse anderer Dienstbenutzer, die das System im gleichen Zeitraum zusätzlich und unvorhersehbar belasten, zu mildern bzw. zu maskieren.

Im Rahmen der damit verbundenen Managementaufgabe darf jedoch nicht übersehen werden, daß kein Mechanismus mit absoluter Zuverlässigkeit arbeiten kann. So können aus verschiedenen Gründen Situationen eintreten, in denen die vom Dienstbenutzer individuell beobachtbare Systemleistung nicht mehr als ausreichend bewertet werden kann:

- Methoden der Ressourcenreservierung in paket- bzw. zellvermittelten Netzen basieren auf Modellen sowohl des zu übertragenden Datenstroms als auch des Übertragungssystems bzw. seiner Komponenten: Verhält sich der reale Verkehr oder das reale Transportsystem abweichend von der Modellvorstellung, können sich die reservierten Ressourcen als nicht ausreichend erweisen.
- Der zu übertragende Datenstrom läßt sich im allgemeinen a priori nicht vollständig beschreiben. Zwar kann während der Übertragung der Datenstrom beschränkt werden, eine solche Beschränkung stellt aber im allgemeinen einen schwerwiegenden Eingriff in den Ablauf der Anwendung dar. Eine solche Lastbegrenzung dient daher typischerweise als letztes Mittel, mit der eine negative Beeinflussung einer anderen Übertragung verhindert werden kann.
- Hardwareausfälle von Netzkomponenten bewirken einen völligen Zusammenbruch der Leistung für alle Kommunikationsbeziehungen, die die ausgefallene Komponente benutzen.

Vor dem Hintergrund dieser Fehlermöglichkeiten muß die oben erwähnte dritte Frage nach den möglichen Zusicherungen des Übertragungssystems gegenüber seinem Dienstbenutzer gesehen werden: So wird für manche Netzentwürfe wie ATM oder TENET [4] angenommen, daß die Wahrscheinlichkeit für die oben aufgeführten Fehlermöglichkeiten bei sorgfältigem Systemdesign vernachlässigt werden kann. In diesen Systemen wird im Zuge des Verbindungsaufbaus ermittelt, welche Ressourcen zur Befriedigung der Ansprüche ausreichend sind. Sind diese verfügbar, so werden sie reserviert und die Übertragung läuft ohne weitere Überwachung ab.

Diese Strategie der Dienstgüteunterstützung kann daher als *Strategie der ermittelbar-ausreichenden Ressourcenreservierung* bezeichnet werden. Das Verfahren verlangt neben der Möglichkeit, alle notwendigen Ressourcen reservieren zu können, offensichtlich eine verifizierte Modellierung von Verkehr und Übertragungssystem, um mit hinreichender Zuverlässigkeit die Reservierungs- und Zugangskontrollentscheidung treffen zu können. Stehen keine ausreichend genauen Modelle zur Verfügung, so muß eine pessimistische Abschätzung durchgeführt werden, die wiederum zu pessimistischen, d.h. überdimensionierten Reservierungen führt. Das verbleibende Risiko, daß aufgrund der oben aufgeführten Fehlermöglichkeiten trotz einer solchen verifizierten Garantie, die Leistung nicht ausreichend ist, wird vollständig auf den Dienstbenutzer abgewälzt.

Auch setzt die genannte Strategie voraus, daß der Dienstbenutzer den erzeugten Verkehr an die modellbedingten Lastbeschreibungsmöglichkeiten des Systems anpaßt, um seinen Teil der gegenseitigen Verpflichtung einzuhalten. Ob diese Strategie daher bei einem breiten Anforderungsspektrum in einem dienstintegrierenden Netz sinnvoll anwendbar ist, erscheint zumindest zweifelhaft.

Eine alternative Strategie zur Realisierung einer Dienstgüteunterstützung ist das *Prinzip des adaptiven Dienstgütemanagements* [5-11]. Bei dieser Herangehensweise werden während der Übertragung die erzielte Dienstgüte sowie weitere Leistungsgrößen der Netzkomponenten und/oder Charakteristika des Verkehrs überwacht. In Abhängigkeit der sich so darstellenden Gesamtsituation wird dann dynamisch regelnd in das Übertragungssystem eingegriffen. Für diese Eingriffe stehen die oben aufgeführten sowie weitere, systemspezifische Mechanismen zur Verfügung. Mit ihrer Hilfe wird adaptiv nicht nur die Zuordnung sondern auch die Art und Weise der Verwendung der vorhandenen Ressourcen geregelt. Das Prinzip kann daher auch als *adaptive Ressourcenverwendung* bezeichnet werden.

Die Zusicherung des Übertragungssystems gegenüber dem Dienstbenutzer besteht nun darin, alles zu unternehmen, damit die Übertragungsleistung die Anforderungen des Dienstbenutzers erfüllt. Die Verpflichtung umfaßt weiterhin, im Falle des Mißlingens eine entsprechende Fehlermeldung abzugeben. In vielen Vorschlägen findet sich auch die Verpflichtung, im Mißlingensfall eine Übertragungsleistung zu zeigen, die – wenn auch inakzeptabel – dennoch eine Restverwertbarkeit für den Dienstbenutzer besitzt (vgl. [9]). Dieses Prinzip kann dabei auf verschiedenen architektonischen Schichten einer verteilten multimedialen Anwendung angewendet werden. So kann z.B. die Videokodierung durch Senkung der Bildwiederholfrequenz an die veränderte Übertragungsgüte des Transportdienstes angepaßt werden.

Durch die andersartige Garantiesemantik erlaubt die Strategie des adaptiven Dienstgütemanagements auch eine Dienstgüteunterstützung in Kommunikationsnetzen, bei denen nicht alle Ressourcen für einen Dienstbenutzer reserviert werden können. Die Reservierung wird vielmehr als eine mögliche Form der Ressourcenverwendung verstanden (vgl. [12]).

1.2 Die Meßaufgabe

Es ist offensichtlich, daß die Aufgabe der Messung in einem Übertragungssystem mit adaptivem Dienstgütemanagement eine besondere Bedeutung besitzt. So folgt aus der ergebnisoffenen Garantiesemantik unmittelbar die Verpflichtung, die Dienstgüte zu überwachen. Ein anderer Teil der Managementaufgabe ist die Entscheidungsfindung, ob zur Aufrechterhaltung einer ausreichenden Leistung einzugreifen ist und welche Maßnahme ergriffen werden muß. Diese Entscheidung kann nur unter Verwendung von Basisinformationen zum augenblicklichen Netzzustand erfolgen, die wiederum durch Messungen zur Verfügung gestellt werden müssen. Für diese Meßaufgabe können einige etablierte Methoden der Leistungsmessung in Rechen- und Kommunikationssystemen eingesetzt werden, wie sie seit langem bekannt sind. Es muß jedoch anhand der besonderen Umstände und Zielsetzung der Meßaufgabe eine Auswahl der Meßmethoden getroffen werden.

Für die Strukturierung eines Dienstgütemanagementsystems ist ein Spektrum von Möglichkeiten denkbar, deren zwei Extreme wie folgt charakterisiert werden können: Ein umfassendes Management interagiert direkt mit dem menschlichen Benutzer bzw. den Teilen der Anwendungssoftware, die die Ansprüche des menschlichen Benutzers auszudrücken vermögen. Es sammelt im Zuge seiner Tätigkeit Informationen für seine Managemententscheidungen aus allen Komponenten der verteilten multimedialen Anwendung und bedient direkt alle Mechanismen des Gesamtsystems – von der Parametrisierung der Videokompression bis hinunter zur Wahl der Puffergrößen in den Vermittlungsknoten.

Das andere Extrem ist eine vollständig dezentralisierte Struktur: Hier verfügt jede elementare Komponente der verteilten multimedialen Anwendung über ihr eigenes Management, das die Mechanismen nach außen hin kapselt. Die Managementaufgabe wird dadurch erfüllt, daß ein Teil der Anwendungssoftware mit einer Menge von übergeordneten Managementkomponenten kommuniziert, die wiederum ihre Teilaufgaben durch Interaktion mit bzw. Delegation an untergeordnete Managementkomponenten erfüllen, etc.

Beide Extreme sind sicherlich unrealistisch, da solche Strukturen zu statisch und/oder zu komplex für eine Umsetzung sind. Vielmehr wird ein Dienstgütemanagementsystem in funktionale Komponenten untergliedert werden müssen, die jeweils bei den zu verwaltenden Komponenten und Ressourcen angeordnet sind. Jeweils eine kleine Gruppe dieser Managementkomponenten oder eine einzelne Komponente decken eine geschlossene Managementdomäne als ihr Einflußgebiet ab. Da ggf. manche Komponenten bzw. Ressourcen des Netzes nicht für ein Management zugreifbar sind, können einzelne Bereiche des Netzes auch keiner Domäne zugeordnet werden. Für die Abgrenzung der Domänen kommt einerseits eine vertikale Schichtung des Gesamtsystems in Frage, aber auch eine horizontale Unterteilung z.B. nach funktionalen, geographischen oder administrativen Gesichtspunkten.

Die Kommunikationsstruktur zwischen den funktionalen Komponenten innerhalb einer Domäne ist geprägt durch die jeweilige domänenspezifische Managementaufgabe. Für eine modulare Komponierbarkeit des Gesamtsystems muß sich die Kommunikation zwischen den Managementdomänen jedoch an einem Rahmenwerk von allgemeingültigen Dienstgütekonzepten orientieren, damit der Entwurfsprozeß für ein solches verteiltes Dienstgütemanagementsystem beherrschbar bleibt.

2 Umfeld und Ziele der Arbeit

Die Dissertation ist Teil einer größeren Forschungsanstrengung, bei der der Einsatz von modellgestützten, adaptiven Fehlertoleranzverfahren zum Zweck der Dienstgüteunterstützung erforscht wurde (vgl. [10, 11, 13-18]). Unter adaptiven Fehlertoleranzverfahren soll hier jede Art der Ausnutzung von Redundanz verstanden werden, die in ihrer Wirkungsweise zur Laufzeit ausgewählt und/oder parametrisiert wird.

Ein Beispiel aus dem Bereich der Datenübertragung ist die dynamische Wahl von Protokollmechanismen wie Rückwärts- und Vorwärtsfehlerkontrolle mittels Wiederversendung bzw. redundanter Codierung. Um Auswahl und Parametrisierung adaptiv treffen zu können, ist es notwendig, den Systemzustand zu erfassen und anhand einer Entscheidungsfindungsvorschrift auszuwerten. Im Rahmen der genannten Forschungsanstrengung werden dabei modellgestützte Methoden verwendet, d.h. die Auswahl und Parametrisierung werden durch Auswertung von Modellen zur Laufzeit in ihrer Wirkung optimiert.

Das Ziel dieser Arbeit ist es, zu untersuchen, wie Basiskonzepte der Dienstgüteunterstützung so weiterentwickelt bzw. präzisiert werden können, damit ein solcher Ansatz in allen Bereichen eines Dienstgütemanagementsystems eingesetzt werden kann, das nach den oben dargestellten Grundsätzen strukturiert ist.

Aus mehreren Gründen soll dabei spezielles Gewicht gelegt werden auf die Frage der Dienstgütespezifikation. So definiert die Dienstgütespezifikation aus Sicht eines Diensterbringers das operative Ziel des eigenen Dienstgütemanagements. Aus Sicht des Dienstbenutzers definiert sie die Ansprüche an das Verhalten unterliegender Diensterbringer, deren Dienst ausgenutzt wird, um die eigene Leistung zu erbringen. Die Möglichkeit des gezielten Einsatzes von Fehlertoleranzmaßnahmen als Methode des Dienstgütemanagements ist aber wiederum an Eigenschaften eben dieses Verhaltens der unterliegenden Diensterbringer geknüpft. Zur adäquaten Beschreibung solcher Eigenschaften müssen nun Begriffe wie *Fehlersemantik* [19, 20] aus dem Bereich der Fehlertoleranz mit Begriffen wie *Degradationspfad* [9] aus dem Bereich der Dienstgüteunterstützung miteinander in Beziehung gesetzt werden.

Um die Aufgabe der Dienstgütespezifikation zu lösen, wird ein Rahmenwerk von allgemeingültigen Dienstgütekonzepten vorgeschlagen, mit denen sich ausdrücken läßt, wie Dienstgüte an den Schnittstellen zwischen Managementdomänen bewertet und in einer Verhandlungskommunikation im Rahmen des Verbindungsaufbaus charakterisiert werden kann. Da das Management und damit die Managementdomänen nicht auf die eigentliche Übertragung paketierter Dateneinheiten beschränkt werden kann, sondern vielmehr auch die anwendungsnahen Komponenten des Gesamtsystems sowie Speicher- und Verarbeitungskomponenten umfassen soll, bezieht sich das Rahmenwerk nicht ausschließlich auf die Konzepte spezieller Übertragungsdienste. Vielmehr ist das Rahmenwerk so ausgelegt, daß eben keine speziellen Dienststrukturen vorausgesetzt werden. Dies eröffnet zugleich die Möglichkeit, die gewonnenen Erkenntnisse und Verfahren auf Managementsysteme außerhalb des Umfeldes von Datenübertragungsdiensten anzuwenden.

Betrachtet man die Ergebnisse der Diskussion in der Literatur zu den beiden ersten oben genannten Fragen nach Bewertungskriterien und Anforderungscharakterisierung, so stellt man fest, daß die bisher verfolgten Dienstgütekonzepte stark auf die paketvermittelte Datenübertragung orientiert und selten eindeutig und widerspruchsfrei formuliert sind. Das vorgeschlagene Rahmenwerk erlaubt es erstmals, die genannten Fragen unabhängig von speziellen Dienststrukturen unter Verwendung formaler Hilfsmittel der Mengen- und Relationentheorie zu beantworten. Das Rahmenwerk orientiert sich dabei an den bereits etablierten Begriffen, die es vereinheitlicht und exakt definiert, so daß die Ergebnisse der bisher geleisteten Arbeit erhalten bleiben. Es wird der Begriff der *Dienstgüteordnung* eingeführt, der als das zentrale Konzept des Rahmenwerks identifiziert wird. Es wird dargelegt, daß für die Ausnutzung adaptiver Fehlertoleranzmaßnahmen zur Bewältigung der Dienstgütemanagementaufgabe nicht nur die Verhandelbarkeit der Dienstgüteschranke, sondern auch die Verhandelbarkeit der Dienstgüteordnung von einem dienstgüteunterstützenden System ermöglicht werden sollte.

Aus der mathematischen Darstellung der Konzepte des Rahmenwerks ergibt sich unmittelbar eine Möglichkeit, Bewertungskriterien und Anforderungen formal zu spezifizieren. Dieses Vorgehen wird anhand eines umfangreichen Beispiels am Ende der Arbeit illustriert.

Neben der Notwendigkeit eines Rahmenwerkes exakt definierter Dienstgütekonzepte wurde im Vorfeld der Arbeit die Klärung der Frage nach Dienstgüte- und Leistungsmessung als Voraussetzung für den Einsatz adaptiver Fehlertoleranzmaßnahmen identifiziert. Auch in diesem Punkt zeigt die Diskussion in der Literatur eine bemerkenswerte Divergenz der vorgeschlagenen Meßkonzepte, -aufgaben und -me-thoden. Zwar wird die Notwendigkeit von Messungen zum Zweck des Dienstgütemanagements von vielen Autoren erkannt, es wird hingegen nur in wenigen Veröffentlichungen detailliert darauf eingegangen, welche Meßgrößen zu erfassen sind und welche Meßmethoden dafür eingesetzt werden können. Auch lassen die wenigen Veröffentlichungen, in denen solche Angaben gemacht werden, eine exakte Zielanalyse, aus der sich die Meßaufgabe ableiten ließe, vermissen.

Ausgehend von den Überlegungen zur ergebnisoffenen Garantiesemantik und den Dienstgütekonzepten des Rahmenwerkes wird daher die Meßaufgabe für ein adaptives Dienstgütemanagement analysiert. Es wird dargestellt, daß sich diese Meßaufgabe in zwei Bereiche aufspalten läßt, deren unterschiedliche Zielsetzungen sowie unterschiedliche Meßgrößendomänen auch die Anforderungen an Meßmethoden und -genauigkeit unterschiedlich bestimmen.

Für die erste der beiden Teilaufgaben, den Test auf Erfüllung der Dienstgütevereinbarung, wird dargestellt, wie aus einer Dienstgütespezifikation, die nach den zuvor eingeführten formalen Methoden des Rahmenwerks aufgestellt wurde, die spezielle Meßaufgabe eines betrachteten Systems direkt abgeleitet werden kann.

Für die zweite Teilaufgabe, die Informationsbeschaffung für das adaptive Management, läßt sich diese Frage nicht ohne Kenntnis der jeweils verwendeten, speziellen Entscheidungsfindungsvorschrift der Managementmethode beantworten. Statt dessen wird die grundsätzliche Problematik dieser Teilaufgabe soweit diskutiert, daß nach einer Festlegung der spezifischen Managementmethode die Meßaufgabe der Informationsbeschaffung strukturiert gelöst werden kann.

Um die praktische Umsetzbarkeit der vorgestellten Methoden zu demonstrieren, wird das Flexible Continuous Media Transfer System, FCMTS dokumentiert. FCMTS ist ein Transportsystem, das als Herzstück verteilter multimedialer Anwendungen in Netzen mit adaptivem Dienstgütemanagement eingesetzt werden kann. Es baut auf einem Vermittlungsdienst mit best-effort Semantik auf und verfügt über die Möglichkeit, durch adaptive Auswahl und Parametrisierung von Protokollmechanismen des Transportprotokolls zur Laufzeit, an wechselnde Randbedingungen wie Laständerungen oder schwankende Leistung des Vermittlungsdiensterbringers angepaßt zu werden. Dazu wird das Konzept der *Mikroprotokollmaschinen* als Strukturierungsprinzip flexibler Protokollarchitekturen eingeführt.

Die Dienstgüteeigenschaften, die durch FCMTS angeboten werden, sind nach den eingangs beschriebenen Methoden der Dienstgütespezifikation exakt spezifiziert. FCMTS erlaubt es erstmals, nicht nur die einzuhaltende Dienstgüteschranke, sondern auch die unterstützte Dienstgüteordnung nach den Wünschen des Dienstbenutzers zu variieren. Das dokumentierte System verfügt über eine Meßinfrastruktur, die es erlaubt, Leistungsgrößen des unterliegenden Vermittlungssystems zu erfassen, das sich aufgrund seiner best-effort Semantik einem regelnden Management entzieht. FCMTS bietet somit die Infrastruktur, um sowohl ein adaptives Dienstgütemanagement innerhalb einer Transportschichtmanagementdomäne aufzubauen, als auch ein solches adaptives Dienstgütemanagement in der Managementdomäne des Dienstbenutzers optimal zu unterstützen.

Die Untersuchung geeigneter modellgestützter Entscheidungsfindungsmethoden im Rahmen eines adaptiven Dienstgütemanagements ist nicht Thema dieser Arbeit. Diese komplementäre Aufgabe bleibt den weiteren Arbeiten des umfassenden Forschungsvorhabens vorbehalten. Auch die im FCMTS in Form von Mikroprotokollmaschinen implementierten Methoden der Vorwärts- und Rückwärtsfehlerkorrektur stellen nur Beispiele für den Einsatz adaptiver Fehlertoleranzmaßnahmen dar. Weitere Fehlertoleranzverfahren in anderen Managementdomänen des Gesamtnetzes werden dadurch nicht ausgeschlossen. Die Arbeit bietet die Methoden und eine prototypische Implementation, um darauf aufbauend weitere Untersuchungen durchzuführen.

3 Resultate der Arbeit

3.1 Dienstgütekonzepte in konventionellen Dienstgütearchitekturen

Zu Beginn der Arbeit [1] wird das Problemfeld der Dienstgüteunterstützung, wie es in der Literatur diskutiert wird, anhand der speziellen Anforderungen bei der Übertragung kontinuierlicher Mediendatenströme dargestellt. Dazu werden verschiedene Ansätze zur Bewertung der Dienstgüte sowie mögliche Garantiesemantiken und eine Klassifikation vorgeschlagener Umsetzungsmechanismen dargelegt. Es wird gezeigt, daß viele der vorgeschlagenen Abstraktionen Defizite in ihrer Klarheit aufweisen, was ihre Eignung für den Aufbau von adaptiven dienstgüteunterstützenden Transportsystemen stark einschränkt. Speziell die Frage der Festlegung geeigneter Dienstgüteparameter sowie eine übergeordnete Zusammenfassung der vorgeschlagenen Begriffe zur gezielten Auswahl einer Dienstgüteunterstützungsstrategie müssen noch als offene Probleme angesehen werden.

3.2 Vereinheitlichung von Dienstgütekonzepten mit Hilfe eines formalen Ansatzes

Es wird ein formales Rahmenwerk von Begriffen der Dienstgüteunterstützung eingeführt. Die Begriffe werden so gewählt, daß sie weitestgehend mit den bereits in der Literatur etablierten übereinstimmen, sich aber durch eine allgemeingültigere Definition auch auf andere Problemfelder anwenden lassen.

Neben einer natürlichsprachlichen Beschreibung der Begriffe werden mathematisch-formale Definitionen in der Notation der Cantor'schen Mengenalgebra gegeben. Diese formalen Definitionen erlauben es, Dienstgüteeigenschaften von Diensterbringer-/Dienstbenutzersystemen durch die Angabe entsprechender Mengen und Relationen formal exakt zu spezifizieren. Dies eröffnet gleichzeitig die Möglichkeit, mit Hilfe konventioneller mathematischer Methoden, Aussagen über komplexere Eigenschaften eines so spezifizierten Systems formal herzuleiten.

Um die Aufgabe der Formulierung einer Spezifikation von Dienstgüteeigenschaften zu erleichtern, werden drei Methoden präsentiert, die die Komplexität dieser Aufgabe reduzieren: *parametrische Spezifikation, schrittweise Spezifikation* und *hierarchische Spezifikation.*

3.3 Dienstgüteunterstützung durch ein adaptives Management

Es wird dargestellt, wie der flexible Einsatz von Fehlertoleranzmaßnahmen als Basismechanismus für ein adaptives Dienstgütemanagement dienen kann. Es wird an verschiedenen Beispielen erläutert, wie die Verhandelbarkeit der angebotenen Dienstgütevereinbarung in direkter Beziehung zur bedarfsgerechten Nutzung der Ressourcen sowie der optimalen Wahl der Redundanzmaßnahmen und des Redundanzgrades steht.

Weiterhin wird die ergebnisoffene Garantiesemantik diskutiert, die besser als die Semantik der verifizierten Garantie geeignet ist, ein effizientes Diensterbringersystem mit adaptivem Dienstgütemanagement zu implementieren, da sie – anders als die verifizierte Garantiesemantik – unabhängig von den Ursachen einer eventuellen Dienstgütedegradation ist.

Die besonderen Probleme und Möglichkeiten beim Übergang zwischen den Schichten einer geschichteten Diensterbringerarchitektur werden dargestellt und dabei darauf hingewiesen, daß das in der Literatur viel diskutierte Problem der Dienstgüteabbildung tatsächlich eine zweistufige Lösung verlangt. Anhand des Anwendungsfeldes der Transportdienste in paketorientierten Datennetzen wird erläutert, wie die Flexibilisierung von Protokollmechanismen eingesetzt werden kann, um Eingriffsmöglichkeiten für ein adaptives Dienstgütemanagement im Sinne der zuvor geführten Diskussion zu bieten. Abschließend wird auf die Notwendigkeit einer fortlaufenden Dienstgüteüberwachung mittels Messung hingewiesen.

3.4 Meßkonzepte für ein adaptives Dienstgütemanagement

Es wird untersucht, wie Meßverfahren für Kommunikationsnetze für verschiedene Zwecke in der Vergangenheit eingesetzt wurden. Neben den klassischen Aufgaben des Netzwerkmanagements und der Leistungsevaluation werden auch Ansätze dargestellt und kritisch hinterfragt, die im Kontext der Dienstgüteunterstützung publiziert worden sind.

Daran anschließend wird mit Hilfe einer Zielanalyse die Meßaufgabe präzisiert. So wird herausgestellt, warum Messungen in diesem Kontext durchzuführen sind, und welche Meßgrößen – zumindest potentiell – zu erfassen sind. Ausgehend von diesen Ergebnissen wird in einem weiteren Schritt diskutiert, welche Meßmethoden prinzipiell für die Erfüllung dieser Aufgaben geeignet sind und wie sich die Gesamtaufgabe der Messung in Teilschritte untergliedern läßt. Die Untergliederung stellt gleichzeitig ein architektonisches Gerüst für die Implementierung einer Meßkomponente dar, wie sie im weiteren Verlauf der Arbeit anhand eines konkreten Beispiels illustriert wird.

3.5 Beispielanwendung: Das FCMT-System

Eine detaillierte Anforderungsanalyse für ein Transportsystem für kontinuierliche Mediendatenströme wird durchgeführt. Dabei wird auch auf die speziellen Anforderungen an den Rechtzeitigkeitsbegriff bei der Übertragung MPEG-kodierter Videodatenströme eingegangen. Die Analyse beinhaltet die Diskussion der anzubietenden Dienstgütevereinbarungen entsprechend des zuvor eingeführten formalen Rahmenwerks.

Es wird eine Systemarchitektur vorgestellt, die geeignet ist, die Anforderungen effizient umzusetzen. Die vorgestellte Architektur ist gleichzeitig in der Lage, ein adaptives Dienstgütemanagement sowohl durch die Bereitstellung von Dienstgütemeßwerten als auch durch Eingriffsmöglichkeiten zur Laufzeit zu unterstützen. Die Parametrisierung und/oder der Austausch von Mikroprotokollmaschinen als zentraler Mechanismus der Rekonfiguration wird eingeführt und seine Möglichkeiten diskutiert.

3.6 Dienstgütemessung im FCMT-System

Es wird dokumentiert, wie die zuvor identifizierten Meßaufgaben im Beispielsystem FCMTS durch eine geeignete Meßinfrastruktur bewältigt werden. Dabei werden die Meßverfahren ausgehend von der Spezifikation der möglichen Dienstgütevereinbarungen entwickelt sowie ihre Implementation im Rahmen des Beispielsystems beschrieben.

Eine Reihe von Meßexperimenten werden dokumentiert, die die Leistungsfähigkeit und Validität der Meßinfrastruktur belegen. In einem abschließenden Experiment wird die Wirkungsweise eines adaptiven Dienstgütemanagements, das auf der Auswahl und Parametrisierung von Transportprotokollmechanismen basiert, illustriert.

In Anhängen zur Dissertationsschrift [1] wird zum einen die Spezifikation der Dienstgüteeigenschaften für den FCMT-Diensterbringer nach den Konzepten des Rahmenwerkes dokumentiert.

Zum anderen werden zwei grundlegende Methoden des software monitoring bezüglich ihrer Eignung für die Meßaufgabe des Tests auf Erfüllung der Dienstgütevereinbarung miteinander verglichen.

4   Ausblick

Die Arbeit bietet die Grundlage für vielfältige weitere Forschungsaktivitäten im Bereich des Dienstgütemanagements. Auch wenn das vorgestellte Rahmenwerk von Dienstgütebegriffen ausreichend ist, die erörterten Fragen zu behandeln, so können Erweiterungen neue Aspekte zugänglich machen. An erster Stelle ist hier die Einführung von σ-Algebren über den Teilmengen der Sitzungsmenge mit jeweils identischer Last zu nennen. Dadurch läßt sich für eine gegebene Last die Eintretenswahrscheinlichkeit einer spezifischen Reaktion oder auch einer Menge von Reaktionen formal ausdrücken. So läßt sich das Konzept der Fehlerwahrscheinlichkeit z.B. zur Bewertung des Nutzens einer Managemententscheidung formal definieren. Da diese Wahrscheinlichkeit abhängig von der Last ist, ergibt sich auch die Möglichkeit, eine totale Ordnungsrelation auf der Menge der Lasten aufzustellen. Diese stellt eine Bewertung des Risikos für den Diensterbringer dar, einen Fehler zu erzeugen. Die Betrachtung unterschiedlicher Sitzungsmengen, die nach der Dienstgüteordnung Fehler abgestufter Schwere darstellen, schlägt wiederum die Brücke zu den etablierten Konzepten der Fehlersemantik – jedoch unter Einbeziehung der spezifischen Last.

Eine weitere wichtige Aufgabe ist die Weiterentwicklung der Spezifikationsmethode für Dienstgüteeigenschaften. Die in dieser Arbeit verwendete Notation ist zu allgemeingültig, als daß sie eine kompakte Beschreibung der relevanten Eigenschaften erlaubte. Hier gilt es, Methoden der formalen Spezifikation von Datenübertragungsdiensten so weiterzuentwickeln, daß ihre Semantik eine Abbildung auf die Mengen und Relationen des Rahmenwerks erlaubt. Eine solche Spezifikationstechnik wäre dann jedoch auf diese Dienste eingeschränkt; für die Anwendung des Rahmenwerks auf anders geartete Dienste muß wieder auf die hier verwendete Notation zurückgegriffen werden oder es müssen andere, entsprechende Spezifikationsmethoden entwickelt werden.

Die Verfügbarkeit der umfassenden prototypischen Implementation des Flexible Continuous Media Transfer System erlaubt es nunmehr, die bisher nur theoretisch entwickelten Verfahren für ein modellgestütztes adaptives Dienstgütemanagement in die Realität umzusetzen und ihre Wirksamkeit praktisch zu untersuchen. Dies gilt einerseits für die Managementaufgabe innerhalb der Managementdomäne der Transportschicht: Hier sind geeignete Modelle zur Beschreibung der Wirkungsweise der bereits implementierten Mikroprotokollmaschinen aufzustellen und ihre Verwendbarkeit zur Optimierung der erzielten Dienstgüte zu untersuchen. Auch muß untersucht werden, ob und wie die vorhandenen Mikroprotokollmaschinen in ihrer Funktionalität optimiert werden können und ob weitere Mikroprotokollmaschinen entwickelt werden sollten.

Auch die Fragestellung des domänenübergreifenden Dienstgütemanagements kann nun anhand des lauffähigen Systems praktisch untersucht werden. So wäre insbesondere die Entwicklung geeigneter Managementschnittstellen zwischen den Managementkomponenten der verschiedenen Domänen nach den Grundsätzen des formalen Rahmenwerkes ein sinnvoller nächster Schritt zum Aufbau einer umfassenden Managementarchitektur.

Literatur

1. Richter, Jan-Peter: *Spezifikations- und Meßmethodik für ein adaptives Dienstgütemanagement*, Dissertation, Fachbereich Informatik, Universität Hamburg, Shaker Verlag, Aachen, 2000.
2. C. Aurrecoechea, A. T. Campbell, and L. Hauw: „A Survey of QoS Architectures", *Multimedia Systems*, Vol. 6, No. 3, Special Issue on QoS Architectures, pp. 138-151, ACM/Springer, May 1998.
3. A. Hafid, G. v. Bochmann and R. Dssouli: „Distributed Multimedia Applications and Quality of Service: A Review", *Electronic Journal on Networks and Distributed Processing*, Vol. 2, No. 6, pp. 1-50, 1998.

4. D. Ferrari, A. Banerjea, and H. Zhang: „Network support for multimedia – A discussion of the Tenet Approach", *Computer Networks and ISDN Systems*, Vol. 26, No. 10, pp. 1267-1280, July 1994.

5. C. Schmidt, M. Zitterbart: „Towards Integrated QoS Management", *Proceedings of the First International Workshop on High Performance Protocol Architectures HIPPARCH `94*, Sophia Antipolis, France, December 1994.

6. I. Busse, B. Deffner, and H. Schulzrinne : „Dynamic QoS control of multimedia applications based on RTP", *Computer Communications*, Jan. 1996.

7. J.-F. Huard, I. Inoue, A. A. Lazar and H. Yamanaka: „Meeting QoS Guarantees by End-to-End QoS Monitoring and Adaptation", *Workshop on Multimedia and Collaborative Environments of the fifth IEEE International Symposium on High Performance Distributed Computing(HPDC-5)*, Syracuse, NY, August 1996.

8. M. Zitterbart: „User-to-User QoS – Management and Monitoring", in: W. Dabbous and C. Diot [eds.]: *Protocols for High Speed Networks V*, Proceedings of the 5th Int. Workshop on Protocols for High Speed Networks (PfHSN96), Sophia Antipolis, France, October 28-30, 1996.

9. M. Fry, V. Witana, P. Ray, and A. Seneviratne: „Managing QoS in Multimedia Services", *Journal of Network and Systems Management – Special Issue on Multimedia Network/Service Management*, Vol 5, No. 3, 1997.

10. B. E. Wolfinger: „Modellgestütztes Dienstqualitätsmanagement in heterogenen, dienstintegrierten Kommunikations- und Rechnernetzen", *20. Europäische Congressmesse für Technische Kommunikation (ONLINE'97)*, Hamburg, 3.-7. Feb. 1997.

11. H. De Meer: *QoS Support for Multimedia Communications: An Internet Perspective*, Habilitationsschrift in Vorbereitung, Universität Hamburg, Fachbereich Informatik, 2000.

12. S. Damaskos, A. Gavras: „A Simplified QoS Model for Multimedia Protocols over ATM", in: S. Fdida [ed.]: *High Performance Networking, V (C-26)*, pp. 241-257, Elsevier Science B. V (North-Holland), 1994.

13. B. E. Wolfinger: „On the Potential of FEC Algorithms in Building Fault-tolerant Distributed Applications to Support High QoS Video Communication", *ACM Symp. on Principles of Distributed Computing (PODC '97)*, Santa Barbara 1997.

14. J.-P. Richter und H. De Meer: „Modellbasiertes QoS Management am Beispiel MPEG-kodierter Videoströme", *Workshop Anwendungsunterstützung für heterogene Rechnernetze*, Freiberg / Sachsen, 30.3. – 31.3. 1995.

15. J.-P. Richter and H. De Meer: „Adaptive MPEG video coding in the presence of failures as an example for quality of service management", *Proceedings of EWDC-7, 7th European Workshop on Dependable Computing*, University of Twente, April 19-21, 1995.

16. H. De Meer: „Adaptive Quality of Service Management: A Model-Based Approach", *10th European Simulation Multiconference*, Budapest, 2.6. – 6.6. 1996.

17. J.-P. Richter and H. De Meer: „Towards Formal Failure Semantics for QoS Support", *Proceedings of the IEEE INFOCOM `98*, San Francisco CA, March 29 - April 2, 1998.

18. Chr. Langmann und S. Weitendorf: *Dienstgüteüberwachung im IP-basierten Transportsystem FCMTS (Flexible Continuous Media Transfer System)*, gemeinsame Diplomarbeit, Universität Hamburg, Fachbereich Informatik/TKRN, 1999.

19. F. Cristian: „Understanding Fault-Tolerant Distributed Systems", *Communications of the ACM*, Vol. 34, No. 2, pp. 57-78, February 1991.

20. F. Cristian: „Abstractions for Fault-Tolerance", in: K. Duncan, K. Krueger [eds.]: *Linkage and Developing Countries – Information Processing `94, Proceedings of the IFIP 13th World Computer Congress*, Hamburg, Elsevier Science B. V., 1994.

Service Separation and QoS in ATM Networks: The RCC+ Multiplexer

Dirk Abendroth

Department of Communication Networks, AB 4-06, Technical University of Hamburg-Harburg, Denickestr. 17, D-21073 Hamburg, Germany (e-mail abendroth@tu-harburg.de; Tel.: +49 40 42878 3249; FAX: +49 40 42878 2941).

Abstract. Providing service separation and quality of service guarantees requires the use of scheduling algorithms in the switches and network interfaces. We present the RCC+ Mux, a hardware efficient Rate Controlled Cell Multiplexer that has the capablity to provide explicit bandwidth reservation guarantees and thereby an excellent service separation. The RCC+ Multiplexer is simulated in the presence of self-similar traffic and compared to the FIFO queue, the Worst-case Fair Weighted Fair Queueing plus (WF^2Q+) scheduler, and the already existing RCC Multiplexer. Moreover we point out the most favourable and critical characteristics of the RCC+ Multiplexer.

1 Introduction

Integrated services networks support multiple services and are faced to the problem of ressource sharing among applications. Many applications rely on the ability of the network to privide quality of service (QoS) guarantees. The most important issue in designing integrated services networks is the choice of the packet service discipline at queueing points. The service discipline is defined by a scheduling algorithm which must be designed to meet the QoS requirements of all customers (sessions, flows, connections). A FIFO queue works properly only if all customers cooperate, which means that all connections adhere to the bandwidth share reserved. Otherwise well behaving streams might be affected heavily by other session's traffic characteristics, experiencing delays and losses. In order to meet the QoS requirements of all flows a scheduler has to isolate misbehaving flows and to share the bandwidth among the competing flows fairly according to their reservations under the condition of optimal link utilization and low implementation complexity.

Generalized Processor Sharing (GPS) assumes infinitely devisible packets (referred to as a liquid model) and multiplexes traffic of several connections onto a single line. A GPS scheduler serves all sessions at the same time, each according to its reserved rate or bandwidth share respectively. Bandwidth left over by idle sessions is distributed among backlogged [1] sessions in proportion to their reservations. The normalized service, which is the work performed by the server for a

---

[1] a session is called backlogged when it has one or more packets buffered in the switch throughout the time of consideration, otherwise it is called empty

certain connection normalized by its reservation, is the same for all backlogged sessions. GPS provides perfect flow isolation, offers the same normalized service to all backlogged sessions, is optimally fair but has an unacceptable high calculation complexity.

In real networks packets have finite length and we have to drop the above assumption of infinitely divisible packets. This leads to the ideal packet switching schedulers or alternatively ideal Packet Fair Queueing (PFQ) schedulers namely Weighted Fair Queueing (WFQ) and Worst-case Fair Weighted Fair Queueing (WF^2Q).

With WFQ a GPS system is simulated to determine the set of backlogged sessions, their current service rates and completion times using the concept of virtual time [1]. For each arriving packet a finishing potential (FP) is derived from the current value of the virtual time. The arriving packet is timestamped with the FP, containing the instant of time at which the arriving packet would have finished service in the corresponding GPS server simulated in parallel. The timestamped packets are transmitted in increasing order of finishing potentials. The resulting scheduler (WFQ) is able to provide the same latency-bound as GPS, with a maximum discrepancy equal to the transmission time of one (maximum size) packet [2], [3] but its fairness properties are much weaker than those of GPS.

As stated above, WFQ has the same upper delay-bound as GPS except for a granularity of one packet transmission time. Unfortunately this does not hold for lower bounds and WFQ can be far ahead of GPS in terms of finishing potentials. This might cause bursty output traffic or an oscillation of the service rate with respect to a single connection. Based on this grievance Worst-case Fair Weighted Fair Queueing (WF^2Q) was defined as an alternative ideal fair packet scheduling discipline. WF^2Q is identical to WFQ exept for an additional condition: the WF^2Q scheduler admits only packets for transmission that have already started (and possibly finished) receiving service in the corresponding fluid server (GPS) [4], [5], [6].

WFQ and WF^2Q need to simulate a GPS server in parallel and the calculation of the virtual time might become prohibitively expensive with increasing number of connections. The key problem of a scheduling discipline is the trade-off between delay, fairness and low implementation complexity. The WF^2Q+ scheduler approximates the ideal packet scheduling disciplines WF^2Q by replacing the virtual time with a piecewise linear function with slope one and, if neccessary, recalibration with the minimum starting potential among all backlogged sessions [7], [8], [5].

The WF^2Q+ scheduler is equivalent to the shaped Starting Potential Fair Queueing (sSPFQ) scheduler which was published by Stiliadis and Varma in [1], [9] and belongs to the popular Latency Rate $\mathcal{LR}$ class [10], [11], [12].

In this paper we present the RCC+ Multiplexer, a scheduler for high-speed switching in ATM networks with low implementation complexity which provides service separation, QoS and explicit bandwidth guarantees. We compare its performance to that of a FIFO queue, the Worst-case Fair Weighted Fair Queueing plus (WF^2Q+) scheduler and the already existing RCC Multiplexer.

2 RCC Multiplexer

In contrast to WF^2Q+, the Rate Controlled Cell Multiplexer (RCC Mux) is a hardware oriented scheduler that addresses to approximate the GPS directly without taking care of a virtual time function [13]. The general structure of an RCC Mux is given in Figure 1. For each connection there is a Periodic Token-

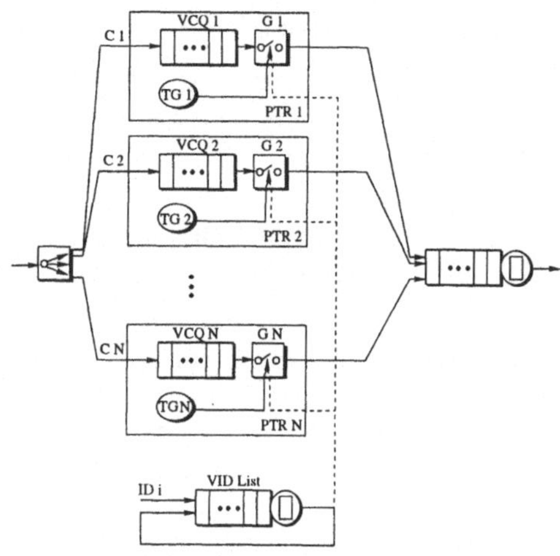

Fig. 1. General Structure of an RCC Multiplexer

based Regulator (PTR) containing a FIFO queue (Virtual Connection Queue, VCQ) , a Token Generator (TG) and a Gate (G) to be triggered by the dedicated TG. The arriving packets are fed into the corresponding VCQs . The TGs work as CBR sources each with the reserved rate associated with the respective connection. Each time a TG generates a token and thereby triggers the gate, one packet from the VCQ is forwarded to the common output queue. The output buffer is emptied by a server with a rate that is equal to the constant transmission rate of the link. If all sessions are backlogged at each instant of time, this description is complete and the structure is obviously able to make explicit bandwidth reservations. If the output queue is empty and a token is sent to a gate dedicated to an empty VCQ at the same time, the next time slot might stay unused (residual slot). The VCQ Identifier (VID) list distributes residual slots among all backlogged session to improve the link utilization similar to a GPS system that distributes the excess bandwidth among all backlogged sessions. When a packet arrives at the i-th VCQ an ID_i is enqueued to the VID list but there can be at most one ID for each session in the VID list. When a residual slot occurs the VID list searches for the first ID dedicated to a non-empty queue, removes all IDs up to and including the concerned one and sends a token to the selected session's gate. Notice that a triggered VCQ might be empty irrespective of the ID in the VID list.

Assuming a heavily loaded system, a residual slot is a rare event and there will be arrivals at all VCQs regularly. For this reason the VID list will contain most of the VC's IDs. In this case the VID list operates very similar to a Round Robin scheduler irrespective of any bandwidth reservations. This behaviour is obviously not very close to that of GPS. In Section 3.3 we will present an alternative method to distribute residual slots more fairly than with the VID list.

3 RCC+ Multiplexer

In the following we present some improvements of the RCC Mux leading to a new scheduler which was named RCC+ Mux.

3.1 Desynchronization of Token Generators

The question of buffer dimensioning of the output queue leads to the phase relations of the token generators. If all N virtual connections (VCs) are backlogged and all TGs trigger the corresponding gates exactly at the same time, i.e. the same time slot, N packets will be forwarded to the output queue simultaneously and the packet of one VC has to wait at least N-1 slots for beeing served. The number of VCs in ATM nodes might be very high so that there is a serious need to desynchronize the TGs. The degree of freedom we can make use of is to determine the instant of time at which each token generator starts generating tokens incessantly. Once having started, a TG is sending equally spaced tokens. Let $t = 0$ be the instant of time when we start to consider the system and let $T_1 \leq T_2 \leq \cdots \leq T_V$ be the VC's reserved periods. The pseudo code below determines a delay Δ_i for each VC_i representing the instant of time when the TG_i starts sending tokens. Let $T_{max} = max_i\{T_i\}$ be the maximum VC's period which is equivalent to the reciprocal value of the minimum reserved rate. The period of the arriving superposed CBR data streams is denoted by $T = lcm_{\forall i}\{T_i\}$ [2] and $e_s^{T_{max}}$ is a unit vector of length T_{max} with only one non-zero element at position s. The vector $\delta^{T_{max}}$ of length T_{max} is initialized to zero and will be used to observe the maximum arriving packet pattern at the output queue.

```
for i = 1 through N
```

$$\Delta_i \quad = min\left\{p \middle| \delta_p^{T_{max}} = 0\right\} - 1$$
$$t_{max}^i \quad = \left\lfloor \frac{T_{max}-(\Delta_i+1)}{T_i} \right\rfloor$$
$$\delta^{T_{max}} = \delta^{T_{max}} + \sum_{t=0}^{t_{max}^i} e_{t \cdot T_i + \Delta_i + 1}^{T_{max}}$$

```
end
```

---

[2] lcm$\{\cdot\}$: least common multiplier of $\{\cdot\}$

The code above searches for the first position p in $\delta^{T_{max}}$ which has a zero element, determines the first VC to start sending tokens in this slot and adds the CBR pattern of the first VC to the occupancy vector $\delta^{T_{max}}$ and repeats these steps for all other VCs. $t^i_{max} + 1$ is the number of VC_i packets that fit into the period of consideration T_{max}, taking into account the delay Δ_i associated with session i. Assuming a stable system it is sufficient and reasonable to perform the pseudo code for all VCs over a period of T_{max} instead of T because every VC should start sending tokens at latest before the first period T_{max} has passed by. The desynchronization algorithm avoids simultaneous arrivals at the output queue as far as possible and thereby results in an optimally flat packet arrival pattern. Subsequently the delays caused in the output queue and the over all delays are minimized by this desynchronization algorithm. This algorithm especially takes care of reservations that are multiples of one fixed unit (e.g. 64 $\frac{kbit}{sec}$). It is reasonable to avoid collisions as long as possible: for very long periods T the set of backlogged sessions might have changed before the first simultaneous arrivals occur and the algorithm is initialized again. Furthermore the arrival pattern considered is the maximum arrival pattern that *might* occur so that simultaneous arrivals at the output queue become a very rare event. It is close to intuition that we can make use of the occupancy vector δ when tracking the above algorithm for a whole period T with given delays Δ_i:

```
for i = 1 through N
```

$$\tau^i_{max} = \left\lfloor \frac{T-(\Delta_i+1)}{T_i} \right\rfloor$$

$$\delta^T = \delta^T + \sum_{\tau=0}^{\tau^i_{max}} e^T_{\tau \cdot T_i + \Delta_i + 1}$$

```
end
```

Taking into consideration the constant service time of the output server (link) the output queue's buffer occupancy can be derived easily in a recursive way:

$$b(0) = 0 \tag{1}$$

$$b(s) = \left[b(s-1) + \delta^T_{s-1} - 1 \right]^+, \qquad s = 1, \cdots, T \tag{2}$$

$$b_{max} = max_{1 \leq s \leq T} \{b(s)\} . \tag{3}$$

The buffer occupancy (upon arrival) in time slot s, $b(s)$, can be derived from the buffer occupancy in the previous slot, the arrival pattern in the previous slot and the deterministic transmission (service) time of one time slot (see (2)). In (1) the initial buffer occupancy is set to zero. If the cyclic condition $b(T) = b(0)$ does not hold one has to perform the loop once more with initial condition $b(0) = b(T)$. The stability of the system ensures that cumulative behaviour (overlapping) is limited to only one following period. (3) returns the maximum buffer occupancy and answers the question of buffer dimensioning in order to avoid packet losses in the output queue.

3.2 Extension to Float Periods

The RCC Mux was restricted to bandwith reservations of integer periods of slots so far. Unfortunately this corresponds to discrete valid bandwidth shares. It is evident that admitting float periods for the TGs would solve the problem but additonal to that the forwarded packets should be synchronized to the ATM clock. We propose to apply the ceiling function to the multiples of the float periods to get proper trigger times. The ceiling function can be implemented easily, does not increase the algorithm's complexity and it is compatible to the RCC structure, the desychronization algorithm and the analytical derivation of the buffer occupancy (see above). To adapt the calculation of delays Δ_i of the desynchronization algorithm to float periods one has to supplement the ceiling function correspondingly. Furthermore the period $T = lcm_{\forall i}\{T_i\}$ of the superposed signal might become much larger when passing the gates in the case of float periods [14]. Nevertheless all improvements work properly with the above extensions.

3.3 Residual Slot Scheduler (RSS)

There is no common agreement on how to measure the fairness of a scheduler. Benett and Zhang have proposed a Worst-case Fairness Index (WFI) that measures the maximum additional time a packet has to spend in the scheduler because the scheduler does not adhere to the reserved bandwidth, and this normalized to the respective reserved rate [4]. On the other hand Golestani proposed the Service Fairness Index (SFI) that measures the maximum difference between the normalized services provided by the scheduler to any pair of continuously backlogged sessions [15].

Packets arriving at a VCQ of an RCC Mux structure are served with the reserved rate instantaneously and do not experience any further delay than in a WFQ algorithm. Therefore the WFI is determined only by any additional delays introduced by the output queue. The desynchronization algorithm above minimizes the output queue's buffer occupancy, the additional delays and the WFI. Notice that the WFI does not take into account the distribution of excess bandwidth. Both indices WFI and SFI are determined by the worst-case behaviour of the scheduler. Especially in the case of SFI we believe that an average fairness in terms of the same normalized service (like in GPS) is more important than to minimize the maximum difference. In the following we propose to replace the VID list by a prescription that distributes residual slots among the active sessions in proportion to the reserved bandwidth shares so that all normalized services are the same like in GPS. Pay attention to the fact that the favourable behaviour in respect of WFI holds irrespective of the distribution of the excess bandwidth.

```
interval = 0
for (i = all VCs)
   if (VCQ_i not empty)
       interval = interval + 1/T_i
   end
end


Random = uniformly distributed random number in [0,1]
Random = Random * interval

upper = 0
for (i = all VCs)
   if (VCQ_i not empty)
       upper = upper + 1/T_i
       if (Random < upper)
          winnerVC = i
          exit for-loop
       end
   end
end
```

The pseudo code above builds first an interval between zero and an upper bound that is equal to the sum of the bandwidth shares of all backlogged sessions. Then the code generates a pseudo random number that is uniformly distributed in [0, 1] and after multiplication with the upper interval bound is uniformly distributed in the interval calculated before. Each session is collated to a subintervall which is proportional to the reserved bandwidth share. Starting at zero and proceeding by the reserved bandwidth shares the code determines the session that gets the residual slot. Figure 2(a) shows an example with five backlogged and three empty sessions. The sum of the bandwidth reservations of all backlogged sessions is equal to 0.6. The intervals are marked by the number of the session associated. In case of a uniformly ditributed random number in [0, 0.6] each session gets residual slots in proportion to its reserved share considering 'enough' residual slots. Because of the granularity of one packet the word 'enough' is determined by the given reservations and not by the scheduler (especially not by this scheduler). We did not specify the way to generate the random numbers for the Residual Slot Scheduler (RSS) as proposed above. One possibility is to generate random numbers independently of residual slots and to keep them in a queue, a heap, or a stack and to take one in case of a residual slot. The effort for checking the whole interval for the winner session might become quite high with increasing number of connections. In this case we propose to skip some of the connections with the smallest shares, to reduce the algorithm's complexity. If so, it has to be found a reasonable compromise between calculation complexity and fairness. Nevertheless each session gets its reserved bandwidth share. The RCC Mux combined with the improvements presented in this Section was called RCC+ Mux. Figure 2(b) comprisingly shows the structure of the RCC+ Mux including

separate entities for the RSS and the desynchronization algorithm. The extension
to float periods can be integrated with the gates or TGs.

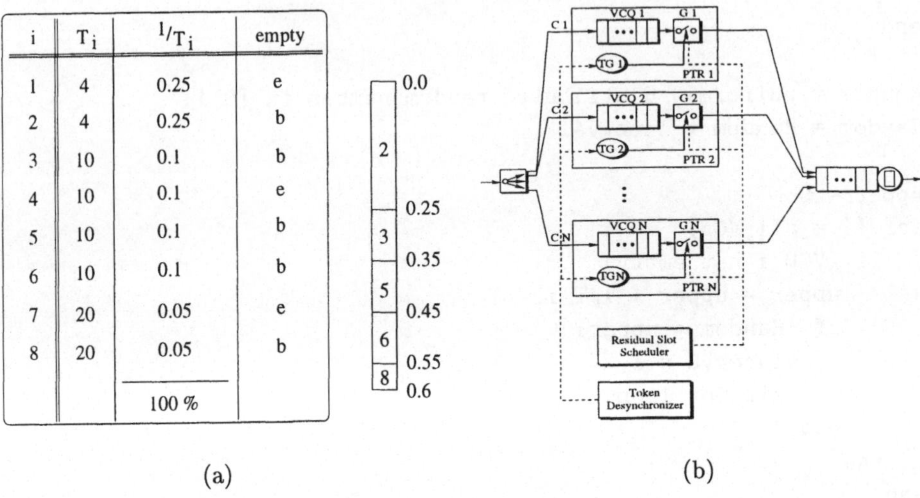

(a)   (b)

Fig. 2. Residual Slot Scheduler, Example (a) and General Structure of an RCC+ Multiplexer (b)

4   Simulation Results

The schedulers presented have been simulated with Ptolemy [16], [17], [18] which
contains an event driven simulator (discrete event domain). The aim was to
prove that the schedulers provide QoS and service separation and to compare
them among themselves and to a FIFO queue. Our scenarios are based on a
CBR source that perfectly adheres to its reserved bandwidth share, with a background traffic that is varied from Poissonian to self-similar. We assume a 1 $\frac{Gbit}{sec}$
link and a foreground traffic (CBR) that has a 1 $\frac{Mbit}{sec}$ reserved rate. The remaining bandwidth is shared equally among seven background connections. The
reservations are assumed to be overdimensioned so that the utilization is less
than 100% for each session and the entire system. We have additionally assumed
one misbehaving source sending two and a half times the reserved rate. The
whole scenario including bandwidth reservations, utilization per session and the
entire system's utilization can be seen in Table 1. In this publication we restrict
ourselves to self-similar background traffic with hurst parameter[3] of 0.8.

---

[3] measure of self-similarirty, bounded between 0.5 and 1, high values of hurst parameter signify serious self-similarity and vice versa

connection	reserved bandwidth share	relative utilization	resulting traffic load
$VC1$	14, 27%	70%	9, 99%
$VC2$	14, 27%	70%	9, 99%
$VC3$	14, 27%	70%	9, 99%
$VC4$	14, 27%	70%	9, 99%
$VC5$	14, 27%	70%	9, 99%
$VC6$	14, 27%	70%	9, 99%
$VC7$	14, 27%	250%	35, 68%
$VC8$	0, 1%	80%	0, 08%
$\sum_{i=1}^{8} VC_i$	100%		95, 7%

Table 1. Simulation scenario, VC8 is foreground, VC1 through VC7 background traffic, VC7 is misbehaving

In the following we suppose TG8 to be synchronized to the foreground traffic stream. As a first result we found that contrary to other schedulers overdimensioning of reservations is harmful for the RCC and RCC+ Mux and causes additional delays [14]. Figures 3 and 4 show the inter departure times and delays of the VC8 data stream fed into a FIFO queue (a), a WF^2Q+ scheduler (b), and an RCC+ Mux (c). The results for a FIFO queue (a) demonstrate the influence of self-similar background traffic. The interdeparture times are distributed over a broad range and serious delays occur regularly. The WF^2Q+ scheduler (b) provides inter departure times in a well shaped gaussian curve and bounds the delays in a negative exponential manner to a value well below. Figures 3(c) and 4(c) demonstrate the RCC+ Mux's capability to provide explicit bandwidth reservation guarantees. Inter departure times and delays actually are ideally distributed delta functions for an RCC+ Mux.

The buffer occupancies for the RCC Mux and the RCC+ Mux are shown in Figures 5 and 6. All VCQs have been bounded to a size of 200. The RCC Mux generates buffer occupancy distributions for VCQ 1 through 6 that are close to negative exponential but, on account of the background traffic's self-similarity, have very long tails and losses (Figure 5(a)). The RCC+ Mux avoids losses, see Figure 6(a). VC 7 is misbehaving and consequently there are lots of losses in VCQ7 for the RCC Mux (Figure 5(b)) but the RCC+ Mux can stabilize even the buffer occupancy of the misbehaving VC (Figure 6(b)), hence, improving the link utilization. The reason for this improvement lies in the desynchronization algorithm that pulls down the output buffer's occupancy distribution to zero (Figures 5(c) and 6(c)). Recalling that residual slots can be assigned only if the output queue is empty and an empty VCQ is triggered, the RCC+ Mux distributes residual slots more often and thus relieves the input buffers (VCQs).

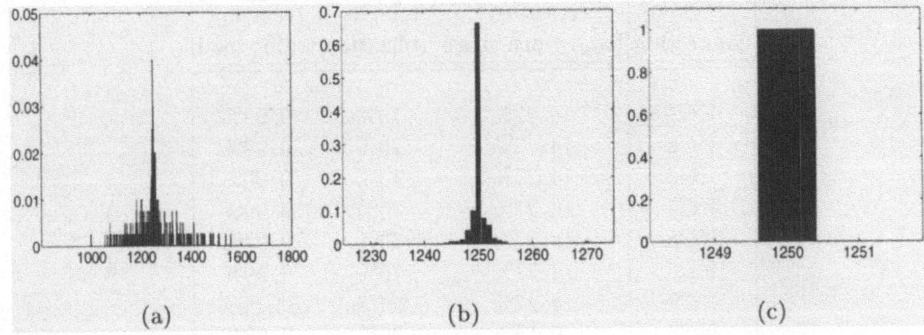

Fig. 3. Inter Departure Times of VC8: FIFO Queue (a), WF^2Q+ Scheduler (b) and RCC+ Mux (c)

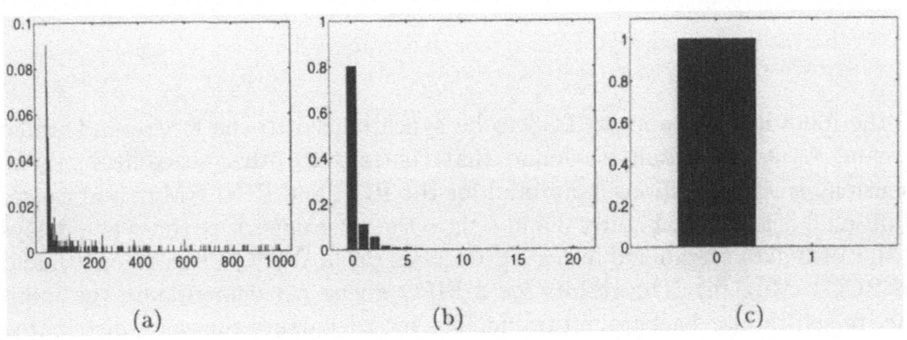

Fig. 4. Delays of VC8: FIFO Queue (a), WF^2Q+ Scheduler (b) and RCC+ Mux (c)

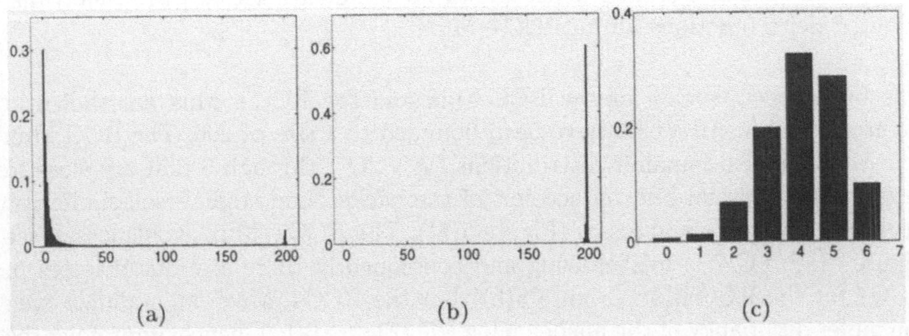

Fig. 5. RCC Mux, Buffer Occupancies: VCQ1-VCQ6 (a), VCQ7 (b) and Output Queue (c)

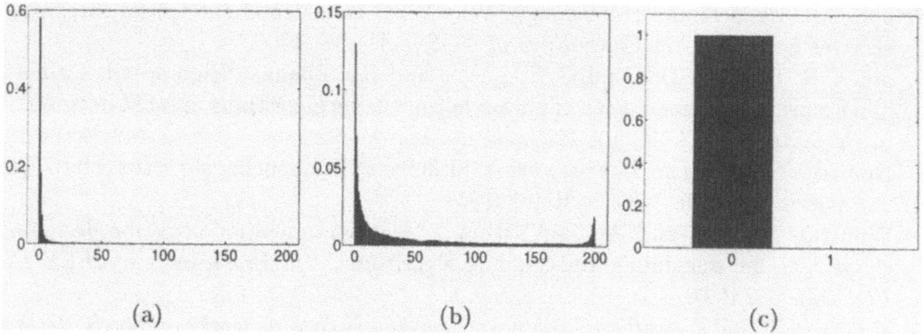

Fig. 6. RCC+ Mux, Buffer Occupancies: VCQ1-VCQ6 (a), VCQ7 (b) and Output
Queue (c)

5   Conclusions

We introduced a new WFQ scheduler that provides QoS by excellently separating flows. The RCC+ Multiplexer was derived from the RCC Multiplexer by adding a desynchronization algorithm, making an extension to reservations of arbitrary bandwith shares and replacing the VID list by a Residual Slot Scheduler that distributes excess bandwidth more fairly. The RCC+ Multiplexer was shown to provide explicit bandwidth reservation guarantees. The simulations prove the superior behavior of the RCC+ Multiplexer in comparison to the RCC Multiplexer in terms of buffer occupancies, delays, fairness and generality. We pointed out that overdimensioning of bandwidth reservations for an RCC or RCC+ Multiplexer might cause additional delays. Moreover we demonstrated the superior behaviour of the RCC+ Multiplexer in comparison to the popular WF^2Q+ scheduler.

References

1. Anujan Varma and Dimitrios Stiliadis, "Hardware implementation of fair queuing algorithms for asynchronous transfer mode networks," in *IEEE Communications Magazine*, 1997.
2. A. Parekh, *A generalized processor sharing approach to flow control in integrated services networks.*, 1992.
3. A. Demers, S. Keshav, and S. Shenker, "Analysis and simulation of a fair queueing algorithm," in *Proceedings ACM SIGCOM '89*, 1989, pp. 3–12.
4. Jon C.R. Bennett and Hui Zhang, "WF2Q: Worst-case fair weighted fair queueing," in *Proceedings of INFOCOM '96*, 1996.
5. Sašo Stojanovsky, *Traffic management over APON and superPON access networks*, 1999.
6. Donpaul C. Stephens, Jon C.R. Bennett, and Hui Zhang, "Implementing scheduling algorithms in high-speed networks," in *IEEE JSAC Special Issue on High Performance Switches/Routers*, 1999.

7. Jon C.R. Bennett and Hui Zhang, "Why WFQ is not good enough for integrated services networks," in *Proceedings of NOSSDAV '96*, 1996.

8. Jon C.R. Bennett, Donpaul C. Stephens, and Hui Zhang, "High speed, scalable, and accurate implementation of packet fair queueing algorithms in ATM networks," in *Proceedings of ICNP '97*, 1997.

9. Dimitrios Stiliadis and Anujan Varma, "Efficient fair-queueing algorithms for ATM and packet networks," Tech. Rep., 1995.

10. Dimitrios Stiliadis and Anujan Varma, "A general methodology for designing efficient traffic scheduling and shaping algorithms," in *Proceedings of IEEE INFOCOM '97*, 1997.

11. Dimitrios Stiliadis, *Traffic scheduling in packet-switched networks: analysis, design, and implementation*, 1996.

12. Dimitrios Stiliadis and Anujan Varma, "Latency-rate servers:a general model for analysis of traffic scheduling algorithms," in *Proceedings of IEEE INFOCOM '96*, 1996, pp. 111–119.

13. Koohong Kang, Bart Steyaert, and Cheeha Kim, "Service separation in ATM networks using a hardware efficient rate-controlled cell multiplexer," in *Proceedings of the International Teletraffic Congress ITC-16*, 1999, vol. 3a.

14. Dirk Abendroth, "Untersuchung der Leistungsfhigkeit von WFQ-algorithmen zur Sicherung von Service-Separation und QoS-Garantien in ATM-Netzen," Diploma thesis, Communication Networks TU Hamburg-Harburg, 2000.

15. S. Golestani, "A self-clocked fair queueing scheme for broadband applications," in *Proceedings of IEEE INFOCOM '94*, 1994, pp. 636–646.

16. Berkeley, University of California, *The Almagest - Volume I, Ptolemy 0.7 Users Manual*, 1997.

17. Berkeley, University of California, *The Almagest - Volume II, Ptolemy 0.7 Programmers Manual*, 1997.

18. Berkeley, University of California, *The Almagest - Volume III, Ptolemy 0.7 Kernel Manual*, 1997.

19. Dimitrios Stiliadis and Anujan Varma, "Frame-based fair queueing: A new traffic scheduling algorithm for packet-switched networks," 1995.

20. James W. Roberts and Jorma T. Virtamo, "The superposition of periodic cell arrival streams in an ATM multiplexer," in *IEEE transactions on communication, february 1991*, vol. 39, pp. 298–303.

Index der Autoren

A
Abeck......103, 229
Abendroth......479
Augustin......103

B
Baier......255
Battaglia......35
Becker......103
Beigl......81
Bohn......305
Böger......147
Braun......315
Brose......233

C
Carle......21
Charzinski......377
Cihal......359

D
Dolling......229
Drobnik......159

E
Eberhardt......187
Erfurth......315

F
Faust......247
Feil......403
Feuerhelm......229
Fischer......117
Franz......415
Frick......81
Friedmann......103

G
Gellersen......81
Gran......255
Griffel......325
Guardado......35

H
Harbaum......349
Hartenstein......279

Hauser......215
Heidtmann......201
Hinz......259
Hördt......187

I
Imhoff......455

J
Jocher......47

K
Kabatnik......93
Kahmann......237
Karjoth......305
Kaspar......47
Kassler......279
Keller......425
Kellerer......391
Kerse......201
Key......3
Kiefer......233
Killat......35
Koster......369
Kramp......369
Krautgärtner......279
Krieger......159

L
Lin......241
Lindemann......291
Link......251
Lukas......247
Luttenberger......251
Lübbehusen......341

M
Matthes......159
Mayerl......229
Mühlhäuser......359
Müller-Wilken......325

N
Niedermeier......279
Nochta......103
Noffke......233

P
Paepcke 141
Pählke 59
Petras 439

Q
Quendt 47

R
Richter 467
Ritter 173
Rossak 315
Rothermel 215
Rueß 187

S
Sailer 93
Schauer 229
Schäfer 59
Schiller 59
Schmidt 81
Schrader 279
Stauch 127
Sties 391
Stümpfle 403
Stüttgen 349
Suchanek 201

T
Thümmler 291
Tolksdorf 127

U
Unterschütz 241

V
Vogel 241

W
Walther 117
Wehrle 173
Welzl 359
Wolf 173, 187
Wolfinger 201
Wu 69

Z
Zaddach 201
Zander 21
Ziegert 265
Zirpins 325
Zisowsky 255
Zitterbart 69, 147, 349
Zseby 21